ANDREWS UNIVERSITY SEMINARY
DOCTORAL DISSERTATION SERIES
VOLUME IV

THE HORN-MOTIF

IN THE HEBREW BIBLE AND RELATED
ANCIENT NEAR EASTERN LITERATURE AND ICONOGRAPHY

by
MARGIT L. SÜRING

ANDREWS UNIVERSITY PRESS
BERRIEN SPRINGS, MICHIGAN

Copyright © 1980
by
Margit L. Süring

BL
604
.H6
S90
1980

Dedicated with love to my sister Viola and
my friends Leona and Meeri

TABLE OF CONTENTS

LIST OF ILLUSTRATIONS vii
LIST OF ABBREVIATIONS xviii
ACKNOWLEDGEMENTS xxiv
INTRODUCTION 1

    Posing the Problem 1
    Aim and Methodology 2
    Limitations 4

Chapter

  I. REVIEW OF LITERATURE 5

      Horns on Altars 6
      The Bull Concept of Yahweh 15
      "Horn" Symbol in OT Apocalyptic 19
      The "Horns" of Moses 24
      Task 36

  II. COMPARATIVE PHILOLOGY OF THE ROOT QRN 38

      The Root QRN in Sumerian and Ancient Near
        Eastern Semitic Languages 38
        "Horn" in Sumerian 38
          Preliminary Considerations 38
          The Meaning of the Sumerogram SI 40
        Qarnu in Akkadian 58
          Preliminary Considerations 58
          The Meaning of Qarnu 60
        QRN in Ugaritic 70
          Preliminary Considerations 70
          The Meaning of Qrn 74
        QRN in Aramaic 81
          Preliminary Considerations 81
          The Meaning of קרן (קרנא) 83
            The Official Aramaic 84
            The Middle Aramaic 86
            Onomastic Usage 88
            The Aprocrypha 90

Chapter

  II. (Continued)

          Qarn in South-Arabic   95
              Preliminary Considerations   95
              The Meaning of Qarn قَرْنٌ
                 (pl. qurun قُرُونٌ)   97
          Qrn in Biblical Hebrew   102
              Preliminary Considerations   102
              The Meaning of קֶרֶן   104
          Summary and Evaluation   111

 III. HORN-MOTIFS IN NON-BIBLICAL SOURCES   117

          Non-Literary, Literary Texts and Iconography . .   117
              Non-Literary Texts   118
                  Mesopotamia   118
                      Literal Meaning   118
                      Literal-Extended Meaning   122
                      Purely Extended Meaning   123
              Literary Text and Iconography   125
                  Gods--in Literary Texts   125
                      Sumer and Akkad   125
                      Babylonia and Assyria   142
                      Syria   155
                      Anatolia   161
                      Ugarit   166
                      South-Arabia   172
                      Egypt   179
                      Sinai   187
                  Priests and Kings   192
                      Sumer and Akkad   192
                      Assyria and Babylonia   210
                      Syria   219
                      Anatolia   224
                      Ugarit   230
                      South-Arabia   237
                      Egypt   243
                  Soldiers   261
                      War-helmets   261
                  Kudurru/i-stones   264
                  Ziggurats and Altars   270
                      Mesopotamia   270
                      Syria   277
                      Anatolia   284
                      South-Arabia   286
          Summary and Evaluation   292

Chapter

IV. HORN-MOTIFS IN BIBLICAL SOURCES   300

    Literal Meanings of Horns   302
        On the Animal   302
        As a Musical Instrument   303
        As a Vessel   306
        On the Altar   308
    Literal-Extended Meanings of Horns   313
        Cultic Context   313
        Political Context   317
        Sociological Context   323
    Purely Extended Meanings of Horns   325
        Hymnic Texts   325
        Prophetic Texts   363
        Apocalyptic Texts   383
        The Horns of Moses   422
        Special Usages   432
            Idiomatic Usage   433
            Onomastic Usage   435
    Evaluation and Summary   438

SUMMARY AND CONCLUSION   446

APPENDICES   463

  A. Chart A - Occurrences of קרן in
      Biblical Aramaic   465
  B. Chart B - Occurrences of קרן in
      Biblical Hebrew   467
  C. Chart C - Structural Occurrences of קרן in
      Biblical Hebrew   473
  D. Table 1 - Occurrences of "Horn" in
      the Hebrew Bible   477

BIBLIOGRAPHY   479

LIST OF ILLUSTRATIONS

1. A Horned Deity Battling the Legendary Seven-headed Monster. Shell Plaque from ca. 2600 B.C. After Suzanne M. Heim, Ladders to Heaven, p. 10, fig. 4. . . 127

2. The Seven-headed Dragon Attacked by the Gods Wearing Horned Headdresses. Seal Impression from the Akkadian Period (ca. 2360 B.C.). After Othmar Keel, The Symbolism of the Biblical World, p. 54, fig. 52. 128

3. "Horned" Gods Engaged in Building Activities. Stone Cylinder Seal from the Late Akkadian Period (ca. 2254-2154 B.C.). After Heim, Ladders to Heaven, p. 10, fig. 5. 129

4. So-called "Sündenfall-Zylinder" Seal. Neo-Sumerian Period (ca. 2000 B.C.). After Martin A. Beek, "Baum," BHH, 1:207, fig. 3. 129

5. The Victorious King Narâm-Sin Wearing the Horned Helmet and Trampling His Enemies under His Feet. Sandstone Stela from Susa 23rd. Century B.C. After Yigael Yadin, The Art of Warfare in Biblical Lands, 1:150. 131

6. The Mythological Zû Captured and Deprived of His Divine Emblem--the "Horned" Headdress. Seal Impression from the Akkadian Period. After Henri Frankfort, Cylinder Seals, pl. XXXI, fig. 6. 135

7. Tiara of Nannar with the "Moon-crescent" Emblem Balancing on the Knob of the Tiara. From the Epoch of Ur-Nammu, ca. 2113-2096 B.C. After L.-H. Vincent, "La Représentation Divine Orientale Archaïque," Mélanges Syriens, 1:378, fig. 3. 139

8. An Attacking Bull with a "Horned" God as His Target. The Seal, Which Is from the Akkadian Period, is Enshrouded in a Mysterious Mythological Context. After Frankfort, Cylinder Seals, pl. XXII, fig. f. . . 140

9. Headdresses from the Early Dynastic and Akkadian Periods. After Rainer M. Boehmer, "Hörnerkrone," RLA, 4:432. 141

10. The Great Hammurabi in Front of Šamaš Who Is Depicted Sitting on His Throne. The Sun-god Is Wearing the Multiple "Horned" Headdress. After Frankfort, The Art and Architecture of the Ancient Orient, p. 65. . . 144

11. King Nabu-apal-iddin of Babylon, Led by a Priest and Accompanied by a Tutelary Deity, Enters into the Presence of Šamaš in the Sun-temple at Sippar (ca. 885-828 B.C.). After Keel, The Symbolism of the Biblical World, p. 174, fig. 239. 145

12a. The Sun-god Equipped with a Saw in His Left Hand and with Rays Emerging from His Shoulders Rises from Between the Mountains with a Powerful Leap. The Sun-god as Well as the Other Gods Wear "Horned" Headdresses. Keel, The Symbolism of the Biblical World, p. 23, fig. 9. 147

12b. Šamaš, the Sun-god, Dispelling Darkness, Marduk, the Victor of Chaos and Ea, the Wise Lord of the Depths. All Three Gods Wear a Headdress with Multiple Pairs of Horns. Keel, The Symbolism of the Biblical World, p. 48, fig. 43. 147

13. The Martial Goddess Ištar Depicted Standing on Her Lion, and Equipped with Weapons. She is Wearing the Feather-crown on Her Head. Marvin H. Pope, "The Saltier of Atargatis Reconsidered," in Near Eastern Archaeology in the Twentieth Century, p. 183, fig. 7. 148

14. The Goddess Nanna, Receiving the King and His Daughter, is Depicted with the Typical Feather-crown Worn by Goddesses. This Kudurru of Melishipak, Found at Susa, Originates from the Kassite Period. After Martin A. Beek, Atlas of Mesopotamia, p. 137, fig. 259. 150

15. This Unidentified God Has Traditionally Been Interpreted as the Storm-god. Equipped with Lightnings, and Wearing a Combined Horn- and Feather-crown, He Rides His Holy Bull. A Basalt Stela from Arslan Taş from the End of the 8th Century B.C. After Kurt Galling, BRL, p. 102, fig. 30. 151

16. Marduk, the Babylonian God, Depicted with a Feather-crown While the Dragon Resting at His Feet Wears Two Pointed Horns. After Beek, Atlas of Mesopotamia, p. 139. 151

17. The Young God Marduk with a Horned Helmet, Fighting a Winged Monster Which is Also Depicted with Two Pointed Horns. Relief from the Palace of Aššurnassirpal II at Nimrud. After Eckhard Unger, "Mischwesen," RLV, Vol. 8, pl. 61, fig. 3.   152

18. Neo-Assyrian and Neo-Babylonian Headdresses. After Rainer M. Boehmer, "Hörnerkrone," RLV, 4:432.   152

19. The Winged Disk as the Symbol of the Sun-god Aššur Depicted in a War-like Attitude and with a Horned Helmet on His Head. After Morris Jastrow, The Civilization of Babylonia and Assyria, pl. XXXI, fig. 2.   153

20. The Warlike Sun-god Aššur, Together with Conspicuous Bulls, Depicted on the Banner of Khorsabad   153
    After Ludolf Malten, "Der Stier in Kult und Mythischem Bild," Jahrbuch des Deutschen Archaeologishen Instituts 43 (1928):100, fig. 13.   153

21. An Unknown God with a Combined Horn- and Feather-crown Standing on a Fictitious Animal (a Mixture of Lion, Bull and Bird). Limestone Relief from Aššur. After Bruno Meissner, "Grundzüge der mittel- und neubabylonischen und der assyrischen Plastik," Der alte Orient, 15:133, fig. 224.   154

22. A Winged Human-headed Bull decorated with Three Pairs of Horns on His Headdress (a Combined horn- and Feather-crown). From the Palace of Sargon II, ca. 721-705 B.C.). After Alexander Heidel, The Babylonian Genesis, fig. 13.   155

23. A Winged Human-headed Bull from the Palace of Aššurnassirpal at Calah (ca. 800 B.C.). After Bruno Meissner, "Grundzüge der mittel- und neubabylonischen und der assyrischen Plastik," Der alte Orient, 15:103, fig. 177.   160

24. A Guardian at the Entrance to Aššurnassirpal's Palace at Nimrud. This Genius Combines the Body of a Lion, the Wings and Breast of an Eagle and the Human Head Crowned with Three Pairs of Horns. After Beek, Atlas of Mesopotamia, p. 92, fig. 177.   157

25. The Storm-god, Riding on His Bull, is Depicted Last in the Row among the Symbolic Signs (cf. fig. 15). Stela of Esarhaddon from Zinjirli. After Wm. J. Hinke, A New Boundary Stone of Nebuchadrezzar I from Nippur, p. 89, fig. 26   158

26. The Storm-God Adad Depicted with a Feather-crown on His Head and Equipped with a Three-Forked Lightning in His Right Hand and in His Left Reins Attached to Fictitous Animals. After Beek, Atlas of Mesopotamia, p. 139. 159

27. Procession of Gods Riding on Their Holy Animals. From a Rock Relief at Maltaya. After Karl Frank, Bilder und Symbole babylonisch-assyrische Götter, p. 2, fig. 1 . 159

28a. Three Shrines with Tiaras Showing how the Horns Meet in Front. Rock Relief of Sancherib at Bavia. After Wm. J. Hinke, A New Boundary Stone of Nebuchadrezzar I from Nippur, p. 88, fig. 25. 160

28b. Sargon and an Officer Standing in Front of a God Wearing the Peculiar High Headdress. The Four Pairs of Horns Can Be Seen in Side view. After James B. Pritchard, ed., ANEP, p. 199, fig. 609. 160

29. Various Types of Hittite Cone-formed Headdresses--All with the Upward Bent Horn in the Front. After Kurt Bittel, Rudolf Naumann, and Otto Heinz, Yazilikaya Architektur, Felsbilder, Inschriften und Kleinfunde, p. 105, fig. 31. 163

30. A Relief Showing a Cone-formed Cap with Six Horns in Profile. Hittite Rock Relief from Yazilikaya. After Bittel, Naumann, and Heinz, Yazilikaya Architektur, Felsbilder, Inscriften und Kleinfunde, p. 87, fig. 29. 165

31. An Attacking Bull Depicted in Bold Relief from Hüyük. After Bittel, Naumann, and Heinz, Yazilikaya Architektur, Felsbilder, Inschriften und Kleinfunde, p. 160, fig. 65. 165

32. The Seated Figure Has Traditionally Been Interpreted as the Old Canaanite God El. A Stela from Ugarit. From the Latter Part of the 13th Century, B.C. After Kurt Galling, BRL, p. 100, fig. 30. 167

33. Baʿal, the Young Storm-god from Ugarit, Wearing a "Horned" Headdress. After Hans-Fredrich Weiss, Baʿal," BHH, 1:175 167

34. Tešub, the Hittite Storm-god, Depicted with a Pointed Headdress Decorated with Two Horns--Like the Horns of a Gazelle--in the Front of His Helmet. After Heinrich Otten, "Teschup," BHH, 3:1954. 171

35. The Apis Bull Wearing a Sun-disk between His Horns. After ANEP, p. 190, fig. 570. 180

36. The Goddess Hathor in the Form of a Cow and Wearing
    a Sun-disk between her Horns. A Sandstone Statue
    from Deir el-Bahri. After <u>ANEP</u>, p. 136, fig. 389. . .   183

37. The Sun-god Seated between the Horns of the Great
    <u>jht</u> (= <u>Ahet</u>) Cow. After Malten, "Der Stier in Kult
    und Mythischem Bild," p. 95, fig. 7.   184

38. The Sun-god Holding the Horn while Riding on the
    Ahet Cow (Fayûmpapyrus). After Malten, "Der Stier
    in Kult und mythischem Bild," p. 96, fig. 8.   184

39. Dancing Gods. The Figure to the Left Probably
    Depicts a Bull-god, Whereas the One to the Right May
    Represent the Cow-goddess Hathor. A Rude Drawing on
    a Pithos from Kuntillet Ajrud. After Ze'ev Meshel,
    "Did Yahweh Have a Consort?" <u>BARev</u> 5 (1979):35. . . .   188

40. The Cow and Suckling Calf-motif Depicted at Kuntillet
    Ajrud--a Well-known Motif in the Syro-Phoenician
    World of the 9th Century B.C. After Ze'ev Meshel,
    "Did Yahweh Have a Consort?" <u>BARev</u> 5 (1979):61. . . .   190

41. A Cow Tenderly Nursing Her Calf. A Furniture Inlay
    Carved in Ivory from Arslan Taş, Syria, ca. 900-700
    B.C. After Norma Kershaw, "The Bible Comes to Life
    at the Jewish Museum," <u>BARev</u> 3 (1977):45   190

42. A Cow and Suckling Calf-motif. Ivory Carving Dis-
    covered at Nimrud (Ancient Kallah) in Northern Syria
    in the Palace of the Assyrian King Shalmaneser III
    (859-824 B.C.). After Ze'ev Meshel, "Did Yahweh
    Have a Consort?" <u>BARev</u> 5 (1979):61.   191

43. The Nude Figures May Represent Priests. Early Seal
    from the Uruk Period. After Frankfort, <u>Cylinder Seals</u>,
    pl. III, d.   195

44. (Upper Part) A Ritual Motif Depicting Two Naked Priests
    in Front of Their Gods. The "horned" Headdress,
    Symbolizing Divinity, Is Clearly Noticeable. Engraved
    Limestone Tablet. (Lower Part) Ordinary Citizens
    Bringing Their Sacrifice. After Carl Bezold, <u>Ninive
    und Babylon</u>, p. 33.   196

45. A Ritual Motif with a Single Ministering Priest in
    Front of His God. Limestone Tablet from Nippur.
    After Bezold, <u>Ninive und Babylon</u>, p. 33.   197

46. A Deity Holding Gudea by the Hand and Introducing Him
    to the High God. All Three Deities are Depicted as
    Wearing Headdresses with Horns. After Meissner,
    "Grundzüge der altbabylonischen Plastik," <u>Der alte
    Orient</u>, 15:42, fig. 68.   199

47. Gudea, Ensi from Lagaš, Wearing a Plain, Round Cap without Horns. After ANEP, p. 150, fig. 430. 199

48. Ur-Ningirsu, Son of Gudea, Depicted with a Cap Similar to That of His Father. After ANEP, p. 151, fig. 434. 200

49. The Well-known Hammurabi Wearing a Round Cap without Horns. After ANEP, p. 151, fig. 437. 200

50. Deity, King and Priest Equipped with Tools in Attempt to Lay the Foundation Stone for a Temple. A Part of a Frieze in the Relief Stela of Urnammu from Ur. After Alfred Jeremias, Handbuch der altorientalischen Geisteskultur, p. 73, fig. 63. 201

51. The Headdress of the God (?), Sitting on the Throne, Is Plain, Round and Simple Compared to the Two Female Figures Wearing "Horned" Headdresses. The Worshiper Is Shaven. After Bezold, Ninive und Babylon, p. 16. . 207

52. A Goddess, with a "Horned" Headdress, Leading a Worshiper to an Enthroned King. A Cylinder Seal from the Ur III Period. After ANEP, p. 222, fig. 701. 208

53. The Moon-God Nanna, with a Headdress Decorated with Four Pairs of Horns, Sits Enthroned While Ur-Nammu of Ur (2000-1955 B.C.) Offers Libation to a Tree Which Symbolizes This Particular God. After Keel, The Symbolism of the Biblical World, p. 136. 208

54. A Kudurru of Marduk-apal-iddina II Showing the Presence of the Gods Depicted through Symbols. After Hinke, A New Boundary Stone of Nebuchadrezzar I from Nippur (cf. 28a), p. 72, fig. 20. 214

55. The Many Layers of Horns on the Headdresses, Placed on the Miniature Shrines, Represent Probable High Gods. A Stone Tablet of King Nabû-apal-iddina from the Early 10th Century B.C. After Hinke, A New Boundary Stone of Nebuchadrezzar I from Nippur, p. 23, fig. 9. 215

56. Sargon II, Depicted on a Limestone Sculpture, with a Miter-like Headdress without Horns. After Hinke, A New Boundary Stone of Nebuchadrezzar I from Nippur, p. 23, fig. 9. 216

57. Two Winged Men (Priests?) Kneeling on Both Sides of the Holy Tree. The Headdresses Are Decorated with Horns. After Bezold, Ninive und Babylon, p. 118, fig. 110. 217

58. A Winged Man (Priest)? with a Bird-mask? (or a Protective Genius) Touching King Aššurnassirpal II (Not Depicted Here). After ANEP, p. 202, fig. 617.   218

59. The "Priest-Prince," Seated on His Throne, Is Depicted with a Low, Round Cap. Behind the Seated Ruler Is Shown a Figure with Upward-pointed Lateral Horns. After Carney S. Gavin, The Glyptic Art of Syria-Palestine, p. 138.   222

60. Tuthalija IV, the Son of Hattušili III, Has Himself Depicted as a God by Wearing the Emblem of the Gods-- a Cap with Horns. He is Shown to the Extreme Left on a Seal from Ras Shamra, ca. 1250-1220 B.C. After Claude F.-A. Schaeffer, Ug. III, p. 21, fig. 26.   230

61. Priests, Dressed in Animal Masks, with Horns, Making Sacrifices. From a Haematite Cylinder Seal Found at Ras Shamra. After Claude F.-A. Schaeffer, The Cuneiform Texts of Ras Shamra-Ugarit, pl. 10, fig. 2.   232

62. The Ibexes (Wild Goats) with Accentuated Horns Seem to Carry a Symbolic Design. Relief-work on a Door-post at the Temple of ʿAttar dū-Qabd at Qarnāwu (South Arabia). After Hartmut Gese, Maria Höfner and Kurt Rudolph, Die Religionen Altsyriens, Altarabiens und der Mandäer, p. 311, fig. 9.   243

63. The Upper Part of a Fragmentary Plate Palette Outlined by a Bull, Aggressively Attacking a Man. After Keel, The Symbolism of the Biblical World, p. 87, fig. 105.   245

64. Bullheads with Horns Depicted on the Upper Part of the Famous Narmer Slate Palette. After ANEP, p. 93, fig. 297.   246

65. Narmer, the First King of the United Kingdom of Egypt, Depicted under the Symbol of an Aggressive Bull Trampling upon His Enemy and Breaking through the Wall of a City with His Horns. From a Slate Palette from Hierankopolis. After ANEP, p. 93, fig. 297. . .   246

66. Bronze Figure of Apis, the Bull-god from Memphis, Depicted with a Disk between His Horns--(Sacred to the Moon According to Older Sources). After J. Gardner Wilkinson, The Manners and Customs of the Ancient Egyptians, 3:88, fig. 520.   251

xiii

67. (a) The White Crown of Upper Egypt; (b) the Red Crown of Lower Egypt; (c) the Double Crown of the United Kingdom. After Adolf Erman, Life in Ancient Egypt, p. 60. 252

68. The Royal Helmet (Kheperesh). After Erman, Life in Ancient Egypt, p. 62. 252

69. The Young King Tuet-ʿAnch-Amun, of the 18th Dynasty, Seated on His Throne, Wearing the Royal Helmet, Gives Audience to the Governor of Ethiopia. After Erman, Life in Ancient Egypt, p. 63. 253

70. This Kind of Peculiar Headdress (without Horns) Was Worn by Kings and Queens Alike. Queen Hat-shepsut, from Deir el-Bahri. After ANEP, p. 136, fig. 388. . . 254

71. (a) The Ram-headed God, with the Horns of Khnûm Standing Out at the Sides, and with the Horns of Amen Curling around the Ears, Shows a Fusion of Two Originally Distinct Gods. (b) The twisted, Lateral Horns are Typical of Khnûm, the Ram-headed God Amen at Thebes. The Cult Penetrated to the Oasis of Jupiter Ammôn about the Beginning of the New Kingdom. After J. Gardner Wilkinson, The Manners and Customs of the Ancient Egyptians, 3:3, pl. 18 (#1). . 255

72. Alexander the Great Was Hailed as the Son of Zeus Ammon, Assuming to Himself the "Incurvated" Horns of the God of Thebes (Coinage). After John W. McCrindle, The Invasion of India by Alexander the Great, p. 48, fig. 4. 256

73. Hathor, the Mistress of Merriment and Dance, and the Goddess of Love; When Depicted as a Woman She is Wearing on Her Head a Pair of Horns within Which Rests the Solar-disk. After Anthony S. Mercatante, Who's Who in Egyptian Mythology, p. 54. 257

74. Hathor, the Goddess of Love, Depicted under the Symbol of a Cow and with the Sun-disk Enclosed between the Horns. After George Hoyningen-Huene, Egypt, p. 107. 257

75. The Horn-motif Emphasized on a Small Artifact from the Grave of Rech-me-reʿ. From the Time of Thutmose III and Amenophis II. (Figs. 75-85, After Kurt Sethe, Untersuchungen zur Geschichte und Altertumskunde Aegyptens, 4:16, fig. 31; 4:31, figs. 71, 72; 4:32, fig. 75; 4:35, figs. 86, 88; 4:36, figs. 93, 96; 4:37, figs. 100, 101; 4:5, fig. 2. 257

76. The Horn-motif from the Grave of Zen. From the
    Time of Thutmosis IV. 258

77. The Horn-motif from the Grave of I-me-sib. From
    the Time of Ramses IV. 258

78. The Horn-motif from a Relief. From the Time of
    Thutmosis III (Karnak). 258

79. The Horn-motif from the Grave of Har-em-hab. From
    the Time of Thutmosis IV. 258

80. The Horn-motif from the Grave of Mer-i-reʿ. From
    the Time of Amenophis IV. 259

81. The Horn-motif on a War Booty. From the Time of
    Sethos I (Karnak). 259

82. The Horn-motif on a Bronze Basin with Cover. From
    Etrurien. 259

83. The Horn-motif on a War Booty. From the Time of
    Sethos I (Karnak). 259

84. The Horn-motif on a War Booty. From the Time of
    Ramses II (Karnak). 260

85. The Horn-motif, Probably from the Grave of
    Rech-me-reʿ. From the Time of Thutmosis III and
    Amenophis II. 260

86. Soldiers of the Allied Sea Peoples Wearing Horn-
    topped Helmets, or Feather-topped Helmets. Re-
    constructed Relief from Medinet Habu (from the 20th
    Century). After Yadin, The Art of Warfare
    in Biblical Lands, 2:250. 262

87. Bronze Helmet Found at Zenjirli--Probably from the
    Early Assyrian Period. After Felix.von.Luschan,
    Die Kleinfunde von Sendschirli, p. 75, fig. 83. . . 265

88. Bronze Helmet Found at Zenjirli--Probably from the
    Early Assyrian Period. After von Luschan, Die
    Kleinfunde von Sendschirli, p. 75, fig. 84. 265

89. Warriors Engaged in an Attack on a City, Wearing
    Crest-helmets. From the Time of Sargon II (721-
    705 B.C.). After Yadin, The Art of Warfare, 2:422. . 266

90. A Single Warrior Depicted with a Crest-helmet. After
    Yadin, The Art of Warfare, 2:423. 267

91. A Peaked Cap with a Pair of Horns is Depicted in the Row of Symbols. From the Kilamu Orthostat. After Yigael Yadin, "Symbols of Deities at Zinjirli, Carthage and Hazor," p. 201, fig. 1. 268

92. The Horned Cap on the Bar-Rakkab Orthostat at Zinjirli. After Yadin, "Symbols of Deities at Zinjirli, Carthage and Hazor," p. 206, fig. 4. 269

93. The Horned Cap Symbol Depicted on the Ördek-burnu Monument. After Yadin, "Symbols of Deities at Zinjirli, Carthage and Hazor," p. 210, fig. 7. . . 270

94. The Horned Cap and the Janiform Head was the Particular Symbol of Baal-Semed. (The "Horned" Cap Alone Depicted Baal in General.) After Yadin, "Symbols of Deities at Zinjirli, Carthage and Hazor," p. 215, fig. 10. 270

95. The Ahaz-Ezekiel Altar as It Has Been Conjectured. After Keel, The Symbolism of the Biblical World, p. 145, fig. 194. 274

96. Two Bull-heads with Horns Are Supposed to Have Decorated the Last Stage of This Depicted (Reconstructed) Temple-tower. From an Assyrian Bas Relief. . After George Smith, The Chaldean Account of Genesis, p. 169. 275

97. A Variety of Horned Altars from Syria and Palestine:
    a-i: The Square-cornered Altars (Type I) 279
    j-q: The Pinnacle-like Edge on the Square Altar (Type II) 279-80
    r-s: A Bull-head Depicted in Relief on These Two Altars, of Which -r- Represents the Square Type, Whereas -s- Represents the Round Pillar Type of Altar (Type III). 280
    t: A Bull-head Depicted on a Square Altar. 280
    After Kurt Galling, Der Altar in den Kulturen des Alten Orients, pls. 17-36.

98. Horned Incense Altar from Megiddo. After ANEP, p. 192, fig. 575. 281

99. A Limestone Altar with Its Knobs or Horns Broken Off. From Gezer ca. 600 B.C. After Hugo Gressmann, AOB vol. 2, pl. 177, fig. 444. 282

100. A Horned Altar from Beer-sheba with a Snake Engraved on One of Its Corner Stones. From the 8th Century B.C. After Hershel Shanks, "Yigael Yadin Finds a Bama at Beer-sheva," BARev 3 (1977):10. 283

xvi

101. Sabaean Altar with the Crescent-motif. (Figs. 101-107 after Adolf Grohmann, Göttersymbole und Symboltiere auf Südarabischen Denkmälern, pp. 38-39, figs. 83-87.). 287

102. Sabāean Altar with the Crescent-motif. 287

103. Sabaean Inscription from Domâr with the Crescent-motif. 288

104. Sabaean Relief from Domâr with the Crescent-motif. . . 288

105. Sabaean Altar from Mârib with the Crescent-motif. . . 288

106. Sabaean Altar with the Crescent-motif. 288

107. Sabaean Altar from Girʾân with the Crescent-motif. . 289

108. Sabaean Altar with the Horns of a Symbolic Animal Strongly Emphasized. After Grohmann, Göttersymbole und Symboltiere auf Südarabischen Denkmälern, p. 62, fig. 166. 290

109. A Small Mussel Table from Tello, ca. 3800 B.C. After Grohmann, Göttersymbole und Symboltiere auf Südarabischen Denkmälern, p. 57, fig. 144. 291

110. Crowns of Various Dynasties in Ancient Times. After Boehmer, "Hörnerkrone," RLA, 4:432. 293

111. Occurrences of קרן in Biblical Aramaic Compared with Some Other Ancient Translations 464

112. Occurrences of קרן in Biblical Hebrew Compared with Some Other Ancient Translations 466

113. Structural Forms of קרן in Biblical Hebrew 471

xvii

LIST OF ABBREVIATIONS

AAA	--	Annals of Archaeology and Anthropology
AASOR	--	Annual of the American School of Oriental Research
AB	--	Anchor Bible
AfO	--	Archiv für Orientforschung
AfOSupp	--	Archiv für Orientforschung: Supplement
AHW	--	Soden, Wolfram von. Akkadisches Handwörterbuch. 2 vols. Wiesbaden: Otto Harrassowitz, 1965-72.
AJSL	--	The American Journal of Semitic Languages and Literature
AJT	--	American Journal of Theology
AnOr	--	Analecta Orientalia
ANEP	--	Pritchard, James B., ed. Ancient Near Eastern Pictures. Princeton, NJ: Princeton University Press, 1954.
ANET	--	Pritchard, James B., ed. Ancient Near Eastern Texts Relating to the Old Testament. 3d ed. Princeton, NJ: Princeton University Press, 1969.
AnSt	--	Anatolian Studies
AOAT	--	Alter Orient und Altes Testament
AOB	--	Altorientalische Bilder zum Alten Testament
APOT	--	Charles, Robert H., ed. The Apocrypha and Pseudepigrapha of the Old Testament. Oxford: At the Clarendon Press, 1913.
ARI	--	Albright, William F. Archaeology and the Religion of Israel. Baltimore: Johns Hopkins Press, 1942.
ARM	--	Archives royales de Mari

ArOr	--	Archiv Orientální
ARW	--	Archiv für Religionswissenschaft
ATD	--	Das Alte Testament Deutsch
BA	--	Biblical Archeologist
BARev	--	Biblical Archaeology Review
BASOR	--	Bulletin of the American School of Oriental Research
BHH	--	Reicke, Bo, and Rost, Leonhard, eds. Biblisch-historisches Handwörterbuch. 3 vols. Göttingen: Vandenhoeck & Ruprecht, 1962-64.
BHS	--	Biblia Hebraica Stuttgartensia. Edited by K. Elliger, and W. Rudolph. Stuttgart: Württembergische Bibelanstalt, 1967-77.
Bib	--	Biblica
BKAT	--	Biblischer Kommentar Altes Testament
BRL	--	Biblisches Reallexikon
CAD	--	Assyrian Dictionary of the Oriental Institute of the University of Chicago. Edited by Miguel Civil, Ignace J. Gelb, A. Leo Oppenheim and Erica Reiner. Chicago: Oriental Institute, 1956-.
CAH	--	Cambridge Ancient History
CANES	--	Corpus of Ancient Near Eastern Seals in North American Collections. Washington, D.C.: Pantheon Books, 1948.
Cat. cyl. or.	--	Delaporte, Louis J. Catalogue des cylindres orientaux.
CBQ	--	Catholic Biblical Quarterly
CIS	--	Corpus Inscriptionum Semiticarum
CTA	--	Corpus des tablettes en cunéiformes alphabétiques
DAI	--	Dissertation Abstracts International. Ann Arbor: Xerox University Microfilms.
DISO	--	Jean, Charles-F. and Hoftijzer, Jacob. Dictionnaire des inscriptions sémitiques de l'ouest. Leiden: E. J. Brill, 1965.

DJD	--	Baillet, M., Milik, J. T., and R. de Vaux, eds. *Discoveries in the Judaean Desert of Jordan*. Oxford: At the Clarendon Press.
EncJud	--	*Encyclopedia Judaica*. Jerusalem: Keter Publishing House, 1971.
FZPhTh	--	*Freiburger Zeitschrift für Philosophie und Theologie*
HAT	--	Handbuch zum Alten Testament
Hex	--	Field, Fridericus, ed. *Origenis Hexapla*. Hildesheim: Georg Olm, 1964.
HKAT	--	Handkommentar zum Alten Testament
HTR	--	*Harvard Theological Review*
HUCA	--	*Hebrew Union College Annual*
HWB	--	Delitzsch, Friedrich. *Assyriches Handwörterbuch*. Leipzig: J. C. Hinrichs, 1975.
IB	--	*Interpreter's Bible*
ICC	--	International Critical Commentary
IDB	--	*Interpreter's Dictionary of the Bible*. Edited by George A. Buttrick. 4 vols. Nashville: Abingdon Press, 1976.
IDBSupp	--	*Interpreter's Dictionary of the Bible: Supplementary Volume*. Edited by Keith Crim. Nashville: Abingdon Press, 1976.
JAOS	--	*Journal of the American Oriental Society*
JBL	--	*Journal of Biblical Literature*
JCS	--	*Journal of Cuneiform Studies*
JEA	--	*Journal of Egyptian Archaeology*
JNES	--	*Journal of Near Eastern Studies*
JST	--	*Journal of Semitic Studies*
KAI	--	Donner, Herbert, and Röllig, Wolfgang. *Kanaanäische und aramäische Inschriften*. 3 vols. Wiesbaden: Harrassowitz, 1966.

KAR	--	Keilschriftexte aus Assur religiösen Inhalts
KAT	--	Kommentar zum Alten Testament
KB	--	Keilinschriftliche Bibliothek
LKA	--	Ebeling, Erich, ed. Keilschrifttexte aus Assur. Berlin: Akademic Verlag, 1953.
LXX	--	Septuaginta
MT	--	Masoretic Text
MVAG	--	Mitteilungen der vorder-asiatisch-ägyptischen Gesellschaft
NBD	--	Douglas, J. D., ed. The New Bible Dictionary. Grand Rapids: Wm. B. Eerdmans, 1962.
NCB	--	New Century Bible
NCE	--	New Catholic Encyclopedia
NIV	--	New International Version of the Holy Bible
NSI	--	Cooke, George A. A Textbook of North-Semitic Inscriptions. Oxford: Clarendon Press, 1903.
NTT	--	Norsk Teologisk Tidskrift
Or	--	Orientalia
OrSuec	--	Orientalia Suecana
OT	--	Old Testament
OTL	--	Old Testament Library
PRU	--	Le Palais royal d'Ugarit
RA	--	Revue d'Assyriologie et d'Archéologie Orientale
RB	--	Revue biblique
RGG	--	Die Religion in Geschichte und Gegenwart
RHA	--	Revue hittite et asianique
RLA	--	Reallexikon der Assyriology
RLV	--	Reallexikon der Vorgeschichte
RSV	--	Revised Standard Version

S²	--	Codex Sinaiticus (2d correction).
SBP	--	Langdon, Stephen. *Sumerian and Babylonian Psalms*
SL	--	Deimel, Anton, ed. *Šumerisches Lexikon*
Sym	--	Symmachus
Syr	--	Lagarde, Paulo, de. *Bibliothecae Syriacae*. Göttingen: Luederi Horstmann, 1892.
TDNT	--	*Theological Dictionary of the New Testament*. Edited by Gerhard Kittel. Translated by Geoffrey W. Bromiley. Grand Rapids: Wm. B. Eerdman, 1964-77.
TH	--	Sjöberg, Åke. *The Collection of the Sumerian Temple Hymns*. Locust Valley, NY: J. J. Augustin, 1969.
THAT	--	*Theologisches Handwörterbuch zum Alten Testament*. Edited by Ernst Jenni and Claus Westermann. Munich: Kaiser, 1971.
Theod	--	Theodotion
ThR	--	Theologische Rundschau
TZ	--	Theologische Zeitschrift
UF	--	Ugarit-Forschungen
Ug	--	Ugaritica
UL	--	Gordon, Cyrus H. *Ugaritic Textbook*. Rome: Pontificium Institutum Biblicum, 1949.
UMBS	--	University Museum Babylonian Section
UT	--	Gordon, Cyrus H. *Ugaritic Literature*. Rome: Pontifical Biblical Institut, 1965.
VT	--	Vetus Testamentum
VTSupp	--	Vetus Testamentum, Supplements
WZKM	--	Wiener Zeitschrift für die Kunde des Morgenlandes
ZA	--	Zeitschrift für Assyriologie
ZAW	--	Zeitschrift für die alttestamentliche Wissenschaft

ZDMG -- Zeitschrift der deutschen morgenländischen Gesellschaft

ZDPV -- Zeitschrift des deutschen Palästina-Vereins

ZKT -- Zeitschrift für katholische Theologie

ACKNOWLEDGEMENTS

As the finishing touch is placed on my dissertation I feel greatly indebted to a number of people. I am particularly grateful to Dr. Gerhard G. Hasel for suggesting this fascinating topic for my dissertation and for his help and valuable suggestions in the process of investigation. His willingness to sacrifice his precious time in careful supervision of my research and in criticizing my outline and writing was much appreciated and a great source of encouragement. Thanks go to him also for sharing his views in some of the areas related to my topic, which will be available for the public in his forthcoming publications.

To Drs. William H. Shea and William G. Johnsson, members of my committee, I also present my thanks: to Dr. William Shea for his helpful hints, especially in the field of iconography, and for his readiness to share some of his views from forthcoming publications; and to Dr. William Johnsson, who read the entire manuscript and offered valuable criticism. My thanks go to Dr. Thomas H. Blincoe, Dean of Andrews Theological Seminary, for his interest in my research and for his initiative in working out a plan for securing financial support; and to Andrews University for tuition scholarships. I also express my gratitude to the committee of Th.D. Scholarships of the General Conference of Seventh-day Adventists for their willingness to secure financial support throughout my stay at the University.

To Dr. Leona G. Running a special thanks for her initiating and specific interest, in the first place, to make it possible for me to take up and pursue my theological training at this particular Seminary. With her financial and moral support my dream came true!

I am very much indebted to all the members of the faculty and the Seminary student body for their friendship and cheerful encouragement all along the way.

As the James White Library has been the anvil where my dissertation was forged into shape, I want to express my thanks to the staff of the library in its various departments.

To Aune Ainsalo goes the credit for the illustrative drawings, and to Mrs. Meeri Virtanen a special thanks for her faithfulness and willingness to spend many late hours arranging the iconographic material, for editing assistance and checking footnotes and bibliography. Also to Jim Brower, who copied the cuneiform signs into the final copy, I express my thanks. To Joyce Campbell and Catherine Cash, who willingly overworked typing the final copy, I express my sincere thanks. There are many, many others I am indebted to, whose names I cannot mention, but I express my thanks at this hour and say, you all helped to make my dream come true--and therefore my thanks to all of you. Thanks be to God!

INTRODUCTION

Posing the Problem

What is the meaning of the word "horn" in the Bible? Beginning with the present century an increasing number of scholars have attempted a variety of answers. But in spite of all the suggestions regarding the horn-motif in all its complexity major issues remain unresolved. Does the "horn" refer to animals, to "wings" or perhaps to the "rays of the sun"? What is known of the origin of horn(s)? Do they originate from maṣṣēbôt ("standing stones") or from bull-horns? What is the relationship of the "horns" of the altar and the ancient ziggurats? Are the "horns" and the masweh ("mask" or "veil") of Moses connected with the ancient tradition of ritualistic performance of the oracle-priest in the Near Eastern context? Does the metaphorical usage of the term "horn" indicate the strength and fertility of the bull? Are the various expressions "safety," "victory," "exaltation," "pride," "branch," "lamp," or some other unexpressed concept to be considered as synonyms of the term "horn"? Are the singular, dual, and plural forms of the same term to be used interchangeably, always expressing the same import, or does each form carry a basic connotation that will advance the interpretation of the word "horn" along certain guidelines?

These are certainly valid and appropriate questions when we consider that the term "horn" and its motif have been touched upon nearly one hundred times in the Bible. The Bible is full of symbols and motifs expressing both general and particular ideas or truths, but when a symbol or motif is not adequately understood, the idea or truth it presents may be lost. The horn-motif is but one of the many motifs that need investigation in various contexts in Scripture.

The non-biblical sources plead urgently for the same elucidation of the horn-motif in its symbolic quality. What is the relationship between the word "horn" and the crescent of the moon? The reference to the recurrent moon-sickle is found in all Semitic cognates and in other ancient languages of the Near East. Are the words "arm," "wing," "rebel," "warrior," or other terms synonyms of the word "horn"? The options are many but there is no comprehensive work to synthesize available evidences.

To this day no compendium is obtainable of the various horn-motifs in the Bible, nor is there any comprehensive study elucidating that same motif in ancient literature and iconography. No consensus has emerged in prior fragmentary studies as to the meaning, origin and function of "horns" in ancient Near Eastern cultures, and even less so in ancient Israel. The need for a more thorough investigation of the horn-motif in its various shades of meaning (and especially in its extended meaning) is long overdue. This fact alone is a sufficient reason to justify this study.

Aim and Methodology

The current interest in ancient Near Eastern backgrounds for biblical studies necessitates a more careful assessment of the term "horn" and its various associations. We will in this study attempt to investigate the term "horn" in the Hebrew Bible in order to elucidate its meaning in the variety of contexts where it appears. This involves a careful philological and contextual study of the word "horn" in its various literal, literal-extended, and purely extended semantic ranges and meanings. Attention will be given to the external form of the word "horn," depending on number and gender in its immediate and larger contexts. This aspect is expected to supply an added guideline that could be helpful in determining the original meaning of the term "horn."

The main procedure in our approach of investigating the "horn" and its "motif" has therefore to begin with a review of literature indicating what selective issues of the horn-motif have been discussed in this century. This will be our concern in chapter one. The next step will be an attempt at a philological study with the word "horn" in the focal point. We have chosen to begin the second chapter by examining the usage and meaning of "horn" in the ancient Sumerian language and then to proceed with the ancient Semitic cognate languages. The third chapter will be devoted to obtaining evidence from ancient Near Eastern literature of how the word "horn" was used in ancient times and to substantiate in part the literary usage with illustrative iconographic material. In the fourth and last chapter the unique Hebrew Bible with its nearly one hundred examples of the usage of "horn" will be searched in order to get a fair view of the biblical connotations of "horn" in various contexts. A summary and conclusion chapter in which we hope to reassess the meaning of the horn-motif in the ancient

Near Eastern world, and especially in biblical contexts, will round
off the study of the horn-motif.

Limitations

This investigation does not claim to exhaust the abundance
of non-biblical material. Ancient Near Eastern literature and
iconography rather have been utilized with the basic principle of
selectivity in mind. Typical samples from various contexts, on a
comparative basis, will elucidate the usage of the term "horn" both
in the Near Eastern and in Israelite culture. It is hoped that
these examples, as well as the biblical text itself, will contribute
to the understanding of the word "horn" in the Bible, Israelite
literature sui generis.

It should also be pointed out that although an all-inclusive
view of the Old Testament passages with reference to the term "horn"
has been aimed at, not every passage has been explored to its limits,
by any means. However, it is hoped that this investigation will
stimulate further studies along the line followed in this dissertation
with the purpose of disclosing ancient motifs and hidden symbols.

CHAPTER I

REVIEW OF LITERATURE

In this chapter we will briefly explore the understanding of the horn-motif as it has been brought to the forefront by scholars since about the turn of the century. The starting point marks the apex of the "history-of-religion" school as well as of Pan-Babylonianism. These schools have had a clear-cut influence not only at the cultural--but also at the religious--level, a fact which is strongly reflected in literature pertaining to these areas.

This review does not deal with commentaries generally, because these will be more extensively consulted in chapter four. The review is intended chiefly to give a view of the trend of scholarship today with reference to the horn-motif which is of interest in this dissertation.

A new note was struck by the pioneers in form criticism, Hermann Gunkel and Hugo Gressmann, and it became the keynote for succeeding scholars with a continuous stream of sophisticated literary analyses in various genres of biblical texts.[1] This has had its influence upon the study of the horn-motif.

The aim has certainly been to clarify obscure passages where obsolete and enigmatic expressions present a crux in the context.

---

[1] Robert R. Wilson, "Prophecy and Ecstasy: A Reexamination," JBL 98 (1979):321.

The word קרן in its various contexts challenged scholars to assess
its meaning but the result was often more confusing than convincing.

William E. Addis, for instance, at the threshold of our
century expressed his view concerning the altar and its horns in
the following words:

> At the four corners on the top were four projections called
> "horns." Possibly they represent, as [Bernhard] Stade has
> suggested, the beginning of an attempt to carve the altar stone
> into the form of an ox, which symbolized the power of Yahweh.[1]

Such was the general outset of belief and working hypothesis
of scholars who articulated their views. With this view from the
previous century we will briefly note the various major interpretations in our present century. Only a few "highpoints" will be
pointed out from the trend of scholarship that they may be viewed
in regard to the concept of "horn" and its meaning.

Horns on Altars

Hugo Gressmann in 1908 wrote an account entitled Die
Ausgrabungen in Palästina und das Alte Testament.[2] Considering the
origin of altars, Gressmann takes the view that these were nonexistent
at first because Napflöcher and later the maṣṣēbôt ("sacred pillars"
or "standing stones") were used as altars. This he proves by saying
that when the altar and maṣṣēbâ began to separate as two distinct

---

[1] "Altar," Encyclopaedia Biblica (London: Adam and Charles
Black, 1899), 1:124. Addis also refers to William Robertson Smith,
who regards the 'horns of the altar' as a modern substitute for the
actual horns of sacrificial victims, such as the heads of oxen which
are common symbols on Greek altars (Religion of the Semites, p. 436)
as quoted by Addis (n. 2).

[2] Tübingen: Verlag von J. C. B. Mohr [Paul Siebeck], 1908).

objects, they still remained closely connected with each other in that the maṣṣēbâ was placed either <u>on</u> the altar or <u>behind</u> it. And so Gressmann comes to the conclusion that Johann G. Eichhorn was right in saying that the horns were only vestiges originating from the maṣṣēbôt which were originally placed on the altar.[1] This statement seemed supported by the archaeological finds at that time,[2] which do not show any real horns but, to the contrary, show knobs on the four corners of the altar; these could be depicted just as well by the Hebrews as "mountains" instead of horns.[3] According to Gressmann, then, there is a development in Israelite religion, from primitive to more advanced, comparable to neighboring religions.[4]

Isidore Scheftelowitz in 1912 wrote a very detailed article on horns.[5] As for the horns of the altar, Scheftelowitz takes the view that they were the symbol of holiness. In many cultures the

---

[1] Eichhorn's oral statement to Gressmann; see the latter's Die Ausgrabungen, p. 28. This view was later expressed in standard works. So Gressmann "Altar," in RGG³ (Tübingen: J. C. B. Mohr [Paul Siebeck], 1909), 1:373; Kurt Galling, "Altar II In Israel," RGG³ (Tübingen: J. C. B. Mohr [Paul Siebeck], 1957), 1:254. Idem, Der Altar in den Kulturen des alten Orients (Berlin: Karl Curtis Verlag, 1925), p. 59; idem, "Altar," IDB (New York: Abingdon Press, 1962), 1:97.

[2] Gressmann is referring especially to the altar found at Gezer; see R. A. Stewart Macalister, The Excavation of Gezer 1902-05 and 1907-09 (London: John Murray, 1912), 2:424.

[3] Gressmann, Die Ausgrabungen, p. 28.

[4] According to Gerhard F. Hasel, one of the distinctive features of the History-of-religion school is to consider "evolution as the magic key to unlock all the secrets of history" (Old Testament Theology, p. 29)--a concept which is clearly reflected in Gressmann's view and in others of the same opinion.

[5] Isidore Scheftelowitz, "Das Hörnermotiv in den Religion," ARW 15 (1912):451-87.

altar of sacrifice was adorned with literal horns--bull's or ram's horns. This decoration was the recognizable sign that the altar was the appointed food table for the gods.[1] Also the Israelites had an altar with four horns on which the blood of the sacrifice was smeared (gestrichen). The horns, therefore, were the most holy place of the altar. Scheftelowitz then goes on to mention the ornaments of the altars in other cultures and in a footnote says that Bernard Stade, in speaking about the history of Israel, puts together the horns of the altar and the godhead in the form of a bull.[2] Scheftelowitz considers that the horns of the gods, shrines, and altars constantly signify the horns of an animal (a bull or ram or the like) and that they are symbols of strength and force.[3]

Andreas Eberharter in 1927 took up the question of horns not so much from the external point of view but rather from an internal viewpoint. In other words he is concerned with the role of the horns in the ritual of the OT and in religious thought. With him the meaning of the symbol of horns is emphasized. Consequently Eberharter links the horns to the theological question of atonement, which he discusses on the basis of the texts from the Pentateuch. And so he raises the important question: How did the Hebrews come to the point

---

[1] Throughout the years there has been noticeable disagreement among scholars in regard to "the table," "the altar," "the maṣṣēbôt," and "the horns." Often imprecise definitions or disregard of their function have caused confusion. Martin Noth (Exodus A Commentary [Philadelphia: The Westminster Press, 1962], p. 215), however, made a clear distinction between "the table" and "the altar."

[2] Scheftelowitz, p. 473, n. 3.

[3] Scheftelowitz, "Das Hörnermotiv in Religionen," p. 466.

of ascribing such a meaning [as of the atonement] to the horns?[1]
The next concern, according to Eberharter, is to find whether there
is a basis in the Scripture for this custom. Eberharter concludes
that the altar is mentioned in the oldest documents of the Old
Testament. But not until Exod 20:24-26 is there any specific rule
as to how the altar should be built. It is clearly stated that it
should be built of earth or, in case it were built of stones, un-
hewn stones should be used. And so, according to Eberharter, where-
ever in the priestly code the erection of the altar is mentioned, it
appears as no striking, unusual innovation that the corners of the
altar should have horn projections.[2] Eberharter further points out
that the altar with horn projections meets us in the ancient Near
Eastern context already in vague antiquity. From there, he says,
it was no doubt adopted into the Hellenistic and Roman world.[3] But
this does not answer the question: Whence did the Hebrews take over
this tradition? Did the Hebrews take over the horn projections from
another culture or did they originate from their ancestors? Eberharter notes that there seems to be no unity among scholars on this
point. Furthermore there seems to be uncertainty on the part of the
few who have attempted an explanation.

It seems that Eberharter is trying to say that the horns on
the altar are but a natural outcome of a religious conception. Because

---

[1] Eberharter, "Das Horn im Kult des Alten Testamentes,"
ZKT 51 (1927):395.

[2] See Eberharter's discussion (ibid., p. 396).

[3] Ibid.

God is strong and powerful (as a bull or a wild ox) it is but natural to apply the horns, which naturally were the symbol of power and strength, to the altar which symbolized God in general.

Eberharter's view conforms more or less to the historical-critical views of Gressmann, Immanuel Benzinger,[1] and Kurt Galling.

The same historical-critical view is held by William F. Albright who sees a clear relationship between the ziggurats and the "horned" altars. Albright says,

> The cosmic symbolism appears clearly in the four horns, or rather four mountains, if we may judge from the four "horns" on an altar at Petra.[2]

Thus the scholarly opinion in the first quarter of this century remained more or less at a status quo where the views of the "history-of-religion" school prevailed though modifications of that opinion can be noticed.[3]

---

[1] For Immanuel Benzinger's view, see his Hebräische Archäologie, 3d. ed. (Leipzig: Eduard Pfeiffer, 1927), pp. 320-28. Benzinger especially emphasizes the maṣṣēbâ as the "phallus-symbol."

[2] "The Babylonian Temple-Tower and the Altar of Burnt-offering," JBL 39 (1920):141 (This article is, however, concerned with the altar-hearth and the Ziggurat rather than with "horns." Albright's view is included only because of his outstanding position as an archaeologist). The "horns" of the ziggurats have, by many scholars, been looked upon as analogous to the horns of the altars in Biblical context. For a description of ziggurats, see Martin A. Beek, Atlas of Mesopotamia (London: Thomas Nelson and Sons, Ltd., 1962), pp. 142-43; Theodor Dombart, "Die Zikkurat-Darstellung aus Ninive," AfO 3 (1926):177-81.

[3] Though there were also scholars in this period who refrained from imposing cultural concepts from surrounding nations on the Israelite religion, these concepts were often expressed in a purely descriptive manner as can be noticed from dictionary and encyclopedia articles (Harold M. Wiener, "Altar," The International Standard Bible Encyclopaedia [Grand Rapids: Wm. B. Eerdmans Publishing Co., 1939], 1:106-10; W. Shaw Caldecott, "Altar In Worship," ibid., pp. 110-12, idem, "Horns of the Altar," ibid., 3:1422; Eckhard Unger, "Altar," RLA [Berlin: Walter de Gruyter & Co., 1932], 1:73-75;

Herman T. Obbink, in the second quarter of this century, was not satisfied to be passively silent. He disagreed openly with Eichorn, Gressmann, and Galling and criticized especially Galling's work Der Altar in den Kulturen des alten Orients giving several reasons why he disagreed about the horns being originally maṣṣēbôt.[1] Obbink's arguments were convincing and certainly justified and were further developed by later scholars. Obbink was not, however, able to disassociate himself from the "history-of-religion" school interpretation. Instead he referred to Scheftelowitz as a support for the concept of the origin of horn and a meaning that was fit for a symbol of horn and used it as one of the arguments against Galling.[2]

It was not until the third quarter of this century that a clarification of the functions of the maṣṣēbôt and the "horns" was attempted on a more systematic basis.

Paul W. Lapp, a young archaeologist, in 1963 attempted a

Georg H. Karo, "Altar B. Ägäischer Kreis," RLV [Berlin: Walter de Gruyter & Co., 1924], 1:108-9; Günther Roeder, "Altar C. Ägypten," ibid., p. 109; Peter Thomsen, "Altar D. Palästina-Syrien," ibid., pp. 109-11; Eckhard Unger, "Altar, E. Vorderasien," ibid., pp. 111-12; Kurt Galling, "Altar," Biblisches Reallexikon, HAT, vol. 1 [Tübingen: Verlag von J. C. B. Mohr (Paul Siebeck), 1937], pp. 13-22; idem, "Altar," in IDB (New York: Abingdon Press, 1962), 1:96-100; Andreas Reichert, "Altar," BRL, 2d ed. [Tübingen: J. C. B. Mohr (Paul Siebeck), 1977], pp. 5-10). An explanation as to meaning or origin of horn was, however, still unexpressed.

[1] Obbink criticizes especially the terminology used vis à vis the placement of the horns (maṣṣēbôt): "next to the altar," "against it," "on top of it," "at the four corners of it;" "The Horns of the Altar," JBL 56 [1937]:45.

[2] See Obbink's development of arguments against Galling (ibid., pp. 44-45).

broad typology classification in order to describe the maṣṣēbôt.[1]
He distinguishes three basic types: the square- the round-, and
the slab-type of pillars. In his discussion he equates the maṣṣēbôt
with stelae. This precise, though limited, definition was a great
step forward in distinguishing the horns of the altar from the
maṣṣēbôt.[2]

A further step along this line was taken almost a decade
later when Carl F. Graesser presented the results of his research of
the maṣṣēbôt or sacred pillars.[3] Already Obbink had categorized the
pillars as to their function: some pillars were for the dead, some
were boundary stones, some votive tablets, some memorial stones, etc.,
but still he admits that "the precise nature and purpose of very few
of them is completely assured."[4] Graesser enlarges upon the typology
classification suggested by Lapp and categorizes the maṣṣēbôt under
five headings: "slab, round, obeliskoid, rude, and square."[5]
Furthermore, Graesser traces the etymological origin of maṣṣēbâ
from the root nṣb (נצב) "to stand upright" which indicates, as

---

[1] "The 1963 Excavation at Ta'annek," BASOR 173 (1964):35-37.

[2] Ibid., pp. 36-37. (It had thus taken nearly three quarters of a century to remove a deep-rooted misconception and misinterpretation.)

[3] Studies in Maṣṣēbôt, Ph.D. dissertation, Harvard University, 1969.

[4] Obbink, "The Horns of the Altar," p. 45.

[5] Studies in Maṣṣēbôt, p. 298.

Graesser has also pointed out, that "the maṣṣēbâ is an upright stone which serves as a marker."[1]

It is quite evident that this systematic, helpful study by Graesser has finally separated the "horns" and the maṣṣēbôt as being widely apart both in position and in function, not to speak of their external features. The maṣṣēbâ "had a hoary pedigree in Canaanite sanctuaries but no secure place in Yahweh's house."[2]

Many of the altars discovered in Palestine and Syria[3] are apparently (with or without horns) connected with pagan worship[4]--or perhaps with a distorted Yahweh worship.

The "horned" altar recently found at Beer-sheba with the snake symbol on one of its corner-stones may indicate snake-worship, which, in spite of suppression, persisted among the Israelites as late as the 8th century B.C.[5]

However, that the Eichhorn-Gressmann-Galling concept still is

---

[1] Ibid., p. 298; for the function of maṣṣēbôt, prohibition of use in Israel, etc., see further Graesser's discussion (ibid., pp. 299-307).

[2] Ibid., p. 297.

[3] The altars are discussed by Galling (apart from his magnus opus: Der Altar [1925] and in RGG³) in IDB 1:96-100, s.v. "Altar;" cf. also Yohanan Aharoni, "Arad: Its Inscriptions and Temple," BA 31 (1968):2-35 (esp. pp. 18-23); and idem, "The Horned-Altar of Beer-Sheba," BA 37 (1974):2-6; Yigael Yadin, "Beer-sheba: The High Place Destroyed by King Josiah," BASOR 222 (1976):5-17.

[4] George E. Wright, for instance, in regard to the altar of incense from Megiddo (8th cent. B.C.) says that it "probably belongs to the pagan religion of Baal, and not to the orthodox Israelite worship" ("'Sun-Image' or 'Altar of Incense'," BA 1 (1938):9-11.

[5] Yohanan Aharoni, "The Horned Altar of Beer-Sheba," BA 37 (1974):4; cf., idem, "Horned Altar for Animal Sacrifice Unearthed at Beer-Sheba," BARev 1 (1975):1, 8-9, 15 (2 Kgs 18:1-4).

alive in the minds of certain scholars is evident from Aharoni's remark: "Some scholars believe that they [the horns] were substituted for original maṣṣēbôt standing on the corners of the altar."[1] A primitive, animistic concept seems to be reflected by LaMoine Ferdinand DeVries concerning the horns of the altar when he writes that they "in addition to symbolizing strength and durability, also symbolized the dwelling-place of the deity, the holy mountain."[2] DeVries sees the horns as significant "because of the role played by the bull in ancient Near Eastern religions, including the religion of Israel."[3] DeVries, however, restricts himself to the period of the judges (ca. 1050-1000 B.C.) and is therefore chronologically to be placed before the altar of Beer-sheba discovered and described by Aharoni.

John P. Brown has also touched upon the symbol of horn in a recent article[4] which reveals his one-sided concept of horn(s) in the Bible as always depicting the horns of an animal, for he expresses his surprise that "the horn is also the symbol of a woman's strength (1 Sam 2:1)."[5] This surprising aspect can be completely

---

[1] Ibid., pp. 4-5.

[2] DeVries seems to lean on William F. Albright ("The Babylonian Temple-Tower and the Altar of Burnt-offering," p. 141) for this interpretation--a concept which per se is of pagan origin-- see DeVries, "Incense Altars from the Period of the Judges and their Significance," DAI 36 (1975/76):355-A; (cf. also idem, Ph.D. dissertation, Southern Baptist Theological Seminary, 1975, pp. 156-61).

[3] Incense Altar from the Period of the Judges and their Significance, Ph.D. dissertation Southern Baptist Theological Seminary (Ann Arbor: University Microfilms International, 1975), p. 259.

[4] "The Sacrificial Cult and Its Critique in Greek and Hebrew," JST 24 (1979):159-73.

[5] Ibid., p. 173.

eliminated if another tradition could be recognized--a tradition running parallel with the concept emphasized above.

A new investigation is needed in order to break out of the circulus vitiosus which is caused by present interpretations. There may be other avenues yet to be explored for a discovery of the meaning of "horns" on altars.

The Bull Concept of Yahweh

The old position of Hermann Gunkel, still entertained by his followers, is that the picture given in Ps 75:11 and elsewhere is taken from the wild ox (a well-known symbol among the Babylonians). Gunkel writes:

> . . . das Bild ist vom Wildochsen (Ps 92:11) hergenommen, der mit hoch aufgerichtetem Horn in der Fülle seines Kraftgefühls, der Gegner herausfordern, dasteht, ein Bild, das auch den Babyloniern bekannt ist.[1]

Mitchell Dahood is of the same opinion and says that "the image of the bull's horns recurs throughout this psalm [Ps 75]."[2] Dahood's proof is based on the assumption that $^{\jmath e}lohē\ ya^\zeta aqōb$ is a "toned-down" title probably based on an older reading $^{\jmath}ab\bar{\imath}r\ ya^\zeta aqōb$ which Dahood in turn translates "the Bull of Jacob."[3] In regard to Ps 132:2, 5, Dahood says,

---

[1] Die Psalmen (Göttingen: Vandenhoeck & Ruprecht, 1968), p. 327; So also Hans Schmidt, Die Psalmen, HAT, vol. 15 (Tübingen: J. C. B. Mohr [Paul Siebeck], 1934); Hans Joachim Kraus, Psalmen, BKAT, vol. 15 (Neukirchen Kreis Moers: Neukirchener Verlag, 1961), p. 522; this concept is very deep-rooted among scholars in general.

[2] Psalms II, AB (Garden City, N.Y.: Doubleday & Company, Inc., 1968), p. 216.

[3] Ibid.; as 'proof-texts' for his hypothesis Dahood cites Gen 49:24; Isa 1:24; 49:26; 60:16; Ps 132:2, 5; cf. William L. Holladay, A Concise Hebrew and Aramaic Lexicon of the Old Testament (Grand Rapids: Wm. B. Eerdmans, 1971), p. 2.

The recurrence of this title ["The Mighty of Jacob"] in vs. 5, together with the impressive list of archaic forms and usages registered in these Notes, suggest that ʾabīr yaʿaqōb, "the Mighty of Jacob," is related more closely to the occurrence of this title in the eleventh-century Gen 49:24 than to the later use in Isa 49:26 and 60:16. In Ugaritic ibr, "mighty," is used to designate things of unusual strength, such as a stallion or an ox.[1]

This reference to the Ugaritic language makes it implicit that the concept of אביר יעקב has been interpreted in light of Near Eastern cultures. It is also implicit that the emblem of strength and fertility in neighboring cultures imposed upon Israel's יהוה concept. However, standard Bible commentaries[2] translate the expression ʾabīr yaʿaqōb, "the Mighty One of Jacob," a fact which

---

[1] Psalms III, p. 243.

[2] See, for instance, C. F. Keil and F. Delitzsch, The Pentateuch, Biblical Commentary on the Old Testament (Grand Rapids: Wm. B. Eerdmans, n.d.), p. 407; Delitzsch, Biblical Commentary on the Psalms, Biblical Commentary on the Old Testament (Grand Rapids: Wm. B. Eerdmans Publishing Company, 1959), pp. 307, 310-11; idem, Biblical Commentary on the Prophecies of Isaiah (Grand Rapids: Wm. B. Eerdmans, 1900), 1:103; idem, 2:273-74, 419; Ephraim A. Speiser, Genesis, AB (Garden City, N.Y.: Doubleday & Company, 1960), p. 369; Cuthbert A. Simpson, "The Book of Genesis," IB (New York: Abingdon Press, 1952), p. 822; R. B. Y. Scott, "The Book of Isaiah," IB (New York: Abingdon Press, 1956), p. 177; James Muilenburg, "The Book of Isaiah," IB (New York: Abingdon Press, 1956), pp. 578, 704; Hans Wildberger, Jesaja, BKAT (Neukirchen-Vluyn: Neukirchener Verlag, 1965), p. 63 (Wildberger places not only אביר ישראל as a synonym for אביר יעקב but also אלהי ישראל and (קדוש/ש ישראל); Charles August Briggs, A Critical and Exegetical Commentary on the Book of Psalms, ICC (Edinburgh: T. & T. Clark, 1951), p. 469; John Skinner, however, though he translates אביר יעקב "Strong One of Jacob" he comments that "it is reasonably suspected that the Mass. changed the punctuation to avoid association of ideas with אביר 'bull,' the idolatrous emblem of Yahwe in N Israel. Whether the name as applied to Yahweh be really a survival of the bull-worship of Bethel and Dan is another question; אביר (strong) is an epithet of men (Judg 5:22, Job 24:22; 34:20; Jer 46:15; 1 Sam 21; etc.), and horses (Jer 8:16, 47:3, 50:11) much more often than of bulls (Ps 22:13, 68:31, 50:13, Isa 34:7), and might have been transferred to Yahweh in its adj. sense," A Critical and Exegetical Commentary on Genesis, 2d. ed., ICC (Edinburgh: T. & T. Clark, 1951), p. 531 (n. on Gen 49:24).

indicates that the "Strong One of Jacob" is to be considered a poetic title of Yahweh. A contrary concept is foreign to Israelite religion.

Apostate Israel had already worshipped the bull or golden calf at Sinai (Exod 32:1-21). Although some scholars would consider the bull-worship, on account of bull-worship in the Transjordanian countries, to have been practiced by Israelites not earlier than their confrontation with Baal-Peor,[1] it has been argued that since Yahweh had as his symbol the ark, the bull concept does not fit in the period of Israel's wilderness wanderings. The bull was part of the former religion. For the Canaanites bull-worship and Baʻal-cult could not be separated.[2]

Othmar Keel-Leu has in a recent work strongly suggested that the suffix "his" (קרניו) in Deut 33:17 refers to יהוה.[3] Keel-Leu also says that the concept of יהוה as a bull was prohibited at the latest since the ninth century B.C.[4] This view indirectly suggests

---

[1] Otto Eissfeldt, "Lade and Stierbild," ZAW 58 (1940-41):201.

[2] Ibid., cf. H. T. Obbink, "Jahwebilder," ZAW 47 (1929): 264-74. Obbink draws the inference from Hadad-Ramman that יהוה was not only worshipped as standing on a bull (pedestal) but the bull itself was worshipped as God (p. 269). Cf. also Manfred Weippert ("Gott und Stier," ZDPV 77 [1961]:93-117) who also points out the Ugaritic and Akkadian affinities, and the worship of the bulls as gods. Ludolf Malten again tracing the bull in cult and mythology starts off with Egyptian cult and cosmogonic speculations. Worship of both bull and cow was from antiquity introduced in several places and given personal names like "Apis," "Hathor," and which cult no doubt exercised an influence on the Israelites while in Egypt; "Der Stier in Kult und mythischem Bild," Jahrbuch des deutschen Archäologischen Instituts 43 (1928):92.

[3] Wirkmächtige Siegeszeichen im Alten Testament, Orbis Biblicus et Orientalis, 5 (Freiburg [Switzerland]: Universitätsverlag Freiburg, 1974), p. 126.

[4] (Cf. Exod 32; 1 Kgs 12:28f.; Hos 8:4-6; 13:2; Ps 106:19-21 as cited by Keel-Leu, ibid., p. 126.)

that this concept had been prevailing up to that time.[1] Keel-Leu conceives the bull-images put up by Jeroboam in Bethel and Dan (1 Kgs 12:25-33) not only as podia but as representatives of divine power.[2]

Zeʼev Meshel's recent article "Did Yahweh have a Consort?"[3] presumes the possibility of Israel having been under Egyptian influence rather than Syrian, Ugaritic, or even Akkadian when they departed from God at Sinai. Meshel points to the crude drawings on the pithoi found at Kuntillet Ajrud forty miles south of Kadesh-Barnea (and west of the Arabah) that give a hint in that direction. He points out that "the faces and ears of the two figures on the left resemble a cow or calf."[4] The horns and the ears were especially conspicuous on the cow deity of Egypt.[5]

The bull concept which is so closely related to our particular study of horns requires a separate study, however, therefore cannot be pursued in this dissertation.[6] It seems clear from these

---

[1] This statement, of course, has to be applied to the period of Jeroboam I, who originated the idol-worship on a nationalistic basis. Nowhere is the concept of the true God as a bull supported in the Hebrew Bible.

[2] Ibid., p. 129; Keel-Leu here refers to Manfred Weippert's study, "Gott und Stier," pp. 93-117.

[3] BARev 5 (1979):24-35.

[4] Ibid., p. 31. Although Meshel is unable to identify the woman playing the lyre and the figure to the left, he makes some connections with Egypt for he identifies the middle god as Bes--originally an Egyptian demi-god (p. 30).

[5] So Malten, "Der Stier in Kult und mythischen Bild," p. 93.

[6] Because of its close relationship to the particular investigation of horn, a dissertation on such a topic would make an excellent complement to a study of the nature here elucidated.

few allusions to the topic, nevertheless, that the bull concept both in cult and mythology has influenced people's thinking not only in the ancient past but still today.

"Horn" Symbol in OT Apocalyptic

The question of the identification of the fourth beast in Dan 7:7, 8 has occupied the minds of scholars and Bible students for many centuries. The fourth beast, different from all others, was recognizable because its ten horns made it appear diverse from all the previous beasts. The Sibylline oracle also speaks of ten "horns," but without identifying them.[1] The interpretation of the eagle vision[2] in IV Ezra 11:1-2:1-2 has been the basis for later interpretations, the majority of which diverge from the interpretation given by the heavenly messenger to Daniel and instead accept the concept of Greece or the Seleucid Kingdom as the fourth empire.

Thus these bygone non-canonical writings have been used as norms for the interpretation of both beasts and horns in the book of Daniel.[3] A glance at articles which have been produced in this

---

[1] The Sibylline Books (Book III, Lines 397-400) APOT, ed. Robert H. Charles (Oxford: At the Clarendon Press, 1913), 2:386.

[2] "And he [the Spirit] said unto me: This is the interpretation of the vision which thou hast seen. The eagle which thou sawest come up from the sea is the fourth kingdom which appeared in vision to thy brother Daniel; [but it was not interpreted unto him as I now interpret it unto thee or have interpreted it]." Charles commenting upon the passage, says, "This is a particularly clear and interesting case of the way in which apocalyptic prediction was reinterpreted and reapplied. It is interesting to note that in the Talmud (T.B. Abodā Zārā Ib), Dan 7:23 (i.e., the fourth kingdom) is interpreted of Rome" (ibid., p. 613, n. 11).

[3] All this, in spite of the fact that Charles has pointed out "that a close examination of the details of the vision and its interpretation reveals many grave difficulties" (ibid., 2:612, xii. 36-39).

century indicates that the Grecian or Seleucid interpretation predominates.

Denis Buzy may be used as a typical example for those scholars that identify the "little horn" in Dan 8 with the "eleventh horn" in Dan 7. He builds upon the interpretation of Saint Jerome, suggesting that the "little horn" is to be identified with Antiochus Epiphanes.[1] In harmony with many other scholars Buzy, too, makes an attempt to identify the ten horns. Starting with Alexander the Great he points to Antiochus Epiphanes as the eleventh king of the Seleucids.[2]

Walter Baumgartner presents a review of the scholarly opinion concerning the book of Daniel--especially in regard to the interpretation of the fourth beast.[3] On the basis of Harold H. Rowley's work[4] Baumgartner sees the interpretation of the fourth kingdom as the Roman empire as a rejected concept.[5] The Diadochi are seen henceforth as the fourth kingdom in Baumgartner's opinion.[6]

Sigfried Morenz, a representative of the apocalyptic interpretation of "horn," writes more recently:

---

[1] "Les symboles de Daniel," RB 15 (1918):410.

[2] Ibid., p. 417.

[3] "Ein Vierteljahrhundert Danielforschung," ThR 11 (1939): 201-28.

[4] Darius the Mede and the Four World Empires in the Book of Daniel (Cardiff: University of Wales Press Board, 1959).

[5] "Ein Vierteljahrhundert Danielforschung," p. 202.

[6] Ibid., pp. 202-3; Baumgartner recognizes the two views of opinion in regard to the interpretation of the fourth beast: those who consider the fourth empire to be that of Alexander, and those who consider it to be that of the Diadochi.

> Als einziges von den geschauten Tieren ist das vierte
> gehörnt. Mehr noch: Hörner sind das eigentlich Kennzeichnende
> dieses Ungeheurers. Kommt das von ungefähr? Da muss man sich
> zunächst freilich gegenwärtig halten, dass das Horn in der Welt
> des AT selbst und im Alten Orient überhaupt ein Sinnbild der
> Macht ist. Der Sprachgebrauch zeigt, dass im Horn die Kraft
> eines Wesens gesammelt vorgestellt ist; so können Hörner ganz
> für sich allein mächtige Reiche versinnbilden (Sach 2:1ff.),
> und in letzter Linie geht das gewiss auf den Stiergott und
> Stierkönig zurück, der in Mesopotamien und Ägypten ikonographisch
> und Titular fassbar ist.[1]

Interestingly enough Morenz is one scholar who seems to recognize also another tradition:

> Auf einem anderen, hier nicht zu bestimmenden Wege wurde
> auch das Horn des Altars zum Sitze der höchsten Wirkungsmacht;
> wer den Altar Jahwes als Asyl aufsucht, umklammert seine Hörner,
> und der Psalmist preist das "Horn des Heils," wenn er den
> Asylschutz Jahwes rühmt (2 Sam 22:2 = Ps 18:3).[2]

Morenz, however, does not follow up on this insight. He poses the question, "why had the beast of the Seleucids horns?"[3] His attempt at an answer leads him to numismatic representations of the Seleucid kings.[4]

André Caquot sees the four empires as Babylonia, Media, Persia, and Greece and interprets the monstrous fourth beast as Leviathan, the primitive chaos monster.[5] He follows Otto Eissfeldt who considers the beast with the seven heads in the Ugaritic epics (the ltn) as a prototype of the Biblical Leviathan (לויתן). Caquot, with his background in mythological texts, also sees mythology represented in Daniel's vision.[6] Actually he sees the cosmology of the

---

[1] "Das Tier mit den Hörnern, ein Beitrag zu Dan 7:7f." ZAW 63 (1951):152.

[2] Ibid.   [3] Ibid.   [4] Ibid.

[5] "Sur les quatre bêtes de Daniel 7," Semitica 5 (1955):6.

[6] Ibid., p. 7.

Babylonians represented in the four beasts. It is in the four directions of the compass that Daniel places the four empires: Babylonia in the south, Media in the north, Persia in the east, and Greece in the west.[1] Caquot, however, does not discuss the horns.

M. Delcor pays attention to structural patterns in his study of Dan 7,[2] and, in harmony with Caquot, discusses the mythological background as well as the chorographic astrology (i.e., the signs of the Zodiac).[3]

Urs Staub, in a recent study concerning the beast with the horns in Dan 7, takes the well-noted view of the same as representing the Grecian-Macedonian empire.[4] He points out that this nameless beast which emerges from the sea has been identified, in recent commentaries, with the Grecian-hellenistic power.[5] Following

---

[1] Ibid., p. 9.

[2] "Les sources du chapître 7 de Daniel," VT 18 (1968):290-94.

[3] Delcor's main interest lies in the concept of the "Ancient of Days," whom he discusses at length (ibid., 300-312).

[4] This study, "Das Tier mit den Hörnern. Ein Beitrag zu Dan 7:7f." FZPhTh 25 (1978):351-97, is a revised article based on Staub's Lizenziatsarbeit Die Tiervision im Danielbuch. Eine motivgeschichtliche und ikonographische Untersuchung zu Dan 7:2-8. Lizenziatsarbeit, Freiburg Universität, 1977.

[5] Staub refers inter alia to J. Göttesberger, Das Buch Daniel, Die Heilige Schrift des Alten Testamentes, eds. F. Feldmann and H. Herkenne, VIII/2 (Bonn, 1928), p. 54; Norman W. Porteous, Daniel A Commentary (Philadelphia: The Westminster Press, 1965), p. 86; Otto Plöger, Das Buch Daniel, KAT 18 (Gütersloh, 1965), 116; D. Karl Marti, Das Buch Daniel, Kurzer Hand-Commentar zum Alten Testament, vol. 18 (Tübingen, 1901); G. Behrmann, Das Buch Daniel, HKAT, pt. 3: Die prophetischen Bücher, III/2 (Göttingen, 1894, 44), p. 45; Aage Bentzen, Daniel, HAT K/19 (Tübingen (2) 1952, 59), p. 65; André Lacocque, The Book of Daniel (Atlanta: John Knox Press, 1979), p. 141; Martin Noth, "Das Geschichtsverständnis der altestamentlichen Apokalyptik," in Gesammelte Studien zum Alten Testament.

Morenz, he emphasizes the numismatic material of the Seleucid kings. Enlarged illustrations of "horned" kings of the Seleucid empire (on coins) aid in identifying the ten horns on the fourth beast.[1] A new emphasis in Staub's research is his far-fetched view of the "war-elephant" as the fourth beast.

> Auf jeden Fall machen es die ikonographischen Motive der hellenistischen Münzprägungen wie auch die Texte der Makkabäerbücher wahrscheinlich, dass der Verfasser von Dan 7 im bisher unbekannten Elephanten, besonders wenn er dazu noch zu kriegerischen Zwecken abgerichtet worden ist, das "Wappentier" des griechisch-makedonischen Reiches sah.[2]

It may be assumed that Staub sees in the Elephantphalanx a fulfillment of Dan 7:7. He expresses himself particularly on the cryptography in the following words:

> Zerrissen die drei früheren Weltmächte die von ihnen unterjochten Länder wie Raubtiere, so war eine Elephantphalanx, die wie eine lebendig gewordene Stadtmauer auf einem Schlachtfeld alles niedertrampelte, eine gute Chiffre für das gewaltige hellenistische Staatensystem.[3]

From these few highpoints it may be seen that the dominating view about the ten horns in Dan 7 is that of the ancient Sibylline oracle. "In the Sibyllines 'the man clad with the purple cloak' is

---

Theologische Bücherei, Neudrucke und Berichte aus dem 20. Jahrhundert, vol. 6 (München, 1960), p. 269f. and K. Koch, "Spätisraelitisches Geschichtsdenken am Beispiel des Buches Daniel," in Historische Zeitschrift 193 (1961):16 (as referred to by Staub [with our imprints added], "Das Tier mit Hörnern," p. 359, n. 21).

[1] For a helpful review of the various standpoints of scholars in regard to the identification of these kings, see Staub's chart in four columns, "Das Tier mit den Hörnern," p. 364; for the numismatic representatives of the Seleucid king, see ibid., pp. 368-69, 372-73.

[2] Staub, "Das Tier mit den Hörnern," p. 395; cf. also pp. 389-94.

[3] Ibid.

Antiochus Epiphanes."[1] By and large discussions concerning the fourth beast, or the ten horns, aim to identify the tenth horn--or the eleventh--as Antiochus.[2] Voices to the contrary are rarely articulated. For this reason it may be stated that recent interpretations have seen no essential change apart from details. A fresh approach is needed. It seems quite reasonable in an age of renewed study in apocalyptic to expect that an intense study of the horn-motif will lead to new discoveries and open up new directions for interpretation.

The "Horns" of Moses

The "horns" of Moses in Exod 34:29-35 have caused much perplexity, as can be clearly noticed already from the time of Jerome in the fourth century A.D. He must certainly have pondered over the meaning as he had at least two versions available, the Septuagint and the Aquila, when he prepared his own Latin translation.[3] He had to choose between the two expressions: the abstract "glorified" in the Septuagint and the literal "horned" in the Aquila version. His having chosen the literal rendering "horned" is believed to indicate that Jerome "equates glorified with horned."[4]

It is, however, not only the locution qāran ʽor pānāw that

---

[1] Robert H. Charles, A Critical and Exegetical Commentary on the Book of Daniel (Oxford: At the Clarendon Press, 1929), p. 168.

[2] See Staub, "Das Tier mit den Hörnern," p. 364.

[3] Ruth Mellinkoff, The Horned Moses in Medieval Art and Thought (Berkeley: University of California Press, 1970), p. 77, has in an excellent way set forth Jerome's preference (Aquila) in translating the Vulgate.

[4] Ibid., p. 78.

caused misconception but also the word maswēh which occurs as a hapax legomenon in Exod 34:33-35.

Gressmann's "history-of-religion" school background led him to strike a note that still echoes. He argues that although it cannot be proved with certainty that masks were used in the Israelite cult, it would appear from Exod 34:29-35 that such are assumed.[1] According to Gressmann the מסוה implies a usage similar to that of the Egyptian tradition where cult masks were used. Or perhaps it is in line with Arabic tradition where masks were also used at religious feasts and festivities.[2] The Arabic word maschara "der Scherz," gives us the word "mask" (masquerade).[3] Does the context of the narrative of Exod 34 indicate that Moses was a mummy in need of a mask or that he was engaged in a masquerade of any kind? Moses, as the story indicates, was very much alive and displeased with the people who engaged in such frivolity.[4] Gressmann finds the solution in the gloss teraphim[5] which he considers to be understood as a "Gottesbild" or a "Maske."[6]

Julian Morgenstern criticizes Gressmann as having "far

---

[1] "Teraphim," ZAW 40 (1922):76.   [2] Ibid., pp. 78-82.

[3] Ibid., p. 70; cf. Khalil M. Saad, Centennial English-Arabic Dictionary of the American Press, ed. Paul Eerdman (1926), p. 541.

[4] The people eating and drinking and playing is referred to in Exod 32:6, 19. The Sitz im Leben is the same in ch. 34, but the people's attitude was different. With reverent awe did they look upon the shining face of Moses.

[5] See Gen 31:19, 34, 35.

[6] Gressmann, "Teraphim," p. 98.

overshot the mark" and for being too geistreich in working out "a hypothesis of the wearing of sacred masks by priests in ancient Israel, while consulting the oracle."[1] Morgenstern, after a lengthy discussion trying to refute Gressmann's arguments, presents his own conclusion that Moses in the course of time became almost a demi-god in the Israelite tradition and "whose face shines almost like Yahwe's with a radiance that defies all mortal vision."[2]

Many follow Gressmann's suggestion that the "strahlende Gesicht" of Moses is to be understood as his wearing a "golden mask."[3] Anton Jirku takes this position when he writes:

> Mit seiner Erscheinung, bei der er Hörner trägt, jagt Mose seinen Landsleuten einen solchen Schrecken ein, dass er immer eine Hülle (maswae) umnimmt, wenn er mit seinen Landsleuten spricht, um ihnen den göttlichen Willen zu verkünden. . . . Es ist klar, dass es sich hier nur um eine mit Hörnern versehene Gesichtsmaske handeln kann.[4]

Fritz Dumermuth takes up the question anew about the shining face of Moses.[5] He feels that the explanation given by most scholars has a rationalistic aftertaste and their interpretations often reach the borderline of phantasy.[6] He criticizes not only Gressmann and Jirku but points out how absurd and unreal is the position of Bernardus D. Eerdman[7] who writes:

---

[1] "Moses with the Shining Face," HUCA 9 (1925):4, n. 9.

[2] Ibid., p. 27.   [3] See Gressmann, "Teraphim," pp. 83-84.

[4] "Die Gesichtsmaske des Mose," ZDPV 67 (1944):43.

[5] "Moses strahlendes Gesicht," TZ 17 (1961):241-48.

[6] Ibid., p. 241.

[7] The Covenant at Mount Sinai (Leiden: Burgerskijk & Niermans, 1939). As we have not had an opportunity to consult this work by Eerdman we are here dependent on Dumermuth's critical view.

Die sogenannte "Theophanie" am Sinai sei ein gemeinsam von den midianitischen Wüstenschmieden und Mose inszeniertes Schauspiel gewesen, um Moses autorität vor dem Volk zu begründen.[1]

Further on, still quoting Eerdman:

Heimlich hätten diese Midianiter auf dem Sinai gewaltig rauchende Feuer angezündet, in Deckung mit allen möglichen Instrumenten Lärm gemacht und Gottes Stimme nachgeahmt.[2]

Furthermore, Eerdman explains in regard to Exod 34:29-35 that when Moses, for the sake of his role, had to stay around in the dense smoke, his face got hardened like horn:

Die Wirkung, die die Hitze des Feuers auf die Haut ausübt, besteht darin, dass diese wie Krokodilshaut auszusehen beginnt. So berichten uns die ägyptischen Papyri und erklären, weshalb die Ägypter die Anwesenheit eines Schmiedes nicht liebten.[3]

Dumermuth, on the other hand, presumes that the meaning of qrn must be interpreted here in its context from the phrase qāran 'ōr pānāw, "to become shining." The presupposition that the narrative in Exod 34:29-35 must originate from the explanation that Moses used to put on a mask[4] on his awe-inspiring face when he returned from having spoken with Yahweh is but an etiological explanation for the usage of cult masks in Israel, i.e., if the presumption would be true. However, Dumermuth points out that we have no data for masks being used in the Yahweh cult. It is therefore very questionable whether

---

[1] Bernardus D. Eerdman, The Covenant at Mount Sinai (Leiden: Burgerskijk & Niermans, 1939), p. 22 as quoted in Dumermuth, p. 241.

[2] Ibid.

[3] Eerdman, as quoted in Dumermuth, pp. 241-42.

[4] Dumermuth points out that the Hebrew word maswēh must be translated in context. The meaning of "mask" is completely to be rejected as the word in the context simply means "Bedeckung" (ibid., p. 242).

Exod 34:33-35 may be accepted as indicating the use in Israel of this custom prevailing among surrounding nations.[1]

Elmer G. Suhr wrote an article in which he emphasizes the "theophany of Moses."[2] Suhr would not only have the face of Moses shining; he would apply shining to the whole body.[3] His analogies are drawn from mythology. The key parallel is found in "the glorification or transfiguration of Siegfried."[4] Suhr writes,

> After slaying the dragon and bathing in its blood, his skin became "horned," and loth as some may be to rank him with Moses, the fact remains that he is a messiah, although on a different plane.[5]

Suhr also infers that

> The dragon had some invulnerable quality which was passed along to the hero with its skin, and in this case no one has ever . . . identified such a feature with a pair of horns on the head.[6]

Suhr continues with parallels of Achilles, who always remained invincible until he was slain by Paris, "whose arrow was guided by the god of the sun,"[7] and with Krishna, who also "took on the horned skin of the serpent to cope with the monster, and revealed his divinity in terms of a transfiguration."[8]

In spite of the fact that Suhr attempts to defend the "shining" of Moses, he is completely given over to mythology as one more passage, in addition to the ones quoted above, will clearly indicate. He writes:

---

[1] Ibid., p. 243.

[2] "The Horned Moses," *Folklore* 74 (1963):387-95.

[3] Ibid., p. 387. [4] Ibid., p. 390. [5] Ibid.

[6] Ibid. [7] Ibid. [8] Ibid.

> One more manifestation we must consider: the skin of Moses was not only horned but also included the implication of shining light, which can be accounted for by the light and heat of the sun permeating the body of the dragon or the lunar shadow. Most dragons, in whatever context they appear, are saturated with fire, they pour forth flames from the mouth, thereby scorching the earth and spreading pestilence.[1]

In conclusion Suhr says,

> While Michelangelo misinterpreted the horned skin of Moses, I see no reason why we should accuse the Hebrew scribe of an error; he evidently wrote in good faith and with conscious intent; our only regret lies in our ignorance of the context from which he drew his information.[2]

Suhr places the story of Moses on the level of Grecian mythology.

In the year 1968 Jack M. Sasson traces the bovine symbolism in Exodus.[3] He poses a question that had already been asked by Julius Lewy nearly a quarter of a century earlier:[4] "How are the two traditions [one worshiping Sin, the other of Yahweh] combined in the present narrative?"[5] Sasson presents his own view by saying,

> In this one vestige of a suppressed cult, this one single depiction of a horned Moses, symbolizing the old pagan faith, being brought face to face with the God of the new creed, YHWH asserts his dominance. . . . From then on, there is no

---

[1] Ibid.   [2] Ibid., p. 395.

[3] "Bovine Symbolism in the Exodus Narrative," VT 18 (1968): 380-87.

[4] The article "Traces of the Worship of the Moon God Sin among the Early Israelites" was organized and published by Andrew F. Key who gives full credit to the late Julius Lewy to whom the merit for the interesting article is due. Lewy points out, for instance, that the name Sinai "would suggest that it was the place of revelation of the moon god." JBL 84 (1965):23.

[5] Sasson, "Bovine Symbolism in the Exodus Narrative," p. 387; the question posed here by Sasson is challenging and certainly needs further investigation, especially in view of the recent discoveries at Kuntillet Ajrud.

more mention of horns, no more mention of veils, Monotheism triumphs, at least for the time being.[1]

In spite of the interesting suggestions brought forth by Sasson, his conclusion that "through Moses, a direct link to Sin, God of the Harranite Terah, seems to have been maintained,"[2] is open to serious doubt.

Vassos Karageorghis makes it quite clear that bull cult was prevalent in Cyprus already in the Early Bronze Age (third millennium B.C.).[3] Karageorghis also shows that not only in Cyprus but also in the whole Aegean world "the head of the sacrificed bull played an important part in religious ritual, especially during the second millennium B.C."[4] This was the case also in the Near East where the idea of fertility in connection with the bull appeared even in prehistoric times.[5] It is in connection with the ritualistic services, then, that Karageorghis assumes that the mask had its origin. He writes,

> The idea of entering into a direct association with the god by putting on the divine image led to the invention of masks which were worn during religious rituals.[6]

Karageorghis, however, is not able to support his hypothesis with literary evidences. He comments, ". . . we have ample archaeological evidence that this custom did exist during the Late Bronze Age."[7]

---

[1] Ibid., p. 387. [2] Ibid.

[3] "Notes on Some Cypriote Priests Wearing Bull-Masks," HTR 64 (1971):261-70.

[4] Ibid. [5] Ibid.

[6] Ibid. [7] Ibid., p. 262.

George E. Mendenhall combines the mask with the Akkadian melammū and puluḫtu;[1] he does not make the parallel with the maswēh but with the ʽanan, saying, "ʽanan is the mask, and the fire the garment of flame called puluḫtu in Akkadian."[2] Mendenhall presents his hypothesis after having carefully studied both Egyptian and Mesopotamian literature. He says, for instance, concerning melammū, that it is "the word label for a most complex conceptualization of divine and royal glory. . . ."[3] Mendenhall further says:

> The melammū itself as glory cannot really be seen, all that can be seen is the visible mask with which the melammū is identified because the mask has the functional effects necessary to the melammū.[4]

He also sees the melammū--later called epiphany (or manifestation of deity)--already as a very complex concept during the Bronze Age.[5]

The approach of Karl Jaroš is philological.[6] He refers to Rabbi Raschi's Commentary Exodus[7] which says: "קרן is an expression connected with the word קרנים 'horn,' and the phrase קרן עור the light-'horned' is used here because light radiates from a point and projects like a horn."[8] Jaroš emphasizes that Martin Noth[9]

---

[1] See A. Leo Oppenheim, "Akkadian pul(u)ḫ(t)u and melammu," JAOS 63 (1943):31-34.

[2] The Tenth Generation; The Origins of the Biblical Tradition (Baltimore: The Johns Hopkins University Press, 1973), p. 59.

[3] Ibid., p. 53.   [4] Ibid.   [5] Ibid.

[6] "Des Mose 'strahlende Haut'," ZAW 88 (1976):275-81.

[7] Pentateuch with Targum Onkelos, Haphtaroth and Prayers for Sabbath and Rashi's Commentary, trans. M. Rosenbaum and A. M. Silbermann et al. (London: Shapiro, Vallentine & Co., 1946), p. 196.

[8] Jaroš, "Des Mose 'strahlende Haut'," p. 276.

[9] Das Zweite Buch Mose, Exodus, 3d. ed., ATD 5 (Göttingen: Vandenhoeck & Ruprecht, 1965), p. 220; as we have not had access

and Umberto Cassuto[1] and almost all modern exegetes follow this guideline.[2] Jaroš interprets the Qal in the Exodus passage on the basis of Ps 69:32 where the Hiphil participle expresses the causative meaning of "producing horns." According to this norm the Qal would have to mean "to have horns"--a fact which Jaroš also points out. In the same way Jaroš argues that the dual qarnayim in Hab 3:4 does not mean "a pair of rays," but "a pair of horns."[3]

This philological study defends the assumption that Moses, to be sure, wore a face-mask with horns but the idea was suppressed already in the P document "by use of the phenomenon of the 'shining face'."[4]

Staub plainly presents his position on the issue here discussed:

> Die gehörnte Gesichtsmaske, die Mose bei seiner Begegnung mit Gott auf dem Sinai trug und die er verhüllen musste, um das Volk nicht zu erschrecken (Exod 34:29f. 35), stellt eine weitere Verbindung zwischen Jahweh und dem hörnertragenden Stier her.[5]

---

to the English edition Exodus: A Commentary (Philadelphia: Westminster [1962]), we cite the German edition. Noth here takes the same view as Gressmann in regard to the "teraphim" (that they originally were face-masks).

[1] A Commentary on the Book of Exodus (Jerusalem: Magnes Press, 1967), pp. 448-51; according to Cassuto the verb qāran "shine" is derived from the noun qeren in the sense of a "ray of light," in accordance with Hab 3:4. Cassuto further says, "According to the belief of the Mesopotamian peoples a radiant brightness (melammu) shone from the faces of the gods, which resembled in shape those of human beings and were differentiated from the latter by this very radiance. The Israelite prophet does not actually refer to the 'face' of the Lord, but only to His radiance" (p. 448).

[2] Jaroš, "Des Mose 'strahlende Haut'," p. 276.

[3] Ibid., pp. 276-277.   [4] Ibid., p. 289.

[5] "Das Tier mit den Hörnern," p. 367.

From the foregoing four sections in this review of research we may adduce the following observations:

1. <u>The "horns" of the altar</u>. The hypothesis of a development from primitive to advanced concepts in religion is reflected in the nineteenth century interpretation of Bernhard Stade. His theory was modified by Hugo Gressmann who no longer emphasized the carving of the altar stone into the form of an ox in order to symbolize the power of God; he rather considered the horns of the altar as vestiges of maṣṣēbôt.

This theory was questioned by Herman T. Obbink and finally disproved by Paul W. Lapp and Carl F. Graesser. Thus the old Eichhorn-Gressmann-Galling hypothesis of the horns of the altar as vestiges of maṣṣēbôt which dominated the thinking of scholars for about seven decades, can no longer be held. It may be asserted that the function of the maṣṣēbôt has been solved,[1] but the question of the function and meaning of the "horns" still calls for an answer.

2. <u>The bull-concept of Yahweh</u>. Scholars in general conceive the bull concept of Yahweh as a relic of antiquity--but a real one. Israel had its bull-gods. The ʾabîr yaʿaqōb and other epithets confirm the scholarly position that Yahweh was considered a bull in an early period. The bull concept of Yahweh is not a

---

[1]Carl F. Graesser still expresses uncertainty as to the specific function of certain pillars, but the classification he makes confirms the purpose of these upright stones primarily to serve as a marker. As for the function Graesser describes them under the headings of "commemorative, memorial, legal, and cultic;" see Carl Frank Graesser, <u>Studies in Maṣṣēbôt</u>, pp. 298-99.

myth, however. It was a real situation in Israel's history, i.e., as late as the first millennium B.C. It seems, however, evident that bull worship originated in other cultures and was accepted into Israel in a time of apostasy.

3. "Horn" symbolism in OT apocalyptic. The question of the interpretation of the "horn" symbol in Dan 7 is closely connected with an understanding of the fourth beast. Both concepts are part of the symbolism of apocalyptic. Most scholars assert to find the right key in the Apocrypha and Pseudepigrapha.

During the first quarter of our century the aim of critical scholarship was to analyze and scrutinize the text of Daniel and to inquire about the trustworthiness of historical material.[1] A part of this attempt was to investigate the prophecy of Daniel in relationship with the time of the Diadochi and specifically in regard to Antiochus Epiphanes.[2] The identification of the fourth beast with the ten horns became a burning question. The critical debate came pretty much to an end when the learned Harold H. Rowley presented his views.[3] Henceforth the Diadochi (or the Alexandrian empire) was regarded as the fourth-empire--symbolized by the fourth beast with the ten horns.

---

[1] Many of these discussions are not relevant in regard to our particular study, but see Baumgartner, "Ein Vierteljahrhundert Danielforschung," pp. 201-02.

[2] For a list of scholars discussing this particular view see ibid., p. 202.

[3] Darius the Mede and the Four World Empires in the Book of Daniel, pp. 95-136.

Most recent commentaries[1] and articles[2] follow the suggestions of Rowley.

4. The "horns" of Moses. The question of the "horns" of Moses has closely been tied up with the question of the mask. Both the Qal form qāran and the noun maswēh are hapax legomena. The history-of-religion school, with Gressmann being a main representative, finds the solution in the socio-cultural context. Though Gressmann admits that the usage of a mask cannot be proven in Israel, the narrative in Exod 34:29-35 is said to assume such a concept. The ancient usage of a mask is believed to be implied in the gloss about the teraphim referred to in the pericope of Jacob in Genesis.

Various extreme views with much phantasy have been put forth.[3] The "horns" of Moses, being likened to those of the bull are regarded by certain scholars as a curious relic from antiquity, revealing religious practices and cultic ceremonies from prerecorded time. Although the usage of a mask in cultic ceremonies is not explicitly mentioned in ancient Israel, there is enough evidence to assume such a tradition. The "shining" face of Moses is accordingly

---

[1] See, for instance, John J. Collins, The Apocalyptic Vision of the Book of Daniel (Missoula, MT: Scholars Press, 1977); Louis F. Hartman and Alexander A. Di Lella, The Book of Daniel, AB (Garden City, NY: Doubleday & Company, Inc., 1978); André Lacocque, The Book of Daniel (Atlanta: John Knox Press, 1979).

[2] See, for instance, Urs Staub, "Das Tier mit den Hörnern, 351-97, et al.

[3] Dumermuth refers especially to B. D. Eerdman (The Covenant of Sinai [Leiden, 1939]) for an extreme rationalistic view, but other more "sober" scholars also sided fully with Gressmann. So Anton Jirku, "Die Gesichtsmaske des Mose," ZDPV 67 (1944-45): 43-45; Martin Noth, Exodus: A Commentary (Philadelphia: The Westminster Press, 1962), p. 267, et al.

for a number of recent scholars an etiological explanation in a context where bull worship and the usage of masks were suppressed.[1] At present scholars tend to explain the "horns" of Moses, i.e., his shining face, on an etiological basis.

Task

On the basis of this review of literature it has become apparent that the horn-motif has never been fully investigated. On the contrary the horn-motif has been discussed only in selected areas.

Some scholars have concentrated their study on the origin and meaning of the "horns" of the altar. Many of these studies are based on archaeological discoveries or else discuss the symbolical function of "horns." Other authorities have been preoccupied with the "bull-motif" and the "horns" of the bull-gods. There are also those who have focused their interest on horn-symbolism in Old Testament apocalyptic. Still others have considered the "horns" of Moses as an all-inclusive theme of that same motif.

The various views brought forth indicate that there is no consensus of scholarly opinion in regard to the complex motif of "horns." Many lines of thought and conclusions are contradictory. The horn-motif has never been studied on a comprehensive basis. Such a study seems now mandatory on the basis of new ancient Near Eastern materials and the biblical connections and contributions.

---

[1] See especially, Jaroš, "Des Mose 'strahlende Haut'," pp. 275-81.

We therefore attempt in this study to meet the new challenges. The questions of origin, meaning, and literal and non-literal connotations of the term "horn" and the "horn-motif" call for investigation. This involves philological, iconographic and literary studies in the cultural surroundings of the ancient Israelites and in the literature of ancient Israel itself.

CHAPTER II

COMPARATIVE PHILOLOGY OF THE ROOT QRN

The Root QRN in Sumerian and Ancient Near Eastern Semitic Languages

This chapter is designed to present a brief linguistic basis for the usage of the term "horn" in some of the ancient languages. The general purpose of this dissertation is to deal with the horn-motif in ancient Near Eastern contexts. We attempt to discover the origin, usage, and meaning of the term "horn" and its symbolic connotations from the earliest time possible. In order to achieve this we will engage in a terminological investigation, beginning with the Sumerian language. This will be followed by a study of the Akkadian, Ugaritic, Aramaic, and South-Arabian linguistic evidences. Finally the Hebrew root will be investigated. A concise introduction before each section will provide a condensed history of the language.

"Horn" in Sumerian

Preliminary Considerations

Old Babylonian copies of Sumerian literary texts were brought to the attention of scholars about the turn of the century[1]

---

[1] William W. Hallo, "Toward a History of Sumerian Literature," in Sumerological Studies in Honor of Thorkild Jacobsen on his Seventieth Birthday June 7, 1974, Assyriological Studies, no. 20 (Chicago: University of Chicago Press, 1976), p. 181. Hallo gives the

and since then publications began to appear. The cuneiform writing is generally considered as an invention of the ancient Sumerians, though some recent scholars propose a substrate theory.[1]

Many early Sumerologists have been reluctant to accept evidences of a highly developed structure of the language.[2] However, Wilfred G. Lambert and other later scholars have proved that by 3000 B.C. the Sumerian civilization had a full-fledged sign list; by 1800 B.C. they had dictionaries of pronunciation, and by 800 B.C. lexical texts, commentaries, analysis of the Sumerian verb, and "other philological materials."[3]

Nevertheless, there are still graphic, lexical, and grammatical problems to solve. Thorkild Jacobsen says:

> The field of Sumerian Grammar is not one in which one can move with much confidence. The Sumerologist who examines his presuppositions knows only too well how many unknowns enter into his slightest decisions. How unproven, perhaps unprovable, are even his most fundamental assumptions about the writing and about the spoken forms it can and cannot symbolize.[4]

---

arbitrary date 1873. Since we are primarily concerned with the literary texts, we prefer a later date that is compatible with the discovery of the Fara texts (1902, 1903) as a more relevant date for this particular purpose. Cf. also Thorkild Jacobsen, "Samuel Noah Kramer: An Appreciation," AOAT 25 (1976):xii-xvi.

[1] Marvin A. Powell, Jr., "Sumerian Area Measures and the Alleged Decimal Substratum," ZA 62 (June 1973):172.

[2] Samuel N. Kramer, "A Matter of Method in Sumerology," AJSL 49 (1932/33):229-47 (esp. n. 64).

[3] Wilfred G. Lambert, "A Catalogue of Texts and Authors," JCS 16 (1962):59. On account of the Ebla tablets this date has to be pushed back considerably.

[4] "About the Sumerian Verb," in Studies in Honor of Benno Landsberger on his Seventy-fifth Birthday April 21, 1965, Assyriological Studies, no. 16 (Chicago: University Press, 1965), p. 71.

Whatever one presumes in regard to the origin and the structure of the Sumerian script, one thing seems self-evident, namely a long history of oral transmission before the language adapted itself to writing.[1] The tradition of the text comprises "antiquity, longevity and continuity" that supersede any other language.[2] This fact makes the study of the Sumerian script and language very important.[3]

The Meaning of the Sumerogram SI

The Sumerogram ⌐╤Υ (SI) is supposed to have a paleographic development of eight steps. Anton Deimel, who proposes this view, does not, however, refer to any source in order to substantiate his theory.[4] According to him the basic meaning of SI (with pronunciation si) is qarnu.[5] For the syllables gišši

---

[1] For the problem of "written" or "oral" see, for instance Jørgen Læssøe, "Literacy and Oral Tradition in Ancient Mesopotamia," in Studia Orientalia Ioanni Pedersen 70th Anniversary Nov. 7, 1955 (Copenhagen: Einar Munksgaard, 1953), pp. 205-18. So also Bendt Alster, Dumuzi's Dream, Aspects of Oral Poetry in a Sumerian Myth (Copenhagen: Det Kongelige Bibliotek, 1972), pp. 15-27.

[2] Hallo, "Toward a History," p. 182.

[3] A new importance of the Sumerian script is advocated by Giovanni Pettinato. In speaking of the importance of the Ebla documents he emphasizes "a sound grasp of the Sumerian language as well as of the cuneiform system of writing in the third millennium." "The Royal Archives of Tell Mardikh," BA 39 (May 1976):50. (According to Pettinato's assertion, 80 percent of the Ebla tablets are Sumerian and only 20 percent Paleo-Canaanite.)

[4] Anton Deimel and P. Gössmann, ŠL, 3rd. ed. (Rome: Pontificum Institutum Biblicum, 1947), Part I, p. 42. (The third edition of this work is consistently used unless otherwise clearly indicated.)

[5] Ibid. (The spelling qarnu will be used interchangeably with ḳarnu, depending on sources referred to.)

(-si) ma₂, 𒋛 𒋛 𒋛𒁹 (𒋛) Deimel gives the meaning ḳarnāte elippi.[1] For the sign 𒋛𒁹 (ma-a = elippu) Deimel comments, "Urbild und Grundbedeutung ein Schiff (mit hornartig aufsteigendem Vorderteil)."[2]

A brief analytical study will illustrate how the concept of SI was used among the Sumerians.

Jacob Klein, for instance, says that SI "refers to the towering, horn-shaped stem and stern on the magur-boat, which is well illustrated on cylinder seals."[3]

There are several examples of má-gur meaning "rundes Schiff."[4]

---

[1] Ibid., Part III, vol. 1, p. 180; cf. Part II, vol. 1, p. 289 (112.96 [cf. #112.99]); cf. also Friedrich Delitzsch, Sumerisches Glossar (Leipzig: J. C. Hinrichs, 1914), p. 236; Stephen Langdon, A Sumerian Grammar and Chrestomathy (Paris: Paul Geuthner, 1911), pp. 27, 31. Langdon points out that confusion of the meaning of the sign 𒋛 si (and other signs) arose through the elision of the final consonants--a process which resulted in a large number of homophones. See, for instance, François Thureau-Dangin, Les Homophones Sumériens (Paris: Paul Geuthner, 1929), p. 28.

[2] Deimel, ŠL, Part II, vol. 1, p. 312 (112.1).

[3] Šulgi D: A Neo-Sumerian Royal Hymn (Ph.D. dissertation, University of Pennsylvania, 1968), p. 137 (1.260).

[4] Jacobsen points out that má and má-gur₈ mean "boat" or "barge" and are used to designate Nanna's vessel. (Jacobsen disagrees with Kramer's translation [gufa] and says that "one cannot travel upstream in a gufa; Nanna travels from Ur to Nippur in the story dealt with." "Sumerian Mythology: A Review Article," JNES 5 (1946):130. (Cf. Kramer's Sumerian Mythology [Philadelphia: University of Pennsylvania Press, 1944], pp. 47-49); Falkenstein also translates ma-gur₈-an-na-gim "wie das Himmelsschiff (leuchtest)." "Ein sumerisches Kultlied auf Samsujiluna," ArOr 17 (1949):217, 219 (line 62); cf. also Deimel, ŠL, Part II, vol. 1, p. 312 (122.14); ma-gu-ur = ma-ku-ru "rundes Schiff," Leo A. Oppenheim, Catalogue of the Cuneiform Tablets of the Wilberforce Eames Babylonian Collection, American Oriental Series, Vol. 32 (New Haven, CT: American Oriental Society, 1948), p. 161; etc.

With the determinative $^{(giš)}$má-gur₈ was used as an epithet of the moon-god.[1] The equation of ᵈmá-gur₈ with "nann[aru] 'Leuchte,' 'Licht,'" shows that má-gur₈ signified the new-moon sickle.[2] The etymology of má-gur₈ is, however, according to Åke Sjöberg, quite unproductive.[3]

Here the present writer would observe that the "unproductive etymology" is, no doubt, due (at least in part) to the fact that SI never means ship (boat). It is true, as Deimel points out, that the signs for SI (⊢≡𒌋𒌋) and ma₂ (⊢≡𒌋𒌋𒌋) are very similar even in the oldest texts.[4] Deimel therefore assumes that SI may refer to the picture of a ship, the front stem (prow) of which does not end in an animal head--as with the sign ma₂--but in a horn.[5] It was, on the other hand, the magur-boat [ma₂ = ship; gur₈ = bull] that ended in an animal head.[6] The concept of "bull" as an epithet for a god in ancient time was probably the reason why the magur-boat was used in the moon-cult referring to the "rundes Schiff" and, furthermore, as an epithet of the moon-god ⊢𒌋𒌋𒌋 ⊣𒌋 ⊢𒌋 / ⊢𒌋𒌋𒌋 (⊢𒌋) ᵈma₂-gur₈.[7]

---

[1] Åke Sjöberg, Der Mondgott Nanna-Su'en in der Sumerischen Überlieferung (Uppsala: Almqvist & Wiksell, 1960), p. 27.

[2] Ibid.   [3] Ibid.

[4] Deimel, "Recensioner," Or 6 (1937):268.

[5] Note that ^{giš}si-má₂ ⊢𒌋𒌋 ⊢𒌋𒌋𒌋 (⊢𒌋) = qarnu elippi, Deimel, SL, Part II, vol. 1, p. 289 (112.99).

[6] Deimel, "Recensiones," p. 274.

[7] Deimel, SL, Part III, vol. 1, p. 158; cf. Part II, vol. 1, pp. 312-13 (122.14-17).

For the introductory words to the Sumerian version of the story of the creation of Moon and Sun, Hermann Wohlstein gives the translation:

> Als An, Enlil und Enki, die grossen Götter, in ihrem unwandelbaren Entschluss das Schiff des Mondes eingesetzt hatten, die Mondsickel erglänzen zu lassen und den Mond ins Leben zu rufen, und als sie ihn als Wahrzeichen des Himmels und der Erde eingesetzt hatten, . . .[1]

For si-sar Deimel gives 𒋛𒊬 karnû--a passive participle construction of si.[2] He also lists 150 combinations (less frequent) in which the homophone si occurs as one part of the ideogram. The scope of these usages is momentous, but the meaning of all these occurrences is unfortunately not known.[3] Also Kurt Jaritz records several examples with "Bedeutung unbekannt."[4]

These "unknown" meanings arouse the curiosity of scholars and many conjectural interpretations have been suggested. But there is still no homogenous explanation. The meaning of si in many of these combinations is still obscure and the context often ambiguous--no matter whether one reasons out of the word to the context or vice versa.[5]

---

[1] "Die Gottheit An-Anu in Sumerisch-Akkadischen Urzeitsmythen," In memoriam Eckhard Unger Beiträge zu Geschichte, Kultur and Religion des Alten Orients (Baden-Baden: Valentin Koerner, 1971), p. 56.

[2] Deimel, ŠL, Part III, vol. 1, p. 180; cf. Part II, vol. 2, p. 289 (112.108).

[3] Ibid., Part II, vol. 1, pp. 286-93.

[4] Schriftarchäologie der altmesopotamischen Kultur (Graz: Akadamische Druck-und Verlagsanstalt, 1967), pp. 55-57; cf. also Rykle Borger's Akkadische Zeichenlisten (Neukirchen-Vluyn: Neukirchen Verlag, 1973), pp. 31, 32.

[5] Bendt Alster, Studies in Sumerian Proverbs, Mesopotamia 3, Studies in Assyriology (Copenhagen: Akademisk Forlag, 1975), p. 100.

A typical example is found in one of the old Sumerian hymns treated by Sjöberg.[1] This article is actually a continuation of a previous article written by him.[2] In the first hymn the greatness of Nergal is acclaimed with awe inspiring terms:

> Powerful Nergal, in heaven and earth (line 4)
> . . .
>
> Nergal, his greatness covers heaven and earth
>   to their outer limits (line 11)
> . . .
>
> Nergal, great dragon, covered with blood,
>   drinking the blood of living creatures (line 16)
> . . .
>
> Lord, who like his own father Nunamir, has the
>   power to create life (line 18)
> . . .
>
> It is within your power to determine destiny,
>   to render judgment and to make decision, (line 20)
> . . .
>
> You are standing (like) a lusty wild bull,
>   your great horn has smitten them (line 49)[3]

Sjöberg, however, admits that he does not understand the passage.[4] It is the context and not the construction of si-gal-zu which here offers the crux. The grammatical combination si-gal-zu is not hard to analyze by itself, as it is a normal chain-word

---

[1] "Miscellaneous Sumerian Hymns," ZA 63 (1973/74):1-55. This particular hymn is called: An Adab-song to Nergal with a prayer for King Šuilišu of Isin (p. 1).

[2] "Hymns to Meslamtaea, Lugalgirra and Nanna-Suen in Honour of King Ibbisuen (Ibbīsin) of Ur," OrSuec 19-20 (1970-71):140-70.

[3] The transliteration of line 49 reads: am-ma-az-za ba-ši-gub-bé-en si-gal-zu bi-tu$_x$ (=HUB); "Miscellaneous Sumerian Hymns," p. 4 (translation p. 7).

[4] Ibid., p. 12.

built on a noun (i.e., noun [si] + adjective [gal] + pronoun [zu]) and has been translated by Sjöberg in a literal sense. There are, however, other combinations of ideograms with si (as one component) reflecting a completely different meaning, for instance, that of "splendor" or "radiance."[1] Sjöberg refers to sources which indicate a clear connection between "horn" and "light."[2] Si-mú, for instance, could be an epithet for a god or goddess; as an epithet for Nanna (si-mú-kù-an-na . . .) "reines (helles) Licht des Himmels."[3] Sjöberg seems to think that behind this translation lies the concept of the "horns" of the moon.[4] He also refers to Stephen Langdon who translates si še-er-zi ^{d}utu-mul-mul-la-gim to Akkadian qarnāšu kīma šarūr ^{d}šamsi ittananbiṭu "seine [Enlils] Hörner sind Strahlenglanz des Sonnengottes, der immer wieder leuchtet."[5]

---

[1] Ibid., pp. 11, 12 on this point: si-múš-bi ma-az-ma-az = šarūrša ḫitbuṣ "her splendor is exuberant" (speaking of the goddess Inanna-Ištar, LKA 23.2, pp. 14, 15), and si-ma-az-bi u₄-è-a-gin_x mul-ma-al "whose exuberant radiance shines like the rising sunlight" (speaking of Marduk); see Louis J. Delaporte, Cat. cyl. or. 299, pp. 4-5; Bendt Alster, Studies in Sumerian Proverbs, p. 8, considers the possibility of the disappearing and returning Venus star as constituting the basic pattern in all Inanna myths; cf. Stephen Langdon, Sumerian and Babylonian Psalms (Paris: Paul Geuthner, 1909), esp. pp. xvi-xvii.

[2] Sjöberg, Der Mondgott, p. 144.

[3] For si-mú 𒋛𒈬 qarnû "mit Hörnern versehen" or "gehörnt," Sjöberg (ibid., p. 143) refers to Deimel SL, Part II, vol. 1, p. 289 (112.108); cf. Part II, vol. 1, p. 289 (112.110): ^{d}si-mu-a 𒋛𒈬𒀀 ( ) Sumerian "die Gehörnte" = ^{d}Ištar kakkabi "Ištar der Sterne."

[4] Sjöberg, Der Mondgott, p. 143.

[5] S. Langdon, IVR 27, 2, 5-6 (see SBP 220 xviii 5-6) as cited by Sjöberg, ibid., p. 144.

Furthermore, according to Sjöberg si-mus, "Glanz," is verified several times in the Old Babylonian texts.[1]

The context is here very important, as, of course, it always is when one carries on philological study.[2] Klein, for instance, translates am-zi am-gal-sè tu-da-gim si-mus-gú-nu-me-èn "you are adorned with splendid horns like a fecund ox, which was born to be a great ox."[3] In his commentary Klein says: "Judging from the context, si-mus is here to be translated 'splendid horns,' in the concrete sense of the word, and not 'radiance, splendor' as usual."[4] Klein thus is affirmative that si-mus in most cases has to be understood in a figurative sense. As an example of this latter usage, Klein refers to an Ur Lament: áb-mah-bi si-mùs-bi-ta ba-(ra-)an-dab₅-bé-es si-bi ba-ra-an-ku₅ "Its noble cows were seized by their splendid horns, their horns were cut off."[5]

The major source of imagery utilized by Sumerian poets was the animal kingdom.[6] Figurative speech was a sign of the sophisticated literary text just as it is today. Wolfgang Heimpel, in his very unique and helpful study, groups figurative speech into

---

[1] SBP 220 xviii 5-6 as quoted by Sjöberg, Der Mondgott, p. 144.

[2] Bendt Alster, The Instructions of Suruppak, Mesopotamia 2. Studies in Assyriology (Copenhagen: Akademisk Forlag, 1974), p. 8; cf. Claus Wilcke, "Philologische Bemerkungen zum Rat des Šuruppag," ZA 68 (December 1978):199-200.

[3] Šulgi D: transliteration p. 66 (1:29), translation p. 82 (1.29).

[4] Ibid., p. 103.   [5] Ibid.

[6] Wolfgang Heimpel, Tierbilder in der Sumerischen Literatur Studia Pohl, 2 (Rome: Päpstliches Bibelinstitut, 1968), pp. 1-4; so also Alster, Studies in Sumerian Proverbs, p. 12.

metaphors, comparisons, parables, images (similes), etc. He explains their usages and gives examples from each category.[1] Actually the only unknown genre among Sumerian poets was allegory.[2]

Metaphors are often found in proverbs,[3] but by the frequent use of figurative speech the original meaning was easily lost and the unique character of the whole metaphor became obscure. At what particular stage in the process of transmission this happened, however, is hard to determine.

Sometimes a saying may be ambiguous, as for example, "Ich (d. i. Inanna) bin ein Wisent, der im Gebirge die Hoerner erhebt" (alim kur-ra si! gùr-ru-me-en).[4] The gods (and goddesses) were in antiquity often given the epithet ox, and the gods were frequently depicted with horns.[5] There is, however, an equal possibility that si could refer to the moon.[6]

Another interesting example is given by Heimpel:

Seine (d.i. des Tempels Ki^jur) Mauerwerk ist rotglaenzendes Edelmetall. Es besitzt eine Fundamentplatte aus Lapislazuli. Wie ein Ur erhebt es in Sumer vielspitzig leuchtend die Hoerner. Alle Laender senken davor das Haupt.[7]

---

[1] Heimpel, Tierbilder, pp. 11-53.   [2] Ibid., p. 53.

[3] It is noticeable that a variety of domestic animals are used in proverbs, whereas wild animals seem to belong to the genre of myth; Alster, Studies in Sumerian Proverbs, p. 12.

[4] Heimpel, Tierbilder, p. 78. (The spelling with -e- to indicate "Umlaut" has been used interchangeably with the Umlaut spelling throughout the whole dissertation.)

[5] Klein, Šulgi D: transliteration p. 66, translation p. 82 (1:29).

[6] Ibid., p. 103 (1:29).   [7] Heimpel, Tierbilder, p. 83.

All the countries seem to have accepted the lordship of Sumer at this time; at least this is our conclusion from these boastful words. Samuel N. Kramer also refers to the same myth and says: ". . . the Kiur of the Ekur of Nippur, raises its shining horns over Sumer 'like a wild ox'."[1]

The Sumerian ideogram si-mul has been translated on a noun basis by Benno Landsberger with "Sternhorn."[2] But si-mul can also be used as a compound verb. Si-mul-di can mean both "zerhornen" and "leuchten von den Hoernern," and for the Sumerians the meaning of the two went together and could not be separated from each other.[3] Also one has to count on the fact that the Akkadian translation on si-mul-mul (below) is not literal but figurative.[4] "(Enlil), der wie ein ungestuemer Ur einmal dort im Bergland lagert, dessen Hoerner wie das Licht Utu's gleissen."[5]

A whole series of combinations with si is rendered in Akkadian with the word šarūru ("Glanz"), especially the combination si-mùs-gun.[6] In another example, ^{d}utu-gá-nun-ta-è-a-gim si-múš ḫa-ma-ab-gùn-gùn, the context seems ambiguous. Heimpel gives the

---

[1] Kramer, "Sumerian Similes," JAOS 89 (1969):6.

[2] Die Fauna des Alten Mesopotamien nach der 14. Tafel der Series Ḫar-ra Ḫubullu (Leipzig: S. Hirzel, 1934), p. 11.

[3] Heimpel, Tierbilder, p. 85.   [4] Ibid., pp. 85-86.

[5] Ibid., p. 110. (The translation is from the Akkadian text because the Sumerian text is corrupted; the gim in [mul-mul-la-gim] indicates that a metaphor is being used in this passage).

[6] Ibid., pp. 86, 89; cf. also p. 87 (si-mùs-gú-nu-me-en "funkelnde, gekruemmte [Hoerner]).

translation: "Wie bei Utu, der aus seinem Gemach kommt, moege er mir [d.i. Enmerkar] die geschwungenen Hoerner funkeln lassen."[1]

The horns in the literal sense were indicative of the strength of the Ur or "Auerochs," but no less so of the glowing horns of a god or perhaps of the moon. The omens of the moon were, of course, used in antiquity in all kinds of "Beschwörungstexte," and whoever had such an omen applied to his life and fortune had the great gods against him.

Heimpel also proposes that whenever the occurrence of the Sumerogram á is used in connection with horned animals, it refers to "horn" in a literal sense.[2] The Akkadian translation for á (of the bull) may be either qarnu or èmūqu.[3] Heimpel says further: "Es ist mir ausserdem kein Beleg bekannt, der fuer á 'Vorderfuss (eines Tieres) fordert'."[4]

---

[1] Ibid., p. 88; cf. p. 137 where Heimpel seems to indicate an apotropaic usage: "Die 'geschwungenen Hoerner' beziehen sich hier entweder auf Tempelzinnen oder auf die typisch elamische Uebung, am Tempel Hoerner anzubringen." Landsberger refers to the antelope (gazelle) as existing already in pre-dynastic era: "Auffällig sind die langen geschwungenen Hörner auf Siegeln der vordynastischen Perioden." "Geschwungenen Hörner" probably means "twisted horns;" cf. Landsberger's Die Fauna, p. 90; cf. also Encyclopedia Britannica (1977), s.v. "Antelope," by Leonard Harrison Matthews.

[2] Heimpel, Tierbilder, p. 93.

[3] Ibid., (Emūqu = Armkraft, Macht, Gewalt). Heimpel does not agree with some modern translations which give the meaning "Vorderfuss." So, for instance, Adam Falkenstein, "Untersuchungen zur sumerischen Grammatik (Fortsetzung)," ZA 47 (1942-43):181-223. Falkenstein holds that the Sumerian by the expression á-íl-íla "das Bild eines mit den Vorderfüssen aufbäumenden Stieres vor Augen hatte, ein Bild, das die frühe Glyptik ausserordentlich dargestellt hat" (p. 211). Falkenstein, however, admits that "anderseits ist die in den akkadischen Übersetzungen bezeugte Auffassung sicher schon in altbabylonischer Zeit vertreten, da UMBS V 103 Rs. 7 die Gleichung á = qarnum bietet" (p. 211); cf. also Falkenstein, "Sumerische Religiöse Texte," ZA 56 (1964):44-129 (esp. p. 52) ". . . das Getier, die Vierfüssigen der Steppe liessen sie zur Zierde vorhanden sein."

[4] Tierbilder, pp. 93-94.

Also Alster provides an example of the usage of the Sumerian á:[1] as á.zi na-ab-bal-e šu-uš im-ši-nigin in which á.zi na-ab-bal-e constitutes an idiom and can be translated, according to Alster, "Do not curse with violence." Later on the idiom á.zi was no longer understood and was replaced by á-zu (your arm).[2] If this interpretation is valid, it would show that the metaphor was the more ancient usage and when, in the course of time, the metaphorical meaning was lost the replacement of a literal expression was not the term "horn" but "arm" in this particular tradition. This is significant because this deliberate choice seems to indicate that the words "horn" and "arm" were equivalent locutions whereby to express the metaphor of "power." Furthermore, it seems evident that two different traditions are expressed in these terms: one tradition referring back to the power of an animal as the source of strength, i.e., the horns, and another tradition referring back to the power of a being (human or divine) as the source of strength, i.e. the arm.

There are other scholars who have observed a similar usage of à (i.e., with the meaning of "arm"). So, for instance Edmund I. Gordon who gives a typical example of the usage of á as follows: da-ga nam-kù-zu ᵈlamma á bí-ib-gar. Gordon suggests the following translation: "(When) reason was perseverant (?) the

---

[1] The Instructions of Suruppak, transliteration, pp. 36, 55 (#55), translation and notes pp. 37, 72 (#55).

[2] See Robert D. Biggs, Inscriptions from Tell Abu Ṣalābīkh (Chicago: University Press, 1974), p. 14, as cited by Alster, The Instruction of Suruppak, p. 87 (#55).

guardian-genius reinforced it (literally placed its strength [or 'arm'] upon it)."[1] In modern terms, Gordon suggests: "God helps them that help themselves" or "Man proposes, God disposes."[2] This example (and many others) shows that Heimpel takes a too one-sided view giving only one literal alternative ("horn") for the Sumerian á. However, we agree with Heimpel that in the context of "bull" the translation "horn" and not "Vorderfuss" is to be preferred.

The compound logogram si-sá (𒋛𒁉) = ašāru "to be in order," (išaru "straight," "right") and the (𒐕 𒋛𒁉) níg-si-sá = mīšaru, mēšaru, "righteousness"[3] are some of the pregnant expressions with si which are hard to explain etymologically though the meaning is known. (The word níg-si-sá is attested already as early as in the dynasty of Lugalbanda.)

In the text about the gods Claus Wilcke records the following passage of transliterated text:

. . . lugal(-e) nì-si-sá (-é) ki-ág nì-erím-e hul-gig
^{d}su′en-e nì-si-sá(e) ki-ág nì-erím-e hul-gig nì-si-sá-e
ša-e sà- *húl-la si-sá(bi) ša-ra-an (*Var. da-a-DU.)

Wilcke gives the following translation:

---

[1] Sumerian Proverbs (Philadelphia: The University Museum [University of Pennsylvania], 1959), p. 51 (#1.19); cf. p. 194 (#2.28).

[2] Ibid., p. 51 (1.19).

[3] Theo Bauer, Akkadische Lesestücke (Rome: Pontificium Institutum Biblicum, 1953), 3:4; cf. Rykle Borger, Akkadische Zeichenliste, Alter Orient und Altes Testament--Sonderreihe, vol. 6 (Neukirchen-Vluyn: Neukirchener Verlag, 1971), p. 31 (#112).

> Herr, der die Gerechtigkeit liebt, der das Böse hasst,
> Su^jen, der die Gerechtigkeit liebt, der das Böse hasst.
> Die Gerechtigkeit bereitete dir geradewegs Herzenfreude.[1]

The word "righteousness," which here occurs three times, is used with an abstract meaning, and the present writer sees here an indication of a divine attribute. It certainly seems that si has something to do with "righteousness," if Wilcke is right in his translation.

There may be other passages that would perhaps benefit from a translation based on an abstract rather than a concrete meaning.

Sidney Smith in an article written as long ago as 1933,[2] presented a suggestion for the translation of "pukku" and "mekku"[3] in the well-known Gilgameš Epic which has not had any large response in the scholarly world, as far as the present writer is aware. There are several ideas worth noting in this article.[4] Smith points out that the same ideogram in Sumerian may refer to different things.[5] He also notes that "pukku" and "mekku" are partly synonyms.[6] Furthermore, Smith shows that "giš zuraḫ is equated not only with mekū but also with lab (𒋃𒀭𒌅)-ba-na-a-tu."[7]

---

[1] Das Lugalbandaepos (Wiesbaden: Harrassowitz, 1968), pp. 76, 77.

[2] "b/pukk/qqu and mekku," RA 30.4 (1933):153-68.

[3] These debated words occur also in the Ištar Epic, referred to by Smith (ibid., p. 163).

[4] Since we have to rely completely on reading Sumerian only in translation, we depend fully on Smith in the remarks below.

[5] Smith, "b/pukk/qqu and mekku," p. 154.

[6] Ibid., p. 155.   [7] Ibid.

This instrument is mentioned in Sennacherib's famous description of his siege operations in Palestine. ina šukbus aramme u qitrub šupi mithuṣ zuk šepe pilši mīksi u labbannate alme akšud . . . labbanātu must mean trumpet.[1]

Smith also observes that there is another ideogram which is equivalent to both labbanātu and mekū, namely ^{giš}GEŠTIN which is to be read karan ["horn"?] (this has been shown by Deimel).[2] Furthermore, Smith points out that karan ["horn"?] had two parts, the pattu and the kizallu. In the Ištar Epic kizallu is applied to a musical instrument. Smith, however, remarks that "the attempt to connect this word with Semitic languages breaks down . . . the Sumerian original must be looked for elsewhere."[3] Smith then refers to the syllabary published by Bruno Meissner[4] where ^{giš}ZAL with the reading gizzal or gissal is given in the following Akkadian equivalents: hasisu, nišmu, qūlu, qālu, utequ, p/bukku (variant p/buqqu).[5] Smith

---

[1] Ibid.

[2] ŠL 15.227 and Knudtzon, el-Amarna, 22, I 36, II 54, III 45 as cited by Smith (ibid., p. 155); It is interesting to find the sign ⌂⌐⌐ ⌐⌐⌐ ⌐⌐ ⌐⌐ (⌐) til-la-tum, ḫu-un-na-tum, having the meaning "Weinrebe" ("branch," "shoot of a vine") and also the meaning labbanâtu "Breschemaschine" (a machine breaking through and with the figurative meaning "to break the back of a thing"). The same Sumerian sign also means mekû "Breschestange," "a pole or stick to break with" (see Deimel, ŠL, Part II, vol. 1, p. 62 (#15.227). Deimel also gives the logogram gi-eš-tin (= Geštin) ⌐⌐⌐ (= ka-ra-nu) with the meaning of "Rebe," "Wein" ŠL, Part II, vol. 1, p. 436 (#210.2) and Part III, vol. 1, p. 45 (geštin).

[3] Smith, "b/pukk/qqu and mekku," p. 156.

[4] Beiträge zum assyrischen Wörterbuch (Chicago: The University of Chicago Press, 1931), II, 89, 65ff. as cited by Smith (ibid., p. 156).

[5] Smith, "b/pukk/qqu and mekku," p. 156.

draws the conclusion that "gizzal meant in the opinion of the scribe an instrument that causes attention," and adds, "not a bad description of a trumpet or horn."[1] Smith is also making us aware of another important point, namely, that although gizzal ordinarily was thought of as being an object of wood, it "may be thought that gizzal in this connection does not mean an object of wood, but is abstract; indeed Deimel suggests this."[2]

The association of trumpets and horns with lament is known from the ancient culture of Mesopotamia as well as among other cultures, and this has also been emphasized by Smith. He also makes an interesting suggestion[3] in this connection when he says that the lament might have begun: "Divine karan [horn?] of heaven."[4] The context of the lament refers to a special day. Alexander Heidel translates Tablet XII, 56, 57 of the Gilgameš Epic: "Father [Enlil], on the day that my pukku fell into the underworld and my mikkú fell into the underworld." According to our understanding the locution "this day" refers to a particular day in a context which may refer to an explicit or definite day in history.

---

[1] Ibid.   [2] Ibid.

[3] According to the wish of Smith, this suggestion is subject to all necessary reserve (p. 166).

[4] Ibid.; the lament of the lost "pukku" and "mekku" in the Gilgameš epic takes on a new interest if something abstract was meant rather than an object of wood (see "The Epic of Gilgameš," Table XII in ANET³, pp. 97-99); cf. Kramer, "The Epic of Gilgameš and its Sumerian Sources," JAOS 64 (1944):7-23 (esp. pp. 19-23); Alexander Heidel, The Gilgamesh Epic and Old Testament Parallels, 2d. ed. (Chicago: The University of Chicago Press, 1949), p. 97. Our conjectural guess would be that ^{giš}E.AG (ideogram for mekku) might be a synonym for KA.DI (the logogram is used in the Gudea,

Si with reference to music has been attested in several texts. Robert D. Biggs, for instance, has attested several occurrences of si in the Abu Ṣalābīkh tablets.[1] Biggs points out that the Abu Ṣalābīkh Text 281[2] has several occurrences of gù si ba₄.ra "sounded the horn" while the Fara text has gù si ba.ra.[3]

Fadhil A. Ali has published a Sumerian text[4] which substantiates that si was used for "blowing the horn." The text deals with a court decision. A merchant by the name Urshul had lost a seal which was provided with his signature and the "bailiff" was to announce this publicly. The text informs that "the bailiff went to the streets and blew the horn, obviously to draw people's attention to the announcement."[5]

Cylinder A, VI, 25 as a parallel to giš ellag, see Smith's discussion on p. 165; cf. also the beginning of the Gilgameš lament, Smith, p. 166) and refer to an abstract divine gift that had been lost and for that reason was lamented. Åke Sjöberg, in The Collection of the Sumerian Temple Hymns (TH no. 33) in Texts from Cuneiform Sources, vol. 3 (Locust Valley, NY: J. J. Augustin, 1969), p. 41 translates ᵈKA.DI lugal-BIR-an-na-ke₄ "Ištaran, the . . . king (lord) of heaven. (For SI-DI = išaru, mešaru, see G. Howard, Clavis Cuneorum sive Lexicon signorum assyriorum [London: Apud H. Milford, 1904-33], p. 237.) The avenues for translating "pukku" and "mekku" are far from being exhausted. The matter needs further clarification before one can draw a definitive conclusion. It has to be admitted that the text is difficult and the true meaning elusive.

[1] "The Abū Ṣalābīkh Tablets," JCS 20 (1966):73-88. These tablets are of great importance for many of the texts are duplicates of texts from Fara. These two text-collections can therefore serve as mutual controls (ibid., p. 88).

[2] This text is in many ways similar to text Fara 2, no. 40, which is an important literary text (ibid., p. 81).

[3] Ibid.

[4] This text has been reconstructed from five duplicates; see Fadhil A. Ali, "Blowing the Horn for Official Announcement," Sumer 20 (1964):66.

[5] Ibid.

The transcript of this particular passage reads:

<u>nimgir-e</u> <u>sila-sila-a</u> <u>si</u> <u>gù</u> <u>ba-ni-in-ra</u>
<u>lú-na-me</u> <u>nig-na-me</u> <u>ugu-na</u> <u>li-bí-in-tu-ku</u>

"the bailiff blew the horn [<u>si</u>] in the streets,
(so that) no one may have any claim against him."[1]

Kramer provides a similar example from one text of the Gilgameš Epic.[2] Realizing that he once must die like all mortals, Gilgameš determines to raise up a name for himself, and he sets out on his journey to a far-away "Land of the Living" felling its cedars and bringing them to Erech. The apparent success prompted Gilgameš to "act joyfully," for the passage reads:

He brings into the . . . of the mountains,
Who felled the cedar, acted joyfully,
The Lord Gilgamesh, acted joyfully,
In his city, as one man, he . . .[3]

The last line reads in transcript:

<u>uru</u> ^{ki}-<u>na</u> <u>lu-as-gim</u> <u>si-ka</u> <u>ba-ni-in-ra</u>[4]

To "sound the horn" was thus an ordered procedure of announcing important events--whether of negative or of positive contents.

To sum up briefly what has been said of the meaning of <u>SI</u>, the present writer would appeal to Henry Ward Beecher's statement: "The soul without imagination is what an observatory would be with-

---

[1] Ibid., pp. 66, 67.

[2] "Gilgamesh and the Land of the Living," <u>JCS</u> 1 (1947):10 (line 48). (This epic was formerly called "Gilgamesh and Huwawa.")

[3] Kramer, ibid., p. 11 (lines 45-48).

[4] Kramer points out the variations (<u>am</u> for <u>gim</u> and <u>ga</u> for <u>ka</u> [ibid., p. 11, nos. 45, 46], cf. the correction and completion of the translation by Ali: <u>uru</u>^{ki}-<u>na</u> <u>lú-as-gin</u>$_x$ <u>si</u> <u>gù</u> (var. <u>ga</u>) <u>ba-ni-in-ra</u> "In his city, (the people gathered) as one man when he (Gilgamesh) blew the horn." ("Blowing the Horn," p. 68, n. 3).

out a telescope."[1] With this statement as a "security" we would point out, first of all, that the magur-boat, whether in reference to a ^{giš} má-gur with an animal head at the prow or to ^{d}má-gur as an epithet, should not be confused with the si(-si)-ma₂, which according to its sign-combination [ideogram] refers to a boat [ship] ending in a horn.[2] Secondly, the elision of the final consonant [sig -g = si], which at some early stage in the development of the language took place and resulted in a large number of homophones, has no doubt a great responsibility in the many "unknown" meanings of SI in compound logograms.[3] Thirdly, the Moon-god and the Bull (ox) epithets referred to in various translations describing the gods (and kings) with horns seem to be interdependent on each other. The SI with the meaning of "light" or "radiance," no doubt refers to the moon while the SI in certain combinations refers to the literal horns of a bull (ox). This latter usage seems in many instances to be metaphorical. Fourthly, the abstract usage of SI requires further investigation and every specific compound logogram [ideogram] would have to be investigated and its usages analyzed.[4] Fifthly, SI was also used as referring to the instrument of horn used to proclaim a message of importance or a joyful victory.

---

[1]Cited in the New Dictionary of Thoughts, A Cyclopedia of Quotations, ed. Tryon Edwards, et al. (Standard Book Company, 1966), p. 292.

[2]Cf. p. 4, and n. 19 (above).   [3]Cf. n. 11.

[4]Because of the large amount of SI combinations (150 variations according to Deimel, SL, Part II, vol. 1, pp. 286-93 [112:1-150]) a thorough investigation offers an opportunity of research for another dissertation.

Qarnu in Akkadian

Preliminary Considerations

The term Akkadian was used during the last century by many scholars as applying to the Sumerian language.[1] Rykle Borger adds the information, "Mit 'akkadisch' ist der sumerische Hauptdialekt gemeint, mit 'sumerisch' Emesal."[2] In light of the knowledge we have of the usage of these two dialects, the above statement would have to be interpreted with the meaning that Akkadian was the administrative and business language whereas the Emesal (Sumerian) was used for literary purposes.[3] This split of the Sumerian (Akkadian) language would thus be even more abrupt than when we today speak of "Umgangssprache" and "Hochdeutsch" in Germany or of "nynorsk" and "bokmål" in Norway. In any case, scholars who define the Emesal language as the "women's language"[4] apparently define the term Emesal needlessly rigidly.

---

[1] So, for instance, Paul Haupt in his presentation at the 5th Internationalen Orientalisten-Congresse in Berlin 1883 in his lecture: Die akkadische Sprache (Berlin: A. Asher & Co., 1883), cited in Handbuch der Keilschriftliteratur, ed. Rykle Borger (Berlin: Walter de Gruyter & Co., 1967), 1:185.

[2] Borger, Handbuch der Keilschriftliteratur, 1:185.

[3] William F. Albright called the Emesal an "obscure dialect." ARI (Baltimore: Johns Hopkins Press, 1942), p. 45; for further discussion see, for instance, Johannes J. A. Van Dijk, La Sagesse Sumero-Accadienne (Leiden: E. J. Brill, 1953), pp. 89, 99; Edmund I. Gordon, Sumerian Proverbs, p. 13; Claus Wilcke, "Formale Gesichtspunkte in der sumerischen Literatur," in Sumerological Studies, p. 207, and Stephen Liebermann, The Sumerian Loanwords in Old-Babylonian Akkadian, Harvard Semitic Studies, no. 22 (Missoula, MT: Scholars Press, 1977), p. 33.

[4] This view has now been nearly universally abandoned. So, for instance, Igor M. Diakonoff, "Ancient Writing and Ancient Written Language," in Sumerological Studies, pp. 113-16. Eme-KU is now the current term for "Akkadian" (the main dialect) while Eme-SAL has maintained its technical term for the literary language.

The older conception of Sumerian and Akkadian with reference to dialects is here left aside and we use the term Akkadian to include also the two main dialects into which the Semitic Akkadian language split: the Assyrian and the Babylonian.

In spite of various systems of subdividing the eras of the Akkadian civilization and in spite of different concepts as to linguistic terminology, it is generally agreed that the Akkadian language has a Semitic structure in contrast to the non-Semitic Sumerian language.[1]

In spite of the fact that with the heyday of the Babylonian culture we stand on firmer ground,[2] there are still various theories in regard to the origin, transmission, and development of the Akkadian language.

Hard as it is to determine where and when the Akkadian script took form, it seems certain, however, from a historical-chronological viewpoint to suggest that by the time of the Sargonic age (ca. 2500-2200 B.C.), the taking over of the Sumerian Script for writing Akkadian was already in full swing.[3]

---

[1] So, for instance, Jerrold S. Cooper, "Sumerian and Akkadian in Sumer and Akkad," Or 42 (1973):239; cf. Gene M. Schramm, "The Semitic Languages: An Overview," in Current Trends in Linguistics, ed. Thomas A. Sebeok (The Hague: Mouton, 1970), 6:257-60; Edward Ullendorff, "Comparative Semitics," in Current Trends, p. 264.

[2] Adam F. Falkenstein and Wolfram von Soden, Sumerische und akkadische Hymnen und Gebete (Zürich: Artemis-Verlag, 1953), Einführung, p. 7.

[3] Von Soden, Das Akkadische Syllabar, p. xxx.

The Meaning of Qarnu

The basic meaning of qarnu is horn.[1] This meaning has been attested in various cuneiform texts from the Old Assyrian and Old Babylonian time and through the Middle-Assyrian and Middle-Babylonian period right down to the neo-Assyrian and neo-Babylonian time.

Qarnu is used in the literal sense referring to domestic horned animals;[2] it is also used of horn with decorative purpose,[3] etc.

We also find the word qarnu attested in legendary texts originating already partly from the Sargonic period and from a later time. A classical example is the text of the "Legend of Naram-Sin," copied by T. G. Pinches. Here the apparent idiom qá-ar-na-am qá-ar-na-am "Horn (an) Horn [? Seite an Seite?]" provides an example of a literal-extended usage.[4]

Most frequently, however, the word qarnu occurs in mythological context. In the sixth tablet of the Gilgameš Epic,[5] the

---

[1] Wolfram von Soden, AHW (Wiesbaden: Otto Harrassowitz, 1965-1972), 2:904; Friedrich Delitzsch, HWB (Leipzig: J. C. Hinrichs, 1896; reprint ed., Leipzig, 1975), p. 597; Carl Bezold, Babylonisch-Assyrisches Glossar (Heidelberg: Carl Winter, 1926), p. 247; Theo Bauer, Akkadische Lesestücke: Glossar (Rome: Pontificium Institutum Biblicum, 1953), 3:27.

[2] Leo A. Oppenheim and F. Louis Hartman, "The Domestic Animals of Ancient Mesopotamia According to the XIIIth Tablet of the Series ḪAR-ra = ḫubullu," JNES 4 (1945):152-77.

[3] Franz Köcher, "Ein Inventartext aus Kār-tukulti-Ninurta," AfO 18 (1957-58):300-13.

[4] Hans Gustav Güterböck, "Keilschrifttexte nach Kopien von T. G. Pinches," 11. Bruchstück eines altbabylonischen Naram-Sin Epos," AfO 13 (1934-41):46-50 (Transliteration, p. 46, line 7; translation, p. 47).

[5] R. Campbell Thompson, The Epic of Gilgamesh (Assyrian version), Text, Translation, and Notes (Oxford: At the Clarendon Press, 1930), p. 41 (lines 168-70).

Bull of Heaven is described as having horns.[1] The gods in antiquity bore the epithet ox (bull) or lion (or other epithets) and this was especially true of Enlil, who was regarded as the "supreme"[2] god already in Sumerian time and throughout the Old Babylonian time when Sumerian and neo-Sumerian epics, myths, and legends were especially treasured. In the very first line of the Šulgi Hymn (C), for instance, the epithets "Wild Bull" and "Lion" are attested.[3]

The mythological usage of horn is not restricted only to gods but is applied to demons, mixed creatures, serpents, etc.[4]

A much disputed usage of qarnu comes from the Old Babylonian time and has been translated by many scholars with the meaning of "skirt" or "hem of a dress." All the instances here referred to come from Mari or nearby areas. George Dossin, for instance, working with a cuneiform fragment which proved to be a letter from the royal palace in Mari, writes:

---

[1] For a translation, see Ephraim A. Speiser, "Akkadian Myths and Epics: The Epic of Gilgameš," in ANET³, p. 85.

[2] "Enlil, dont la souveraineté sur les dieux est suprême, . . ." Edmond Sollberger and Jean-Robert Kupper, Inscriptions royales sumériennes et akkadiennes (Paris: Les éditions du Cerf, 1971), p. 223.

[3] So in Giorgo Raffaelo Castellino Two Šulgi Hymns (BC), Studi Semitici, vol. 42 (Rome: Istituto Di Studi Del Vicino, 1972), p. 249; cf. also "Sumerischer Hymnus auf Enlil" (translated by Hartmut Schmökel) in Religionsgeschichtliches Textbuch zum Alten Testament, ed. Walter Beyerlin (Göttingen: Vandenhoeck & Ruprecht, 1975), pp. 124-30; see esp. p. 125 where the epithet "der Löwe" is used.

[4] For horns on gods, see, for instance, Eckhard Unger, "Götterbild," in RLV (Berlin: Walter de Gruyter & Co., 1926), vol. 4, pt. 2; for specific gods see under particular entries (ibid.); Karl Frank, Bilder und Symbole Babylonisch-assyrischer Götter (Leipzig: J. C. Hinrichs, 1906), pp. 1-32. For horn on demons, mixed creatures, serpents, etc. see RLV under respective entries.

Judging by the type of script it seems that Zimri-Lim rather than Iasmah-Adad had been the receiver. The sender is a 'servant' of the king of Mari and as he affirms his faithfulness in the service of his master it is not possible that it is a question of a ruling prince in some city of Mesopotamia of the North but rather an area located on the route from Mari to the land of the Hittites.[1]

The primary interest (for our purpose) is, however, not so much the "Hattusa" as the expression [ù] (?) q[a]-ra-an ṣubât Ia [. . .] which Dossin translates "et (?) le pan du vêtement de Ia . . ."[2] In his commentary on the text Dossin refers to other letters from Mari wherein the same expression is found:

qaran ṣubât X ṣabâtum and qaran ṣubât X wuššurum "saisir ou (re)lâcher la corne du vêtement, c'est-à-dire le pan du vêtement de quelqu'un." Le geste de la saisie du pan du manteau exprime la soumission, le geste de l'abandon du pan du manteau la defection. Ce sens ressort des passages suivants: (1') ki-a-am iq-bu-ni[m um-ma šu-nu-ma] (2') qa-ra-an ṣú-ba-at Zi-i[m-ri-li-im] (3') [ṣa]-ba-at ša qa-bi-šu e-pu[úš] Ils s'exprimèrent ainsi: "Saisis le pan du vêtement de Zimrilim; exécute ses ordres."[3]

The aspect of submission on the part of the one touching the skirt of his master's garment is clearly brought out in the passage in the translation given.

Hildegard Lewy, referring to the above text by Dossin, says that the texts from Mari use qaran ṣubatim "horn of garment" in the sense of sissiktu or qannu.[4] She further is of the opinion that qannu is a variant of qarnu "horn."[5] Assimilation of -r- into -n-

---

[1] "Une mention de Hattusa dans une lettre de Mari," RHA 35 (1939):70, line 1 (freely translated).

[2] Ibid., pp. 70, 71.   [3] Ibid., p. 72.

[4] "The Nuzian Feudal System," Or 11 (1942):313, n. 2.

[5] Ibid.

would thus have taken place (perhaps only locally under the impact of the Amorite language).[1] As a support for her view, Lewy refers to similar orthographic phenomena (where assimilation has occurred): annabu "hare" and arnabatum "female hare."[2] Lewy also points out that since "qannu is to qarnu as annu 'sin' . . ."[3] is to arnu 'sin' . . ."[4] and . . . in the Fellîḫi dialect, Aramaic qarnâ 'horn' is replaced by qanná, . . . this conclusion is all the more likely.[5] The old custom of making an impression with the hem of one's garment on the document when a purchase took place, and that before witnesses, is well attested.[6]

François Thureau-Dangin in 1912 published an important text concerning a copper tablet dated to an intermediate era between the epoch of Agade and Dynasty III of Ur. From the correspondence we learn that Arišen was a vassal of Zimri-Lim. His relationship to Zimri-Lim is revealed in the following words: ". . . u_4-mi-em an-ni-em qa-ra-an ṣubat Zi-im-ri-li-im [iṣ]-ba-at . . ." which Charles F. Jean has translated, "Depuis ce jour où (Arišen) s'est

---

[1] Heteroclitic stems were known, for instance, in the Anatolian languages of which the best known today is the Hittite language. See Albrecht Goetze, Kleinasien (München: C. H. Beck, 1957), pp. 56, 57.

[2] "The Nuzian Feudal System," p. 313, n. 2; cf. Joseph A. Fitzmyer, The Aramaic Inscriptions of Sefîre, Biblica et Orientalia, no. 19 (Rome: Pontifical Biblical Institute, 1967), p. 50 (Sf. I A 33).

[3] Delitzsch, HWB, p. 102.   [4] Ibid., p. 135.

[5] Lewy, "The Nuzian Feudal System," p. 313, n. 2.

[6] Ibid.

soumis à la puissance de Zimri-Lim. . . ."[1] However, Jean gives the literal translation in a footnote as follows: "(Arišen) a saisi 'le bord' du vêtement de Zimri-Lim," and refers to Paul Koschaker for the explanation.[2]

Koschaker in a brief article[3] points out that the garment of a person in a unique way represents the individual. It is a "Persönlichkeitssymbol," which in the long run may lie as the basis for a magical concept. Thus garment is equal to personality and change of garment equal to change of personality. Both of these concepts operate not only in law but also in magic, superstition, religion, and cult. But as a rule, only a certain part of the garment is used, and, indeed, qannu and sissiktu. The meaning of these words is debated. Koschaker reservedly suggests (with a "vielleicht" sentence) qannu to mean "Gewandsaum" (border, hem) and sissiktu to mean "Gewandzipfel" (corner of a garment). Whatever the translation, there seems to be no fundamental contrast in their juristic usage. For the sake of curiosity the following statement by Koschaker is of interest as he writes: "So ist Ablegen, Wegnehmen des Gewandes, Abschneiden des qannu oder sissiktu Verstossungssymbol

---

[1] "Arišen dans les lettres de Mari," Semitica 1 (1948):19, 20; cf. also André Finet, "Lettres de Iawi-ilâ," (148.8) in ARM XIII: Textes Divers (Paris: Paul Geuthner, 1964), p. 155, who also translates q[a-ra]-an ṣubat "le bord du vêtement;" Donald J. Wiseman, "Abban and Alalaḫ," JCS 12 (1958):124-29 takes the same position, i.e., by seizing the horn of another king's garment one forfeited his former privileges.

[2] Ibid., p. 20, n. 1.

[3] "Kleidersymbolik in Keilschriftrechten," Actes du 20e Congrès International des Orientalistes Bruxelles 5-10 Septembre 1938 (Louvain: Bureaux du Muséon, 1940), pp. 117-19.

(altbabyl. Recht, Nuzi, Ras Šamrā, heth. Gesetze)."[1] Koschaker explains that the same tradition is enforced in society where the rejected child or the separated wife, by laying aside the garment, lawfully becomes a new person and thus a stranger to the hitherto existing family. Also the custom of chasing away the adultress naked from her home belongs to this tradition.[2]

As for qannu being a variant of qarnu, Ephraim A. Speiser takes a completely contrary view. Building his opinion on Koschaker, Speiser admits the old Akkadian tradition of the "hem of garment" serving as an extension of one's personality, and by the very act signifying "surrender to punishment in case of non-compliance,"[3] he does not agree with Lewy's view of qannu being equated with qarnu "horn," "corner." Speiser offers two weighty reasons why he cannot accept Lewy's view: first, qarnu alone does not designate "hem of garment" (only in connection with ṣubat), and second, the laws of Eshnunna have established the occurrences of kannum with the initial -k-.[4] As for the first objection, Alster's warning against a too literal translation[5] is here appropriate,

---

[1] Ibid., pp. 117-18.

[2] Eduard Dhorme, Georges Dossin, A. Schott and P. O. Schaumberger agree with Koschaker on his views and translation in "Kleidersymbolik" (ibid., p. 119).

[3] "Palil and Congeners: A Sampling of Apotropaic Symbols," in Studies in Honor of Benno Landsberger on his Seventy-fifth Birthday April 21, 1965, Assyriological Studies, no. 16 (Chicago: University Press, 1965), p. 393, n. 32.

[4] Ibid.

[5] Alster, The Instructions of Suruppak, pp. 7-8.

especially as the context clearly suggests an idiom being used. As for the second objection, we have no sure answer: perhaps it is an orthographic misspelling or variation in the Eshnunna laws (though this explanation seems vague). More clarity is needed here. But if the evidence has to be based on numbers, it seems that too many pros outweigh Speiser's cons.

Qarnu with reference to the moon occurs frequently in astrological and omen texts. The edges of the sickle of the moon were in antiquity considered as the horns of the moon, and, accordingly, most dictionaries and glossary lists include the "horns of the moon" under the entry qarnu.[1]

The concept of the horns of the moon originated in the Sumerian kingdom, because of the moon-god Sin that was worshiped in Ur and in Harran. The Babylonians, for the purpose of astrological calculations, made minute observation of the phases of the moon. Later the omen predictions were connected with this particular science.

Reginald C. Thompson shows that the omens were deduced "from all the celestial bodies known to them, . . . but the Moon was the chief source. . . ."[2] The "sharpness" or "bluntness" of the horns was important; whether the horns were equal or unequal, etc. A few "predictions" cited by Thompson may serve as examples:

---

[1] So Bezold, Babylonisch-assyrisches Glossar, p. 247, von Soden, AHW, 2:904, Bauer, Glossar, 3:27; and Delitzsch, HWB, p. 597.

[2] Reginald C. Thompson, The Reports of the Magicians and Astrologers of Nineveh and Babylon (London: Luzac and Co., 1900), 1:xxiv.

If the horns are pointed, the king will overcome whatever he goreth . . . ; When the Moon rideth in a chariot the yoke of the king of Akkad will prosper; When the Moon is low at its appearance, the submission [of the people] of a far country will come to the king.[1]

Not only the "horns" of the moon were of importance in the omen texts but equally important was the Agû Apir. The agû here refers to the fullness of the moon and is probably derived from the Sumerian aga or mer.[2] The agû of the moon was apparently seen as the crown (halo) of the moon-god Sin. On several seals the gods are represented as having two bull horns, instead of the moon sickle, on the head. Deimel expresses his belief that these might mean the same as the new moon horns, in which the "Tiara" (aga = agû) of the moon-god was seen.[3]

The incantation texts also refer to the "Light of Heaven," most probably with reference to the moon.[4] Also the prophylactic figures in Babylonian rituals of exorcism are well known. They served the purpose of warding off calamities and expelling evil influences. A figure of clay or wood was first used in the ritualistic cult process before finally being taken to the house where the rituals of purification continued. It was eventually buried as the protector of the house.[5]

---

[1] Ibid.   [2] Unger, "Diadem und Krone," RLA, 2:209.

[3] Deimel, "Zur Erklärung sumerischer Wörter und Zeichen," Or 13 (1944):333.

[4] So, for instance, Erica Reiner, Šurpu: A Collection of Sumerian and Akkadian Incantations IX, 1-29 in AfOSupp 11. Ed. Ernest Weidner (Graz: Im Selbstverlage des Herausgeber, 1958), p. 48.

[5] Oliver R. Gurney, "Babylonian Prophylactic Figures and Their Rituals," AAA 22 (1935):31-35.

Sidney Smith, referred to by Oliver R. Gurney, translates sibitti ṣalmê ilāni sibitti ša iṣbi-ni agê ramani-šú-nu ap-ru lu-bu-uš ramāni-šú-nu labšu: "Seven statues of the seven gods, of tamarisk-wood, crowned with their proper head-dresses and clad in their proper garments."[1] The agê is used with the meaning of "headdress" with the addition that bands of copper encircled their heads.[2] Further details say: karnāt erî šak-nu "(and furnished with copper horns, . . ."[3] The same attire and weapons are repeated later on in the text.[4] The horns, no doubt, gave extraordinary power to the prophylactic figure and guaranteed success in the ritual.

From these examples presented it is apparent that qarnu in Akkadian basically has the same meaning as the Sumerian SI. It is used in the literal sense in which the meaning is self-evident. The word is also used with a literal-extended meaning, in idioms, for instance, as the "Legend of Naram-Sin" shows. Most frequently, however, qarnu occurs in mythological contexts with a purely extended meaning. Various mythological beings--mostly gods and goddesses--are described as wearing horns. The epithet "Bull" applied to the gods also provides the framework of the horn-motif alluding to the fact that it was the bull's horns that exerted an almost magic influence on this ancient people.

---

[1] Text KAR 298 translated and commented upon by Smith is together with other texts included in Gurney's article (ibid.). The particular passage (298.21) shows how the headdress and garment played an important role in magic (Gurney, pp. 66, 67).

[2] Ibid. [3] Text KAR 298.24 (ibid., p. 67).

[4] KAR 298.31, 33 (ibid., pp. 68, 69).

A new interesting usage seems to have originated among the West-Semites, for especially from Mari come several texts using qarnu with the meaning of "skirt" or "dress-hem." It is often used in legal contexts where it takes on the connotation of an "extreme limit" or "utmost point" as representative for wholeness or completeness--the whole of a garment, for instance. When the hem of the garment was used to make an impression on a legal contract (instead of a seal), it represented the whole garment and its owner. Probably under Amorite influence the anomalous spelling of qannu occurs and proves the tendency of assimilation in West-Semitic dialects.

The usage of horns with reference to the moon is persistent both in mythological and omen texts. In the former case qarnu very frequently takes on the meaning of "light" or "radiance," while in the latter it refers to the literal "horns" of the moon (i.e., the sickle), and it is in this context we find the many omen texts with their credulous explanations.

At the close of this section, in which we have discussed the meaning of qarnu, we refer to Erica Reiner who makes the following remark about the Akkadian language:

> Since it is written with special characters which have to be painfully learned and whose combinations seem inexhaustible, every text takes on the character of a puzzle, of a secret code to be deciphered, and hence acquires either a kind of mystique--it remains, ultimately, elusive and unattainable--or a pompous and pedantic apparatus to justify a reading or an interpretation.[1]

---

[1] "Akkadian," in *Current Trends in Linguistics*, ed. Thomas A. Sebeok (The Hague: Mouton, 1970), 6:293.

In spite of all these impedimenta (which apply not only to Akkadian but also to its "precursor," the Sumerian) we have attempted to explore the usage and meaning of qarnu. We conclude that the basic meaning of qarnu is "horn;" but, as in any other language ambiguity may in certain cases occur and especially so in metaphorical usages.

QRN in Ugaritic

Preliminary Considerations

Many great textual discoveries have come about in a fortuitous way rather than by planned systematic search, and the Ras Shamra texts belong to this former category. Since 1929, when the first expedition to Ras Shamra under the leadership of Claude F.-A. Schaeffer was undertaken, a continuous stream of tablets has come to light[1] which, especially in the first decade, created great excitement. The enthusiasm among Ugaritic scholars still exists half a century later. In 1969 Mitchell Dahood wrote:

> Driver's prediction "The pan-Babylonian theories of Haupt and his contemporaries have long passed away, half forgotten unlamented, thanks to their extravagances; and the pan-Ugaritism of the present age will go the same way" . . . as yet shows no signs of being fulfilled."[2]

Arvid S. Kapelrud, some years earlier, expressed the same opinion that the Ras Shamra discoveries cannot be underestimated by anyone who is fully aware of the fact that hardly anything

---

[1] Cyrus H. Gordon, UT, AnOr, 38 (Rome: Pontifical Biblical Institute, 1965), p. 1.

[2] Mitchell Dahood, "Ugaritic-Hebrew Syntax and Style," UF 1 (1969):15.

definite was known of the site before the excavation.[1]

Up to the time of the discovery of the Ugarit tablets, the documentary evidences from Canaan,[2] apart from the biblical references, had been confined to certain "Phoenician royal inscriptions, and the Egyptian papyrus of Wen-Amon."[3]

J. William Jack points out the value of the evidences concerning the religion in Syria and Palestine in the premonarchical era.[4] Another valuable evidence from Jack's point of view is that the Ras Shamra texts contradict the premise of the "Reuss-Graf-Wellhausen school," namely, that "the Israelites could not have had documents at their disposal written before the epoch of the kings."[5] Jack even quotes a statement from a personal letter written by René Dussaud:

> C'est une révolution complète de l'exégèse des temps prémosaïque. Ces récits n'ont pas été inventés de toutes pièces au temps des rois de Juda et d'Israel; ils reposent sur des événements réels. . . . L'hypercriticisme subit une sérieuse défaite: les textes ont plus de valeur qu'on ne l'a parfois pensé. . . . Pour la première fois Ras Shamra fournit une documentation externe.[6]

---

[1]Arvid S. Kapelrud, The Ras Shamra Discoveries (Norman, OK: University of Oklahoma Press, 1963), p. 3.

[2]For a rather comprehensive discussion of the importance and impact of the Ras Shamra discovery in regard to literature and linguistics as well as in other aspects, see Albright; "The Old Testament and Canaanite Language and Literature," CBQ 7 (1945):5-31.

[3]John Gray, "Canaanite Kingship in Theory and Practice," VT 2 (1952):194.

[4]The Ras Shamra Tablets and their Bearing upon the Old Testament. Old Testament Studies, no. 1 (Edinburgh: T. & T. Clark, 1935), p. 6.

[5]Ibid.   [6]Ibid., p. 7.

The identification of the ancient city of Ugarit[1] from the second millennium B.C. presented no difficulty, for the name occurs several times in the texts discovered. Ugarit is also known from the Tell el-Amarna letters and is attested from the archives of Zimri-Lim and also appears in the Hittite texts from Boghazköy.[2] For the latest identification the Ebla texts might seem prospective, but so far there is no evidence. With the short geographical distance between Ebla and Ugarit, we may conjecturally assume that one day the verification will appear.

The geographical location of the "Fennel Mound"[3] or "Fennel Head"[4] lay not far from the sea, between two brooks.[5] From this ancient site the peak of Jebel Aqra can be seen towards the north and may perhaps give a hint where gr̂ spn in Ugaritic mythology was to be found.[6]

The excavations at Ras Shamra revealed that Ugaritic had been a city where cosmopolitan influences had made their impact. A variety of languages were represented in that ancient city--Egyptian hieroglyphs, Akkadian syllabic script, Cypriote, Hittite script,

---

[1] Goetze, "Is Ugaritic a Canaanite Language?" Language 17 (1941):127, n. 2.

[2] Kapelrud, The Ras Shamra Discoveries, p. 5.

[3] Ibid., p. 3.

[4] Albright, "The Old Testament," CBQ 7 (1945):7.

[5] Ibid.

[6] Kapelrud, Discoveries, p. 4; Jack, The Ras Shamra Tablets, p. 20; Bruce M. Metzger, "Himmlische und irdische Wohnstatt Jahwes," UF 2 (1970):146; Ulf Oldenburg, The Conflict between El and Baʿal in Canaanite Religion (Leiden: E. J. Brill, 1969), p. 78.

etc.,--but by far the most important and most significant was "the local alphabetic script. . . ."[1]

Enthusiastic scholars drew some too-hasty conclusions as to the origin, location, and affinity of Ugaritic which later had to be revoked.[2] The linguistic classification of Ugaritic has been a matter of dispute since the decipherment of the text in 1930. Dahood pointed out that it is a "widely held view that Ugaritic is a Canaanite dialect"[3] and that "the closest affinity is to biblical Hebrew."[4] The first part of the statement is no doubt "winning the day," but the latter part of the statement may perhaps suffer radical inflation as the publication of the Ebla tablets progresses. The pros and cons may have to be weighed carefully once more. Still it is in this much disputed and distinct language that the bulk of Ugaritic literature was written.

As the texts from Ras Shamra among other material and texts also presented a fairly large bulk of mythological material, epics and poems, etc., it has been possible at least in part to shed light and to "resurrect" the history of the enigmatic culture that hitherto had been alluded to only in a few sources. Though the tablets were

---

[1] John Gray, The Legacy of Canaan. VTSupp 5 (Leiden: E. J. Brill, 1965), p. 3.

[2] Ibid., p. 106.

[3] Mitchell Dahood, Psalms I, AB (Garden City, NY: Doubleday & Company, Inc., 1966), p. xviii.

[4] Dahood also says that "Ugaritic has taken its place as a major language (or more properly a dialect of Canaanite) in the Semitic family of languages" (ibid.). Ullendorff points out that Ugaritic must be considered "the principal manifestation of second millennium North West Semitic" ("Comparative Semitics," p. 265).

written in the latter half of the second millennium B.C., the myths inscribed seem to originate from a much earlier time.[1]

There are several myths, legends, or sagas which have already become "classics" in the Ugaritic corpus of literature. The legends of Krt[2] and the legend of Aqht belong to the bulk that were first translated. Some scholars' opinions are that Krt is a saga and not a myth. The reason is that the Krt tablets contain historical information which is real and not fictitious.[3] The Baʻal and ʻAnat cycle is by far the largest composition that presents purely mythological material but in a fictitious context.

The Meaning of Qrn

Cyrus H. Gordon designates the primary meaning of the Ugaritic

---

[1] Though the mythological texts appear to date from the Ugaritic period, the intrinsic evidences suggest a much earlier date. Gray, for instance, suggests their origin to be ca. four centuries earlier. See his "Canaanite Kingship," pp. 194-95. Albright expresses a similar view in Yahweh and the Gods of Canaan (London: The Athlone Press, 1968), pp. 4-5 and n. 9. Frank Cross shares the views of his teacher, Albright, Canaanite Myth and Hebrew Epic (Cambridge, MA: Harvard University Press, 1973), p. 113. So also Oldenburg, The Conflict, p. 3 and Jack, The Ras Shamra Tablets, p. 6.

[2] Gray takes the name to be a passive participle karut from krt (כרת) "to cut off." See his "Canaanite Kingship," p. 196, n. 1 and The Legacy of Canaan, VTSupp 5 (1965), p. 132, n. 1.

[3] The majority of scholars would maintain a historical nucleus in the Krt "saga," but Sigmund Mowinckel, for instance, regards the poem as a pure cultic myth and with no historical association ("Immanuelsprofetien Jes 7 Streiflys fra Ugarit," NTT 12 (1941): 129-57); i.e., Krt is not a historical king but an Adonis-figure, a dying and rising vegetation-deity. In other words, the poem is a "mytisk heltesagn." Gray belongs to the majority of scholars who sees Dnʲel as being obscured by "the mythological accretions," but he is convinced that the story of Dnʲel "is not a myth but a saga." See his "Canaanite Kingship," p. 196; cf. also Baruch Margalith who elaborates on these two schools represented and their positions, "Studia Ugaritica II: Studies in Krt and Aqht," UF 8 (1977):137-14 (esp. pp. 137-45).

qrn to mean "horn."[1] Joseph Aistleitner denotes the same meaning.[2] The cognates of qrn are attested by the Hebrew qeren, the Aramaic qarnā, the Ethiopian qarn and the Akkadian qarnu, as Aistleitner has pointed out.[3]

Richard E. Whitaker in his work[4] gives a complete list of all the Ugaritic texts published in Corpus des tablettes en cunei- formes alphabétiques, Le Palais royal d'Ugarit II, Le Palais royal d'Ugarit V, Ugaritica V, Ugaritica VI, and Ugaritic Textbook.[5] Amazingly enough the word "qrn" does not occur in the Ugaritic texts more than a dozen times: twice in the plural form, three times in the dual form, and seven times in the singular form.[6]

As some of the texts are too fragmentary and, therefore,

---

[1] UT (1965), p. 481.

[2] Wörterbuch der Ugaritischen Sprache 2d rev. ed., Philologisch- historische Klasse, vol. 106, pt. 3 (Berlin: Akademic-Verlag, 1965), p. 283.

[3] Ibid.

[4] A Concordance of the Ugaritic Literature (Cambridge, MA: Harvard University Press, 1972); G. Douglas Young's Concordance of Ugaritic, AnOr, 36 (Rome: Pontificium Institutum Biblicum, 1956) has also been consulted, but because its usage is limited to the texts of Gordon, we follow Whitaker's Concordance for text- references.

[5] The CTA, ed. by Andrée Herdner (Paris: Imprimerie Nationale, 1963), the PRU II, ed. by Charles Virolleand (Paris: Imprimerie Nationale, 1968); Ug V, ed. by Jean Nougayrol, et. al. (Paris: Imprimerie Nationale, 1968); Ug VI, ed. by André Parrot, et al. (Paris: Mission de Ras Shamra, 1969); and UT, ed. Cyrus H. Gordon (Rome: Pontifical Biblical Institute, 1965).

[6] Some of these occurrences with an apparent singular form have been translated as a dual form; so, for instance, 76:2, 21, 22 and 75:2.40 (Gordon, Ugarit and Minoan Crete [New York: W. W. Norton & Company, Inc., 1966], pp. 89, 93).

give no light on the usage of horn, they will not be discussed per se.[1]

Charles Virolleaud has translated a couple of texts describing Baʿal: the first one describes him with horns and tail[2]--the context is rather degrading, for the young god is splashing in his own dung and urine. The other text describes Baʿal sitting on his mountain--also in this text is he described with two horns.[3] The dual form (qrnm) is used in both of these texts.

One of the Aqht texts[4] presents a plural: adr.qrnt.byʿlm. mtb[ ]m. Gordon translates the passage: "The mightiest horns from wild goats"[5]--showing an ordinary plural with a literal meaning.[6] The other Aqht text[7] has probably a reference to the horn of the moon:

---

[1] These texts are 2001.2.10 and 1176.8 (Whitaker, A Concordance, p. 556); The word sbʿt (in the phrase qrn sbʿt) has been translated by Gordon with the meaning "full" or "satisfied." He also gives as cognates the Hebrew שבע with the meaning "full," "satiated," "satisfied" (according to William L. Holladay, A Concise Hebrew and Aramaic Lexicon of the Old Testament [Grand Rapids: Wm. B. Eerdmans, 1971], pp. 348-49), the Syriac ܣܒܥ, the Arabic شبع and Ethiopic ሰብዕ, (šebū) (UT [1965], p. 487 [# 2380]).

[2] "Les nouveaux textes mythologiques et liturgiques de Ras Shamra," Ug V, transliteration p. 547 and translation p. 549.

[3] Ibid., transliteration, p. 557 and translation p. 558.

[4] 2 Aqht 6:22 (Whitaker, A Concordance, p. 556).

[5] Gordon, Ugarit and Minoan Crete, p. 127; idem, UL, p. 90; cf. Godfrey R. Driver, Canaanite Myths and Legends, Old Testament Studies, no. 3 (Edinburgh: T. & T. Clark, 1956), p. 55.

[6] The other occurrence (Virolleaud, "Les nouveaux textes," p. 592 [13.30] gives a similar literal meaning of qrnt ("un mouton aux cornes," p. 593).

[7] 3 Aqht 4:10 (Whitaker, A Concordance, p. 556); cf. Gordon UT (1965), p. 249.

ik. al. yhdt. yrh.b[. . .]
b qrn ymn h.b anst[. . .],[1]

"How will he not renew the moon
[ ] with its right horn?[2]

Of the remaining two texts, the text (75:2, 40) qrnh.km.gb [, . . .][3] has been translated by Gordon "his horns like [ ],"[4] but the following lines are badly mutilated and the context is therefore unclear. Text (75.1, 30) bhm.qrnm (31) km.trm. wgbtt (32) km. ibrm has been translated by Gordon as follows: "On them are horns like bulls and humps like buffaloes. . . ."[5] This text will be referred to again in chapter three.

The most debated text is, however, 76:2, 21, 22 from the "Baʿal and ʿAnat" cycle.

qrn.d bat k.btlt. ʿnt
qrn.d bat k bʿl.ymšh.[6]

The crux of the passage is, of course, how to translate the d bat and the msh in the bicola.

Gordon translates qrn.d batk "the horns of thy strength."[7]

---

[1]For the sake of the context also line 9 has been copied (i.e., 3 Aqht 4:9).

[2]Gordon, Ugarit and Minoan Crete, p. 129; idem, UL, p. 92. The moon-worship is known, for instance, from a Ugaritic temple hymn "celebrating the marriage of the goddess Nikkal to the Moongod;" Dahood, Psalms I, p. xix.

[3]Whitaker, A Concordance, p. 556.

[4]Ugarit and Minoan Crete, p. 93; Gordon, UL, p. 55.

[5]Gordon, Ugarit and Minoan Crete, p. 91; idem, UL, p. 54.

[6]Whitaker, A Concordance, p. 556; cf. Gordon, UT (1965), p. 182.

[7]UL, p. 50; so also in Ugarit and Minoan Crete, p. 89 (Gordon's opinion is that the goddess ʿAnath has wings and with help

Harold L. Ginsberg gives the same translation as Gordon although he questions the translation.[1] Ginsberg is also hesitant as to the translation of the verb ymšh, as the question mark after "anoint" shows.[2]

Driver translates qrn.d batk "the horn of thy prowess."[3] Other translations have been proposed since then. Edward Lipinski, in a learned article opposing Dahood,[4] gives a literal translation.[5]

The pivot of the whole problem is the qrn and the mšh,[6] and it is evident from the context that the one is dependent on the other. Bernard Couroyer points out that Dahood sees the clue in Ezek 28:14, because Dahood points out that Kᵉrûb mimšaḥ [כרוב ממשח] is rendered correctly by the Vulgate "cherub etentus" ("le chérubin aux ailes étendues").[7] The root is mšh (משח), the

---

of them flies to meet Baʻal in the field). The translation of d batk is not so easily solved. (In Hebrew דבאך is a hapax legomenon [Deut 33:25]; see William L. Holladay, A Concise Hebrew and Aramaic Lexicon, p. 66).

[1] "Baʻl und ʻAnat," Or 7 (1938):8 (line 21); cf. Ginsberg's translation "Ugaritic Myths," in ANET (1969), p. 142 (ii, 21) where d batk is left untranslated.

[2] "Baʻl und ʻAnat," p. 8 (line 22).

[3] Canaanite Myths and Legends, pp. 116, 117 (ii, 21, 22).

[4] "Ugaritic Lexicography," Mélanges Eugène Tisserant 1 (1964): 81-102 (esp. pp. 94, 98).

[5] "Les conceptions et couches merveilleuses de ʻAnath," Syria 42 (1965):44-73 (esp. 44, 69-71) (Lipínski's literal translation; Tes deux cornes vigoureuses, ô Vierge ʻAnath, tes deux cornes vigoureuses, Baal les oindra).

[6] B. Couroyer, "Corne et Arc," RB 73 (1966):517.

[7] Ibid.

Akkadian mašāhu "ausmessen," (to measure [out]).[1]

At this point Dahood draws the conclusion that the semantic connection between "mesurer" and "étendre" is clear in mtḫ, which in Hebrew means "étendre" and in Ugaritic is the name of a measure of length (Längenmass). Dahood's translation therefore reads:

> Your wings of strength, O virgin Anath,
> your wings of strength will Baal spread out,
> Baal will spread them out for flight.[2]

And so Dahood concludes that the goddess needs wings (rather than "horns") to fly.[3]

Couroyer then sums it up by saying, "Si l'on interprete mšḫ par 'eténdre,' il faut nécessairement voir en qrn des ailes."[4] But he also admits that this reasoning has not convinced Lipinski, who considers Dahood's translation too free and also points out that "corne" in the meaning of "wings" has not yet been attested.[5]

André Caquot, Maurice Sznycer, and Andrée Herdner in Textes

---

[1] Von Soden, AHW, 2:623; Aistleitner, Wörterbuch der ugaritischen Sprache, p. 198 (# 1707 mtḫ = Längenmass").

[2] Couroyer, "Corne et Arc," RB 73 (1966):517; cf. Dahood, "Ugaritic Lexicography," p. 95.

[3] Dahood, ibid.

[4] "Corne et Arc," RB 73 (1966):517; cf. bʿl knp Text 9:6 (Gordon, UT, p. 162), "Baʿal of the wing" (?) which might give a vague support for the translation (bʿp) "pour voler" (Oldenburg, The Conflict, p. 79; cf. also tšu knp (Text 76:II, 10, 11) The Virgin ʿAnat lifts wing, She lifts wing . . . , Gordon, UL, p. 50, and, Ugarit and Minoan Crete, p. 88.

[5] Couroyer's discussion "Corne et Arc," p. 518.

Ougaritiques[1] go back to the literal translation, and Wilfred G. E. Watson leans heavily on this recent and excellent French translation as he translates the ambiguous passage from the Baʽal cycle:

> Your butting (?) horns, O Virgin Anath,
> your butting (?) horns Baal will anoint,
> Baal will anoint them against weariness.[2]

The translation of the last line according to Watson "depends on relating ʽp to Hebrew ʽyp/ʽwp, 'to be weary,' and provides consistent imagery."[3] If this translation is correct (or rather preferable), it will justify Lipinski's view, though Lipinski does not focus on the bʽp as Watson does. Watson also gets support for his theory by quoting OT texts (1 Sam 2:10, Ps 92:11-12, and Ps 132:17-18).[4]

Let us sum up the usage of qrn in the Ugaritic texts. It is evident that the word qrn occurs in the dual, plural, and singular forms. It has been shown that the plural is used in a literal sense, i.e., of horns on animals.

In the description of the god Baʽal with his horns, the dual is being used which, of course, is to be expected. The context,

---

[1] André Caquot, Maurice Sznycer, and Andrée Herdner, eds. and trans., Textes Ougaritiques; vol. 1, Mythes et Légendes (Paris: Edition du Cerf, 1974), p. 284.

[2] Watson, "Ugaritic and Mesopotamian Literary Texts," UF 9 (1977):277.

[3] Ibid.; cf. עיף from the root יעף (be weary) and (to fly); William L. Holladay, A Concise Hebrew and Aramaic Lexicon, pp. 271, 268.

[4] Watson, "Ugarit and Mesopotamian Literary Texts," p. 277.

however, is mythological and the interpretation of such texts is therefore often debated.[1]

The singular is used, for instance, with a literal meaning in reference to the horn of the moon (one horn only).[2] The much debated passage in the "Baʿal and ʿAnat" cycle presents a singular form with an option of a singular or dual interpretation, depending on the understanding of the context.

Further study will eventually solve the problem of ʿAnat's "horns," but at the present time we can only briefly state that the singular form occurs in the text, but the correct translation is still debated.

QRN in Aramaic

Preliminary Considerations

At the end of World War I, Emil G. Kraeling said that "the history of the Arameans cannot yet be written."[3] In spite of the fact that archaeology has made some very important discoveries since that time, it does not even yet seem possible to write a veritable, factual history. The ongoing excavations since the time of Kraeling's remark have not been rewarding enough in this respect. It is true that before 1947 there already existed a vast amount of ossuary and sepulchral inscriptions as well as inscriptions on monuments and

---

[1] Cf. Text 75:1, 30 and Gordon's translation, Ugarit and Minoan Crete, p. 91; Gordon, UL, p. 54.

[2] See 3 Aqht 4:10 (Whitaker, A Concordance, p. 556); translation in Gordon, Ugarit and Minoan Crete, p. 129; idem, UL, p. 92.

[3] Aram and Israel (New York: Columbia University Press, 1918), p. 1.

stelae, on papyri and clay, and even inscriptions in silver and bronze, but these were no evidence of what Edgar J. Goodspeed has called "creative" Aramaic literary writing. Goodspeed says: "It cannot be too often insisted that Hebrew must be distinguished from Aramaic, oral composition from written, and translation from creative writing."[1] Nor did the abundance of administrative texts add much "creativity" to the task of writing a history of the Arameans apart from the fact that it gave evidence of the widespread usage of Aramaic as a "language of diplomacy and commerce."[2]

All the numerous evidences of the Aramaic language were overshadowed in 1947 by the discovery of the Dead Sea Scrolls at Qumran and surrounding caves. These evidences were, however, more of a local nature as they pertain only to Palestine. Among the very latest texts in Aramaic of any importance are those found at Deir ʽAlla twenty years later.[3]

The dawn of Aramean history is dated by several scholars to the third millennium B.C. This was already Kraeling's view more than half a century ago.[4] It was also Raymond A. Bowman's view two decades later;[5] more recently, Arthur Jeffery in 1962 has expressed

---

[1] *New Chapters in New Testament Study* (New York: Macmillan, 1937), p. 165.

[2] Raymond A. Bowman, "Arameans, Aramaic and the Bible," *JNES* 7 (1948):65.

[3] For a handbook of Aramaic texts of the Qumran collection at the present, see Joseph A. Fitzmyer and Daniel J. Harrington, *A Manual of Palestinian Aramaic Texts* (Rome: Biblical Institute Press, 1978) and for the Deir ʽAlla Texts, see J. Hoftijzer and G. Van der Kooij, *Aramaic Texts from Deir ʽAlla* (Leiden: E. J. Brill, 1976).

[4] *Aram and Israel*, p. 3.

[5] Bowman, "Arameans, Aramaic and the Bible," *JNES* 7 (1948):67.

the same opinion.[1] A contrary view has been expressed by Abraham Malamat, professor of ancient Jewish and biblical history at the Hebrew University.[2]

Though the origin of the Arameans is partly obscure, their language and its development is fairly well known, especially from the time of the first millennium B.C. when Aramaic in script is first attested.[3] Jonas C. Greenfield quite recently has presented a synopsis on the Aramaic language and its dialects.[4] The most recent articles discussing exhaustively and informatively, not only the Aramaic language and its dialects, but also the problems pertaining to these questions, have been presented by Eduard Y. Kutscher. He also discusses the contributions of various scholars in the field of Aramaic linguistic studies since 1939.[5]

The Meaning of קרן (קרנא)

The Aramaic word קרן with its emphatic form קרנא has a

---

[1] "Aramaic," in IDB (New York: Abingdon Press, 1962), 1:186, cf. Bowman's article "Arameans," in IDB, 1:190.

[2] "Aram, Arameans," EncJud (Jerusalem: Keter Publishing House, 1971), 3:254.

[3] See Bowman's article, "Arameans, Aramaic and the Bible," pp. 65-90 (especially pp. 70-87).

[4] "Aramaic," IDBSupp, pp. 39-44.

[5] Eduard Y. Kutscher starts his review of Aramaic scholarship by referring to Franz Rosenthal's historical division of the Aramaic language. He, however, follows the division as suggested by Joseph A. Fitzmyer. See Kutscher's articles, "Aramaic," in Current Trends of Linguistics, ed. Thomas A. Sebeok (The Hague: Mouton, 1970), 6:347-77 and "Aramaic," in EncJud, 3:259-87. Kutscher follows up his review until 1970.

triliteral root identical with the Hebrew, of which the basic meaning is "horn."[1]

As far as we have been able to ascertain, the Old Aramaic dialect gives no evidence of the word "horn."

The Official Aramaic. The Official or Imperial Aramaic which, according to the late Eduard Y. Kutscher, includes the time-period from 700-300 B.C.[2] offers, no doubt, the richest source material, but even here any reference to the word "horn" is scanty indeed.

The bulk of judicial documents shed no light on the particular motif of "horn." Nor do the "literary" texts contribute anything to the meaning of qrn. The "documents" of whatever kind they may be are, furthermore, mostly in too fragmentary shape to yield any length of text, and though Aramaic epigraphical material spread wide because of its importance as a lingua franca (in the

---

[1] Francis Brown, Samuel R. Driver and Charles A. Briggs, eds., A Hebrew and English Lexicon of the Old Testament (Oxford: Clarendon Press, 1907, reprinted, 1976), p. 1111; Holladay, A Concise Hebrew and Aramaic Lexicon of the Old Testament, p. 420; Charles-F. Jean and Jacob Hoftijzer, DISO (Leiden: E. J. Brill, 1965), p. 266; Ludvig Koehler and Walter Baumgartner, Lexicon in Veteris Testamenti Libros (Leiden: E. J. Brill, 1958), p. 1120; Frants Buhl, Wilhelm Gesenius' Hebräisches und Aramäisches Handwörterbuch über das Alte Testament (Berlin: Springer-Verlag, 19 9), p. 924; Marcus Jastrow, A Dictionary of the Targumim, the Talmud Babli and Yerushalmi, and The Midrashic Literature (New York: Pardes Pub. House, Inc., 1943), 2:1422-23; D. Gustaf H. Dalman, Aramäisch-Neuhebräisches Handwörterbuch zu Targum, Talmud und Midrasch (Göttingen: Eduard Pfeiffer, 1938), p. 391; D. Eduard König, Hebräisches und aramäisches Wörterbuch zum Alten Testament (Leipzig: Dieterich'sche Verlagsbuchhandlung, 1936), p. 599; Julius Fuerst, A Hebrew & Chaldee Lexicon to the Old Testament, trans. Samuel Davidson (Leipzig: Bernhard Tauchnitz, 1867), p. 1260; also the sister language the Syriac substantiates ܩܪܢܐ as having the basic meaning of "horn;" Karl Brockelmann, Lexicon Syriacum (Hildesheim: Georg Olm, 1966), p. 697; and J. Payne Smith, ed., A Compendious Syriac Dictionary (Oxford: Clarendon Press, 1903; reprint ed., 1957), p. 520.

[2] "Aramaic," EncJud, p. 260.

north as far as Sardis, in the south to the oasis of Tema, in the south-west to southern Egypt and in the east to Persia)[1] there is no evidence of the word qrn in the source material investigated.

Herbert Donner and Wolfgang Röllig record, however, one single instance of qrn.[2] The date is uncertain but probably originates from the period of the Middle Aramaic and will be discussed below.

The only documents of some length written in Official or Imperial Aramaic (formerly called Chaldee)[3] are the Old Testament passages: Dan 2:4b-7:28; Ezra 4:8-6:18; and 7:12-26.[4] An investigation with the help of a concordance[5] shows that in this work qrn is used altogether fourteen times: Dan 3:5, 7, 10, 15; 7:7, 8 [four times], 11, 20 [twice], 21, and 24. (See below.)

קרן (simple basic form)	1x	Dan 7:8
קרנא (emphatic singular)	5x	Dan 3:5, 7, 10, 15; 7:11
וקרנא (emphatic singular with waw)	2x	Dan 7:20, 21
בקרנא (emphatic singular with -ב-)	1x	Dan 7:8
וקרניך (dual[6] with waw)	1x	Dan 7:7

---

[1] "Aramaic," EncJud, pp. 260-61.

[2] KAI 2d ed. (Wiesbaden: Otto Harrassowitz, 1966), 3:22.

[3] Kraeling, The Brooklyn Museum Aramaic Papyri (New Haven: The University Press, 1953), p. 4.

[4] To make the list of Aramaic passages complete one can add Jer 10:11 and two words in Gen 31:47; the former passage is a controversial one because of its orthography, and the latter one contains only two words: Yegar-sahadûthaʾ.

[5] Solomon Mandelkern, Veteris Testament Concordantiae Hebraicae Atque Chaldaicae (Leipzig: F. Margolin, 1925), p. 1342.

[6] The dual may be used for the plural. See Franz Rosenthal, A Grammar of Biblical Aramaic (Wiesbaden: Otto Harrassowitz, 1968), p. 24.

קרניא (dual emphatic)　　　　　2x　Dan 7:8, 20
וקרניא (dual emphatic with waw)　1x　Dan 7:24
בקרניא (dual emphatic with -בְ-)　1x　Dan 7:8

A simple chart (appendix A) shows the forms which occur in the book of Daniel and indicates the number of times a particular form is used.[1]

The term "horn" is used with a literal meaning in chapter three with reference to a musical instrument, originally a ram's horn;[2] whereas chapter seven uses qrn as referring to literal horns on animals. Beyond these usages the symbolical description shows that the meaning of horn(s) is used also in a symbolical sense. For a right understanding of the horn(s) an analogous symbolical interpretation in accordance with the writer's (Daniel) own explanation is demanded.[3] Some of these texts will be further discussed in chapter four.

The Middle Aramaic. The Middle Aramaic comprises the period from 300 B.C. to the early centuries A.D.[4] The attestations from this period present a more or less "corrupt Aramaic," as Kutscher has pointed out.[5] Kutscher also asserts that the Aramaic

---

[1] The chart is based on Mandelkern (ibid.).

[2] The emphatic state קרנא (as well as other instruments in the emphatic state) reveal the Oriental origin, whereas the instruments of Greek origin are left without definite article (ibid.).

[3] Gerhard Hasel, "Biblical Interpretation," p. 21 in North American Bible Conference, 1974. Notebook prepared by the General Conference of Seventh-day Adventists Biblical Research Committee.

[4] Kutscher, "Aramaic," p. 260.　　　[5] Ibid.

inscriptions of Jerusalem, the Nabatean Aramaic, the Palmyrenean Aramaic, the Onkelos translation of the Bible (the Targum), the Dead Sea Scrolls, and other documents all seem to belong to this period. "The Uruk document"[1] which dates from this period is the only Aramaic document written in cuneiform,[2] but the Uruk document does not attest the word "horn;" and with the exception of religious texts the same quiescency is spread over the whole corpus of Aramaic texts from this period. The few exceptions detected are more or less of liturgical kind.

An example is given by James A. Montgomery and presents an obscure context. It is an incantation text of which the text in question has one passage saying: "I adjure thee, the angel which descends from heaven--there being kneaded (something) in the shape of a horn [קרן], on which honey is poured. . . ."[3] Montgomery comments on the text:

> . . . in the present case a "horn" (symbol of power?), probably a cone of wax or the like is kneaded, and honey poured upon it, with which we may compare the antique anointing of the sacred stone or <u>bethel</u>, wherein the suppliant literally "smooths" the face of the deity (Heb. חלה).[4]

Montgomery's interpretation and equation with a Hebrew tradition[5]

---

[1] Cyrus H. Gordon, "The Aramaic Incantation in Cuneiform," <u>AfO</u> 12 (1937-1939):105-17.

[2] Kutscher, "Aramaic," p. 260.

[3] James A. Montgomery, <u>Aramaic Incantation Texts from Nippur</u>, The Museum Publications of the Babylonian Section (Philadelphia: University Museum, 1913), 3:174 (no. 12, line 5).

[4] Ibid., p. 176.

[5] Montgomery is apparently comparing this antique anointing with the story that occurs in the much older Jacob tradition (Gen 28:11-22, esp. vv. 18-19).

is farfetched; he, however, assumes that behind the incantation text and the magical idea idolatry probably had its basis.[1]

Donner and Röllig list a Punic text of late date with a reference to "horn."[2] The date for this text may be from the third century or the early part of the second century B.C.[3] The inscription (on stone blocks) was found in Marseilles in 1845, and as the same kind of stone blocks occur in Carthage it is suspected that they originally belonged to a temple there. The context presents some kind of tariff that had to be paid for various animals that were presented as offerings. It is in this context that the text discussed says, "for a calf whose horns are still lacking, . . ."[4]

Onomastic usage. The onomastic usage of gods in personal names is attested throughout history, from the early Sumerians down to the late Aramaic-speaking people. Jürgen K. Stark has presented a case in which the word "horns" occurs. Among other

---

[1] Ibid.

[2] Donner and Röllig, KAI 2:83 (# 69.5); (cf. 3:22); cf. also Charles-F. Jean and Jacob Hoftijzer, DISO, p. 266. We follow Jean and Hoftijzer here, though Punic (late Phoenician) should be classified as Canaanite.

[3] Rosenthal, "Canaanite and Aramaic Inscriptions," The Marseilles Tariff (Temple of Baʻl-[Zaphon]), in ANET (1969), pp. 656-57.

[4] Ibid., Jacob Hoftijzer in DISO (Leiden: E. J. Brill, 1965), p. 266; for the text see CIS, Inscriptionum Phoeniciae (Paris: C. Klineksiek, 1881), 1:165, for a transliteration e.g., Mark Lidzbarski, Handbuch der nordsemitischen Epigraphik (Weimar, 1898; reprint ed., Hildesheim: Georg Olm, 1962), p. 428 (line 5); Cooke, NSI (Oxford: At the Clarendon Press, 1903), p. 163 (text #42.5; translation, p. 113).

names he lists <u>qryn</u> as a one-word name with the meaning of "horn"[1] (diminutive, <u>qutail</u> form).

Hermann Ranke already at the beginning of this century said:

> Personal names are more than mere labels. It is a feature of our present age with its immense technical achievements and the small importance of the single individual . . . that human beings, . . . are simply counted and called by numbers. . . . It was different in times gone by, when names were still living, as it were, coined anew each day, and referred by their meanings to the occasion upon which they were given. These names, preserved through centuries and millenniums . . . tell us to-day about their bearers. They tell what they accomplished and what they believed; they tell how they lived and suffered; they even allow us sometimes to catch a glimpse of their most intimate every-day life. We have only to listen and to understand.[2]

Samuel I. Feigin discusses a particular text--a purchase contract for real estate--originating from Abu-Jamous (near Babylon), a place "where but few tablets have been discovered."[3] The text presents one of the witnesses ^{d}Adad-qar-na-a-a dumu Ib-ni-^{d}Adad "Adad-qarnaia, the son of Ibni-Adad."[4] Feigin gives a literal meaning to the name ^{d}Adad-qar-na-a-a "My horns are Adad."[5]

---

[1] Stark's sources are primarily Arabic, Syriac, Palmyrene and other dialects of Aramaic, Personal Names in Palmyrene Inscriptions (Oxford: Clarendon Press, 1971), pp. 49, 110; cf. Herbert B. Huffmon, Amorite Personal Names in the Mari Texts (Baltimore: The Johns Hopkins Press, 1963), p. 259, et al.

[2] Hermann Ranke, Early Babylonian Personal Names, vol. 3, in The Babylonian Expedition of the University of Pennsylvania, Series D: Researches and Treatises, ed. H. V. Hilprecht (Philadelphia: University of Pennsylvania, 1905), p. 1.

[3] "A Purchase Contract from the Time of Samsu-Iluna," JAOS 55 (1935):284.

[4] Ibid., transliteration p. 291 (line 18), translation p. 293.

[5] Ibid., p. 288; cf. Johann J. Stamm, Die Akkadische Namengebung (Darmstadt: Wissenschaftliche Buchgesellschaft, 1968), p. 212 (idem. MVAG 44 [1939]:212). The occurrence of ^{d}Adad-qar-na-a-a testifies also to the importance of the Storm-god Adad in this area.

The Aprocrypha. The didactic work the Book of the Jubilees (29:11) quotes karnaim (a dual form) in an onomastic reference.[1] The tradition of this place name (according to this apocryphal work is attested before the Jacob Cycle came into existence. The background for the story of the passage in question is, in fact, the encounter between Laban and Jacob on the mountain of Gilead, and thereafter follows this explanation:

> But before they used to call the land of Gilead the land of the Rephaim; for it was the land of the Rephaim, and the Rephaim were born (there), giants whose height was ten, nine, eight down to seven cubits. And their habitation was from the land of the children of Ammon to Mount Hermon, and the seats of their kingdom were Karnaim and Ashtaroth, and Edrei, and Mîsur, and Beon. And the Lord destroyed them because of the evil of their deeds; for they were very malignant, and the Amorites dwelt in their stead, wicked and sinful, and there is no people to-day which has wrought to the full all their sins, and they have no longer length of life on the earth.[2]

After this etiological explanation the author of the Book of the Jubilees takes up the narrative of the Jacob Cycle anew. It appears that Astarothcarnaim (Vulgate) at first was only one city[3] but later on was apparently split into two cities.[4] Karnaim was

---

[1] Robert H. Charles, APOT, 2 vols. (Oxford: Clarendon Press, 1913), 2:57.

[2] Ibid.

[3] Cf. Gen 15:5 in BHS, eds. K. Elliger and W. Rudolph (Stuttgart: Deutsche Bibelstiftung, 1967-77); Genesis, ed. John W. Wevers, in Septuaginta Vetus Testamentum Graecum (Göttingen: Vandenhoeck & Ruprecht, 1974), 1:160; Septuaginta 3d ed., ed. Alfred Rahlfs (Stuttgart: Priviligierte Württembergische Bibelanstalt, 1935), p. 18; and Joseph A. Fitzmyer, The Genesis Apocryphon, Biblica et Orientalia, 18a (Rome: Biblical Institute Press, 1971), pp. 70, 71 (21:29).

[4] Cf. The Septuagint Version of the Old Testament with an English Translation (London: Samuel Bagster and Sons, Ltd., 1884),

captured by Judas Maccabeus and the temple of Atargatis was burned and twenty-five thousand persons massacred at this historical battle.[1]

Robert H. Charles expresses the view that in the historic account of the wars of the Maccabees, the translation of κέρας is a "Hebraism."[2] Avoiding this "Hebraism" he translates, for instance, the passage of 1 Macc 2:48 as an idiom: ". . . neither suffered they the sinners to triumph."[3] In his "commentary" on this verse Charles compares this passage to the idiom found in Ps 75:5, giving evidence of the figurative meaning of horn--the figure of strength.[4]

---

p. 15; cf. Das Buch der Jubiläen oder Die Kleine Genesis unter Beifügung des revidirten Textes der in der Ambrosiana aufgefundenen lateinischen Fragmente sowie einer von Dr. August Dillman aus zwei äthiopishen Handschriften gefertigten lateinischen Übertragung, ed. Hermann Rönsch (Amsterdam: Rodopi, 1970), p. 138 (Jub. 29:11). (All this prelude to the Jacob cycle took place probably in the era of the ancient city kingdom.); cf. also Josh 12:4, 5; 13:12; Deut 3:8-10.

[1] 1 Macc 5:43-44; 2 Macc 12:27 in Charles, APOT, 1:85; 2:149.

[2] Robert H. Charles, APOT, vol. 1 (see note on 1 Macc 2:48). Emil Kautzsch expresses the view that the First Book of the Maccabees (which is of special interest because of the references to qrn) seems to have a Hebrew Vorlage, though the writer might have been an Aramaic-speaking scribe living in the Hebrew "atmosphere" while translating the work into Greek (Die Apocryphon and Pseudepigraphen des Alten Testaments [Hildesheim: Georg Olms Verlagsbuchhandlung, 1962], 1:25).

[3] Charles, APOT, 1:79.

[4] Ibid., n. 48; Bruce M. Metzger gives a translation analogous in meaning: "They never let the sinner get the upper hand" (Apocrypha [New York: Oxford University Press, 1965], p. 226).

In the remaining five passages (1 Macc 9:1, 12, 15, 16; 2 Macc 15:20) Charles translates κέρας with "wing" (a military term).[1]

From these examples it seems evident that by this time the word qrn had taken on a more definite, warlike connotation. "Wing" or "flank" was a proper term to describe the "set-up" of a certain part of the army on the battlefield. On the other hand, the figurative usage seems to maintain its meaning in harmony with earlier literary usages.[2]

The same figurative meaning is also pressured in the wisdom literature from about the same period, namely, in the apocryphal work, the Book of Sirach.[3] All the qrn texts in Sirach (47:5, 7, 11; 49:5) contain "Hebraism" in the same way as the First and Second Books of the Maccabees.[4] The apparent meaning of "horn" in the context is "strength" or "power."

The apocalyptic part of the Books of Enoch contain several passages speaking about horn(s). The Book of Dreams contains some

---

[1] Charles, APOT, 1:96, 97, 153; Metzger agrees in his translation with the exception of the last text (2 Macc 15:20) where he has chosen the synonymous term "flank" (ibid.); Emil Kautzsch, in his German translation, agrees with Charles and Metzger translating qrn (κέρας) "Flügel;" Die Apocryphen, 1:57, 58, 118.

[2] Cf. Charles, APOT, 1:74 (1 Macc 2:48).

[3] For the approximate date of the work (the last quarter of the second century B.C.) see Charles, APOT 1:293. The word παππος with the meaning of "grandfather," or "ancestor" [i.e. an ancestor beyond the grandfather] would make it possible to ascribe the work to an earlier date.

[4] Charles is dependent on the OT for his understanding of "horns," as his many references to OT texts show. See his APOT, 1:495, n. 5.

of this apocalyptic material, and the one passage referring to horns (Enoch 89:43-44) is preserved in Aramaic.[1]

The word בקרנוהי occurring twice in v. 43 has in the Vatican fragment[2] κερατίζειν the first time and "ἐν τοῖς κέρασιν" the second time.[3] Milik translates the phrase דכרא דך שרי לנגחה בקרנוהי as follows: "And that ram began to butt with his horns," and the phrase ולמרדף בקרנוהי "and to pursue with his horns." Milik is thus retaining the literal usage of קרן.[4]

Charles, again avoiding the literal concept of "horn" (which he considers as a "Hebraism"), has the following translation (quoted in its whole context): "And that ram began to butt on either side those dogs, foxes, and wild boars till he had destroyed them all."[5]

As the Book of Dreams contains "apocalyptic" material, the symbols have to be interpreted accordingly. Most scholars interpret

---

[1] Josef T. Milik, The Books of Enoch Aramaic Fragments of Qumran Cave 4 (Oxford: Clarendon Press, 1976), pp. 41, 42; for a translation, ibid., p. 224 and Charles, APOT, 2:254.

[2] The edition by M. Gitlbauer Die Ueberreste griechisher Tachygraphie im Codex Vaticanus Graecus 1809 (extract from Die Denkschriften der philosophische-historischen Classe der Kaiserlichen Akademie der Wissenschaften, xxviii), 1st fascicle, Vienna, 1878, pp. 57 (syllabic transcription) and pp. 94-5, no. xvi as cited by Milik, The Books of Enoch, p. 224, n. on Enoch 89:43-4.

[3] The Aramaic phrase לנגחה בקרנוהי is expressed through the Greek infinitive κερατίζειν in one word and is used several times in the Septuagint; cf. κερατίζοντα = מנגח [Piel pt. from the root נגח "to gore"] in Dan 8:4; see Milik's discussion (ibid., pp. 224-25).

[4] Ibid.   [5] Charles, APOT, 2:254.

this apocalypse <u>vaticinium ex eventu</u>, placing it at the time of the Macabees, and interpret the "ram" as Judas Maccabeus, the hero of the Emmaus and Bethsur.[1]

Unfortunately, the passage of Enoch 90:6-12, which also refers to "horn(s)," is not preserved in its original Aramaic. Charles has a translation of this "apocalypse" which, according to his interpretation, concerns the period from the Graeco-Syrian domination to the Maccabean revolt.[2] Charles interprets the "horned lambs" as the Maccabeans and the "great horn" as Judas Maccabeus. Thus, according to Charles, this particular apocalypse must have been written before Judas' death in 160 B.C.[3] Emil Kautzsch and other recent scholars are apt to place the Book of Enoch on the whole at a much later date and some parts of it as late as in the Christian era.[4]

The Book of Enoch and the Book of Daniel have been equated as the most important pre-Christian documents which have influenced Christian thinking. It is, however, important to keep in mind that the first one is a non-canonical book while the latter is canonical. The intricate and confusing elements of the former book are probably weighty reasons why the book is left outside the Canon of the Protestant Christian Church.

The Dead Sea Scrolls, as far as Aramaic is concerned, are of fragmentary kind, as Kutscher has pointed out.[5] Even the longest

---

[1] Milik, <u>The Books of Enoch</u>, p. 45.

[2] Charles, <u>APOT</u>, 2:257.   [3] Ibid., n. 9.

[4] Kautzsch, <u>Die Apokryphen</u>, 2:224.

[5] Kutzscher, "Aramaic," p. 268.

of them, the Genesis Apocryphon, is silent upon the question of "horn,"[1] apart from the onomastic reference of Ashteroth-Karnaim.[2]

To sum up, then, the Aramaic evidences for the usage of qrn show that the main bulk of evidences come from the biblical source of the Book of Daniel from the period of the Imperial Aramaic. The usage in chapter three testifies to a literal meaning of "horn" as a musical instrument--probably a ram's horn was used. The other evidences from chapter seven give a purely extended meaning to the word, i.e., the context requires a symbolic understanding of "horn(s)."

The Middle Aramaic shows also a scanty collection of evidences. The literal usage in ritual context comes from a Punic text and from an incantation text (an artificial "horn"). The onomastic usage shows evidences of a long tradition of qrn being used both as a personal name and as a place name. The apocryphal works: The First and Second Books of the Maccabees point to the fact that the word "horn" had also received a warlike connotation in certain contexts, although it maintained its metaphorical meaning of "power" and "strength" in other connections.

Qarn in South-Arabic

Preliminary Considerations

From time immemorial Arabia has been divided into North

---

[1] Ibid.

[2] Joseph Fitzmyer, The Genesis Apocryphon of Qumran Cave 1 (Rome: Biblical Institute Press, 1971), pp. 70, 71 (Text 21:28, 29), Commentary, p. 164 (line 28).

and South. The vast desert with its glowing sand formed a natural barrier, especially in the east, but also the distinctly opposite way of life and the widely different character separated two races.[1] It is the people of the South (i.e., Yemen or Arabia Felix) that are first mentioned in history as the bearers of ancient civilization, while the people of the North (the Hijaz and the Najd) were still living their nomadic life.[2]

The story of the civilization of the most influential of all the kingdoms in South Arabia is tied up with the biblical story of the Queen of Sheba (Saba') visiting King Solomon. On the basis of this story it is evident that the kingdom existed at least that early (ca. 1000 B.C.), but probably much earlier.

The rather recent exploratory group of the American Foundation for the Study of Man started its work in Maryab (Marib), the great capital of the bygone kingdom of the Sabeans.[3] How suspecting the local government was in regard to strangers can be seen from the fact that before Albert Jamme, Wendell Phillips, and others arrived, only three Europeans had ever visited the place, and that in the nineteenth century.[4] In the same way and to the same end both F. V. Winnett and W. L. Reed testify when they write in the Preface of their book: "Prior to the beginning of the twentieth century only

---

[1] Reynold A. Nicholson, A Literary History of the Arabs (Cambridge: University Press, 1966), p. xvii.

[2] Ibid.

[3] A. Jamme, Sabaean Inscriptions from Mahram Bilqîs (Mârib) (Baltimore: The Johns Hopkins Press, 1961), p. ix.

[4] Ibid.

fifteen Europeans are known to have visited northern and central Arabia."[1]

Reynold A. Nicholson points to the fact that the "Bedouins of the North spoke Arabic," and thereby he means the language of the pre-Islamic poems and the Koran;[2] whereas the people of the South "used a dialect called by Muhammadans 'Himyarite'. . . ."[3]

More recent scholars, as, for instance, G. Lankester Harding, speak of three main dialects of the North: Lihyanite, Safaitic, and Thamudic, and four main dialects of the South: Hadrami, Minaean, Qatabanian, and Sabaean.[4] The most recent article on the South Arabian Epigraphic has been presented by Wolf Leslau.[5]

In this brief study only a few random examples from the South Arabic dialects will be referred to.

The Meaning of Qarn قَرَن
(pl. qurun قرون)

The word qarn in the modern Arabic language comes from a tri-literal root قرن , just as in Aramaic and Hebrew. Edward W.

---

[1] Ancient Records from North Arabia (Toronto: University of Toronto Press, 1970), p. vii.

[2] Nicholson, A Literary History of the Arabs, p. xvii.

[3] Ibid.

[4] An Index and Concordance of Pre-Islamic Arabian Names and Inscriptions (Toronto: University of Toronto Press, 1971), p. 5. Sabatino Moscati adds the Awsanian to the list of South-Arabian dialects. See his An Introduction to the Comparative Grammar of the Semitic Languages (Wiesbaden: Otto Harrassowitz, 1964), p. 14.

[5] "Ethiopic and South Arabian," in Current Trends in Linguistics, ed. Thomas A. Sebeok (The Hague: Mouton, 1970), 6:467-27.

Lane in his Lexicon gives several meanings:[1]

قَرَنَ (qarana [verb]) He connected, coupled, or conjoined, (a thing with a thing).

أَقْرَنَ (āqrana [verb]) He gave (of a thing two by two) [or one thing after another]

قِرْن (qern [noun, sing. masc.]) One who opposes, or contends with, another, in science, or in fight; an opponent; a competitor; an adversary, an antagonist: or one's equal, or match, in courage, or generally, one's equal, match, or fellow. (This construction with kesr is used when relating to fighting and the like.)

قَرْن (qarn [noun, sing, masc.]) One's equal in age, generation (of men), people (of one time). (When relating to age the construction is with fet-h); the part of the head (of a human being) which in an animal is the place whence the horn grows; side, upper side, of the head: temporal ridge, edge (of the middle and main part of the head), on the right (and) on the left.

أَقْرَنُ (āqranu [participle]) Horned; having horns.[2]

The only one pertinent to our study is the qern (قِرْن [with kesr]) as the discussion below will show.

In the South-Arabic text collection Albert Jamme has transcribed and translated a text which speaks about "Rabbšamsum Yazid and [his] brother [Karibʿata ʾAsʿad . . .]" who dedicated a statue of bronze to "ʾIlumquh Tahwân, master of ʾAwwâm."[3]

ʾIlumquh was the moon-god to whom the temple of ʾAwwam south-

---

[1] An Arabic-English Lexikon (London: Williams and Norgate, 1893; reprint ed. in U.S.A., 1956); cf. G. W. Freytag, ed., Lexicon Arabico-Latinum (Halle, Germany: C. Z. Schwetschke and Sons, 1837), p. 500; F. Steingass, English-Arabic Dictionary (London: Crosby Lackwood and Sons, 1882), p. 181. The modern Arabic usage and meaning of qarn probably more or less reflects the ancient South-Arabic meanings of the same word and has therefore here been included. South-Arabic references have been studied from transliterated passages.

[2] Ibid., vol. 1, pt. 8, pp. 2987-88.

[3] Sabaean Inscriptions from Maḥram Bilqîs (Mârib) (Baltimore: Johns Hopkins Press, 1961), p. 84 (#559, lines 1-4); for the transliteration p. 83.

east of the city was dedicated. The moon-god (who is known by other names in local contexts)[1] was here the patron of the city (Marib) as well as the whole Sab state.[2]

In this statue inscription ʲIlumqah is being praised because "He has helped and assisted their lord ʲIlsaraḥ Yaḥḍub, king Sabaʲ and Raydân, . . ."[3] The inscription tells how Karibʲil and "his tribes and his army were destroyed from the citadel ʲAsʲay and Qarnnahân as far as ʿArwastân and Ẓalmân and Hakrabum. . . ."[4]

From the same collection of inscriptions from South-Arabia is found a text (Ja 576) inscribed on a yellowish-grayish sandstone telling about ʲIlsarah Yahdub and Yaʲzil Bayyin, the two brother kings of Sabaʲ who dedicated to the national moon-god statues in brass giving praise for his help and assistance to ʲIlsarah Yahdub, who was able to defeat the armies and tribes rising up against him in war.[5] A rather long account follows telling about

---

[1] For the South-Arabian divinities, see Jamme, "Le panthéon sud-arabe préislamique d'après les sources épigraphiques," in Le Muséon 40 (1947):57-147. For the various local moon gods see Ditlef Nielsen, Der sabäische Gott Ilmukah (Leipzig: J. C. Hinrichs, 1910), pp. 56, 57.

[2] Jamme, Sabaean Inscriptions, p. 3.

[3] Ibid., (#578) text, p. 83, and translation, p. 84.

[4] The strange form wqrnnhn (#578, line 9) is actually a nominal form (a place name); see Jamme, Sabaean Inscriptions, p. 83 (cf. p. 423) (translation, p. 84); cf. Jamme's notes (line 9), p. 85. The onomastic usage of qrn with a slightly different spelling (karnawu [the capital of the Minaean kingdom]) is attested, for instance, by Otto Weber, "Studien au südarabischen Altertumskunde," MVAG 6.1 (1901):1-43, and "Eine neue minäische Inschrift (Glaser 1302)," MVAG 6.2 (1901):1-34. The spelling according to the first reference is κάρνα or κάρνανα and according to the letter karnâwu.

[5] Jamme, Sabaean Inscriptions, pp. 68, 70 (lines 13, 14).

the raids and vanguards of ʾIlsarah and how he was helped by ʾIlumqah and "so was given over to them 'every rebel' [kl qrn]. . . ."[1]

In the inscription (Ja 643) qrn takes on the verbal form. Jamme translates the phrase wqrn/wqh/mlk/sbʾ "and rebelled against [what] had ordered the king of Sabaʾ" showing the verbal expression "rebelled."[2] In the next line, lqrn/bhmt [an idiom] has the meaning "to attack."[3] Actually, lqrn/b equals lqrn/ʿly.[4] Gonzague Ryckmans translates from the Kawkab (Kaukab) (1/6) the following phrase wbn/dkyhw/mlkn/lqrn/ʿly/nqrn/bn as follows: "Et c'est lui que le roi avait placé comme chef pour combattre contre Nagran d'entre, . . ."[5] which supports Jamme's statement.

In another statue inscription, also dedicated to ʾIlumqah Tahwan, the qrn (prefixed -l-) takes on, not the ordinary meaning of "to attack," but of "to head for, proceed to."[6] This makes it clear that Jamme sees the verbal qrn as having the basic meaning of "to attack."[7]

Jamme gives the same translation of qrn in a long historical text from Bi'r Hima. In this text kqrn/bʿly means "fought against,"

---

[1] Ibid., p. 70 (line 13).

[2] Ibid., pp. 142, 143 (lines 22, 23).   [3] Ibid. (line 23).

[4] Ibid., p. 144 (commentary, lines 22, 23).

[5] "Inscriptions süd-arabes" (Kawkab 1/6) in Le Muséon X in 66 (1953):295-303 (esp. pp. 297-300, line 6).

[6] Jamme, Sabaean Inscriptions, pp. 167, 168 (line 12).

[7] Jamme, Sabaean and Hasaean Inscriptions from Saudi-Arabia, Studi Semitici, 23 (Rome: Istituto di Studi del Vicino Oriente, 1966), pp. 39-41 (Ja 1028).

while qrn/bʿm means "fought with."[1] Jamme commenting on mqrn says: "the root qrn means 'to make war against someone,'" and the noun means "warrior, rebel."[2]

It seems quite clear then, according to Jamme's studies, that aside from the onomastic usage, the Arabic qarn in its verbal form has taken on a clear military, warlike connotation.

The inscription Ja 566 introduces the dynasty of Fariʿum Yanhub, "the most illustrious among South-Arabian dynasties."[3] The coregents are mentioned by Jamme in his transcription and translation of Ja 574 and Ja 576.[4] Jamme, however, gives a rather late date to this dynasty. The late date is based on synchronism, "viz. ʾIlsarah and Aelius Gallus in 24 B.C."[5] The late date for the Fariʿum Yanhub dynasty does not entirely determine the usage of qrn for

---

[1] For the first usage (fought against) see transliteration (#1028, line 6), ibid., p. 40 (translation p. 41); for the second usage ("fought with" or "fought along with") see transliteration (#1031, a, line 3), p. 56.

[2] Jamme, Sabaean Inscriptions, p. 861 (line 39); cf. also C. Conti-Rossini, Chrestomathia arabica meridionalis epigraphica edita et glossario instructa (Rome: Istituto per l'Oriente, 1931), p. 234 A.

[3] Jamme, Sabaean Inscriptions, p. 308. The full name of the dynasty was Ianiatite-Hamdânid dynasty of Fariʿum Yanhub (p. 309).

[4] Ibid., p. 60 (Ja 574, line 1), p. 67 (Ja 576, line 1). Jamme refers to Fariʿum Yanhub as advanced in years when he (shortly after his coronation) appointed his two sons as co-regents. ʾIlšaraḥ Yahḍub may have been the kbr "leader" perhaps already before his father became king. ʾIlšaraḥ's brother was "a simple partaker in some royal duties;" see ibid., p. 309.

[5] See Jamme's chart in Sabaean Inscriptions, pp. 390-91; cf. Jamme's discussion, pp. 308-43 (the date is uncertain and hard to determine).

military expeditions and on the whole in warlike context as a late "innovation."

The South-Arabic inscriptions, scanty as they are, prove that apart from its onomastic usage the word "horn" (similar to Aramaic usage) was pertinently used in battle context. There is a difference, however, for in Arabic qrn as a noun means "warrior" or "rebel" adversary, antagonist, and the like, and as a verb it takes on the meaning of "to attack," i.e., either fighting "against" someone, or fighting "with" someone, depending on the preceding preposition.

Therefore, whatever date we decide on for the South Arabian inscriptions, they prove, as Jamme has shown, that the concept of "horn" had received a strong negative forcefulness in the South Arabian context, even surpassing the Aramaic forte of terms.

Qrn in Biblical Hebrew

Preliminary Considerations

The earliest and most enduring Jewish literary production is the Hebrew Bible, or if we wish to emphasize the various writers, the "books" of the Bible. The one specific characteristic of the Hebrew Bible is that it is the foundation for all other Jewish religious literature which can be considered to be directly or indirectly an outgrowth of the Hebrew Bible. One can therefore agree with Israel Davidson that Hebrew literature ("the outgrowth") is chiefly "religious literature."[1] And so the Hebrew Bible compared

---

[1] "Literature, Hebrew," The Jewish Encyclopedia (New York: Funk and Wagnalls Company, 1904), 8:109.

with the literature of other cultures and also in comparison to "the outgrowth" is unique as to both content and style. It is rightly a unique piece of literature without any equivalence anywhere.

The "easiest" way to establish the date and origin of the various books is to rely on internal evidences of content and on information given by the writers themselves. It may, however, be pertinent to express the opinion held by many scholars that even the Hebrew Bible may have a long oral tradition as its basis before it was presented in writing. How far back this oral transmission goes may be hazardous to speculate about. Did it perhaps already exist as early as the earliest literature transmitted, or does it perhaps even go beyond these to prehistoric times? Can it be that the similarity of content of literature in some cultures (in spite of existing and obvious divergences) does reflect a common original source? We may still have to wait for further evidences; if not Ebla, some other (still unexcavated) tell in the near or distant future may reveal the enigma concealed below the heaps of dust and rubbish.

The task of the linguistic investigation of Biblical Hebrew is necessarily built on the Hebrew Bible which comprises the main corpus of Hebrew texts. Chaim Rabin's recent article (1970) gives a helpful overview of the Hebrew language and its development as well as of the text itself as we have it today. However, Rabin points out that, in spite of various dictionaries and grammars, none of them gives a complete survey of the views and arguments advanced in books and learned journals over the last half-century regarding the meaning and etymology of Biblical Hebrew words.[1]

In other words,

No discipline of Hebrew semantics exists which could be compared with the work done in those languages [i.e., Latin and Greek].[2]

With these preliminary remarks we proceed attempting to investigate the usage and meaning of קרן based on standard lexicons.

The Meaning of קרן

According to the standard lexicons,[3] the tri-literal root qrn in Hebrew has the basic meaning of "horn." Brown, Driver, and Briggs in their lexicon signify קרן to be a feminine nown [a Segolate].[4]

The literal meaning of "horn" is pertinent to a ram (איל), Gen 22:13; and Dan 8:3, 6, 7, 20; and (of goat) Dan 8:5, 8, 9, 21; of oppressors in Israel (under the figure of rams), Ezek 34:21; and of nations, Zech 2:2, 4 (figurative usage).[5] The qrn is further

---

[1]Chaim Rabin, "Hebrew," in Current Trends in Linguistics, ed. Thomas A. Sebeok (The Hague: Mouton, 1970), 6:304-45.

[2]Ibid.

[3]The following lexicons have been consulted: Brown, Driver, and Briggs, A Hebrew and English Lexicon (reprint ed. 1976), p. 901; Holladay, A Concise Hebrew and Aramaic Lexicon, pp. 325-26; Koehler and Baumgartner, Lexicon in Veteris Testamenti Libros, pp. 356-57; Buhl, Wilhelm Gesenius' Hebräisches und Aramäisches Handwörterbuch über das Alte Testament (17th ed.), p. 729; König, Hebräisches und aramäisches Wörterbuch zum Alten Testament (6th and 7th eds.), pp. 420-21; Fuerst, A Hebrew & Chaldee Lexicon to the Old Testament (3d ed.), pp. 1259-60.

[4]A Hebrew and English Lexicon, p. 901.

[5]Cf. also the figurative usage in Deut 33:17, Ps 22:2, Ps 92:1, Mic 4:13, 1 Kgs 22:11 (2 Chr 18:10), as cited from Brown, Driver and Briggs, A Hebrew and English Lexicon, p. 901.

used as oil-flask (1 Sam 16:1, 13; 1 Kgs 1:39) and as wind-instrument (Josh 6:5).[1]

The term qrn is also used in a number of texts which convey a metaphorical or symbolic meaning; i.e., as a symbol of strength (2 Sam 22:3 [= Ps 18:2]); or denoting increase of might and dignity (1 Sam 2:1, 10; Lam 2:17; Ps 75:11; 89:18, 25; 92:11; 112:9).[2] The qrn is also used with a negative connotation in Lam 2:3, Jer 48:25, and Job 16:15.

The term qrn is used of the horn-like projections at the corners of the altar (Amos 3:13; Jer 17:1; Ezek 43:15, 20; Ps 118:27; and the texts in Exodus and Leviticus pertaining to the building of the sanctuary and the service connected with it).[3]

Other usages of the term qrn include a reference to a hill (Isa 5:1); and the meaning of "rays"--at his side (Hab 3:4).[4]

The verbal form קָרַן (Qal) is used only in Exod 34:29, 30, 35 and (Hiphil participle) in Ps 69:32.[5]

The term qrn occurs in the Hebrew Bible eighty-two times. Solomon Mandelkern lists the word qrn in nominal forms a total of seventy-five times and in verbal forms four times, altogether

---

[1] Ibid.

[2] Cf. also 1 Chr 25:5 and Ps 148:14; Brown, Driver, and Briggs, A Hebrew and English Lexicon (1976), p. 902.

[3] To this group of texts Brown, Driver, and Briggs, A Hebrew and English Lexicon also places 1 Kgs 1:50, 51, and 2:28 where the horns of the altar in the sanctuary comprise the place of refuge; cf. ibid., p. 902.

[4] Ibid.   [5] Ibid.

seventy-nine times.[1] Mandelkern excludes from his enumeration the combined forms (in which qrn is one component) in Gen 14:5 and Job 42:14 as well as the second occurrence in Exod 27:2. Gerhard Lisowsky[2] gives the corresponding figures: nominal forms seventy-one times and verbal forms four times, altogether seventy-five times.[3] (See table 1, appendix D.)

Two charts have been prepared to give a swift overview of the occurrences of qrn in the Hebrew Bible: the first one (see appendix B), primarily to help find all the references to qrn in the Old Testament, has been prepared in sequential order according to their occurrences, but without any indication of morphological or contextual structure. The Sefarim Hizonim (Apocrypha), usually of unknown authorship, and the noncanonical apocalyptic works, mostly pseudonymical in nature, are not considered as part of the Hebrew Bible in this study.[4] The chart has been prepared on the

---

[1] Veteris Testamenti Concordantiae Hebraicae Atque Chaldaicae (Leipzig: F. Margolin, 1925), p. 1049.

[2] Konkordanz zum Hebräischen Alten Testament (Stuttgart: Württ. Bibelanstalt, 1958), pp. 1283-84.

[3] Compare the list of occurrences of "horn" in the Hebrew Bible according to Mandelkern, Lisowsky, and our chart (pp. 467ff).

[4] All the apocryphical and pseudepigraphical references of κέρας cited by Edwin Hatch and Henry A. Redpath in A Concordance to the Septuagint and the Other Greek Versions of the Old Testament (Graz: Akademische Druck-und Verlagsanstalt, 1954), 2:759-60, have been thoroughly investigated and many of these references even referred to (especially in the Aramaic section of this chapter). Furthermore the Talmudic literature (the Mishna and Midrash) have been carefully investigated but are not included in this study: the foremost reason is that they do not, from a philological point of view, shed any particular light on qrn, and secondly, although the oral tradition may be placed in B.C. the written text does not appear until ca. 200 A.D.

basis of the <u>Biblia Hebraica Stuttgartensia</u> in the first column and with Aquila, Symmachus, Septuagint,[1] and Theodotion in parallel columns. In the last column the Syriac has been cited.[2]

The second chart (see appendix C) is an attempt to group the term qrn according to its external structure (morphologically). The texts provided with an asterisk indicate that although the morphological structure may suggest a certain meaning, the context seems to indicate another meaning. These are "problem-texts" and will be referred to in chapter four where elucidations of context will be presented.

This chart reveals three basic guidelines which, however, must not be overemphasized.

1. The feminine plural construct (with or without suffix and/or prefix) is used mostly in Exodus and Leviticus and in a few other references which deal with the "horns of the altar."

2. The dual (absolute or construct) is used when the context refers to horns of animal (ox or ram), whether with a literal or metaphorical meaning (idioms or symbols).

3. The singular usage is the most frequent but at the same time the most difficult to classify. As there is only one

---

[1] The Septuagint according to the <u>Origenis Hexaplorum</u>, edited by Fridericus Field (Hildesheim: Georg Olms, 1964); the <u>Migne Patrologia Graeca</u> (Paris: J. P. Migne, 1862); and <u>Septuaginta</u>, edited by Alfred Rahlfs (Stuttgart: Privileg. Württ. Bibelanstalt, 1935) have been the basic tools for the Greek section. However, the Göttingensis and the Cambridge editions have been consulted for every specific text as well as Henry Barclay Swete, <u>The Old Testament in Greek</u> (Cambridge: University Press, 1934).

[2] For the Syriac <u>Bibliothecae Syriaca</u> edited by Paulo de Lagarde (Göttingen: Luederi Horstmann, 1892) has been consulted.

word in Hebrew to express various concepts of horn, it is but natural to assume that misconception and ambiguity could arise. The structural analysis shows that systematic efforts were put forth to solve this practical problem. The "compound" construction is one way of solving this uncertainty. The nominal word that follows qrn qualifies the meaning. So, for instance: קרן מואב (Jer 48:25), קרן ישעי (Ps 18:3), or the more tangible meaning of קרן השמן(את)-, (1 Sam 16:13), (ב)קרן היובל (Josh 6:5), etc. In idiomatic expressions, a preceding verb, for instance, is a helpful construction. So, for instance, (אל)-תרימו קרן (Ps 75:5) "do not lift up your horn." The singular form with various suffixes is also used mostly in idiomatic expressions or in poetry.

There are some irregularities that occur and these are indicated with an asterisk at the respective text-reference; in order to avoid repetition, these will be dealt with in chapter four where elucidations of context will be presented.

It seems clear that on a structural basis the term qrn already seems to fall into several categories, and thus a clue is provided for avoiding potential misconceptions (which have only grown and expanded with the lapse of time). The various meanings can be expected to stand out in bold relief when such basic guidelines are applied. It is, however, important to emphasize that in order to reach a satisfactory clarification, the word has to be studied in its context. Even then other complications may affect the deduction. Some attempt at suggestive interpretations will be alluded to in chapter four.

Edwin Hatch and Henry A. Redpath have recorded κέρας translated from קרן sixty-seven times.[1] A few references of κέρας in Hatch and Redpath's Concordance are from other Hebrew words as, for instance, κέρατα είχε (once) translated from the Hebrew מקצוע (מקצע) (Ezek 41:22) meaning "cornerpost" (or altar),[2] and (once) from the word חזות (Dan 8:8) meaning "conspicuousness."[3]

Some uncertain passages, for instance, 1 Kgs 2:29--κατέχει τῶν κεράτω τοῦ θυσιαστηρίου (supported by the Syriac but not by the Hebrew) do not add to or subtract from the understanding of קרן. The same is the case with the text in Jer 48:12 (in the Septuagint 31:12) τὰ κέρατα αὐτοῦ συγκόψουσι. The last reference presents a corrupt text according to the apparatus in Biblia Hebraica Stuttgartensia and is unimportant as a reference.

The Dead Sea Scrolls which have lent such valuable information contain in but one instance the usage of qrn "in context," namely, Fragment E 1, Pss 118:25-29; 104:1-6, which James A. Sanders adds as a "postscriptum" to his collection The Dead Sea Psalms Scroll.[4] This fragmentary text is in part preserved and reconstructed and reads as follows:

---

[1] A Concordance to the Septuagint and the Other Greek Versions of the Old Testament, 2:759-60.

[2] Brown, Driver, and Briggs, A Hebrew and English Lexicon, p. 893; cf. Hatch and Redpath, A Concordance, 2:760.

[3] Ibid., 2:303; cf. Ludwig Köhler, "Zu Jes 28:15a und 18b," ZAW 48 (1930):227-28.

[4] (Ithaca, New York: Cornell University Press, 1967), post-scriptum 160, 161.

אל [= lacunae] ויאר לנו אסורי חג בעבותים

[lacunae]צרות המז בח

Sanders has translated the text:

The Lord is God, and he has given us light. ᵃThe festal animals are bound with ropes,ᵃ [up to the hor]ns of the altar![1]

The word קרנות has been restored on the basis of the Masoretic Text.[2]

Summing up the evidences of the usage and meaning of the word קרן in the Hebrew Bible we find that this word is used in singular, dual and plural forms. The external structure of the word seems important because in these expressed forms three basic guidelines for interpretation can be detected (see appendix C). As the chart shows, each particular form alerts the reader to a certain prospective meaning. Thus we presume that the three variant forms may in themselves present a key which, of course, can be effectively used only in contextual study that will serve as a control.

At this stage of our investigation, therefore, we are not able to present more than a tentative conclusion to this particular section. We express this conclusion in the form of a conjectural suggestion: It appears that more than one tradition may be represented in the various genres that flow together in the Bible. No final conclusion can be presented until the horn-motif is more

---

[1] Sanders points out that this translation is only in the Qumran text. The RSV (MT) translates, "Bind the festal procession with branches," (ibid., p. 161 a . . . b). (Ps 118:27.)

[2] The text will be referred to anew in chapter four.

thoroughly studied in contextual setting. This we attempt to do in chapter four.

Summary and Evaluation

The root qrn is found not only in Hebrew but also in the major Northwest and East Semitic languages as well as in Sumerian. Its literary usage reaches as far back as evidences of script lead us. It is fairly certain that its usage even goes beyond to prehistoric time, as has been alluded to already and which will be discussed more fully in the next chapter.

The most fascinating evidences of our study of the term and its ancient usages in script go back to the Sumerian culture. The sign SI with the meaning "horn" occurs rather frequently in Sumerian texts. It occurs as a simple logogram, in compound logograms, and in chain-words.[1] The Sumerian culture embodies a rich mythology, a heritage from prehistoric time. A mythological description does not necessarily mean a flight of fancy but rather a creative imagery based on reality (or realities) or some "historical" happening.

A stylistic feature of Sumerian literature is this "creative" imagery (especially animal imagery, as the work by Wolfgang Heimpel

---

[1]The present writer, depending on Arno Poebel, Grammatical Texts (Philadelphia: University Museum, 1914) and Adam Falkenstein, Das Sumerische, Handbuch der Orientalistik, vol. 2, no. 1 (Leiden: E. J. Brill, 1959), uses the word logogram for a sign expressing a chief idea, for instance -e- "house," lugal "king," si "horn," etc. Compound logograms or ideograms are, for instance, si-mul "horn," "Sternhorn," "star," "ray of light," má-gur$_8$ "epithet for moongod," while a chain-word involves grammatical constructions, for instance, é-gal-la-ni, "his great house."

shows). Whether these pictorial descriptions have been produced ad hoc for a particular case or whether they already belonged to the tradition when the Sumerian script developed has been the debate of scholars since knowledge of the Sumerian language came on firm footing a few decades ago. It is a fact, however, that symbols used as epithets of animals meet us abundantly in literary genres, for instance, the epithets of ox, wild ox, gazelle, lion, etc. A symbol, however, is not the reality but points to it. Albert Einstein's reminder of caution is appropriate here: "Most mistakes in philosophy and logic occur because the human mind is apt to take the symbol for reality."[1]

As has been shown, the basic meaning of SI is qarnu "horn," and there are about 150 compounds with the SI sign.

Heimpel has shown how á (a completely different sign)[2] can mean "horn" or "arm" and by extension "strength."[3] Si-mul[4] (a compound) can be "justified lexically by the use of Sumerian si," "horn," to mean "ray, shaft of light."[5] Cooper has pointed out that this is a later mistranslation by the Akkadians.[6] Cooper adds, "The misinterpretation of these phrases

---

[1] Cosmic Religion (New York: Covici-Friede, 1931), p. 101.

[2] See Thureau-Dangin's list of homophones in Les homophones Sumériens, p. 1.

[3] Heimpel, Tierbilder, p. 93.

[4] Translated "Sternhorn" by Landsberger, Die Fauna, p. 11.

[5] Cooper, Book Review: Tierbilder (by W. Heimpel), JNES 30 (1971):149.

[6] Ibid.

in contexts demanding a meaning 'horn' indicates the degree to which the Sumerian images had faded."[1] That many of these "mistranslations" were intentional in order to convey the meaning of these figurative devices seems, however, reasonable. The obsolescence of words because of homonomy was but a natural development and may give an explanation for misinterpretation and mistranslation.

Cooper noted how, for instance, the Sumerian gud [𒄞] with the meaning of "ox" (the domestic alpu) was in many bilingual passages translated qarrādu "hero," or, in another example am [𒀄] "wild ox" was translated bēlu "lord." So also alim "bison" was translated kabtu "weighty, important," etc.[2]

Heimpel suggests two alternatives: "Es liegt also entweder eine semantische Entwicklung von 'Ur' zu 'Herr' vor, oder aber ein Homonym am mit Bedeutungen 'Ur' und 'Herr.'"[3] But both are problematic.[4]

The next step of development seems to be the semantic extension from a specific animal epithet to a general term for might and majesty, i.e., in terms of a divine quality. Here we would consider the interesting study of Smith with reference to the meaning of b/pukk/qqu and mekku in the Gilgameš Epic (Tablet XII). No consensus has yet been reached as to the meaning of these two

---

[1] Ibid., p. 150.   [2] Ibid.

[3] Heimpel, Tierbilder, p. 19.

[4] See further Heimpel's discussion, ibid.

elusive terms. The suggestion offered by Smith that giš ZAL (with the reading gizzal or gissal), one of the Akkadian equivalents of the term b/bukku (variant b/buqqu), may indeed not refer to an object of wood but rather carry an abstract meaning, is significant.[1] If the word b/buqqu carries an abstract meaning (although its literal equivalent would be horn) then we would here have a divine attribute being referred to under the symbol of horn. In our opinion the context of the narrative favors an abstract rendering of the words b/bukku and mekku. The tragedy lamented would thus refer to divine qualities lost in the Garden of Uruk referred to in this particular Epic. Smith suggests that the lament of the lost b/bukku and mekku may have begun, "O, divine karan of heaven." This, of course, is a pregnant phrase, open to all kinds of options. As we are not competent to explore all the variances and nuances of meanings we have to leave the question open and hope that one day the true meaning of pukku and mekku will be unraveled.

There are still many other "unknowns" connected with the Sumerian si which need to be solved.

The Akkadian texts using the term qarnu reflect clearly the meaning of horn, both in its concrete aspect and in its figurative usage in mythological contexts where Akkadian is depending on Old Sumerian literary texts. A new aspect is brought forth in the latter part of the second millennium when the heteroclitic qannu (with assimilation -r- and -n-) came into use (perhaps under the

---

[1] Smith, "b/pukk/qqu, mekku," p. 156.

impact of the Amorite language.)[1] The hem, as the "outermost corner" of the garment, represented the whole of the garment which in turn represented the individual or owner of the garment. The concept of laying aside of the garment representing the loss of the old status will be dealt with in more detail in chapter three.

The "horns" of the moon is a concept that occurs in the languages of the ancient Near East. However, confusion of the signs si (𒋛) and má (𒈣) has resulted in the concept of the magur-boat to be confused with "horn." The "rundes Schiff," the ma-gur₈ boat, originated in the Sin-cult, and very popular in Sumer, spread from there to all surrounding nations. However, the qarnu with the meaning of "horn" should not be confused with ma with the meaning of "ship" or "boat."

The Assyrian culture in the last quarter of the second millennium eliminated at times mythological concepts from their literature. The Ugaritic literature from several centuries earlier still clung to mythological concepts and had a rich mythological bulk of literature. The usage of animal epithets is very common in Ugaritic just as it was among the early Sumerians. The Ugaritic culture, however, created its own pantheon but at the same time accepted gods from other cultures to be included. The debate concerning ʿAnat's "horns" may be an indication of a link between Ugaritic and the use of qrn in Aramaic and South-Arabic, where the word is deprived of its mythological aura. The hostile connotation is, however, preserved.

---

[1]Lewy, "The Nuzian Feudal System," p. 313, n. 2.

One striking observation is brought out in the standard lexicons dealing with Biblical texts, namely, the uniformity of evidences that in spite of many analogous usages the "horns" of the moon are completely lacking in the materials of the Hebrew Bible. No text is known in the Hebrew Bible that uses the term qrn for the concept of the "horns" of the moon. Is this phenomenon purely accidental or reflecting a different culture? It seems to be significant that all surrounding cultures discuss the "horns" of the moon in close association with the "horns" of the bull just as though the two expressions were synonymous.

The opening words in James Barr's work[1] are worth considering: "The Hebrew manuscript text of the Old Testament shows a high degree of uniformity." Although we have not been ultimately concerned with textual criticism in this dissertation, Barr's words are still appropriate. The uniformity of the Hebrew manuscripts in the usage of the term qrn is discernible throughout the Old Testament, giving evidence of the various works drawing on one and the same tradition.

It has to be emphasized that the ancient Near Eastern languages serve as "windows" through which elucidative concepts of various traditions can be obtained. The final control for the meaning of a term is the contextual setting of the linguistic-syntactic connection within its literary unit and the setting within the piece of literature in which it occurs.

---

[1] *Comparative Philology and the Text of the Old Testament* (Oxford: At the Clarendon Press, 1968), p. 1.

CHAPTER III

HORN-MOTIFS IN NON-BIBLICAL SOURCES

Non-Literary, Literary Texts and Iconography

In this chapter we attempt to examine the horn-motifs in non-literary and literary contexts as well as in iconographical contexts by means of available material from ancient Near Eastern sources.

A careful investigation of non-literary texts (business documents, administrative texts, lexical lists, and the like) gives rather meager results as to the usage of "horn," but occurring samples, for the sake of reference, have been included. It seems, however, proper in this chapter to place the main emphasis on literary texts (myths, epics, hymns, prayers, etc.) where "horns" with reference to gods, priests, kings, soldiers, ziggurats, and altars make a more suitable context.

It is, however, not the purpose here to analyze the texts either historically, grammatically, or literarily (in the narrow sense of the word); such analyses have already been made and they still continue to be made by competent scholars who are specialists in their fields.

The foremost interest here is to retrace the motifs of "horn" in contextual settings in order to detect (if possible) the origin for its innumerable occurrences in the ancient Near East. Secondly the purpose is to recover, if possible, the original meanings and usages of the word. Some mythological material has therefore been pondered rather extensively.

Iconography (monuments, stelae, statues, seals, etc.) will be referred to all along in order to make the presentation more relevant and realistic.

Owing to the fact that both texts and iconography with reference to "horn(s)" are to be numbered by the hundreds and even thousands, the material to be examined, by necessity, has to be selective. The principle of selection has been made with the purpose of obtaining a variety of genres and cultural specimens on both a diachronical and geographical basis.

Non-Literary Texts

Mesopotamia

We have not been able to trace the motif of horn in non-literary sources from the Early Dynastic Period. The source material from the earliest prehistorical periods that does exist is non-verbal, yet eloquently illustrative, namely, the seals and other small sculptures (terracotta). But the motif of "horn" in seals seems to be framed in mythology and ritual and for this reason this kind of source material will have to supplement the section of literary texts as far as this is possible.

Literal meaning. The word "horn" in its literal meaning is attested in several lawcodes:[1] The Lipit-Ishtar

---

[1] The non-literary context can be debated here as the stylistic approach in the prologue and epilogue of the law codes

Lawcode,[1] The Laws of Eshnunna,[2] The Code of Hammurabi,[3] and, finally, The Hittite Laws.[4]

The lawcode by Lipit-Ishtar (#36) attests the literal usage of horn in the following paragraph: "If a man rented an ox (and) broke its horn, he shall pay one-fourth of (its) price."[5] The particular passage in the Eshnunna law reads:

> If an ox is known to gore habitually and the authorities have brought the fact to the knowledge of its owner, but he does not have his ox dehorned, it gores a man and causes (his) death, then the owner of the ox shall pay two-thirds of a mina of silver.[6]

---

may be classified as literate. This overlapping has been considered but the classification has been maintained because of the "administrative" function of the law. Some scholars, however, question the legislative purpose and function of the law codes and see them primarily as "royal apologia and testaments." So, for instance, Jacob J. Finkelstein, "Ammiṣaduqa's Edict and the Babylonian 'Law Codes'," JCS 15 (1961):103.

[1] Samuel Noah Kramer, The Sumerians (Chicago: The University of Chicago Press, 1963), pp. 336-40; The "Lipit-Ishtar Lawcode," in ANET³ (Princeton, NJ: Princeton University Press, 1969), pp. 159-61.

[2] Albrecht Goetze, "The Laws of Eshnunna," in ANET³, pp. 161-63.

[3] Theophile J. Meek, "The Code of Hammurabi," in ANET³, pp. 163-80. Meek gives the date 1728-1686 B.C. for this lawcode. It was at the very beginning of his reign that Hammurabi promulgated his lawcode (p. 163). Jacob J. Finkelstein takes the opposite view and says that "it is generally recognized that the Laws of Hammurabi . . . could not have been compiled except in the last years of his reign, after he had accomplished all the conquests enumerated in his prologue;"Ammiṣaduqa's Edict and the Babylonian 'Law Codes'," p. 101.

[4] Albrecht Goetze, "The Hittite Laws," in ANET³, pp. 188-97.

[5] Kramer, The Sumerians, p. 339; also idem, "The Laws of Eshnunna," in ANET³, p. 161.

[6] Goetze, "The Laws of Eshnunna," in ANET³, pp. 161-63 (#54); cf. the transliteration, Goetze, "The Laws of Eshnunna Discovered at Tell Harmal," Sumer 4 (1948):63-102. Goetze indicates

A similar content is found in the Hammurabi law where it says:

> If a seignior's ox was a gorer and his city council made it known to him that it was a gorer, but he did not pad its horns (or) tie up his ox, and that ox gored to death a member of the aristocracy, he shall give one-half mina of silver.[1]

The Hittite lawcode records the following rule (first part):

> If anyone breaks the horn or the foot of an ox, he shall receive that (animal) and give one in good condition to the owner of the ox.[2]

All these instances deal with the horns of oxen and therefore attest a literal and unambiguous usage.

Towards the end of the second millennium the literal usage is attested, for instance, in The Annals of the Kings of Assyria.[3] The story of Tiglath-Pileser I, king of Assyria (1115-1077 B.C.) recorded on a cylinder tells how the king boasted of having brought into subjection "forty-two lands and their princes,"[4] while in the desert in the country of Mitanni, Tiglath-pileser, "the valiant hero," with his own spear killed four wild bulls. About these incidents he says, "Their hides and their horns unto my city of Ashur

---

with a question mark (?) the uncertainty of la pa-si-ir-ma (#54), p. 91. Also the translation "dehorned" has been italicized to indicate the uncertainty (ANET[3], p. 163).

[1] Meek, "The Code of Hammurabi," in ANET[3], p. 176 (#251).

[2] Goetze, "The Hittite Laws," in ANET[3], p. 192 (#74).

[3] Ernest A. Wallis Budge and Leonard William King, eds., Annals of the Kings of Assyria . . . in the British Museum, Vol. 1 (London: Trustees of the British Museum, 1902). This text (like the lawcodes) may by some scholars be considered a literary text. Overlapping seems unavoidable.

[4] Ibid., p. 82 (col. VI, lines 38-39).

I brought."[1] Tiglath-pileser brought with him the most valuable parts as trophies of his heroic deed. The literal meaning of "horns" is obvious in the context.

The same literal usage is attested by Jørgen A. Knudtzon in a dowry-list sent from Tušratta, King of Mitanni, to Thutmose IV, who was to marry Tušratta's daughter.[2] All the various kinds of horns, karan rimi ["wild bull"], karnu ša alap ["mountain bull"] karnu lu-lu-t[u]m [?], and karan a-i-gal-lu-ḫu [?] were to be covered with gold.[3] The dowry was impressive not only due to the enormous amount of gold used,[4] but also, probably, because horns in all their variety were treasured items in Egypt--perhaps a symbolic greeting was attached to this gift.

The value of horns even in natura without a gold-covering is seen from "a fictitious letter purporting to be addressed by none other than Gilgamesh, the famous hero of the epic and legendary king of Uruk (Erech). . . ."[5] The king, in this letter, "requests his correspondent to go to a certain mountain (or country) and send him various animals, precious stones, metals, and other commodities,

---

[1] Ibid., p. 85 (col. VI, lines 68, 69).

[2] Die El-Amarna-Tafeln (Aalen: Otto Zeller, 1962).

[3] Ibid., 1:208-11, 214, 215.

[4] According to the record, ca. thirty-five pairs of horns were covered with gold (ibid).

[5] Oliver R. Gurney, "The Sultantepi Tablets VI, A Letter of Gilgamesh," AnSt 7 (1957):127. Although this document is a letter Gurney would not classify it as such, for he says that it "can hardly be compared as literature," (p. 127) and for this reason it is here classified with non-literary documents.

. . ."[1] The fictitiousness of the letter is, of course, revealed in the fantastic and absurd quantity which Gilgameš requests. The text includes the usual foreboding prognostics of severe retribution should the correspondent fail to fulfill the request. The manuscript lists <u>inter alia</u>: <u>L lim pùre^meš šum/tak-d/ti-ri šá ṣu-pu-ru bu-un-nu-ú qar-nu šal-mu</u> "50,000 . . . calves with hooves in good condition and horns intact."[2] The calves here mentioned are only a part of the king's demand: altogether over 400,000 animals are mentioned and in addition to butter, wine, lentils, wood, etc. Anyway the horns had to be "intact," i.e., undamaged.

Jean Bottéro in his translation of some economic and administrative texts has attested the usage of "horn" as a vessel: 1 <u>GAL siḷ-ri-im qarnim kaspum ša qi-iš-ti Ha-ab-du-Ma-lik</u> "1 vase-à-boire en 'corne-coupée,' du cadeau (fait) à Ḫabdu-Màlik."[3]

<u>Literal-extended meaning</u>. An unusual meaning of the word <u>qarnu</u> is attested from a time prior to Hammurabi (i.e., from the early second millennium). J. R. Kupper has transcribed and translated some of the letters comprising the diplomatic correspondence of Baḫdi-Limm [the servant of Zimri-Lim] and the following passage from the fragmentary text is here quoted:

<u>[k]i-a-am iq-bu-ni[m um-ma-a-mi]</u>

---

[1] Ibid., p. 127. [2] Ibid., pp. 128, 129 (line 19).

[3] Jean Bottéro, <u>Textes Economiques et Administratifs</u>, vol. 7 of ARM, ed. André Parrot and Georges Dossin (Paris: Imprimerie Nationale, 1957), p. 44. (The onomastic usage of Qarni-Lim [personal name] is attested in the same text [Rev 117.5]). Also Text 119:1 (ibid., p. 46) and Text 219, 3.4.6 (ibid., p. 110) present similar usages.

qa-ra-an ṣú-ba-at Zi-i[m-ri-Li-im]
[ṣ]a-ba-at ša qa-bi-šu e-pu-úš
ù Zi-im-ri-Li-im mâras-sú
li-iṭ-ru-dam-ma šar-ru-tam
i-na Ka-ra-na-a(ki) li-pu-ús
a-na qa-bi-e ma-ti-ia qa-ra-an ṣú-ba-at
be-lí-ia aṣ-ba-at be-li qa-ti la i-na-pa-as.[1]

Unfortunately, the wider context is fragmentary. The immediate context, however, shows that in the early second millennium the usage of the word "horn" in Mari had an extended meaning of edge (skirt or flap) of a garment, as Kupper's translation reveals:

> ils m'ont parlé [comme il suit]:
> "saisis le pan du vêtement de Zi[mri-Lim],
> exécute ses ordres;
> quant à Zimri-Lim, qu'il envoie
> sa fille et qu'il exerce
> la royauté à Karanâ.
> Selon l'ordre de mon pays, j'ai saisi le pan du vêtement
> de mon seigneur; que mon seigneur ne repousse pas ma main!"[2]

To grasp the "horn" or edge of the garment of the king, then, according to this text from Mari, conveys the meaning of a submissive attitude vis à vis the attitude of the servant to his king and a minute execution of his will.

Purely extended meaning. The word "horn" could also take

---

[1] J. R. Kupper, "Correspondance de Baḫdi-Lim prefet du palais de Mari," ARM, vol. 6, eds. André Parrot and Georges Dossin (Paris: Imprimerie Nationale, 1954), p. 42 (26 Rev.).

[2] Ibid., p. 43 (26 Rev.); cf. also i-na qa-ra-an si-ba-ti-su "A la pointe de sa vieillesse," conveying the meaning of "the extreme limit," i.e., "at the tip (end, edge, point) of his old age. . . ." Georges Dossin and Andre Finet, "Correspondance Feminine," ARM, vol. 10, eds. André Parrot and Georges Dossin (Paris: Paul Geuthner, 1978), 10:94, 95 (57 Rev.).

on an extended meaning that may seem unrelated to its literal and basic value.

Edmond Sollberger, in the Glossary of his work[1] commenting briefly on the Sumerian word si (written SI), gives the meaning išaru "fair, just."[2] For the usage of ensi (written PA.TE.SI, in which the compound SI comprises one link), Sollberger refers to several examples[3] but cautiously remarks that "the interpretation of si is far from certain.[4]

The other example given by Sollberger concerns the same homophone si, but written su₄ (occasionally spelled si). In the compound ᵈnin-si₄-an-na the variation si and su₄ (si₄) shows that at some early time confusion between the two homophones must have taken place.[5]

This observation by Sollberger shows that Arno Poebel was

---

[1] The Business and Administrative Correspondence under the Kings of Ur in Texts from Cuneiform Sources (Locust Valley, NY: J. T. Augustin, 1966), 1:166 (#607).

[2] Ibid.; for this meaning of si cf. CAD, 7:224, s.v. "išaru;" cf. also Anton Deimel who lists the meaning išaru in the third place of frequency usage ŠL 3d. ed. (Rome: Pontificium Institutum Biblicum, 1947), Part III, vol. 1, p. 180; cf. also Stephen Langdon, The Annals of Ashurbanipal: A Glossary in English and German and Brief Notes Semitic Studies Series, vol. 2 (Leiden: E. J. Brill, 1903), p. 42 (#88), who gives the sign 𒐊𒌷 for išêru.

[3] Sollberger, The Business and Administrative Correspondence, p. 116 (#201).

[4] Ibid., p. 166 (#607).

[5] The si₄ = SÂMU (red, brown) and su₄ = PILÛ: PILÛTU (red, brown) actually have the same sign 𒐊𒌷 (see Deimel ŠL, Part III, vol. 1, pp. 177, 180). Knut Tallqvist gives Nin-qun-an-na [bēlit eqī ša samē] as a synonym for ᵈNin-si₄-an-na with the meaning "die rote Herrin des Himmels." See his Akkadische Götterepitheta, Studia Orientalia 7 (Helsinki: Akateeminen Kirjakauppa, 1938), pp. 417, 407.

certainly right when he said that the Sumerian text "has by no means been carefully transmitted."[1] Poebel, on the basis of the already existing material (1914), says, "the process of decay seems to have set in during the later period of the first dynasty in Isin"[2]--i.e., in the first century of the second millennium B.C.

From these few examples of nonliterary texts which give evidence of both literal, literal-extended, and even allude to a purely extended meaning, we have to turn to a more fruitful field of literary texts and iconography.

Literary Text and Iconography

Gods--in Literary Texts

Sumer and Akkad. There are two main sources from which to study ancient traditions of horns in relation to gods: literary texts and iconography. The former pertain to historical time although the plots described can go back into primeval history. For the ancient Sumerian history we are dependent mostly on early second millennium but there are even some third millennium cuneiform copies.[3] Iconographic material, on the contrary, may authentically and originally represent early third millennium (perhaps even fourth

---

[1] Historical Texts, Publications of the Babylonian Section, (Philadelphia: University Museum, 1914), vol. 4, pt. 1, p. 68.

[2] Ibid.

[3] See William W. Hallo's discussion "Toward a History of Sumerian Literature," in Sumerological Studies in Honor of Thorkild Jacobsen on His Seventieth Birthday June 7, 1974, Assyriological Studies, no. 20 (Chicago: University Press, 1976), pp. 181-203.

millennium)[1] mythological and/or religious concepts and may do so apart from any text. It is for this reason that iconography becomes very valuable not only for this early period but also for later periods when contemporary texts may substantiate that the interpretation is correct.

It is interesting to notice that the horn-motif is present on cylinder seals appearing in Sumer from a very early time.[2] The motif is, however, not horns on gods but on animals in scenes which may eventually depict ritual contexts.

Edith Porada, for instance, in The Collection of the Pierpont Morgan Library, refers to a composite monster with a "two-pointed" headdress, a scene which she suggests may be connected with a mythological scene; the interpretation of the scene is, however, enigmatic.[3]

---

[1] So, for instance, Edith Porada, ed., The Collection of the Pierpont Morgan Library in CANES, The Bollingen Series, 14 (Washington: Pantheon Books, 1948), vol. 1, pt. 1, p. 1.

[2] The history of seals and the questions pertaining thereto are not discussed per se in this dissertation. However we have consulted a number of works prepared by specialists in this field to get a general perception of the motif of horns in various periods: Rainer M. Boehmer, Die Entwicklung der Glyptik während der Akkad-Zeit (Berlin: Walter de Gruyter & Co., 1965); Louis J. Delaporte, Catalogue des cylindres orientaux (Paris: Ernest Leroux, 1910); Henri Frankfort, Cylinder Seals (London: Macmillan and Co., 1939); Carney E. S. Gavin, "The Glyptic Art of Syria-Palestine," (Ph.D. dissertation, Harvard University, 1973); Anton Moortgat, Vorderasiatische Rollsiegel (Berlin: Gebrüder Mann, 1966); Hans Henning von der Osten, Ancient Oriental Seals in the Collection of Mr. Edward T. Newall (Chicago: University Press, 1934); Edith Porada, ed., The Pierpont Morgan Library, vol. 1, pts. 1-2 of Corpus of Ancient Near Eastern Seals in North America Collections (Washington: Pantheon Books, 1948); William H. Ward, The Seal Cylinders of Western Asia (Washington: Carnegie Institution, 1910; reprint ed., n.p.: Columbia Plansgraph Company, 1919).

[3] CANES, vol. 1, pt. 1, p. 11 (cf. pl. X, fig. 62). The figure in front of the shrine is clearly depicted with horns. The seal is, according to Porada, from the Early Dynastic II Period.

A very clear representation from the Early Dynastic III Period (ca. 2600 B.C.) is depicted not on a seal but on a shell plaque. According to this motif a single god is confronting a seven-headed dragon in battle. The god wears a headdress with horns and has already wounded or cut one of the dragon's heads (fig. 1). Although the horn-motif on gods was not common on seals in the early Dynastic periods, it was certainly known from the Early Dynastic III Period.

Fig. 1. A horned deity battling the legendary seven-headed monster. Shell plaque from ca. 2600 B.C.

Since the gods of Mesopotamia were all conceived in human shape, it was impossible to distinguish a god from a human in iconography unless the former were distinguished by a special attire. From the Jemdet Nasr period (ca. 2900 B.C.)[1] the horned crown first appeared and remained the distinct divine attribute throughout ancient history.[2]

---

[1] This date is given by H. W. F. Saggs, The Greatness That Was Babylon (New York: Hawthorn Books, Inc., 1962), p. 184.

[2] Henri Frankfort, Cylinder Seals (London: Macmillan and Co., 1939), p. 32.

The same motif of a battle with the dragon is depicted on a seal from the Akkadian period (ca. 2360 B.C.). The seal has apparently another tradition behind it than the shell plaque with the dragon motif above, for the seal depicts the seven-headed dragon, attacked by the gods, having four of the seven heads already mortally wounded (fig. 2). This seal depicts also two onlookers with caps on their heads but no horns.

Fig. 2. The seven-headed dragon attacked by the gods wearing horned headdresses. Seal impression from the Akkadian period (ca. 2360 B.C.).

Classical is a cylinder seal from the Akkadian period (ca. 2254-2154 B.C.) depicting the gods engaged in a building enterprise. It presents a motif from time immemorial when gods had to toil for their daily bread. Some of the gods are presented with the Akkadian style of headdress (low cap with lateral horns [fig. 3]). There are many seals from the Akkadian period representing motifs from earlier periods and therefore they may rightly belong to two periods.[1]

---

[1] Cf. the various seals in James Pritchard, ed., ANEP, (Princeton, NJ: Princeton University Press, 1954), pp. 221-22 (#686-700).

Fig. 3. "Horned" gods engaged in building activities. Stone cylinder seal from the late Akkadian period (ca. 2254-2154 B.C.).

Another presentation of a "simple" motif is the so-called "Sündenfall-Zylinder" seal (fig. 4). This particular seal belongs to the Neo-Sumerian period or, to use Eckhard Unger's identification, to the time of Hammurabi (ca. 2000 B.C.).[1] Unger sees two deities with "Hörnermütze" seated on either side of the "Lebensbaum" and a serpent standing on its tail behind the figure on the left.[2]

Fig. 4. So-called "Sündenfall-Zylinder" seal. Neo-Sumerian period (ca. 2000 B.C.).

---

[1] Unger sees the "Lebensbaum" as having several traditions; the oldest one already from the time of the dynasty of Akkad, and the latest from the time of Hammurabi; "Lebensbaum," RLV, ed. Max Ebert (Berlin: Walter de Gruyter & Co., 1926), 7:261-62.

[2] Scholars do not agree on this identification. Alexander Heidel refers to this seal by saying that it was "formerly supposed to represent the Babylonian tradition of the fall of man;" The Babylonian Genesis, First Phoenix ed. (Chicago: University Press, 1963), caption to fig. 17 [last page]. Martin Beck in 1962 does not

Without discrediting this interpretation, we would reconsider the discarded option as worth considering anew, if for nothing else than for its traditional labeling. Only the right-hand figure is clearly depicted as having horns. Furthermore, this being seems to be more masculine in contours than the one on the left. Also the fact that the serpent is depicted as standing behind the left-hand figure would indicate a possibility of this representing the biblical Eve, while the right-hand figure may represent Adam in the primeval story told in Genesis. Though there is a considerable time-gap that separates the iconography from the later text, the two presentations should be reconsidered as possibly compatible on the basis of at least two weighty reasons: first, the vast material, both literary and iconographic, that offers parallels with the Hebrew Bible, and secondly, because so many scholars at the present take seriously into account a long-existing tradition of oral transmission.[1]

As for the style of the horns depicted on the right-hand figure, they seem to reflect the very ancient type of protruding lateral horns (fig. 5).[2] The cap itself, apart from the horns,

---

express his opinion either pro or con; he simply labels the seal: "Der sog. 'Sündenfall Zylinder';" "Baum," in BHH (Göttingen: Vandenhoeck & Ruprecht, 1962), 1:207 (seal #3).

[1] So, for instance, Jørgen Laessøe, "Literal and Oral Tradition in Ancient Mesopotamia," in Studia Orientalia Ioanni Pedersen 70th Anniversary Nov. 7, 1955 (Copenhagen: Einar Munksgaard, 1953), pp. 205-18; and Bendt Alster, Dumuzi's Dream, Aspects of Oral Poetry in a Sumerian Myth (Copenhagen: Det Kongelige Bibliotek, 1972), pp. 15-27.

[2] Cf. the headdresses worn by gods on the "battle with the dragon" motif (figs. 5 and 8 below).

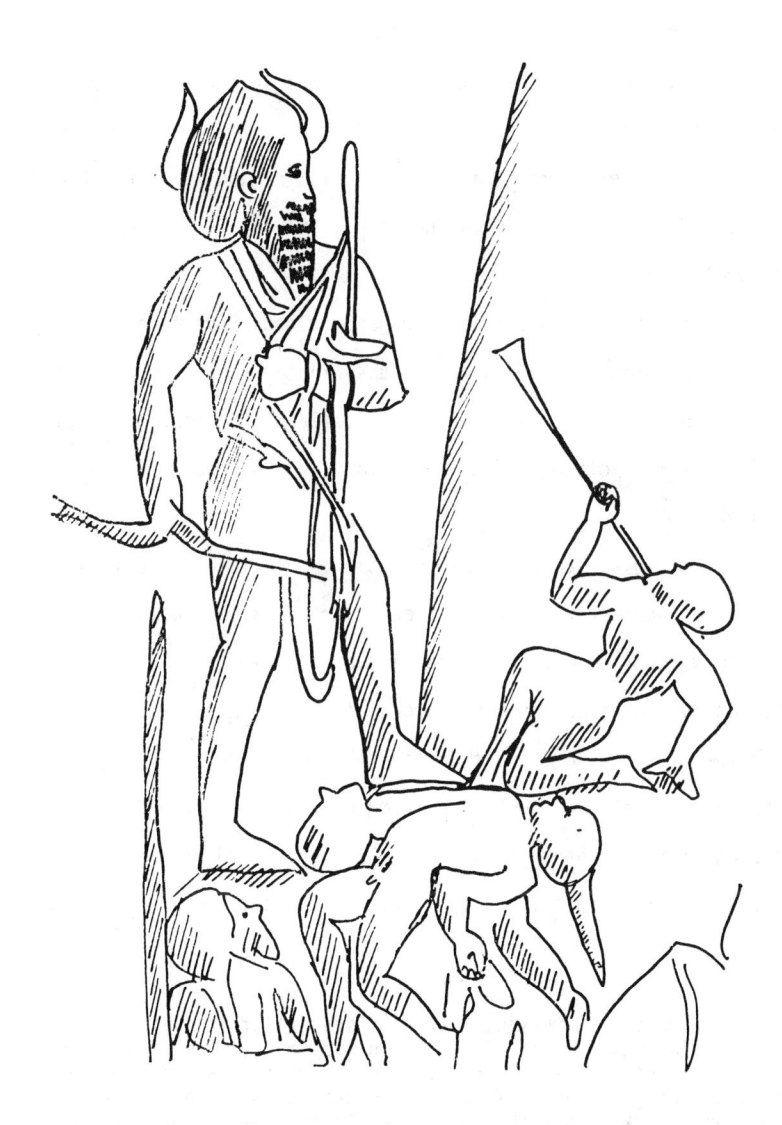

Fig. 5. The victorious King Narâm-Sin wearing the horned helmet and trampling his enemies under his feet. Sandstone stela from Susa 23rd. century B.C.

seems to be more flattened on the "Sündenfall-Zylinder" than the headdress that Narâm-Sin wore.[1]

It is, however, well to remember that iconographic seals can be ever so bewildering unless they may be verified by synchronous texts and/or other forms of art. With this in mind we cannot pinpoint the details of the seals, nor can we be dogmatic concerning the interpretation.[2]

Many other horn motifs in regard to gods may be relatively easy to understand (though none are easy in the narrow sense of the word, as we do not know what the seal-cutter had in mind), but the complex motif is often hard to understand and the real meaning is elusive.

E. Douglas Van Buren has pointed out that it was unimportant for the seal-cutter whether the events were depicted in the precise order in which they once occurred; it was more important to maintain "the connecting thread running through the whole narrative."[3] This would then, of course, result in the fact that a particular representation was not limited to one theme only but had embedded in it allusions to other happenings or events, past or future--in other words a "complex" motif. The primary aim seems to be to produce a

---

[1] Cf. figs. 4 and 5 above.

[2] Carney E. S. Gavin, a present specialist on cylinder seals in the Syria region, says: "Most divinities on cylinders cannot be precisely identified and even the horn mitre, our basic criterion for determining whether a figure represents a god or a mortal, remains but a working hypothesis." "The Glyptic Art of Syria-Palestine," p. 3.

[3] Van Buren, "Akkadian Sidelights on a Fragmentary Epic," Or 19 (1950):159.

continuous narrative--a sequence of ideas. Van Buren has fittingly expressed it thus:

> The desire to depict a series of successive events induced the Akkadian artists to borrow certain forms from mythological cycles the iconography of which was already formalized, and mold them into a new pictorial image to illustrate the continuation of the narrative.[1]

Some of these "complex" motifs seem to belong to a certain group of seals depicting some particular myth. So for instance Van Buren refers to the myth related in Enuma eliš (Tablet VI) telling how the rebel Qingu and his followers fought against the other gods.[2]

This myth, then, may substantiate the seals depicting the contest series which, although they differ considerably, have one thing in common: they "seem to illustrate passages from the legend of Zû which have not been fully perceived."[3] Furthermore Van Buren says, "They all [the seals] depict a great bird of prey or a superhuman being with ornithological characteristics."[4]

It is also of significance that Van Buren classifies the story of Zû as a legend--not a myth.[5]

This classification then, if correct, would suggest that the ancient seal-cutters might have recognized a true kernel in the story, although the artists borrowed certain forms from mythological cycles of which the iconography had already been shaped, only to mold the

---

[1] Ibid., p. 160.

[2] Ibid. For a translation of Enuma eliš [Tablet VI] see, for instance, Ephraim A. Speiser, "Akkadian Myths and Epics," in ANET³, pp. 68-70.

[3] Van Buren, "Akkadian Sidelights," p. 160.

[4] Ibid.   [5] Ibid.

events into a new form and, perhaps, with new pictorial images. This process is then to be seen not as a simple motif but as a complex one--a presentation of successive events.

Among the various traditions of Zû there is one that gives a faint reflection of a religious motif. Van Buren refers to the legend as follows:

> Zû beheld the insignia of the Enlil-ship, the tiara of lordship, and the tablets of destiny, and coveted them in his heart. To himself he said: "I will take the tablets of destiny and authority over the gods. My throne will I establish."[1]

The theft which was considered a <u>casus belli</u>[2] caused a discussion in the assembly among the gods. Anu, the spokesman, challenged several of the gods, but according to the legend the god hesitated because of the fear and dread that the Zû-bird had evoked. Van Buren writes,

> The mention of his name is usually accompanied by the qualifying adjective "evil." Zû, "the evil storm-bird," was a fallen divinity who became a powerful demon able to change his shape at will, for there are hints that he could assume successively the guise of a man, a lion, and a bird.[3]

That the Zû-bird was finally captured and his horned cap removed seems apparent from both legends and seals.[4]

---

[1] Ibid., pp. 162-63. The story seems to be parallel to the story told in the prophetic tradition of the prophet Isaiah (14:12-14). Iconography representing a bird-figure on the ancient seals from the third millennium B.C. may or may not refer to this myth; cf. Unger "Mischwesen," §18 in <u>RLV</u> (8:201).

[2] Thomas Fish, "The Zû Bird," <u>Bulletin of the John Ryland's Library Manchester</u> 31 (1948):167.

[3] Van Buren, "Akkadian Sidelights," pp. 163-64.

[4] These are various versions of the hero who finally overcame the foe. For instance, Ephraim A. Speiser, "The Myth of Zu," in <u>ANET</u>[3], pp. 111-13; Wilfred G. Lambert, "The Gula Hymn of Bulutsa-

According to Van Buren there is even a more archaic representation of what seems to be the final phase of the struggle with emphasis on Zû's being captured, for this seal depicts a herald standing ready to proclaim the successful outcome of the conflict.[1] Furthermore, Van Buren says.

> An echo of this ancient tradition is preserved in an Assyrian text which relates that the divine herald announced to the god Ashur: "Zû is captured," and was at once told: "Hasten, unto all the gods announce the tidings."[2]

It is at this stage, then, that the removal of the horned cap takes place[3]--a *fait accompli* authenticated by both literature and iconography. Especially the pictorial representation is interesting: the capturing of Zû (depicted as a bird-man with a bird's tail) who is brought to judgment before Ea. All the gods wear caps with horns, but Zû is deprived of his crown (fig. 6). According to Van Buren,

Fig. 6. The mythological Zû captured and deprived of his divine emblem--the "horned" headdress. Seal impression from the Akkadian period.

---

rabi," Or 36 (1967):105-29 and Van Buren, "Akkadian Sidelights," pp. 159-74. The respective heroes in these versions are Lugalbanda, Ninurta, and Marduk.

[1] Van Buren, "Akkadian Sidelights," pp. 172-73.

[2] Ibid., p. 173.   [3] Ibid., p. 171.

The outward and visible sign that kingship was conferred upon a deity was the crown placed upon his head. Moreover, as token of divinity and kingship, the loss or fall of the horned cap pretended the loss, or at least a diminution of divine ascendency.[1]

Zû had many monstrous followers described in various genres of ancient Near Eastern literature. Erich Ebeling, for instance, has translated a text telling about a dream which a king of Aššur had and in which he describes his descent into hell. The whole story, which is told partly in the third person [he] and partly in the first person [I], gives a horrifying description of the retinue of Zû.[2]

One of the followers of Zû is described as being "in the shape of a bull"[3] and, when referred to in later text, was apostrophized "O Bull! offspring of Zû art thou."[4]

This is a rather strong indication that dZU.EN (the Sîn of a later tradition), the moon-god of Ur with the particular epithet "Bull" was one of Zû's close followers.

The definite origin of bull-worship is enigmatic, but it is evident from later traditions that the bull is connected with the Sîn culture. The connection of Sîn with the earlier ZU (su) is a rather strong etymological evidence that there must have occurred a

---

[1]Van Buren, "Concerning the Horned Cap of the Mesopotamian Gods," Or 12 (1943):323.

[2]Erich Ebeling, Tod und Leben nach der Vorstellung der Babylonier (Berlin: Walter de Gruyter & Co., 1931), p. 1.

[3]Van Buren, "Akkadian Sidelights," p. 164.

[4]Ibid.

confusion of homophones (inter alia si and su) at an early stage in the transmission of the text.[1]

Jimmy J. M. Roberts points out that the divine name Su'en is normally written dEN.ZU in the Old Akkadian period.[2] The Sumerian EN-ZU actually means "Lord of Knowledge" from En 𒂗 "lord" and Zu 𒍪 "to know"[3] (also in a bad or negative sense).

Maurice H. Farbridge suggests that the name of the moon-god Sin "may be a contraction of an original Si-in, which, in turn, may be equivalent to the form En-Zu inverted."[4]

Roberts supports this theory of Farbridge in his further discussion of the anagram dZU.EN[5] (once with determinative and a second time without it), in which he points out that "this variant orthography is also supported by the old Assyrian writings su_2-en and su_2-in as well as by the later development of Sin."[6]

---

[1] Cf. Stephen Langdon's suggestive remarks, A Sumerian Grammar and Chrestomathy (Paris: Paul Geuthner, 1911), p. 31, and Deimel, SL, Part III, vol. 1, p. 177 (su_4) and p. 180 (si_4).

[2] The Earliest Semitic Pantheon (Baltimore: The Johns Hopkins University Press, 1972), p. 50.

[3] Deimel, ŠL, Part III, 1:92, 118.

[4] Studies in Biblical and Semitic Symbolism (New York: Ktav Publishing House, Inc., 1970), p. 190.

[5] Roberts points out that "one should probably assume that the writing dEN.ZU was viewed as an anagram in Akkadian context to be read as dSU_2-en. Thorkild Jacobsen notes that dEN.ZU as an anagram was "comparable to e.g. GAL:LU for lu-gal; ZU-AB for ab.zu [house of knowledge] and was read dsu.en;" see further the discussion by Jacobsen in his article "Early Political Development in Mesopotamia," ZA 52 (1957):93, n. 3; cf. Morris Jastrow, The Civilization of Babylonia and Assyria (Philadelphia: J. B. Lippincott Company, 1915), pp. 222-23.

[6] The Earliest Semitic Pantheon, p. 50.

Several epithets of Sîn might infer not only that the Moon-cult was maintained at Ur but also that it originated there:

^dSin-sar-Urim^{KI} "Sin ist König von Ur" (KU 1514), ^dSin-ra-im^{KI} "Sin liebt Ur" (VAB 5, no. 206, 9), ^dSin-ri-im-Urim^{KI}

"Sin ist der Stier (=Held) [?] von Ur" (VAB 5, no. 41, 8-9).[1]

There are similar epithets from the later Assyrian time which substantiate the theory that it is the god of a nation or a city who is the "Bull." Johann J. Stamm refers to an epithet Aššur-rīm-nišīšu "Aššur ist der Stier seines Volkes,"[2] which seems to substantiate the bull-god theory. Stamm is, however, hesitant as to its meaning, for in the same breath as he cites the epithet he adds "obwohl der Sinn dieser Aussage noch unklar ist."[3]

It is, however, of interest to find that as early as the old Akkadian period Su'en was identified with Nanna, the Sumerian city-god of Ur.[4] The tiara of the moon-god is depicted with four pairs of horns (fig. 7).[5]

---

[1] Johann J. Stamm, Die akkadische Namengebung (Darmstadt: Wissenschaftliche Buchgesellschaft, 1968), p. 227.

[2] Ibid., p. 228.

[3] Ibid. (Stamm, on account of the ambiguity suggests a metaphorical meaning of the word rimu--perhaps with the meaning of "hero;" cf. his analogous suggestion for the Sin-god [ibid., p. 227]).

[4] Roberts, The Earliest Semitic Pantheon, p. 112, n. 408.

[5] Othmar Keel says, "The bull's horns are widely used . . . in the ancient Near East. . . . The Mesopotamian gods wear horned caps as a headcovering. Up to four sets of horns may be arranged on top of each other." The Symbolism of the Biblical World, trans. Timothy J. Hallet (New York: The Seabury Press, 1978), p. 86.

139

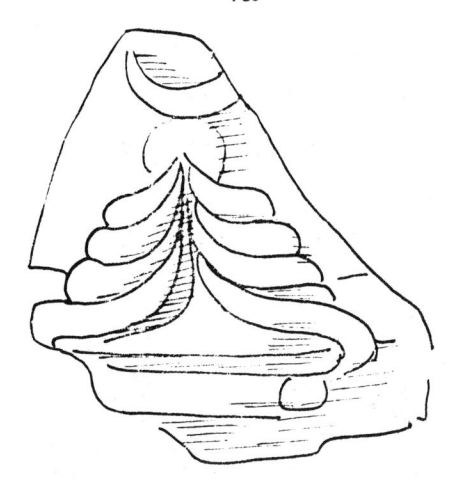

Fig. 7. Tiara of Nannar with the "moon-crescent" emblem balancing on the knob of the tiara. From the epoch of Ur-Nammu, ca. 2113-2096 B.C.

There are several versions of the bull in iconography. Van Buren describes the framework of these seals where the bull, in the midst of "ravening winged monsters," is pictured in an attacking position with a god as the target (fig. 8). The divinity of the god on one of these seals is indicated by the horns which deviate slightly in style from the typical designs of lateral horns in the Akkadian period. There is no literary source to substantiate the interpretation of this seal;[1] therefore we are limited and must depend on conjectural suggestions. Van Buren, however, remarks that these seals do not originate from the well-known tradition of the Gilgameš epic, but "must illustrate a kindred legend in which a

___

[1] Henri Frankfort, Cylinder Seals (London: Macmillan and Co., 1939), p. 132.

bull symbolized a destructive force of nature."[1] Furthermore, when we consider the theme of the epic of Gilgameš, it appears to be essentially of a secular nature, whereas the motif presented on this particular seal quite clearly appears to be of a religious nature.

Fig. 8. An attacking bull with a "horned" god as his target. The seal, which is from the Akkadian period, is enshrouded in a mysterious mythological context.

It is inevitable, therefore, to conclude that at an early time (perhaps in the Early Dynastic II period) before the Early Dynastic III period there might have been a forceful attempt to establish a universal rulership of the moon-god (represented as an attacking bull, a mountain-god, with a god as his target). The seals of these kinds speak eloquently in favor of such a conclusion though we cannot include any details.

In the Akkadian period several styles of headdresses developed. Some show close connection with the early predynastic periods

---

[1] Van Buren, "Akkadian Sidelights," p. 168. Keel also speaks of the "aggressive" bull, but not as a "destructive force of nature," but as representing the victorious ruler. . . ." The Symbolism of the Biblical World, p. 86.

having still some vegetable element in the midst of the horns, but on a flat cap (fig. 9, Akkadian a). Others show clearly the new-moon sickle supported by the tips of a pair of horns bent toward each other (fig. 9, Akkadian b).

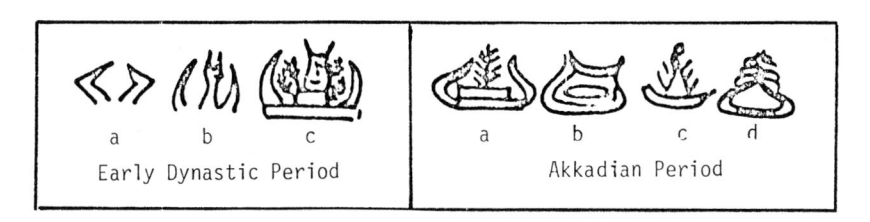

Fig. 9. Headdresses from the Early Dynastic and Akkadian periods.

The connection between the bull-horns and the new-moon sickle becomes clearer as one compares the style of the old Sumerian headdresses with the Akkadian ones. Although, according to Rainer M. Boehmer, it is not until Akkadian time that we can with certainty identify the new-moon sickle on the bull's horns, the same motif in a more cautious way is already present in the old Sumerian types (fig. 9, Early Dynastic, a, b, c).

Even if we question the validity of Boehmer's hypothesis,

> Neben einfachen "Hörnern," die hier erstmalig menschenartigen Wesen aus dem Kopf wachsen und sie so als Götter erkenntlich machen [for example "Early Dynastic" a] kommen Kronen auf mit pflanzlichen Elementen in der Mitte.[1]

there may be a kernel of truth in it.[2]

---

[1] Rainer M. Boehmer, "Hörnerkrone," in RLA (Berlin: Walter de Gruyter, 1972-75), 4:432.

[2] E. Douglas Van Buren would rather see the horns being imagined "as encircling the head of divinity rather than springing out of it" [as Boehmer thinks]. See Van Buren's article "Concerning the Horned Cap of the Mesopotamian Gods," Or 12 (1943):319.

We see the evidence of an authority (perhaps by usurpation) coming to prominence and receiving homage as a deity at this time. His chosen visible symbol was the new-moon sickle. Universal rule by such a god of authority was liable to be accepted universally, as the emblem also was of a universal kind. There might have been a religious crisis before such an attempt could succeed. The old creative gods, Anu, Enlil, and Enki, and those gods lesser in rank, giving polytheistic flavor to worship, still had their function as national gods, though the usurper attempted a universal rule.

Babylonia and Assyria. Throughout Mesopotamian history polytheism flourished. The pantheon was great and the national gods competitive. Best known, of course, is the astral triad: Sin, Šamaš, and Ištar. In Babylonia, however, Sin came to prominence in the neo-Babylonian period (especially under Nabonidus). Many hymns dedicated to Sin originate however from the Akkadian period. E. Guthrie Perry in Hymnen an Sin[1] gives a sample of the authority of Sin.

> Herr, Herrscher unter den Göttern, der im
>   Himmel und Erde allein gross ist!
> Vater, Nannar, Herr, Gott Anšar, Herrscher
>   unter den Göttern, . . .
> Kräftiger junger Stier mit starken Hörnern,
>   vollkommenen Gliedmassen,
>   lasurfarbenem Bart, voller
>   Üppigkeit und Fülle. . . .[2]

It is evident that Sin wore the "Herrschermütze" or

---

[1] Hymnen an Sin (Leipzig: J. C. Hinrichs, 1907) gives the hymn also in Sumerian and Akkadian transcripts. Only fragmentary verses have been selected.

[2] Perry, Hymnen an Sin, p. 5.

"Kopfbinde" as a sign of authority.[1] Furthermore, Sin is described in this hymn with authority over all, the begetter of all.

> Gewaltiger Anführer . . .
> der da öffnet die Tür des Himmels,
> Licht schafft allen Menschen;
> Vater, Erzeuger von allem . . .
> Im Himmel, wer ist gross? Du, du allein bist gross!
> Auf Erden, wer ist gross? Du, du allein bist gross![2]

Šamaš, the son of Sin, was however, the god who rose to prominence in Babylonia along with Marduk and Ištar. The importance of Šamaš, as the guardian of law and justice, can be understood on account of the elevated place he has on the well-known stela of Hammurabi. On this diorite stela Šamaš is depicted sitting on a throne and wearing the multiple horned headdress (fig. 10) while Hammurabi, the king, stands before the throne in an attitude of worship.[3] The same multi-horned headdress is attested a millennium later on a stone building inscription found at Abu Habba on the

---

[1] Ibid. The "Kopfbinde" was perhaps the headdress for liturgical purpose emphasizing religious authority. The phrase, "Herr der Kopfbinde, glänzender" is translated from the Sumerian umun mèn ZUBU-na "be-lum a-gi-e sú-pu-ú. The umun mèn "be-lum a-gi-e" is not hard to understand. The crux is the Sumerian logogram ZUBU ZUB (GAMLU) = Sichel, Krummschwert (see Deimel, SL, Part III, vol. 1, p. 118). ZUBU again is enigmatic. It might be a synonym for KA + ZU (see Deimel, SL (1947), Part I, p. (60) with KA = Antlitz (see Ibid., Part III, vol. 1, p. 139). ZU has already been discussed, but see ibid., p. 118 (i.e., Part III, vol. 1). The ideograph is enigmatic and further study may give light on the quotation.

[2] Perry, Hymnen an Sin, p. 1.

[3] William H. Ward points out that Hammurabi does not stand in front of the god "'receiving the law,' as it has generally been described, in memory of the way Moses received the tablets of the law from Jehovah on Mount Sinai, but in the ordinary attitude of worship." The Seal Cylinders of Western Asia, p. 100.

Fig. 10. The great Hammurabi in front of Šamaš who is depicted sitting on his throne. The sun-god is wearing the multiple "horned" headdress.

Euphrates (near Sippar [fig. 11]). The engraved inscription gives credit to Nabu-apal-iddin (885-828 B.C.) for having restored the temple of Šamaš which had been destroyed by enemies. The god Šamaš is depicted in a similar way as on the Hammurabi stela and with a similar headdress. The three astral symbols, perhaps, give recognition to both Sin and Ištar as well. The three figures in front of Šamaš are of dwarf size compared to the god. Two of them wear turban-like headdresses without horns; the third one wearing the horned headdress may perhaps represent a priest, for his dress differs from the other two.

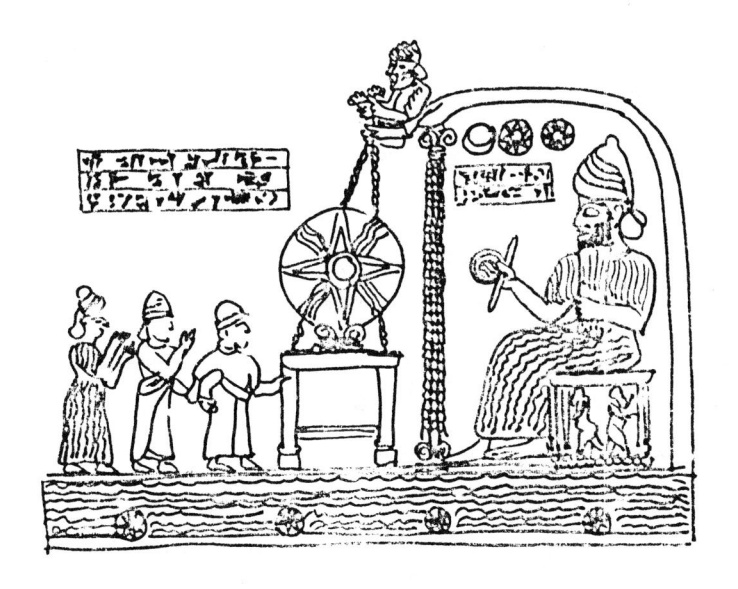

Fig. 11. King Nabu-apal-iddin of Babylon, led by a priest and accompanied by a tutelary deity, enters into the presence of Šamaš in the sun-temple at Sippar (ca. 885-828 B.C.).

The headdress of Šamaš maintained for so long in Babylon may have originated from the type of tiara that Nannar, the moon-god, wore in the time of Ur-Nammu (fig. 7 above). Another explanation, of course, may be that both were astral gods and closely related, and this relationship may be reflected in their headdress (unless it is purely accidental).

The sun-god Šamaš is often represented on seals with rays springing up from his shoulders, a horned headdress on his head and a notched sword or a saw in his hand. He either sits on a "mountain" or places his right foot on a "mountain" (fig. 12 a and b). The god Šamaš is the most popular and the most worshiped of all the gods of the Babylonian pantheon. Another observation is that his worship was not local but general.

It may be noted in this connection that also Ištar, the third astral deity (Venus) also wears horns, according to the name si-sar-a[1] "die Gehörnte" given to her. Ištar was the daughter of Anu and sister of Marduk[2] and had several positions to fill. She was martial and valiant but also the goddess of lust and love. She was the goddess of mankind, but also the mistress of heaven.[3] Scores of names indicate her popularity. Some of the better known were: Bêlit-Šamê "Himmels-herrin," In-na-na (Sumerian), Nin-an-na "Herrin des Himmels," Nûr-ilê "Licht der Götter," Si-du-ri, sù(d)-ud-da-ám "Himmelslicht," etc.[4] From the Ištar hymn Karl Frank refers to the following description of Ištar:

---

[1] Tallqvist, Akkadische Götterepitheta, p. 332.
[2] Ibid.   [3] Ibid., pp. 333, 335.   [4] Ibid., p. 331.

Fig. 12a. The sun-god equipped with a saw in his left hand and with rays emerging from his shoulders rises from between the mountains with a powerful leap. The sun-god as well as the other gods wear "horned" headdresses.

Fig. 12b. Šamaš, the sun-god, dispelling darkness, Marduk, the victor of Chaos and Ea, the wise lord of the depths. All three gods wear a headdress with multiple pairs of horns.

Agū ina qaqqadiša aki kakkabi

"Eine Herrscher-krone (trägt sie) auf
ihrem Haupte gleich einem Sterne."[1]

Farbridge gives this description of Ištar:

> On her head is a crown of feathers, her right hand is raised; whilst in her left hand she holds the top of a bow fixed in the ground. Fortunately, all doubt as to whom the figure represents is removed by the inscription ṣalam Ishtar (image of Ishtar) underneath [fig. 13].[2]

Fig. 13. The martial goddess Ištar depicted standing on her lion, and equipped with weapons. She is wearing the feather-crown on her head.

---

[1] Karl Frank, Bilder und Symbole babylonisch-assyrischer Götter (Leipzig: J. C. Hinrich, 1906), p. 18.

[2] Farbridge, Studies in Biblical and Semitic Symbolism, p. 168. Ištar's feather crown with a star on top identifies her as an astral goddess. For another presentation of Ištar (or ʿAnat?) see André Parrot, ed., Studia Mariana (Leiden: E. J. Brill, 1950), vol. 4, Plate 7. The head of Ištar, in this colorful painting from the palace at Mari, is unfortunately damaged. It is uncertain whether the headdress represents the same style. The posture of Ištar, with one leg on the lion (Ištar's holy animal), is, however, similar in both depictions.

Some scholars see Ištar as fertility goddess being symbolized through the well-known motif of a cow with a suckling calf. Franz V. M. Cumont has expressed the significant opinion that every god was regarded as a bull and every goddess as a cow "in so far as they bear lunar character."[1]

The feather-crown that she wears seems to have been normally worn by female deities even in the Old Babylonian time. A typical example can be seen on the kudurru of Meli-shipak (fig. 14) found at Susa from the Kassite period.[2] Beneath the astral symbols (Ištar, Sin and Šamaš) is shown the goddess Nanna sitting on her throne and decorated with a feather crown. The king holding his daughter's hand is with her approaching the goddess.

Contrary to the sole feather-crown worn by goddesses, a combined horn and feather crown (fig. 15) was worn by the gods in the same era. (This style was still found in Syria at a somewhat later time.)

Marduk as a sun god was (like Šamaš) promulgating justice and right. As a ruler and victor over the sea-monster, Marduk is

---

[1] Franz V. M. Cumont, Die Mysterien des Mithra (Leipzig: B. G. Teubner, 1923), p. 89.

[2] Meli-Shipak (Meli-Shikhu) was a successful Kassite King ruling (1188-1174 B.C.) in Babylon. The Kassite rulership was, however, approaching its final eclipse and with the rulership of Enlil-nādin-ahki the fierce struggle between the Elamites and Babylonians was brought to its last phase. With the death of Enlil-nādin-ahki (who died in exile) the successful regime of the Kassites which had lasted for nearly six-hundred years, was brought to its end; Donald J. Wiseman, "Assyria and Babylon ca. 1200-1000 B.C.," in CAH[3], (Cambridge: At the University Press, 1975), vol. 2, pt. 2, pp. 466-47; cf. René Labat, "Elam and Western Persia," ibid., p. 487.

Fig. 14. The goddess Nanna, receiving the king and his daughter, is depicted with the typical feather-crown worn by goddesses. This <u>kudurru</u> of Melishipak, found at Susa, originates from the Kassite period.

represented with a feather-crown and is in full regalia while the two-horned dragon rests at his feet (fig. 16). On another illustration where Marduk is still fighting with the monster Tiamat, the headdress of the god is not a feather-crown, but a helmet-like headdress with three pairs of horns (fig. 17), which would indicate a neo-Assyrian style in the Boehmer classification (fig. 18 Neo-Assyria <u>a</u>).

The symbol of Aššur, the winged sun-disk, is well-known, but perhaps less known is the picture of the sun-god Aššur within the sun-god symbol. The headdress is not the feather type, but is

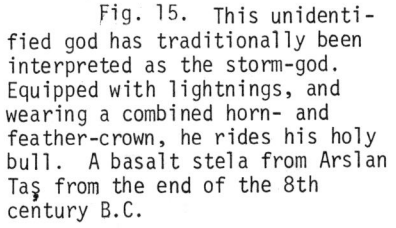

Fig. 15. This unidentified god has traditionally been interpreted as the storm-god. Equipped with lightnings, and wearing a combined horn- and feather-crown, he rides his holy bull. A basalt stela from Arslan Taş from the end of the 8th century B.C.

Fig. 16. Marduk, the Babylonian god, depicted with a feather-crown while the dragon resting at his feet wears two pointed horns.

152

Fig. 17. The young god Marduk (?) with a horned helmet, fighting a winged monster which is also depicted with two pointed horns. Relief from the palace of Aššurnassirpal II at Nimrud.

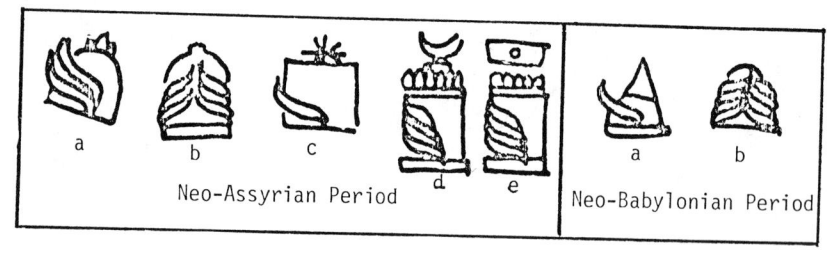

Fig. 18. Neo-Assyrian and Neo-Babylonian headdresses.

rather a helmet-like headdress with several horns (fig. 19 [cf. fig. 20])--a type reminiscent of the headdress of Marduk while he was still engaged in fighting (fig. 17 [above]). Also Aššur is presented in a fighting position with his bow stretched, ready to shoot his arrow. This symbol is rather fitting for Assyria, the greatest military power of the ancient world.[1] "By the might of

---

[1]Morris Jastrow, The Civilization of Babylonia and Assyria (Philadelphia: J. B. Lippincott Company, 1915), p. 230.

Ashur" is a conventional phrase in many historical and votive inscriptions of Assyrian kings.[1]

Fig. 19. The winged disk as the symbol of the sun-god Aššur depicted in a warlike attitude and with a horned helmet on his head.

Fig. 20. The warlike sun-god Aššur, together with conspicuous bulls, depicted on the Banner of Khorsabad.

The combined feather and horn crown (fig. 21) is also known from a limestone relief from Aššur. Unfortunately, the god wearing this headdress is not known, but he is shown standing on a bull, which suggests that the god might be a weather god. The emblems of the sun and moon deities are also conspicuous. The crown itself has at least three pairs of horns encircling it.

The same type of headdress is also seen on a winged human-headed bull from the palace of Sargon of Assyria (ca. 721-705 B.C.).

---

[1] Ibid.

154

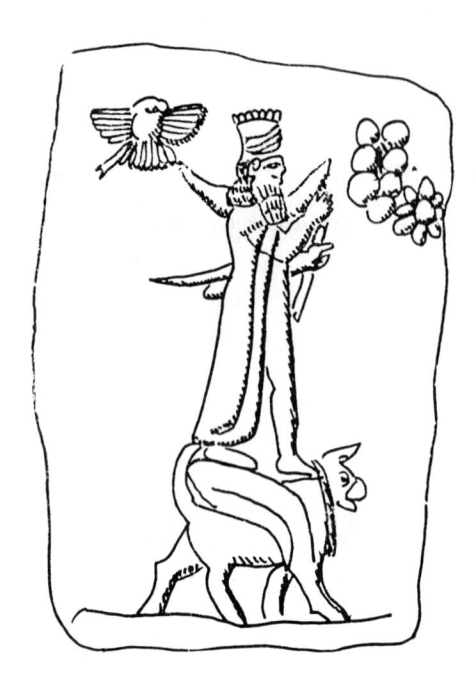

Fig. 21. An unknown god with a combined horn- and feather-crown standing on a fictitious animal (a mixture of lion, bull and bird). Limestone relief from Aššur.

Fig. 22 shows the fabulous guardian with a crown decorated with three pairs of horns and with feathers on the top part.[1] Another type is the crown of the gate-bull at Aššurnasirpal's palace at Calah (northern Nimrud twenty-two miles south of Nineveh [fig. 23]). This giant representation from circa a century earlier has no feather-crown but a round cap and only one pair of horns--but the bull ears are rather conspicuously emphasized. A third type comes also from the doorway at Aššurnasirpal's palace (883-859 B.C.). Here the turban is higher and encircled with three pairs of horns

---

[1] A particular feature of these combined feather- and horn-crowns is that the horns are encircling the headdress (instead of protruding from it) and approaching each other in the front.

meeting in the front (fig. 24), but there is no indication of feathers.[1]

Fig. 22. A winged human-headed bull decorated with three pairs of horns on his headdress (a combined horn- and feather-crown). From the palace of Sargon II, ca. 721-705 B.C.).

Syria. The excavation at Zinjirli[2] at the end of the last century and early years of the present century has greatly enriched the collections of iconographic material. The kudurri, stelae, and monuments represent the first-millennium god-concept in a forceful but often ambiguous way.

---

[1]This guardian has a body of a lion, wings and breast of an eagle, and a human head.

[2]See Mark Lidzbarski, "Eine phönizische Inschrift aus Zendschirli," Ephemeris für Semitische Epigraphik, vol. 3 (Giessen: Alfred Töpelmann, 1915), pp. 218-38; see Felix von Luschan, Ausgrabungen in Sendschirli 5 in Mitteilungen aus den orientalischen Sammlungen, vol. 15 (Berlin: Walter de Gruyter & Co., 1945).

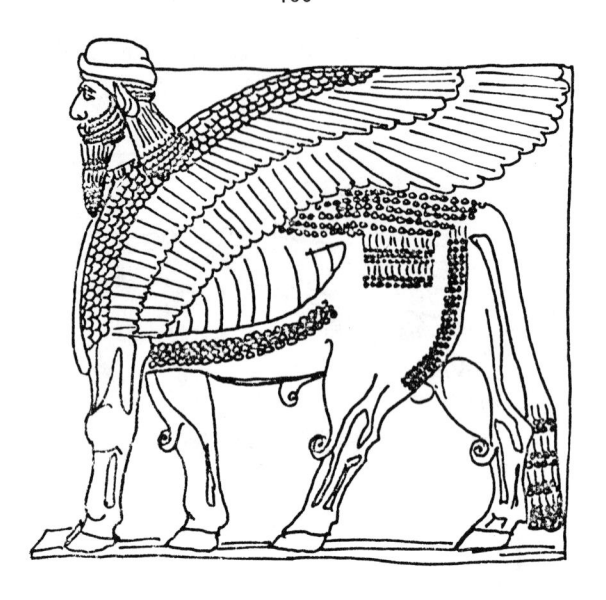

Fig. 23. A winged human-headed bull from the palace of Aššurnassirpal at Calah (ca. 800 B.C.).

One of the best known gods in the collection of monuments from Zenjirli is the god Ramman.[1] On the Esarhaddon stela (fig.

---

[1] Ramman, "the Thunderer" or "Bellowing" or "Roaring One," is the title of Adad analogous to Nannar which is considered the title of Sin; so, for instance, Ulf Oldenburg, The Conflict between El and Ba'al in Canaanite Religion (Leiden: E. J. Brill, 1969), p. 59; Jack R. Conrad, The Horn and the Sword (Westport, CT: Greenwood Press, 1957), p. 101. Adad, the storm-god, was also known as Hadad in Syria (Oldenburg, The Conflict, p. 65); as for the name Hadad, Oldenburg points out (p. 65) that in Akkadian it was expressed by the logogram of the storm-god IM, whose first value is šâru "wind" (Deimel, ŠL, Part III, vol. 1, pp. 134 and 79). Oldenburg's investigation of the logogram IM in the Mari-texts and its attested reading as A(d)-du is worth noticing. Oldenburg also affirms the reading Addu of the logogram IM by referring to a cuneiform list of gods: dAd-du = dIM Mar^ki "Adad = the storm-god of the land of Amurru." Roberts substantiates Oldenburg's theory of Addu equating the Sumerian Iškur (dIM). Addu is the pre-Sargonic orthography whereas the assimilation of -dd- to -nd- (Ad[d]u/Anda) is attested in the West. "Adad is attested as the syllabic spelling in Ur III, but

Fig. 24. A guardian at the entrance to Aššurnassirpal's palace at Nimrud. This genius combines the body of a lion, the wings and breast of an eagle and the human head crowned with three pairs of horns.

---

this vocalization is not attested and may not have been in use in the earlier period." See further discussion by Roberts, The Earliest Semitic Pantheon, pp. 13-14; Georges Dossin, "Les archives épistolaires du palais de Mari," Syria 19 (1938):115, n. 3 as quoted in Ulf Oldenburg, The Conflict, p. 65. For the confusion between the two semi-divine beings Zû and Im-dugud (Imgig), see Van Buren, "A Problem of Sumerian Art," AfO 10 (1967):246.

25) Ramman is presented (last in the row) holding his lightning fork and standing on an ox.[1]

Fig. 25. The storm-god, riding on his bull, is depicted last in the row among the symbolic signs (cf. fig. 15). Stela of Esarhaddon from Zinjirli.

Ramman or Adad usually wears either a simple feather-crown (fig. 26) or a combined feather-and-horn crown (fig. 15 above).

There are many other high gods and goddesses represented at Zenjirli. On the rock relief from Maltaya (fig. 27) all the seven gods riding on their holy animals[2] and with their peculiar headdresses have been identified as Babylonian-Assyrian deities.[3] All

---

[1] The other gods have been identified (from left to right): Aššur (Anu) standing on two animals, Bêlit seated on a lion, Ellil standing on a dragon (similar to that of Anu); Wm. J. Hinke, A New Boundary Stone of Nebuchadrezzar I from Nippur (Philadelphia: MacCalla & Co., Inc., 1907), p. 89, n. 1.

[2] Sin, the moon-god, and Adad, the storm-god, are the only gods in the whole procession having a bull as their pedestal.

[3] See Frank's description in Bilder und Symbole, pp. 2-3.

the headdresses, a high cylindric form with several rows of horns (starting from the side and meeting in the front) seem to reflect the neo-Assyrian style (fig. 18, neo-Assyrian, d-e above). On a fragment from a rock relief of Sennacherib at Bavia (fig. 28a), also from Zenjirli, these same cylinder-formed headdresses with three pairs of encircling horns meeting at the front can be seen (cf. also fig. 28b).

Fig. 26. The storm-god Adad depicted with a feather-crown on his head and equipped with a three-forked lightning in his right hand and in his left reins attached to fictitious animals.

Fig. 27. Procession of gods riding on their holy animals. From a rock-relief at Maltaya.

Fig. 28a. Three shrines with tiaras showing how the horns meet in front. Rock relief of Sancherib at Bavia.

Fig. 28b. Sargon and an officer standing in front of a god wearing the peculiar high headdress. The four pairs of horns can be seen in side view.

Anatolia. In the excavation at Çatal Hüyük in 1961-63 under the guidance of James Mellaart, an unexpected, advanced, pre-Hittite civilization was brought to light in the history of Anatolia. According to Mellaart we are here faced with a remarkably advanced civilization--a center of art and crafts, a center of agriculture and stockbreeding, a center of religion and business; in short, a cultural and religious center--which disproves, once more, Julius Wellhausen's theory of development from primitive to advanced. Mellaart gives a completely opposite picture of this major Neolithic site.

The sanctuaries and shrines show "piles of aurochs' skulls, horns and scapulae."[1] These were found together with obsidian and flint weapons, clay figures, etc. It seems that Mellaart equates the aurochs and the wild bull (Bos primigenius).[2]

Bruno Meissner speaks of the two species as related.[3] Benno Landsberger speaks of three distinct species: the wild ox (rimu), as the aurochs (Bos primigenius); the bison (Bison europaeus), which served as a prototype for the bull-colossi in Assyria; and the Arni-Büffel (Bob bubalus), as völlig verschwunden.[4] William H. Ward points out that in the time of Gilgameš (ca. 2500 B.C.), Eabani, the friend of Gilgameš, wears the horns of the bison and

---

[1]James Mellaart, Çatal Hüyük: A Neolithic Town in Anatolia (New York: McGraw-Hill Book Company, 1967), p. 78.

[2]Ibid., p. 65.

[3]"Assyrische Jagden," Der alte Orient (46) 13 (1911):6.

[4]Die Fauna des alten Mesopotamien nach der 14. Tafel der Serie ḪAR-RA = ḪUBULLU (Leipzig: S. Hirzel, 1934), p. 89.

not the horns of the buffalo of the swamp district of lower Babylon. Ward says, "Later [after the time of Gilgameš], in the time of Sargon, the buffalo takes the place of the bison, as a more dangerous animal. . . ."[1]

The bull-horns, which are presented in drawings in Mellaart's work, seem to represent a variety of species--a fact that may point to the long period of time in which the bull-worship existed.[2] As there are no signs of the bull-horns being equated to the "horns" of the moon, we may conclude that this early Anatolian cult (pre-Hittite) precedes the early prehistoric era of Mesopotamia, as discussed above. Further investigation and clarification of bull-species seem necessary in order to grasp the cultural and religious affinities between these two cultural cradles.

Yazilikaya rock reliefs east of Boghaz-köy, representing the later Hittite civilization of Anatolia, present *in situ* the peculiar high cylinder-formed tiaras of the Hittite goddesses in "Reichstil."[3] The twelve gods in the procession (depicted in relief on the west wall of the rock chamber) seem to be identical.[4] A variation of gods and goddesses is depicted by the north wall and the east wall--gods on the former and goddesses on the latter--in one of the rock chambers. Their headgear is typically Hittite. Other

---

[1] *The Seal Cylinders of Western Asia*, p. 63.

[2] See Mellaart, *Çatal Hüyük*, p. 52.

[3] Ekrem Akurgal, *Die Kunst der Hethiter* (München: Hirmer Verlag, 1976), p. 85; cf. pls. 76, 77.

[4] Ibid., plates 86, 87.

gods (the sword-god and the Šarruma, the god of protection, for instance) are presented with headdresses similar to those already mentioned.[1]

Many headdresses, though they appear alike, differ from one another--not indiscriminately but distinctly--and reveal to which deity each particular headdress belongs. The one, upward, bent horn (fig. 29) over the forehead, however, is typical of all the high pointed caps belonging to gods.

Unfortunately the true meaning of many of the gods and their symbols is still unclear. For instance, concerning the "sword-god" Ekrem Akurgal says,

Fig. 29. Various types of Hittite cone-formed headdresses --all with the upward bent horn in the front.

> Noch unklar ist die Bedeutung des Schwertgottes, der wegen der Vielzahl der Hörner und der Götterideogramme, die seine Spitzmütze schmücken, als eine wichtige Gottheit angesehen werden muss. Das Relief ist zwar nichts anderes als die Umsetzung eines Kleinkunstmotives in die monumentale Dimension, doch in der Vorstellung des Schwertgottes muss ein tiefer religiöser Sinn gesucht werden.[2]

Among all the uncertainties that still exist in the relatively "new" Hittite culture, there are still many gods that have been identified. Akurgal, for instance, points out that the main god in the Hittite pantheon is the weather-god (or storm-god) whose

---

[1] Ibid., Plates 82, 84.

[2] Akurgal, Die Kunst der Hethiter, p. 87.

name is always written with the ideogram of the Mesopotamian Adad (IM). The Hittite name, however, is still unknown--only the ending -una is known at the present.[1] Ulf Oldenburg notes that the name of the storm-god in Luwian was called Tarḫunt. The Hurrian name Tešub is more familiar, and it is known that he was identified with Hadad.[2]

On Hittite monuments the storm-god is usually depicted as a warrior with a club as his weapon (fig. 30). Kurt Bittel, the highly qualified scholar in Hittite rock reliefs and inscriptions, presents two close-up relief presentations on which the weather-god is presented. The high pointed cap with horns in stages to the top can be studied both in profile and from the front.[3]

One interesting feature that meets us wherever the storm-god appears is his holy animal, the bull. The chariot of the storm-god is drawn by two bulls; they are analogous to Sheri and Hurri, "Day and Night," of the Hurrian mythology.[4] The attacking bull was also a motif known in Anatolia (fig. 31), although Akurgal sees this motif as originally neither Hittite nor Anatolian, but arising and being transmitted in various ways from Mesopotamia via Syria to Anatolia.[5]

---

[1] Ibid., p. 49. [2] Oldenburg, The Conflict, pp. 64, 65.

[3] Kurt Bittel, Die Hethiter (München: C. H. Beck, 1976), pp. 184 and 228, figures 207 and 264, respectively. Both stelae are from the 13th century B.C. (on one of the stelae the weapon of the storm-god is a spear).

[4] So, for instance, Oldenburg, The Conflict, p. 65.

[5] Ibid., p. 85.

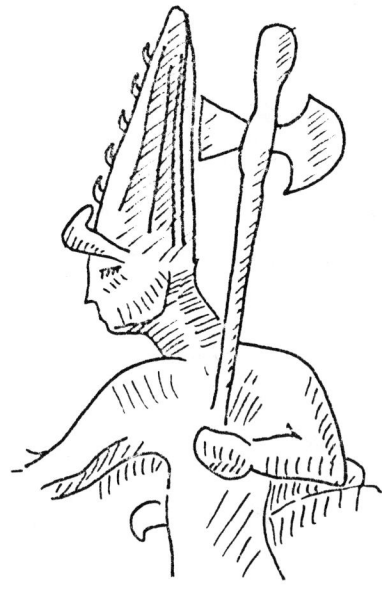

Fig. 30. A relief showing a cone-formed cap with six horns in profile. Hittite rock relief from Yazilikaya.

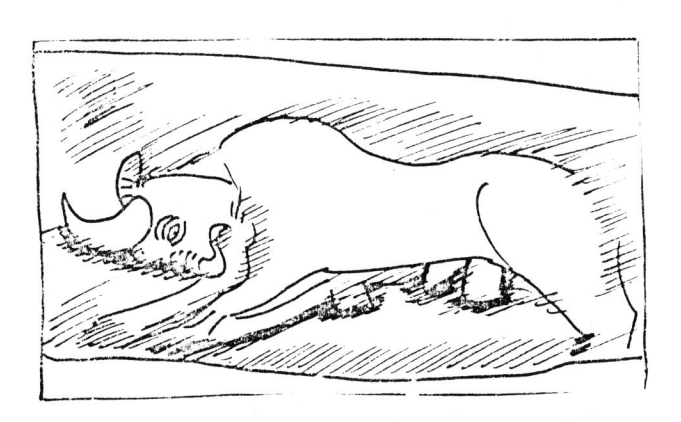

Fig. 31. An attacking bull depicted in bold relief from Hüyük.

Akurgal clearly says that "during the last phase of the Anatolian prehistoric period Hattian culture [pre-Hittite, i.e., Early Bronze Age, c. 2500-2000 B.C.] achieved contact with the Mesopotamian world and received a fresh impetus."[1] This cult must have been located in Central and Southern Anatolia where the leading divinities in the Hittite pantheon (the sun-goddess of Arinna, her spouse, the weather-god, and other gods and goddesses) date from the Hattian age.

Jack R. Conrad has pointed out that in Anatolia the supreme god was the god "who ruled over rain, lightning and thunderstorm."[2] This supreme god has from time immemorial among the Hittites been considered to be a wild bull. It is therefore of significance that "the Hittites never bestowed divinity upon any other animal but the bull."[3]

The Hittites, however, developed an anthropomorphic conception of the "bull-weather-god" (Tešub), and he is so depicted on many seals and carvings, as has already been discussed.

Ugarit. Several of the Canaanite and Phoenician gods have come to light since the Ras Shamra excavation began (1929). The old Canaanite god El, who was deposed in favor of the young god Baʽal, and the latter are both well known from iconography (figs. 32 and 33).

---

[1] Ekrem Akurgal, The Art of the Hittites (New York: Harry N. Abrams, Inc., n.d.), p. 24.

[2] The Horn and the Sword, The History of the Bull as Symbol of Power and Fertility (Westport, CT: Greenwood Press, 1973), p. 96.

[3] Ibid., p. 97.

167

Fig. 32. The seated figure has traditionally been interpreted as the old Canaanite god El. A stela from Ugarit. From the latter part of the 13th century B.C.

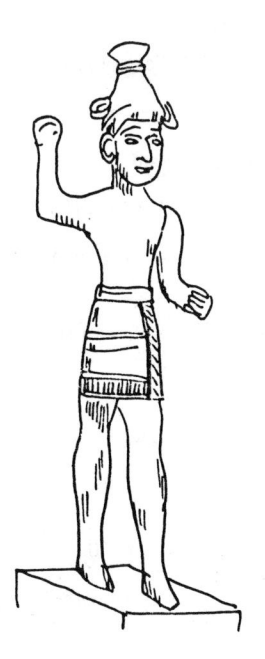

Fig. 33. Baʽal, the young storm-god from Ugarit, wearing a "horned" headdress.

That Baʿal from Ras-Shamra obtained the characteristics of Hadad is shown by the epithet <u>rkb ʿrpt</u> "Rider of the Clouds."[1] As the thundering god, Hadad never left the clouds because with them "he came and went." Baʿal's dominion is far more extended, for as the head of the Ugaritic pantheon, he becomes the <u>zbl bʿl arṣ</u> "Prince, Lord of the Earth."[2]

Oldenburg, referring to the great Baʿal-ʿAnat Cycle,[3] summarizes the apex of the epic in these words:

> When Baʿal has gone down hunting in the meadow of <u>šmk</u> Virgin ʿAnat lifts her wing and flies after Baʿal. When Baʿal sees ʿAnat approaching, dancing, he falls deeply in love with her, and from their intercourse a bull is born to Baʿal.[4]

As for Baʿal's relationship to Asherah, Oldenburg says "they [Baʿal and Asherah] probably were believed to provide fertility magically, by sexual intercourse."[5]

The immediate result of these relationships, then, was in the first place a "monster" born, and in the second relationship "fertility"--features that are always consistent with bull worship

---

[1] Cyrus H. Gordon, <u>UT</u>, Analecta Orientalia 38 (Rome: Pontificial Biblical Institute, 1965), Text 51:III, 11, 18; V:122; 1 <u>Aqht</u>:I, 43-44.

[2] Gordon, <u>UT</u> Text 49:I, 14-15; 49:III, 3, 9, 21.

[3] Gordon, <u>UT</u>, Text 76.

[4] Oldenburg, <u>The Conflict</u>, p. 116; That the virgin ʿAnat also wore horns has been shown already in chapter 2, pp. 29 and 30. Cf. Godfrey R. Driver, <u>Canaanite Myths and Legends</u> (Edinburgh: T. & T. Clark, 1956), p. 115 (ii, 10, 11), <u>tšu.knp.blt.ʿn[t]</u> <u>tšu.knp.wtr bʿp</u>, "The virgin Anat lifted up (her) wing(s), she lifted up her wings and went off flying."

[5] Ibid.

in one or another form or with gods that are related to Sin the moon-god and the "Bull of Heaven."

Conrad has expressed himself also in regard to the Palestinian and Phoenician gods and says in regard to Baʻal: ". . . like all other bull-gods of the Near-East, he [Baʻal] was a god of fertility and, like many of them, was a storm-god as well."[1]

This description, then, places Baʻal in the line of the same bull-tradition known all over the Levant. Loren R. Fisher and F. Brent Knutson discuss an interesting text that "will have a sustained impact upon studies of the Hebrew Bible."[2] The obverse side of the text in translation is here quoted:

> (1) Baal returns because of the throne to his mountain,
> Hadd, the She[pherd], (2) because of
> the Flood to the midst of his mountain,
> (Yea), the god of Ṣapan to the [midst of] (3) the
> mountain of (his) victory.
> . . .
> (5) His head is wonderful.
> Dew is between his eyes.
> (6) Of hostility speaks his leg
> (even) [his] horns (7) which are upon him.
> His head is descending from the heave[ns],
> (8) [from the ten]t of the bull.
> There is his mouth like two cloud[s].[3]

For the expression "of hostility speaks his legs" Fisher points out that "to speak with the foot" is no compliment. Fisher further says,

---

[1] Conrad, The Horn and the Sword, p. 101.

[2] "An Enthronement Ritual at Ugarit," JNES 28 (1969):157-51.

[3] Ibid., pp. 158-59.

Another interesting passage is Dan 7:20, where a horn is described as having eyes and a mouth that speaks (ממלל). In our text it is not only the leg but the horns that speak.[1]

Though Fisher indicates that it is possible to translate qrn[h] (7) [ ]dt. ʿlh "his grandeur [which is upon him]" instead of "(even) [his] horns which are upon him,[2] we, however, see the context as favoring the translation given.

Another reason for maintaining the given translation is that Baʿal--as is well known--is presented with horns (fig. 33 above).

Claude F.-A. Schaeffer says: "The iconography of Baʿal on the stele (fig. 34) and his description in the texts agree in every detail."[3]

Baʿal, identified with the Phoenician Hadad, the Syrian-Hittite Tešub, and other storm-gods, was certainly one of the most remarkable deities of the Ras Shamra pantheon. It was not so much that he was a "god of the heights, storms and rains" that made him so exceptional, it was rather his horns that added to his fame. Schaeffer says that Baʿal was "endowed with the strength of a bull, striking and destroying his enemies with his horns;" and adds, "This explains the presence of the mysterious horns that rise from the frontal of the helmet worn by Baʿal."[4]

---

[1] Ibid., p. 159, n. 15.   [2] Ibid.

[3] Claude F.-A. Schaeffer refers to the "stele showing the god Baal brandishing a club and holding a stylized thunderbolt ending in a spear-head" (fig. 35) which shows Tešub with the forward pointed horns (gazelle-horns?); The Cuneiform Texts of Ras Shamra-Ugarit (London: Oxford University Press, 1939), p. 64; (so also in Ug 2 [1949]:121-30).

[4] Ibid., pp. 63-64.

Fig. 34. Tešub, the Hittite storm-god, depicted with a pointed headdress decorated with two horns--like the horns of a gazelle--in the front of his helmet.

Arvid S. Kapelrud sees Baʻal's horns clearly "made in the shape of a bull's horns."[1] Kapelrud also says that Baʻal was identified with the bull--"the bull stood for Baal, and Baal for all the bull meant in ancient thought."[2] The fact that Baʻal is pictured in the texts several times in the role of a bull does not make void the fact that El, the ancient Canaanite god, was pictured with horns and described as a bull.[3] Schaeffer says,

_____

[1] Baal in the Ras Shamra Texts (Copenhagen: G. E. C. Gad, 1952), p. 20.

[2] Ibid., p. 21.

[3] So, for instance, in the well known passages from the "Baʻal--ʻAnat cycle" (the text is cited in its context). Gordon, UT 76:II, 1-35; 67:V, 15-25; 76:III, 2-25; the passage in 75:II, 40 is badly mutilated as Gordon indicates in his transcript (above) and in his translation UL (Rome: Pontificium Institutum Biblicum,

The Canaanites of Ras Shamra symbolized the idea of force, and especially the force of procreation, by a bull. It is therefore not surprising to find that in some of the texts the god El appears in hypostatic form as Shor-El or the Bull-El. It is in the form of a mighty bull that El is found in union with Asherat-of-the-Sea, the chief goddess and mother of the gods. The decisive passage, a sort of annunciation, reads thus: "The hand of El the King will lay hold of you, the love of the·Bull-El will strike you blind."[1]

Although the epithets[2] of the "Ugaritic El" reveal that he was a god of high position, it was, however, Baʿal who was the best known god in the Ugarit pantheon.[3] Both El and Baʿal, in spite of their "bull-nature," are best known in their anthropomorphic form. Baʿal, for instance, though performing a double function just as the bull-god of almost any country, was mostly depicted in an anthropomorphic form similar to that of Tešub, Adad, Hadad, Ramman, and El.

South-Arabia. South-Arabia developed its own pantheon of gods and goddesses, many of which meet us in other cultures and under different names.

The astral element was predominant in the Arabic religion and especially in South-Arabia. According to Ditlef Nielsen the three

---

1949), p. 55 and also in <u>Ugarit and Minoan Crete</u> (New York: Norton & Company, Inc., 1966), p. 93. The word <u>qrnh</u> is however well preserved, but the context is not clear but <u>may</u> refer to Baʿal, for he is spoken of in the text (cf. 7:II, 5, 23, 25, 32, 34, 55). Cf. also Kapelrud, <u>Baal in the Ras Shamra Texts</u>, p. 20; Kapelrud, <u>The Violent Goddess Anat in the Ras Shamra Texts</u> (Oslo: Universitatsforlaget, 1969), p. 43.

[1] <u>The Cuneiform Texts of Ras Shamra-Ugarit</u>, p. 60.

[2] For some of his epithets, see Oldenburg, <u>The Conflict</u>, pp. 16-22.

[3] Ibid., p. 69.

gods the Moon, the Sun and Venus, are mentioned in Qatabanian inscriptions and bear the respective names Wadd, ʲAṯirat, and Malik. Nielsen says:

> Da wir nun wissen, das Wadd den Mondgott bezeichnet und ʲAtirat oder ʲAṯrat, die Gemahlin Wadd's, die Sonnengöttin, so liegt es nahe in Malik den Venusgott zu sehen.[1]

Gonzague Ryckmans basically agrees with Nielsen that the stellar and lunar deities (both of masculine gender) play a preponderant role among the southern Arabs.[2] Ryckmans also points out that the origin and character of the numerous divinities of South-Arabia are far from being clear, and many divine names have remained up to now indecipherable mysteries.[3]

The celestial bodies were not impersonal nature objects, but, as it is common in mythology, they were considered as personal beings.[4]

All over Arabia the moon-god was the main god. Though the "North-Semitic people" also embraced the astral religion, their religion appears to be a sun-religion in contrast to the old Arabic religion which must be designated as a moon-religion. The most frequently used name for the moon-god among the Sabaeans was Ilmukah,

---

[1] Ditlef Nielsen, Handbuch der altarabischen Altertumskunde (Copenhagen: Arnold Busck, 1927), vol. 1, Die altarbische Kultur, p. 233.

[2] Ryckmans, however, disagrees with Nielsen in regard to the hypothesis of the exclusive primitive triad which Ryckmans thinks is far from verified; Les Religions Arabes Préislamiques (Louvain: Publications Universitaires, 1951), p. 41.

[3] Ryckmans, ibid., p. 21.

[4] Nielsen, "Die äthiopischen Götter," ZDMG 66 (1912):591. Idem, Die altarabische Kultur, p. 213.

in Maʿin Wadd, in Qataban ʿAmm, and in Hadrami Sin.[1]

The nature of the moon-god is not exhausted with the name Ilmukah because there are other names as well as nicknames, and every new name found in various texts designates a new trait of character, a new aspect of his nature, or a new function in his relationship to humanity. The function of the moon-god as an oracle-god which was exercised in the Sabaean temple was, however, only a peripheral manifestation; the god himself dwells in heaven and reveals himself to humanity during the night in the light of the moon.[2]

Further elucidation of the god Ilmukah can be expected from other names, though most of them unfortunately are enigmatic, as has already been pointed out.[3] Nielsen points out that

---

[1] Ryckmans vocalizes the word Ilmukah differently to be pronounced ʿAlmaqah, but he holds that the exact meaning of the name is unknown (Les Religions Arabes Préislamiques, p. 42). For a great number of other proposed readings see Nielsen, "Der sabäische Gott Ilmukah," MVAG 14 (1909):62 (cf. pp. 38-39). A tempting suggestion that Ilmukah would mean "Gott des Gebotes" and be identical with אל אמר or אלה אמר is proposed by Nielsen. He also suggests that as the Minaean amar ("befehlen") corresponds to the Sabaen kahat or mukah, there is a possibility that the divine name Il-amr may be the Minaean form of Il-mukah; see further, Nielsen, "Der sabäische Gott Ilmukah," p. 38. We see here a possible relationship to the north-Syrian god Hadad who also was called Ilumer (> ʾilu "god" and the Sumerian word mer/wer "wind," "rainstorm" (cf. Oldenburg, The Conflict, p. 60. The Minaean god Wadd is frequently given the appellative "père" (Ryckmans, Les Religions Arabes Préislamiques, p. 43). To the Qatabanian moon-god ʿAmm (also ʿAmân) was also given the epithet "beau-père," (ibid.). The term Sin marks the idea of recurrence according to Ryckmans who says, "One would gladly see here all the lunar cycles constituting a year, as Warakh ["month"] among the Qatabanians indicates all the lunar phases constituting a month;" ibid., p. 44.

[2] Nielsen, "Der Sabäische Gott Ilmukah," p. 50.

[3] Cf. p. 173 (above).

Der Name תור, taur "Stier" ist aber deutlich genug und gibt einen unzweideutigen and direkt Beleg dafür, dass Ilmukah einer von den vielen semitischen Namen des Mondgottes ist.[1]

Nielsen further says,

In ähnlicher Weise, wie schon D. H. Müller gesehen hat, der sabäische Hauptgott Ilmukah . . . auch Taur genannt; und dieser Name ist wegen der Hörner des Neumondes ein gewöhnliches semitisches Epithet des Mondgottes.[2]

It is in this way, then, that Nielsen finds the explanation of the schematically presented bull-heads on the monuments.[3] For instance, he presents this interesting thought:

Der Neumond ⌣ wird als "Hörner" qarni bezeichnet, Enuma eliš Taf. V Z.16, und diese Hörner sind Stierhörner, denn er heisst "jugendkräftiger Stier buru mit gewaltigen Hörnern," IV.R.9, also sind im Neumond Stierhörner offenbart wie im Stierbilde des Tierkreises ein Stierkopf ∀. Auf den südarabischen Denkmälern sind einfache Darstellungen vom Neumonde und Stierköpfe nicht selten. Der Neumond ruht häufig auf einer konischen Figur und ein Stern, wahrscheinlich die Venus, strahlt über ihm, während die Stierköpfe meistens so hart stilisiert sind, dass man sieht, der Künstler habe kein lebendiges Tier abbilden wollen, sondern entweder den himmlischen Stierkopf oder die göttlichen Neumondshörner, wozu sich dann mehr oder weniger von einem in groben Konturen gehaltenen Stierkopf gefügt hat, um den Gedanken anzudeuten, dass die Mondsichel hier nicht als Bogen, sondern als Hörner und zwar Stierhörner aufzufassen sei. Man bekommt den Eindruck, als ob diese ornamentalen Stierköpfe mit den "gewaltigen Hörnern" sich aus dem einfachen Neumondsymbol entwickelt haben.[4]

It seems evident that the horns of the new-moon and the bull's horns in some way must resemble each other. The iconography

---

[1] Nielsen, "Der sabäische Gott Ilmukah," p. 51.

[2] Ibid., pp. 51-52.

[3] Ibid., cf. also Hartmut Gese's description of Ilmukah (ʿAlmaqah) and other gods of South-Arabia (Die Religionen Altsyriens, Altarabiens und der Mandäer (Stuttgart: W. Kohlhammer, 1970), pp. 242-53.

[4] Nielsen, Die altarabische Mondreligion (Strassburg: Karl J. Trübner, 1904), p. 110.

on the cylinder seals may give some suggestion as to what kind of bull is referred to.

Ward informs us that in the more archaic cylinder seals (of Western Asia) the Bison bonasus is the "bull" of the older nomenclature. The horns of this kind of bison "are short, rounded inward and slightly backward, quite different from the longer and more upright horns of the ancient aurochs, which is figures in Cretan art."[1]

In older seals, then, Gilgameš, for instance, "is represented as in a fight with the bison . . ."[2] in the period immediately following the archaic, Gilgameš fights the buffalo of the swamps-- quite a different animal.[3]

> The Babylonian name for bison was rimu (Hebrew reʲem). The archaic sign for alpu, ox, was ⊽, and that for rimu was ⊽, in which the three inclosed wedges are the sign for mountain, so that the meaning was the bull of the mountains, a proper definition of the rimu or bison.[4]

Ward also says that the bison may have been included "in the meaning of buru (Hebrew bôr), which was connected with the moon-god Sin, probably because of his horns, which are moon-like."[5]

---

[1] Ward, The Seal Cylinders of Western Asia, p. 414.

[2] For a depiction of this "divine bull," see ibid., p. 59 (fig. 141).

[3] According to Ward, then, the bison with short round horns is the more archaic one and the representation of the buffalo of the swamps (with longer horns) is of a later type; ibid., p. 414.

[4] Ibid., for a depiction of a bull with his left foot stepping on a "mountain" see, for instance André Parrot, ed., Studia Mariana, Documenta et Monumenta, ed. W. F. Albright and A. de Buck (Leiden: E. J. Brill, 1950), pl. 1.

[5] Ward, The Seal Cylinders of Western Asia, p. 414; cf. various depictions of bulls, i.e., figs. 84-93.

"In the epic of Gilgameš Eabani wears the horns of the bison and not of the buffalo,"[1] i.e., the bull-Bison is the Bison bonasus and the water-buffalo is Bos bubalus.[2]

It seems evident that a particular kind of bull whose horns resembled those of the moon-sickle lies behind the identification of the bull with the new-moon. Although we cannot with certainty identify the particular bull, we have to recognize that the picture of the moon-god Sin, as the new-moon sickle, spreading its light to mankind is rather a romantic presentation in disguise, whereas the attacking, wild, and feared type of god seems to be the real and original nature of the moon-god. Nielsen asserts that

> In der Tiersymbolik ist der Stier wegen den Hörner, die an den Hörnern des Neumondes erinnern, vorzugsweise das heilige Tier des Mondgottes.[3]

We would rather change the sentence around and say that it is rather on account of the "horns of the moon" (the moon-sickle) being a reminder of the bull's horns that the attacking and fierce

---

[1] Nielsen says, "Wenn der Neumond als Stier aufgefasst wird und der Vollmond als menschliches Gesicht, so wird der zu- oder abnehmende Mond ein Stier mit menschlichen Gesichte, ein 'Stiermensch' wie Ea-bani im Gilgameš--Epos." And he continues, "Nun hat der Mondgott ja ausserdem Flügel und ist mit einer Tiara bedeckt, das vollständige Mondsymbol, wie es auf assyrischen Denkmälern abgebildet ist, . . ." Die altarabische Mondreligion, pp. 113-14. Nielsen's theory is creative and in the present writer's mind, just as probable and certain as any other suggested theory as to the meaning of the bull colossi.

[2] Ward, The Seal Cylinders of Western Asia, p. 65.

[3] Nielsen, Die altarabische Kultur, p. 214.

bull, the aurochs, the Hebrew re^jem (or the representative force that the moon-god stands for) has been seen fit to present himself under the disguising nature of romanticism, of being a light to mankind. In reality the Sin Cult was an attempt to establish the moon-cult on a universal basis.[1]

Hildegard Lewy says "that the moon was the prototype of a universal god in contrast to the various national deities. It is visible everywhere. . . ."[2] It was the prototype of a universal god that inspired the Akkadian kings to create a universal empire on the same basis. But moon-worship, though early, does not appear to have been the dominating one at first; the creative or high gods Anu, Enlil, and Enki were the foremost gods in the old Sumerian community, whereas the astral gods may be the result of a religious revolt, the circumstances of which are enshrouded in mystery. South-Arabia, however, seems to have embraced the moon-cult fully and totally, and its connection with the bull seems also established (whether on account of the bull's horns being analogous to the new moon or the new moon being analogous to the horns of the wild bull cannot with certainty be established at the present).[3] Still, in no other culture so far studied is the evidence of a moon-cult so

---

[1] Van Buren, "Akkadian Sidelights," Or 19 (1950):168.

[2] Lewy, "Assyria c. 2600-1816 B.C.," in CAH[3] (Cambridge: At the University Press, 1971), vol. 1, pt. 2, p. 736.

[3] The topic calls for further investigation.

clearly brought forth as it is in the South-Arabian culture. That the moon-cult and the bull-cult are analogous looks quite obvious.

Egypt. The religion of Egypt is complicated and the animal cult as we know it from literary and iconographical sources seems to be the only fair starting point in dealing with the god-concept of the Egyptians. When we endeavor to narrow down this concept to get an understanding of gods with horns, the worship of bull and cow come to the foreground.

The four well-known bull-gods which have received proper names are: Apis from Memphis, Mnevis from Heliopolis, Buchis from Hermonthis, and Montu or Month from the Theban district.[1]

Hans Bonnet places the Apis cult at the beginning of historic time, although later tradition has partly attributed the introduction of its cult to a king of the first dynasty or second dynasty and even as late as the second half of the eighteenth and twentieth dynasties (1580-1085 B.C.) of the New Kingdom.[2]

The Apis-bull is usually depicted with a sun-disk and a serpent (Uräus) between the horns (fig. 35).

The Mnevis cult (in likeness to the Apis cult) is not attested before the eighteenth dynasty, though the cult must be much older.

---

[1] Ludolf Malten, "Der Stier in Kult und mythischen Bild," in Jahrbuch des deutschen Archäologischen Instituts 43 (1928):92; cf. Hans Bonnet, respective "Apis," "Mnevis," "Buchis," and "Montu," in Reallexikon der ägyptischen Religionsgeschichte (Berlin: Walter de Gruyter & Co., 1952).

[2] Bonnet, "Apis," ibid., p. 46.

180

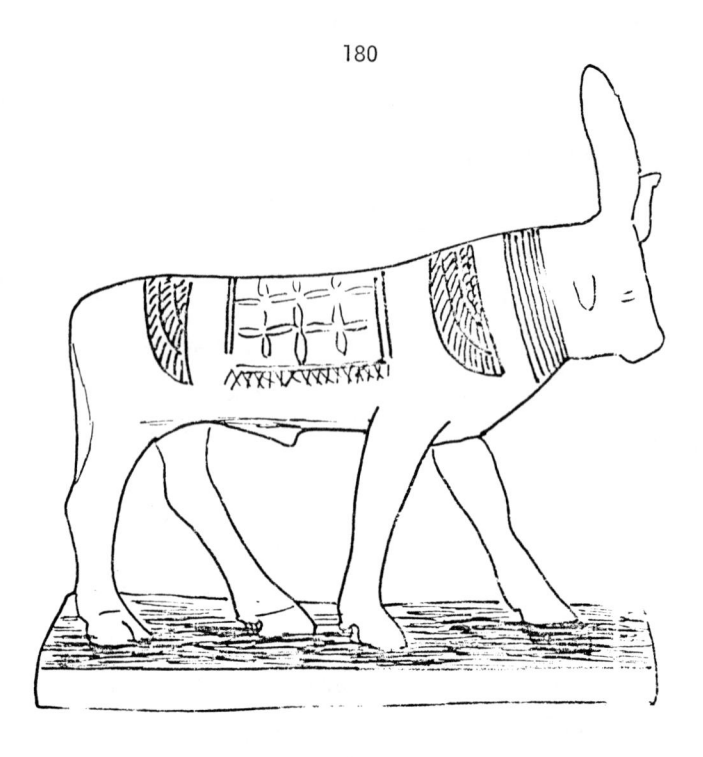

Fig. 35. The Apis bull wearing a sun-disk between his horns.

Already in the time of the Old Kingdom the "Bull from Heliopolis"[1] is mentioned. Whether Mnevis is meant or not, or perhaps a Heavenly Bull which is subordinate to the sun-god or perhaps the sun-god itself, is hard to determine.[2] Bonnet, however, argues that the Mnevis cult existed independently of the sun-cult and probably placed the procreative power of the bull at the center point of service.

---

[1] Pyramidentexte 716 in Die altägyptischen Pyramidtexte, 4 vols., ed. Kurth Heinrich Sethe (Leipzig: J. C. Hinrichs, 1908-22), as quoted by Bonnet, "Apis," in Reallexikon der ägyptischen Religionsgeschichte, p. 468.

[2] Bonnet, "Mnevis," in Reallexikon der ägyptischen Religionsgeschichte, p. 468.

On monuments Mnevis is recognized by the highly arched neck and he usually wears a sun-disk between the horns.[1]

The holy bull Buchis from Hermonthis goes back to the Ptolemaic time when the Egyptian sign for bull (Bh) was attested. Bonnet points out that in spite of many attempts the meaning of the sign has never been adequately explained. Like Mnevis, Buchis functions as "lebende Seele" or as "Herold" of Re. In addition he is often given the epithet "Atum whose pair of horns is on him" and, thereby, is often equated to the sun-god.[2] Buchis usually carries the sun-disk and the ostrich plumes.[3]

Before the introduction of Amun, Montu (Mn-tw) was the main god of the Theban district. He was worshiped as lord not only in the old capital Hermonthis but also in the neighborhood districts Medamud and Tuphium as well as in the younger capital of the district, Thebes--here perhaps in the district of Medinet Habu.[4]

Montu is represented by a falconhead which is crowned by a sun-disk and a high pair of feathers. The growing importance of the bull is shown in the fact that in later times Montu is occasionally presented with a bull head.[5]

---

[1] Ibid., p. 469; for a depiction of the Mnevis bull, see for instance, Zeitschrift für ägyptische Sprache und Altertumskunde 72 (1967):pl. 8.

[2] Bonnet, "Buchis," Reallexikon des ägyptischen Religionsgeschichte, pp. 126-27. Cf. Robert Mond and Oliver H. Myers, The Bucheum (London: Oxford University Press, 1934), 2:1-57 (esp. pp. 7-9 and pp. 40-46).

[3] Mond, The Bucheum, 2:45.

[4] Bonnet, "Montu," in Reallexikon der ägyptischen Religionsgeschichte, p. 475.

[5] Ibid., pp. 476-77.

All the bull-gods seem more or less to have a solar-nature. Herodotus, for instance, says,

> This Apis, or Epaphus, is a calf born of a cow that can never conceive again. By what the Egyptians say, the cow is made pregnant by a light from heaven, and therefore gives birth to Apis.[1]

The cow-god Hathor, the Heavenly Queen, was also worshiped in Egypt. Analogous to the bull-gods, Hathor too wears the sun-disk between the horns (fig. 36).

It is at the horns and in connection with the horns that the symbolism takes place. This is revealed in both mythological trains of thought and in iconography. Ludolf Malten notes that in the mythological world of ideas the Heavenly Cow was thought of as a daily bringing forth of the sun-god.[2] There are hints which allude to the fact that he (the sun-god) was considered as a young calf, but mostly he is represented as a human child or as a young man sitting between the horns of the Heavenly Cow (fig. 37) or riding on her back (fig. 38). The fact that the young sun-god is depicted as having a firm right-hand grip on one horn is significant. Malten indicates that the symbolism is likely to take place on the horns, and the iconographic representations confirm this assumption.[3]

Not only is the cow goddess represented with horns but she

---

[1] Herodotus 3.28.

[2] Malten, "Der Stier in Kult und mythischen Bild," p. 96.

[3] Ibid.

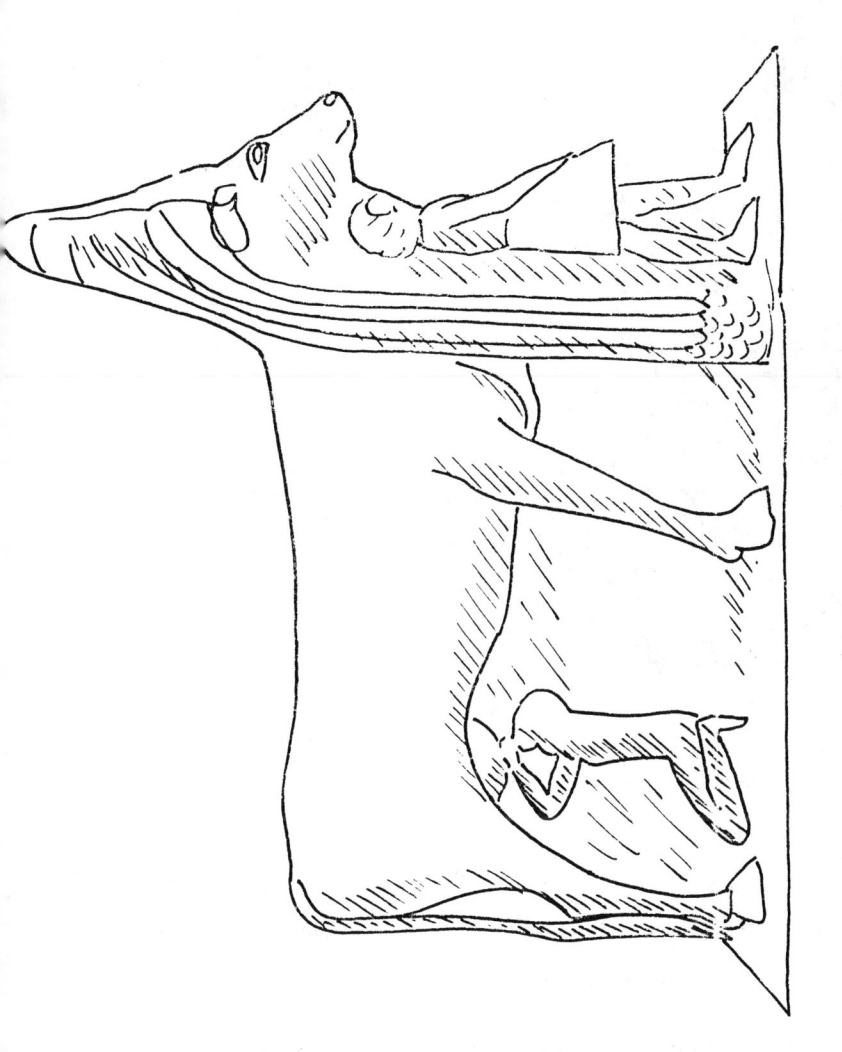

Fig. 36. The goddess Hathor in the form of a cow and wearing a sun-disk between her horns. A sandstone statue from Deir el-Bahri.

Fig. 37. The sun-god seated between the horns of the great j̲h̲t (= Ahet) cow.

Fig. 38. The sun-god holding the horn while riding on the Ahet cow (Fayûmpapyrus).

is also recognizable through the big ears of a cow and is presented with a human face.[1]

It is because the Egyptian religion was zoomorphical (in contrast to the Mesopotamian anthropomorphic god-concept) that iconography between the two cultures differs so widely. In Egypt it is

---

[1] Sethe, Urgeschichte und älteste Religion der Ägypter, no. 4. Abhandlung für die Kunde des Morgenlandes, vol. 18 (Nendeln, Lichtenstein: Kraus Reprint, Ltd., 1966), p. 26 § 32, n. 3.

with the horned animals that the divinity is expressed, and that is one reason why the god-concept and divinity in Egypt is so closely connected with the bull. In other words, it appears that the bull-worship is Egypt originates from the animal cult whereas in Mesopotamia it originates from a mythic concept.

In the Theban theology Amon wore the name the "Hidden One."[1] There are many complicated ideas involved in the various theological systems that are hard to grasp. Some of these ideas and decrees of gods are expressed in hymns. Only one passage from such a hymn, representing the creed of the religion of Amon-Re, kings of the god, will be quoted here:

> This venerable god, Lord of all Gods, Amon-Re,
> . . .
> Venerable Power . . . creative power,
> out of whose form came into being every form,
> he who came first into being, besides whom nothing exists.
>
> He who gave light to the earth, for the first time with
> the disk. Light, Radiating One, when he appears, men
> live. When he sails the sky, he is not weary, early in
> the morning his work is already fixed.
> . . .
>
> Divine God who found himself, who made heaven and earth
> in his mind. Ruler of Rulers, Great One of the Great,
> greater than the gods.

---

[1] Amon was not originally a Theban divinity (the god of the region was the falcon-headed Montu of Hermonthis) and he did not, in fact, appear in Thebes until the eleventh dynasty (at the beginning of the Middle Kingdom) and became then in theological speculations the divine principle of creation and of life. See Alexander Piankoff, *Mythological Papyri*, Bollingen Series 40, (New York: Pantheon Books, 1957), vol. 3, pt. 1, p. 11. Piankoff also says, "It is generally accepted at the present, that Amon, the Hidden One (many other names were used in Litany) was one of the four or eight divinities of Hermopolis, where they personified the chaos before the creation of the world" (ibid.).

Young Bull with sharp horns, before whose mighty name
the Two Lands tremble. Eternity carries his might while
he reaches the end of everlastingness.
. . .

Lord of Might, Holy Power, Hidden One by the rays of his
body. His right and left eye, the disk and the moon, the
sky and the earth are full of beauty of his light.[1]

From a political point of view the period of the twenty-first dynasty presented a picture of decay. Although in the North Egypt was ruled by the Pharaoh and the High Priest of Amon ruled in the South, one may say that neither of them ruled, but the god Amon himself, "the Young Bull with sharp horns," was the ruler.[2]

According to Jaroslav Černey "the Twenty-first Dynasty is, still, a particularly obscure period in Egyptian history,"[3] a time period of circa one hundred and thirty years, or between the death of Ramesses XI (ca. 1085 B.C.) and the accession of Sheshonq I, the founder of the twenty-second Dynasty (ca. 945 B.C.).[4]

There is something in this obscurity that reminds one of the time of Gudea in the second dynasty of Ur, when, as Legrain expresses it, "the name of the Moon god was a mystery,"[5]--a time when the Sin-rulership, apparently, was established at Ur and an attempt was made to promulgate it as a universal religion.

---

[1]Ibid., pp. 13-14.   [2]Ibid., pp. 9, 13, 19.

[3]"Egypt: From the Death of Ramasses III to the End of the Twenty-first Dynasty," in CAH[3], vol. 2, pt. 2, p. 643.

[4]Ibid., p. 646.

[5]Leon Legrain, The Culture of the Babylonians from Their Seals, The Collections of the Museum Publications of the Babylonian Section, vol. 14 (Philadelphia: University Museum, 1925), p. 65.

The strange cult that thus meets us in the zoomorphical presentation of the gods in Egypt makes it clear that the horns of the animal gods played an important role in both the ritual and the magical. Bull-worship and moon-cult may have been predominant in prehistoric time and "enforced" in the period of the twenty-first dynasty. But sun-worship also started quite early as iconographic material attests: the sundisk between the horns.

Sinai. A very recently discovered, crude, iconographic representation from Sinai shows two figures seemingly dancing with each other while a third figure (a seated woman) is playing the lyre (fig. 39 [extreme right]). The figure of this seated, playing woman has been placed on the front cover of Biblical Archaeology Review[1] with the startling question: "Did Yahweh have a Consort?" perhaps as a suggestive answer to the question. The article dealing with this intriguing topic is written by Ze'ev Meshel, of Tel Aviv University, who has excavated at Kuntillet Ajrud, the place where the pithoi with these "blasphemous" pictures and the religious inscriptions were found.[2] This discovery has received quite a lot of attention, not the least because of the "blasphemous concept" of these pictures possibly representing Yahweh and His Consort! These ancient Hebrew and Phoenician inscriptions contain, apart from the names of El and Yahweh, also "the names of pagan gods and goddess like Ba'al and Ashera."[3]

---

[1] Ze'ev Meshel in BARev 5 (1979):24.

[2] Ibid., pp. 24-35.   [3] Ibid., p. 27.

188

Fig. 39. Dancing gods. The figure to the left probably depicts a bull-god, whereas the one to the right may represent the cow-goddess Hathor. A rude drawing on a pithos from Kuntillet Ajrud.

Meshel makes a tentative suggestion that the lady with the lyre may be the Consort of Yahweh while the central figure is "the god Bes (fig. 39 above) . . . with his genitals (or tail) exposed between his legs."[1] As for the figure to the extreme left, Meshel describes it vaguely.

Marvin H. Pope follows Meshel in identifying the central figure with the Egyptian god Bes. The larger figure to the left he sees as representing YHWH.[2]

---

[1] Ibid., p. 30.

[2] Marvin H. Pope, "YHWH and his AŠRT," paper presented to the American Oriental Society, St. Louis, April 26, 1979.

William H. Shea has adopted the view[1] that for the central figure the Egyptian goddess Hathor presents a much better candidate than does the god Bes.[2] Shea presents some weighty reasons for this theory: Hathor was the patron goddess of Sinai (and thus not far from Kuntillet Ajrud) where the Egyptians had large turquoise mines. Hathor, in Egyptian iconography, was depicted as a cow (fig. 36 above), and the central figure depicted on the pithos from Kuntillet Ajrud seems to have both a cow's head and cow's ears (fig. 39 above). Furthermore, both the central figure and the one playing a lyre have "mammary orbs."[3] Thus, if they are females, as it seems, it appears that the dangling object between the legs of the central figure must be a tail (not a phallus). Shea also informs us that "the typical hairdo is missing from this figure at Kuntillet Ajrud,"[4] but it is certain that the dancing couple wear some kind of headgear. It is possible that the one to the left (the larger figure) may have "horns" on his head; the drawing is, however, too crude to get a clear perception of what the "artist" might have had in mind.

As for the bovine motif, a cow suckling her calf (fig. 40)

---

[1] We express our sincere gratitude to Prof. William Shea for his readiness to share his views and for letting us use his materials, an article entitled "The Date and Significance of the Israelite Settlement at Kuntillet Ajrud," forthcoming in BA.

[2] We have also adopted this view as a much more plausible view than the one presented by Meshel and Pope.

[3] Shea, "The Date and Significance of the Israelite Settlement at Kuntillet Ajrud," p. 4.

[4] Ibid., p. 5.

presented on the same pithos, it also has its analogy in Egypt, though it is a well known motif also in the Syro-Phoenician world (fig. 41). Shea says:

Fig. 40. The "cow and suckling calf-motif" depicted at Kuntillet Ajrud--a well-known motif in the Syro-Phoenician world of the 9th century B.C.

Fig. 41. A cow tenderly nursing her calf. A furniture inlay carved in ivory from Arslan Taş, Syria, ca. 900-700 B.C.

Hathor has been found in a related pose in Egypt, the main difference being that the one suckling was not a calf but apparently a crown prince, presumed to be Amenhotep II.[1] [Cf. fig. 36.]

---

[1] Ibid. (fig. 36 above).

The motif of cow and calf depicted on an ivory plaque excavated at Nimrud (Calah) in Assyria (fig. 42) Shea sees as ultimately of Egyptian origin.[1]

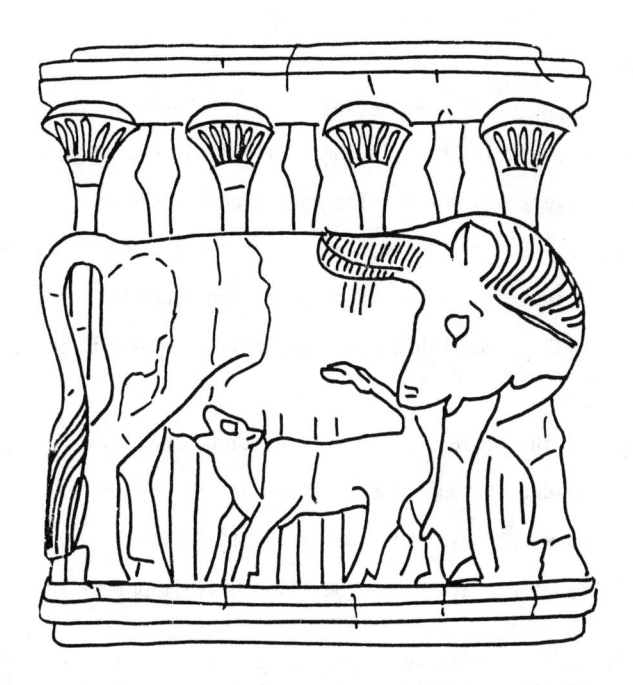

Fig. 42. A cow and suckling calf-motif. Ivory carving discovered at Nimrud (ancient Kallah) in northern Syria in the palace of the Assyrian King Shalmaneser III (859-824 B.C.).

The bull-god and his Consort depicted at Kuntillet Ajrud, if they do represent YHWH and his Consort (the cow-goddess Hathor!), are indeed "a thoroughly blasphemous notion," as Meshel observes.[2]

---

[1] Shea's conclusion in this respect is due to the fact that the cow and the calf stand in front of a lotus thicket; ibid., p. 5.

[2] "Did Yahweh Have a Consort?" p. 27.

The crude drawing testifies strongly to the idolatrous surroundings of a little nation trying to uphold a true concept of God which was completely contrary to the concept of the bull and what it stood for.

Priests and Kings

Sumer and Akkad. According to Gunnar Landtman there existed no proper priesthood in the earliest history of cult. In other words "everybody invoked the gods each for himself."[1] Landtman further says: "A remarkable feature in the history of priesthood is the combination of priestly functions with royal authority."[2] This remarkable combination is attested in early Sumerian history.

But if the offices have to be distinguished Sumerologists generally consider the government of the en ["governor" or "high priest"] to have preceded the one of lugal[3] ["king"].

Leo Oppenheim avoids any detailed definitions of the term

___

[1] "Priest, Priesthood," Encyclopedia of Religion and Ethics (New York: Charles Scribner's Sons, 1919), 10:279; This view by Landtman, of course, presupposes a polytheistic god-concept from the very beginning of human history. There is, from our point of view, a possibility that both a monotheistic and a polytheistic tradition existed side by side.

[2] Ibid., p. 280.

[3] For the terms en and lugal, see Deimel, ŠL, Part III, vol. 1, p. 93 (cf. p. 92 and p. 31 § 30), and Part III, vol. 1, pp. 154 and 39. (The en, as Deimel shows, may come closest in translation by the word "governor" while lugal actually means "great man"). Samuel H. Hooke says that "in the Early Sumerian period INSI [or ENSI] alternates with the title LUGAL, literally 'great man,' which we translate 'king';" Myth, Ritual and Kingship (Oxford: Clarendon Press, 1958, reprint ed., 1960), p. 25 (cf. also p. 26).

en (-si)[1] and lu (-gal) because he feels the relationship evolving between the two titles to be "too complex and as yet too ill-defined. . . ."[2] Still, Oppenheim's own translation gives a clue of the original status of en and lugal as he translates the respective terms "high priest" and "king."[3] It must, however, be pointed out that neither the Sumerian nor the Akkadian language presents a term that can be equalized for the concept of "priest" as it was known in the later Hebrew cultic setting.[4]

Thorkild Jacobsen gives the following helpful information:

> Umun and its Eme-ku equivalent en are translated in Akkadian by bêlum or, when they denote the human spouse of a deity, by enu/entum.[5]

As for the translation of enu/bêlum into English Jacobsen says,

> The traditional English rendering "lord" would be happier if it had preserved overtones of its original meaning "bread-keeper" for the core concept of en is that of the successful economic manager. The term implies authority, but not the

---

[1] For ensi see Tallqvist, Akkadische Götterepitheta, pp. 493, 156 (pa-te-si [ensi^{si}]), and p. 34 (iššakku [si, ensi^{si}], viceroy, governor). Theophilus G. Pinches nearly twenty years before Tallqvist pointed out that the "patesi namely iššakku was generally a kind of viceroy, under a royal ruler (lugal-šarru, 'king'), . . ." See "Priest, Priesthood (Babylonia)," Encyclopaedia of Religion and Ethics, ed. James Hastings (New York: Charles Scribner's Sons, 1919), 10:285.

[2] Ancient Mesopotamia (Chicago: The University of Chicago Press, 1964), p. 99.

[3] Ibid.

[4] Johannes Renger, "Untersuchungen zum Priestertum in der altbabylonischen Zeit," ZA 58 (1967):112.

[5] Jacobsen, "The Myth of Inanna and Bilulu," JNES 12 (1953): 180 (n. 41).

authority of ownership, a point on which it differs sharply from bêlum. . . .[1]

Furthermore, Jacobsen points out that the authority of en is of a charismatic kind depending on the endowed gift from above to handle the economic management.[2]

The function of an en in the complex temple community of ancient Sumer was thus partly of a practical and partly of a religious nature. He was the "lord" with the overtone of a "bread-keeper" and in this respect the mediator between the people and their god(s).

As for the "priestly" dress in the early Sumerian period nothing definitive is known and tentative suggestions must remain more or less conjectural. Henri Frankfort makes such a guess, for instance, in regard to an early seal from the Uruk period. Frankfort suggests that the nudity of the figures (fig. 43) "may, by analogy with Early Dynastic times, be taken to mark them as priests.[3] No garment appears on the figures (except for the second figure from the left). Their heads appear completely shaven. Frankfort

---

[1] Ibid., n. 41 (pp. 180-81).

[2] The reference to authority (implied in en) seems to have a closer relationship to the Hebrew basic and original meaning of בעל than to the Babylonian Bêl; cf. Lewis B. Paton, "Baal, Beel, Bel," Encyclopaedia of Religion and Ethics, 2:283, 284.

[3] Cylinder Seals, p. 19; cf. Frankfort, "The Last Predynastic Period in Babylonia," revised and rearranged by Lewis Davis, CAH³, vol. 1, pt. 2, p. 78 where Frankfort says, "In Early Dynastic times priests were often naked when officiating." E. Douglas Van Buren also interprets the "nudity" as a pictorial conception formulated in the second Early Dynastic Period; "Akkadian Sidelights," p. 159; cf. for a contrary view Martin A. Beek, Atlas of Mesopotamia, p. 67, caption to fig. 132.

sees the presentation--an act of sacrifice [some woven stuff is brought as an offering]--as part of a larger ritual. Frankfort also sees the boat and its figures (behind the sacrificers) as a reminder of Gilgameš trying to reach "the depths of the primeval waters in his search for the plant of life." Although the interpretation of the picture is speculative, Frankfort is affirmative that the seal-cutter in his presentation of this motif is concerned "with ritual, not with myth."[1]

Fig. 43. The nude figures may represent priests. Early seal from the Uruk period.

Another presentation with a similar motif (a nude priest in front of his god [fig. 44]) engraved on a limestone tablet comes from Nippur. The upper part of the tablet presents the naked ministering priests bringing their gifts to the horned deity seated on a throne. The lower part presents what are probably ordinary

---

[1]Cylinder Seals, p. 19. Cf. also Frankfort in Sculpture of the Third Millennium B.C. from Tell Asmar and Kalājah (Chicago: University Press, 1939) which presents some of the published iconographical material from the Iraq expedition in the Diyālā region. Plates 21-23 present statues of typical shaven priests with bare upper chest (not nude, however); cf. a presentation of a man with hair and beard (Pl. 20, for instance).

Fig. 44. (Upper part) A ritual motif depicting two naked priests in front of their gods. The "horned" headdress, symbolizing divinity, is clearly noticeable. Engraved limestone tablet. (Lower part) Ordinary citizens bringing their sacrifice.

citizens bringing their gifts with a ram and a goat. (The difference in horns is beautifully brought out). Fig. 45 presents a similar scene but with only one ministering "priest" depicted. The god may be Enki (Ea) as plants seem to be sprouting from his headgear.[1]

Carl Bezold indicates that the limestone tablets come from the Assyrian-Babylonian time, but the motif may represent an already

---

[1]Carl Bezold, Ninive und Babylon, 4th ed., Monographien zur Weltgeschichte, 18 (Leipzig: Velhagen & Klasing, 1926), p. 33.

then ancient tradition.[1] Many of these early "mediator" motifs may, however, depict kings or lesser gods rather than "priests."

Fig. 45. A ritual motif with a single ministering priest in front of his god. Limestone tablet from Nippur.

In the Mesopotamian civilization kingship was one of the basic concepts. There the kingship (not the king) was divine. The ancient tradition, preserved in the Sumerian King List,[2] relates the descent of kingship from heaven:

[me]n nam-lugal-la an-ta e_{11}-d[è(?)]-a-ba
[gi]ššibir giš[gu-za][7] nam-lugal-la an-ta e_{11}-a-ba

"When the crown of kingship was lowered from heaven,

---

[1] Ibid., p. 164.

[2] Jacobsen, The Sumerian King List, Assyriological Studies, no. 11 (Chicago: University Press, 1939).

when the scepter and the throne of kingship were lowered from heaven."[1]

For the Sumerians and their successors, kingship (and even the royal insignia or emblems) was an institution that existed before and independently of the human king.[2] The iconography supports this hypothesis in a remarkable way. Not only early seals but early statues from the early second dynasty seem to agree.

Gudea, viceroy of Lagaš (of the second dynasty), for instance, is presented either bareheaded (fig. 46) or with a round, flat headdress without horns (fig. 47), and so is his son Ur-Ningirsu (fig. 48) and even Hammurabi (fig. 49).

It seems evident from these few but significant examples that the horns are missing from the ruler's headgear, no matter whether he was an *en* (or *ensi*) or a *lugal*. Fig. 50 shows the headgear of a god, a king, and a priest in a very illustrative way. The crowns were for the gods, as also the many seals from early time periods show. It is, however, to be noticed that even Gudea, *patesi* [viceroy] of Lagaš, ca. 2450 B.C., was deified after his death.[3]

---

[1] Ibid., p. 58.

[2] H. W. F. Saggs, The Greatness That Was Babylon (New York: Hawthorn Books, Inc., 1962), p. 359.

[3] So, for instance, Arthur S. Tritton, "King (Semitic)," Encyclopaedia of Religions and Ethics, 7:726. Tritton also says that Dungi, the second king of the dynasty of Ur (ca. 50 years after Gudea) always describes himself as god, and a temple is built to his honor. Ward has dated a cylinder of Dungi, King of Ur, to ca. 2450 B.C.--a date which would show that he ruled before Ur-Nammu (Ur-engur) (ca. 2113-2096 B.C.) the founder of the Third Dynasty of Ur; and also states that Dungi was the son of Urbaga; Seal Cylinders of Western Asia, p. 22.

Fig. 46. A deity holding Gudea by the hand and introducing him to the high god. All three deities are depicted as wearing headdresses with horns.

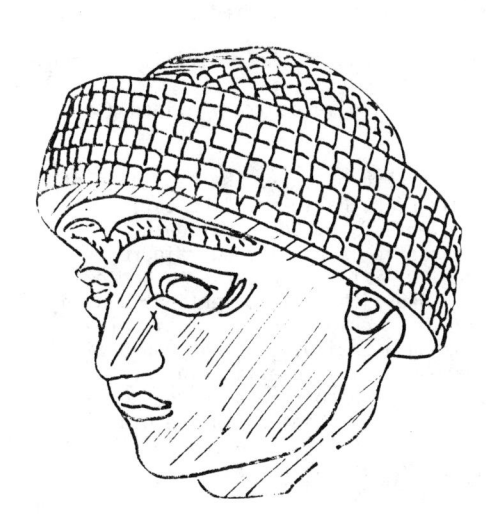

Fig. 47. Gudea, ensi from Lagaš, wearing a plain, round cap without horns.

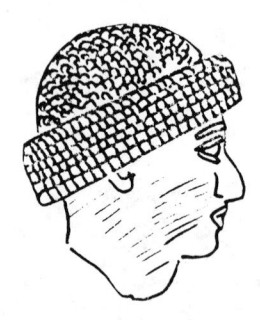

Fig. 48. Ur-Ningirsu, son of Gudea, depicted with a cap similar to that of his father.

Fig. 49. The well-known Hammurabi wearing a round cap without horns.

It is true that some early Sumerian literature speaks of Gilgameš and Dumuzi,[1] for instance, as being deified and we might expect them to wear horned crowns as signs of their divinity. Iconography from this early period, however, gives contrary evidence.

---

[1] Gilgameš, the fifth king of Erech, marks the beginning of the Early Dynastic III period; Max E. L. Mallowan, "The Early Dynastic Period," in CAH^3, vol. 1, pt. 2, p. 244. Mallowan assigns the kings of the Early Dynastic II as "shadowy figures." Dumuzi, the fourth ruler of Erech, will therefore have to be comprised in this category (ibid.). Åke Sjöberg also mentions a hymn to the temple é-mùš in Badtibira whose chief god is Dumuzi. There is, as is well known, a Dumuzi among antediluvian kings ^{d}dumu-zi si-pa "Dumuzi the shepherd," (Jacobsen, The Sumerian King List, p. 72) who was king of Badtibira. Sjöberg also refers to the deified Dumuzi of Uruk (-Kulaba) who appears as a shepherd in the Old Babylonian texts, and he therefore does not exclude the possibility of the two being identical; The Collection of the Sumerian Temple Hymns in Texts from Cuneiform Sources, vol. 3 (Locust Valley, NY: J. J. Augustin, 1969), p. 9.

Fig. 50. Deity, king and priest equipped with tools in attempt to lay the foundation stone for a temple. A part of a frieze in the relief stela of Urnammu from Ur.

Ward, who has devoted a whole chapter in his work[1] to early mythology of Gilgameš, has presented many early designs (perhaps from

---

[1] The Seal Cylinders of Western Asia, pp. 59-79.

4000 B.C.) which depict Gilgameš and his friend Eabani and the Divine Bull, against whom Gilgameš, according to the myth, was engaged in battle. Gilgameš (mostly presented *en face*) never wears horns. Ward says about Gilgameš, "He has two curls each side of his head, instead of later three. . . ."[1] Also in the earliest seals Gilgameš is depicted in nudity while seals from a later time present him with a girdle cord.[2]

Contrary to Gilgameš, Eabani always is depicted with horns, and Ward even observes that the horns are specifically those of the bison and not of the buffalo. Ward also points out that in the same way the human-headed bull always has the horns of a bison and never those of a buffalo.[3] Ward sees a geographical importance in this distinction, whereas we see a significant mythological-religious analogy here that could not be represented in the *Bos bubalus* (water buffalo). Only the horns of the *Bison bonasus* (bison) had horns analogous to the "horns of the moon."[4]

In several Sumerian temple hymns[5] the word *men* (crown) is

---

[1] Ibid., p. 59; for drawings of Gilgameš, Eabani and the Divine Bull see Ward's collection, ibid., pp. 59-75, figs. 141-201.

[2] Cf., for instance, the depiction of Gilgameš in seal no. 141 (p. 59) (of earlier time) and no. 159 (p. 65) (of a later time) in Ward's collection (ibid.).

[3] Ibid., pp. 63, 66.   [4] Ibid., p. 66.

[5] As it is impossible in this dissertation to cite all the literary works, only a few random samples have been chosen to represent this particular genre of hymns and epics. We would refer to Åke Sjöberg's Introduction in *The Collection of the Sumerian Temple Hymns*, vol. 3, for an annotated collection of hymns. (According to Sjöberg, two of the temple hymns in his collection date from the Ur III period and the rest of them are Old Babylonian copies [p. 7]); see also Hallo, "Toward a History," pp. 181-203.

used. So, for instance, Åke Sjöberg translates a hymn where the ancient Eridu is given this epithet, eridu^ki sag-men-gál "O Eridu with a crown on your head!"[1]

In another example men is used to give the epithet to "the wide heaven" men-an-dagal-la.[2] The sag-men is also applied to a king:

en ù-tu sag-men gá-gá su-na ì-gal
"The (new) born lord, she [Mother Nintu] sets the crown (on his head), he is (secure) in her hand."[3]

There is also another word mùš-zi which Sjöberg translates muš-crown (lustrous like).[4] The muš is uncertain but might denote a kind of headgear--perhaps of lapis lazuli.[5]

Nowhere is the word si (horn) applied (with the literal meaning of the word) to the king. However, si in compounds is used in a metaphorical sense. So, for instance, one of the old hymns says

nun-zu am-gal am-si á-ni-šè húl-la
sùn-si-mú si-mùš-a-ni-šè húl-la
"Your prince (is) a great wild ox, an elephant? who
   rejoices at his strength,
A wild bull with horns, who rejoices at his . . ."[6]

---

[1] Sjöberg, TH no. 1, line 13 (p. 17); cf. commentary on line 13 (p. 53), in The Collection of the Sumerian Temple Hymns.

[2] Ibid., TH no. 8, line 115 (p. 23).

[3] Ibid., TH no. 39 line 503 (p. 46); cf. commentary on line 503 (p. 143) and on line 13 (p. 53).

[4] Ibid., TH no. 39, line 502 (p. 46).

[5] Ibid., TH no. 39, line 498 (p. 46) and commentary, pp. 141-142; cf. also TH no. 7, line 95 (p. 22) and commentary, p. 73.

[6] Wolfgang Heimpel points out that the original meaning of am-si is "Ur mit (langen) Hoernern." Furthermore, Heimpel asserts that the Romans in a similar way designate the elephants as

Narâm-Sin, the fourth king of the Sargonic dynasty, who ruled (2254-2218 B.C.), is the Mesopotamian king who first deviated from the old tradition and had himself deified.[1]

According to Hildegard Lewy, the importance of the kings of Akkad "was the creation of a universal empire, comprising what later princes used to call kiššat matati, 'the totality of the countries.'"[2] It was this idea that had as its prototype and origin the cult of the moon, for the moon was a universal god in contrast to the national deities.[3] Although much of the story of Narâm-Sin is legendary, his historical reality is archaeologically and historically attested.[4] The unique inscription on his stela from Susa begins,

---

"lukanischen Ochsen;" Tierbilder in der sumerischen Literatur, Studia Pohl, 2 (Rome: Pontificium Institutum Biblicum, 1968), p. 73. This tradition is a strong evidence that am-si was used not to refer to elephants, but to wild oxen with horns. We see the original meaning ("Ur mit [langen] Hoernern") as more suitable in the context (apparently not the bison but the buffalo).
Ibid., TH, no. 11, lines 151, 152 (p. 26); cf. commentary, p. 82 where Sjöberg agrees with Heimpel by saying, "It is uncertain if am-si means "elephant" in all quoted passages."

[1] Jacob Klein in his dissertation (Šulgi D: Neo-Sumerian Royal Hymn, University of Pennsylvania, 1968) points out that not only Narâm-sin but also Šar-kali-šarri of the Old-Akkadian dynasty were "the first kings to use the 'preposed' and 'apposed' divinity titles (p. 13, n. 6).

[2] "Assyria, c. 2600-1816 B.C., in CAH³, fol. 1, pt. 2, pp. 735-36.

[3] Ibid., p. 736.

[4] Ibid., p. 739. Oliver R. Gurney, "The Sultantepe Tablets," in AnSt 5 (1955):94-95, 98-99; Jacob J. Finkelstein, "The so-called 'Old-Babylonian Kutha Legend'," JCS 11 (1957):83-88. (The narrator of the story is not a king of Kutha, but Narâm-Sin of Akkad [p. 83]).

(ilu)[Na-r]a-am(ilu) ÊN.ZU da-num . . . Si-dur . . .
Sa-tu-ni Lu-lu-bi-im [ki] ip-ḫu-ru-m[a]

Narâm-Sin, le puissant, . . . (prince) de Sidur . . .
Satuni, (prince) de Lulubi, . . .[1]

Well known are the protruding horns on Narâm-Sin's helmet-like headgear (fig. 5 above).[2]

Following the example of Narâm-Sin there are but a few kings in the neo-Sumerian kingdom who were deified. Šulgi, the son of Ur-Nammu, who ruled over Elam and Ansham as well as over Sumer had this vain glory of deification attached to himself. C[yril] J. Gadd in his history remarks that "vain glory and popular superstition supported it [the deification]." Furthermore, Gadd points out that "this assumption of divinity coincided with the great expansion in the middle years of Shulgi."[3]

Leon Legrain notes that Ibi-Sin, the last king of the third dynasty of Ur, was also deified.[4] The same kind of honor was bestowed upon Lipit-Ištar, the fifth king of the dynasty of Isin, who was the promulgator of the neo-Sumerian law-code ca. 1850 B.C.[5]

---

[1] Vincent Scheil (O.P.) "Stèle de Naram-Sin," Mémoirs de la Délégation en Perse (Paris: E. Leroux, 1900), pp. 52-56.

[2] (Fig. 5 above); not only the horned helmet but also the giant figure of Narâm-Sin, in comparison to the other figures of submissive and degraded size, bring out the idea of a superhuman being, a deified king.

[3] So Cyril J. Gadd, "Babylonia c. 2120-1800 B.C.," CAH³, vol. 1, pt. 2, p. 619.

[4] Historical Fragments, Publications of the Babylonian Section, vol. 13 (Philadelphia: University Museum, 1922), pp. 35-36.

[5] Samuel N. Kramer, The Sumerians (Chicago: The University Press, 1963), p. 336.

as well as on other kings of the Isin dynasty.[1]

Jacob Klein has proved that actually all the kings of the Isin Dynasty were deified, for they all took over the divinity title.[2]

Legrain, describing a seal of Ibi-Sin presented to Sag-Nannar-zu, priest of Enlil,[3] points out that the scene (on the seal) represents "the introduction of a person to a seated king or deity."[4] The smiles on their faces imply favor of the king. The question that arises: how to interpret the seated figure wearing a turban? has been discussed by Legrain. The seated figure might represent either the deified king or Sin, the patron god.[5]

The seal is unique in its design.[6] It may indicate that the headdress of the king, though he was deified, was traditionally the same as all the Sumerian rulers from Gudea to Hammurabi, or that the gods (if the seal represents a seated god) wore turbans like kings (no female figures wear turbans).[7] Legrain, however, says,

---

[1] There is, as far as we have been able to investigate, no iconographic representation of either Šulgi or Lipit-Ištar. Only by the determinative do we recognize their deification. So, for instance, Martin A. Beek, Atlas of Mesopotamia (London: Thomas Nelson, 1962), p. 54.

[2] Šulgi D: A Neo-Sumerian Royal Hymn (Ph.D. dissertation, University of Pennsylvania, 1968), p. 13, n. 6.

[3] Legrain, Historical Fragments, p. 35.

[4] Ibid., p. 37.   [5] Ibid., p. 40.

[6] We have not had possibility to study this particular seal nor its clay relief (see Legrain, ibid., pp. 34-41) which presents king Ibi-Sin with turban (no horns) and beardless. Legrain says, "Our clay relief is nearly the only known example where the seated god is beardless" (p. 40).

[7] Legrain, Historical Fragments, pp. 39-40.

Strong literary tradition speaks of the horns of Sin, which may be simply the symbol of the crescent moon and of his long, dark, lapis-lazuli beard. All seal cylinders and impressions of the seals of the school of Ur represent the seated god wearing the turban and with a long beard hanging on his breast [cf. figs. 51 and 52 and cf. fig. 53]. Our clay relief is nearly the only known example where the seated god is beardless.[1]

Legrain is strongly of the opinion that the seal does not represent a god but a deified king, for he says:

The large, set eyes, the high cheek bones, the curved nose, the thin lips, the firm and round chin complete an interesting attempt to portray King Ibi-Sin, the last king of Ur, with a necklace and arm-band as becomes his majesty.[2]

Fig. 51. The headdress of the god (?), sitting on the throne, is plain, round and simple compared to the two female figures wearing "horned" headdresses. The worshiper is shaven.

A fragment of an octagonal prism gives additional light regarding Ibi-Sin.[3]

---

[1] Ibid.   [2] Ibid., p. 41.

[3] The main part of the text is here referred to as it is presented by Legrain in his translation which he has published in a column parallel to the text in transliteration (<u>Historical Fragments</u>, p. 81).

Fig. 52. A goddess, with a "horned" headdress, leading a worshiper to an enthroned king. A cylinder seal from the Ur III period.

Fig. 53. The moon-god Nanna, with a headdress decorated with four pairs of horns, sits enthroned while Ur-Nammu of Ur (2000-1955 B.C.) offers libation to a tree which symbolizes this particular god.

Dubkiag-Nannar, son of Nanni,
let shine the horn [si] (exalted) of Tummal
Ninlil into Tummal was brought up,
A fourth time Tummal was ruined.
Ur-Engur built the temple ekur,
Dungi, Son of Ur-Engur,
let shine the horn [si] of Tummal,
Nin-lil into Tummal was brought up.
A fifth time Tummal was ruined.
By . . . of Ibi-Sin
when King Ibi-Sin,
was elected by oracles as priest of the
temple: "the great heavenly bull,"
priest of Inanna at Uruk . . .[1]

Ibi-Sin was a priest as well as a deified king according to this text. The determinatives indicate that he was a priest-king. The epithet "the great heavenly bull" seems here to apply to him in his office of priest.

It is especially the horns of the ox that comprise the metaphorical picture when applied to a king, prince, or priest. Another example will substantiate this theory. Hallo refers to a hymn to Enlil[2] in which the king appointed for Enlil is given the epithet "fierce ox"[3] (gu_4-bàn-da). On the reverse side are attested the words:

lugal-en gal-di-an-na
sag-me-en-kù
. . .
gu_4-e si-gar-re

Oh lofty king, distinguished one of heaven
Oh holy headband(?)
. . .
Oh ox, horned one[4]

---

[1] Cf. ibid., n. 2.

[2] The hymn is an Old Babylonian version according to an Old Babylonian Catalogue, referred to in Hallo's article, "On the Antiquity of Sumerian Literature," JAOS 83 (1963):169.

[3] Ibid., p. 170 (i, 5).   [4] Ibid., p. 170 (Rev, iii, 33, 34, 36).

Hallo translates *lugal-en* "Oh lofty king" instead of the literal "king-priest," but whatever he was, a king, a priest, or a "king-priest," he was the horned bull or ox.

The designation "bull" in ancient civilization was both "sacred and dignified," according to Jack R. Conrad's analysis.[1] Conrad expounds his view by saying

> . . . strength was something that all bulls yet few men had . . . to the extent that man possessed it, to that extent he was a bull whether he appeared to be or not. In most cases, to be a great king or leader was to be anointed by the bull-god, as was Sargon I, the son of the bull-god such as Gilgamesh, or the bull-god himself as were the Pharaohs.[2]

Assyria and Babylonia. By the time of the kingdom of Assyria the ancient Sumerian terms *lugal* and *en* had fused completely. The Assyrian king was the high priest of the god Aššur.[3] Some of the earlier kings of Assyria did not claim the title of king for themselves. Ashur-dan I (1179-1134? B.C.), for instance, contented himself with the title "Prince" (*ishakku* [*iššakku*, *iššiakkum*]), an Akkadinized form of the Old Sumerian *Ensi* [*PA.TE.SI*].[4] At a later time Ashurbanipal (668-626 B.C.) still in a certain measure, upholds the same tradition that comprises the *iššakku* concept, for

---

[1] *The Horn and the Sword* (New York: E. P. Dutton and Co., Inc., 1957, reprint ed. Westport, Connecticut: Greenwood Press, 1973).

[2] Ibid., p. 106.

[3] Oppenheim, *Ancient Mesopotamia*, p. 99.

[4] H. W. F. Saggs, *The Greatness that Was Babylon* (New York: Hawthorn Books, Inc., 1962), p. 86; for *iššakku* = *si*, *ensi*[si] see Tallqvist, *Akkadische Götterepitheta*, p. 34.

he calls himself "offspring of Ashur and Belit."[1] Some insight can also be derived from scenes depicted on seals from the Old Assyrian period. Hildegard Lewy refers to such a seal, belonging to Sharrum-kēn [Sargon I of Assria], which presents a deity seated on a throne and wearing the horned crown.[2] The lunar crescent including the sun-emblem is also depicted in front of the seated god, thus identifying him with Aššur. Lewy does not identify any priest on this seal, but she sees the other figure with a horned crown and a sheepskin frock (like Aššur, the supreme god), and who holds the king by his hand as a "lower deity." This lower deity Lewy identifies as the moon-god because of the lunar crescent behind his head. Lewy sees the introduction of the king by the moon-god into Ashur's presence as significant evidence of Sin being the royal family's patron god in the Neo-Assyrian period and already playing a preponderant role in Assyrian state religions in the Old Assyrian period.[3] In the capacity of priest the king performed sacrifices and was able to influence both temple and cult.[4]

The circumstances in Babylon were different, however, because the traditional cult from Old Babylonian time lived on and

---

[1] A. S. Tritton, "King (Semitic)" in Encyclopaedia of Religion and Ethics, 7:726.

[2] For a discussion of this particular seal (ibid.), pp. 710-11 and 760; for a depiction, Julius Lewy, "Die Keilschriftquellen zur Geschichte Anatoliens," Nachrichten der Giessener Hochschulgesellschaft 6 (1925), fig. 4, as cited by Hildegard Lewy, "Assyria, c. 2600-1816 B.C.," p. 767.

[3] Lewy, ibid. (That the moon-god had several priests in his service is however known, though not evident on this particular seal.)

[4] Oppenheim, Ancient Mesopotamia, p. 99.

influenced the whole policy differently than in Assyria. The Babylonian king, for instance, was restricted in his priestly performances--only once a year was he admitted into the cella of Marduk, and on that occasion he had first to put aside his royal insignia.[1] The power of the priests in Babylonia was far more deeprooted than in Assyria.[2] However, both cultures, and especially that of Assyria with its terror-striking policy, incorporated the old Sumerian concept of pul(u)ḫ(t)u and melammū, to which Oppenheim has alluded.[3] Oppenheim says: "The well-known phrase of the Assyrian historical inscriptions: pulḫu melammu šarrûtia isḫup or iktum "the terror (and) the glory of my royalty threw down (or: covered) (my enemies) . . ."[4]

> The king as representative and likeness . . . of the gods, also has such an aura which constitutes the divine legitimation of his royalty. This melammu is bestowed upon him when he becomes king . . . yet he could lose his divine support . . . when his melammu disappears it becomes known that he is no longer king "by the grace of God."[5]

---

[1] Ibid.

[2] For a study of the priesthood in the Old Babylonian kingdom, see Renger, "Untersuchungen zum Priestertum in der altbabylonischen Zeit," ZA 58 (1967):111-88; for an older source of both the Sumerian and Babylonian tradition of priests and priesthood (Theophilus G. Pinches, "Priest, Priesthood," Encyclopaedia of Religion and Ethics, ed. James Hastings [New York: Charles Scribner's Sons, 1919], 10:284-88).

[3] Melammu was probably a pre-Sumerian term meaning "awe-inspiring luminosity" or something of the like; Oppenheim, Ancient Mesopotamia, p. 98; cf. also Oppenheim's article, "Akkadian pul(u)ḫ(t)u and melammu," JAOS 63 (1943):31-34.

[4] Ibid., p. 31.

[5] Ibid. According to Oppenheim such an aura or melammu denotes a characteristic attribute of the gods consisting a dazzling aureole or nimbus which surrounds the divinity (ibid.). Oppenheim

Oppenheim also observes that the first iconographic representations of this nimbus are as late as the neo-Assyrian period.[1] This "nimbus" or "halo" cannot, however, be seen in the relief presentations of the kings of Assyria and Babylonia, neither on kudurri nor on stelae nor on statues, not even the peculiar horned headdress--in fact, the Assyrian headdress is more like a miter.[2] The "nimbus" or "halo" of a god may be indicated, however (see, for instance, fig. 19). (See figures 54, 55, and 56.)

In his work Carl Bezold[3] has included a presentation of an artwork in relief from the time of Aššurnasirpal (884-860 B.C.). The motif presents two winged figures facing each other and kneeling on either side of the "holy tree"; the figures are dressed and have horns on their headdresses (fig. 57). Bezold's interpretation of the kneeling figures is that they are priests. An even more "fanciful" interpretation is given to a figure with a bird's head

---

mentions that pulḫu and melammu are often considered synonymous expressions, but in religious texts there is a difference which always is maintained. The word pul(u)ḫ(t)u denotes a kind of supernatural garment and the word labāšu "to clothe" is nearly always used in connection with pul(u)ḫ(t)u, while melammû has the meaning of like supernatural headgear and is used with the verb našû "to wear." Oppenheim further says that the pulḫu-garment is conceived as "a wrap of flames and fire" and melammû as a "peculiarly shaped sparkling."

[1] Ibid., p. 31, n. 1.

[2] Cf. figs. 54, 55, 56, 57, and 25 for samples of Babylonian and Assyrian headdresses worn by well-known kings.

[3] Ninive und Babylon, p. 118, and the caption to fig. 110 in Bezold's word reads: "Stilisierter heiliger Baum mit zwei geflügelten Männern (Priestern). Relief aus der Zeit Aššurnassirpals." Cf. Pritchard's interpretation of a similar motif, "A winged deity . . . at each side of a stylized tree, relief of Ashurnasirpal II from Nimrud," ANEP, p. 214, fig. 656.

(fig. 58), for its caption reads: "Geflügelter Mann (Priester) mit Vogelmaske."[1]

Fig. 54. A kudurru of Marduk-apal-iddina II showing the presence of the gods depicted through symbols.

---

[1] Bezold, Ninive und Babylon, p. 118 (fig. 110); cf. Pritchard's caption, "A protective genius, . . ." ANEP (1954), p. 202, fig. 617. (The motif of "holy tree" and related questions are not relevant per se in this connection.) Samuel H. Hooke in Myth, Ritual and Kingship (Oxford: Clarendon Press, 1958); Ivan Engnell, Studies in Divine Kingship in the Ancient Near East (Oxford: Basil Blackwell, 1967), have inter alia dealt with these issues.

Fig. 55. The many layers of horns on the headdresses, placed on the miniature shrines, represent probable high gods. A stone tablet of King Nabû-apal-iddina from the early 10th century B.C.

Isidore Scheftelowitz also gives a "fearful" picture of the priests. He says:

> Die Priester, welche die Stelle der Götter vertraten nahmen bei zeremoniellen Ausübungen die äussere Gestalt der Götter an, die sie repräsentierten. Daher trugen die sumerischen und babylonischen Priester zwei Hörner auf ihrer Kopfbedeckung.[1]

---

[1] "Das Hörnermotiv in den Religionen," ARW 15 (1912):472. (Scheftelowitz is referring to Stephen Langdon for this information [n. 5]; we have not had access to Langdon's work).

Scheftelowitz is here probably referring to the ašipu priest performing magic rituals and incantations.[1]

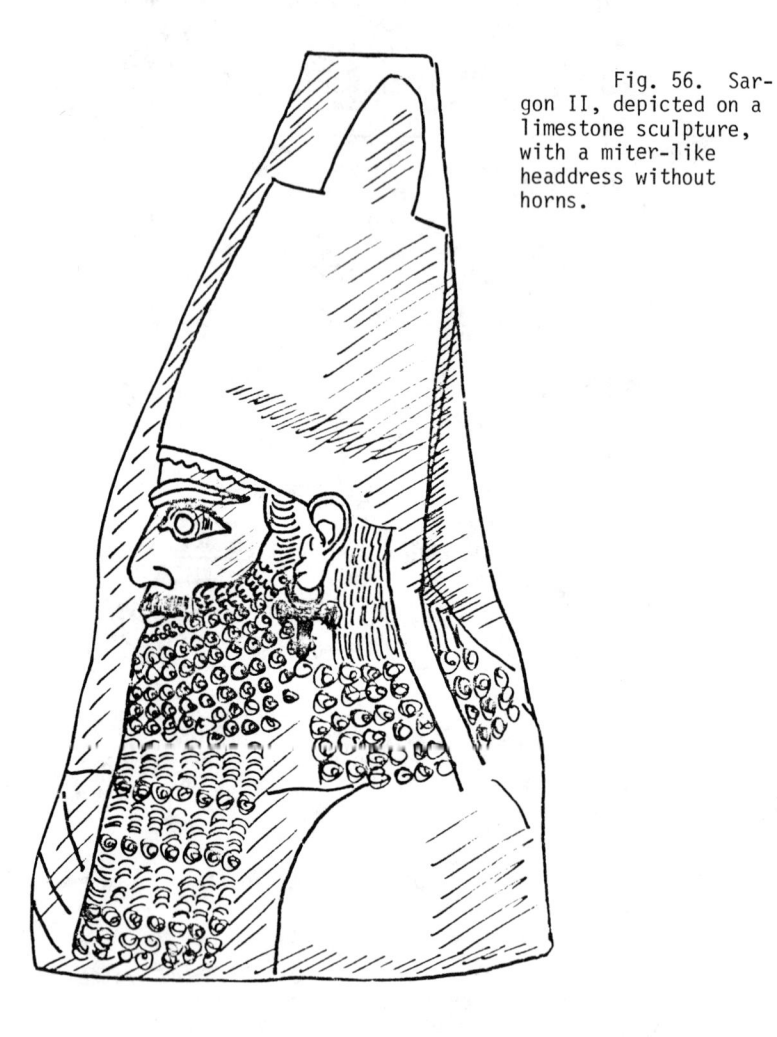

Fig. 56. Sargon II, depicted on a limestone sculpture, with a miter-like headdress without horns.

---

[1]Ibid.; cf. Pinches, "Priest, Priesthood (Babylonian)," p. 286.

Fig. 57. Two winged men (priests?) kneeling on both sides of the holy tree. The headdresses are decorated with horns.

In summary it may be said that the concept of priests and priesthood has always played a significant role wherever any nation has had an established cult of worship. The magnificent temple construction and the large pantheons from earliest Sumerian culture and up to neo-Assyrian and neo-Babylonian time are evidences enough that an elaborate system of rituals existed in which the function of the priests was important. The king in ancient Sumer as well as the king in the Assyrian kingdom often assumed the role of the priest, thus influencing the religion and cult. In Babylonia, the king had a more restricted function in cult and ritual except for the akîtu festival in which both priests and king played a significant role in ceremonies and specific rituals.[1] On the whole, it may be said that

---

[1] The strange ceremonies performed by the king in the hieros gamos act in Esagila on the akîtu or New Year festival have been treated more or less by all ancient Near Eastern historians and will therefore not be dealt with here. It is only to be observed here that many scholars still cling to the theory of Marduk as dying and

the Assyrian and Babylonian priesthood followed the ancient Sumerian pattern, but necessary changes were made to suit their own culture, which in its core likewise was a heritage from old Sumeria.

Fig. 58. A winged man (priest)? with a bird-mask? (or a protective genius) touching King Aššurnassirpal II (not depicted here).

---

rising again at the akîtu festival, a theory which makes the king, who in the act of hieros gamos assumes the god's role, also to be identified as a dying and rising "god" in this particular ceremony. The old theory by Sir James Frazer is, however, untenable today as H. W. F. Saggs, The Greatness That Was Babylon, p. 301; Edwin M. Yamauchi, "Tammuz and the Bible," JBL 84 (1965):283-90, and others have shown.

Syria. The evidences of priests and kings from this area, generally termed Syria,[1] are scanty, and therefore the reconstructive task is contextually risky. The tendency of imposture of one culture upon another when the available material is meager is always bidding and a strict distinction between "imposing" and "reality" must be maintained.

Ivan Engnell, for instance, has pointed out that in the northwest Semitic area (as in other cultures) the king was directly called "son of the god, and the god father of the king."[2] Engnell also notes that in the Amarna age the king calls the high god his father:

^{d}šamaš a-bū-šú damku or ana ^{d}Samši abī šarri beliia

"the sun-god his gracious father," and "to the sun-god, the king's father, my lord."[3]

Well known also is the case of king Meša from Moab who calls himself בן כמש, "the son of Kemoš," or the royal name Ben Hadad from Damascus.[4]

Engnell goes even a step further showing that the king was not only the son of the god but was identical with the god: šarru

---

[1] Syria is not here restricted to any particular geographical area but is used in a broad sense of West-Semitic cultures.

[2] Studies in Divine Kingship in the Ancient Near East, p. 80.

[3] Ibid., cf. Samuel A. B. Mercer, The Tell El-Amarna Tablets, 2 vols. (Toronto: Macmillan Company, 1939), 2:480-81 and pp. 484, 485 (147:8, 58); and Jørgen A. Knudtzon, Die El-Amarna Tafeln, 2 vols. (Aalen: Otto Zeller, 1964), 1:608-611. Both Mercer and Knudtzon neglect to translate the determinative for "god." This has been corrected by Engnell (above).

[4] Engnell, Studies in Divine Kingship, p. 80.

^{d}Šamaš dārītum "The king is the sun-god eternally." In fact, the king was not only identical with the sun-god but also with the "atmospheric high god Adad."[1] A very clear example where the king is identified simultaneously as Šamaš and Adad has been pointed out by Engnell: šarru bēliia kīma ^{d}Šamaš kīma Addi ina šame atta "O, king my lord, (as) Šamaš, (as) Adad in heaven art thou."[2]

It is also probable that the king was the high priest par excellence in analogy with other cultures. There are some texts that hint of this. From a letter of Abdi-Hiba of Jerusalem to the king of Egypt, we quote from Mercer's translation:

> [T]o the king, my lord, my sun, [sa]y.
> Thus saith Abdi-Hiba, thy servant:
> At the feet of the king, my lord, seven times and seven times I fall down.
> . . .
>
> Verily, I am not a regent;
> I am an officer of the king, my lord.
> Behold, I am a shepherd of the king, . . .[3]

In his translation Jørgen A. Knudtzon has italicized the words "Offizier" and "Hirt," probably with purpose of emphasizing the original titles ^{amêlu}u-e-u and ^{amêlu}abu.[4] Engnell notes that "the

---

[1] Ibid., p. 81 ina 7 ana šēpē b[ēl]iia Addiia amkut "seven times at the feet of my lord, my Addu, I fall down." Cf. Mercer, The Tell El-Amarna Tablets, 1:224, 225 (52:3, 4) and Knudtzon, Die El-Amarna Tafeln, 1:320, 321 (52:3, 4).

[2] Ibid.; cf. Mercer, The Tell El-Amarna Tablets, 2:488, 489 (149, 6.7); Knudtzon, Die El-Amarna Tafeln, 1:614, 615 (149, 6.7).

[3] Mercer, The Tell El-Amarna Letters, 2:715; cf. Knudtzon, Die El-Amarna Tafeln, 1:869. For the cuneiform text see pp. 714, 868 respectively.

[4] Knudtzon, Die El-Amarna Tafeln, 1:868, 869.

former is an Egyptian priest-title, and the latter the Semitic רעה rō'aē 'shepherd'."[1] He gives other examples of the "sacred" shepherd title: <u>inter alia</u> he points out that king Meša probably was a high priest and that the same can be said of Zakir of Ḥamath.[2] As for the deification of the king, the evidences are few, but they give indications that the same tradition of a deified king exists.[3]

Iconography, however, substantiates the theory of a priest-king, as Carney E. S. Gavin, the specialist on Syrian seals, has shown. Gavin, in his dissertation, refers to a seal belonging to Šarrum-ken, (Sargon) I, the son of Ikunum and grandson of king Erišum.[4] The inscription of the seal reads:

^{d}Šarrum-ken PA.TE.SI ^{d}A-šur mer I-[kunim], PA.TE.SI ^{d}A-[šur]

"Šarrum-ken, Priest--Prince of Aššur, son of Ikunum, Priest--Prince of Aššur."[5]

The seal impression which is depicted in Gavin's dissertation shows a seated figure with a low and rounded cap (fig. 59).[6]

---

[1] Studies in Divine Kingship, p. 86.   [2] Ibid., p. 87.

[3] Whether the king was deified already in his lifetime is a question that we have to leave unanswered though we may not be far from the truth if we assume that this might have been the case also in Syria. Evidences, however, are lacking.

[4] Gavin, "The Glyptic Art of Syria-Palestine" (Ph.D. dissertation, Harvard University, 1973), pp. 135-39. This seal has been discussed pp. 208-11 (above).

[5] Ibid., p. 139; cf. Georg Eisser and Julius Lewy, "Die altassyrischen Rechtsurkunden vom Kultepe," (part 4), MVAG 35 (1935): 100-01 (# 327); cf. also Lewy, "Some Aspects of Commercial Life in Assyria and Asia Minor in the Nineteenth Pre-Christian Century," JAOS 78 (1958):89-101.

[6] It seems that Lewy has erred in her description (CAH^3, vol. 1, pt. 2, pp. 767-68), for she describes the seated king wearing a

The symbol of the moon (the sickle) with a sundisk is depicted in front of the seated figure. One figure stands before the "Priest-prince" and behind him is another figure with well-formed, upward-pointed, high horns.[1]

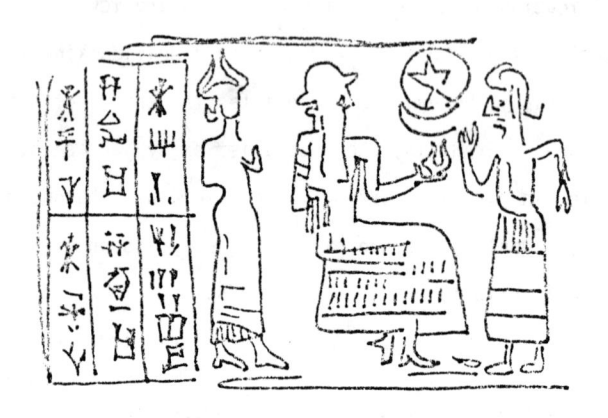

Fig. 59. The "Priest-Prince," seated on his throne, is depicted with a low, round cap. Behind the seated ruler is shown a figure with upward-pointed lateral horns.

On the basis of its motif, the seal appears to be very old-- the date ca. 1910 B.C. according to the historical reconstruction by Hildegard Lewy.[2] In the present writer's opinion it seems to convey the same tradition of the headdress of certain kings in Mesopotamian

---

horned cap, whereas the seal shows a low rounded cap. The figures in front and behind the seated figure have, on the contrary, been presented with horns. The king whom the deity, in front of the god, is supposed to lead, is not shown on the seal impression.

[1] Gavin, The Glyptic Art of Syria and Palestine, p. 138.

[2] As referred to by Gavin (ibid., p. 139); cf. also Lewy, "Assyria, c. 2600-1816 B.C.," pp. 752-69.

art (Gudea of Lagaš and Hammurabi of Babylon, for instance) which are presented with a round cap. There is also the possibility of the seated figure being the moon-god himself--usually identified by his round cap (fig. 51 above) and his long, dark, lapis-lazuli beard.[1]

Syria has been the melting pot of many cultures, so a direct influence from Mesopotamia in the second millennium is therefore tenable. Yigael Yadin's studies of the monuments at Zinjirli, Carthage and Hazor give abundant evidences, for instance, of the spread of the moon-cult into the West-Semitic world. There seems to be a clear religious-cultural connection between the great cultural focal points not only within Syria, but with the cultural centers outside its borders.[2]

It is to be hoped that Tell Mardikh will, in years to come, constitute an oasis that will fertilize and nourish our vague and limited comprehension of Syrian culture and religion. At present we can propose only conjectural hypotheses at the best and assume, on analogy of the Mesopotamian culture and religion, that the Syrian religion basically conformed to the same pattern.

As for the Seleucid kings of later times, it is well known that several of them are depicted with horns. Alexander the Great

---

[1] So, for instance, Ward, The Seal Cylinders of Western Asia, p. 109, and Legrain, Historical Fragments, p. 40 (see fig. 52 above).

[2] Yigael Yadin, "Symbols of Deities at Zinjirli, Carthage and Hazor" in Near Eastern Archaeology in the Twentieth Century, ed. James A. Sanders (Garden City, NY: Doubleday & Company, Inc., 1970), pp. 199-231.

is depicted with ram's horns, thus emphasizing his divine origin, and with the diadem around his head, shows that he was a world-ruler.[1] Urs Staub records a prayer by Alexander in connection with his visit at the shrine in the Libyan desert: "Ich weiss, dass du meine Hörner auf meinem Haupt hast wachsen lassen, dass ich die Reiche der Erde zerstosse."[2]

The picture of Seleukos I Nicator with helmet and bull-horns is probably an idealized portrait of Alexander.[3]

The depiction of "horn" per se is nothing new, for that symbol had been in use at this particular time for about two thousand years. The one thing "new" is the horn attached to the diadem--probably to insinuate (not the deification as in Mesopotamia) the intrinsic divinity of the king, as in Egypt.

Furthermore, the depiction of Alexander the Great with ram's horns indicates clearly that the author of Daniel was not influenced by the depiction of the Seleucid kings on the coins; his imagery must have had another source as he presents Alexander not as a ram but as a goat (Dan 8:5).

Anatolia. Oliver R. Gurney, Assyriologist and Hittite scholar, points out that "the Hittite king was not only leader in

---

[1] See Urs Staub, "Das Tier mit den Hörnern" (a revised article based on Staub's Lizenziatarbeit: Die Tiervision im Danielbuch: Eine motivgeschichtliche und ikonographische Untersuchung zu Daniel 7:2-8 [Freiburg (Switzerland), 1977]), FZPhTh 25 (1978):374.

[2] Ibid., p. 370, n. 71.

[3] Cf. the horns of Ptolemaios I and Soter and Lysimachos (ibid., p. 369, figs. 3 and 4).

war and supreme judge but also chief priest of the national cults."[1]

Albrecht Goetze, in his translation of the "Plague Prayers of Mursilis" shows how Mursilis, the Hittite king and son of Suppiluliumas (about third quarter of the 14th century B.C.) directs his prayer to the Hattian storm-god (the main deity of the Hittites) and other Hattian gods urging them to drive forth the plague from Hattiland.[2] In this prayer Mursilis says, "I have become the priest of the gods."[3] Thus it is evident that also in the Hittite kingdom the offices of kingship and priesthood were united in one person.

As for the divinity of the king, in the role of that particular office or as an officiating priest, there is no evidence in the Hittite text. Gurney, to the contrary, remarks that "the fact that the Hittite king 'became a god' at death" . . . shows that there is no trace of a cult of living kings.[4] Gurney also says that

> In theory the king was the steward appointed by the weather-god of Hatti to administer his estate, and must render homage to him by constant prayer and sacrifice.[5]

As early as 1954 Hans Gustav Güterbock, the well-known Hittitologist, presented the same theory on the role of the king and for this purpose refers to the following statement from the Hittite Text.[6]

---

[1] "Hittite Kingship" in *Myth, Ritual and Kingship*, ed. Samuel H. Hooke (Oxford: Clarendon Press, 1958), p. 105.

[2] ANET³, pp. 392-96.   [3] Ibid., p. 396.

[4] Gurney, "Hittite Kingship," pp. 119, 121.

[5] Ibid., p. 121.

[6] *Istanbul Arkeoloji Müzelerinde Bulunan Boğazköy Tabletleri* I, no. 30; trans. Albrecht Goetze, JCS 1 (1947):90-91.

The land belongs to the storm-god, heaven and earth with
the people belong to the storm-god. And he made the Labarna,
the king, his deputy (maniyaḫḫatallaš) and gave him the
whole land of Ḫattusa. The Labarna shall govern the whole
land.[1]

Güterbock commenting on the text, says:

In accordance with this theocratic view of kingship, we
find that the Hittite king was not deified during his lifetime; he only "became god" when he died.[2]

Furthermore, Güterbock brings out that ". . . there is not a single text referring to the cult of the living king that could be compared to those of the Third Dynasty of Ur."[3]

Instead of the king being considered divine, just the contrary seems to be true for, as Güterbock rightly pointed out, "in the countless cult texts the king worships the gods as a human being, and in the prayers he addresses them as his lord and calls himself their slave."[4] In the same way as in Mesopotamia, it was the king's duty to care for the cults of the god, to maintain the provision for temple and images of gods and perform in similar ways.[5]

As a priest (even as high priest at the spectacular New Year feast analogous to the akítu festival in Babylon) the king was the channel through which his people approached deity. In the role of priest the king makes certain preparations.[6] Goetze has made clear

---

[1] Güterbock, "Authority and Law in the Hittite Kingdom," supplement to JAOS 17 (July-September 1954):16; Albrecht Goetze, "Critical Reviews," JCS 1 (1947):91.

[2] Ibid.   [3] Ibid., p. 17.   [4] Ibid.

[5] Goetze, Kleinasien 2d rev. ed. 3. Abschnitt, 1. Unterabschnitt of Kulturgeschichte des alten Orients (München: C. H. Beck, 1957), p. 150.

[6] Goetze, who in an article, "The Priestly Dress of the

that the king puts on at least two things: "he puts on his ornaments" and "he puts the ceremonial garment o[n himself?]."[1]

Nothing is said of the priest's headwear--unless the kušiši has something to do with the king. However, it seems, according to Goetze, that it is not "attached to the headdress, but wrapped around the shoulders like a cape. This veil or shawl, then, is to be identified with the kušiši."[2] Goetze says "the kušiši must be the long gown that both queen and king wear in virtually identical fashion, the veil or cape being the main difference."[3] No headdress with horns is referred to in the priestly attire.

Kurt Bittel in his detailed study of Yazilikaya comes to the conclusion that the headdress of the gods and the king did not differ basically. He says,

> Wir haben damit einen weiteren Beleg dafür, dass die Kopfbedeckung der Könige, soweit es sich um Darstellungen

---

Hittite King" (JCS 1 [1947]:176-85) refers to the Hittite texts which describe the opening of a new day "and the putting on of 'ornaments' and 'garments,'" does not make clear whether this "putting on" refers to the king in quality of priest or high-priest. "The opening of a new day referred to by Goetze is however marked by the opening of the halentu-house" (a term not yet defined accurately) which suggests that a ceremony of infrequent occurrence (perhaps a yearly New Year fest or the like) may be referred to.

[1]Goetze, "The Priestly Dress of the Hittite King," JCS 1 (1947):177.

[2]The kušiši (kureššar) is used in the genitive case in an example referred to by Goetze, which would indicate that the kureššar could refer to the material from which it was made (genitive of source) or the larger garment of which the kureššar is a part (perhaps an ablative or partitive). The kureššar, however, is a garment characteristic of women, something like a long veil or shawl spreading out from a "polos"; ibid., p. 178.

[3]Ibid., p. 179.

kultischen Inhaltes handelt, nicht grundsätzlich verschieden ist.[1]

Güterbock, however, brings out a particular detail which is worth noticing in this connection, namely, that the title "My Sun" is used for the king.[2] He furthermore points out that "since the word 'sun' is, in cuneiform, necessarily spelled with the determinative for 'god,' this title has been taken as evidence for the divine character of the Hittite king."[3]

Ekrem Akurgal, a recent scholar in Hittite art, shows that the kings in the "Grossreichzeit" (13th century B.C.) are always depicted with a calotte-formed headdress.[4] Akurgal refers to the best examples being attested in the reliefs at Alaça Hüyük and Yazilikaya. He says furthermore, that the Hittite texts inform us that the king can wear the horns only when he is presented as a deified ruler, i.e., after his death.[5]

Güterbock, in turn, notes, however (already two decades before Akurgal's work was published), that although in the reliefs of the Empire the king wears the same costume as the Sun-god--"round cap, long gown, and curved staff"[6]--the title "My Sun" already

---

[1] Kurt Bittel, Rudolf Naumann, and Otto Heinz, eds., Yazilikaya, Wissenschaftliche Veröffentlichung der deutschen Orientgesellschaft 61 (Leipzig: J. C. Hinrichs, 1941), p. 107; cf. also p. 108.

[2] Güterbock, "Authority and Law in the Hittite Kingdom," p. 16.

[3] So, for instance, Ivan Engnell, Studies in Divine Kingship, p. 60, and Cyril J. Gadd, Ideas of Divine Rule in the Ancient East (Schweich Lectures) (London: Oxford University Press, 1948), p. 48.

[4] Die Kunst der Hethiter, p. 81.   [5] Ibid.

[6] Güterbock, "Authority and Law in the Hittite Kingdom," p. 16.

occurs in the Old Kingdom, i.e., "at a time when contacts with Egypt seem unlikely."[1]

It is therefore hard to explain the tradition of the "round cap" so different from the high-pointed, horn-decorated cap, typical of the Hittite culture. As was discussed in the section on Mesopotamia, the "round cap tradition" is already prevalent in Sumer in the time of Gudea from Lagash and in the time of Hammurabi from Babylonia.

There is no way, however, to put forth a theory that the Hittite culture deviated from the Mesopotamian or Egyptian pattern in regard to kingship, for Akurgal brings forth evidences to the contrary. He says:

> Es scheint jedoch, dass am Ende des Grossreiches auch der orientalische Brauch, die Könige schon bei Lebzeiten zu vergöttlichen in Hattusa Eingang gefunden hat. Tuthalija IV [1250-1220 B.C.] [the son of Hattusili III] hat sich im grossen Kultraum des Heiligtums von Yazilikaya wie Gott, auf Bergen, darstellen lassen. . . . Auffallend ist ferner, dass derselbe König auf seinem Siegel, das in Ras-Schamra gefunden worden ist, eine Göttermütze mit Hörnern trägt.[2]

Thus Akurgal basically disagrees with Güterbock and even apart from the evidence of the title "My Son," presents a rather strong evidence for deification of the king in his lifetime by indicating this from the seal impression (fig. 60).

It is also to be remembered that the Hittite cultural evidences are relatively "new," and therefore new discoveries with a sequentially new interpretation of texts and iconography are to be

---

[1] Ibid.

[2] Akurgal, *Die Kunst der Hethiter*, p. 57, fig. 64.

expected. These proleptic new evidences may still widen our conception of the Hittite culture with its vast pantheon, royalty, and priesthood.

Fig. 60. Tuthalija IV, the son of Hattušili III, has himself depicted as a god by wearing the emblem of the gods--a cap with horns. He is shown to the extreme left on a seal from Ras Shamra, ca. 1250-1220 B.C.

Ugarit. As we endeavor to study the concept of the king and the priest in Ugaritic context, the much debated issue of whether cult or myth is the special character of the Ras Shamra texts will not be dealt with here.[1]

---

[1]Engnell in his study has included a comprehensive review of the scholarly opinion in regard to this question (Studies in Divine Kingship in the Ancient Near East, pp. 73-110); cf. also Arvid S.

Until quite recently only a few of the kings of Ugarit were known. The temples excavated comprise the period 2100-1500 B.C.[1]

Kenneth A. Kitchen, who in a recent study has reconstructed the king list of the Ugaritic kings,[2] also refers to a period before the dynastic king (mlk) when the principal officiant, in some ancient cult contest, invokes a series of names (the Assembly of Didaru)[3] which are all summed up in the words rpʾim qdmym "the shades/saviours of old."[4] These were distinct from the later "kings" and may, as Kitchen points out, suggest a "primeval antiquity" before the king of the first dynasty Yaqaru(m).

Another interesting thing that Kitchen presents is the list of deceased dynastic rulers showing that all the deceased kings were deified.[5] This brief information given by Kitchen gives us a basis for the foundation of the kingship in Ugarit.[6] It certainly seems

---

Kapelrud, Baal in the Ras Shamra Texts (Copenhagen: G. E. C. Gad, 1952), pp. 13-19.

[1] Arvid S. Kapelrud, "Ugarit," IDB 4:729.

[2] "The King List of Ugarit," UF 9 (1977):131-42; cf. John Gray, "Sacral Kingship in Ugarit," Ug 6 (1969):289-302 (especially pp. 298-300).

[3] For dit/dam, see Kitchen, "The King List of Ugarit," pp. 141-42 (perhaps a tribal ancestor of Keret's clan).

[4] Ibid., p. 141.

[5] The king list comprises a minimum of thirty kings if the list was prepared under the time of the thirty-first (and last) king, Ammurapi, according to the information given by Kitchen, "The King List of Ugarit," p. 133.

[6] The assumptions of Kitchen that "Ugarit is now probably attested as one centre among many others in the archives of Ebla of c. 2300 B.C." ("The King List of Ugarit," p. 142), is however, not yet proved--though the Ebla tables may conceal this fact.

that the concept of deification had spread right across from the Mesopotamian culture over Syria and to the Mediterranean Sea. But again, these are as yet not evidences for deification of the king during his lifetime.

As for the priests and priesthood, Engnell says that the "shepherdship" has long been suspected to be of a sacral nature because the Arabic and Akkadian etymologies give certain hints in that direction.[1]

The vast pantheon and the two temples discovered at Ugarit[2] (dedicated to Baʿal and his father Dagon) suggest that a great staff of priests was necessary to maintain the cult. Iconography comes to our assistance here also. A haematite cylinder-seal depicts priests with animal masks (fig. 61). Kapelrud describes the scene on the seal as follows:

> There are two groups of them [the priests]. In one group two priests, one of them wearing a goat's mask, are preparing a sacrifice for the solar emblem, supposed to be that of El. In the other group one of the priests wears a bull's mask. Here the sacrifice is brought to a bull's head, without doubt the symbol of Baal.[3]

Fig. 61. Priests, dressed in animal masks, with horns, making sacrifices. From a haematite cylinder seal found at Ras Shamra.

---

[1] Engnell (Studies in Divine Kingship, p. 87) is depending on James Montgomery, "Notes on Amos" (JBL 23 [1904]:94) for this conclusion. Montgomery sees a relationship between the Assyrian nakidu and the Hebrew נגיד (shepherd and prince).

[2] Kapelrud, Baal in the Ras Shamra Texts, p. 17.

[3] Ibid., p. 21.

Kapelrud gives importance to the fact that the priests wear masks,[1] because he understands in this tradition something more than just an everyday offering scene. He sees in this an evidence that a cult drama is going on. Kapelrud does not want to "prove" his theory but he refers to different religions in the ancient Near East where the priests usually wear masks during cultic performances. He gives the following description:

> In the cultic dramas the stages in the incessant struggle between gods and their enemies are given. The enemies are pictured as dangerous monsters, and the priests who play those parts wear awful, fear-rousing masks, while the priests who are acting in the gods' parts wear masks symbolizing certain gods (and in some religions these masks are just as awful as those of the enemies).[2]

Kapelrud draws his conclusion saying, "The Ugaritic cylinder-seal shows that there is all reason to believe that similar cult-dramas have been performed also in ancient Ugaritic religion."[3] For evidence of this, he turns to an enigmatic text[4] and feels the text itself giving the clue. He says: "The 'eaters,' aklm, and the 'devourers,' ʿqqm, are mentioned as gods, wearing horns like bulls and humps like steers."[5] Then Kapelrud makes the connection with the cylinder-seal and says, "The aklm and the ʿqqm were the priests dressed in animal hides and masks, of which bull's heads and hides are especially mentioned.[6]

---

[1] Ibid., p. 22. [2] Ibid. [3] Ibid.

[4] See, for instance, Gordon UT (1965), 75:I, 26-33 (translation in Gordon, Ugarit and Minoan Crete [NY: W. W. Norton & Company, Inc., 1966], p. 91).

[5] Kapelrud, Baal in the Ras Shamra Texts, p. 23; cf. also his later treatment of the same text (75:I, 26-33) "Baal and the Devourers," Ug 6 (1969):319-32.

[6] Kapelrud, Baal in the Ras Shamra Texts, p. 23; cf. the

Though Kapelrud's explanation seems simplified, Gordon gives certain support through his added information as to ʽqqm "'devourers' having bulls' horns, buffaloes' humps and Baʽal's face."[1] In his translation of this text Gordon notes, "Such creatures--partly bovine, partly anthropomorphic--are to be compared with the Mesopotamian 'Bull of Heaven' and the Cretan Minotaur."[2]

Gordon does not explain what he means by the expression "such creatures," but if he means the ritual priests he does not state it explicitly--not even implicitly unless one happens to know exactly to what he refers.

The cultic drama with the masked figures had, of course, a special meaning, but what was the meaning? Engnell sees in the cultic performances "an expiatory sacrifice, where the god-king, substituted by the bull, brings about the atonement by his 'vicarious suffering'."[3]

Kapelrud, on the other hand, brings out the importance of the fertility cult analogous to the akîtu cult in other cultures--

---

similar view of Theodor H. Gaster, "The Harrowing of Baal, A Poem from Ras Shamra," Analecta Orientalia 16 (1937):41-48, and Engnell, Studies in Divine Kingship, p. 127; cf. also Nicolas Wyatt's view, "Atonement Theology in Ugarit and Israel," UF 8 (1976):415-30 (especially pp. 418-22).

[1] Gordon, UT, Glossary, p. 460 (1909); for aklm, ibid., p. 357 (158).

[2] Gordon, Ugarit and Minoan Crete, p. 91, n. 39; in Gordon's previous translation, UL (1949), this note was not included.

[3] Engnell, Studies in Divine Kingship, p. 127. This same strange interpretation is reflected also in Nicolas Wyatt's presentation, "Atonement Theology in Ugarit and Israel," where he sees Baʽal as a substitute for the sin of the world (expressed in primitive theology); UF 8 (1976):415-30.

in Assyria, Babylonia, and in other nearby countries.[1]

John Gray, discussing the status and function of the Ugaritic king, refers to a short text[2] which interestingly enough deals with the status of the king in form of his titles.[3]

Roland de Vaux has suggested the possibility that these titles refer not to the king but to the "heir apparent" and infer that this text might enumerate "the royal titles roughly corresponding to the titles of the young priest in Isa 9:5 [Masoretic Text]."[4]

Gray sees some of the titles--especially the title b'l ṣdq "Upholder of Right" or "Legitimate Prince"--as bringing the kingship at Ugarit "into direct contact with royal ideology in Mesopotamia and Israel."[5] The general consensus among scholars is that this text is but one of the many that "helps elucidate the subject of kingship in Canaan."[6] Engnell, for instance, "assumes a uniform pattern of royal ideology as valid throughout the ancient Near East."[7]

---

[1] Kapelrud, Baal in the Ras Shamra Texts, pp. 27-43.

[2] See Claude F.-A. Schaeffer, Le palais royal d'Ugarit II Mission de Rash Shamra, vol. 7 (Paris: Imprimerie Nationale, 1957), pp. xvi-xvii.

[3] An enumeration of the titles in transcript and English translation is given by Gray, "Sacral Kingship in Ugarit," p. 289.

[4] R[oland] de V[aux] ["Bulletin--Ras Shamra"] RB 65 (1958): 635-36.

[5] Gray, "Sacral Kingship in Ugarit," p. 290.

[6] Ibid.

[7] As quoted by Gray (ibid., p 292). (Engnell is not alone in

There are, however, scholars who seriously question a uniform pattern throughout the history of Mesopotamia.[1] It seems evident, for instance, that the status of the kings in Canaan was "limited by their subordination to their Egyptian or Hittite overlords."[2] In Gray's opinion the ideal kingship is illustrated not in these caricature vassal relationships but in the royal legends of Krt and Aqht in "the heroic age."[3]

Gray, who seems to attempt to defend a close affinity between the Ugaritic texts and the Bible, sees the king as the "servant" (ʽbd, ǵlm) of El[4] and as the representative of the people par excellence "for which he is set aside by the rite of anointing."[5] Although the proofs for anointing are farfetched, it seems evident that the king of Ugarit was considered a priest and as such "Krt himself performs sacrifice."[6]

---

holding this opinion. It is well known that his colleagues of the "Myth and Ritual" school take the same view and with certain variations the predecessors of the History-of-religion school have similar views with some deviating emphases.)

[1] Karl F. Euler, "Königtum und Gotterwelt in den altaramäischen Inschriften Nordsyriens," (ZAW 56 [1938]:272-13) is one of the contemporaries of Engnell that questions the conception of divine kingship among the Arameans in Syria in the Iron Age.

[2] Gray, "Sacral Kingship in Ugarit," p. 293.

[3] Ibid., pp. 294-95.

[4] Cf. Isa 42:1-4; 49:5-6; 52:13-53:12 as cited by Gray, "Sacral Kingship in Ugarit," p. 296.

[5] Ibid.

[6] Corpus 14 = UT krt, 156 ff, as cited by Gray, "Sacral Kingship in Ugarit," p. 296.

The function of the priest was, however, vastly different from the Israelite priests, for Gray refers to the function of the priest saying,

> We believe <u>qua</u> priest king <u>Dn^{j}el</u> officiates at certain fertility rites. He prays for rain and dew in a drought, ineffectively as it proves and he performs a rite of imitative magic. . . .[1]

Concerning the main function of the priest, Gray goes on to say, "his office is significantly associated with a sacred guild (<u>mrz $^\zeta$</u>) of dispensers of fertility, obviously functioning as priests."[2] The water-pouring rite was another of the important priestly functions tied up with magic.[3]

The priest-king tradition known from other cultures thus seems to have been accepted also in Ugaritic culture. The priests were subordinate to the king. It was the king, assuming the priestly role, who was the key figure in the many cultural rites and especially in the important fertility rite, akin to many other cultures. No one studying Ugaritic art is unaware of that fact and will certainly agree with Kapelrud that "the religious cult at Ugarit was of a decidedly fertility character."[4] The many nude goddesses of fertility give a silent testimony as to the character of Ugaritic religion.

<u>South-Arabia</u>. The many temples in South-Arabia (Mârib-temple one of the best known) testify to a deep-rooted religious

---

[1] Corpus 19 = <u>UT 1 Aqht</u>, 39-42 as cited by Gray (ibid.); see also Gray, "Sacral Kingship in Ugarit," p. 296.

[2] Ibid., p. 297.   [3] Ibid.

[4] Kapelrud, <u>Baal in the Ras Shamra Texts</u>, p. 20.

attitude among the Arab people.[1] Unfortunately, we do not know much of their religion but, as already alluded to, Nielsen points out that their religion was an astral religion.[2] Also in South-Arabia, as in Mesopotamia, religion stands in close connection to mythology, and through the myths we can perceive something of the god concept that prevailed in antiquity in various cultures.

Nielsen notes that the three gods that repeatedly meet us in South-Arabian inscriptions are Wadd, ʾAtirat, and Malik, and Malik apparently refers to the Venus-god.[3] Furthermore, Nielsen sees this assumption important, for he continues: "Als Beiname eines Gottes ist Malik nur im Lichte des altarabischen Königs-Kultus zu verstehen."[4] Nielsen, however, does not lose himself in idealistic speculations, for he says, "Der Begriff und der Name 'König' ist natürlich auf Erden entstanden und sekundär auf himmlische Wesen übertragen worden."[5]

The cult of the king becomes understandable as we follow Nielsen's presentation:

> Nun wissen wir aus den Inschriften, dass der König im alten Arabien und von den Abessiniern als Gott verehrt wurde, [6]

---

[1] Nielsen refers to an inscription telling about "the king building and restoring the temple of Wadd and ʾAtirat and the sanctuary (Mahtan) of Malik," Die altarabische Kultur, p. 233.

[2] Idem, Studier over, old arabiske indskriften Rejserne til Sydarabien, Landets ældste historie (København: Det Schønbergske forlag, 1906), p. 123.

[3] Nielsen, Die altarabische Kultur, p. 233.

[4] Ibid.   [5] Ibid.

[6] This statement assumes, as far as we understand Nielsen's

wahrscheinlich als der irdische Repräsentant des ʿAttar,
als der inkarnierte, der fleischgewordene Venusgott. Der
Venusgott ist vom Himmel auf die Erde niedergestiegen,
und hat in der Person des Königs Wohnung genommen. Die
Inkarnation geschieht wohl schon bei oder vor der Geburt
des Königs, indem der arabische König nicht in gewöhnlicher
Weise wie andere Menschen geboren ist, sondern von
göttlicher Herkunft ist.[1]

The triad of gods was considered as a family in which the Venus star was the son. Nielsen tells us that the king also belongs to this family:

Zu dieser Götterfamilie gehört auch der König, denn als
Venusgott ist er, wie es wiederholt in den Inschriften
ausgesprochen wird, der Sohn des Mondgottes.[2]

If Nielsen is right, the philosophy behind the kingship is astonishing, for further on he says,

Die arabische Königsmythologie führt endlich zu der
Annahme, dass Malik ein Venusbeiname sei. Denn wenn der
König ein Sohn des Mondgottes und der Sonnengöttin ist, so
kann er wohl nur diesen Titel tragen kraft seiner Würde
als Stellvertreter des Venusgottes, denn nur dieser ist
der erstgeborene Sohn des Mondgottes. Der himmlische
Venusgott ist also, so zu sagen, mit dem irdischen König
identisch, und nur ihm kommt daher der Name Malik "König"
zu.[3]

Nikolaus Rhodokanakis agrees in principle with Nielsen about the South-Arabian concept of kingship, for he says, *inter alia*, that

---

presentation, that deification of the king already during his lifetime was a tradition among both the Arabs and the Ethiopians.

[1]Ibid.

[2]Ibid. For the many inscriptions Nielsen refers to in this connection he cites the following sources (p. 234, n. 1): J. Halévy, Revue Sémitique 11 (1903):58-62; Mark Lidzbarski, Ephemeris für semitische Epigraphik 2 (1903-1907):382-86; H. Derenbourg, Nouveaux textes Jemenites. No. 3; Enno Littmann, Deutsche Aksum-Expedition, vol. 4 and his own works in ZDMG 66 (1912):589-600, and 68 (1914):705-18.

[3]Nielsen, Die altarabische Kultur, p. 234.

the king of the Sabaeans was thought of as the representative of God on earth; he was his son and his function was to administer the land--in other words, he was his steward.[1] Rhodokanakis also points out that the king needed no deification, for as the son of the national god he was already in his lifetime a divine being.[2]

In spite of the ideology of the king, the Sabaeans at the same time perceived their government relationship very realistically: "deren Könige hatten das mulk, die Macht."[3]

Not until the time of mukarrib Karibʲil Watar II (ca. 410 B.C.) is the ruler title "king" (mlk) used.[4] It is therefore to be assumed that somewhere around that time the transfer to a secular rulership took place. Another evidence that the political situation alters is the fact that at about the same period we find, in addition to Saba, the states of Qatabān (in the south) and Maʿin (in the north).[5]

The first historically proved mukarrib was Yitaʿ ʲamar in the time of Sargon II (ca. 720 B.C.).[6] Gese mentions that the title mkrb mukarrib (or makrûb) is traditionally translated "Priesterfürst," but the real meaning is still unclear.[7] The title is not

---

[1] "Dingliche Rechte im alten Südarabien," WZKM 37 (1930):122.

[2] Ibid., p. 124.   [3] Ibid.

[4] Gese, Hartmut; Höfner, Maria; and Rudolph, Kurt. Die Religionen Altsyriens, Altarabiens und der Mandäer. Die Religionen der Menschheit. Vol. 10, pt. 2 (Stuttgart: W. Kohlmanner, 1970), p. 240.

[5] Ibid.

[6] For information concerning date of historical events we are following Gese (ibid.), p. 240.

[7] Gese, Die Religionen, p. 241; cf. Nielsen, Die altarabische Mondreligion (Strassburg: Karl J. Trübner, 1904), p. 4.

much clearer in the later periods of the Qatabanian and Hadrami kingdoms where the mukarrib and malik are used side by side.[1] In the kingdom of Maʿin, on the contrary, the title mukarrib is unknown, for the title mlk is used exclusively.[2]

Because of the title change from mukarrib to malik Gese draws the conclusion that the oldest government form known was theocracy; the national god was the actual ruler.[3] Everything in the land is the god's property and everything happens according to his will. The earthly ruler is only an executor of the will of his god and a mediator between god and man.[4]

Regarding the question whether mukarrib was a cultic profession or not, there exist several opinions. Gese, however, points out that if we consider the governmental rule in Saba as theocracy, then during the mukarrib period there existed actually no difference between "cultic" and "secular," for, in a certain sense, all the activities of the theocratic ruler had a cultic character.[5]

In Qataban the situation was different, for here the South-Arabic inscriptions clearly prove that the mukarrib was a cultic profession, as his title reveals. The mukarrib calls himself "Erstgeborener des ʿAnabāy und Ḥaukam des Orakelbefehls und der Willenentscheidung."[6]

---

[1] Gese, Die Religionen, p. 281.

[2] Ibid., p. 288.   [3] Ibid., p. 240.

[4] The government form outlined by Gese is basically the same as that of Old Sumeria.

[5] Gese, Die Religionen, p. 347.

[6] Ibid; cf. also Maria Höfner, "War der sabäische Mukarrib

The priests were employed for the many services that took place in the temples, but evidences for this are meager. In Saba we know only of the rašu (ršw) "priests." This title is always followed by the name of the god whom the priest served. Other titles occur--none of them actually relevant for our study, and one of these titles is qayn (qyn) which, according to Gese, has the meaning of "steward." Another title is qāzir with the meaning "der festzitzt, bestimmt." The function of all these priests is, however, unknown.[1]

In contrast to the rich iconographic material from Mesopotamia, the South-Arabic cult appears to be pictureless in that the figurative conceptions of the gods were only symbolically mentioned. Nielsen reminds us, however, that we still do not know what the soil is hiding as no systematic digging has taken place.[2] The iconographic material that does occur seems to be expressed in symbols, but not in direct and plain representation of the gods or kings or priests. The overemphasized horns on the ibexes (wild goats) which decorate the doorposts of the temple of ʿAttar dū-Qabd at Qarnāwu are typical of this kind of symbolism (fig. 62).

The Arabian world has succeeded in hiding its real face from time immemorial, and it will take a tremendous effort to lift its veil and uncover its secrets.

---

ein "Priesterfürst"? WZKM 54 (1957):77 (Festschrift F. H. Junker), as cited by Gese (ibid.).

[1]Gese, Die Religionen, p. 349; the same word (rašu) is also used as a professional title in Qataban (ibid., p. 349).

[2]Nielsen, Die altarabische Mondreligion, p. 118.

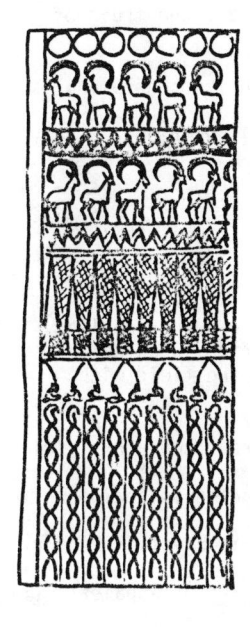

Fig. 62. The ibexes (wild goats) with accentuated horns seem to carry a symbolic design. Relief-work on a doorpost at the temple of ʿAttar dū-Qabd at Qarnāwu (South Arabia).

Egypt. From the very beginning of kingship in Egypt, divinity was considered the king's prerogative. The king was not an "adopted" son of the god as in Mesopotamia; he was born very god himself.[1]

Gerald A. Wainwright says, "Nothing is more certain than that the Pharaoh was divine."[2] Engnell also says,

> The king is divine from birth or even in a pre-natal existence. The crown prince is begotten by the god--

___

[1] Samuel H. Hooke, Myth, Ritual and Kingship, p. 75.

[2] The Sky-Religion in Egypt (Cambridge: University Press, 1938), p. 14. Adolf Erman already several decades earlier had expressed the same view when he said that "the king was actually as much a divinity as were any of the gods," and "the divinity of the kings belongs to the primitive dogmas of Egypt," A Handbook of Egyptian Religion, tran. A. S. Griffith (New York: E. P. Dutton & Co., Ltd., 1907), p. 37.

corporalized in the king--and the queen . . . the fruit of a ἱερός γάμος.[1]

On account of this divinity from birth the conclusion is that "the god is the king's father."[2] Engnell describes briefly the duty of the king who is described as "god on earth." He says, "He is a victorious warrior who subdues all external enemies."[3] Then he goes on to say:

> The king, himself being a young bull, a devouring lion, attacks the foes as a storm, a consuming fire, when he makes them feel the power of his hand and fills the field with their dead bodies.[4]

This brief description is enough to prove that this violent, attacking force described in metaphorical language is analogous to one of the earliest representations of a king in Egyptian history, namely, Narmer, as he is represented on the verso of a palette (fig. 63). On both sides of the palette the upper corners are decorated with bull-heads with the horns (fig. 64), as it seems, rather heavily emphasized. On the lower part of the verso, king Narmer himself is presented in bull-form, attacking and trampling his enemy and

---

[1] Engnell, Studies in Divine Kingship, p. 4.

[2] Engnell (ibid.) refers here to Wainwright, who gives an example that "the divine Pharaoh did impersonate the gods, at least on some occasion[s]" (Wainright, The Sky-Religion in Egypt, p. 52). Wainright in his footnote (n. 4) to the statement (given above) says, ". . . Hatshepsut's father was Tethmosy I [Tuthmose], yet her 'bodily' father was Amûn, . . . This could not have been unless Tethmosy I had impersonated the god, and in fact we are told in the crudest language how Amûn 'made his form like the majesty of this husband, the king Okheperkere (Thutmose I), etc., etc.', . . ."

[3] Engnell, Studies in Divine Kingship, p. 12.

[4] Ibid.

pushing through the walls with his horns (fig. 65).[1] On the recto side King Narmer is presented in human form wearing the white crown of Upper Egypt. This well-known picture does reveal some of the Egyptian ideology of kingship. The horns on the bull apparently represent the attacking, brutal, and authoritative force of the king in bull form.[2]

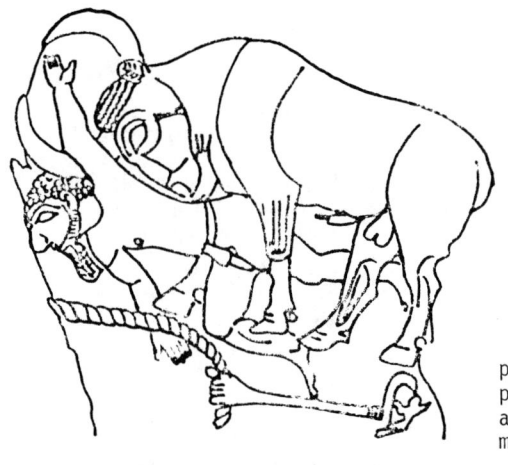

Fig. 63. The upper part of a fragmentary plate palette outlined by a bull, aggressively attacking a man.

---

[1] Malten's view is here presented. See his "Der Stier in Kult und mythischem Bild," p. 97. Archibald H. Sayce also points out that "among the Egyptians . . . the Pharaoh was symbolized under the form of a bull at the very beginning of history." The Religion of Ancient Egypt (Edinburgh: T. & T. Clark, 1913), p. 111.

[2] Thutmose III, for instance, was given the epithet, "Mighty Bull." Cf. John A. Wilson, "Egyptian Historical Texts," ANET[3], pp. 234-35; cf. also Alan Gardiner, Egypt of the Pharaohs (Oxford: Clarendon Press, 1961), p. 51. The same ideology existed still in the time of Merneptah, for in a victory hymn it says about the king:
"Der kräftige Stier,
der die Feinde mordet,
Schön am Kampfplatz,
sein Stoss (wie) die Sonne,
Die das Gewölk verscheucht,
das Aegypten bedrohte.
Adolf Erman, Aegypten und aegyptisches Leben im Altertum, new

Fig. 64. Bullheads with horns depicted on the upper part of the famous Narmer slate palette.

Fig. 65. Narmer, the first king of the United Kingdom of Egypt, depicted under the symbol of an aggressive bull trampling upon his enemy and breaking through the wall of a city with his horns. From a slate palette from Hierankopolis.

There are also other hints that bull-cult and the connected moon-cult existed in Egypt in prehistoric times. Eberhard Otto points out that already in the prehistoric time the palette-art from the region of Abydos[1] presented star-decorated bull-heads and a peculiar sign on jars (earthen vessels) which seems to picture a bull

---

revised edition by Hermann Ranke (Tübingen: J. C. B. Mohr, 1923), p. 469. The same epithet of "Bull" was also given to Ramses II (p. 644).

[1] For the presentation of ancient animal-palettes with the emphasized horn-motif on the bovines, see Otto, Beiträge zer Geschichte der Stierkulte in Aegypten, Untersuchungen zur Geschichte und Altertumskunde Aegyptens, vol. 13, ed. Herman Kees (Hildesheim: Georg Olms,1964), pls. nos. 1, 2, 3 (the last one presents the Narmer Palette).

carrying the sun-disk between its horns (compare fig. 37 above).[1]

Otto also points out that very early the Egyptians connected the bull with a cosmic and especially with an astral idea, although it is not possible to account in detail for the manner in which this took place.[2]

The pyramid of Unas also gives hints about the importance of both the bull and his horns. Unas, the last king of the Fifth Dynasty of Egypt, ruling ca. 2375-2345 B.C., was probably a contemporary of Sargon the Great of Akkad.[3] The inscriptions in this pyramid describe how, after death, Unas was to pass through different stages in his process of regeneration--these stages were symbolized by identifications with different gods.[4] During his travel, and with the destiny to appear before the gods, the king was to utter certain phrases in which, <u>inter alia</u>, the words "bulls" and "horns" occur rather frequently.[5]

The "Bull of Heaven" which we find in the Unas pyramid inscription and in other Pyramid-texts gives a hint to the then existing importance of the moon-god.[6]

---

[1] Ibid., p. 3.   [2] Ibid.

[3] Alexander Piankoff, <u>The Pyramid of Unas</u>, Bollingen Series 40 (Princeton: University Press, 1968), 5:8.

[4] Ibid., p. 6.

[5] Piankoff refers to several of these expressions: (ibid., p. 17 § 504, p. 19 §§ 513, 516, p. 22 § 470, p. 24 § 481, p. 29 270 [the strong horn of the antelope], p. 31 § 280, p. 32 §§ 282 and 283); cf. the horns of Tešub (fig. 34 [above]) which might be an imitation of the horns of an antelope (gazelle).

[6] <u>The Ancient Egyptian Pyramid Texts</u>, trans. R. O. Faulkner (Oxford: Clarendon Press, 1969) is the most recent English edition.

In one of the Pyramid texts it says, ". . . for I am that eye of yours which is on the horns of Hathor. . . ."[1] Samuel A. B. Mercer, commenting on the text, says,

> The eye of the sun-god stood for the sun-god himself, and here the deceased king being identified with the eye of the sun-god was identical with the sun-god himself.[2]

Another utterance, also identifying the king with the sun-god, says:

> The king is the Bull with radiance in the midst of his eye, the king's mouth is hale through the fiercy blast and the king's head through the horns of the Lord of Upper Egypt. The king controls the god, the king has power over the Ennead, the king makes lapis-lazuli grow. . . .[3]

Mercer says that "the bull as well as the falcon stood for royal might in all periods of Egyptian history."[4] As for the "flaming breath" and "the horns" [of the bull], Mercer says that these render him [the king] immune.[5] Some of these incantation texts are rather enigmatic in their expressions. One such phrase says, "A vulture has become pregnant with the King in the night at your horn, O contentious (?) cow."[6]

The commentary and notes are concentrated. The present writer has used this edition side by side with Samuel A. B. Mercer's The Pyramid Texts in Translation and Commentary, 4 vols. (New York: Longmans, Green and Co., 1959). This is an older edition but the notes are more comprehensive.

[1] The Ancient Egyptian Pyramid Texts, p. 132 (Utterance 405).

[2] The Pyramid Texts in Translation and Commentary, vol. 2, p. 347.

[3] The Ancient Egyptian Pyramid Texts, p. 101 (Utterance 319).

[4] The Pyramid Texts, vol. 2, p. 243.

[5] Ibid.

[6] The Ancient Egyptian Pyramid Texts, p. 122 (Utterance 352).

Mercer commenting on the text says that

> Here the personage addressed is the heavenly goddess, Nut, as a pregnant cow; but not as mother of the deceased king. The king is said to be on her horn, that is, in the west, Nut's hind legs being in the east where the sun-god was daily born.[1]

To be "on her horn" in this case then takes on a simple explanation when the idiom of the myth is clear. For still another utterance[2] we quote the following passage:

> Hail to you, Bull of Rēʿ who has four horns, a horn of yours in the west, a horn of yours in the east, a horn of yours in the south, and a horn of yours in the north! Bend down this western horn of yours for me that I may pass.[3]

Mercer, commenting on this particular text, says that

> The expression "four horns" is to be taken symbolically like the "four horns" of Zach 1:18 or the "ten horns" of Dan 7:7 and Rev 13:1. . . . The guardian ox of Rēʿ . . . inclines his horn when he is favourable to the voyager; otherwise he must be forced to open the passage.[4]

Otto expresses his belief that the "Bull of Heaven" refers to a star constellation.[5] Furthermore, he says that the planet Saturn was called so: "Horus, Stier des Himmels, und als

---

[1] The Pyramid Texts, vol. 2, p. 277; cf. figs. 37, 38 (above).

[2] Similar enigmatic incantation texts occur in the Collection of Pyramid Texts, but as they give no particular light on the question of "horn" they will not be commented upon here. These passages are found on p. 58 (Utterance 246), p. 62 (Utterance 251), pp. 132-33 (Utterance 254), and p. 211 (Utterance 548) in The Ancient Egyptian Pyramid Texts.

[3] The Ancient Egyptian Pyramid Texts, p. 93 (Utterance 304).

[4] The Pyramid Texts, vol. 2, p. 221. (Mercer discusses the bull of Reʿ in Excursus 19 "Bull in the Pyramid Texts," ibid., vol. 4, pp. 77-79.)

[5] Beiträge zur Geschichte der Stierkulte in Aegypten, p. 3.

stierköpfiger Gott oder Falke dargestellt."[1] And interestingly enough, he also says, "Dieselbe Bezeichnung findet sich für den Mond, und auch die Winde heissen 'Stiere des Himmels'."[2]

It is also amazing that during the Eighteenth Dynasty of Egypt the Apis-bull is placed on coequality with the heliopolitanean Atum and, so presented, he often wears the sun-disk (fig. 66). It is of interest that Apis is connected with Atum and not with Re. In Memphis the proto-sun-god Atum was especially connected with the sinking sun in the West. The relationship between Apis and Atum is expressed through the connection of the name Apis-Atum in the phrase [hieroglyphs] "Apis-Atum, dessen Hörner auf ihm sind."[3]

Egypt is usually referred to as a country of the sun-god Re, and the title of the king "the Son of Re" is attested already from the Fourth Dynasty.[4] Whether the moon-god or the sun-god was the original god with an established worship system is hard to

---

[1] Ibid.

[2] Ibid. E. A. Wallis Budge points out that "at one period Osiris was identified with the moon." Osiris and the Egyptian Resurrection (London: Philip Lee Warner, 1911), 1:384). Budge also points out that the moon is addressed "bull, that groweth young in the heaven each day." (De Iside, chapter 43, as cited by Budge, ibid., p. 385 and p. 384, n. 1); Adolf Erman thinks that the Egyptians assigned to the moon-god (the representative of Rēʿ) a far lesser importance than to the sun-god. See further Erman's discussion of the moon-god, who in spite of his lesser rank, was the god of all wisdom and learning (A Handbook of Egyptian Religion, trans. A. S. Griffith [New York: E. R. Dutton & Company, 1907], p. 11).

[3] Otto, Beiträge zur Geschichte des Stierkulte in Aegypten, p. 27.

[4] Sethe, Urgeschichte und älteste Religion der Ägypter, p. 174.

determine. The question has been much debated.[1]

Fig. 66. Bronze figure of Apis, the bull-god from Memphis, depicted with a disk between his horns--(sacred to the moon according to older sources).

Aylward M. Blackman says that we can trace "the association of the Egyptian kings with the sun-cult back to the Second Dynasty."[2] This statement by Blackman, then, leaves open the possibility that in the first dynasty and in the proto-dynastic period the moon-cult might have been prevalent.[3]

It is, however, certain that much fusion of the gods took place in Egypt as well as elsewhere. It has already been pointed out that Apis and Atum fused and so did Amon and Re, to mention some well-known instances. Alfred Wiedeman, for instance, refers to a hymn to Amon-Re showing the fusion of the two gods.[4] Part of the hymn reads:

---

[1] For a discussion on this topic, see, for instance, William J. Perry, "The Cult of the Sun and the Cult of the Dead in Egypt," JEA 9 (1925):191-200 and Aylward M. Blackman, "Osiris the sun-god? A Reply to Mr. Perry," JEA 9 (1925):201-205.

[2] "Osiris or the Sun-god?" JEA, 9 (1925):204.

[3] This is our conclusion which would, then, account for the bull motif on the Narmer and other palettes. Further investigation and excavation may bring clarity on the matter.

[4] Religion of the Ancient Egyptians (London: H. Grevel & Co., 1897), pp. 111-13.

Wake in health (?), Min Amen
Lord of the Everlasting, maker of Eternity,
Lord of adorations dwelling in Thebes,
Established with thy two horns, fair of face,
Lord of the uraeus crown, exalted by the two feathers,
Beautiful of diadem [exalted one], of the white crown of upper
Egypt, the kingly land and the two uraei are his (?).
He is adorned (?) in his palace with the sekhet crown, the
   Nemmes cap, and Kheperesh helmet
Fair of face, he seizeth the Atef crown, . . .[1]

Figures 67-70 depict various headdresses mentioned in the hymn.

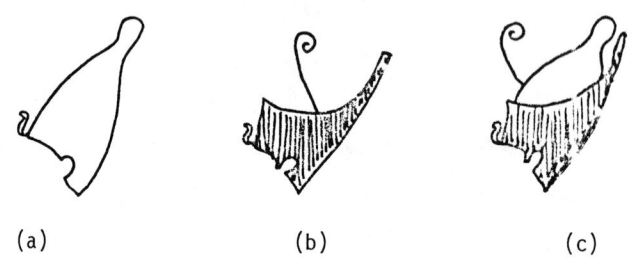

(a)   (b)   (c)

Fig. 67. (a) The white crown of Upper Egypt; (b) the red crown of Lower Egypt; (c) the double crown of the United Kingdom.

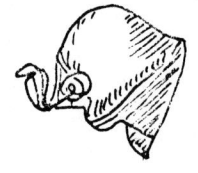

Fig. 68. The royal helmet (Kheperesh).

Wiedeman gives a description of Amen Râ:

Amen Râ is generally figured in human form; . . . is crowned with the sun disk and two long feathers, which rise

---

[1] This particular passage quoted below is from the hymn to Amon Râ which begins "Praise to Amen-Ra (ibid.). Amen = "The Hidden One" (ibid., pp. 108, 114). The Atef crown was a tall cap with a pair of horns and a pair of feathers (resembling the white crown); cf. ANEP, p. 187 (fig. 557); for the white, the red, and the double crown, see fig. 67, and for the royal helmet (Kheperesh), figs. 68, 69 (cf. fig. 70).

either from a stiff cap, or else from a pair of ram's horns
. . . he has the horns of a ram, because in Thebes he was
supposed to be incarnate in a ram.[1]

Fig. 69. The young king Tuet-ʿAnch-Amun, of
the 18th dynasty, seated on his throne, wearing the
royal helmet, gives audience to the governor of
Ethiopia.

Wiedeman also refers to a fusion between the gods of Amen and Khnûm having taken place in iconography; he says,

---

[1] Wiedeman, Religion of the Ancient Egyptians, pp. 118-19.

> . . . the horns represented as standing out at the sides are not those of Amen, but those of Khnûm . . . in representation of the god with these horns a combination has taken place of the gods Amen and Khnûm, originally distinct: the horns of Amen curl round the ear.[1]

Samples of these are shown in figures 71a and b.

Fig. 70. This kind of peculiar headdress (without horns) was worn by kings and queens alike. Queen Hat-shepsut, from Deir el-Bahri.

Although we know that Egyptian religion from the remote past was polytheistic and the many gods needed many temples, we actually know very little of the priesthood in the prehistoric and the time of the Old Kingdom. It is not actually until the New Kingdom that we get more verified information. And even then when we know about three great priesthood centers (Heliopolis, Memphis, and Thebes) and we know that the king served as a High Priest and that on account of

---

[1] Ibid., p. 119, fig. 71b shows Khnûm with both kinds of horns on his head; (it was the characteristic "incurvated horns" of the god of the god of Thebes that Alexander the Great more than a thousand years later assumed when he caused himself to be hailed as "the son of Zeus Ammôn," as the coins from the Hellenistic time prove [ibid., p. 120]; cf. fig. 72).

his many duties had an elaborated priesthood for the increasing temples that were built, we still do not know any particular details about the particular garments or headdresses of the priests.[1]

(a)

Fig. 71. (a) The ram-headed god, with the horns of Khnûm standing out at the sides, and with the horns of Amen curling around the ears, shows a fusion of two originally distinct gods.

(b) The twisted, lateral horns are typical of Khnûm, the ram-headed god Amen at Thebes. The cult penetrated to the oasis of Jupiter Ammôn about the beginning of the New Kingdom.

(b)

---

[1]Hermann Kees, Das Priestertum im Ägyptischen Staat vom neuen Reich bis zur Spätzeit, Probleme der Ägyptologie, vol. 1 (Leiden: E. J. Brill, 1953) and idem, Die Hohenpriester des Amun von Karnak von Herihor bis zum Ende der Äthiopenzeit, Probleme der Ägyptologie, vol. 4 (Leiden: E. J. Brill, 1964) are both very

Fig. 72. Alexander the Great was hailed as the son of Zeus Ammon, assuming to himself the "incurvated" horns of the god of Thebes (coinage).

The headdress of the king in Egypt was completely different from the horn-decorated headgear of Mesopotamia. Though the Egyptian texts speak about horns, these refer mostly to the bulls' or rams' horns, not to the headdress of the king, in spite of the fact that he was considered a god.

It was probably because the Egyptian religion was zoomorphic that often when an anthropomorphic figure of a god was presented, the god or goddess was presented with an animal's horns. Hathor, for instance, may have an anthropomorphic figure, but the cowhorns or ears are present to identify her (figs. 73 and 74). The horns of Amon and Khnum had their particular type (figs. 71 and 72 above). The kings of Egypt are represented with peculiar crowns that differ completely from those of any other country.[1]

The Egyptian religion was so embued with zoomorphical god-concepts that even small art-works in abundance reflect particular gods. Some of these art-works are depicted in figures 75-85 where rams, gazelles, and bulls are represented.

---

detailed concerning the political Sitz im Leben and Chronology, but both works deal with later periods; the first one starting with the New Kingdom. Adolf Erman, for instance, also gives some insight into the functions of the priests but this information is also from the time of the New Kingdom (Life in Ancient Egypt [London: Macmillan and Co., 1894], ch. 4).

[1] Cf. for instance figs. 67-70 [above].

257

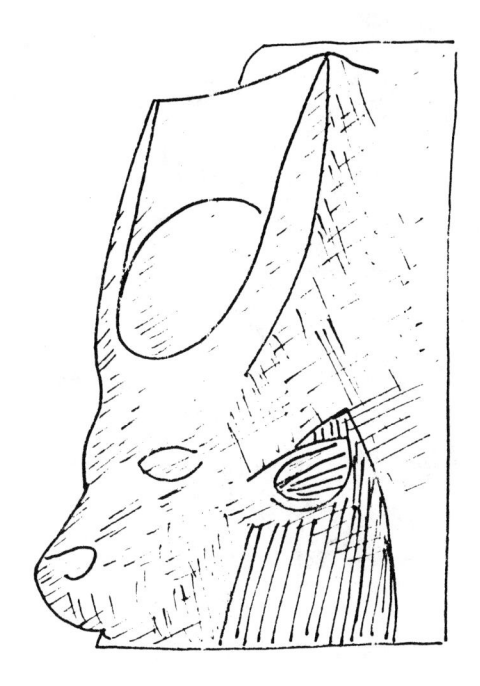

Fig. 73. Hathor, the mistress of merriment and dance, and the goddess of love; when depicted as a woman she is wearing on her head a pair of horns within which rests the solar-disk.

Fig. 74. Hathor, the goddess of love, depicted under the symbol of a cow and with the sun-disk enclosed between the horns.

Fig. 75. The horn-motif emphasized on a small artifact from the grave of Rech-me-re'. From the time of Thutmose III and Amenophis II.

258

Fig. 76. The horn-motif from the grave of Zen. From the time of Thutmosis IV.

Fig. 77. The horn-motif from the grave of I-me-sib. From the time of Ramses IV.

Fig. 78. The horn-motif from a relief. From the time of Thutmosis III (Karnak).

Fig. 79. The horn-motif from the grave of Har-em-hab. From the time of Thutmosis IV.

Fig. 80. The horn-motif from the grave of Meri-reʿ. From the time of Amenophis IV.

Fig. 81. The horn-motif on a war booty. From the time of Sethos I (Karnak).

Fig. 82. The horn-motif on a bronze basin with cover. From Etrurien.

Fig. 83. The horn-motif on a war booty. From the time of Sethos I (Karnak).

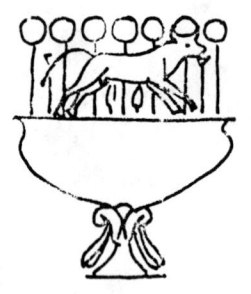

Fig. 84. The horn-motif on a war booty. From the time of Ramses II (Karnak).

Fig. 85. The horn-motif, probably from the grave of Rech-me-reꜥ. From the time of Thutmosis III and Amenophis II.

This discussion, by necessity, has been mixed with a presentation of the gods. In other words there is an overlapping which is unavoidable due to the fact that the king-ideology in Egypt is different from elsewhere. In Egypt the king was not and needed not to be deified, for he was god from the very beginning of his birth.[1]

There is, therefore, a strange mixture of zoomorphic, anthropomorphic, and symbolical peculiarities reflected in the presentation of kings and gods as we find nowhere else. The astral symbols together with their "hidden" horn-symbolism give a faint reminder of a relationship with other religions in other countries (of which the South-Arabian religion may be the closest). But though

---

[1] One difference between king and god is pointed out by Erman: "While Amon, Rêꜥ, Osiris, and Horus are called the great gods, the king as a rule had to be content with the appellation, the good god (Life in Ancient Egypt, p. 58).

there might exist some kind of connection between various countries in the field of astral religion at an early prehistoric period, this "universal" religion in Egypt took expression in a strange and unique way. This trend of religion cannot, in our opinion, be explained without penetrating thoroughly into the speculative philosophy that governed the ruling class who through their administrative rules, in turn, dominated the society. In the whole system that governed Egypt there lies a hidden mystery that has not yet been uncovered.

Soldiers

War-helmets. The headdress of soldiers, in the various cultures discussed, present a rather meager contribution. We have been able to obtain only sporadic information.

Yigael Yadin in his work The Art of Warfare in Biblical Lands[1] presents a reconstruction of a relief at Medinet Habu (near Thebes) from the 20th Dynasty, i.e., in the time of Ramses III (1192-1160 B.C.). In the sea battle the Sea-peoples' vessels depicted with "high stern and prow terminating in duck-heads"[2] can easily be distinguished from the Egyptian crescent-shaped vessels with prow depicting a lion's head. The Sea-peoples' vessels are manned by Philistines with feather-topped helmets and by allied Sea-peoples wearing horn-topped helmets (fig. 86).

And so it can be assumed that during various periods the

---

[1] (New York: McGraw-Hill Book Company, Inc., 1963), 2:340-41.
[2] Ibid., 2:340.

armies favored special shapes and ornaments for their helmets.[1] Yadin, for instance, also shows how in an earlier period (in the time of Ramses II) a certain group of the Sea-peoples (the Sherdens) wore disk-and-horn-topped helmets[2]--perhaps indicating their loyalty as mercenaries in the Egyptian army to Egypt and to Hathor.

Fig. 86. Soldiers of the allied Sea peoples wearing horn-topped helmets, or feather-topped helmets. Reconstructed relief from Medinet Habu (from the 20th century).

Herodotus, in describing the vast army of Xerxes marching towards the Hellespont, gives a vivid picture of the army comprising 1,700,000 entities (or perhaps only infantry?). In any case, the vast mixed host gathered from various nations must have presented pageantry on a grand scale and perhaps without equivalence in antiquity.

Exactly what kind of helmet and helmet-decoration Herodotus had in mind, when he wrote, "καὶ κέρεα προσῆν βοὸς χάλκεα, ἐπῆσαν

---

[1] Ibid., 1:15. [2] Ibid., 2:248.

δὲ καὶ λόφου"[1] (and horns of oxen wrought in bronze thereon, and crests withal) cannot be determined. It is, however, apparent that he tries to paint the pageantry in vivid colors. In addition to the horns of oxen wrought in bronze, the helmets were also decorated with λόφοι (crests).

About the headdress of the Assyrians Herodotus says, "περὶ μὲν τῇσι κεφαλῇσι εἶχον χάλκεά τε κράνεα,"[2] and the Sacae (Scythians) again wore κυρβασίας (tall caps).[3]

There is, however, more than half a millennium between the Sea-peoples on the one hand and the pageantry of Xerxes and Herodotus on the other hand. Herodotus was born ca. 484 B.C., just before the Persian king Xerxes started to prepare his great European invasion and he probably wrote his work sometimes between 464-477 B.C. At this time as well as in the Persian time, the "Hörnerkrone" had already become unimportant. An exception is the Egyptian crown of the genius on a gate-relief in Pasargade.[4] We must therefore assume that the army with the soldiers wearing horn-decorated helmets, consisted of people with an old tradition that was no longer current in the time of Xerxes and still more archaic in the time of Herodotus.

As a general remark it can be said that there is a paucity

---

[1] Herodotus, Book VII, 76 (p. 386) in the Loeb Classics.

[2] Herodotus, Book VII, 63 (pp. 378-79) in the Loeb Classics.

[3] According to Liddell & Scott, A Greek-English Lexicon (Oxford: At the Clarendon Press, 1940), 1:1012; the κυρβασία (ἡ) was a Persian bonnet or hat "with a peaked crown, probably much like the tiara;" A. D. Godley translates κυρβασίας "tall caps" (Herodotus, Book VII, 64 (p. 379).

[4] Boehmer, "Hörnerkrone," p. 434.

of material giving adequate descriptions of horn-motifs in military contexts. In the remote antiquity of the Sumerians, at the dawn of civilization, the horns were precisely the symbol of divinity, and no ordinary human being was supposed to apply this insigne for himself. Gadd even assumes that later traditions following Narâm-Sin, who unrestrainedly attributed to himself the blasphemous title "the god of Agade," possibly attached to him some of the stories of downfall in his later years as evidences of punishment by the offended gods.[1]

The war-helmet from the early Assyrian time (Kassite period) is depicted as a modification of the Sumerian helmet (figs. 87 and 88). The helmet in the neo-Assyrian period was a crest-helmet (figs. 89 and 90) which deviated completely from the horn-decorated helmet of Narâm-Sin (fig. 5 above) and from the helmets of the Sea-people depicted at Medinet Habu (fig. 86 above).

Kudurru/i-stones

Before the proper <u>Kudurru/i</u> in the time of the Kassite dynasty made their appearance, other monuments, or even doorsockets and threshholds of temples, served as boundary-stones.[2] Apart from the text inscribed, all kinds of symbols stand out in relief, especially on the <u>kudurri:</u> animals and monsters with horns, shrines

---

[1] "The Dynasty of Agade and the Gutian Invasion," <u>CAH</u>³, vol. 1, pt. 2, p. 441.

[2] So, for instance, in William J. Hinke's description of various types of boundary stones in <u>A New Boundary Stone of Nebuchadrezzar I from Nippur</u> (Philadelphia: University of Pennsylvania, 1907), p. 4.

with tiara, the crescent, stars, maces with various tops, vulture head, etc.[1]

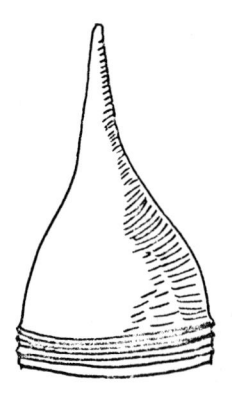

Fig. 87. Bronze helmet found at Zenjirli--probably from the early Assyrian period.

Fig. 88. Bronze helmet found at Zenjirli--probably from the early Assyrian period.

It is remarkable, however, that nowhere is the horn presented as an independent symbol. The horns occur always as part of a headdress (horned cap or tiara--on kudurri this crown is placed on a shrine or on a "divine" being, or on an animal, either natural or mythological). The subdued dragon, which often occurs in mythological representations, is often pictured as having sharp horns on its head. In the same way the snake is often presented with horns. Animals like bulls, gazelles, etc., are, of course, represented with horns, in both natural and mythological contexts.

---

[1]For illustrations and "descriptions" see ibid., passim; Hinke has also provided a list of twelve symbols and their counterpart gods (ibid., p. 88).

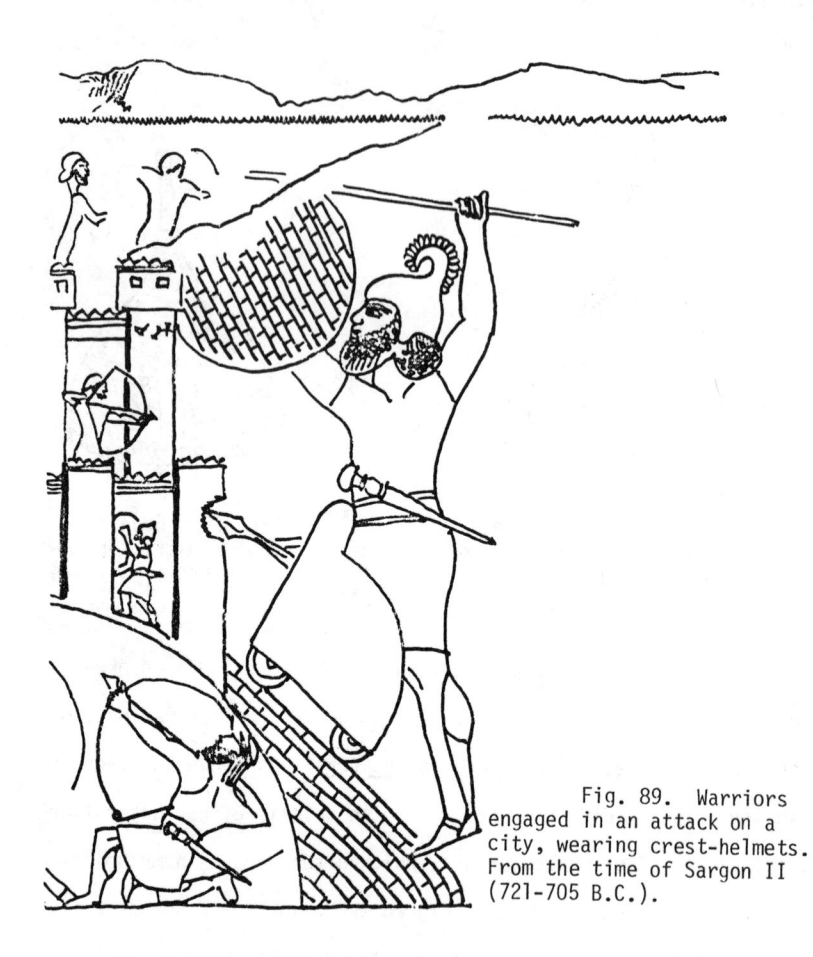

Fig. 89. Warriors engaged in an attack on a city, wearing crest-helmets. From the time of Sargon II (721-705 B.C.).

The horned cap (tiara) still occurs after the Kassite period in the Iron Age. The Zinjirli stela is here of particular interest. The Kilamu inscription (from the second half of the 9th century B.C.),[1] which is the earliest of the Zinjirli monuments, presents

---

[1]The date is given by Yigael Yadin in his article, "Symbols of Deities at Zinjirli, Carthage and Hazor," <u>Near Eastern Archaeology in the Twentieth Century</u> (Garden City, NY: Doubleday &

both names and symbols of gods. Three particular gods are mentioned in this inscription:[1] Baal-Ṣemed = of Gabbar, Baal-Ḥamman = of BHM, and Rakkab-El = Lord (Baal) of the House (i.e., Kilamu's dynasty).

Fig. 90. A single warrior depicted with a crest-helmet.

The monument, however, has four symbols carved at the head of the orthostat.[2] The very first symbol on this slab is "a peaked cap with pair of horns" (fig. 91).

Company, 1970), pp. 200-31 (see especially p. 200). J. Halévy seems to opt for a slightly earlier date though he does not pinpoint it; "Eine phönizische Inschrift aus Zendschirli," Ephemeris für semitische Epigraphik, ed. Mark Lidzbarski (Giessen: Alfred Töpelmann, 1909-15), 3:222.

[1] Yadin, "Symbols of Deities," p. 200.

[2] The difficulty of interpretation has been observed by Yadin, who refers to several of his predecessors' attempts as having led up "a blind alley" (ibid., p. 202).

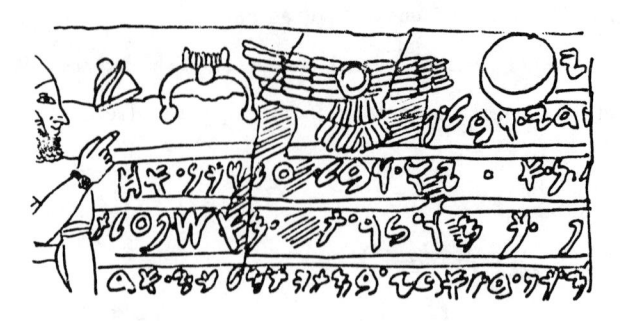

Fig. 91. A peaked cap with a pair of horns is depicted in the row of symbols. From the Kilamu orthostat.

Yadin suggests that the central symbol, the winged sun-disk, is ascribed to El himself, the supreme god "in the Mesopotamian, Canaanite and Hittite pantheon."[1] Yadin further suggests that the second element, "Rakkab," was symbolized by the yoke (Rakkab-El being the god of Kilamu and his dynasty).[2] His explanation would thus agree with Hinke's interpretation of two or three figures constituting one symbol.[3]

This interpretation receives confirmation from the seal-impression of King Bar-Rakkab, son of Panamu, of whom, no doubt, the principal god was Rakkab-El.[4] On the seal both symbols appear: the yoke and the winged disk.

The name Baal-Ṣemed, unlike Baal-Ḥamman, is mentioned in no

---

[1] The second symbol: Bow-shaped object (the extremities pointing downward and terminating in a knob). The third symbol: the winged sun-disk, and the last one, the crescent with a full-moon disk (p. 201).

[2] Ibid., p. 202.   [3] Hinke, A New Boundary Stone, p. 77.

[4] Yadin, "Symbols of Deities," p. 203.

other inscription, and therefore the identification of Baal-Hamman would give the clue to the remaining symbol. From the Phoenician-Punic cultural realm in North Africa, Yadin obtains the evidence of the crescent with disk as being the symbol of Baal-Ḥamman.[1] Thus "the first symbol (the horned cap) must necessarily be identified with Baal-Ṣemed."[2]

Furthermore, unlike Herbert Donner (and Wolfgang Röllig),[3] Yadin also identifies the janiform head in a similar way as the horned cap, i.e., with Baal-Ṣemed. Yadin says,

> The horned cap [cf. figs. 92 and 93] is the general symbol of the various "Baals," including Baal-Ṣemed; whereas the janiform head with the horned cap [fig. 94] is the symbol peculiar to Baal-Ṣemed.[4]

The janiform head on a mace would perhaps indicate duality, a weapon of double nature.

Fig. 92. The horned cap on the Bar-Rakkab orthostat at Zinjirli.

This condensed investigation, though far from exhaustive, indicates that the horns were used on war-helmets in various

---

[1] Ibid., pp. 204, 205.   [2] Ibid., p. 205.

[3] KAI 2:234-36 (#217).

[4] Yadin, "Symbols of Deities," p. 210.

cultures--probably as a means of protection and a symbol of strength. The need of strength was nowhere so prompted as in precarious situations and the horns apparently symbolized the god that was believed to be strong enough to give the fighting soldier complete victory.

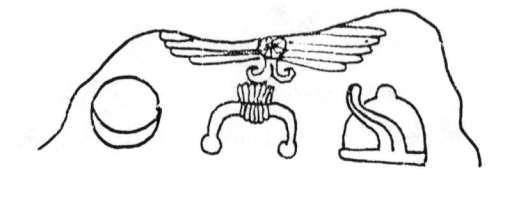

Fig. 93. The horned cap symbol depicted on the Ördek-burnu monument.

Fig. 94. The horned cap and the janiform head was the particular symbol of Baal-Şemed. (The "horned" cap alone depicted Baal in general.)

Ziggurats and Altars

　　Mesopotamia. Paul Lohmann discusses in detail many altars from the Sumerian and the Akkadian time period and gives the iconographic source material for the altars discussed.[1] He expresses

---

　　[1] Paul Lohmann, "Der Altar im altbabylonischen Kulturkreise"

himself strongly on the question concerning the horns of sacrificial animals (in the Babylonian-Assyrian cult), saying that the horns were in no way attached to the altar.[1] The vast corpus of Babylonian-Assyrian literature does not refer to such a concept, nor are they depicted in that way.[2] If ever horns are mentioned, Lohman perceives them being mentioned in connection with a sacred building, i.e., temple horns which are "erected like the horns of a bull" and which may be considered "Eck-Akroterien."[3]

The reason we are briefly discussing the ziggurats is because they were "originally comparable to the bamoth or high places which the Old Testament mentions as scenes of worship."[4] Beek points out that "the name 'ziggurat' which was given to these towers is connected with a verb meaning 'to rise up high'."[5] The particular feature of the ziggurat is--as is well known--the many stories and stairways. If these are missing it may be debatable whether the simple terraces (especially the more archaic) were ziggurats at all.[6] The names[7] of these ziggurats indicate that they

---

and "Der assyrische Altar" in Kurt Galling, Der Altar in den Kulturen des alten Orients (Berlin: Karl Curtius, 1925).

[1] Lohmann, "Der assyrische Altar," p. 47.

[2] Ibid. [3] Ibid.

[4] Beek, Atlas of Mesopotamia, p. 143.

[5] Ibid., p. 142. [6] Ibid.

[7] The ziggurat at Borsippa was called E-ur-me-im-imin-an-ki or "the house of the seven leaders of heaven and earth" or, as Beek points out, a reference to the sun, the moon, and the five planets which determine the lot of macrocosm and microcosm alike." The ziggurat in Nippur, Larsa, and Sippar, "people spoke of E-dur-an-ki,

were regarded as connecting links between the earth below and the heaven above.

In the relatively recent Pan-Babylonia era (ca. 1900-1920) it was emphasized that the biblical burnt-offering-altar--handed down from exilic times--"reflects Mesopotamian cosmic ideas."[1] William F. Albright, who points out this Pan-Babylonian heritage within the Hebrew Bible, seems to regret that Johannes de Groot and Kurt Galling have missed this point.[2]

Referring to the summit of the altar (Ezek 43:13-17) which was crowned by four "horns" at its four corners, Albright remarks that most scholars have incorrectly explained the ʾarʾel or harʾel to mean "hearth of God."[3] He is also almost certain that the ʾrʾl (vocalization uncertain) is derived from the Akkadian arallu or arallû and has a dual sense of "underworld" and "mountain of the

---

"the house of the link between heaven and earth." The ziggurat at Babylon (the most famous one) was called E-temen-an-ki, "the house of the foundation of heaven and earth." The ziggurat built in Ashur was called E-kur-ru-ki-shar-ra, "the house of the mountain of the universe" (ibid., p. 143).

[1] William F. Albright, ARI (Baltimore: Johns Hopkins University Press, 1942), p. 150.

[2] Ibid.; cf. Johannes de Groot, Die Altare des salomonischen Tempelhofes (Stuttgart: W. Kohlhammer, 1924) and Kurt Galling, "Altar," in BRL, 2d. ed. (Tübingen: J. C. B. Mohr [Paul Siebeck], 1977) and Galling ["Ein Beitrag"] in Hezekiel Handbuch zum Alten Testament, 3d. by Alfred Bertholet (Tübingen: J. C. B. Mohr [Paul Siebeck], 1936), 13:152-55.

[3] Albright, ARI, p. 151. Galling discusses the arallu in Babylonian temples and אריאל [a terminus technicus] in the Hebrew temple as referring to the uppermost parts of the altar where the fire was lighted (Bertholet, Hezekiel, p. 153), and only in BRL does he discuss the horns of the altar (p. 19). It seems apparent that neither of the scholars accepted the Pan-Babylonian "cosmic ideas."

gods," i.e., "the cosmic mountain in which the gods were born and reared."[1] Albright also sees in the expression "bosom of the earth" an exact equivalence to the <u>irat erṣiti</u> or <u>irat kigalli</u> "bosom of the earth, bosom of the underworld"[2]--phrases used in the inscriptions of Nebuchadnezzar when Etemenanki, the temple-tower of Marduk in Babylonia, was built.[3]

It is only within this Mesopotamian background that Albright sees the description of Ezekiel (cf. fig. 95) as intelligible, for the Mesopotamian temple-towers and their summits, the <u>ziggurats</u>, were also adorned with four "horns." This is known "both from inscriptions and monumental representations."[4]

Theodor Dombart discusses the <u>ziggurat</u> presentation on the relief from Nineveh, and comparing it with the depiction of the Nebo-tower on a <u>kudurru</u>,[5] refers to the inscriptions on the

---

[1] Ibid. (In contrast to the summit ʾrʾl the lowest stage of the altar was set on a foundation-platform called 'bosom of the earth' (ḥeq ha-ʾareṣ) [ibid., p. 150].

[2] Ibid., p. 152.

[3] W. Andrae, <u>Mittleilungen der deutschen Orient-Gesellschaft</u> no. 71 (1932), pp. 1 ff. as cited by Albright, ibid., p. 218, n. 90.

[4] Albright, <u>ARI</u>, p. 152. Albright refers to the Rassam Cylinder of Sardanapalus, vi:29, and the <u>ṣît shamshi</u> of <u>Shilkhak-in-Shushinak</u>, king of Elam in the 12th century B.C. (Hugues Vincent, <u>Canaan d'après l'exploration récente</u> [Paris: J. Gabalda, 1907], p. 144) which exhibits two stage-altars or temple-towers (?) each with four broken-off "horns" at the four corners of the top stage (ibid., p. 218, n. 91).

[5] This <u>kudurru</u> is preserved in the British Museum (Br. Mus. 90850) and in spite of its crude drawings it has helped in reconstructing the Susa-<u>ziggurat</u> presented on the Nineveh relief (Theodor Dombart, "Die Zikkurat-Darstellung aus Ninive," <u>AfO</u> 3 (1926):175-81 passim).

so-called Rassam cylinder[1] which reads:

> Die zikkurat von Susa, welche mit Steinverkleidung von Lapislazuli ausgeführt war, zerstörte ich; ihre Hörner, ein Fabrikat von heller Bronze, brach ich ab.[2]

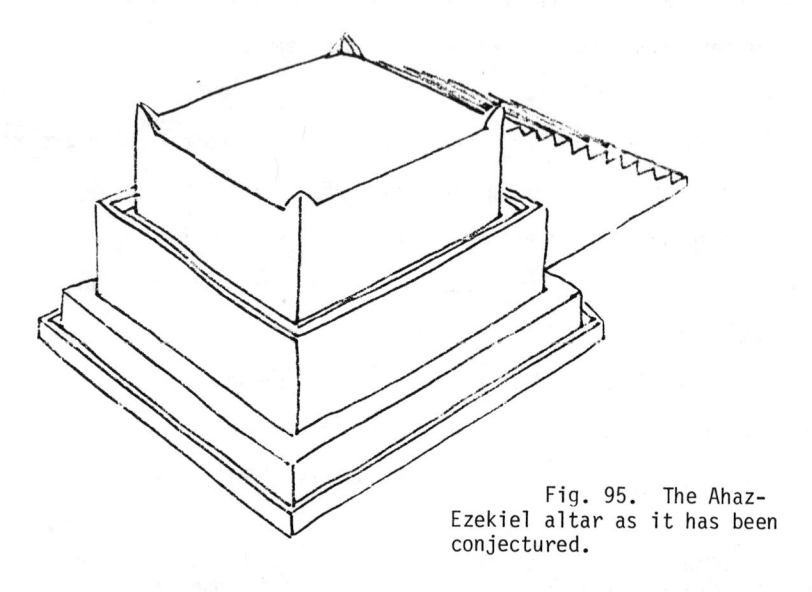

Fig. 95. The Ahaz-Ezekiel altar as it has been conjectured.

The word karne e meš "horns" is used in the transliterated text and, as the context shows, must grammatically be understood as referring to the horns (?) of the ziggurats. Maximilian Streck, however, suggested that karnê may refer to the projecting corners of the tower with the meaning of "pinnacles."[3]

---

[1] The Rassam-cylinder col. VI, 27-29 as cited by Theodor Dambart, ibid.

[2] The Susa ziggurat was finally destroyed by Aššurbanipal; Dombart, "Die Zikkurat-Darstellung aus Ninive," p. 180; cf. Bruno Meissner, Babylonien und Assyrien (Heidelberg: Carl Winter, 1920-25), 1:312.

[3] Cf. the German translation of the Aššurbanipal text (k. 7673) col. VI, 27-29 (by Maximilian Streck) in Vorderasiatische

Dombart refers to several reconstructions[1] of the relief from Nineveh on which two bull-heads with horns can be seen on the very top terrace (fig. 96). Dombart follows closely the reconstruction of Smith, and Dombart himself has retraced the bull-heads on the top terrace with the horns clearly depicted.

Fig. 96. Two bull-heads with horns are supposed to have decorated the last stage of this depicted (reconstructed) temple-tower. From an Assyian bas relief.

All these reconstructions are based on subjective

Bibliothek 7:52-53, n. 4. (We see in this interpretation a tendency of imposture of a later cultural design on a much earlier one, i.e., from Hebrew to Elamite culture.)

[1] George Rawlinson's reconstruction in 1862 (not complete), George Smith's in 1876 (complete), Charles Chipiez' in 1884 (incorrectly reduced); Dombart, "Die Zikkurat-Darstellung aus Ninive," p. 177 (fig. 1); Rawlinson's reconstruction of the uppermost terrace shows the whole crest depicted with "horns" (pinnacles?)--no bull-heads can be seen. See Dombart, "Das Zikkuratrelief aus Kujundschik," ZA 38 (1929), p. 43, fig. 3.

interpretation, for the annals of Aššurbanipal do not speak of bull-heads on the top of the ziggurat. The only information that the Rassam Cylinder gives is that the terrace of the ziggurat was covered with lapis-lazuli and the horns were of shining copper.[1] The record of Aššurbanipal, however, does not exclude the possibility of bull-heads (with horns) on the terrace of the ziggurat, but this is an argumentum ex silentio.

It is considered that the ziggurats are of a relatively late date; in fact, they compound a characteristic feature of the later Babylonian architecture.[2] The ziggurat of Susa, however, may have been of a much earlier date, though it was not destroyed until the time of Aššurbanipal (668-626 B.C.).

Though it is an argument from silence, it is very possible that these ziggurats were decorated with horns (in the form of bull's horns) for it would otherwise be hard to understand all the hymnal references to horns. The old Sumerian hymns, for instance, repeatedly mention "the horns of E-kur"--a fact alluded to already in chapter II. From very early times these horns may have been cast in bronze, or at least covered with bronze or gold, for they are always described as "shining."[3]

Isidore Scheftelowitz "has pointed out that the horns of gods, shrines and altars do invariably signify the horns of an

---

[1] Cf. p. 274.

[2] Frankfort, "The Last Pre-Dynastic Period in Babylonia" (revised and re-arranged by Lewis Davies) in CAH[3], vol. 1, pt. 2, p. 84.

[3] See, for instance, in chapter II, p. 48.

animal, a bull, a ram etc., and that they are symbols of strength and force. . . ."[1]

This investigation of horns on altars in Mesopotamian context brings a negative result. It is evident that only the ziggurats were decorated with horns. This evidence comes primarily from literature: foremostly from Old Sumerian hymns. The classic example of Aššurbanipal breaking off the "horns" refers, not to an altar, but to a ziggurat.

The Ezekiel temple and the $^{j}r^{j}l$ have been explained, not on any account that attests any horns on altars, but rather on the basis of the horns of the ziggurat. The altar and the ziggurat were, however, two different constructions and served different purposes; the assumption by Albright that only within this Mesopotamian background, the description of Ezekiel becomes intelligible, is in our opinion overemphasized (if not wrong).

Syria. Syria as used here is the geographical designation applied in a broad sense with a West-Semitic connotation.[2] Kurt Galling categorizes the altars of Syria from an archaeological point of view into: stone altars (block altars and hewed altars),

---

[1] Quoted by Herman T. Obbink, "The Horns of the Altar in the Semitic World, especially in Jahwism," JBL 56 (1937):45. Stanley A. Cook in his book, The Religion of Ancient Palestine (London: Oxford University Press, 1930), p. 29, says, "Horns were a symbol of strength, superhuman power, and deity. As emblems of divine rank they are found on gods, genii, and great kings; as many as four pairs of horns indicating special pre-eminence."

[2] We feel free to apply Kurt Galling's definition of the West-Semitic cultural area to include geographically the region between Egypt and the Euphrates (Der Altar in den Kulten des alten Orients [Berlin: Carl Curtius, 1925], p. 54).

rock-level altars with basin holes (Napflöchern), dressed-block altars (the rock cube altar and the step altar [Würfel-altar and Stufenaltar] portable altars, horned altars, and maṣṣēbôt altars).[1] Only the horned altar is of interest here.

Galling has recorded not less than fifty-three horned altars in the Syro-Phoenician area[2] and has classified the horned altar into three subtypes: Types I and II, built in a quadratic form, and Type III, in a round shaft form ("pillar" form).[3] These various types may be most adequately studied through iconography. Galling has depicted all three types of the horned altar (fig. 97a-t).[4] LaMoine Ferdinand DeVries has worked on incense altars (limiting himself to the period of the judges) and assumes that the symbol of horns--in addition to the traditional meaning of power and strength--points out the dwelling place of the deity[5]--thus revitalizing the ancient animate view. An incense altar from Megiddo which dates from the 8th century B.C. is also depicted with horns (fig. 98). In the early years of this century another horned altar was found in Gezer at the excavation under the direction of R. A. Stewart Macalister.[6] This limestone altar, which dates from ca.

---

[1] Galling, Der Altar, pp. 59-68.

[2] Ibid., p. 65.   [3] Ibid.

[4] All of them represent the square form except for 97s which represents the "pillar" form.

[5] LaMoine Ferdinand DeVries, Incense Altars from the Period of the Judges and Their Significance, Review in Dissertation Abstracts International 36 (1975/76), p. 355-A.

[6] The Excavation of Gezer, (London: John Murray, 1912), 2:424.

279

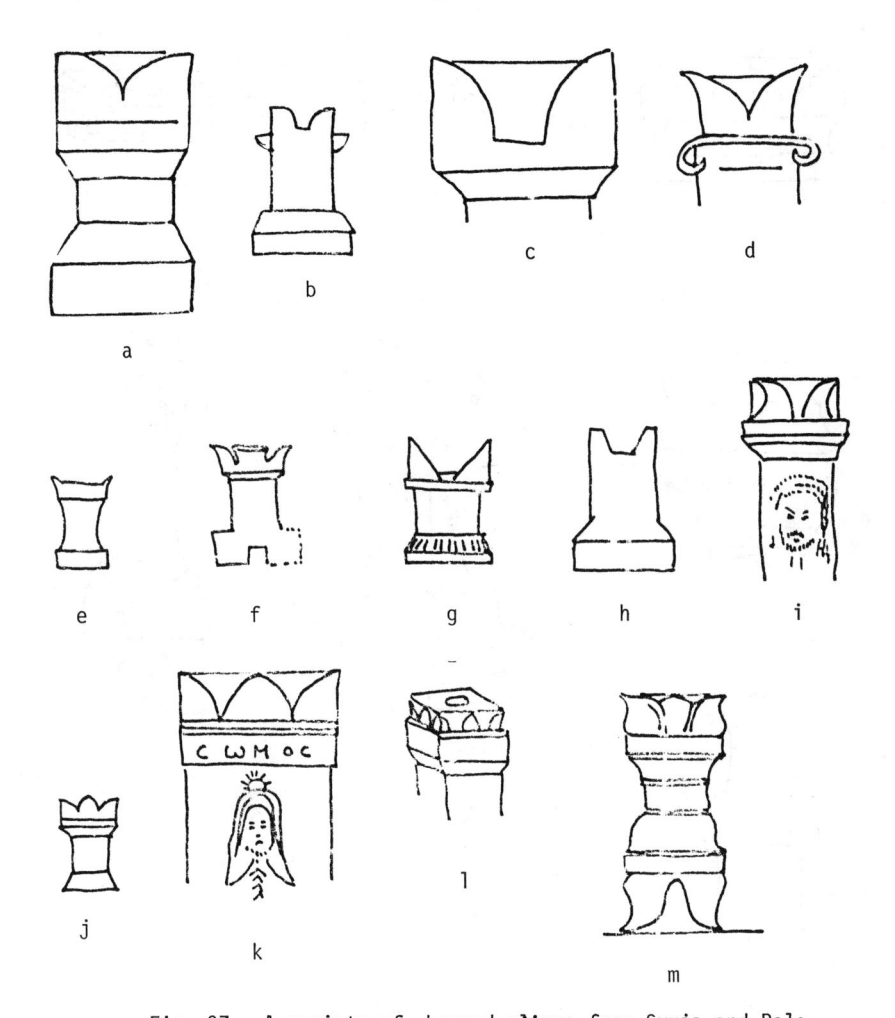

Fig. 97. A variety of horned altars from Syria and Palestine.
Figs. 97a-97i. The square-cornered altars (Type I).
Figs. 97j-97q. The pinnacle-like edge on the square altar (Type II)

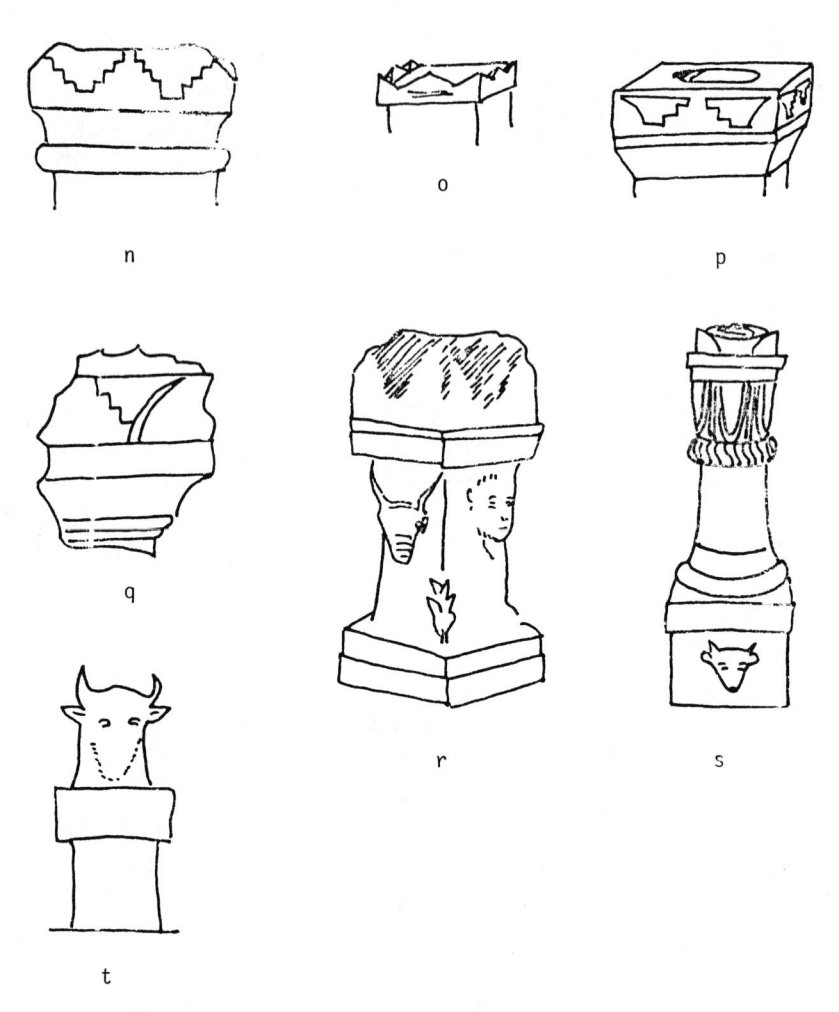

Fig. 97 continued. A variety of "horned altars from Syria and Palestine.
    Figs. 97r-97s. A bull-head depicted in relief on these two altars, of which -r- represents the square type, whereas -s- represents the round pillar type of altar (Type III).
Fig. 97t. A bull-head depicted on a square altar.

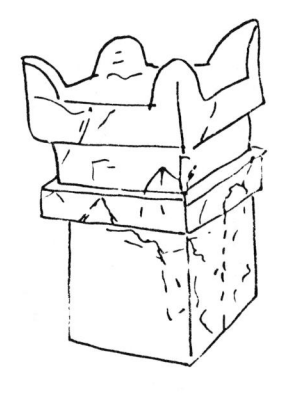

Fig. 98. Horned incense altar from Megiddo.

600 B.C.[1] shows as the most interesting detail "the prolongation upwards of the angles into four knobs," doubtless the "horns" of the altar (fig. 99).

A horned altar was rather recently discovered (1973) at Beer-sheba.[2] Yohanan Aharoni, describing this altar of well-smoothed ashlar masonry, says that three of the four corners were presented intact; "this altar unlike the Arad altar was not preserved in situ but had been re-used as part of a repaired wall."[3] A unique feature of the Beer-sheba altar is the twisted snake engraved on the corner stone . . ." (fig. 100).[4] The snake was an ancient symbol of fertility widely dispersed throughout the Near

---

[1] Ibid.; (Hugo Gressmann assumes the altar to originate from a much earlier time [AOB 2, p. 123]).

[2] Yohann Aharoni, "The Horned Altar of Beer-sheba," BA 37 (1974):2.

[3] Ibid., pp. 2-3; cf. Y. Yadin, "Beer-sheba: The High Place Destroyed by King Josiah," BASOR 222 (1976):5-17.

[4] The faint tracing of a snake on the lower right stone may be seen on this picture.

East.[1] This altar at Beer-sheba is particularly of interest inasmuch as only one burnt-offering altar has been found earlier in Palestine, namely, the one in the Arad temple.[2]

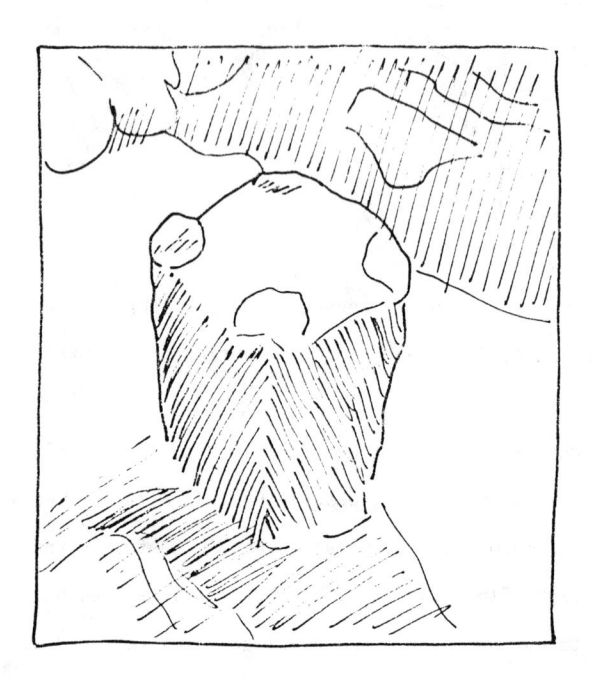

Fig. 99. A limestone altar with its knobs or horns broken off. From Gezer ca. 600 B.C.

Galling also speaks briefly about some of the altars which wear a bull's head as relief-decoration. According to Galling this

---

[1] Aharoni, "The Horned Altar of Beer-sheba," p. 4.

[2] Aharoni, "Arad: Its Inscriptions and Temple," BA 31 (1968):2-35; for the stone-built altar and the crescent-shaped bamah see especially pp. 19-21 and fig. 14. The altar had been covered with plaster but the corners were not preserved. Aharoni thinks that the altar may originally have had horns (Aharoni, "The Horned Altar of Beer-sheba," p. 2).

kind of altar has been found along the coast of Syria and Palestine: from Byblos and Gerasa in the north over Kades-Naphtali and Samaria and Hauran down to Petra.[1]

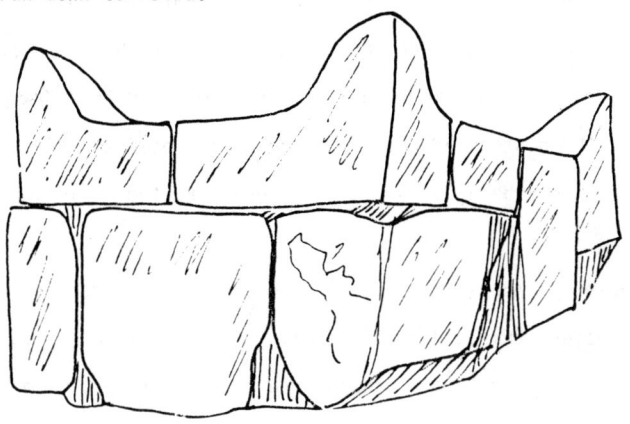

Fig. 100. A horned altar from Beer-sheba with a snake engraved on one of its corner stones. From the 8th century B.C.

Concerning these altars Stanley A. Cook says that they are "widely distributed."[2] He also points out that "sometimes a bull's head is placed on the altar."[3] This bull has been interpreted as the local god Ṣalm (identified with Saturn--Baal Ḳarnaim).[4]

Cook particularly points out that the Syro-Hittite or

___

[1] Galling, Der Altar, p. 66.

[2] The Religion of Ancient Palestine in the Light of Archaeology (London: Oxford University House, 1930), p. 28.

[3] Ibid., (cf. figs. 98r, 98s, and 98t [above]).

[4] Cook, The Religion of Ancient Palestine in the Light of Archaeology, p. 28, n. 5; so also Malten, "Der Stier in Kult und mythischem Bild," p. 119.

North-Syrian seals with their bull-motifs,[1] which might represent bull altars, may be illustrations of the Molech cult of Palestine.[2]

The bull altars, however, represent another tradition, as the horns on these altars are not on the altar but on the bull. The horns on the altar have been interpreted by Galling from the point of view of the history of religions and with Hugo Gressmann's assumption of the horns being originally maṣṣēbôt, as the valid interpretation.[3]

However, there are several scholars who have reacted strongly against this old traditional, but certainly wrongly, established view. With the passing years and with more archaeological light enlightening the topic, other opinions have been presented. During the last decade Carl F. Graesser, in his dissertation, "Studies in Maṣṣēbôt,"[4] has clearly refuted Gressmann's claim [above] advanced by Galling.

Anatolia. Once more we find that the literary evidence, this time from Anatolia, is too meager to provide a sure basis for discussion. Steven Diamant and Jeremy Rutter have tried to establish a relationship between the Minoan "horns of consecration" and the Anatolian hybrid evidences.[5] Since the time of Sir Arthur Evans'

---

[1] Cook, The Religion of Ancient Palestine, p. 29.

[2] Ibid.; cf. Ward, The Seal Cylinders of Western Asia, pp. 307-10.

[3] Galling, Der Altar, pp. 58-59, 67; Galling, "Altar II in Israel," RGG³, p. 254; cf. also Gressman, AOB (1926), 2:133.

[4] Ph.D. dissertation, Harvard University, 1969.

[5] "Horned Objects in Anatolia and the Near East and Possible

discoveries of the "horns of consecration" at Knossos, at the beginning of this century, several interpretations of the objects have been presented, but none of the theories are as yet unitedly accepted.[1] And yet, on the other hand, Diamant and Rutter have suggested that excavations since about the middle of this century strongly hint to the fact that "the Minoan 'horns' have their origin in Anatolia and that the object's function, originally at least, was a pot-support in a hearth."[2] The "altars" or "shrines" may have been tied up with the usage of hearth and thus utilized domestically.[3] Anyhow, though some of those horns might have had partly a cultic function,[4] certainly many a hybrid form had, as it seems, only a purely domestic usage.[5]

Ward has pointed out another tradition of "horns" in connection with altars, and he also uses iconographic evidences as support for his theory.[6] The bull-altars indicated by Ward[7] are typically

---

Connections with the Minoan 'Horns of Consecration'." Anatolian Studies 19 (1969):147-77.

[1] Ibid., p. 1.

[2] Ibid., p. 147; as a curiosity to be mentioned is the fact that we came to the same conclusion by studying the works of Arthur Evans, The Palace of Minos, 4 vols. (London: Macmillan and Co., 1921-33).

[3] Ibid., pp. 167, 170; (most of the "horned" objects in Anatolia originate from the Early Bronze period).

[4] Ibid., p. 3.   [5] Ibid., p. 176.

[6] Seal Cylinders of Western Asia, pp. 307-13.

[7] Cf. p. 100 and nos. 436 and 437 (ibid.).

Cappadocian.[1] Edith Porada gives an objective description of these seals,[2] while Ward has attempted an interpretation which, if correct, may indicate that the worship of the bull claimed human victimes[3]--a tradition which might have been suppressed and concealed at a later time. Too little is known to draw any definitive conclusions.

South-Arabia. The altar (i.e. incense altar) in South-Arabia has a clear connection with the moon-cult. There seems to be no other alternative to interpret the many new-moon motifs that appear on the altars. Adolf Grohmann has presented several Sabaean altars with the new-moon sickle as a prominent part of the relief decoration (figs. 101-107). It is amazing how dominant the motif is. Nikolaus Rhodokanakis also refers to these altars[4] but he also refers to the Stelenaltar.[5] It is in connection with these Stelenaltäre that Rhodokanakis mentions the Steinbocke (capra ibex) which especially among the Sabaeans was holy to the god ʲAlmaḳah, and which appear so often on the inscription stones.[6]

It seems that the moon-god in Arabia not only had several

---

[1] A comparison between Ward, The Seal Cylinders of Western Asia (seals nos. 965-75) and Edith Porada, The Collection of the Pierpont Morgan Library in CANES, pls. 127 and 128 (nos. 852-61) makes it clear that seals from the same tradition are being discussed.

[2] Porada, The Collection of the Pierpont Morgan Library in CANES, vol. 1 (Text), pp. 108-109.

[3] Ward, The Seal Cylinders of Western Asia, pp. 309-10.

[4] Rhodokanakis mentions both incense altars and fire-altars (Kohlenpfanne) "Altsabäische Texte, II," WZKM 39 (1932):183-84.

[5] Ibid., p. 192.   [6] Ibid.

names[1] but also several symbolic animals: the bull, the antelope (gazelle), and the wild-goat seem to be represented the most. The excavation at Maḥram Bilqis clearly shows that ʾAlmaqah, the moon-god of the Sabaeans, was the national god at this central sanctuary.[2]

Fig. 101. Sabaean altar with the crescent-motif.

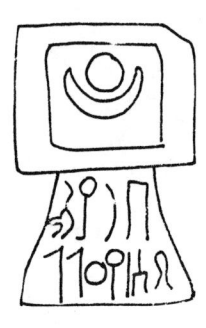

Fig. 102. Sabaean altar with the crescent-motif.

---

[1] For some of these names see Nielsen, "Der sabäische Gott Ilmukah," MVAG 14 (1910):51, 57, 58, 62.

[2] Gese, Die Religionen, pp. 261-62.

Fig. 103. Sabaean inscription from Domâr with the crescent-motif.

Fig. 104. Sabaean relief from Domâr with the crescent-motif.

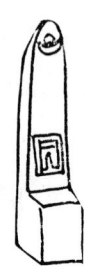

Fig. 105. Sabaean altar from Mârib with the crescent-motif.

Fig. 106. Sabaean altar with the crescent-motif.

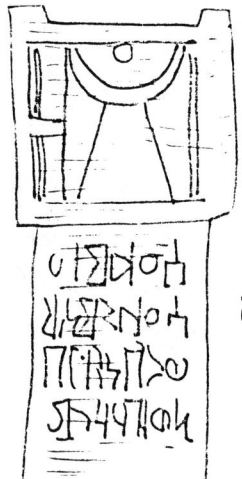

Fig. 107. Sabaean altar from Ğir'ân with the crescent-motif.

From the numerous votive inscriptions at the entrance of the temple it becomes obvious that the temples were dedicated to ʲAlmaqah, the "Herr von ʲAwwām."[1] At later times he is given the title, "ʲAlmaqah ṯahwān und Stier des Baʿlslandes, Herren von ʲAwwām und Ḥarun."[2] It seems, however, that while the bull was the holy animal of ʲAlmaqah at ʲAwwām, the antelope was the particular holy animal at Ḥarun.[3] The wild goat (capra ibex) is also a holy animal

---

[1] Ibid., p. 261. [2] Ibid.

[3] It is not known where the temple of Ḥarūn is situated, but according to Gese, it probably was not very far from ʲAwwam (ibid., p. 262). As a curiosity it may be mentioned that still today in Hadrami is a stele capital preserved that originates from Husn al-ʿUrr, an antique temple ruin. On one side antelopes in various positions can still be seen, and in between a human figure with a staff in his hand and antelope-horns or a whole antelope mask on his head. This figure, says Gese, reminds one of the dancer which still today in Hadrami exercises antelope (gazelle) dances while wearing antelope horns on his head--probably a rest from an old cult-exercise, which might be presented on the capital. In the same way antelope horns attached to a building may probably still serve as apotropaion; cf. Scheftelowitz, "Das Hörnermotiv in den Religion," p. 473.

of the moon-god ʲAlmaqah,¹ though in Qarnāwu this animal decorates the door-post of the temple dedicated to ʲAttar dū Qabd (fig. 62 above). A Sabaean altar shows clearly the extremely bent horn (fig. 108) on a wild-goat. Grohmann has also included in his collection a small mussel table which he labels in the caption "Muscheltäfelchen aus Tellô" and ascribes to the pre-Sargonic period, i.e., before 3800 B.C.² The horns on this well-designed, ancient little art work present, interestingly enough, the horns as a complete replica of the sickle of the moon (fig. 109).

Fig. 108. Sabaean altar with the horns of a symbolic animal strongly emphasized.

It is worth noticing that whether the horns were those of the bull or those of the wild goat the association with the new-moon is clearly brought out.³ In some way it may be said that these

---

¹Gese, Die Religionen, p. 32.

²Grohmann, Göttersymbole und Symboltiere auf Südarabischen Denkmälern, p. 57.

³The horns of the antelope (gazelle) which are rather

animal horns are synonyms of the horns of the new-moon. Nielsen, referring to a cylinder-seal, says, "folgender Siegelcylinder lehrt, dass die Hörner auf dem Stierköpfe Neumondshörner sind."[1] Nielsen also refers to a South Arabian altar fragment on which a bull head is depicted, thus confirming his theory.[2] Furthermore, Nielsen points out that it has to be noted that the new-moon (the sickle) is designated with the word qarni "horns."[3] Nielsen has expressed his conclusion concerning this phenomenon: "Man bekommt den Eindruck, als ob diese ornamentalen Stierköpfe mit den 'gewaltigen Hörnern' sich aus dem einfachen Neumondsymbol entwickelt haben."[4]

Fig. 109. A small mussel table from Tello, ca. 3800 B.C.

As far as we have been able to investigate from available

---

straight seem to depict only the attacking phase of the god. The god Nergal which has his equal in Rešep and Tešub is depicted with these kinds of horns; cf. William J. Fulco, S.J., The Canaanite God Rešep, American Oriental Series 8 (New Haven, CT: American Oriental Society, 1971), p. 67; cf. also the drawn picture of Tešub fig. 35, Knut Tallqvist, Akkadische Götterepitheta, pp. 389-95, and Roberts, The Earliest Semitic Pantheon, p. 48.

[1] Nielsen, Die altarabische Mondreligion, p. 111.

[2] This fragment is, according to Nielsen, preserved in Vienna (ibid.).

[3] Ibid., p. 110. [4] Ibid.

sources, horns on the altar do not appear in the South Arabic culture. On the contrary, the new-moon sickle, as a symbol of a bull's or a goat's horns, is abundantly represented, indicating that in South Arabia the two were synonymous.

Summary and Evaluation

A careful investigation of ancient Near Eastern non-literary, literary, and iconographic material has revealed the astonishing fact that the horn-motif is present from the very beginning of history--even from prehistoric time. Especially the Sumerian literary sources--temple hymns with praise to the various gods--reveal this fact. The culture of the Two Rivers presents the various gods of their pantheons with horned headdresses that vary slightly from culture to culture and from one era to another.

Rainer M. Boehmer has graphically shown these variations (differences and similarities) as he traces the evidences of the horned crown (Hörnerkrone) in art from as far back as the Mesilim-time (early Dynasty II). Boehmer's assumption: "Neben einfachen Hörnern, die hier erstmalig menschenartige Wesen aus dem Kopf wachsen und sie so als Götter erkenntlich machen, . .", however, sounds rather strange and appears conjectural.[1] The examples from periods that follow (fig. 110) are verified over and over again through various iconographic material which so abundantly illustrates the cultural, the religious, and partly the political world of the ancient Near East.

---

[1] Boehmer, "Hörnerkrone," in RLA 4:432.

293

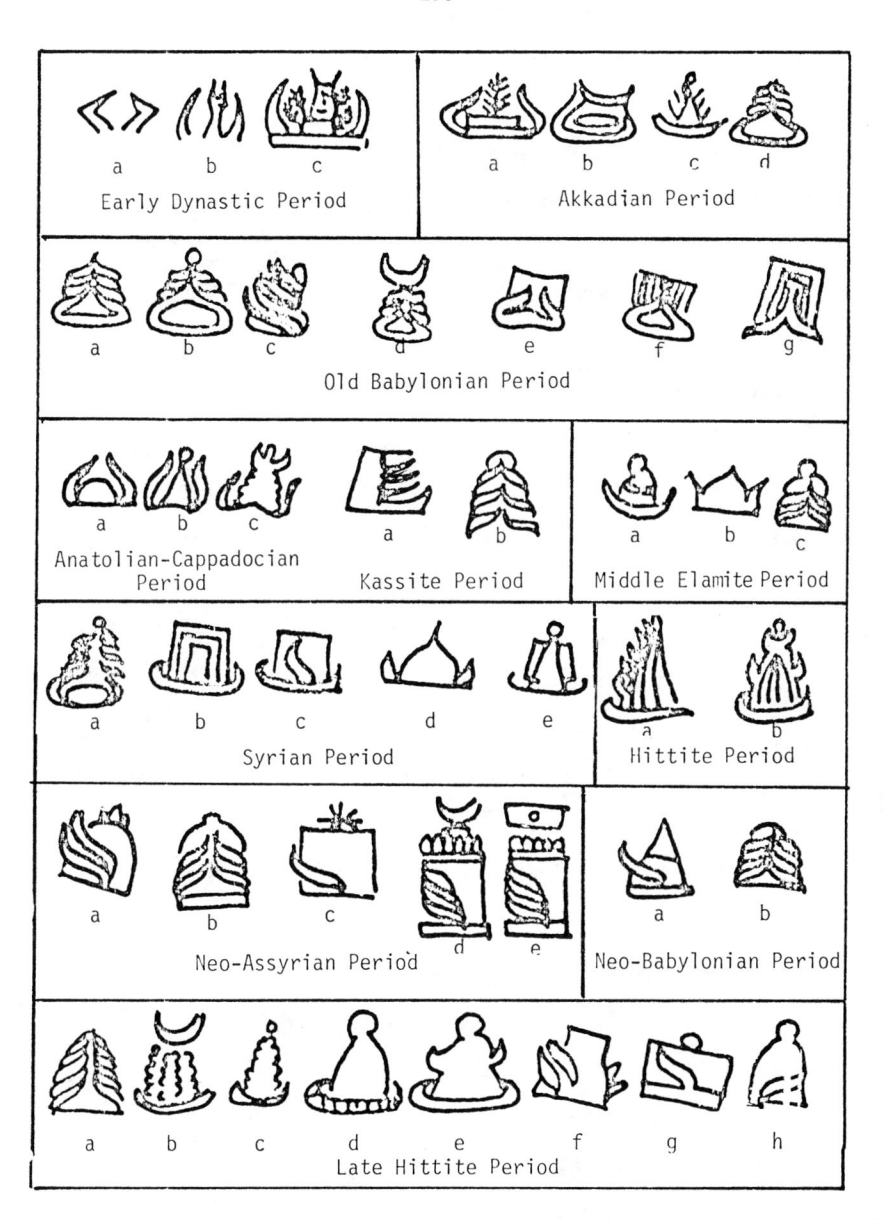

Fig. 110. Crowns of various dynasties in ancient times.

The Sumerian period by necessity has awakened the keenest interest in our mind due to the fact that (if not mistaken) it is somewhere in the old Sumerian context that the basic cultural pattern for most of the ancient civilizations of this area was set.

This study so far has further shown that the "horned" headdresses on the gods are attested in all of the Near Eastern cultures that we have so far investigated. South-Arabia with a pictureless religion (of anthropomorphic forms) is an exception, and Egypt is partly so with a zoomorphic god-concept.

The horn-motif is clearly brought out whether the headdress or cap is depicted with one pair or several pairs of horns. The caps with multiple pairs of horns may, as it seems, indicate a higher rank of a god. The headdress of the moon-god Sin (Nannar), for instance, is depicted with four pairs of horns--probably to indicate not only the high rank but also the universality of the cult. The "four corners of the earth" became almost an idiomatic expression in the Assyrian annals of the kings as they boasted about the extent of their kingdom. The locution "the four corners of the earth" was a fit expression to describe a universal empire. Hildegard Lewy points out that "the idea of a universal empire . . . had its origin in the cult of the moon. . . ."[1] When this universal coup d'état took place cannot with exactness be determined, but from the investigations made by Lewy we presume a pre-Sargonic era--perhaps even as far back as the Early Dynastic II period.

The iconographic depiction on a seal of an attacking bull

---

[1] Hildegard Lewy, "Assyria c. 2600-1816 B.C.," p. 736.

with a "horned" god as his target may reflect this ancient tradition
(perhaps alluding to a confrontation between the true universal God
and an usurper). The seal, however (see fig. 8) is enshrouded in a
mysterious mythological context. Even the legend of the Zû-bird
seems to be tied up with the story of a fallen deity and a bull as
his offspring. In spite of only a tentative reconstruction of
events in regard to the pregnant mythological material, we are on
firmer ground when we say that many nations and people accepted the
universal cult of the moon-god. Especially South-Arabia was under
the influence of this cult, and the same penetrates to neighboring
countries, and remains of the cult have been shown in Anatolia,
Egypt, and elsewhere.

Furthermore, the early evidences of the horn-motif makes it
necessary to place the origin of the motif back in prehistoric time.

All the astral gods were important, but it is evident that
the moon-god was considered the personalized "father" of the astral
family and the procreator of all things. As such he was the symbol
of power and fertility. The sun was considered the "mother" and
Venus the "son" of that same family.

Furthermore, the concept of melammu as a pre-Sumerian concept, suggests that the meaning of melammu goes beyond the suggested
meaning of "mask," which we know to have been in use in the Late
Bronze period and even in the Early Bronze period. Oppenheim says
that the melammu, an "awe-inspiring luminosity," was of divine origin.

> This radiance is shared by everything endowed with divine
> power . . . it may be noted that this supernatural glamour

could be granted by the principal divinities and withdrawn again.[1]

Moreover, Oppenheim says,

> A king could be endowed with godlike appearance and power. Yet he could lose his divine support . . . šarru me-lam-ma-šu i-m-is-s[i-šu] . . . his melammu will turn from him.[2]

The primeval story of Adam and Eve, which, according to some scholars, is substantiated by the Sündenfall-Zylinder seal, also suggests a state of original bliss or a "Golden Age" when

> . . . there was no snake, there was no scorpion,
> There was no hyena, there was no lion,
> There was no wild (?) dog, nor wolf,
> There was no fear, no terror. . . .[3]

We presume this time to have coincided with the time when "luminous light" covered the couple in the Garden of Eden. The primeval story in Genesis indicates, in likeness with ancient mythological sources, that at a critical point something was lost--probably something relating to divine nature. This is the conclusion we draw on the basis of the fact that the primeval account states that after the "fall" man and woman became naked (Gen 3:7)--apparently deprived of a nimbus or aureole that covered them. The two strands of traditions (the king losing his melammu, and the couple in the Garden losing their luminous light garment) have a point of contact in the luminous light that surrounded them. To be wrapped in a garment of flames of fire seems in mythological context to refer to a

---

[1] A. Leo Oppenheim, "Akkadian pul(u)ḫ(t)u and melammu, JAOS 63 (1943):31. Oppenheim considers melammû to be a pre-Sumerian term; Ancient Mesopotamia, p. 98.

[2] Oppenheimer, JAOS 63 (1943):31.

[3] Samuel N. Kramer, "Man's Golden Age: A Sumerian Parallel to Genesis 11:1," JAOS 63 (1943):193.

supernatural, luminous garment which was considered as divine, invincible, victorious, etc. The supernatural headgear was analogous to the garment in its sparkling light.

In the religious sphere the tragic event of something lost, and with nakedness as a result, is clearly stated in the primeval narrative, but no clarifying details can be worked out. The beams of light have in many instances been likened to "horns" of the sun. The early Sumerian concept of si with the meaning of "light" and "glory" seems to support that this is one meaning of the term "horn."

As for the headdress of the priests, the present evidences are too vague and too sporadic to be able to present a set pattern. We have seen that cultic masks were used in many cultures when the priest was engaged in magic performances. It is therefore expedient to exercise the eloquence of silence at the present, hoping for new and more concrete evidences in a near future.

In regard to the motif of horns on the altars, the evidences so far have been of the negative kind. The ancient ziggurats may have had bull-horns, although no clear iconographic evidence can be presented; only ancient hymnology refers clearly to horns (of bronze and gold), not on altars but on temple-towers. A few examples of bull-heads with horns attached to the side or on top of the altar can be shown, but these cannot be considered horns of the altar in view of the exact meaning of the expression.

The most abundant evidences of horns on altars can be found on the hewn stone altars found in Syria and especially in Palestine. None of these, however, are normative for horned altars as presented in the Bible. On the contrary, they are all of the "prohibited" type of altars.

Although we agree with Obbink in many aspects, especially when he points out the misinterpretation of Gressmann and Galling in regard to the horns which they consider to originally have been maṣṣēbôt, we do challenge the following statement by Obbink:

> The horns of the altar are emblems of the god, not only in Palestine, but also in Mesopotamia, Syria and the entire Near East. They are found on the top of the headdress of the gods, on the top of shrines and on altars. In all instances, I contend, they have precisely the same meaning.[1]

Our investigation indicates clearly that nowhere else than in Syria and Palestine do we find altars with horns. The temples, shrines, or ziggurats did not serve the same purpose and cannot be called altars.

This leads thus to the simple conclusion already expressed by George Rawlinson, that "horns were not usual adjuncts of altars."[2] Furthermore, Rawlinson says that they indeed "seem to have been peculiar to those of the Israelites. . . ."[3] This statement then

---

[1] "The Horns of the Altar in the Semitic World, especially in Jahwism," p. 43; cf. Hugo Gressmann, "Altar," RGG, ed. Hermann Gunkel (Tübingen: J. C. B. Mohr [Paul Siebeck], 1909), 1:373; and Kurt Galling, "Altar: II, in Israel," RGG3, ed. Kurt Galling (Tübingen: J. C. B. Mohr [Paul Siebeck], 1957), 1:253.

[2] George Rawlinson, Genesis & Exodus, The Pulpit Commentary, (Grand Rapids: Wm. B. Eerdmans, 1977), 1:269 (on Exod 27:2). On the basis of the present investigation of the horns on the altar, the assertion by Julius Fuerst that "other nations too [i.e., apart from Israel] had altars with horn[s]" has to be considered invalid. A Hebrew and Chaldee Lexicon to the Old Testament, trans. Samuel Davidson (Leipzig: Bernhard Tauchnitz, 1867), p. 1259.

[3] Ibid.

impels us to investigate the horn-motif in the Hebrew Bible, which by many scholars has been categorized as a manuscript _sui generis_ in the corpus of ancient Near Eastern literature.

CHAPTER IV

HORN-MOTIFS IN BIBLICAL SOURCES

In this particular chapter we will confine ourselves to an investigation of the usage of the horn-motif as it occurs in the context of the texts of the Hebrew Bible. This special motif occurs in most of the books of the Hebrew Bible and is thus present in the three divisions of the Hebrew Scriptures--the Torah, the Nebi'im, and the Kethubim.

We will categorize the material into respective groups that seem to convey the same specific meaning or analogous meaning in given contexts. In other words, our investigation begins with the literal meaning of the word "horn." The subsections of this part of our study deal with horns on animals, horns as vessels, horns as musical instruments, and horns of the altars. The second section discusses the literal-extended meaning of the horn-motif in cultic, political, and sociological contexts. The third section discusses the purely extended meaning in the context of hymnic, prophetic, and apocalyptic texts. A fourth section comprises the much-debated passage in Exod 34:29, 30, 35 referring to the "horns" of Moses. A short summary and evaluation of the horn-motif in the Hebrew Bible rounds off this part of the study.

As has been mentioned, this method of categorizing the material is far from being the only and exclusive one. It is rather hoped that this division will be helpful in providing an overview of the unique material in the Hebrew Scriptures which presents the horn-motifs in various contexts and various genres.

The main tools in this chapter are: for text--Biblia Hebraica Stuttgartensia;[1] for translated text--The Revised Standard Version (RSV);[2] for comparison--the Septuaginta.[3] Unless otherwise indicated, these three Bibles are used throughout. When other versions are consulted (especially in problem areas) this is clearly indicated. Such versions are those of Aquila, Symmachus, and Theodotion's versions in the Origenes' Syriac Hexapla,[4] the Septuaginta Göttingensis,[5] the Cambridge,[6] and the Swete editions,[7] the Biblia Sacra Vulgata,[8] and other editions and versions.

The linguistic-philological investigation with its Hebrew charts (appendices B and C) has already been referred to in

---

[1] Edited by K. Elliger and W. Rudolph (Stuttgart: Deutsche Bibelstiftung, 1967-77).

[2] 2d rev. ed. (New York: American Bible Society, 1952).

[3] 3rd ed. Ed. Alfred Rahlfs (Stuttgart: Privileg: Württ. Bibelanstalt, 1949).

[4] Ed. Fridericus Field (Hildesheim: Georg Olm, 1964).

[5] Septuaginta Vetus Testamentum Graecum. Auctoritate Academiae Scientiarum Göttingensis editum (Göttingen: Vandenhoeck & Ruprecht, 1974).

[6] The Old Testament in Greek, eds. Alan England Brooke and Norman McLean (Cambridge: University Press, 1906).

[7] The Old Testament in Greek, ed. Henry Barclay Swete (Cambridge: University Press, 1930 [reprint ed.]).

[8] Biblia Sacra iuxta Vulgatam versionem, ed. Robertus Weber (Stuttgart: Württembergische Bibelanstalt, 1969).

chapter II. The charts include every occurrence of the term "horn" in the Hebrew Bible and form the basis of this chapter.

Literal Meanings of Horns

On the Animal

A very basic meaning of the word horn confronts us in the very first book of the Torah. The story in which the "horns" is attested is found in the Abraham cycle telling how God commanded Abraham to sacrifice his son and that he was prevented by a voice at the moment of sacrifice. After this dramatic experience Abraham lifted up his eyes and looked "and behold, behind him was a ram caught in a thicket by his horns" (והנה־איל אחז בסבך בקרניו) (Gen 22:13)[1] The text presents qrn in a dual construct form; it is used to refer to the literal "horns" of the ram.[2]

Julian Morgenstern, in his comment upon this text, says,

---

[1] The animal איל means ram (male sheep) and is so used in this case. William L. Holladay, A Concise Hebrew and Aramaic Lexicon of the Old Testament (Grand Rapids: Wm. B. Eerdmans, 1971), p. 12. (In other contexts the same word may have a metaphorical meaning.)

[2] The problem in this text is not the usage of horn but the translation of אחר (ʾaḥar). Mitchell Dahood criticizes the emendation to אחד (ʾeḥād) suggested by David Noel Freedman, "Genesis" in: The New American Bible (Paterson, NJ: St. Anthony Guild Press, 1970) as cited by Dahood, "Northwest Semitic Notes on Genesis," Bib 55 (1974):76. Dahood says, "F [Freedman] misses the humor in 22, 13, wahinnēh ʾayil ʾaḥar, 'and behold there was another ram' (the first being the sacrificial Isaac!) and, following some versions and many commentators, he emends ʾaḥar, 'another,' to banal ʾebād, 'one.' To express 'one' no number is needed, especially in a masterful account with no superfluous words. Hence the emendation ʾeḥad must be rejected. . . ." (Dahood, ibid., p. 79). The RSV translation of אחר "behind him" is no doubt an attempt to present a "neutral" translation even before the problem was acute. The problem of ʾaḥar does not, however, impinge upon the literal translation of "horns"-- a translation which has not been questioned.

And on Rosh Hashonah, our sacred New Year's Day, the
blast of the Shofar reminds us of Abraham's sacrifice, and
of God's promise to him. According to tradition, the Shofar
was first made from the horn of the very ram which Abraham
sacrificed in place of Isaac. Therefore the Shofar on New
Year's Day proclaims, unto Israel and all mankind, peace and
forgiveness, and a new period of life and faith in God.[1]

There is, of course, no support in the Scriptures for this Jewish tradition. It may, however, provide a hint that the horn of an animal (ram) was used as a "musical" instrument from an early time in the history of Israel.

As a Musical Instrument

The horn of an animal was used in Mesopotamia at a very early time to proclaim solemn events or joyful messages.[2] In the Hebrew Bible the horn of a ram, used as a "musical" instrument, is first attested in Josh 6:5. The first phrase of the text reads: ויהי במשך בקרן היובל‏--"When they make a long blast with the ram's horn, . . ." John J. Lias proposes that though the word "horn of jubilee" is used, it does not necessarily mean that of a ram's horn.[3] Holladay, however, gives the meaning of יובל (יבל) as ram, i.e., קרן יובל "ram's horn" (as wind instrument).[4]

---

[1] The Book of Genesis, A Jewish Interpretation (New York: Schocken Books, 1965).

[2] Cf. ch. II, p. 55, n. 5, and p. 56, n. 1 (above).

[3] Joshua: Exposition and Homiletics, The Pulpit Commentary (reprint ed., Grand Rapids: Wm. B. Eerdmans Publishing Company, 1977), p. 98.

[4] A Concise Hebrew and Aramaic Lexicon, p. 130. See also Francis Brown, Samuel R. Driver, and Charles A. Briggs, A Hebrew and English Lexicon of the Old Testament (reprint ed., Oxford: Clarendon Press, 1976), p. 385; Julius Fuerst, A Hebrew and Chaldee Lexicon to the Old Testament (Leipzig: Bernhard Tauchnitz, 1867), p. 532 et al. In Exod 19:13, referred to by Lias, the qrn is not used at all but

Lia's observation, however, may create some confusion, especially when we observe that שופר is used in all other instances in the same chapter (i.e., Josh 6:4, 5, 8, 13). Furthermore, it seems that šôpar is connected with the verb תקע (תקע ב) "blow" (a wind instrument, e.g., šôfār) while ḳeren hay-yôḇēl is connected with the verb משך. A trumpet (שופר) could, however, be made of either a ram's horn, if with יובל is meant a ram (Josh 6:5), or of metal (bronze or silver), but in the latter case the shape was straight (not bent) and the Hebrew חצצרה was used.[1]

Martin Noth gives a clarifying general statement of the horn [Widderhorn] when he comments on Josh 6:4.

> שופר, im Hebräischen nur noch in der Bedeutung von "Horn" als Blasinstrument, dann ganz allgemein von "Blasinstrument" bekannt, ist ursprünglich aus dem Sumerischen stammende, und als Lehnwort in das Akkadische übergegangene Bezeichnung einer später ausgestorbenen Wildschafspezies. . . .[2]

As for the word יובל Noth says, "יובל, ursprünglich vielleicht 'Leiter (der Herde),' Widder (so noch [v.] 5) dann ebenfalls = Widderhorn. . . ."[3] Hans W. Hertzberg points out that חצצרה is a straight wind instrument made of metal, while שופר the phrase is יהיה במשך היבל, "When the trumpet sounds a long blast." Cf. v. 16: וקל שפר חזק מאד, "and a very loud trumpet blast." The conclusion that קרן היובל would refer to an instrument made of horn lies very near. It is not, however, thereby indicated that the instruments at Sinai and in the wilderness were made of bronze or something else, but this may be the case as the qrn is not used. It is an argument from silence, however.

[1] Cf. Holladay, A Concise Hebrew and Aramaic Lexicon, p. 114.

[2] Das Buch Joshua, HAT (Tübingen: J. C. B. Mohr [Paul Siebeck], 1938), p. 16.

[3] Ibid.

Posaune is "ein gekrümmtes Instrument."[1] This makes it clear that the חצצרה and the שופר originally were different instruments. Hertzberg, however, treats the שופר היובל and the קרן היובל Josh 6:4, 5) as synonyms.[2]

John Gray, commenting upon the šôperôt hay-yôbelîm, says,

> The ram's horn was either yôbel or ḵeren hay-yôḇēl. Šôpār is here equated with the ram's horn. The word may be connected with the Assyrian šapparu, a kind of wild goat or sheep; cf. Arabic sawāfir, wild sheep.[3]

Though J. Albert Soggin does not deal particularly with the meaning of the šôpār or the qeren, his translation confirms the concept that the trumpets were made of rams' horns.[4]

We may, therefore, with certainty conclude that the wind instrument referred to in Josh 6:5 (קרן היובל) was made of animal horn rather than of metal (חצצרה).

John Bright also takes this view, for he says,

> Seven priests escorting the ark and blowing seven trumpets of rams' horns are to lead the march. Such horns, which were not metal "trumpets," were used in battle and also to signalize state occasions.[5]

A play on words (with an added meaning) is not, however, excluded, although that is not directly implied.[6] The many different

---

[1] Die Bücher Joshua, Richter, Ruth (Göttingen: Vandenhoeck & Ruprecht, 1953), p. 39.

[2] Ibid., p. 40.

[3] Joshua, Judges and Ruth, NCB (London: Thomas Nelson Ltd., 1967), p. 75.

[4] Joshua (Philadelphia: The Westminster Press, 1973), p. 79.

[5] "The Book of Joshua," IB (New York: Abingdon Press, 1953), p. 578.

[6] Holladay, A Concise Hebrew and Aramaic Lexicon, p. 395,

translations of this passage[1] seem to indicate some confusion in regard to the exact meaning of קרן היובל.

The only other text in which קרן is used with reference to a musical instrument is in Daniel, where it occurs four times. The morphological structure and the context is repetitive in all four cases (3:5, 7, 10, 15). The translation of קל קרנא "the sound of the horn" seems to convey the same usage of the instrument as in the days of Joshua, i.e., a signaling instrument (a trumpet).[2] The instrument seems to have retained its old name (from the root קרן) though at a later time (at the time of Daniel[?]) it was apparently made of metal. The many Greek versions using σάλπιγγος unanimously seem to support this hypothesis.

As a Vessel

The usage of "horn" as a vessel is sparingly referred to in the Old Testament. However, a few texts from the period of the early kings show that this usage is known in the Bible.

There are only three texts (1 Sam 16:1, 13 and 1 Kgs 1:39) that present this usage of קרן. The context of the two occurrences of קרן שמן in 1 Samuel refer to the anointing of David (i.e., ca. 1000 B.C.), and the instance in 1 Kings refers to the

---

points out that שנה היבל means "year of release," or "jubilee year, inaugurated by blowing the ram's horn" (Lev 25:23). With this in mind, Lias' view may be justified but not stressed.

[1] See chart on Josh 6:5 (appendix B).

[2] Carl F. Keil says that the "קרנא, horn, is the far-sounding tuba of the ancients, the קרן or שופר of the Hebr.;" Biblical Commentary on the Book of Daniel (Grand Rapids: Wm. B. Eerdmans, 1959), pp. 122-23.

anointing of David's son Solomon. In the first instances the prophet performed the anointing and in the last instance the priest. But in both cases the oil-horn (קֶרֶן שֶׁמֶן ; i.e., a vessel made of horn and containing oil)[1] was used. As the anointing of David took place at the command of Yahweh to Samuel, it is implied that the anointing was a confirmation of Yahweh's choice. The context also makes clear that both sacrificing and consecration were preparatory actions and the anointing revealed a charismatic infilling of Yahweh's power in David's life from that day on.

The reference in 1 Kgs 1:39 presents a similar connotation of holiness in connection with the oil contained in the horn, for it was preserved in the tent (הָאֹהֶל) "set up by David for the ark of the covenant upon Mount Zion (2 Sam 6:17)."[2] The preservation of the horn in the holy tent speaks affirmatively to the fact that the horn was used for holy purposes. There are no other texts in the Old Testament referring to the horn being used as a vessel--neither in secular nor in ritual context. On the basis of the usages recorded we may therefore conclude that it is known that the horn as a vessel for oil was used in ritualistic service and for holy purposes.[3]

___

[1] Idem, The Books of the Kings, Biblical Commentary of the Old Testament (Grand Rapids: Wm. B. Eerdmans Publishing Co., 1952), p. 23.

[2] Ibid., p. 24.

[3] There are very few commentators discussing the horn as a vessel for holy usage. The act of anointing, on the other hand, is more frequently discussed and from such discussions the sacred usage of the horn can be inferred. So, for instance, Martin Noth, 1. Könige, BKAT (Neukirchen-Vluyn: Neukirchener Verlag, 1968), p. 24. The painting depicting Samuel anointing David and pouring oil on his head from a horn, referred to by Noth (Carl H. Kraeling, The Excavations at

Whether the horn as a vessel was used in secular context cannot be proved from the Hebrew Bible. Such a usage is not, however, inconceivable.

On the Altar

There are four passages in Exodus and one in Ezekiel which are purely descriptive in regard to the altar. Exod 27:2 and 38:2 describe the altar of burnt offering and Exod 30:2, 3 and 37:25, 26 sketch the altar of incense. Though these altars were of different size,[1] they were constructed similarly in their external form. Both were square and were provided with horns; however, those in the first case were overlaid with bronze, and in the second case they were overlaid with gold. It is interesting, however, to notice that all four texts explicitly point out how the horns were to be made. In every instance it says that "its horns were of one piece with it [the altar]."[2] This repetition must not be overlooked.

Brevard S. Childs observes the fact that "there has been considerable debate as to the appearance, size, and function" of these horns.[3] Childs also refers to modern archaeological research

---

Dura-Europos, Final Report [New Haven: Yale University Press, 1956], vol. 8, pt. 1, p. 66), is of a late date (3d cent. A.D.) and therefore not relevant per se in this context.

[1] The altar of burnt offering was five cubits by five cubits and three cubits high; the altar of incense was much smaller--one cubit by one cubit and two cubits high. (For a discussion of the actual burning place of the sacrifice, see Niels H. Gadegaard, "On the So-Called Burnt Offering Altar in the Old Testament," PEQ 110 (1978):35-45.

[2] Exod 27:2; 38:2; 30:2, 3; 37:25, 26.

[3] The Book of Exodus (Philadelphia: The Westminster Press, 1974), p. 525.

as having shed light on the problem. He does not, however, refer to the works of Paul Lapp or Carl F. Graesser, but mentions the older works of Hugo Gressmann and Kurt Galling.[1] Both of these latter scholars considered the "horns" of the altar to be vestiges of maṣṣēbôt. Rudolf Smend, to whom Childs also refers, represents a more neutral position. It is obvious that he does not commit himself to the view of Gressmann and Galling.[2] Lapp and Graesser have, through their studies, made the horns-maṣṣēbôt-theory obsolete in light of more recent excavations and re-evaluation of the maṣṣēbôt.[3]

The emphasis of the horns being made in one piece with the altar, in our opinion, excludes any possibility of bull-horns (or other horns) being constructed separately and attached to the altar. Carl F. Keil and Franz Delitzsch have, however, suggested that

> These horns were projections at the corners of the altar, formed to imitate in all probability the horns of oxen, and in these the whole force of the altar was concentrated.[4]

This assumption has no support in any of the texts referred to, for none of them speaks of the horns as being made to imitate the horns of oxen or to imitate anything for that matter. What the texts

---

[1] Gressmann, Die Ausgrabungen in Palästina und das Alte Testament (Tübingen: Verlag von J. C. B. Mohr [Paul Siebeck], 1908), p. 28; Galling, "Altar," BRL (Tübingen: J. C. B. Mohr [Paul Siebeck], 1937), vol. 19.

[2] Smend, "Altar," BHH (Göttingen: Vandenhoeck & Ruprecht, 1962), 1:63-65.

[3] Paul Lapp, "The 1963 Excavation at Taʿannek," BASOR 173 (1964):4-44; Carl F. Graesser (Ph.D. dissertation, Harvard University, 1969).

[4] The Pentateuch, Biblical Commentary on the Old Testament (Grand Rapids: Wm. B. Eerdman, 1959), 2:186.

do bring out is that "the horns were of one piece with it [the altar]."[1]

The text in Ezek 43:15 is also descriptive, presenting the altar of burnt offering (Ezek 43:18) in a literal way but with other dimensions than those of the altars presented in Exod 27:2 and 38:2.[2]

Kurt Galling assumes that although the Assyrian relief of the step-tower[3] shows two bull's heads (containing four horns), the horns as an emblem on the step-towers is anomalous rather than normal.[4] On the other hand, Galling sees the equipment of horns on the altar as a well-known pre-exilic tradition.[5]

Keil's brief description reads: "Upon the basis of the חיק,[6] [consisting of earth] . . . there rose the true altar, with its hearth, and the horns at the four corners, noticed in ver. 15."[7]

---

[1]So, for instance, Charles R. Eerdman who says, "The 'horns' of the altar were projections at the four corners. They were of the same piece with the altar itself and not merely added ornaments." The Book of Exodus (New York: Fleming H. Revell Company, 1949), p. 188.

[2]On the question of the hearth from which the horns projected, see William I. Albright, "The Babylonian Temple-Tower and the Altar of Burnt-Offering," JBL 39 (1920):137-42; Walther Zimmerli, Ezechiel, BKAT 13/2 (Neukirchen-Vluyn: Neukirchener Verlag, 1969), pp. 1093-94.

[3]See fig. 97 in chapter III (above).

[4]Kurt Galling, [Ein Beitrag] in Ezechiel, HAT (Tübingen: J. C. B. Mohr [Paul Siebeck], 1955), p. 249.

[5]Cf. Galling, "Altar," BRL (Tübingen: J. C. B. Mohr [Paul Siebeck], 1937), p. 19; cf. idem, "Altar," BRL^2, p. 9.

[6]חיק (according to Holladay, A Concise Hebrew and Aramaic Lexicon, p. 103) is in this connection (Ezek 43:13) an architectural technical term meaning "channel around altar."

[7]Biblical Commentary on the Prophecies of Ezekiel,

The addition, in the RSV the rendering of the horns being "one cubit high," has no support in the major and most important Hebrew manuscripts.[1]

One passage from the Psalms (118:27) must be added to this category of Bible texts. The passage has been much discussed. It is not so much the קרנות "horns" that have caused the discussion, but the previous tricolon (אסרו־חג בעבתים).[2] All, however, agree

---

Biblical Commentary on the Old Testament (Grand Rapids: Wm. B. Eerdmans, 1952), 2:287. Cf. John W. Wevers, ed. Ezekiel 43:13-18) The Century Bible (London: Thomas Nelson and Sons, Ltd., 1969) discussing the altar hearth and the "horns" (pp. 313-14); Walther Eichrodt, Ezekiel: A Commentary (London: SCM Press, 1970), discussing especially the altar of Ahaz--evidently built after the pattern of a Babylonian ziggurat (pp. 557-58).

[1]See BHS (apparatus) on Ezek 43:15. The RSV also points out in the margin to Ezek 43:15 that the Hebrew lacks the phrase "one cubit high;" cf., however (for a contrary view), Jacob Milgrom, "Altar," EncJud (Jerusalem: Keter Publishing House, Ltd., 1971), 2:763.

[2]Bernhard Duhm at the threshold of the present century gave an interpretation according to the view of the prevailing theological school at that time, and many scholars have followed him in his interpretation; Die Psalmen, Kurzer Hand-Commentar zum Alten Testament (Tübingen: J. C. B. Mohr [Paul Siebeck], 1899), p. 264. The pagan concept of חג as a "religious dance" has been followed by several scholars since then. So, for instance, Hermann Gunkel, Die Psalmen, 5th ed (Göttingen: Vandenhoeck & Ruprecht, 1968), p. 510. See also Hans Schmidt, Die Psalmen, HAT (Tübingen, J. C. B. Mohr [Paul Siebeck], 1934), p. 212. Many later scholars cherish the same concept. So, for instance, John H. Eaton, Psalms (London: SCM Press, Ltd., 1967), p. 272. Dahood sees the text as referring to "thanksgiving rites celebrating the recent victory"; Psalms III, AB (Garden City, NY: Doubleday & Company, Inc., 1966), p. 160. Both Kraus and Anderson refer to ḥag by the term 'procession' which is more fitting in a Jewish context and the whole verse has in more recent years been interpreted in light of Mishnah referring to the Feast of the Tabernacles in which the worshippers in procession used to go round the altar; see Hans-Joachim Kraus, Psalmen BKAT 15/2, p. 808; Arnold A. Anderson, The Book of Psalms, 2:804. For a particularly detailed interpretation of Ps 118:27 reflecting the "history-of-religion" school view (from the last century), see Paul Haupt,

with the translation of the קרנות in the last tricolon עד־קרנות
המזבח "up to the horns of the altar."

A possible variant of אמרו in Ps 118:27 is found in Fragment E 1 of a Dead Sea Scroll.[1] The crucial tricola are: . . . אל
ויאר לנו אסורי חג בעבותים [lacunae]נות המזבח. The festal animals are bound with ropes [up to the hor]ns of the altar.[2]
J. J. Stewart Perowne says with regard to the עד־קרנות המזבח:
"The expression is apparently a pregnant one, and the sense is, 'Bind the victim with cords till it is sacrificed, and its blood sprinkled on the horns of the altar'."[3]

The real tradition behind the text is not known and a final interpretation is perhaps not to be pronounced as yet. It seems, however, quite sure that the attempted reconstruction [עד־קר]נות is certain and here as elsewhere it refers to the horns of the altar.

"Schmücket das Fest mit Maien," ZAW 35 (1915):102-9; and for a similar view from the first quarter of the present century, see W. O. E. Österley, "Heilige Tänze," in "Bemerkungen des Herausgebers," by Hugo Gressmann, ZAW 42 (1924):159-60.

[1]For the acquisition of this fragment by Yigael Yadin, see James A. Sanders, The Dead Sea Psalm Scroll (Ithaca, NY: Cornell University Press, 1967), pp. 155-56.

[2]Ibid., Postscriptum 161. The RSV gives the following translation: "Bind the festal procession with branches, up to the horns of the altar." Two mutually exclusive translations are here presented and neither of them can be fully explained in the light of what is known.

[3]The Book of Psalms (Grand Rapids: Zondervan Publishing House, 1976), 2:345; cf. John W. Rogerson and John W. McKay, Psalms (Cambridge, NY: University Press, 1977), p. 87. Even George Rawlinson, The Book of Psalms in The Pulpit Commentary, sees in this text a portrayal of "the procession representing the nation, advancing to dedicate the new temple, and join in the first public service of thanksgiving" (p. 101). His description of the bringing of the

Literal-Extended Meanings of Horns

Cultic Context

This section is actually a continuation of the previous section, for the passages (Exod 29:12; 30:10; Lev 4:7, 18, 25, 30, 34; 8:15; 9:9; 16:18; Jer 17:1; and Ezek 43:20) are all dealing with the same topic, namely, the horns of the altar; though not any more with only the literal meaning of the word, but rather with the literal-extended[1] meaning or signification of the word "horn" in its context.

Most of the passages deal with the horns on the altar of burnt-offering, but Exod 30:10 and Lev 4:7, 18 deal with the horns of the altar of incense. Already in the desert sanctuary we find two altars: the bronze altar, or burnt-offering altar, standing in the courtyard, which was intended for sacrifice. Jacob Milgrom points out that "the most important feature of the bronze altar was its keranot (qeranot) or 'horns'. . . ."[2] The other altar, the gold or incense altar, had its place within the tent or tabernacle.

---

burnt offering to the altar to be fastened to the very horns has received a slant of pagan "gaiety" over it.

[1] The term "literal-extended" is here used with the meaning "to broaden the application or action of the actual word conveying the primary (literal) meaning"; cf. the usages of "literal" and "extend" in Webster's Third New International Dictionary (pp. 1321 and 804 respectively).

[2] "Altar," EncJud, 2:762. Most of the scholars half a century ago sided with the "history-of-religion" school, seeing the horns of the burnt-offering altar as a development obtained from the neighboring cultures. So, for instance, Andrew Eberharter, "Das Horn im Kult des Alten Testament," ZKT 51 (1927):396; Emil Kautzsch, Biblische Theologie des Alten Testament (Tübingen: J. C. B. Mohr [Paul Siebeck], 1911), p. 26; Immanuel Benzinger, Hebräische Archäologie, 3d ed. (Leipzig: Eduard Pfeiffer, 1927), p. 320.

Milgrom says about this much smaller altar,

> Like the sacrificial altar, it contained horns, rings, and staves for carrying and was made of acacia wood. However, it differed from it by being plated with gold, not with bronze.[1]

In regard to the purpose of the incense altar, Milgrom says, "Incense was burned upon it twice daily at the time of the *tamid*, or 'daily,' offering. No other offering but the prescribed incense was tolerated."[2]

The historicity of the incense altar has been questioned among earlier scholars "on the assumption that the burning of incense was not introduced into Israel until the Second Temple. . . ."[3] Archaeology, since the turn of the century, has, as is well known, refuted this kind of criticism, for the many incense altars attested in Canaan give no reason to deny that there was an incense altar also in Solomon's temple. But the question of an incense altar ascribed to the tabernacle is thereby not solved. As Milgrom points out, scholars have been "nearly unanimous in declaring it [the description of the incense altar] an anachronistic insertion based upon the Temple."[4] The main reason is that in the main description of the "inner sancta" (Exod 26) there is no description of this altar. The portrayal in Exod 30:1-10 has therefore been considered as paraphernalia--an objection which Milgrom labels as "fallacious."[5]

---

[1] Ibid., p. 765.   [2] Ibid., p. 766.

[3] Ibid., so also J. Philip Hyatt, *Exodus*, NCB (London: Oliphants, 1971); for a contrary view cf. Georg Beer, *Exodus* HAT (Tübingen: J. C. B. Mohr [Paul Siebeck], 1939), pp. 136-38.

[4] Milgrom, "Altar," *EncJud*, 2:766.   [5] Ibid., p. 767.

Milgrom gives a very reasonable explanation as to why the explanation of this altar is not arranged where the scholars would logically have it to be, i.e., in chapter 26. Milgrom has this to say:

> Indeed, it can be shown that the description of the Tabernacle is divided in two parts: Exodus 26:1-27:19, the Tabernacle in blueprint; and Exodus 27:22ff. and 30:38, the Tabernacle in operation. Since the incense altar is described functionally (Ex. 37:7-8), it therefore belongs in the latter section.[1]

Milgrom brings out further evidences presenting this "other kind of logic." Though these cannot be included here, we refer to his concluding statement, "Therefore, there is no evidence, either textual or archaeological, to deny an incense altar to the Tabernacle."[2]

This clarification by Milgrom helps us to understand in which respect these passages differ from those texts in the previous section (i.e., of the literal meaning). These passages, as Milgrom notes, present the altar, not in blueprint, but in function. For this reason almost every text describes how part of the blood of the bull (the sacrifice) should be put upon the horns of the altar: Exod 29:12; Lev 4:7, 18, 25, 30, 34; 8:15; 9:9; and 16:18. The passage in Ezek 43:20 makes a slight emphasis pointing out that the number of horns were four (one at each corner) even if this is implied from the context already.

Exod 30:10 brings out more forcefully than any of the texts so far discussed, the importance of the horns and their central place in the ritual, for the text says: וכפר אהרן על־קרנתיו

---

[1] Ibid.   [2] Ibid.

אחת בשנה: "Aaron shall make atonement upon its [the altar's] horns once a year." The horns on the altar [here: the altar of incense] did not only obtain a specific place as the object(s)[1] for ritual performance in general, but these projecting parts functioned specifically and conspicuously in an act by the High Priest that figuratively proclaimed the very concept of atonement or cleansing which was the central truth in the Jewish salvation-history.[2] This passage does not refer to the ritual only (of putting blood on the horns), but it states explicitly that "Aaron shall make atonement on its [the altar's] horns" (Exod 30:10). It is on the horns that the symbol takes place. As has already been pointed out, this altar was not the altar of burnt-offering but the altar of incense (Exod 30:1). The atonement that took place was made, however, with the blood of the sin-offering (Exod 30:10).[3] The whole ceremony refers to the ritual performed on the day of atonement.[4]

The last passage in this category that we will deal with is Jer 17:1. The passage as it is recorded in Hebrew is complementary and explanatory vis-à-vis the text in Exod 30:10: חטאת יהודה כתורה . . . על־לוח לבם ולקרנות מזבחותיכם "The sin of

---

[1] Numerically there were four horns, but architecturally or constructively they have to be considered one piece with the altar.

[2] George Rawlinson, referring to Kalisch, says, "The horns were symbolical of power, of protection and help; and at the same time of glory and salvation;" Exodus; Exposition and Homiletics, The Pulpit Commentary (Grand Rapids: Wm. B. Eerdmans Publishing House, 1977), p. 269.

[3] For the prescriptions of ritual in regard to sin offering, see Lev 4.

[4] Cf. Lev 16 and 23.

Judah is written . . . on the tablet of their heart, and on the horns of their altars."[1] Due to the omission of the first few verses in the Septuagint, no control is provided from this source, but the reconstructed texts[2] do not deviate from the Hebrew in regard to the main thrust of the Hebrew record, "the sins of Judah being written or engraved . . . upon the horns of their altars."

The "engraving of the sins on the horns of the altar" as well as the "making of the atonement on the horns of the altar" are both phrases which are constructed in metaphorical terminology. The action performed in regard to the horns implies a deeper and wider meaning of the word than a solitary literal usage. The application of "horns" in the passages discussed (above) asserts as sine qua non a literal-extended usage.

Political Context

There are actually not more than two clear passages that can be categorized in a political context, namely, 1 Kgs 22:11 and 2 Chr 18:10 (and Deut 33:17). The passages are identical in content and almost identical in form. The minor differences occur in orthography: King Zedekiah's name being spelled צדקיה in 1 Kgs 22:11

---

[1] Cf. NIV, which agrees in the translation of RSV though some clarifying synonyms bring out the force of the text more clearly.

[2] For the reconstruction of the missing verses from the Septuaginta, see the apparatus in Septuaginta Vetus Testamentum Graecum: Ieremias Baruch Threni Epistula Ieremiae, ed. Joseph Ziegler. Auctoritate Societatis Litterarum Göttingensis (Göttingen: Vandenhoeck & Ruprecht, 1957), 15:233; cf. Origenis Hexapla, ed. Fridericus Field (Hildesheim: Georg Olms Verlagsbuchhandlung, 1964), 2:616; Biblia Sacra Iuxta Vulgatam Versionem, ed. Robertus Weber Osb (Stuttgart: Württembergische Bibelanstalt, 1969), 2:1189. (As we are not dealing with textual criticism in this dissertation we are not discussing the particular textual problems in regard to the text.)

and צדקיהו (with šûrek as the final vowel) in 2 Chr 18:10. In a similar way we find כלחם (from the root כלה) in 1 Kgs 22:11 and כלותם (with a full ḥôlem) in 2 Chr 18:10.

The controversy that took place between Israel and Syria and which is related in 1 Kings took place nearly one and a half centuries before the Syro-Ephraimitic War (734-733 B.C.).[1] Three peaceful years had marked the relationship between the two countries, when finally Ahab's claim on the ancient Ramoth Gilead[2] became the spark that caused the war that was fatal for Ahab. King Jehoshaphat of Judah who sided with Ahab, in this controversy, promised Ahab full support as an ally, but suggested an inquiry from among the prophets whether there was a "word from the Lord," probably to assure them success and protection (1 Kgs 1:5-10).[3] But before Micaiah, the son Imlah, told the truth, Zedekiah, the son of Chenaanah, gave his

---

[1] See Gerhard F. Hasel, The Remnant, Andrews University Monographs Studies in Religion, Vol. V (Berrien Springs, MI: Andrews University Press, 1974), p. 270.

[2] Ramoth Gilead was the governmental seat of one of Solomon's provinces (1 Kgs 4:13). This site has been "identified by Dalman with Tell el-Ḥusn, south-east of Irbid-Arbela, Palästinajahrbuch des Deutschen evangelischen Instituts Altertumswissenschaft des Heiligen Landes zu Jerusalem, 2d ed. (Berlin: E. S. Mittler, 1913), p. 64, as cited by James A. Montgomery, A Critical and Exegetical Commentary on the Books of Kings, ICC (Edinburgh: T. & T. Clark, 1951), p. 337; cf. Felix M. Abel, Géographie de la Palestine (Paris: J. Gabalda et Cie, 1938), 2:430; William F. Albright, "New Israelite and Pre-Israelite Sites: The Spring Trip of 1929," BASOR 35 (1929): 11; and Nelson Glueck, "Ramoth-Gilead," BASOR 92 (1943):12-14. Glueck sees Tell Rāmîth as identical with Ramoth-gilead, or even, perhaps, Mizpah Gal'ēd.

[3] James A. Montgomery points out the ancient custom of consulting "seers and diviners" to have been customary already in the time of ZKR of Hamath; "Some Gleanings from Pognon's ZKR Inscriptions," JBL 28 (1909):68-69; cf. idem, The Book of Kings, p. 337. For a biblical example see 1 Sam 23:1-5 (David inquiring from the Lord before he went to battle against the Philistines).

prophecy and acted symbolically, probably to impress the kings. The record tells us: ויעש לו צדקיה בן־כנענה קרני ברזל ויאמר כה־אמר יהוה באלה תנגח את־ארם עד־כלתם: "And Zedekiah the son of Chenaanah made for himself horns of iron, and said, 'Thus says the Lord, with these you shall push the Syrians until they are destroyed'" (1 Kgs 22:11). The passage in 2 Chr 18:10 agrees as to the content, as has already been shown. What kind of horns is not told; we know only that they were קרני ברזל "horns of iron," and the Septuagint and the Bibliothecae Syriacae support this reading.[1]

Joseph Hammond in his commentary on 1 Kgs 22:11 says "[Thenius understands that these were iron spikes held on the forehead. . . .]"[2]

Othmar Keel understands the לו in the context of 1 Kgs 22:11 not as reflexive (as it usually has been interpreted) but with the meaning "for him." Zedekiah did not make a cap with iron horns for himself but for the king. The horns transformed the king, as נגח implies, to an invincible, triumphant bull.[3] "With these you shall push the Syrians until they are destroyed" (1 Kgs 22:11). Hammond

---

[1] See chart on 1 Kgs 22:11 (appendix B).

[2] Joseph Hammond, The First Book of Kings, The Pulpit Commentary (Grand Rapids: Wm. B. Eerdmans, 1979), p. 533. Also Carl F. Keil refers to Thenius for the view of the iron horns probably being "iron spikes held upon the head;" The Books of the Kings, Biblical Commentary on the Old Testament (Grand Rapids: Wm. B. Eerdmans, 1952), p. 275.

[3] Keel, Wirkmächtige Siegeszeichen (Göttingen: Universitätsverlag Freiburg, 1974), pp. 131-32.

connects the demonstration of Zedekiah with the old prophecy in Deut 33:17.[1]

בכור שורו הדר לו וקרני ראם קרניו בהם עמים ינגח
יחדו אפסי־ארץ

His firstling bull has majesty, and his horns are the horns of a wild ox; with them he shall push the peoples, all of them, to the ends of the earth.[2]

This interesting text has recently been commented upon by Othmar Keel, who observes that the verb נגח ("to gore") is used literally of horned animals (bull, ram, and he-goat) but metaphorically also of kings. In Israel also, a people or a tribe could take this place. Keel supports his view with Ps 44:6 and Deut 33:17. In the suffix "his" (קרניו) in the latter passage, Keel sees a reference to "Yahweh as the firstborn of bulls."[3]

We have pointed out already in previous chapters that in the ancient Near East those gods wearing a "horned" helmet--crowns or caps--appear also in literature occasionally as bulls (wild oxen). Keel points out that since the time of Šalmaneser III the comparison of the king fighting with the wild ox (not with the domestic ox) appears also in Assyrian inscriptions.[4]

---

[1] Hammond, The First Book of Kings, p. 533.

[2] Cf. the NIV employing the term "gore" instead of "push" (Deut 33:17).

[3] Keel, Wirkmächtige Siegeszeichen, p. 126; so also William A. Wright, "Zedekiah," A Dictionary of the Bible, ed. William Smith (London: Jack Murray, 1863), 3:1836; Keil, The Books of the Kings, p. 275; and James A. Montgomery, A Critical and Exegetical Commentary on the Books of Kings, ICC (Edinburgh: T. & T. Clark, 1951), p. 338.

[4] Keel, Wirkmächtige Siegeszeichen, p. 131.

James A. Montgomery refers to Albert Sanda as having noted "similar ascriptions to Thutmose III and Seti II as 'invincible,' 'a young bullock with horns' "[1] The similarity of titles seems to be more than "accidental," as both seem to have an Egyptian background, for both Joseph and his sons had an Egyptian background and neither Ephraim nor Manasseh had become acquainted with the land of their ancestors at this particular time. It seems, therefore, probable that the bull-title originated in Egypt as far as Israel is concerned.

But who is the "firstborn" that is emphasized in Deut 33:17? Does it refer to a single king only? Keil and Delitzsch translate the verse:

> The first-born of his ox, majesty is to him, and buffalo-horns his horns: with them he thrusts down nations, all at once the ends of the earth. These are the myriads of Ephraim, and these the thousands of Manasseh.[2]

Furthermore, Keil says:

> The "first-born of his (Joseph's) oxen," (shor [שורו], a collective noun, as in chap. 15:19) is not Joshua . . . ; still less is it Joseph . . . , in which case the pronoun his ox would be quite out of place; nor is it King Jeroboam II. . . . . It is rather Ephraim, whom the patriarch Jacob raised into the position of the first-born of Joseph (Gen 48:8ff.).[3]

Keil continues his exegesis:

> All the sons of Joseph resembled oxen, but Ephraim was the most powerful of them all. He was endowed with majesty; his horns, the strong weapon of oxen, in which all their strength is concentrated, were not the horns of common oxen, but horns of the wild buffalo (reem, Num 23:22 [אל מוציאם

---

[1] Montgomery, The Book of Kings, ICC (Edinburgh: T. & T. Clark, 1951), p. 338.

[2] The Pentateuch, p. 506.   [3] Ibid.

ממצרים כתועפת ראם לו] that strong indomitable beast (cf. Job 39:9ff.; Ps 22:22). With them he would thrust down nations. . . . Such are the myriads of Ephraim, i.e., in such might will the myriads of Ephraim arise.[1]

From this detailed exegesis, it becomes clear that the שור (the bullock) and קרניו (his horns) refer to Ephraim and the tribe of Ephraim that rose from him.

At the time of the disruption of the ten tribes from the united kingdom (after David and Solomon), Ephraim and Israel were used synonymously to describe the northern country and its nation.[2] Peter C. Craigie says, "The blessing of military strength is described dramatically in the imagery of a powerful bull, goring its enemies before it."[3] Craigie sees "the metaphorical language

---

[1] "God brings them out of Egypt; they have as it were the horns of the wild ox" (RSV); as can easily be seen from the Hebrew text, the word קרן that is, the word for "horn," is not used here. Instead, the word כתועפת (<תועפה) "horns (of wild ox [cf. Num 24:8]); the most important Greek manuscripts translate the word ὡς δόξα, the Syriac, Targums and the Vulgate translations have bʷšnh = fortitudo; see apparatus in BHS (Num 23:22). Martin Noth thinks that Num 23:22 should be emended on the basis of Num 24:8 in order to fit the description of God "with horns" into the Mesopotamian context where ox-horns were the "symbols of divine power and of divinity in general;" see his Numbers, A Commentary (Philadelphia: The Westminster Press, 1968), p. 187.

[2] We cannot accept the "Homiletics by Various Authors" in The Pulpit Commentary, p. 548 of the two horns (1 Kgs 22:11) representing Ahab and Jehoshaphat, Israel and Judah. The main reason is that the dual here has not to be stressed literally. Although dual is used of things that go in pairs (eyes, hands, etc.) the context shows that the word קרן is not used to describe horns on any animal; it is used in a literal-extended way to convey a broader meaning to it. (Cf. Hans Bauer and Pontus Leander, Historische Grammatik der Hebräischen Sprache [Hildesheim: Georg Olms Verlagsbuchhandlung, 1962], 1:516 [#V] "Wörter, die paarweise vorhandene Körperteile bezeichnen, haben daneben oft eine übertragene Bedeutung.") Secondly, the prophecy in Deut 33:17 is applied to Ephraim [and Israel] not to Judah.

[3] The Book of Deuteronomy (Grand Rapids: Wm. B. Eerdmans, 1976), p. 399.

employed . . . as" reminiscent of other early Hebrew poetry and of Ugaritic poetry.[1]

From a political point of view and with this prophecy to back up his own prophecy, it is no surprise that Zedekiah, the son of Chenaanah,[2] ventured to give a prophecy that would please Ahab.

Sociological Context

There are two particular instances that have to be discussed from the Books of the Kings (1 Kgs 1:50, 51; 2:28) which belong in a sociological context. The instances refer to similar circumstances while the role-players are two different persons.

Adonijah, David's own son (born next after Absalom), "exalted himself" wanting to be king. The only way to succeed was to become a usurper,[3] but as the plot was discovered and Solomon was anointed king instead, Adonijah feared for his life. The passage reads: ואדניהו ירא מפני שלמה ויקם וילך ויחזק בקרנות המזבח "And Adonijah feared Solomon; and he arose and went, and caught hold of the horns of the altar" (1 Kgs 1:50).[4] The story in

---

[1]The passage of Ugaritic that Craigie refers to reads: "Môt is strong, Baal is strong. They gore like buffaloes" (UL 49.VI.17-18); cf. Num 23:22 and 24:8.

[2]William A. Wright gives strong reasons which place Zedekiah among the Baal and Ashtaroth worshippers; "Zedekiah," A Dictionary of the Bible, 3:1836.

[3]Adonijah might have thought that he had a claim to the throne. He was David's fourth son (2 Sam 3:4), but after the death of Ammon and Absalom, Adonijah was probably the oldest son, for Chileab, David's second son, "had most likely died when a child, since he is never mentioned again"; Keil, The Books of the Kings, p. 17.

[4]Cf. vs. 51 with the same context.

the next chapter tells a similar story of Joab the commander-in-chief having supported Adonijah, and who "fled to the tent of the Lord and caught hold of the horns of the altar" (1 Kgs 2:28). In this way both Adonijah and Joab sought refuge at the horns of the altar.

Keil says, in regard to the ancient tradition of asylum right at the altar:

> The altar was regarded from time immemorial and among all nations as a place of refuge for criminals deserving of death. . . . In the horns of the altar, as symbols of power and strength, there was concentrated the true significance of the altar as a divine place, from which there emanated both life and health. . . . By grasping the horns of the altar the culprit placed himself under the protection of the saving and helping grace of God, which wipes away sin, and thereby abolishes punishment.[1]

Martin Noth thinks that above all the "horns" of the altar are the seats of "holiness" and, originally, God's presence.[2]

Without attempting any further spiritual interpretations and ad hoc implications, a brief conclusion of the sociological pattern must be stated. It seems apparent, when comparing Israel with adjacent cultures, that Israel (and Judah) were the only countries in the Near Eastern context that provided asylum at the horns of the

---

[1] Keil, The Books of the Kings, p. 25. We question the validity of Keil's statement that the altar was a refuge for criminals. As far as we have been able to investigate, the asylum right is peculiar only in the sociological context of the Hebrews. This is in harmony also with the next result of this study: only in Syria and Palestine and in the Jordan Valley countries do we find altars provided with horns, a fact that strongly purports the only one "altar-horn" tradition having its center in Palestine. See George Rawlinson, Genesis and Exodus, The Pulpit Commentary, p. 269 (Exposition on Exod 27:1).

[2] Martin Noth, Könige, BKAT (Neukirchen-Vluyn: Neukirchener Verlag, 1968), pp. 28-29.

altar "to the involuntary manslayer who fled for his life from the blood avenger."[1] This is an axiom which by necessity must be true; the lack of horns on the altars among the surrounding nations proves the justification of this axiom, though it is an <u>argumentum ex silentio</u>. It is, however, not to be presumed that the asylum-right for law-breakers did not function in neighboring countries.[2] It only asserts that if it existed, it must have functioned on another basis.

And so the conclusion is that the sociological pattern in Israel and Judah in respect to asylum-right or refuge functions differently from other countries and on this basis presents a unique feature.

Purely Extended Meanings of Horns

Hymnic Texts

The language of poetry is, generally, more dynamic and expressive than ordinary prose. It uses grand and lofty terms that speak to the depth of a man's soul and set his emotions in action in a way different from trivial prose. Furthermore, poetry makes use of figurative speech, probably more abundantly than any other genre of literature. It is, therefore, inevitable that one must understand the meaning of the figurative language in order to be able to grasp the intended meaning.

---

[1] John E. Steinmueller, "Cities of Asylum," <u>New Catholic Encyclopedia</u> (New York: McGraw-Hill Book Company, 1967), 1:993-94.

[2] Michael M. Sheehan, "Right of Asylum," <u>New Catholic Encyclopedia</u> (New York: McGraw-Hill Book Company, 1967), 1:994.

It may be a matter of opinion whether some Hebrew poems are purposely devised with ambiguity in order to make the proper meaning obscure. In our opinion this is not the case. The difficulty lies mostly in our neglect to familiarize ourselves with ancient literature and especially so with that of the Bible, which differs so distinctively from ancient poetry in general. Because of the elusiveness of meaning some scholars resort to emendation. But here William H. Shea's remark gives weight to the contrary, for he says, "Emending poetry not only runs the risk of altering what the poet has said but also the form in which he has said it."[1]

We are, therefore, cautioned to carefulness in interpreting the ipsissima verba of each poem and especially so in those poems which convey a figure of speech. The main passages to be discussed in this category are, apart from Deut 33:17 (discussed above), namely, 2 Sam 22:3; Ps 18:3; and Lam 2:3, 17.

A comparison of 2 Sam 22:3 and Ps 18:3 reveals immediately that the texts are almost tantamount;[2] the first one slightly longer, adding two more epithets and a concluding statement, while the latter text adds a prefix-clause. Samuel H. P. Smith assumes 2 Sam 22 to be the original of the two psalms.[3] Peter R. Ackroyd, a

---

[1] "David's Lament," BASOR 221 (1976):141.

[2] Georg Schmuttermayr calls the two tantamount texts (2 Sam 22 and Ps 18) "Die Doppeltexte;" Psalm 18 and 2 Samuel 22: Studien zu einem Doppeltext (München: Kösel-Verlag, 1971), p. 15. (Unfortunately Schmuttermayr, however, does not deal with קרן ישעי per se.)

[3] A Critical and Exegetical Commentary on the Books of Samuel, ICC (Edinburgh: T. & T. Clark, 1951), p. 379.

recent scholar, takes the position that it is not possible to reconstruct the "original" psalm. Ackroyd says, "A close comparison of the two texts shows small but important differences, though the overall effect is the same."[1]

Hans-Joachim Kraus, pointing out the antiquity of the psalm, observes the fact that all the attributes of Yahweh point to him as the Deliverer and Helper.[2] It is apparent that the term קרן is explicitly combined with salvation in the locution קרן ישעי "the horn of my salvation."

There are strong reasons why the word קרן should not be given a negative connotation in these passages (2 Sam 22:3 and Ps 18:3), i.e., as originating from the figure of speech with reference to a bull.[3]

First, it may be pointed out that 2 Sam 22:2-3 and Ps 18: 1-2, which may be called parallel-texts (Doppeltext), give a vivid presentation of Yahweh where one image follows the other in rapid sequence. Each epithet paints a positive portrait of the Lord,

---

[1] The Second Book of Samuel (Cambridge: Cambridge University Press, 1977), p. 204.

[2] Kraus, Psalmen I, BKAT (Neukirchen Kreis Moers: Neukirchener Verlag, 1961), p. 142; Kraus refers to several scholars who likewise have noticed that the origin of the psalm may well be placed in the 10th century B.C.: Mitchell Dahood is one of the recent scholars who also emphasizes the antiquity of the psalm (Psalms I [Garden City, NY: Doubleday & Company, Inc., 1966]), p. 104.

[3] Older commentators usually take this figure of speech as borrowed from animals (bulls) which have their strength and weapons in their horns. More recent commentators are more careful. Artur Weiser, for instance, says, ". . . the image of the 'horn of salvation' is probably to be understood as a symbol signifying 'strength';" see The Psalms (Philadelphia: The Westminster Press, 1962), p. 188.

apart from the קרן in the epithet קרן ישעי which gives a negative image, if the word קרן is ascribed as originating from the animal kingdom.

Secondly, it may be observed that although the Samuel passage contains the concluding statement מחמס תשעני [1] "thou savest me from violence," the animal horn portrayal in the previous strophe is misguiding (i.e., "the horn of my salvation"). If we maintain the traditional view of horn as a figure of speech pertaining to the animal kingdom, it implies attack, aggressiveness, and eventually killing.[2] The picture is not positively forceful any more but negatively destructive. Such a negative presentation of Yahweh seems out of place in a list of epithets describing exclusively positive traits of characteristics. It is true that another picture of the Lord is presented somewhat later in the same passage portraying the Lord as the supreme victor discomfiting his enemies and as the sole ruler of the universe, but this does not seem to be the concern in the exordium.

Thirdly, the presentation of a saving God is marred if, in order to save, he has to do the saving act by killing. The pagan concept of fighting and battling gods comes through in this kind of exegesis, i.e., à priori assumption of uniformity of Near Eastern cultures.

Ackroyd confirms our view, for his striking comments make a

---

[1] 2 Sam 22:3 (the last bicolon): note that the last couplet in 2 Sam 22:3 is omitted in Ps 18:3.

[2] Perowne, The Book of Psalms, p. 210.

total break with the traditional translation:

> The psalmist piles up words to express divine power and protection. <u>My mountain fastness</u>: an ingenious translation, but the parallel with shield may suggest the more literal "horn of salvation," i.e., my royal saving power.[1]

The animal horn can be a symbol of "strength" and "power," it is true, but hardly a symbol of "protection," as has been the old traditional[2] but incorrect view. Ackroyd has, in our opinion, shown a telescope-like imagination in that he at least dares to break fully the fallacious interpretation connected with pagan imagery.

---

[1] <u>The Second Book of Samuel</u> (Cambridge: Cambridge University Press, 1977), p. 207.

[2] So, for instance, James G. Murphy who ascribes to the horn both an offensive and defensive quality and says that it is used "as a figure for any source of power or protection" (<u>A Critical and Exegetical Commentary on the Book of Psalms</u> [Andover: Warren J. Draper, 1875], p. 144). Bernhard Duhm has rightly pointed out that "'Horn des Heils,' oder der Hilfe ist schwerlich ein rettender Berg . . . ." <u>Die Psalmen</u>, p. 51. Duhm also points out that "horn" is a weapon which depiction is obtained from the horn of the bull, an assumption which we challenge; cf. Charles August Briggs and Emilie Grace Briggs, <u>A Critical and Exegetical Commentary of the Book of Psalms</u>, ICC (Edinburgh: T. & T. Clark, 1952), 141; Albert Barnes, <u>Notes on the Old Testament: Psalms</u> (Grand Rapids: Baker Book House, 1950), 1:147. Later scholars have become more careful and have seen other possibilities than to ascribe the metaphor of horn directly to the animal kingdom. Arnold A. Andersson, for instance, expresses himself somewhat hesitatingly and leaves room for an alternative interpretation, for he says, ". . . the metaphor [of "horn"] was most likely derived from the horns of animals rather than from the horns of the altar"(cf. <u>NBD</u>, p. 537b) and denoting 'my place of asylum' . . . . Werner W. Foerster, '<u>Keras</u>,' <u>TDNT</u>, III, pp. 669ff," Andersson, <u>The Book of Psalms</u>, NCB (London: Marshall, Morgan & Scott, 1972), 1:155. George Rawlinson leaves out the explicit reference to an animal-metaphorical origin of horn though he vaguely implies it for he says, "The horn is the emblem of excellency and might, whence 'salvation' or deliverance comes to those who trust in it;" <u>Psalms</u>, The Pulpit Commentary (Grand Rapids: Wm. B. Eerdmans Publishing Company, 1977), p. 115. Thus Rawlinson does not emphasize the animal metaphor with a negative implication, but retains the positive figure of "horn" meaning "excellence" and "might." (Other synonyms may be proper also depending on the context.)

"My mountain fastness"[1] may appear at first to be a far-fetched interpretation, but an analysis of the phrase gives a certain new nuance to the expression קרן ישעי. The קרן as "mountain" finds some support in the קרן בן־שמן of Isa 5:1 (Isa 26:4 יהוה צור עולמים and other texts). The "fastness" or "fixedness" is, of course, dependent on the translation of קרן as "mountain." The translation brings out the stability and fixity of the mountain, which, of course, must be taken figuratively as the other epithets in the poem.

We would go even a step further and suggest this "fastness" or "fixedness" also in combination with an abstract noun, for example, in combination with ישעי. This suggestion is based on comparison of קרן with the Sumerian SI with the meaning of qarnu and emūqu but also with the purely extended (and abstract) meaning of ašaru (išaru, mišaru[2]), etc. The ambiguous "horn" would get another emphasis if terms like "right of salvation," "justice of salvation," or even "righteousness of salvation" could be used for all these expressions, which are dynamic in quality and may in certain combinations eventually serve as synonyms for "strength" and "power."[3]

---

[1] Ackroyd, The Second Book of Samuel, p. 207.

[2] Anton Deimel, ŠL [3d ed.] (Rome: Verlag des Päpstt. Bibelinstituts, 1934), part III, vol. 1, p. 180; Karnû, malû, išâru (išêru), etc.; cf. Rykle Borger, Akkadische Zeichenliste AOAT, vol. 6 (Neukirchen-Vluyn: Neukirchener Verlag, 1971), p. 31 (#112); Theo Bauer, Akkadische Lesestücke, vol. 3, Glossar (Rome: Pontificium Institutum Biblicum, 1953), p. 4 (ašaru); Wolfram von Soden, Altar (Wiesbaden: Otto Harrassowitz, 1965), 1:392 (išaru, eš(e)ru); CAD (Glückstadt, Germany: J. J. Augustin Verlagsbuchhandlung, 1958), 4:352-63 (ešēru).

[3] This tentative suggestion of ours is subjected to all necessary reserve.

Ackroyd calls "my mountain fastness" an "ingenious translation."[1] He adds, however, that "the parallel with shield [משגבי] may suggest the more literal 'horn of salvation,' i.e., my royal saving power."[2] Furthermore, Ackroyd finds support for this last suggestion in 1 Sam 2:10 "'raise high the head of his anointed prince,' literally 'the horn of his anointed'."[3] We would tentatively suggest: "my royal saving right or righteousness."

Though Ackroyd has deviated from the "traditional" misconception of קרן as, without selectivity, presenting a figure of speech from the animal kingdom, he still agrees with commentators in general that "this psalm is understood as a general reflection on God's delivery of David from the power of all his enemies and from the power of Saul."[4]

These two Scripture references (2 Sam 22:3 and Ps 18:3) provide an important key for the interpretation of other texts with reference to the singular קרן which, as it seems, must be carefully analyzed not only per se but also to its qualifying part (noun or adjective) and not the least in regard to its context.[5]

---

[1] Ackroyd, The Second Book of Samuel, p. 207.

[2] Ibid.

[3] Ibid.; Mitchell Dahood does not comment upon קרן ישעי but gives a literal translation; Psalms I, AB (Garden City, NY: Doubleday & Company, Inc., 1966), p. 104.

[4] Ackroyd, The Second Book of Samuel, pp. 206-7 (as a curiosity it may be pointed out that Ackroyd sees stanza 6 containing a word-play [שׁאול and שׁאאל] that depicts David's arch-enemy and rival for royal power).

[5] We suggest that only a positive interpretation is attached to the word when it refers to Yahweh, and a complete elision

Hannah's Song, 1 Sam 2:1-10, has been identified as a psalm by David,[1] a royal psalm,[2] and even considered a prototype of the Magnificat anima mea Dominum,[3] to mention a few identifications given to it. Scholars have considered the poem as "incongruous to the situation it is supposed to illustrate" and so the name "Hannah's Song" has on this ground been eliminated as inapplicable.[4] Rather, the poem has been considered "in style and tone" to bear the marks of a later age.

Paul Haupt himself took the position that the Son of Hannah

> . . . refers to King Jehoiachin of Judah, who was carried captive by Nebuchadnezzar (597 B.C.) to Babylon where he remained in confinement until Nebuchadnezzar's son and sucessor, Evil-Merodach of Babylon lifted up the head of Jehoiachin out of prison (562 B.C.). . . .[5]

Haupt also says,

> It is a mistake to suppose that the last line of the poem is a subsequent liturgical addition. . . . The final couplet

of animal-metaphor with reference to Yahweh should be observed.

---

[1] [Otto] Thenius' theory (Die Bücher Samuels, 2d ed. [Leipzig: Weidmann, 1842] adopted by Bittcher) that the Song of Hannah is a psalm of David, celebrating his victory over Goliath and the defeat of the Philistines . . . is untenable according to Paul Haupt, "The Prototype of the Magnificat," ZDMG 58 (1904):617-18.

[2] So Peter Ackroyd, The First Book of Samuel (Cambridge: The University Press, 1971), p. 30. Ackroyd also calls this psalm "a song of victory" (ibid.).

[3] Haupt, "The Prototype of the Magnificat," ZDMG 58 (1904):618.

[4] In spite of the MT which plainly states: ותתפלל הנה ותאמר "Hannah also prayed and said" (omitted, however, in Rahlf's Septuagint) some scholars see it as impossible that the poem could have been recited by Hannah. So Haupt, "The Prototype of the Magnificat," p. 618.

[5] Haupt, ibid., p. 618.

refers to Jehoiachin who was regarded as the legitimate king even in his exile.[1]

This kind of interpretation is typical of the historical method with contemporary applications. In this way eschatological allusions or explicit texts could be re-interpreted.

It has been the general trend of even conservative scholars to consider the Song of Hannah to bear the marks of a later age.[2] Julius Ley is one of the few who considered the poem to be archaic.[3]

Keil and Delitzsch point to a sore spot in scholarly presuppositions when they write,

---

[1] Ibid. With the term "subsequent liturgical addition," Haupt refers to the following scholars who have adopted this view: Gustav Bickell, Dichtungen der Hebräer (Innsbruck: 1882), 1:33; August Klostermann, Die Bücher Samuelis undder Könige (Nördlingen: Beck, 1887), p. 5; Abraham Kuenen, Historisch-Kritische Einleitung in die Bücher des Alten Testaments (Leipzig: 1892), p. 48; T. K. Cheyne, The Origin and Religious Contents of the Psalter in the Light of Old Testament Criticism and the History of Religions (London: K. Paul, Trench, Trübner & Co., Ltd., 1891), p. 57, n.e.; Max Löhr, Die Bücher Samuels (Leipzig: 1898), p. 12; K. J. Grimm, Euphemeistic Liturgical Appendixes in the OT (Baltimore: Johns Hopkins University, 1901), p. 3; Hermann Gunkel, Ausgewählte Psalmen (Göttingen: Vandenhoeck & Ruprecht, 1904), p. 238, as cited by Haupt, "The Prototype of the Magnificat," p. 618.

[2] So, for instance, Heinrich Ewald, Die Dichter des alten Bundes, 2d ed. (Göttingen: Vandenhoeck & Ruprecht, 1866), p. 158; Samuel R. Driver, Notes on the Hebrew Text of the Books of Samuel (Oxford, 1890), p. 21, as cited by Haupt, "The Prototype of the Magnificat," p. 629; Eric C. Rust, The First and Second Books of Samuel, The Layman's Bible Commentary (Richmond, VA: John Knox Press, 1961), pp. 82-84; John Mauchline, ed., 1 and 2 Samuel in NCB (London: Marshall, Morgan & Scott, Ltd., 1971), pp. 50-51; William McKane, I & II Samuel (London: SCM Press, Ltd., 1963), pp. 37-38; Hans W. Herzberg, I & II Samuel (Philadelphia: Westminster Press, 1964), p. 29; Ackroyd, The First Book of Samuel (Cambridge: University Press, 1971), pp. 30-32.

[3] Die metrischen Formen der hebräischen Poesie systematisch dargelegt (Leipzig: B. G. Teubner, 1966), p. 172, as cited by Haupt (ibid., pp. 629-30).

The refusal of modern critics to admit the genuineness of this song is founded upon an à priori and utter denial of the supernatural saving revelations of God, and upon a consequent inability to discern the prophetic illumination of the pious Hannah, and a complete misinterpretation of the contents of her song and praise.[1]

Keil and Delitzsch furthermore hold that

. . . it is only by the most arbitrary criticism that it can be interpreted as referring to definite historical events such as the victory of David over Goliath (Thenius), or a victory of the Israelites over heathen nations (Ewald and others).[2]

As for a positive and constructive interpretation, Keil and Delitzsch point out that "Hannah's prayer rises up to a prophetic glance at the consummation of the kingdom of God."

The king, or the anointed of the Lord, of whom Hannah prophesies in the Spirit, is not one single king of Israel, either David or Christ, but an ideal king, though not a mere personification of the throne about to be established, but the actual king whom Israel received in David and his race, which culminated in the Messiah. The exaltation of the horn of the anointed of Jehovah commenced with the victorious and splendid expansion of the power of David, was repeated with every victory over the enemies of God and His kingdom gained by the successive kings of David's house, goes on in the advancing spread of the kingdom of Christ, and will eventually attain to its eternal consummation in the judgment on the last day, through which all the enemies of Christ will be made His footstool.[3]

There are others who agree with Keil and Delitzsch in their presuppositions and interpretation of this particular hymn. R. Payne Smith, for instance, says,

---

[1] Biblical Commentary on the Books of Samuel (Grand Rapids: Wm. B. Eerdmans Publishing Company, 1960), pp. 29-30.

[2] Ibid.; the last mentioned example of the song referring to Jehoiachin (Haupt) must thus be placed in the same category of misinterpretation (according to Keil and Delitzsch).

[3] Ibid.

The last distich [colon] is remarkable. It is a distinct prophecy of David's kingdom, and of the king as the anointed one, but looking onwards to the Messiah, David's greater Son the קרן משיחו (1 Sam 2:10).[1]

Smith further says,

> In claiming for Jehovah, her covenant God, the righteous government of the whole world, she prepares our minds for the corresponding thought of Jehovah being the universal Saviour.[2]

As for the concept of kingship in the pre-monarchial era, Smith points out that "the thought of a king was in no respect alien from the Jewish commonwealth.[3] Smith's concluding remarks lead even one step further, for he says:

> . . . though the present longings of the nation for a king make Hannah's words not unnatural even in their lower sense, yet the truer exposition is that which acknowledges in Israel a people raised up for a special purpose, and the bestowal by God upon its seers for the carrying out of this purpose of the gift of prophecy. And it was this extraordinary gift which bent and shaped the mind of the nation, and filled it with future aspirations.[4]

As it furthermore seems evident that the hymn is a unit both in structure and style[5] there is no reason to separate the last stanza from the poem. When, furthermore, the context seems to require this stanza in order to bring out a dynamic eschatological climax,[6] the best solution is, in our opinion, to accept the text

---

[1]*The First Book of Samuel*, The Pulpit Commentary (Grand Rapids: Wm. B. Eerdmans Publishing Company, 1977), p. 27.

[2]Ibid.   [3]See Smith's discussion (ibid.).   [4]Ibid.

[5]The whole hymn presents (with possibly a few exceptions: the third stanza and the first half of the last couplet in the eighth stanza) a regular synthetic parallelism with beat 3:3.

[6]For various concepts of eschatology, see Sigmund Mowinckel, *He That Cometh* (New York: Abingdon Press, 1954), especially pp. 3, 7f., 14f., 21, 46, 55, 99, 101, 121ff., chapter V passim, pp. 159,

as genuine without rejection of any part or parts.

The "lamentation-texts" (Lam 2:3, 17) with their acrostic device[1] also show occurrences of קרן. The first occurrence is found in the third stanza and the first couplet (second tricolon as follows: גדע בחרי־אף כל קרן ישראל "He has cut down in fierce anger all the might of Israel." The whole of the poem which is a lament[2] presents Zion in a miserable position because of its sins.[3] The lament depicts the Lord as having abandoned the kingdoms of Judah and Israel. "He [the Lord], has cut down [removed] [כל קרן ישראל] all the might of Israel." According to the context the קרן must refer to something that Judah and Israel enjoyed in their days of prosperity. The poem laments this "something" being "cut off" [removed] and the lack that results is sufficient reason for lament.

Some commentators assume that this "something" or the קרן refers to "all the means of defense [especially the fortresses]."[4]

173, 245, chapters VIII-X passim. Additional Notes I, IX, XIII, XIV. Many of these concepts are restricted in meaning. In this dissertation we have accepted eschatology based on the text of the Bible as it appears. We have obtained an acceptable definition from Gerhard Hasel: "Eschatology refers to the future in which God by natural and supernatural means brings about something final which can be within or beyond history and which brings about something new." (The *final* and *new* is a radical change within history and beyond history.)

[1] See David N. Freedman, "Prolegomenon," in George Buchanan Gray, The Forms of Hebrew Poetry ([n.p.]: Ktav Publishing House, 1972), p. xxxvii.

[2] The qina-meter device shows this to be a lament.

[3] See Lam 1 for the background. (The term Zion refers to Jerusalem and the terms Judah and Israel are used "loosely" and interchangeably as synonyms more or less.)

[4] See, for instance, Thomas K. Cheyne, Jeremiah, The Pulpit Commentary (reprint ed., Grand Rapids: Wm. B. Eerdmans Publishing Company, 1977).

This interpretation, which is by no means uncommon, gives, however, an unbalanced and one-sided imaginary perception that seems to unfavorably reflect an à priori thought pattern.

It is surprising to find Bertil Albrektson deviating from the rigid pattern with reference to קרן in the phrase above. Actually, he bypasses it with only a short comment: "This should of course be translated 'all the strength of Israel,' the horn being 'a frequent symbol of strength in the O.T'."[1]

Theophile J. Meek, to whom Albrektson refers, is not slavishly bound to a literal interpretation of just one single word, but pays attention also to the context. He expresses his view as follows:

> In this verse [verse three] Yahweh is described as depriving the nation of strength, of withholding his own help, and then of taking the offensive against it. . . . The might is, lit. the horn, a frequent symbol of strength in the O.T. (again in vs. 17).[2]

Meek does not, however, emphasize nor even bring out any animal metaphor in the context--rather, he seems to be influenced by the context, for he says furthermore:

> The second line reads lit., "He has drawn back his right hand from the face of the enemy," which Ps 74:11 shows must mean that Yahweh has withdrawn his help, symbolized by the right hand, as often in the O.T.[3]

---

[1]Albrektson is more cautious and refers to Theophile J. Meek as the authority on which he bases his opinion for this particular phrase; Studies in the Text and Theology of the Book of Lamentations, Studia Theologia Lundensia 21 (Lund: CWK Gleerup, 1963), p. 89.

[2]Theophile J. Meek,"The Book of Lamentations," IB (New York: Abingdon Press, 1956), p. 17.

[3]Ibid.

Both Meek and Albrektson thus interpret the tricolon כל קרן ישראל "all the strength of Israel," or "all the might of Israel,"-- a translation which in our opinion is preferably balanced. It has to be emphasized, however, that the context brings out that the "might of Israel" was not intrinsically its own but it was dependent on the presence and glory of Yahweh and on his protection and help. The קרן was not of human but of divine quality. This intrinsic interpretation gets support from the structural pattern of the poem, for it is expressing synthetic parallelism of thought although not ad amussim in words.

In our opinion, Kraus has come quite close to the original meaning, though he does not deal with the synthetic extension of thought. He sees that כל קרן ישראל concerns "ganz Israel."[1] He also interprets קרן ישראל as "Kraft Israels" and comments, ". . . das Horn is im AT ein Sinnbild der Siegreich erhöhten Kraft (Ps 75:11, Jer 48:25)."[2]

Although it seems hard to find an exact term to cover the meaning of קרן,[3] the interpretation of this particular tricolon (in its narrow sense) seems to refer to the moral backbone of the nation, i.e., its "power" having been broken due to the fact that

---

[1] Klagelieder (Threni) 3d enlarged ed. BKAT (Neukirchen-Vlugn: Neukirchener Verlag, 1968), p. 42.

[2] Ibid.; Kraus seems to pay more attention to the specific phrase כל קרן ישראל in a more narrow sense to the negligence (more or less) of the immediate context.

[3] It seems that no one term covers all the nuances in which the word קרן may occur. The immediate context and the broader context as well as comparative usages must all the time be kept in view.

(in a wider sense) Yahweh had ceased from favoring his people.

Delbert R. Hillers has translated Lam 2:3 as follows:

> In fierce anger he [the Lord] lopped off the horns of Israel. He turned back his right hand in the face of the enemy, and he burned against Jacob like a fire that consumes on every side.[1]

Hillers explains the phrase "he lopped off the horns of Israel" to mean, "He destroyed all Israel's proud strength."[2] Hiller also agrees with other commentators on the frequent usage of "horn" in the Old Testament as a symbol not only of strength but also of pride.[3] As for the next couplet השיב אחור ימינו "he has withdrawn from them his right hand." Hillers sees the pronouns as "probably" referring to Israel. He says, "God destroys the 'horn' of Israel in 3a, and here turns back Israel's right hand--both parts of the body, symbolic of strength, belong to Israel."[4]

As Hillers' assumption is not unflinching we would suggest both expressions (קרן ישראל and especially the ימינו) to refer, in a primarily and wider sense, to the power or might of יהוה[5] which belonged to Israel as long as the people served Yahweh, but was withdrawn when they obstinately chose their own way. In a narrow

---

[1] Lamentations, AB (Garden City, NY: Doubleday & Company, Inc., 1972), p. 31.

[2] Ibid., p. 36.

[3] Ibid.; Hillers is here dependent on Edouard P. Dhorme, "L'emploi métaphorique des noms de parties du corps en hébreu et en akkadien," RB 29 (1920):465-506 (see especially p. 499 where Dhorme points out the double symbol of horn "the pride" and "the strength").

[4] Hillers, Lamentations, p. 36.

[5] Cf. Meek, "The Book of Lamentations," p. 17.

sense, and secondarily, the קרן seems to refer to the inner strength and attitude of Israel. This interpretation seems to be favored by Kraus (indirectly), for in commenting upon Lam 3:17 he expresses his opinion thus:

> Auch die Schadenfreude des Feindes, die soeben noch in schmerzlicher Schärfe in Erinnerung gerufen wurde, fällt nicht aus dem Plan und der weissagenden Ankündigung Jahwes heraus. Jahwe liess es zu, dass der Feind sich freute. Er selbst liess die Macht (קרן) des Feindes triumphieren.[1]

Kraus is thus alluding to the fact that even the malicious relish of a nation's defeat was not omitted from the proclamation of the purpose of Yahweh. He it is that permits even the "might" (קרן) of the enemy to triumph.

Ps 22 has generally been considered as belonging to the genre of lamentation. It represents a high quality of poetry in the Psalter and makes use of powerful and striking metaphors of a pious one who is pressed in need and is surrounded by hate and scorn.[2] The context is of importance in order to understand the lament of the sufferer.[3]

The psalmist records how the sufferer, in his great need, is praying: הושיעני מפי אריה ומקרני רמים עניתני "Save me from

---

[1] See Kraus in Klagelieder (Threni), p. 48.

[2] Duhm, Die Psalmen, p. 71; Duhm applies the pious one to the poet himself who he thinks was a victim in strife between opposing parties under the late Hasmonean rulers (pp. 68, 71, 72 passim). So also Gunkel, Die Psalmen, 5th ed. (Göttingen: Vandenhoeck & Ruprecht, 1968), pp. 90, 94, et al.

[3] For a discussion, see, for instance, Claus Westermann, "Struktur und Geschichte der Klage im Alten Testament," ZAW 66 (1954):47-74; Kraus, Psalmen 1:176-76, and Ernst W. Hengstenberg, Christology of the Old Testament and a Commentary on the Messianic Predictions (reprint ed., Grand Rapids: Kregel Publications, 1956), 4:298-99.

the mouth of the lion, my afflicted soul from the horns of the wild oxen."

Already Hermann Gunkel conceived the enemies of the sufferer to be compared with powerful bulls. He writes:

> Er [the psalmist] nennt sie "Stärke Basans:" in Basan, einen fruchtbaren Weideland nordöstlich vom Jordan, muss es eine besonders kraftvolle Rinderart gegeben haben, Amos 4:1. Von dem übrigen, ihn verhöhnenden Volke unterscheiden sich diese Gegner durch ihre besonders bittere Feinschaft. . . . Die Tiervergleiche haben für das Empfinden des Altertums nichts Beschimpfendes; vielmehr will der Dichter sagen, dass es sich um mächtige, vornehme Leute handelt, deren Mut furchtbar ist.[1]

Gunkel thus assumes that with animal-parallels are meant mighty and prominent enemies of the individual.

Kraus takes a more negative view in regard to the figurative language, for he says, "In fact it cannot be doubted that the raging hostile people can be described with animal metaphors (Ps 7:3; 10:9f.; 27:2; 35:21f.)"[2] Kraus is more apt to see the enemies in the suffering hymns as representing always demonic powers separating the sufferer from God.[3] Kraus' observation is no doubt a valid one, for it is an undeniable fact that the concern of this particular psalm is

---

[1] Gunkel, Die Psalmen, pp. 91-92.

[2] Kraus, Psalmen, 1:180.

[3] Kraus also refers to ancient exorcism (i.e., magical invocation of spirits) in which disease and injury or harm of any kind were presented as dangerous animals. For further elucidation see works by Sabatino Moscati, Geschichte und Kultus der semitischen Völker: Urban-Bücher, 1953, p. 57f.; George Widengren, The Accadian and Hebrew Psalms of Lamentation as Religious Documents, Diss. Uppsala, 1936 (1937); Adam Falkenstein and Wolfram von Soden: Sumerische und akkadische Hymnen und Gebete, 214, as cited by Kraus (ibid.). See also Sigmund Mowinckel, Psalmenstudien II, Kultprophetische Psalmen (Amsterdam: P. Schippers, N.V., 1961), p. 59.

the "separation from God." This is clearly indicated in the poem. Furthermore, the particular stanza (Ps 22:21) indicates clearly that the same theme is still a matter of relevance. The sufferer wants speedy relief and the vivid description is intensified by forceful imaginary similitudes of wild beasts. Herbert C. Leupold says:

> How extreme the peril was is indicated by the last figure, "from the horns of the wild oxen." This could well mean that the victim envisions himself as being caught up on the oxen's horn and about to be further tossed or gored to death.[1]

George Rawlinson presumes the animal similitudes ('the dogs,' 'the lions,' and 'the strong bulls of Bashan') to comprise the adversaries (the chief persecutors, viewed as a class, or Satan, the instigator) of the sufferer, whom he sees as applicable to Jesus.[2]

Rawlinson's conclusion seems to echo Murphy's typological approach of more than a century ago, for he said:

> This psalm is ascribed to David, and there is no valid reason in the style or matter for questioning this statement. . . . But it is evident that the writer regards the occasion as foreshadowing an event of immensely greater importance. He himself is the historical type of the Messiah who was to come.[3]

Whether one interprets the sufferer here from a historical

---

[1] Exposition of the Psalms (Columbus, OH: Wartburg Press, 1959), p. 303.

[2] The Book of Psalms, pp. 153-54. Leupold Sabourin, who entitles the Psalm, "Passion and Triumph of the Messiah," also interprets the fierce animals as the Sufferer's foes, The Psalms (Staten Island, NY: The Society of St. Paul, 1969), 2:239-41.

[3] Murphy, A Critical and Exegetical Commentary on the Book of Psalms, pp. 169-70.

or typological point of view or even considers it from a prophetical point of view, it seems evident that the imagery of the "horns" presents a negatively forceful imagery. Both the immediate context (of stanza twenty-two) and the broader context presume that the Sufferer has hostile powers surrounding him. This fact then makes us conclude that the imagery of the wild oxen refers to adversaries of one or another kind who press upon the Sufferer.

From a structural point of view the psalm must be considered a unit.[1] The division of the psalm into two main sections--stanzas 1-21 ("The Sufferer 'forsaken by God'" or "the complaint of suffering") and 22-32 ("The Sufferer 'delivered by God'" or "confession of hope")--seems to comprise a natural demarcation on the basis of content.

Ps 75:5, 6 present synonymous usages of the word "horn." The immediate context seems to belong to the genre of Wisdom-literature, but both of the "proverbs" are stated negatively: אל־תרימו קרן למרום and אל־תרימו "Do not lift up your horn on high" and "do not lift up your horn."

Duhm says, "Wie es scheint, redet hier nicht mehr Jahwe, sondern der Dichter."[2] Also Gunkel sees these two stanzas as an exhortation or admonition speech--a form which seldom occurs.[3] Gunkel first makes clear that the "Mahnrede" is directed against "die 'Rasenden,' die Narren . . . die frevlerischen Verächter Jahves,

---

[1] The whole psalm presents throughout an interchangeable pattern of 2:2, 2:3, 3:2, 3:3, 3:4, and 4:3 beats.

[2] Die Psalmen, p. 197.

[3] Die Psalmen (Göttingen: Vandenhoeck & Ruprecht, 1968), p. 327.

Heiden und Heidengenossen, die in wahnsinniger Hoffart das Horn gegen den Höchsten emporheben."[1]

For the figure of speech employed, Gunkel explicitly points out the source with

> . . . das Bild is vom Wildochsen (Ps 92:11) her genommen, der mit hochaufgerichtetem Horn in der Fülle seines Kraftgefühls, den Gegner herausfordern, dasteht, ein Bild, das auch den Babyloniern bekannt ist. . . .[2]

This tune, struck by the history-of-religion school, has continued to sound in most commentaries since that time. So, for instance, Hans Schmidt explicitly says,

> Wehe den Menschen, den Frevlern, den Rasenden, die sich dagegen auflehnen, die meinen, dass sie wie ein Stier ihre Hörner, emporwerfen können gegen "den Felsen," d.h. gegen den Gott, der auf dem Zionfelsen thront.[3]

Some more recent scholars are more careful and avoid explicitly drawing this particular analogy (though they seem to unconsciously imply it). Kraus, for instance, says in regard to the "idiom" אל־תרימו קרן "do not lift up your horn," that it concerns "die רשעים ["the wicked"], die stolz 'das Horn erheben'."[4] As for the meaning of קרן he briefly says, "קרן ist in der altorientalischen Symbolsprache ein Ausdruck für 'Kraft,' 'Macht'."[5]

Dahood also expresses his opinion on the parallelism and admits that the expression "to raise one's horn" is figurative for

---

[1] Ibid.   [2] Ibid.

[3] Die Psalmen, HAT (Tübingen: J. C. B. Mohr [Paul Giebeck], 1934), p. 142.

[4] Psalmen, p. 522.

[5] Ibid.

"to become arrogant." That Dahood has the animal-horn as the basis for this metaphor is implicitly expressed in a comment on the phrase "your horn" (Ps 75:5), for he says: "qāren requires no suffix since it is part of the body."[1]

The difficulty with this text is the grammatical construction (with קרן as the object) in difference to קרן in construction where the word is clearly qualified. It is to be noticed that in this particular chapter all three genders are present, for in vs. 11 both the dual and plural are found.[2] וכל־קרני רשעים אגדע תרוממנה קרנות צדיק: "All the horns of the wicked he will cut off, but the horns of the righteous shall be exalted."

The problem is not easy. It seems clear, however, that the word is used with different emphasis to bring out specific truths embedded in this psalm.

The idiomatic expressions in vss. 5 and 6, though they seem to present an anciently known proverb, cannot give the solution to the problem while pondered in isolation or studied in a vacuum. They have to be seen against the background of the whole psalm. Perowne has observed that the הרים (<רום "lift up") is an "emphatic word" in this psalm. This key-word occurs actually six times

---

[1] Dahood, Psalms II, p. 212. The statement implies, of course, the figure of speech to be drawn from the animal kingdom (though he does not explicitly say so). Dahood attempts to prove his statement from several passages (ibid., p. 45, et al.)--a statement of which we do not question the correctness (in general)--but whether the statement can be enforced with reference to qeren also in Lam 2:3 as Dahood implies, is doubtful; see our remarks above, for in the very next verse (Ps 75:6) the suffix is used on the very same word (קרנכם).

[2] Dahood has keenly observed this fact, but though he notes it as a curiosity he has offered no suggestion for solution.

in this short psalm. Perowne points out that the "lifting up" does not mean "promotion" as it is mainly understood, "but deliverance from trouble; safety, victory."[1] Without disregarding this definition, which no doubt is true as far as it goes, it is, however, only one-sidedly presented. Perowne further elucidates his statement by saying:

> The image, in particular, of lifting up the head or the horn (the last, borrowed from wild beasts, such as buffaloes, etc., in which the horn is the symbol of strength), denotes courage, strength, victory over enemies.[2]

Holladay notes that רום inter alia means "be exalted" with God as the subject while it may mean "be overbearing," "boast," or "be haughty" when man's heart is the subject (or man's eyes).[3] Though the meaning of "horn" often means "strength," as has already been pointed out, the context of this psalm presents the wicked man and his offensive hybris in contrast to God who ultimately is the judge over all: both wicked and righteous. With this in mind the meaning of the idiom does not refer to the strength, courage, and victory of man, but to his attitude--his boastful arrogant attitude--which proves that he has neglected to consider God who is the true שפט who "is putting down" or "lifting up"[4] (cf. 1 Chr 25:5).

In this wider context the idiom in vss. 5 and 6 need not necessarily convey the metaphor of "strength" primarily, though the

---

[1] The Book of Psalms, 2:37.   [2] Ibid.

[3] A Concise Hebrew and Aramaic Lexicon of the Old Testament, p. 335 (רום #2, 4).

[4] The wider context of this psalm places vss. 6 and 7 right in the middle or heart of the psalm showing the real "uplifting" to come from the Lord.

meaning of an arrogant attitude indirectly is attached to that concept which, however, according to this psalm, is based on false assumptions. The climax of the psalm which is embedded in an eschatological framework[1] (vs. 11) portrays the final destiny of two categories of people here contrasted. The Lord himself is the speaker as the verb אגדע (<גדע "cut off") shows. Dahood, for instance, points to the fact that God himself "will destroy the pride and power of the wicked at the final judgment."[2] Dahood, however, fails to explain vs. 11 on which he comments as follows: "The use of dual qarnē in the first colon but plural qarnôt in the second is very curious; the latter perhaps implies more than two horns."[3] Though Dahood does not endeavor to interpret the qarnē or the qarnôt, he has indicated another contrast in the same verse: "The poet apparently contrasts plural rᵉšaʾim, 'the wicked' with singular ṣaddîq, who is God himself."[4]

Though we have to admit that the true meaning of "horns" in

---

[1] We are aware of Sigmund Mowinckel's application of this psalm (Ps 75 [of mythic content]) in a cultic setting and originally used (but not exclusively) at a throne-inauguration occasion; see Psalmenstudien III, p. 49; cf. Hans Schmidt, Die Thronfahrt Jahves am Fest der Jahreswende im alten Israel (Tübingen: J. C. B. Mohr [Paul Siebeck], 1927), pp. 31-36; Weiser, The Psalms, p. 521, who all emphasize the cultic usage. We, whose presuppositions differ from the representative of these schools, see, however, Psalm 75 and especially vs. 11 as primarily eschatological. This remark does not belittle in any way the views of these scholars, for especially Artur Weiser has, in our opinion, given enrichment to the interpretation of Ps 75 (see further, ibid., pp. 522-23).

[2] Dahood, Psalms II, p. 216.

[3] Ibid.

[4] Ibid.

vs. 11[1] is elusive, we think that the difference is not accidental but intentional. A tentative paraphrasing from us would be: "I will break (cut) off the entire power of the wicked ones, but the ones glorified of the Righteous One will be exalted."

Also in Ps 89:18, 25 the קרן is connected with the verb רום "lift up." Murphy has translated קרננו with "our power and prosperity."[2] The context shows that the concern is not in regard to "the horn of the wicked" (as in Ps 75:5, 6), i.e., the arrogant and boastful to whom is given the warning "do not lift up your horn," but in regard to those "who walk in the light of thy [the Lord's] countenance," and upon whom a blessing is pronounced (. . . אשרי יהוה באור־פניך יהלכון, Ps 89:16). Their "horn" (their "power and prosperity") is exalted--not on their own initiative--but on the initiative of the Lord as the contexts show and as the Hiphil confirms.

Artur Weiser places this psalm in a mythical setting and assumes that certain verses are echoes from the ancient tradition of conquest and victory over the powers of chaos.[3]

---

[1]The particular difference of qarnē and qarnôt is not brought out in the RSV nor in NIV; rather they are translated as identical in meaning.

[2]Murphy, The Book of Psalms, p. 478.

[3]The Psalms, p. 592. For a general summary of the scholarly view in regard to this particular psalm see Gösta W. Ahlström, Psalm 89 (Lund: CWK Gleerups Förlag, 1959), p. 17; Sabourin, The Psalms, 2:239-41. As our view does not coincide in any way to the "extremists of the divine-kingship school" in a cultic setting (asserting that the king represented the dying and rising nature deity in this cultic renewal ceremony), the method applied has simply been to let the psalm speak for itself and to interpret it in its own context. According to our personal view the "horn" both in vss. 18 and 25 of

Also Dahood, without directly referring to any ancient mythical tradition, has incorporated the concept of "victory" in his translation of Ps 89:18. "Indeed, you are our glorious triumph, and by your favor you give us victory."[1] In a similar way he translates vs. 25: "Through my Name [Yahweh] he [David] shall be victorious."[2] In his "Notes" Dahood points out the respective literal meaning: "You raise high our horn," and "His horn shall be raised high."[3]

It is not always easy to find a fitting metaphor that fits the context. The two texts (Ps 75:5, 6 and Ps 89:18, 25) briefly analyzed show that the people addressed are diametrical opposites. Although the word "horn" (קרן) is used in all four passages and even the same verb (רום), structure and style, syntax and context (both immediate and broader context) indicate clearly that the people who are addressed are diametrical opposites. The ones addressed are antithetical in attitude, contradictory in behavior, and divergent in status. This, then, leads inevitably to the conclusion that the "idioms" in the respective psalms--identical as they are in many ways (i.e., in the selection of words), must be interpreted as being autonomous expressions. Furthermore, these passages seem to be strongly Messianic-oriented.

In Ps 92:11 we are confronted with a similitude that seemingly places the metaphorical "horn" as originating from the concept of horn in the animal kingdom. The Hebrew text reads: ותרם כראים

---

this particular psalm should be interpreted in a Messianic setting; so also Derek Kidner, Psalms 73-150 (London: Inter-Varsity Press, 1975), p. 322.

[1] Psalms II, p. 309.   [2] Ibid.   [3] Ibid., pp. 315 (#18) and 317 (#25).

קרני בלתי משקן רענן: "But thou hast exalted my horn like that of the wild ox: thou hast poured over me fresh oil."

Murphy has maintained the word reme in his translation and gives as a reason that "the species is uncertain." At the same time he says that it "is supposed to be the wild ox, or a kind of antelope."[1]

Gunkel suggests the reme "nach Art eines Büffels,"[2] and also observes the unusual כראים instead of כראם which would be the usual way of spelling it. The spelling is of interest for if a plural is intended it alters the meaning considerably. It may suggest that not only the "horn" has to be metaphorically interpreted but also the "wild oxen" themselves. It is well known that "bull" and "gazelle" can be a divine epithet or epithets of kings, noblemen, or priests.[3] As it is uncertain that it refers to any animal, and if so, what kind of wild animal,[4] there is a possibility that neither "wild ox" nor "gazelle" nor any other animal is meant. If it is a psalm of David he may perhaps compare himself and his

---

[1] The Book of Psalms, pp. 493-95.

[2] Die Psalmen, p. 410. Gunkel does not, however, specify what kind of "Büffel" he has in mind. The word re'em is sometimes translated as "buffalo." Cyrus H. Gordon, UT (Analecta Orientalia, 38; Rome: Pontifical Biblical Institute, 1965), p. 481.

[3] See, for instance, John Gray, The Legacy of Canaan, 2d rev. ed., VTSupp (Leiden: E. J. Brill, 1965), pp. 227-28.

[4] See Murphy and Gunkel; so also Kraus, Psalmen BKAT, p. 642. Arnold A. Anderson's remark concerning Ps 89:18 may be accounted valid also for Ps 92:10. He says, "In Canaanite religion 'Bull' can be a divine epithet . . . but it is not certain that this fact has any bearing upon the above idiom; The Book of Psalms, NCB (London: Marshall, Morgan & Scott, 1972), 2:638-39.

"strength and prosperity" (which are from Yahweh) with that of the contemporary rulers. If this is the case the passage involves no difficulty. Whatever position one takes as to the proper meaning, the expression כראים conveys a similitude as the -כ- shows. The metaphor of "horn" has been pointed out already.

Herbert C. Leupold refers to the thought that the expression "God has exalted his horn like that of a wild ox" is a typical figure of speech of that time.[1] He says in regard to the metaphor, "The exuberance of strength is the thought conveyed by this comparison. There is nothing of wildness in it, for the Hebrew has but a single term for this creature."[2]

As the same stanza (Ps 92:11) also says, "I have been anointed with fresh oil," Leupold combines this expression with the previous tricolon and says,

> It may be possible that the anointing with fresh oil is to recall (as in 45:7) some joyous occasion for which men would in days of old anoint their face. . . . In other words, his experience tells him that God is in the habit of supplying gladness and strength to those that fear Him.[3]

This interpretation avoids all controversial issues and paraphrases the whole stanza in a beautiful way; and it seems to aim to make the metaphors to convey a spiritual and personal uplifting experience.

Ps 112:9 offers no particular difficulties in light of the application of similar texts (above).[4]

---

[1] For the date of the completion of the Psalter see Leupold, Exposition of the Psalms, p. 8.

[2] Ibid.   [3] Ibid.

[4] Some more recent translations prefer the translation of

352

As for Ps 132, Dahood points out that "commentators agree that the structure of this poem is 'strange,' 'peculiar,' and 'difficult to recognize'."[1] Because of the difficulties of determining its genre the psalm has been classified in at least three different categories: a "Song of Zion," a "Royal Psalm," and a "Liturgy."[2]

Terence E. Fretheim, who has made a literary analysis of this particular psalm, points out several literary evidences that prove the unity of the psalm.[3] Fretheim shows step by step the unity of the psalm[4] and the last two stanzas forming the conclusion: שם אצמיח קרן לדוד ערכתי נר למשיחי אויביו אלביש בשת ועליו יציץ נזרו: "There will I make a horn to sprout for David. I have prepared a lamp for my anointed. His enemies I will clothe

---

"head" instead of "horn" in this particular passage. So, for instance, Dahood, Psalms III, pp. 126, 129 (#9).

[1] Psalms III, p. 241; so also in Terence E. Fretheim, "Psalm 132: A Form-Critical Study," JBL 86 (1967):289.

[2] See Kraus, Psalmen II, pp. 878-83; so also Fretheim, ibid., p. 289. The first genre is advocated by Gunkel, Die Psalmen, p. 565; the second by William O. E. Oesterley, The Psalms, p. 529; Aubrey R. Johnson, Sacral Kingship in Ancient Israel (Cardiff: University of Wales' Press, 1967), p. 17; Aage Bentzen, "The Cultic Use of the Story of the Ark in Samuel," JBL 67 (1948):42; and the third by Kraus, Psalmen, 2:878; Weiser, The Psalms, p. 779; Otto Eissfeldt, "Psalm 132," WO 2 (1954-59): 450-83, as cited by Fretheim, p. 289.

[3] Fretheim, "Psalm 132: A Form-Critical Study," pp. 292-93, points out, for instance, the repetition of words in the psalm as a key to the understanding of the cultic usage of the psalm.

[4] So, for instance, the כי for (stanza 13) being the linking word, there is a close relationship between vss. 11-12 and 13-16; Fretheim, however, sees the psalm as originally served in liturgical context and only in its present form the various parts (used in various ways) have been "put together with consummate skill and with special regard for form and style, with the result that it constitutes a meaningful whole." "Psalm 132: A Form-Critical Study," pp. 298-99.

with shame, but upon himself his crown will shed its luster."

Dahood, analyzing the same poem, finds the language of the psalm extremely archaic. He contends that

> . . . isolated archaic elements do not suffice to mark a poem as early, but the sheer concentration of archaic words, forms, parallelisms and phrases in this textually well preserved poem accords with the contents which point to a tenth-century date of composition.[1]

He translates the conclusion of the psalm as follows:

> There [שם] I will make a horn [קרן] glow, O David, I will trim the lamp [נר], O my anointed! His foes will I clothe with humiliation, but upon him will sparkle his crown.[2]

A brief analysis of this passage shows that קרן and נר stand in parallelism to each other--but not in synonymous parallelism as Dahood assumes,[3] but in synthetic parallelism. It is therefore not necessary to assume (with Dahood) that "qeren would signify a lamp in the shape of an animal."[4]

The second metaphor seems clearly to refer to David as the nēr yisrāʾēl "the lamp of Israel" (2 Sam 21:17). "The burning lamp is a natural metaphor for the preservation of the dynasty; when a man died without offspring, his lamp was said to be put out."[5]

Dahood maintains the literal translation of קרן "the horn," but he implies it to be synonymously parallel with נר and on this basis he points out the verb אצמיח as having the meaning, "I will make glow" (Hiphil) and the verb יצץ in the next couplet to mean "will sparkle."[6]

---

[1] Psalms III, p. 242. [2] Ibid., p. 241. [3] Ibid., p. 248. [4] Ibid.
[5] Ibid.; cf. 1 Kgs 11:36, 15:4; 2 Kgs 8:19; and Prov 13:9.
[6] Ibid., pp. 248-49 (241). Dahood points out the ordinary

According to our opinion, the meaning of "to blossom"--as it traditionally has been translated--would fit better if we maintain the verb אצמיח with the meaning "to sprout" instead of "to blossom." There are other texts that seem to strongly purport the meaning of "sprout" instead of "glow," especially if we maintain a prophetic-Messianic implication to the text.

Murphy translates vs. 17: "There will I raise up a horn for David."[1] He translates the אצמיח "raise up, cause to grow," and קרן a "horn" as "an invincible kingdom."[2] Furthermore, Murphy translates נר "a lamp" and applies it as "a spiritual kingdom of holiness and truth." Murphy sees the great promise of this passage as having its "full accomplishment in the Messiah."[3]

There are others who likewise see a prophetic anticipation in the Davidic promises which are to be fully realized only in Messiah, "the antitypical and true Son of David."[4]

Sigmund Mowinckel is one of the foremost champions to propose the cultic usage of this psalm and only in that setting can it be understandable: "In Ps 132 wird die Lade ausdrücklich als anwesend erwähnt; der Psalm ist nur als Prozessionslied mit der Lade

---

meaning of יצץ "elsewhere always denoting 'to blossom,' here alone meaning 'will sparkle'."

[1] The Book of Psalms, p. 650.

[2] Ibid., p. 652; also Kidner, Psalms 73-150, p. 451 seems to prefer "will blossom" (literal translation of אצמיח) rather than "will shed its lustre."

[3] Murphy, The Book of Psalms, p. 652.

[4] Arthur G. Clarke, Analytical Studies in the Psalms (Kilmarnock: John Ritchie, Ltd., 1942), p. 328.

verständlich."[1] In other words expressed, this statement by Mowinckel refers to this particular psalm as the "text" of a dramatic procession with Yahweh's ark. The cultic search for the ark in Israel would thus correspond to a similar kind of feature in the Babylonian New Year and enthronement drama: the search for "the lost, dead or imprisoned god."[2]

Traditions related to the event described or alluded to in the particular passage belong to the essential background of this category of psalms.

Cuthbert C. Keat translates the verse: "There will I make a horn to sprout forth unto David: I have prepared a lamp for My anointed."[3] For the verb אצמיח ("to sprout forth") Cuthbert refers to Jer 23:5; 33:15 and Zech 3:8; 6:12 where the noun צמח "a sprout" is used of the Messianic king.[4] All four of these texts have the noun צמח "a sprout." Jer 23:5, however, employs the verb קום while Jer 33:15, interestingly enough, uses the same verb as in Ps 132:17, namely, אצמיח (<צמח) "to sprout forth," which fits the context speaking of a "branch." In Zech 3:8 the מביא (<בוא) Hiphil participle is used. Zech 6:12, like Jer 33:15, employs both צמח and יצמח (צמח), יצמח ומתחתיו צמח שמו איש־הנה "Behold the man whose name is the Branch (צמח): for he shall grow up (יצמח) in his place."

---

[1] Mowinckel, Psalmenstudien II, p. 191.

[2] As quoted by Sabourin, The Psalms, p. 253.

[3] A Study of the Psalms of Ascents (London: The Mitre Press, 1969), p. 99.

[4] Ibid.

According to the evidences given by Cuthbert, then, the evidences for אַצְמִיחַ to be translated "I will cause to blossom" or "I will cause to sprout forth" speak in favor for the fact that also in Ps 132:17 the old translation of אַצְמִיחַ "raise up," "cause to grow," "sprout," or "blossom" would fit better, especially if we consider a play on words, i.e., צֶמַח and צָמַח to be involved.[1]

Although Dahood's approach is new and fresh and creatively suggestive, it seems that too many texts speak against the translation אַצְמִיחַ with the meaning "I will make glow." In the same way it seems artificial to press the meaning of קֶרֶן to signify a lamp in the shape of an animal.[2] In light of this discussion, it seems more appropriate to compare the קֶרֶן to צֶמַח, and then the meaning of the passage in Ps 132:17 becomes clear and even brings out the synthetic parallelism in a beautiful and more natural way. We therefore here agree with Murphy that qeren is used with the meaning of "kingdom."[3] The בֵּן referring to the dynasty of David seems to imply a Messianic prophecy--a fact which there seems to be no contextual reason for denying--though eschatology is not explicitly stated.

Ps 148:14, a psalm of praise, seems to confirm Ps 132:17 as a Messianic prophecy.[4] The whole psalm is an exhortation

---

[1] Cf. also Holladay, A Concise Hebrew and Aramaic Lexicon, p. 307.

[2] Cf. Dahood, Psalms III, pp. 249, 248.

[3] Murphy, The Book of Psalms, p. 652.

[4] So also, Clarke, Analytical Studies in the Psalms, pp. 354-55. Kidner implies a similar interpretation, for he says,

(הללו to יה). The climax or apex of the psalm is יהוה expressed in vs. 14 where the reason is given for this exaltation: וירם קרן לעמו "He has raised up a horn for his people."

Bernhard Duhm interprets the קרן (in this הללו יה hymn) to mean "kingdom" and says, "Das 'Horn' (vgl. 132:17) meint wohl das Königtum, sei es (bei der Lesart וירם) das hasmonäische, sei es wenn das Verb futurisch ist, das messianische."[1]

Hans Schmidt considers the metaphor used as "ein merkwürdiges Bild,"[2] but he compares the figure of speech here used to Ps 132:17 and Ps 89:18 which confirms the conception of the horn being none other than Yahweh himself. Others, however, are more cautious and refer to קרן לעמו as with the meaning "the house of David."[3] Some commentators cling to the metaphoric meaning of strength and dare not enlarge upon its meaning.[4]

Ezek 29:21 belongs, no doubt, to this same category of texts. The קרן is preceded by the same verb אצמיח as in Ps 132:17 which suggests an interpretation in harmony with other texts

---

". . . among this people His [God's] glory is redemptive love (14), in raising up a horn for them, i.e., a strong deliverer (Lk 1:69); Psalms 73-150, p. 488; and Delitzsch, Biblical Commentary on the Psalms, 3:316.

[1] Duhm, Die Psalmen, p. 300-301.

[2] Schmidt, Die Psalmen, p. 256.

[3] So, for instance, Oesterley, The Psalms, p. 533; Kissane, The Book of Psalms (Dublin: Browne and Nolan [1964]), p. 593; Gunkel, Die Psalmen, p. 567: Perowne, The Book of Psalms, 2:416.

[4] So Kraus, Psalmen, 2:963, Anderson, Psalms, 2:951, and Rawlinson, The Book of Psalms, p. 408.

employing the same phraseology, referring to a future Branch of David's house.[1]

The word ובקרניכם per se does not have any Messianic connotation, but Ezek 34:21 places it in a Messianic context.[2] To be able to understand the passage it is necessary to pay attention to the main points of the whole chapter. William H. Brownlee observes that "The first ten verses . . . appear to be a post eventum judgment upon the former shepherds of the nation."[3] Brownlee then sees the next section (Ezek 34:11-16) as a counterpart to the indictment expressed in the first ten verses.[4] In the section of hope (Ezek 34:11-16),

---

[1] George A. Cooke (A Critical and Exegetical Commentary on the Book of Ezekiel, ICC [Edinburgh: T. & T. Clark, 1951], p. 330) refers inter alia to Jer 23:5; 33:15 and Zech 6:12 as parallel texts; cf. Walther Zimmerli who is apt to apply the "horn" to a Königs-messianisches Heil, but because no explicit expression to this end is to be found, Zimmerli adopts the interpretation that the judgment over the Yahweh-opposing nation is connected with the advent of a great salvation for God's people; Ezechiel, BKAT 13/1-2 (Neukirchen-Vluyn: Neukirchener Verlag, 1969), 2:721. John W. Wevers also takes a neutral position, saying that the horn is a symbol of strength. He also presumes that the expression "to spring forth" is literally "to sprout forth"--but adds, "a mixed figure." For the "sprouting horn," he refers to Ps 132:17 where (he asserts) it refers to a descendant of David. See Wevers, Ezekiel, The Century Bible (London: Thomas Nelson and Sons, Ltd., 1969), p. 227.

[2] Zimmerli gives allusion to such an interpretation being possible, Ezechiel, 2:841.

[3] "Ezekiel's Poetic Indictment of the Shepherds," HTR 51 (1958):191.

[4] Brownlee here expresses a general traditional view; Brownlee, after studying the chapter in depth, changed his view as to the "hope material," considering it non-genuine on the presumption that "the genuine Ezekiel emerges as a poet of doom;" "Ezekiel's poetic indictment," pp. 200-201. We diverge from Brownlee's view at this point and see the classification (i.e., of any prophet as either a prophet of doom or a prophet of hope) to be

The Lord pledges that he will inaugurate a new order for his sheep whereby he himself will assume the role of the good shepherd and perform the functions neglected by Israel's erstwhile earthly rulers.[1]

Brownlee sees the following section (Ezek 34:17-22) as a supplement promising a firm hand against all recalcitrant elements that may appear in the flock itself. The next two verses he sees as a return to the shepherd theme, "but the Lord is no more Shepherd, but David."[2]

It seems quite evident that the passages in Jer 23 and Ezek 34 refer to the same theme.[3] Joachim Jeremias referring to the ποιμήν-motif says the following:

> In view of the fact that in, e.g., the threats of Jeremiah "shepherds" is also a common term for political and military leaders, it is surprising that there is no single instance in the OT of "shepherd" ever being used in Israel as a title for the ruling king.[4]

---

too rigid a classification and on this presupposition see no valid reason to suppose that the unity of the chapter will undermine the authenticity of the chapter as a whole. Nor does it seem necessary to deprive Ezekiel of the authorship of the hope material in order to recover "for him a strong ethical indictment of exquisite beauty and power;" cf. Brownlee's presupposition (ibid., pp. 200-01 and n. 23).

[1] Ibid., p. 191.

[2] Ibid.; Brownlee says in regard to David, who is mentioned in this shepherd theme (v. 23): "The hope of David as a shepherd in Ezekiel 34:23 represents the later level of Messianic expectation found in Jeremiah 23:5-6, rather than the more general hope of better shepherds in the future found in Jeremiah 23:4" (ibid., p. 200).

[3] The level of various traditions in regard to the prophets Jeremiah and Ezekiel will not be discussed here. For our purpose it is enough to establish the fact that Ezek 34:21 which contains the word קרנים is embedded in a context of hope material. The word קרנים in retrospect is, no doubt, referring to the indictment.

[4] "ποιμήν B. Transferred Usage," in TDNT (Grand Rapids: Wm. B. Eerdmans, 1977), 6:487-88.

Jeremias also observes that "It is quite early said of David that he 'tends' Israel . . . and the people is called by him a flock . . ., but the royal title 'shepherd' does not occur."[1]

In general it may be said that already in Sumerian time the king is described as the shepherd appointed by deity. Jeremias says, "In Babylonian and Assyrian rê'û ("shepherd") is a common epithet for rulers and the verb re'û ("to pasture") is a common figure of speech for "to rule'."[2]

The following remark by Jeremias even more distinctly brings out the difference between the Orient and Israel. He says:

> The distinction from the courtly style of the ancient Orient is even more palpable if we add that in the time of impending disaster "shepherd" still occurs as a title for the ruler, but only for the future Messianic son of David.[3]

Jeremias then proceeds to give further implications of the prophecy in Ezek 34:11-22: "He Himself [Yahweh] will take over the office of shepherd and gather and feed the scattered flock."[4]

The indictment found in Ezek 34:21 is directed not to the "wild beast"[5] (the countries to which Israel as a people had been

---

[1] Ibid., p. 488, n. 30.

[2] Ibid., p. 486.   [3] Ibid.

[4] As quoted by Jeremias (ibid.). Jeremias also says that "with the title 'shepherd' Ez. seeks to guard against a one-sidedly political understanding of the figure of the future ruler, and also to leave the manner of the fulfillment of the promise to God." As for the election of David and the "righteous branch" (צמח צדיק), see Zimmerli, Ezechiel, 2:842.

[5] Brownlee, "Ezekiel's Poetic Indictment of the Shepherd," p. 195.

scattered) but to the "recalcitrant elements that may appear in the flock itself."[1]

The accusation to the "powerful, oppressive members of the community"[2] was pronounced because of the acts of violence committed by the strong and ruling members against the weak and sick in the community. These acts are described in figurative language as a pushing and thrusting "with your horns" (קרניכם).[3] It is also of interest to notice that the verb תנגחו (a *Piel* with the meaning of "butt," "thrust," "knock down") comes from נגח which originally means "gore"[4] (of an ox). It is worth remembering the rule that Hebrew words that go in pairs (dual form) have, besides the natural meaning, frequently a figurative meaning,[5] and that they have to be seen in this passage as a metaphor is self-evident.[6] This metaphor is apparently derived from the goring ox and with the horns (dual) the metaphor seems to convey a negative connotation;[7] often an aggressive act or action forced by selfish or proud motifs.

The more texts that are investigated the more enriched the

---

[1] Ibid., p. 191.

[2] Cooke, The Book of Ezekiel, p. 376.

[3] Dual construct. + suffix 2 m. pl.

[4] So Holladay, A Concise Hebrew and Aramaic Lexicon, p. 226.

[5] Hans Bauer and Pontus Leander, Historische Grammatik der Hebräischen Sprache (Hildesheim: Georg Olms Verlagsbuchhandlung, 1962), 1:516.

[6] So, for instance, Cooke, The Book of Ezekiel, p. 376.

[7] Zimmerli strikingly expresses it,"Die Kranken werden mit den Hörnern angegriffen," Ezechiel, 2:841.

nuances of קרן become. Most of the text-references in this section show that the purely extended meaning presents a real crux in interpretation. The form and structure as well as content and context must be considered and still there is a danger to miss the point, especially if à priori concepts play a dominant role.

The texts here discussed seem to present קרן not with a negative aggressive meaning but with a positive and expectant meaning. They look beyond the present towards the One to come. In other words, they are predictive or prophetic. Also the two texts with negative connotation (Ps 22:22; Ezek 34:21) are predictive or prophetic in character and are found in a Messianic setting. The morphological structure of the word as well as the content and context show, however, that they derive from the more well-known tradition of a goring bull--aggressive and violent in attitude and action. Ps 75, with its several references to קרן, presents several usages and each usage has to be interpreted in its own context. The samples show that the one traditional meaning of "power" and "strength" is too limited to bring out the rich variety of nuances which the poet wants to express.

The undeniable prophetic-messianic setting for most of these texts implies by necessity that there must be at least two main traditions in history from which the word קרן has originated: one positive and one negative. The negative tradition of an aggressive, attacking bull (more often presented in disguise but recognizable by the emblem of the "horns" of the moon giving its beneficial light for humanity) is the predominant one in the general Near Eastern

context. The positive tradition of "horn" common in the Bible, is
alluded to in ancient Near Eastern iconography (early seals) and in
certain epics and hymns. There are allusions to something being
lost on a particular day in history which caused the poetic writer
to express the tragedy in lament. The luminuous light of gods and
kings called melammu and pulḫu may refer to this tradition. So
also other mythological motifs and specific motifs on seals. These
traditions seem to have existed already in a pre-Israelite setting--
in other words, even as far back as in prehistoric times.

Prophetic Texts

Let us turn our attention to Amos 3:14: ונגדעו קרנות
המזבח ונפלו לארץ "and the horns of the altar shall be cut off
and fall to the ground."

William R. Harper points out that "the destruction of the
altars meant in reality the entire abolition of Israel's worship,
and was the greatest blow that could be struck."[1] Amaziah, the king
of Israel, made Amos understand that Bethel is the king's sanctuary,
a temple of the kingdom (Amos 7:14). Harper, therefore, sees the
destruction of the altars (with their horns) as a mark of humiliation of the royal house, as well "as the disappearance of the last
refuge of the people."[2] When fallen to the ground, the horns would
become profaned and no longer fulfill their purpose.[3]

---

[1] A Critical and Exegetical Commentary on Amos and Hosea, ICC (Edinburgh: T. & T. Clark, 1953), p. 82.

[2] Ibid., p. 83.

[3] So Samuel Amsler, who also points out "the day of Yahweh"

Richard S. Cripps sees it "unwise to see a religious significance in Amos' prediction of the fall of the Beth-el sanctuary."[1] He elucidates upon the statement by saying, "The ruin of the shrine is prophesied, not because of evil done there, but, so to speak, incidentally."[2] Why should this destruction be but "incidental"? The word פקדתי (<פקד) with the meaning of "to visit," i.e., with the intention to punish, is a rather strong word and is used twice in this passage (Amos 3:14)[3] The context, therefore, points to a retribution by intention that is about to take place ביום "on that day"--a future day--when Israel will be punished.

James L. Mays puts the finger more directly on the spot when he observes that

> Bethel was the pre-eminent religious centre of Israel in the time of Jeroboam II (7:10-13). . . . Because the very worship carried on at Bethel was at root a rebellion against Yahweh (4:4), the central focus of its cult, the altar (9:1; 2:8) was doomed. . . . The altar would be deconsecrated, and thereby the cult brought to an end.[4]

---

that was to arrive and to bring about this punishment; Amsler, Amos in Commentaire de l'Ancien Testament, 11.a (Neuchatel [Suisse]: Editions Delachaux & Niestle, 1965), p. 192.

[1] A Critical and Exegetical Commentary on the Book of Amos London: S.P.C.K., 1969), p. 164.

[2] Ibid.

[3] Hans W. Wolff has given the following elucidative explanation for the meaning of פקד in the context of Amos 3:2: "Because Yahweh has 'selected' (ידי) Israel for a special task, he must also 'examine' (פקד) its performance. 'Transgressions' being the object of the examinations, the basic meaning of פקד here is expanded so as to connote 'to punish (on the basis of investigation), to hold responsible, in short, 'to requite.' . . . The piercing address shows Amos transmitting to Israel a message from Yahweh, the judge, announcing sentence upon the guilty." Joel and Amos (Philadelphia: Fortress Press, 1977), p. 201.

[4] James L. Mays, Amos (Philadelphia: The Westminster Press, 1976), pp. 69-70.

In regard to the date of the impending events, Hans W. Wolff says, ". . . they will occur at the time when Yahweh punishes the crimes of Israel."[1] In conjunction with the statement above, Wolff also emphasizes that

> The first evidence for total judgment will be that the horns of the altar get hewn off. . . . The horns of the altar, which have been hewn off and have fallen to the ground, provide the witnesses with their first pieces of evidence for the total judgment, just as the tip of an ear serves for the shepherd as proof of the lost animal.[2]

It is of interest to notice that the verb נגדעו (<גדע) is the same as in Jer 48:25 (נגדעה).[3] We see this not as purely accidental but as implying a particular choice or selection of phrases that had wider implications. A contextual study gives the impression that קרן מואב could almost be considered a <u>terminus technicus</u> with reference to the dominion of Moab in a political or national sense, i.e., a kingdom, whereas קרנות almost without exception is found in connection with the altar (קרנות המזבח) and for that reason appears as a <u>terminus technicus</u> with reference to the cult of Israel (at Bethel).

___

[1] Ibid.; Wolff sees in the passage of Amos 3:13 bα a "later addition clearly distinguished from the context" (ibid., p. 111); the threat against Bethel, however (5:5 bβ), Wolff recognizes as coming from Amos himself. We can see no reasonable reason of asserting different dates to the two texts. The simplest way, of course, is to acknowledge both as oracles from the time of Amos and fulfilled in the time of Josiah (ca. 620 B.C.)--more than a century after Amos' prediction (2 Kgs 22:15-16).

[2] Ibid., p. 201.

[3] Both of the verbs expressing <u>Niphal</u> perfect; the first one a plural form and the second a feminine singular form (so Holladay, A Concise Hebrew and Aramaic Lexicon, p. 56).

Micah 4:13 is another problem text in interpretation.[1] The "lack of agreement among cirtical scholars leaves their conclusions open to question."[2] There are other problems involved: that of foremost interest here is the exegesis of the second colon because it contains the word קרן. The particular colon reads: כי־קרנך אשים ברזל, "for I will make your horn iron."

As a general rule the קרנך has been interpreted as dual,[3] although at the same time, most commentators translate it rightly as singular.[4] On the other hand, there are some scholars who both translate and interpret קרנך as a dual. Artur Weiser, for instance, who makes this emendation of the text, understands the symbol of the "Hörner zu Eisen" as a symbol of power. Weiser refers to the

---

[1] The problem of relevance to this text is related to the context in vs. 10. Most scholars believe that chapters 4-7 are two miscellaneous collections later added as supplements, and probably postexilic. In this way the word "Babylon" in vs. 10 can be explained as a vaticinum ex eventu. Others explain "Babylon" as a metonymy standing for Assyria; see also Andrew K. Helmbold's discussion, "Micah, the Prophet," in The Zondervan Pictorial Encyclopedia of the Bible (Grand Rapids: Zondervan Publishing House, 1975), 4:217, 215; T. Miles Bennett, The Book of Micah: A Study Manual (Grand Rapids: Baker Book House, 1968), p. 45.

[2] Hembold, "Micah, the Prophet," 4:214; so also Gleason L. Archer, A Survey of Old Testament Introduction (Chicago: Moody Press, 1964), p. 312.

[3] So, for instance, Rolland E. Wolfe, "The Book of Micah," IB, 6:930.

[4] For the singular usage, see, for instance, Karl Marti, Das Dodekapropheton, Kurzer Hand-Commentar zum Alten Testament, vol. 13 (Tübingen: Verlag J. C. B. Mohr [Paul Siebeck], 1904), p. 285; Arvid Bruno, Micah und der Herrscher aus der Vorzeit (Uppsala: Almqvist & Wiksell, 1923), p. 79; John M. P. Smith, A Critical and Exegetical Commentary on the Books of Micah, Zephaniah and Nahum, Habakkuk, Obadiah and Joel, ICC (Edinburgh: T. & T. Clark, 1959), p. 97; Carl F. Keil, The Twelve Minor Prophets,

passage in vs. 13 as a figure of speech in which the threshing oxen present a metaphor of Israel.[1]

The "threshing" דושי (imperative)--a well-known picture from the Near East--makes it almost compulsory to associate it with the idea of oxen-threshing. J. Miles Bennet describes the well-known "ancient custom of treading out the grain by driving cattle over the straw until it was cut to pieces by the feet of the animals and by threshing instruments drawn by them."[2]

Still there arises the question whether the prophet intends to maintain this figure of "threshing oxen" as a general ramification for his message. The answer must be no. First of all there is no mentioning of "oxen" in the text. This is implied by scholars, but there is actually no warrant for it.

Threshing is present. Thus there is no reason to deny such a pregnant expression. But it seems that the prophet leaves the threshing behind and quickly passes on to the next figure. His active mind expresses dynamic events in more than one metaphor. This rapid change of figures of speech is often detected in poetry in general, and much more so in an oracle of Yahweh. Could it be that already in the next colon the prophet leaves the figure of

---

Biblical Commentary on the Old Testament (Grand Rapids: Wm. B. Eerdmans Publishing Company, 1961), p. 471.

[1] Artur Weiser, Das Buch der Zwölf Kleinen Propheten, ATD, vol. 24 (Göttingen: Vandenhoeck & Ruprecht, 1967), pp. 269, 271.

[2] The Book of Micah, p. 45. (The picture is familiar to everyone who has travelled in the Ancient Near East in harvest time.)

threshing behind and enters upon a new metaphor? Yet in the fourth colon (vs. 13d) we notice that he returns to the figure of threshing by using הדקות (<דקק) with the meaning of "crush" and in this way makes the thoughts correspond. In short, in Mic 4:13b the phrase "your horn" occurs and in 13c the phrase "your hoofs."

If one insists on קרנך as a dual, the "horns" could just as well be applied to the daughter of Zion (maybe in likeness to Ištar or ʾAnat) instead of to an ox which is not even mentioned in the text, but exists as a compulsory idea in our minds, and which is assumed to be present as an ellipsis of thought.

There are others who are aware of this inconsistency in interpretation. Wilhelm Rudolph, for instance, points out that in this context (Mic 4:13) the horns actually have nothing to do with the threshing situation but only convey a general picture of strength.[1] Rudolph, at this point, includes within parentheses also 1 Kgs 22:11--a text speaking of "horns of iron."[2] The question arises unsought: What is the figure involved if the horns do not refer to the threshing ox?

John M. P. Smith, who like Rudolph, notes that "the reference to horns here is foreign to the figure of the threshing-floor," offers the following solution: ". . . the reference of horn . . . introduces a new element into the picture--that of the angry ox

---

[1] Micah-Nahum-Habakuk-Zephanja, KAT, vol. 13 (Gütersloher: Verlagshaus Gerd Mohn, 1975), p. 93.

[2] The text is dealt with on pp. 319-22 (above).

goring the foe."[1] This interpretation which is very common confronts the difficulty of the ox having but one horn. Our study so far has shown that the dual is used when קרן has reference to horns on the animal--either natural horns or horns on an animal to be interpreted as a metaphor (Gen 22:13; 1 Kgs 22:11; 2 Chr 18:10; Deut 33:17; Ps 22:22; Ezek 34:21).

Our present text reads קרנך, but there is, of course, the possibility that a dual may be implied although, for poetical reasons, it is expressed as a singular. This would complicate the interpretation. We would therefore suggest that the expression קרנך should be interpreted as it stands and without emendations. The "horn" may still convey the figure of strength, but instead of emphasizing the brutal strength of a goring ox, it would refer to the inner strength that a right attitude of mind brings about. This in turn would make Yahweh to fulfill his eschatological intentions.[2]

A structural analysis of the oracle, which is expressed in poetic form, shows that it consists of six tricola which can be divided into two parts with a proem and two bicola in each. The second part presents a chiastic pattern with a ballast variant (כל־הארץ). The two parts show the same poetical device: proem and bicola. Furthermore, in both parts, the two bicola express synonymous parallelism. As קרנך ("your horn") occurs in the first

---

[1] Smith, Micah, Zephaniah, Naham, Habakkuk, Obadiah, and Joel, p. 99.

[2] See context in vss. 11-12 and a possible allusion to this interpretation in the והחרמתי in the second tricolon in the second part (i.e., 13e).

bicolon, the second bicolon conveys the same thought (but expressed in other words), namely, when the daughter Zion is empowered with strength, which Yahweh will give, she will stand up and thresh. The crushing of the people may be understood as the work of Yahweh himself,[1] or the concept of corporeality may be involved.

According to subject matter, we should discuss next the text in Jer 48:25, which reads: נגדעה קרן מואב וזרעו נשברה נאם יהוה "The horn of Moab is cut off and his arm is broken, says the Lord."

Wilhelm Rudolph points out that this text employs two metaphors for strength: "horn" and "arm."[2] This observation brings to mind the Sumerian usage of si and á ("horn" and "arm") which both could be used in metaphors to signify "power" or "strength." Rudolph's observation might be incidental but it is still significant. The figures of speech conveyed the important prediction that Moab's power or kingdom will be (is) broken. The reason for the downfall of Moab is given (Jer 48:18-20, 26, 29, 30) as self-exaltation, pride, and insolence. Ps 75:5, 6, for instance, would agree with this interpretation: (ולרשעים) אל־תרימו קרן . . . . ("to the wicked") "do not lift up your horn; . . ."

The context makes it clear that Moab's haughtiness and deplorable fall were interrelated. Keil in his commentary brings out

---

[1] Bennett points out that Micah identified the enemies of God's people with the very enemies of God himself; The Book of Micah, p. 46.

[2] Jeremiah, HAT 12 (Tübingen: J. C. B. Mohr [Paul Siebeck], 1958), p. 260.

a further suggestion that the cities of the tableland, and especially Kerioth and Bozrah, are introduced "as two important towns which maintained the strength of Moab."[1] He seems to connect the two facts, for after he has mentioned the facts of the two important cities, he points out that this significant statement occurs, "The horn of Moab is cut off."[2] It is the same position as that of Rudolph in regard to the two synonymous metaphors for "strength" or "power."

> Horn and arm are figures of power: the horn an emblem of power that boldly asserts itself, and pushes down all that opposes (cf. Ps 75:5, 11); the arm being rather an emblem of domination.[3]

The implication here adds a new dimension to the "horn" as it seems indirectly to refer to the many cities of the tableland of Moab which were its (the nation's) pride. The cities gone--Moab was put to shame, for it was broken, i.e., the kingdom of Moab was destroyed (Jer 48:20).

Ebenezer Henderson regards this particular prophecy in Jeremiah (concerning Moab) as "couched in highly practical language."[4] As for the historical background and fulfillment of this oracle, Henderson says:

> The prophecy was most probably composed on occasion of the part which the Moabites took against the Jews, as

---

[1] Keil, The Prophecies of Jeremiah, in Biblical Commentary on the Old Testament by C. F. Keil and F. Delitzsch (Grand Rapids: Wm. B. Eerdmans Publishing Company, 1960), 2:222 (cf. Amos 2:2).

[2] Ibid. [3] Ibid.

[4] Ebenezer Henderson, The Book of the Prophet Jeremiah and That of the Lamentation (London: Hamilton, Adams, and Co., 1851), p. 230.

auxiliaries to the Chaldeans in the days of Nebuchadnezzar, 2 Kgs 24:2; and its fulfillment is to be referred to their subjugation by the same monarch on his way to Egypt, five years after the destruction of Jerusalem. . . . The prophet then shows, that notwithstanding the proud spirit of the Moabites, engendered by their unvaried prosperity, they should assuredly be conquered . . . and lest any of the cities should cherish the hope of escape, an enumeration of the principal cities that were to suffer is specially given, 18-25.[1]

Other commentators add no further light on this text.[2]

Both oracle and lament together are expressed in a highly poetic language.[3] The context of the oracle seems to add a new dimension to קרן in this text--at least implicitly--that of the horn being a symbol of the cities or city kingdoms which were the pride of Moab, i.e., the nation's pride.

---

[1] Ibid.

[2] Most commentators make a note of Moab's pride as the reason for her fall. So, for instance, Helmut Lamparter, Prophet wider Willen (Stuttgart: Calwer Verlag, 1964), p. 244; Andrew W. Blackwood, Commentary on Jeremiah (Waco, TX: Word Books, 1977), p. 298; Solomon B. Freehof, Book of Jeremiah (New York: Union of American Hebrew Congregations, 1977), pp. 259-60; John Bright, Jeremiah, AB (Garden City, NY: Doubleday & Company, Inc., 1965), pp. 316, 321.

[3] That we have to do with an oracle of Yahweh and a prediction concerning the kingdom of Moab is evident from the context; see, for instance, Jer 48:22: לכו ונכריתנה מגוי "Come, let us cut her off [i.e., Moab] from being a nation." (vs. 8) ריבא שדד אל־ כל־עיר ועיר לא תמלט "The destroyer shall come upon every city, and no city shall escape. (vs 12) לכן הנה־ימים באים "therefore, behold, the days are coming . . . (vs 21) ומשפט בא אל־ארץ המישר "Judgment has come upon the tableland . . ." etc. Jer 31:25 in the Septuaginta reads: κατεάχθη κέρας Μωαβ, καὶ τὸ ἐπίχειρον αὐτοῦ συνετρίβη. The text in the Septuaginta is certainly corrupt; cf. Jer 31:12 "καὶ τὰ κέρατα αὐτοῦ συγκόψουσι." The restored text (Jer 48:25) in 2Q Jer (see Joseph A. Fitzmyer, The Dead Sea Scrolls [Missoula, MT: Scholars Press, 1977], p. 18) = 2Q 13 in DJD, ed. M. Bartlet, Joseph T. Milik, and Roland de Vaux (Oxford: Clarendon Press, 1962), 3:66 (Jer 48:25 = LXX 31:25, line 1) is exactly the same as in BHS. An anakrousis tricolon (3:2:2) with a chiastic thought pattern of incomplete synonymous parallelism is expressed in this oracle. The last colon נאם יהוה is deleted in the Septuaginta.

The third chapter of Habakkuk is regarded as one of the "most beautiful anthems of praise in the Old Testament."[1] The chapter has been labelled as a "psalm" by most scholars (since the time of Gunkel)[2] and even as a "prophecy."[3] A very pertinent view throughout the decades since the turn of the century has been that the "psalm" must have been written by another author than the one writing the first two chapters of the book. Walter R. Betteridge, early in this century, has, however, pointed out that the pieces to which the psalm "bears the most resemblance in form and style are the songs of Deborah (Judges, chap. 5) and the so-called Blessings of Moses (Deut, chap. 33)."[4] Betteridge therefore maintains that "the psalm is from the same hand and brain as the rest of the prophecy."[5]

---

[1] George L. Robinson, The Twelve Minor Prophets (Grand Rapids: Baker Book House, 1926), p. 125.

[2] So, for instance, William A. Irwin, "The Psalm of Habakkuk," JNES 1 (1942):10-40; Sigmund Mowinckel, "Zum Psalm des Habakuk," TZ 9 (1953):1-23; William F. Albright, "The Psalm of Habakkuk," Studies in Old Testament Prophecy, ed. Harold H. Rowley (New York: Scribner, 1950), pp. 1-18.

[3] So, for instance, Walter R. Betteridge, "The Interpretation of the Prophecy of Habakkuk," AJT 7 (1903):647-61; Philippe Béguerie, Le Psaume d'Habacuc (Paris: Editions du Cerf, 1954), pp. 53-84 as quoted by Peter Jöcken, Das Buch Habakuk, Bonner Biblische Beiträge, 48 (Köln-Bonn: Peter Hanstein, 1977), p. 478. Béguerie's concept in regard to Hab 3 says, "Der Psalm Hab 3 steht in Form und Aussage zwischen den Visionen der Propheten Literatur und den eigentlichen Apokalypsen: Er schildert den Triumph Gottes über die bestehende Trübsal." It is a victory that surpasses the temporal. It is a cosmic struggle or fight. Yahweh triumphs over death in crushing Yam (the sea); Das Buch Habakuk, pp. 478-79. John H. Eaton sees the psalm as having "prophetic origin"; see his article, "The Origin and Meaning of Habakkuk," ZAW 76 (1964):166-67.

[4] Ibid., p. 659.

[5] Ibid., p. 661. Today after renewed studies of the

Albright, who divides the Psalm of Habakkuk into four parts, finds analogous repetitive or climactic parallelism in many ancient Hebrew poems. He notes that this one especially has a "close affinity of atmosphere and archaism with the Song of Deborah . . . the Blessing of Moses . . . which may as a whole date from the end of the tenth century."[1]

Duhm expresses his view that the passages (Hab 2:1-3 and 3:2-16) give evidence that the author was, in style and terminology, familiar with the older prophetic-apocalyptic literature, and apart from the Deborah song, reminding us of Micah, Ezekiel, Isa 13, as well as the younger apocalypsis, Daniel, etc.[2]

As for the exegesis in particular of Hab 3:4, Duhm interprets the קרנים as rays and likens them to lightning in accordance with the description in Ezek 1:13 and Dan 7:10.[3] Furthermore, he says, "Der Dual קרנים steht vielleicht, weil die Strahlen je nach rechts und links, paarweise, Flügeln ähnlich, von Jahve ausgehen."[4]

---

relationship of the prophet to the national cult, it is generally considered that there is no need for ascribing the psalm to any other author than the prophet himself; see Jöcken, Das Buch Habakuk, p. 481.

[1] Albright, "The Psalm of Habakkuk," in Studies in Old Testament Prophecy, ed. H. H. Rowley (Edinburgh: T. & T. Clark, 1957), p. 8.

[2] See Jöcken, Das Buch Habakuk, p. 269.

[3] Duhm, Das Buch Habakuk, p. 78.

[4] Ibid.; Duhm, who translates קנים מידו לו "Zu seiner Seite Strahlen," thinks that קרנים is a veiled or cryptic expression for his [Yahweh's] power. Wilhelm Vischer has adopted a similar translation: "Sonnenstrahlen ihm zur Seite" in Der Prophet Habakuk (Neukirchen: Kreis Moers, 1958), p. 32.

375

William A. Irwin points out that the psalm in Habakkuk is concerned with theophany and that "this divine manifestation is in some way related to natural phenomena--lightning, thunder, the storm, earthquake, etc."[1] Irwin refers to several earlier and contemporary scholars who likewise, in the fashion of the prevailing school in the early decades of this century, interpreted the poem in the imagery of a cosmic myth--obviously thinking that this was the intent of the poet long ago.[2]

In harmony, then, with the mythological imagery of surrounding nations, the conception prevailed that "in the oldest form of the poem [i.e., Hab 3] El was the sun-god Shemesh."[3]

Furthermore, the mention of <u>Deber</u> [דבר] and Resheph (רשף)

> . . . recalls a similar procession in the Babylonian account of the Deluge, where Ramman the storm-god has for one of his attendants the female counterpart of <u>Deber</u>, Dibarra, goddess of Pestilence.[4]

Irwin also sees the text in vs. 4 as corrupt and thinks that the peculiar [קרנים מידו לו] "horns from his hand" proves this fact. Irwin apparently sees the קרנים as a weapon, for he refers to vs. 11 to prove that among Yahweh's weapons were light and lightning.[5]

---

[1] "The Psalm of Habakkuk," <u>JNES</u> 1 (1942):10.

[2] Ibid., p. 11.

[3] Henry St. J. Thackeray, <u>The Septuagint and Jewish Worship</u>, pp. 51-52, as quoted by Irwin, "The Psalm of Habakkuk," p. 11.

[4] Ibid.

[5] See Irwin, "The Psalm of Habakkuk," p. 13; so also p. 19, where he points out the strangeness of the third colon. The fourth verse presents a tricolon (3:3). Irwin sees this tricolon in

Albright's translation of Hab 3:3-4 clearly shows that he saw no real basis for the usual rendering "rays" instead of "horns."[1] Albright's translation of the passage reads:

> God approached from the Southland And the Holy One from Mount Paran, His glory covering heaven, While earth was full of His praise. [Yahweh] attacked like a bull (?) Provided with tossing horns, Rejoicing in the day of His triumph.[2]

Mowinckel sees the psalm has having originally a Sumerian-Babylonian origin, though it might have reached the Israelites through the Canaanites, for the creation thought in Ugarit shows influences from the east.[3]

Dahood keeps to the meaning of קרנים as "wings" and he says with reference to Hab 3:3-4:

> Yahweh is pictured as an eagle flying from the south whose extended wings fill the heavens: "His majesty covered the heavens and his brilliance filled the earth. His shining was like the sun, two wings were at his sides (qarnayim miyyādō lō)."[4]

---

isolation as a mark of corruption and sees the strangeness of the third colon as a support for his view. The apparatus in BHS (Hab 3:4) brings out the third colon as probably being a later addition. (For a translation of the whole psalm in which Irwin embodies some of the textual conclusions advanced, see ibid., p. 40, where the more highly conjectural readings have been placed by inclusion within parentheses.)

[1] "The Psalm of Habakkuk," p. 14, n. 1.

[2] Ibid., p. 12.

[3] Jöcken, Das Buch Habakuk, p. 305; for an exhaustive survey of scholarly works dealing with various aspects of the psalm of Habakkuk, see Jöcken, Das Buch Habakuk. (Ferris J. Stephens, for instance, says, "The theophany in Habakkuk 3 lends itself readily to the hypothesis that the background for it was furnished by an ancient Semitic legend, one version of which is found in the Babylonian Creation Epic"; "The Babylonian Dragon Myth in Habakkuk 3," JBL 43 [1924]:290.)

[4] Psalms I, p. 108.

Dahood shows that "the motif of the divine bird of great wing-span is richly documented in Canaanite and biblical literature[1] and has adopted the translation of קרן with wing(s) consistently throughout his writings.

Quite recently, Rembert Sorg has attempted a new approach. He sees the key to Habakkuk's third chapter in three different passages (4bc, 9b, and 13d) which "at least by position are associated with the three Selahs in the chapter."[2] Sorg sees a ritual nexus in these cola of parenthetical character.

As for the first passage, Sorg points out that if one accepts the meaning of "rays" [scilicet of light, from his hand(s), or, side(s)] as a translation for קרן, it would be a hapax legomenon. Sorg is also aware of Dahood's novel version and interpretation: "Two wings were at his sides (garnayim miyyādō lō)" and the literal translation of the Septuagint and the Vulgate kérata/ cornua.[3] Sorg, however, does not in fact accept any of these translations but has suggested his own version "horn-pair," though he feels it is clumsy.[4] One of the reasons that defends this translation is, according to Sorg, "the retrospective singular suffix of ʿuzzāh (its strength)"[5] in the third colon. Furthermore he argues, "In the immediate context, it is something 'handed out' by

---

[1] Ibid.; cf. Dahood's discussion (ibid., p. 107).

[2] In referring to these passages Sorg thinks that "they belong to the original composition and they are an indispensable key to the Sitz im leben which the original composition envisages; but their parenthetic nature lifts them out of the poetic context; Habaqquq III and Selah (Fifield, WI: King of Martyrs Priory, 1968), p. 1.

[3] Ibid.   [4] Ibid., p. 4.   [5] Ibid.

God (in person of Priest or Prophet?) and somehow cryptically bears His name."[1]

Sorg sees the "main light" for his interpretation as coming from vs. 13, "where it is suggested that this 'qarnayim' is carried in a leather-case, slung around the neck."[2] As further support for his interpretation, Sorg refers to Job 16:15 in which text he sees the equal possibility of pointing the singular 'qarni' (according to the Masoretic Text) as a dual with suffix, i.e., 'qarnay.' The second text that gives a close parallel, according to Sorg, is 1 Kgs 22:11. Sorg says: "Of prime importance . . . is the explicit attestation of an artifically made pair of horns, qarnayim, used as a prophetic symbol in formal ceremony."[3]

Thus far he sums it all up and says:

> All the given data point not to a natural set of animal horns, much less to a purely figurative sense, but to a real artifact, representing in miniature a pair of horns. The term "qarnayim" thus emerges in Hab as the specific name of object, small enough to be practically portable in a leather-case suspended from the neck, and hallowed, surely in some way. . . . Not an amulet but a "sacramental."[4]

Sorg continues to bring forth archeological evidences—horn-shaped objects excavated at Gezer, at Tell-el 'Ajjul near Gaza, and at Megiddo—which all seem to originate from various periods.[5]

He informs us that the material of these artifacts is variously gold, silver, electrum, and bronze, although silver was by

---

[1] Ibid.; it is not quite clear from Sorg's statement what is the "immediate context," but probably Sorg is referring to verse 3: אלוה מתימן יבוא וקדוש מהר־פארן.

[2] Ibid. [3] Ibid.

[4] Ibid., pp. 4-5. [5] Ibid., p. 6.

far the most common material. This last information is of interest because it may hint to the fact that the objects were connected with moon-worship.[1] Sorg, however, notes the following:

> Even a reference to the Moon-god allows the horn-interpretation. Along with other gods, the Moon-god (the Accadian Sin = Sumerian Zu-en of the ancient Mesopotamian religion and the Phoenician Yarikh) enjoyed the epithet of "Bull." With some Arabian tribes, a live sacred bull was the symbol (or incarnation) of the Moon-god. Accordingly, the horns of a bull, as much as the pictorial image of the moon in the sky, were emblematic of the god.[2]

Sorg further emphasizes the known fact "that horns were a common symbol of divinity, and of human royalty as well, in the ancient world. They designated power, strength and rank."[3] He further purports that

> . . . the texts of Hab 3:4 and 1 Kgs 22:11, seen in archaeological perspective, show that the Israelites adopted this concrete convention of the ambient culture as a symbol of Yahweh's strength, purified of pagan connotation and idolatry.[4]

In this respect, then, the qarnayim, as Sorg here sees the meaning, belong to Yahweh--not to some horned Baal or Ashtoreth. "It [the word qarnayim] symbolizes His [Yahweh's] strength, communicated to men."[5]

The Psalm in Habakkuk, then, has a long history of various interpretations, only a few of which have been referred to here. Peter Jöcken in his exhaustive study refers to numerous and various

---

[1] On this point see Ditlef Nielsen (Die altarabische Mondreligion [Strassburg: Karl J. Trübner, 1904], p. 104) who discusses the particular colors of the astral deities.

[2] Sorg, Habaqquq III and Selah, p. 11.

[3] Ibid.   [4] Ibid.   [5] Ibid.

prevailing conceptions in the lapse of time.[1]

It is evident from the research of Jöcken that the theophany in Habakkuk was understood, at the beginning of the Christian church, to have had an eschatological-messianic meaning.[2] Later the return to the Sinai theophay and the total ramification of the Exodus and the "Thunderstorm-theophany" followed.[3] Quite a number of scholars have accepted Gunkel's hypothesis advocating a mutual influence of mythology with reference to this particular psalm.[4] Also the school advocating the prophetic visionary description of a future judgment has several known scholars as representatives of this view.[5] Several scholars have promoted the scope of apocalyptics in this theophanic hymn.[6] The cultic scope of the theophany has one of the most well-known precursors in Mowinckel.[7] Claus Westermann and Jörg Jeremias speak about the genre of "Epiphany," respectively, the Song of Victory.[8]

A careful study of the work of Habakkuk shows that the book can, without contention, be regarded as a unit.[9] It has also been

---

[1] Jöcken points out that some three hundred different scholars have investigated this hymn (Hab 3) during the more than 150 years of the history of interpretation; Das Buch Habakkuk, p. 518.

[2] So Aurelius Augustinus, Gottesstaat, xviii, 32, as cited by Jöcken, Das Buch Habakuk, p. 520.

[3] Ibid., pp. 520-21 cites several advocates of these various theophany-theories.

[4] Ibid., p. 521, for scholars who side with this view.

[5] Ibid., p. 561.   [6] Ibid., p. 521.   [7] Ibid., p. 535.

[8] Ibid., pp. 521, 550, and 565.

[9] See Donald J. Moeller, "Habakkuk," in NCE, ed. M. R. P.

considered by most scholars to belong to the genre of Psalmody. The theophanic element in this hymn is also obvious. Actually, the theophany is of cosmic nature that emphasizes a real ἔσχατον.

Sorg expresses the view that "the text presents a vivid description of a prophetic vision. The Prophet is actually seeing and hearing what he tells (vs 2)."[1] On the basis of his presupposition Sorg translates "the whole chapter mutatis mutandis in the prophetic and 'liturgical' present tense."[2]

As with many other passages, Habakkuk with its three chapters also presents a variety of genres. Chapter 3 especially yields material that can be classified into various genres. We consider this eschatological theophany described in terms of an earlier impressive theophany. The message is therefore prophetic--referring to the final eschaton and is expressed in poetical terms. The qarnayim of Yahweh are tied up with his avenging wrath (vss. 4-16). As the wrath of Yahweh is no longer retributive but final, the קרנים of Yahweh, as is often the case where dual is used, refer to the aggressive activity of the Lord to rid the earth of evil--a work that is strange and alien to his character (Isa 28:21). The aggressiveness in activity expressed metaphorically by the dual form can be seen from the usage of the same form in 1 Kgs 22:11 and Deut 33:17.

The discussion whether קרנים should be translated "horns"

McGuire et al. (New York: McGraw-Hill Book Company, 1967), 6:876.

[1] Habaqquq III and Selah, p. 38.   [2] Ibid.

or "rays" has led nowhere. A comparison of various ancient translations does not solve all the problems.

Henry B. Swete has preferred the literal translation and his version of Hab 3:4 follows closely that of Rhalfs. "καὶ φέγγος αὐτοῦ ὡς φῶς ἔσται κέρατα ἐν χερσὶν αὐτοῦ καὶ ἔθετο ἀγάπησιν κραταιὰν ἰσχύος αὐτοῦ."[1]

Codex Barberini presents the following translation: "διαύγασμα φωτὸς ἔσται αὐτῷ κέρατα ἐκ χειρὸς αὐτοῦ ὑπάρχει αὐτῷ ἐκεῖ ἐπεστήρικται, ἡ δύναμις τῆς δόξης αὐτοῦ."[2] Although this version follows the Hebrew text independently of the Septuagint, the particular passage κέρατα ἐκ χειρὸς αὐτοῦ does not alter the thought with reference to qarnayim. The word is still ambiguous.

The Latin version also brings out the literal "cornua" in the following translation: "Splendor eius ut lux erit, Cornua in manibus eius; Ibi abscondita est fortitudo eius."[3]

We see the prophecy in Hab 3 as expressed in poetic language, depicting in a majestic theophany, the coming of Yahweh to judge the world. This conclusion in regard to this psalm can, however, at this stage, be only tentative and suggestive due to the textual problems which scholars for the past three hundred years have tried to solve.

---

[1] The Old Testament in Greek (Cambridge: University Press, 1930), 3:61; cf. Septuaginta, ed. Rhalfs, 2:536.

[2] As quoted by Dom Hugues Bevenot, "Le Cantique d'Habacuc," RB 42 (1933):501; for the antiquity of the codex Barberini and for its independency of the Septuagint, see Jöcken, Das Buch Habakuk, p. 523.

[3] Biblia Sacra iuxta Vulgatam versionem, 2:1410.

Apocalyptic texts

The passages that will be considered in this section are the five occurrences of the term "horn" in Zech 2:1-4 and the several passages in Daniel where the word "horn" occurs, namely, chapters 7 and 8.

The quest for alleged differences of style and content with reference to genre will not be elaborated on per se,[1] due to the fact that this question is closely tied up with the debate of authorship, date, unity of the book and related problems which will not be dealt with here.

In this section we are concerned only with the passage Zech 2:1-4, which from a scholarly point of view belongs to the indisputable section of Zechariah.

It is interesting to find the word קרן used five times in a few verses--plural feminine every time except once in singular, in which instance the usage corresponds to the idiom in Ps 75:5, 6. All the other times the grammatical form of morphological structure is the same as that of references to the altar of sacrifice or altar of incense. A glance at the passage will reveal, however, that the meaning of horns with reference to sacrifice or incense does not fit the context. The word קרנות must therefore mean something else in this passage of Zechariah.

---

[1] For a survey and summary of critical views, see for instance, Roland K. Harrison, "Zechariah, Book of," The Zondervan Pictorial Encyclopedia of the Bible (Grand Rapids: Zondervan Publishing House, 1975), pp. 1042-48; Merril F. Unger, Zechariah (Grand Rapids: Zondervan Publishing House, 1976), pp. 12-14; Joyce G. Baldwin, Haggai, Zechariah, Malachi (Downers Grove, IL: Inter-Varsity Press, 1972), pp. 59-84, and Herbert C. Leupold, Exposition of Zechariah (Grand Rapids: Baker Book House, 1978), pp. 1-13.

A closer investigation shows that even structurally the word used is not constructed in the same way as in Exodus. Apart from Zech 2 we find the feminine plural only once in the absolute form prefixed with -ה-, namely, in Ezek 43:15 where it is used in the phrase הקרנות ארבע. This is remarkable for it shows that there can be no confusion as to the proper meaning if one takes proper heed of the morphological structure and the immediate and wider context.

The first occurrence of קרן in the passage under investigation is in Zech 2:1: ואשא את־עיני וארא והנה ארבע קרנות "And I lifted my eyes and saw, and behold, four horns!" The next phrase also deviates from the literal usage in Exodus, for Zech 2:2 reads: . . . אלה הקרנות אשר זרו את־יהודה . . . . "These are the horns which have scattered Judah, . . ." This same phrase is repeated in Zech 2:4. The last sentence containing the word את־קרנות "the horns," is introduced after the four smiths have entered the scene. The passage reads: ויבאו אלה להחריד אתם לידות את־קרנות הגוים הנשאים קרן אל־ארץ יהודה לזרותה. "And these [the smiths] have come to terrify them, to cast down the horns of the nations who lifted up their horns against the land of Judah to scatter it."

Not in one instance is the construction and immediate context analogous to the constructions and setting of the same word in a literal context in the Hebrew Bible. This already gives us the clue that the reference of the horns cannot be to the altar, nor have reference to literal horns of any kind.

Hans Bauer and Pontus Leander give a guiding principle at this stage:

> Wörter, die paarweise vorhandene Körperteile bezeichnen, haben daneben oft eine übertragene Bedeutung. Die natürliche Bedeutung erscheint im Dual, die letztere im Plural.[1]

The meaning thus must be figurative, a fact which has been realized by scholars in general. W. Emery Barnes, nearly fifty years ago, said in regard to the four horns:

> A horned animal is a not uncommon figure in the O.T. for a strong military power; Num 23:22 (R.V., of Israel); Deut 33:17 (of Joseph); Dan 8:3, 4 (of the Medo-Persian Empire). But in the present passage of Zechariah the vision is barely sketched, not described, and the horns . . . represent the hostile tribes which surround the Jewish community.[2]

Barnes, farther on, identifies these four horns as the Samaritans (on the north), the Ammonites (on the east), the Edomites (on the south), and the Tyrians and the Philistines (on the west)--in a contemporary context.[3]

Frederick B. Meyer presents his application in a wider scope, for he says, "On the north Chaldea, Assyria, and Samaria; on the south, Egypt and Arabia; on the west, Philistia; and on the east, Ammon and Moab."[4] Meyer even goes beyond this scope, saying:

> And it is probable that the Spirit of God looked beyond these to the four great monarchies, which have occupied, and still occupy, the "Times of the Gentiles," and which

---

[1]Historische Grammatik der Hebräischen Sprache des Alten Testamentes, 1:516.

[2]Haggai, Zechariah and Malachi (Cambridge: University Press, 1934), p. 32.

[3]Ibid.

[4]The Prophet of Hope Studies in Zechariah (London: Morgan & Scott, 1952), p. 25.

were represented in the four metals of Daniel's vision, or in the four great beasts, which one after another emerged from the sea.[1]

The use of the number <u>four</u> as an indication of the cardinal points of the compass has been indicated by several scholars in the past. But according to Herbert C. Leupold,

> A new argument on the unity of authorship is offered by Moeller (<u>Einleitung in das Alte Testament</u>, p. 161), which stresses Zechariah's strange predilection for the use of the number <u>four</u> throughout the book. He points out that there are "four times two night visions; four horses; four horns; four smiths; four chariots; four winds; four subordinate clauses (3:7); four persons (6:14); four fast days (8:19); four admonitions (8:9f.); a fourfold guilt (7:13f.); fourfold punishment (8:10); four pronouncements (8:12a); . . . Though no finality can be ascribed to arguments of this sort, they are effective in offsetting counterclaims.[2]

Although this enumeration is used as an argument here for the unity of the book, it is significant even from a metaphorical point of view.

Robert Brunner does not see any difficulty in connection with the symbol four. He says clearly,

> Die Zahl vier meint bei symbolischer Verwendung stets ein Ganzes, ein Universales. Wer nach allen vier Richtungen der Windrose zeigt, meint ja auch die ganze Welt.[3]

Brunner, then, takes the position that any power which attempts to scatter the people of Israel at any time in history is included in this concept of universality.[4] This interpretation appears vague.

---

[1] Ibid.   [2] <u>Exposition of Zechariah</u>, p. 11.

[3] <u>Sacharja</u> (Zürich: Zwingli Verlag, 1960), p. 32.

[4] Brunner thus makes an attempt at a solution to the dilemma of interpretation that occurs in the real historical situation by making the application "timeless." See Brunner's argument in his <u>Sacharja</u>, pp. 34-35.

Merrill F. Unger, on the other hand, takes a more restricted view. He says:

> It is to be noted also that the four horns symbolizing Gentile persecutions of the Jew were successive and not contemporaneous. Only the Persian power existed in Zechariah's day, the Babylonian having passed off the scene some sixteen years previously. The empires of Nebuchadnezzar's colossus (Dan 2:31-45) are seen all at one time, but followed each other in historical succession, as well as the wild beasts of chapter 7:2-13. Prophecy has this perspective aspect which appears here.[1]

Unger furthermore says,

> That Zechariah had the four world empires of the "times of the Gentiles" in mind, rather than a vague reference to the universality of the enmity against Israel by allusion to the "four winds of heaven" or "the four corners of the earth" is further corroborated by the fact that the prophet largely bases his visions and prophecies on revelations already granted to the prophets who preceded him. In this case he shows indebtedness to Daniel, in the sense that the same Spirit who inspired Daniel inspired him in similar vein.[2]

Christian Jeremias presents an opposite view as he takes up the question of totality versus sequential world-powers. Jeremias also sees similarities and points of contact between Daniel and Zechariah and raises the question whether Zechariah's two night visions may present a prototype (Vorform) of Daniel's world-empire

---

[1] Unger, Zechariah, p. 38; Unger also takes the position that zeru (present perfect tense = "scatter") has caused many scholars "to reject Babylon, Medo-Persia, Macedonian Greece, and Rome, and to specify Egypt, Assyria, Babylon, and Persia as Gentile powers which had already overrun Israel and Judah." But Unger emphasizes that "the Hebrew verbal system describes the kind of action, and not past, present, or future tense." And he further says, "the perfect presents finished or completed action either in past, present, or future depending upon the context." As for this particular passage we are discussing, Unger points out that "In line with the scope of all the other night visions, it is certainly preferable to interpret this one as a present perfect" (ibid., p. 37).

[2] Unger, Zechariah, p. 38.

teaching (Weltreichlehre).[1] But although Jeremias sees in this night vision a step towards Daniel's presentation, his conclusion is that in the

> Vierzahl, d.h. der Totalität der Israel feindlichen Mächte die Rede ist. Dabei ist aber eben anders als bei Daniel die Totalität nicht durch 4 bestimmte Reiche repräsentiert, und es geht auch nicht wie dort um den Gang der Geschichte.[2]

It seems an undeniable fact that Zechariah does not give any explicit saying that would identify the four horns as four definite world powers.[3] Nor can we prove that the locution "four horns" implies totality. There may also be a third alternative, namely, that the four "horns" in Zechariah represent neither four successive world powers, nor totality, but, as in Daniel, represent four kings or contemporary kingdoms (Diadochi). This investigation will now consider the rest of the apocalyptic passages which are found in Daniel.

---

[1] Christian Jeremias, *Die Nachtgesichte des Sacharja* (Göttingen: Vandenhoeck & Ruprecht, 1977), p. 162.

[2] Ibid., p. 163.

[3] In passing we point out that since the majority of scholars have accepted Zechariah's night visions as apocalyptic and as coming from the genuine Zechariah, and that the visions were given to him at the date 520 (Zech 1:7), i.e., 520 B.C., it seems but natural that Daniel, another book with apocalyptic genre, could have originated slightly earlier. This sequence of apocalyptic would solve the problem of "totality" or "sequential," for in that case Zechariah might have "drawn" not only upon Jeremiah and Ezekiel but also upon Daniel. Scholars, in general, do not consider such a dating possible; for such a contrary view see, for instance, André Lacocque, *The Book of Daniel* (Atlanta: John Knox Press, 1976), p. 6, who thus may represent the majority of scholars who take this negative view. The question of *pars pro toto* is known from ex-biblical context and the concept has by many scholars been transferred to biblical context as well; see Martin Noth, *The Laws in the Pentateuch and Other Studies* (Philadelphia: Fortress Press, 1966), pp. 194-214. So also Gerhard von Rad, *Old Testament Theology* (New York:

Our attention must turn now to the horn-motif in Daniel. There is a lack of consensus among scholars as to the genre of this book.[1] The same may be said in regard to the unity of the book,[2] the authorship and the date,[3] and the interpretation of content.[4]

Inasmuch as the apocalyptic parts in Daniel are presented in both Aramaic and Hebrew, we will proceed with the investigation of the passages by turning our attention first to the "Aramaic"

Harper & Row, Publishers, 1965), 2:312, n. 25.

[1] The most prevailing view today is that chapters 1-6 represent agadoth, while chapters 7-12 consist of apocalypses. So, for instance, Lacocque, The Book of Daniel, p. 8. In this dissertation the term "apocalypse" is ascribed to chapters 7-12. In this connection it is to be recalled that it was Hermann Gunkel "who gave the classic statement of the mythological background to Dan 7 in his Schöpfung und Chaos in Urzeit und Endzeit (Göttingen: Vandenhoeck & Ruprecht, 1895), pp. 323-35. He traced the imagery in Dan 7 back to the Babylonian Tiamat myth. Many scholars have adopted a mythological interpretation of Dan 7, although with modifications. So, for instance, James Montgomery, A Critical and Exegetical Commentary on the Book of Daniel, ICC (Edinburgh: Clark, 1927), pp. 285-86; Arthur Jeffery, "The Book of Daniel: Introduction and Exegesis," IB (Nashville: Abingdon Press, 1956), 6:451; Norman W. Porteous, Daniel: A Commentary, OTL (Philadelphia: Westminster Press, 1965), p. 98; Aage Bentzen, Daniel, HAT (Tübingen: J. C. B. Mohr [Paul Siebeck], 1937), p. 33; Eric W. Heaton, The Book of Daniel, p. 175; John J. Collins, The Apocalyptic Vision of the Book of Daniel (Missoula, MT: Scholars Press, 1977), p. 159.

[2] Harold Henry Rowley is, no doubt, the foremost and best known champion for the unity of the book of Daniel; see his article "The Unity of the Book of Daniel," HUCA 23 (1951):233-72; for a contrary view, Harold L. Ginsberg, Studies in Daniel (New York: The Jewish Theological Seminary, 1948), p. 23; and Yehezkel Kaufmann, History of Israel's Faith (Tel Aviv, 1956 [in Hebrew]) as cited by Lacocque, The Book of Daniel, p. 9.

[3] Roland K. Harrison, "Daniel, Book of," in The Zondervan Pictorial Encyclopedia of the Bible (Grand Rapids: Zondervan Publishing House, 1975), 2:13-19.

[4] Ibid., pp. 20-21; cf. Stanley B. Frost, "Daniel," IDB, 1:761-68.

passages in chapter 7[1] and then to the "Hebrew" ones in chapter 8.

The problem in chapter 7 is, of course, the identification of the "fourth beast" with the "ten horns" (קרנין עשר לה), "another little horn" (קרן אחרי זעירה) and "and three of the first horns plucked up" (ותלת מן־קרניא קדמיתא אתעקרו) (Dan 7:7, 8).[2]

As for the "fourth beast," two widely recognized views struggle for supremacy: the fourth beast as Greece and the fourth beast as Rome.[3] John E. Thomson expresses himself in regard to this

---

[1] Scholars, in general, consider chaps. 7-12 as a unit. There are some, however, who see chap. 7 as standing apart from the rest, due to it being written in Aramaic. Martin Noth, for instance, considers Dan 7 in its present form as coming from a later period (specifically from the time of Antiochus IV); see Noth, The Laws in the Pentateuch and Other Studies (Philadelphia: Fortress Press, 1967), pp. 212-13, as cited in Bruce W. Jones, Ideas of History in the Book of Daniel (Ph.D. dissertation, Ann Arbor, 1972), p. 39, and n. 23. Harold L. Ginsberg also proposed very strongly that "the two main divisions of the book have a separate origin; see his Studies in Daniel, pp. 38-39; see further, Rowley, "Book Review: Studies in Daniel by H. Louis Ginsberg," JBL 68 (1969):174; Ginsberg, "In Re My Studies in Daniel," JBL 68 (1949):405-06; Rowley, "A Rejoinder," JBL 69 (1950):201-03; Ginsberg, "The Composition of the Book of Daniel," VT 4 (1954):246-75. Rowley defended the unity of the whole book. Others who cannot see the unity of the whole book, however, defend chaps. 7-12 as a unit. So, for instance, John J. Collins, "The Son of Man and the Saints of the Most High," JBL 93 (1974):54; Norman W. Porteous sees chap. 7 as "the heart of the Book of Daniel," see his Daniel: A Commentary (Philadelphia: The Westminster Press, 1965), p. 95. Louis F. Hartman calls chap. 7 the "core of the Book of Daniel"; see Hartman and Alexander A. Di Lella, The Book of Daniel, AB (Garden City, NY: Doubleday & Company, Inc., 1978), p. 208.

[2] Robert H. Charles also points out that "three questions call for consideration," but he does not include the "little horn" among these questions. The four world empires, the ten horns, and the three horns "plucked up" are for him the riddles which need to be weighed carefully; A Critical and Exegetical Commentary on the Book of Daniel (Oxford: Clarendon Press, 1929), p. 166.

[3] The first view has no doubt been the preponderant view,

problem in chap. 7 right to the point when he says, "The identification of the empire intended by this beast [the fourth one] has been the crux of interpreters."[1] The interpretation of the fourth beast is, of course, interrelated to the exposition of the other beasts.[2]

Norman W. Porteous, for instance, points to the fact that many commentators see chap. 7 as drawing heavily upon the imagery of the creation myth.[3] Porteous, however, does not see any notable resemblance of the creatures in Daniel's vision to the monsters of the creation myth; he rather sees them as symbolizing "the brutal nature of the empires with which the Jewish people had to do in the course of the last few centuries of their history.[4]

Martin Noth takes the "totality" view in regard to chap. 7 just as he does in regard to chap. 2.[5] Many of the details are no

---

especially so since the literary criticism more forcefully began to exercise its influence in the theological schools at the end of the 19th century. For a discussion: ibid., pp. 166-69; Harold H. Rowley, Darius the Mede and the Four World Empires in the Book of Daniel (Cardiff: University of Wales Press Board, 1959), especially pp. 61-137; John E. H. Thomson, The Book of Daniel, The Pulpit Commentary (Reprint ed. Grand Rapids: Wm. B. Eerdmans Publishing Company, 1977), p. 211.

[1]Thomson, The Book of Daniel, p. 211.

[2]Inasmuch as a discussion of the various views in regard to the apocalypse of chap. 7 would demand a long drawn-out presentation that would deviate from our specific task, we will only briefly consider some particularly extreme opinions which, however, have had considerable support among scholars.

[3]Daniel, A Commentary, p. 98 (the influence of Hermann Gunkel and Sigmund Mowinckel on Eric Heaton and Aage Bentzen [whom Porteous refers to] is clearly discernible in these kinds of views).

[4]Ibid., p. 99.

[5]Noth says inter alia: "The whole of world history is seen

longer important to the author of Daniel; all that is of significance is the number four, representing "the completed whole, possibly as the four quadrants of the world."[1]

Gerhard von Rad takes a similar view when he says,

> Like the four rivers in Gen 2:10ff. or the four horns in Zech 2:1, the four beasts represent the world in general. In Dan 7:3 an idea that the four beasts came up contemporaneously out of the sea is still clearly visible. This would completely correspond to Zechariah's picture of the four horns.[2]

John J. Collins does not discuss the beasts per se; (he is more concerned with the horns). Collins' hypothesis is that

> The chronological factors in Daniel are not designed to convey a sense of development in universal history but to focus attention on the brief period of the present in which the confrontation between God and the kingdoms of the earth takes place. . . . In this way the chronological framework is made to complement the vertical antithesis between heaven and earth.[3]

---

together, as if it were all happening in the present. For in Dan 7 just as in Dan 2 we have that hovering between the idea of successive empires and contemporary empires, . . . but the text testifies clearly (in Dan 7) to a chronological succession of empires. . . . But we still have at the beginning of the vision the statement that four beasts emerged from the sea--as if it were all one single event." Though a certain tension is noticeable in the exposition of Noth and he tries to thread his way between the two views "sequential empires" or "totality of history" represented by the empires, Noth, as Bruce W. Jones has pointed out in his dissertation, tends to accept the latter. Noth namely sees the author of Daniel as "ignoring the proper chronological order," thus showing that "he is not interested in historical events as such, but only in the displacement of human kingdoms by God's kingdom." As quoted by Jones, Ideas of History in the Book of Daniel, p. 37; cf. Martin Noth, The Laws in the Pentateuch and Other Studies (Philadelphia: Fortress Press, 1967), pp. 121-13.

[1] Noth, The Laws, pp. 204, 206.

[2] Old Testament Theology, trans. D. M. G. Stalker (New York: Harper & Row, 1962-[65]), 2:312, n. 25.

[3] The Apocalyptic Vision of the Book of Daniel Harvard Se-

The chronological predictions, thus, have no function to display any history on the historical level as such; they only "intensify the urgency and so further sharpen the focus on the present." Collins further says,

> By means of the chronological schema, one period of history is designated as the last, and this period is set in immediate contrast to the eschatological kingdom which will follow it.[1]

Collins thus sees the chronological schema of the four beasts as a desire to contrast present and future on the horizontal basis.[2] The revolt of the world-kingdoms, embodied by Antiochus Epiphanes, is therefore designated as the last one and set in contrast to the eschatological kingdom.[3] "The vertical spatial imagery," on the other hand, "contrasts heaven and earth."[4] It is on this level then that the "vertical" imagery of the kingdom of "one like a son of man" confronts us. The focus, according to Collins, is "on the sharp antithesis between the two poles."[5] This focus nullifies the chronological predictions per se--and so does Collins.

---

mitic Monographs, 16 (Missoula, MT: Scholars Press, 1977), p. 162.

[1] Ibid.

[2] Collins is here referring to the immediate future of the kingdom of Antiochus Epiphanes (a demise which is discussed in Dan 7 and 12, ibid., p. 163).

[3] This kingdom of God is manifested either by the dominion of Israel over the nations--but still a historical kingdom with a definite extension in space and time--or "as a heavenly kingdom, which will break into this world at a particular time, but thereafter is not commensurate with space and time as we know them" (ibid.).

[4] Ibid., p. 162.   [5] Ibid.

The more common explanation focuses, however, on the chronological schema which moves on the horizontal level. Stanley B. Frost has pointed out that "the four kingdoms of these visions are the four world empires of Babylon, Media, Persia and Greece."[1] Another classical position takes the position of Rome being the fourth beast in the chronological schema of chap. 7.[2]

---

[1] "Daniel," IDB, 1:762. As already pointed out, most scholars in this century take the fourth beast to be Greece (or the Seleucidian empire). So, for instance, Anthony A. Bevan, A Short Commentary on the Book of Daniel (Cambridge: University Press, 1971), p. 115; Karl Marti, Das Buch Daniel, Kurzer Hand-Commentar zum Alten Testament (Tübingen: Verlag von J. C. B. Mohr [Paul Siebeck], 1901), p. 50; Keil, Biblical Commentary on the Book of Daniel (Grand Rapids: Wm. B. Eerdmans Publishing Company, 1959), p. 228; Montgomery, The Book of Daniel, p. 290; Eric W. Heaton, The Book of Daniel (London: SCM Press, 1956), p. 177; Rowley, Darius the Mede and the Four World Empires in the Book of Daniel, pp. 91-98; Frost, "Daniel," p. 762; Porteous, Daniel, p. 106; M. Delcor, "Daniel 7," VT 18 (1968):299; Lacocque, The Book of Daniel, p. xx; Collins, The Apocalyptic Vision of the Book of Daniel, p. 159 (implicitly expressed); Hartman and Di Lella, The Book of Daniel, p. 213. So also Urs Staub, "Das Tier mit den Hörnern" (Ein Beitrag zu Dan 7:7f.) FZPhTh 25 (1978):351-97. For a contrary view see, for instance, Arno C. Gaebelein, The Prophet Daniel (New York: Publication Office "Our Hope," 1911), p. 75; Leupold, Exposition of Daniel, p. 296; Thomson, Daniel, pp. 211-12. John F. Walwoord, Daniel: The Key to Prophetic Revelation (Chicago: Moody Press, 1971), p. 159; Leon J. Wood, Daniel: A Study Guide (Grand Rapids: Zondervan Publishing House, 1975), pp. 93-94; Harrison, "Daniel," pp. 20-21.

[2] This view is inter alia based on the assumption that "the history of the Median empire precludes such a division"; see Harrison, "Daniel, Book of," p. 29 (cf. Montgomery, whose reasoning is revealed in the following statement: "In cc. 2 and 7 we find a parallelism of a system of four kingdoms, which parallelism is admitted by all. In ch. 2 the four are symbolized by the successive series of metals composing a composite image; in ch. 7 by a series of successive monstrous Beasts. The first of these kingdoms thus symbolized in parallel is admitted by almost all interpreters to be Babylonia, as it is specifically incarnated in the person of Nebuchadnezzar, 2:37ff. Now, analogy requires the identification of the fourth Beast with its successive horns in ch. 7 with Greece as specified in ch. 8. According to the equally specific statements at the end of ch. 11 and the beginning of ch. 12 the predecessor of Greece is the kingdom of Persia, i.e., the third kingdom. The

It is but natural that these two diametrically opposite views are reflected in the interpretation of the "ten horns," the "little horn," and the "three horns, plucked up." In this study we will try to reflect this spectrum as far as it is possible in the ramification of the content.

The "ten horns" of the beast (קרנין עשר לה) (Dan 7:7) are considered to be successive kings according to the first view (the Grecian scheme); they "represent ten individual kings . . . not ten kingdoms, as do the 'four horns' of chap. 8:8."[1] Antony A. Bevan says further: "If therefore the Fourth Beast of chap. 7 is the Greek Empire and the little horn is Antiochus, it follows that the ten horns must be ten predecessors of Antiochus."[2]

Several scholars have made attempts to list the predecessors of Antiochus Epiphanes but no final agreement has been reached along

---

remaining, second kingdom can be nothing else than Media, which according to ancient historiography, as still maintained by historians, e.g., Rawlinson, up to our own day, was one of the Great Monarchies of the ancient Orient"; as quoted by Montgomery, The Book of Daniel, p. 61. Montgomery here refers to the work of George Rawlinson, The Seven Great Monarchies of the Ancient Eastern World, 2d ed. (New York: J. W. Lovell [1875]). The assumption by Montgomery in regard to the Median Kingdom seems to rest, not on carefully built up evidences, but on procedures based on assumptions. The faulty methodology is apparent. For a schematic presentation of the opposite views: see Charles Boutflower, In and Around the Book of Daniel (Grand Rapids: Zondervan Publishing House, 1963), pp. 13-14.

[1]This view is explicitly expressed by Bevan, A Short Commentary on the Book of Daniel, p. 115.

[2]Ibid. Bevan's weakness, however, is that he takes for granted the prevalent view that the "little horn" is Antiochus Epiphanes on the basis of statements pronounced by Porphyry and Ephraim Syrus. As the methodology is incorrect, the conclusion does not give any proofs either for or against.

this line.[1] As it would be too voluminous to expand upon the various views, a view expressed by Arthur Jeffery will note the weakness of such a scheme. He says:

> There is an account of attempts to identify the ten in Rowley. . . . and more recent suggestions in H. W. Obbink . . . , Bentzen . . . , and Linder. . . . Some have included Alexander in the series and others have excluded him. Some have insisted that all must be Seleucids, while others have included those Ptolemies who were important for Palestinian affairs.[2]

It seems that no satisfactory identification for the "ten horns" can be given on the scheme of the Grecian empire.[3]

An investigation of the concept of the "ten horns" on the scheme of the Roman empire shows that the "ten horns" are used with the meaning of "kingdoms" rather than "kings"--or else interchangeably used.[4] Another dissimilarity is that the "ten horns" "are not

---

[1] So, for instance, Bevan, A Short Commentary on the Book of Daniel, p. 116; Marti, Das Buch Daniel, p. 51. For a schematic overview of the views of Ginsberg, Walter Baumgartner, Marti, Rowley, Porteous, Bentzen, and Otto Ploeger, see Urs Staub, "Das Tier mit den Hörnern: Ein Beitrag zu Dan 7:7f." FZPhTh 25 (1978): 364.

[2] Jeffery, "The Book of Daniel," p. 456.

[3] So Jeffery (ibid.); Lacocque, The Book of Daniel, p. 141; Leupold has pointed out the discrepancy of the attempt to interpret the ten kings by filling out the list with potential kings or pretenders: Demetrius (the son and brother of Antiochus Epiphanes) Heliodorus and Ptolemy Philometer; see his Exposition of Daniel p. 297.

[4] Leupold says in regard to the "ten horns:" "This . . . on the basis of vs. 24, refers to ten kings. But . . . it matters little whether we say the ten horns signify ten kings or ten kingdoms, for 2:37 makes allowance for both points of view"; Exposition of Daniel, p. 298; cf. Keil, on vss. 17-27 saying: "In vss. 17 and 18 he [Daniel] gives first a general interpretation of the vision. The words, these great beasts of which there were four, form an absolute nominal clause: 'as for the beasts;' as concerning their meaning, it is this: 'they represent four kings.' The kings are

represented as arising consecutively" but rather the opposite--
"they are simultaneously upon the head of the beast."[1]

Leupold gives the following interpretation of the "ten horns":

> They do not, therefore, aim to picture any ten consecutive kings or kingdoms that grew out of the Roman Empire. They present the totality of the power of the fourth empire as it appeared at any time after it was fully grown. Of [sic] they may just as well portray the total number of those kingdoms into which the Roman Empire ultimately broke up.[2]

That the identification of ten contemporary kingdoms has been a crux interpretum, analogous to the crux interpretum in regard to the ten kings, cannot be denied. Leupold gives a sample of an arbitrary listing.[3] A more realistic division has been suggested by Albert Barnes, but he also presents slight variations proposed by other scholars.[4]

Some would hold the "ten horns" as the symbol of completeness

---

named as founders and representatives of world-kingdoms. Four kingdoms are meant, as vs. 23 shows, where the fourth beast is explained as מלכו , 'dominion,' 'kingdom,'" Biblical Commentary on the Book of Daniel, p. 238. Edward B. Pusey says, "throughout these prophecies the king represents the kingdom, and the kingdom is concentrated in its king. The kings then or kingdoms which should arise out of this kingdom [the fourth beast] must, from the force of the term as well as from the context, be kings or kingdoms which should arise at some later stage of its existence, not those first kings without which it could not be a kingdom at all" Daniel the Prophet (New York: Funk & Wagnalls, 1885), p. 127. Interestingly enough Dan 7:17 (מלכין) reads βασιλεῖαι in the Septuaginta (ed. Rahlfs) 2:914, and in the Theodotion version (ibid.); and regna in Biblia Sacra iuxta Vulgatam Versionem, 2:1359, thus giving some support for the terms "kings" and "kingdoms" being used interchangeably.

[1] Leupold, Exposition of Daniel, p. 322.

[2] Ibid.   [3] Ibid.

[4] Notes on the Old Testament Explanatory and Practical (Grand Rapids: Baker Book House, 1950), 2:83-84.

or fullness. This would then mean that we vainly attempt to identify the "ten horns" in either case: i.e., as ten kingdoms on the Roman scheme or as ten kings on the Grecian scheme. If, as it may well be argued, the Scriptures furnish no clue as to their identity, we should not press the figure.[1]

A similar diversion of interpretation exists with regard to "another little horn" of Dan 7:8. Scholars who accept the Grecian schema see the fulfillment in Antiochus Epiphanes. Lacocque says:

> In the little arrogant horn, we must see Antiochus IV, the personage in view of whom everything which precedes and which follows was written by the Author. . . . It is well known that the king indicated that he was divine by giving himself the name Epiphanes. . . . Antiochus is certainly Evil's ultimate assault against the people of God. Hence the war takes on mythic overtones so that it is even possible to see in the blasphemy of the "little horn" an echo of the same motif in what H. Ginkel [sic] calls the Chaosmythus.[2]

Most scholars, by far, take this view of Antiochus who "usurped the Seleucid power on 3 September, 197 B.C.E."[3] being the fulfillment of this prediction,[4] whether one sees it as a prophecy pre eventum or post eventum.

---

[1] Edward J. Young, The Prophecy of Daniel: A Commentary (Grand Rapids: Wm. B. Eerdmans Publishing Company, 1949), pp. 149-50.

[2] The Book of Daniel, p. 142.

[3] Ibid., p. 141, n. 89.

[4] So Bevan, A Short Commentary on the Book of Daniel, p. 115; Marti, Das Buch Daniel, p. 51; Heaton, The Book of Daniel, p. 177; Bentzen, Daniel, p. 35; Frost, "Daniel," pp. 762, 768. Delcor, "Daniel 7," p. 299, and Le Livre de Daniel, p. 141; Porteous, Daniel, p. 106; Montgomery, The Book of Daniel, p. 60; Jeffery, Daniel, p. 456; Lacocque, The Book of Daniel, p. 141. Hartman and Di Lella, The Book of Daniel, pp. 215-17; Collins, The Apocalyptic Vision of the Book of Daniel, pp. 159-63; (Keil abstains from

The "three horns" that were "plucked up" are also a matter of discussion and the interpretation is closely tied up with the identification of the "little horn." So, for instance, Bevan, referring to previous scholars, attempted to identify the three "horns" as kings and present an acceptable interpretation, but because of the controversial views he gave up and focused the attention on the "One like a son of man."[1]

The other view--accepting Rome as the fourth beast,--presents, of course, a hypothesis that will fit such a scheme. As for the "little horn," these scholars see the fulfillment in the Papacy.[2] However, there are scholars who express their view more

---

explicitly identifying the "little horn," and Rowley presents a status quaestionis, Darius the Mede and the Four World Empires, pp. 98-120. Rowley's conclusion on the basis of his investigation is: "If there is uncertainty as to the precise identification of all the ten horns, there is no uncertainty as to the aptness of the identification of the Little Horn with Antiochus Epiphanes" (p. 120).

[1]Bevan, A Short Commentary on the Book of Daniel, pp. 116-18. Porphyry's view of the three kings--Ptolemy Philometor, Ptolemy Euergetes II, and Artaxias, king of Armenia--was later replaced by the view of Heliodorus, Ptolemy Philometor, and Demetrius Soter, as constituting the three kings. The last triad presented by Bevan constitutes the "kings:" Seleucus Philopator, Heliodorus, and Demetrius Soter (ibid., p. 117). Rowley, who discusses exhaustively this question, has pointed out the wide divergence of opinion in regard to these "uprooted horns." Darius the Mede and the Four World Empires in the Book of Daniel, p. 108. Many recent scholars refrain from discussing the "three horns." One of the few taking up the question is Hartman, but without a final and decisive conclusion; The Book of Daniel, pp. 216-17.

[2]So, for instance, Adam Clarke, The Holy Bible Containing the Old and New Testament with a Commentary and Critical Notes (London: Ward, Lock & Co., 1881), vol. 4 (on Dan 7:8); Barnes, Notes on the Old Testament, 2:57-58; 83-85; Leupold and Young go a step further and purport the final fulfillment in the future. See their respective works: Exposition of Daniel, p. 323 and The Prophecy of Daniel, p. 150. A recent scholar, Desmond Ford, expresses

cautiously and apply the final fulfillment to a future manifestation of Antichrist. In a future personal Antichrist all previous manifestations shall culminate. The interpretation of the "three horns . . . plucked up" has also fluctuated somewhat as may be expected.[1] Many commentators avoid discussing the three horns at all.[2]

The final step in this investigation is to consider the text itself and the context in which it is embedded.[3]

Dan 7:7 makes use of the dual form[4] (קרניך), though the immediate context clearly shows that the plural is meant (קרניך

---

a similar view and uses the explicit locution "apotelesmatic application" in speaking of the future manifestations of Antichrist as matching the prophecy of the little horn in Dan 7 and running parallel with it (Daniel [Nashville, TN: Southern Publishing Association, 1978], p. 174.)

[1]Cf., for instance, Adam Clarke, Commentary and Critical Notes, vol. 4 (on Dan 7:8); Barnes, Notes on the Old Testament, pp. 85-90; Ford, Daniel, p. 152.

[2]For a discussion of the "three horns plucked up," see C. Mervyn Maxwell, "An Exegetical and Historical Examination of the Beginning and Ending of the 1260 Days of Prophecy with Special Attention Given to the A.D. 538 and 1798 as Initial and Terminal Dates. . ." (M.A. thesis, SDA Theological Seminary, Andrews University, 1951).

[3]The attempt here is not to provide an interpretation but to consider the meaning of the word קרן which occurs several times. The translation of the Aramaic in chap. 7 and of the Hebrew in chap. 8 is our own version except where otherwise noted.

[4]Franz Rosenthal indicates that "dual is preserved only in remnants," which thus seems to attest the antiquity of the text. It is well known that dual is used with parts of the body that occur in pairs in nature. Rosenthal, referring to Dan 7:7, says, "In such nouns, the dual may be used for the pl.: קרניך עשר "ten horns" . . . A Grammar of Biblical Aramaic (Wiesbaden: Otto Harrassowitz, 1968), p. 24. This explanation by Rosenthal suggests that the dual, though used in the meaning of plural, may give an allusion to the fact that the prophet perhaps had animals in mind (perhaps bulls). In other ancient languages the (dual) horns on an animal often revealed aggression, hostility, and force.

עשר לה). The following verse (vs. 8) contains the normal plural emphatic construction twice (once prefixed מן). The third usage is the singular קרן. The singular קרן is qualified by two adjectives (זעירה, אחרי) and is to be identified with the "horn" presented in the emphatic form toward the end of the sentence.

It was "another little horn" that arose (סלקח) among them (i.e., the other horns), then further information is given--"three (תלח) of the first horns were plucked out."[1] Furthermore, it is clear from this context that three (i.e., "horns") of the first horns (i.e., the ten horns) were plucked up (אתעקרו, Ithpeel) from before it (in retrospect, the קרן). The last phrase ties up the קרנא־דא with the קרן which must be the antecedent in the context and which agrees in number and gender with the emphatic form.[2] The same emphatic form occurs also in Dan 7:11 where this "another little horn" is speaking. In vss. 20 and 21 the emphatic form of קרן is qualified with the adjectival דכן in both instances; this construction confirms that it is the same "little horn" (here in retrospect) which is the matter of concern. The same "little horn" is also understood by ellipsis where only ואחרי appears in the text (vs. 20). On the contrary, the "ten horns" is written out in full--this time not in dual but in emphatic plural construction

---

[1] The "chiastic concord" does not function in this context for תלח is not used adjectivally but nominally (i.e., independently).

[2] Scholars generally agree with an analysis of this kind, but still the exposition differs among scholars. It seems that à priori assumptions play an unnecessarily great factor in the diversity of opinions.

ועל־קרניא עשר "and concerning the ten horns."

The interpretation of the horns follows in vs. 24, explaining the "ten horns." The context, however, requires a brief look at the previous verse which reads:

> Thus he said: As for the fourth beast, there shall be on the earth the fourth kingdom (מלכו) which shall be different from all the kingdoms (מן־כל־מלכותא). . . .

The next verse begins:

> וקרניא עשר מנה מלכותה As for the ten horns from the kingdom, ten kings (מלכין) shall arise and another (אחרן) shall arise after them; he shall be different from the former ones, and shall put down (bring low) three kings (מלכין).[1]

The passage is of importance in the light of vs. 17 which reads: "These four great beasts which are four kings (מלכין) who shall arise out of the earth."[2] It seems evident, as many scholars have pointed out, that the terms "kings" and "kingdoms" are used interchangeably in the book of Daniel.[3]

It seems clear that the locution "four kings" (Dan 7:17) makes better sense if translated "four kingdoms." Holladay, in

---

[1] The מנה ("from it") carries a prospective suffix which refers to the kingdom מלכותה (fem. sg. emphatic). The kingdom must be the מלכו רביעיא "the fourth kingdom" = the fourth beast (vs. 23). The "chiastic concord" is used in this passage as one would expect, of course, because of the adjectival usage of תלתה. The מלכין is in the absolute state (masculine and plural).

[2] The apparatus in the BHS brings out the Septuaginta as having βασιλεῖαι and the Vulgate as having regna where the MT has מלכין. For the expression מן־ארעא "of the earth" in contrast to מן־ימא "out of the sea," see Leupold, Exposition of Daniel, p. 317.

[3] See Young, The Prophecy of Daniel, p. 157. The term "kings" was the "concrete" expression used in place of the "abstract" kingdom. See also J. Barton Payne, Encyclopedia of Biblical Prophecy (New York: Harper & Row Publishers, 1973), p. 373. Cf. the word "kingship" in Sumerian usage.

fact, accepts this translation, for he points out that the Aramaic מלכין (malkîn) in Dan 7:17 means "kingdoms."[1] So also in Dan 7:23 the word מלכו (singular) means "kingship" or "kingdom," and מלכות, מלכותא (plural emphatic) in Dan 7:23, 24 have the same meaning.[2] Furthermore, the context gives evidence not of individual kings being discussed but kingdoms. It is evident from Dan 7:17, 23-24 that the words "kings" and "kingdoms" are used interchangeably. The focal points in the context of Dan 7 are the kingdoms on a horizontal level as contrasted with the kingdom on a vertical level. We therefore have the right to conclude that the "little horn" which came up among the ten horns is a little kingdom—yet a kingdom of a different kind, for it had eyes and a mouth.

Furthermore, it is apparent that the "little horn" is aggressive, hostile, and forceful, for it says, "that horn waged war with the saints" (Dan 7:21). The nature of the "little horn" is brought forth in the most astonishing terms in Dan 7:8, 20-21, 25. The interpretation of this "little horn" has to find its fulfillment as rising to power among the ten horns, which clearly describe a latter stage of the fourth empire.[3]

---

[1] Holladay, *A Concise Hebrew and Aramaic Lexicon*, p. 411.

[2] Ibid.

[3] The most logical interpretation is, no doubt, an interpretation that is true to the text and at the same time recognizes the historical fulfillment. History makes it clear that the Roman empire fulfilled the prophecy of a fourth world empire as described in the framework of the parallel prophecies in Dan 2 and 7. See Boutflower, *In and Around the Book of Daniel*, pp. 15-22 (especially p. 84); Walwoord, *Daniel the Key to Prophetic Revelation*, pp. 153-63; Barnes, *Notes on the Old Testament*, pp. 79-99. Our presuppositions unite with the unpopular view, but at the same time more

404

Daniel 8 is distinguished from the previous chapter not only by its language but by the symbolic elements (i.e., other kinds of animals). Lacocque says,

> In parallel with chapter 7, the empires are represented as animals, in this case, a ram and a he-goat. In astrological geography, the ram represents Persia (κριός) and Syria is represented by a he-goat (αἰγόκερως). By transposition, the goat here signifies Greece, the adopted homeland, at least on a spiritual plane, of the philhellene Syrian King, Antiochus IV.[1]

Also in this chapter the interpretation of the animals and the horns is crucial. The ram standing on the bank of the canal had two horns (קרנים [dual]) and both horns (dual, emphatic) were high, but one was higher than the other and the higher one came up later (Dan 8:3).

Otto Zöckler, with reference to the ram, says:

> Daniel first sees <u>one</u> ram, איל, standing by the river, The אחד (one) does not here stand for the indefinite article, but is a numeral in contradistinction to the <u>two</u> horns which the <u>one</u> ram has (Keil). Rather it indicates a <u>solitary</u> ram, and not a member of a flock, as is usual with

---

consistent expositions, of the kingdom of Rome representing the fourth empire.

[1] The Book of Daniel, p. 157; so also Bentzen, Daniel, p. 69; cf. Barnes, (Notes on the Old Testament, p. 104) who provides examples of art-evidences which confirm the fact that the goat was the emblem of Macedonia. Barnes also describes how "in one of the pilasters of Persepolis this very event [the Macedonians, upon being threatened with an invasion in 547 B.C. became tributary to the Persians] seems to be recorded in a manner that throws considerable light on this subject. A goat is represented with an immense horn growing out of the middle of his forehead, and a man in a Persian dress is seen by his side, holding the horn with his left hand, by which is signified the subjection of Macedon" (ibid.). We have not been able to verify these art-works, but even if misinterpreted they show that the "one-horned goat" in antiquity must have been used symbolically--as such an animal naturally has two horns.

these gregarious animals. For every ram has of course two horns.[1]

Zöckler further says,

> The vision symbolizes the Persian monarchy as a ram (and afterward the Graecian empire as a he-goat), in harmony with that mode of representation--which prevailed generally in the figurative language of O.T. prophecy and accorded with Oriental modes of conception in general--by which princes, national sovereigns, or military leaders were typified under similar figures; cf. Isa 14:9 ("all the great goats of the earth"), and as parallel with it, "all the kings of the heathen," Jer 1:8; Ezek 34:17; Zech 10:3.[2]

The same usage is attested in non-Biblical sources. We see the אחד significant also as pointing out that the one ram represented one kingdom, a united one, though the two horns (dual) indicate the duality of this one kingdom.[3] If this is correct, then the interpretation of the Medo-Persian kingdom here serves as a key for the parallel passage in the previous chapter, i.e., the kingdom following the Babylonian kingdom [the bear] should be interpreted analogously. In general, the ram has been understood by scholars to mean the Medo-Persian kingdom, the goat the Macedonian (Grecian) empire, and the conspicuous horn to mean Alexander.[4]

---

[1] The Book of the Prophet Daniel, trans. enlarged, and ed. James Strong, in A Commentary on the Holy Scriptures: Critical, Doctrinal and Homiletical, vol. 13 by John P. Lange, trans. Philip Schaff (New York: Charles Scribner's Sons, 1915), p. 172.

[2] Ibid.

[3] Carl Brockelmann says "Die Indetermination, die im allgemeinen unbezeichnet bleibt, wird vereinzelt durch das Zahlwort אחד ausgedrückt, wie איש אחד 'ein Mann,' 1 Sam 1:1; אשה אחת 'eine Frau,' Judg 9:53." Hebräische Syntax (Neukirchen: Kreis Moers, 1956), p. 17; (cf. p. 131).

[4] So, for instance, Robert H. Charles, A Critical and Exegetical Commentary on the Book of Daniel (Oxford: Clarendon Press, 1929), pp. 199, 200.

A close study of Dan 8 also implies the term "horn(s)" being used with the interchangeable meaning of "king(s)" or "kingdom(s)." Interestingly enough, Sir Isaac Newton in commenting upon Dan 8:3 says,

> And the Ram having two horns are the kings of Media and Persia: not two persons but two kingdoms, the kingdom of Media and Persia; and the kingdom of Persia was the higher horn and came up last.[1]

Analogously with the interpretation of the ram, Newton, with reference to the he-goat, concludes:

> The rough Goat, saith Daniel, is the king of Grecia, that is, the kingdom; and the great horn between his eyes is the first King: not the first Monarch, but the first kingdom, that which lasted during the reign of Alexander the great and his brother Aridæus and two young sons, Alexander and Hercules.[2]

The text in Dan 8:8, 9 reads:

⁸וצפיר העזים הגדיל עד־מאד וכעצמו נשברה הקרן הגדולה
ותעלנה חזות ארבע תחתיה לארבע רוחות השמים: ⁹ומן־האחת
מהם יצא קרן־אחת מצעירה ותגדל־יתר אל־הנגב ואל־המזרח
ואל־הצבי:

Then the he-goat magnified himself exceedingly; but when he was strong, the great horn was broken, and instead of it there came up four conspicuous horns toward the four winds of heaven. Out of one of them came forth a little horn, which grew exceedingly great toward the south, toward the east, and toward the glorious land.

Before we consider the specific <u>crux interpretum</u> of vss. 8 and 9, we will briefly consider the "little horn." According to the meaning of "horn" in apocalyptic context, we have here accepted Newton's keen view that the "horn" refers not only to "king" but

---

[1] Isaac Newton, <u>Observations upon the Prophecies of Daniel</u> (London: n.p., 1733), <u>p. 115.</u>

[2] Ibid., p. 117.

rather with the emphasis on "kingdom," and to be sure, a new kingdom, which term, according to our opinion, most clearly expresses the intent of the author.[1]

On this basis, then, it is evident that Antiochus Epiphanes does not fulfil the specific prediction of a "little horn." First, we notice that his kingdom was not a new kingdom, but an old one. Furthermore, his kingdom did not wax great, nor was it great above the other horns; rather, it was weak and tributary to Rome as well.[2]

In respect to the new little horn Newton says:

> The horn was a <u>King of fierce countenance</u>. . . ; that is, he prospered in his practices against the holy people; but Antiochus was frightened out of Egypt. . . the horn was mighty by another's power, Antiochus acted by his own.[3]

This brief comparison brings out a new emphasis that has been overlooked by many scholars.

A <u>crux interpretum</u> in this chapter confronts us in vss. 8 and 9. In vs. 8 the one particular problem is the translation of ותעלנה חזות ארבע תחתיה "and instead of it there came up four conspicuous." The feminine suffix of the preposition תחת refers to a feminine antecedent, which can be none other than הקרן preceding the phrase above and which is qualified with an adjective that

---

[1] This principle of interchangeable usage of the two terms "kings" and "kingdoms" is evident from the interpretation of Daniel himself, as several scholars likewise have observed.

[2] Newton, <u>Observations</u>, p. 123.

[3] Ibid. For other points of dissimilarities between the "little horn" and Antiochus Epiphanes, see ibid., pp. 123-24.

agrees in gender and number.[1] The verb ותעלנה[2] requires a subject which here is expressed by ellipsis, but which on two implications may be assumed to be a feminine plural--first, because of the verb תעלנה, which is feminine; second, because ארבע in the chiastic concord requires a feminine plural noun.[3]

---

[1] Many Hebrew grammars consider קרן as a feminine noun. So, for instance, Heinrich Ewald, Ausführliches Lehrbuch der Hebräischen Sprache (Göttingen: Verlag des Dieterichschen Buchlandlung, 1870), p. 455: Emil Rödiger, Gesenius' Hebrew Grammar, new and rev. ed., trans. Thomas J. Conant (New York: D. Appleton and Company, 1875), p. 197; P. Paul Joüon, Grammaire de l'Hébreu Biblique (Rome: Institut Biblique Pontifical, 1947), p. 411. The Arabs call Alexander the Great by the name Dhū l-Qarnain "the two-horned one" (see, for instance, Richard Bell, The Qur'an [Reprint ed. Edinburgh: T. & T. Clark, 1960], 1:280, 281 [##82, 85, 93]), a fact which Zöckler uses to show that the symbolic vision of Dan 8 did not originate with a pseudo-Daniel, who would have prophesied after the event here predicted and in which not Alexander, but the Medio-Persian empire is represented as "a double-horned ram;" see The Book of the Prophet Daniel in Lange's Commentary on the Holy Scriptures, 13:174.

[2] Qal imperf. 3 plural feminine <עלה "to go up," "ascend;' (here defectively written, for correct spelling see Judg 13:16 ותעלּה [Dageš . . . Forte] or ותעלינה); see Ewald, Ausführliches Lehrbuch der Hebräischen Sprache, p. 794.

[3] It is worth noticing that in both ellipses (Dan 8:8 and 22) the form and structure is the same ארבע תחתיה, in which context the ellipsis is implied. The numerals in Hebrew from three to ten are abstract feminine substantives used in appositional construction with the noun which they enumerate. The feminine form is used with masculine nouns; the masculine is a shorter form used with feminines (see William R. Harper's Elements of Hebrew by an Inductive Method, rev. J. M. Powis Smith (Chicago: The University of Chicago Press, 1968; reprint ed., Berrien Springs, 1975), p. 171. For examples of this usage called "chiastic concord," see, for instance, Job 1:2 שבעה בנים ושלש בנית "seven sons and three daughters," and 1 Kgs 11:31 ויאמר לירבעם קח־לך עשרה קרעים "And he said to Jeroboam, 'Take for yourself ten pieces . . . ,'" Gen 41:2 . . . והנה מן־היאר עלת שבע פרות "and behold, there came up out of the Nile seven cows . . . "; Rödiger, Gesenius' Hebrew Grammar, pp. 179-80; Carl Brockelmann, Hebräische Syntax (Neukirchen Kreis Moers: Verlag der Buchhandlung des Erziehungsvereins, 1956), pp. 75-76; Mayer Lambert, Traité de Grammaire Hébraïque (Hildesheim: Verlag H. A. Gerstenberg, 1972), pp. 211-12; P. Paul Joüon, Grammaire de l'Hébreu Biblique (Rome: Institut Biblique Pontificial, 1947), pp. 262-63.

Another alternative, which is in one way even more probable, is that the subject here could be a dual, but with the vowel pointing indicating a plural. So, for instance, in Dan 8:3 the dual is used, but the vowel pointing is plural, קְרָנַיִם instead of קַרְנַיִם. The same plural-type vowel pointing with dual ending is found on the forms recorded in vss. 6, 7, and 20.[1]

The two ellipses in Dan 8:8, 22 are not anomalous per se, for Carl Brockelmann, for instance, records several examples: 1 Sam 20:16 the object ברית is missing which the verb כרת requires ("to make a covenant"); Gen 18:24 the object עון is missing which the verb נשא requires ("to forgive sins"); and other similar ellipses.[2]

The phrase לארבע רוחות השמים "towards the four winds of heaven" is expressed with the same numeral ארבע (prefixed) and

---

[1] It is hard to explain the plural vowel pointing indicated by the Masoretes in vss. 3 and 6, for the form is dual in both verses and so is the meaning. On the other hand, the plural meaning (indicated by the numeral "four" [ארבע]) in vs. 22, shown by the locution ארבע מלכיות (chiastic concord construction) indicating that also the ellipsis should express the plural (either by a plural form קרנות or a dual with plural pointing קרנים) is easier to understand. However, it seems quite obvious that the pattern of external forms breaks down in apocalyptic context and cannot be constrained. (More exegetical word-studies on a comparative basis are needed here.)

[2] For a more exhaustive list of examples, see Brockelmann, Hebräische Syntax (Neukirchen Kreis Moers: Verlag der Buchhandlung des Erziehungsvereins, 1956), p. 126; cf. also the examples of apodotic ellipses given by Joüon, Grammaire de l'Hébreu Biblique, p. 517. The protasis and apodosis ellipses are, however, more complicated because in these constructions a whole thought is to be understood by implication, whereas in Daniel it is only one word-- and that already qualified by gender and number; the definition "explicit ellipse" could almost be used although it is paradoxical. It is also to be noticed that in Dan 7:20 there is also present an ellipsis: אחרי [קרן] די סלקת.

the רוחות as a feminine plural construct--an authentic chiastic concord.¹ The רוח is here morphologically expressed as a feminine noun, but there are several reasons why, in spite of its morphology, it is considered a masculine. First, the word רוח itself, although mostly used as feminine, occurs also quite often as masculine.² Second, the preposition מן with its masculine plural suffix (in the phrase ומן־האחת מהם) finds its closest antecedent in רוחות, which in this context seems to be considered as masculine in gender in spite of its feminine form. The feminine construction, of course, emphasizes that a metaphor is being used, which is also obvious from the context. This construction which has been considered confusing in gender may not be so complicated as it first

---

¹A similar ellipsis (with the numeral "four") is found in Ezek 10:9, 10:
    ומראיהם דמות אחד לארבעתם (ellipsis)
    כאשר יהיה האופן בתוך האופן

    And for their appearance,
    the four[ellipsis] had the same likeness
    as if a wheel were within a wheel
It is obvious from the context that "the four" refers to "wheels" (אופנים) as an unexpressed but self-evident ellipsis. The chiastic concord can be observed in vs. 9 ארבעה אופנים ("four wheels") with the numeral in feminine and the noun in masculine--this we call an "authentic chiastic concord."

²So Ludwig Koehler and Walter Baumgartner, Lexicon in Veteris Testamenti Libros (Leiden: E. J. Brill, 1958), p. 877; Brown, Driver, and Briggs, A Hebrew and English Lexicon, p. 924; Holladay, A Concise Hebrew and Aramaic Lexicon, p. 334. These words with two genders, when constructed in feminine, refer to metaphorical usage. See, for instance, Rödiger, Gesenius' Hebrew Grammar, p. 197; Lambert, Traité de Grammaire Hébraïque, p. 73. The word רוח as a masculine noun is attested, for instance, in Isa 57:16; Ps 78:39; Eccl 12:7; 2 Chr 18:20. The very last reference is of interest because the verb יצא (Qal imperfect 3m sg) preceeds הרוח--the very same verb that confronts us in Dan 8:9.

seems, especially when we consider the following grammatical statement:

> Through a weakening on the distinction of gender, which is noticeable elsewhere . . . and which probably passed from the colloquial language into that of literature, masculine suffixes (especially in the plural) are not infrequently used to refer to feminine substantives.[1]

Third, it is very doubtful if one can speak of a word (noun) being antecedent which is not even expressed but only alluded to through an ellipsis. The given grammatical construction, then, gives us but one choice for the antecedent to מהם, namely, the word רוחות.

The האחת, though feminine in its morphology, may in the same way as מהם refer to רוחות (above), and the masculine priority of gender would thus explain also the verb יצא which stands in that same gender.

The meaning of יצא is not used, however, in the meaning of "growing out" (of one of the four horns), as many scholars have interpreted the word.[2] The basic meaning is "to go out" or "come forth" (in Qal), with the causative similar meaning in Hiphil.[3]

---

[1] Emil Kautzsch and Arthur E. Cowley, Gesenius' Hebrew Grammar, 2d. ed. (Oxford: Clarendon Press, 1976), p. 440; (this statement by Kautzsch and Cowley is applied inter alia to Dan 8:9), cf. also p. 459 (#144) with reference to the masculine as prior gender.

[2] So, for instance, Young, The Prophecy of Daniel, p. 170; although he suggests immediately afterwards "as it stands it can probably best be translated, there went forth a little horn and by emending two letters we get another horn, a little one." So also Hartman and DiLella, (The Book of Daniel, p. 235) say, "The small horn is pictured as sprouting out of one of the he-goat's four 'conspicuous' ones. . . ."

[3] Ernst Jenni, "יצא jṣ' hinausgehen," Theologisches

Gerhard F. Hasel has fittingly expressed his result of analyzing the verb יצא in the book of Daniel. He writes:

> The idea of horizontal expansion is expressed by the verb yāṣa' in the first part of vs. 9. Every usage of a form of yāṣa' in the book of Daniel expresses a movement from a direction of the compass or from a fixed position to another.[1]

The phrase יצא קרן־אחת is closely connected with the phrase ומן־האחת מהם. An alleged confusion of gender is apparent in both phrases. The solution suggested in regard to the first phrase may serve as an analogous exposition to the second one of the Hebrew sentence.[2] One phrase involves a verb (יצא), the other is the suffix (הם) with the preposition מן.

As for the masculine form of the verb יצא, Kautzsch and Cowley state that ". . . not infrequently . . . masculine forms are used in referring to feminines. . . ."[3]

Ronald J. Williams also points out that a verb preceding the

Handwörterbuch zum Alten Testament, eds. Ernst Jenni and Claus Westermann (München: Chr. Kaiser Verlag, 1971), 1:755-62; Köhler and Baumgartner, Lexicon in Veteris Testamentis Libros, pp. 393-94.

[1]"The 'Little Horn,' the Saints and the Sanctuary in Daniel 8," Studies in the Sanctuary and the Atonement, ed. Arnold Wallenkampf (Washington, D.C.: General Conference of Seventh-day Adventists, 1980), forthcoming. Hasel cites the following passages, all in the book of Daniel, where יצא expresses this predominant idea of going/moving/coming-forth concept: Dan 9:22, 23; 10:20; 11:11, 44.

[2]Cf. p. 411 (above). Keil says that "the masculine forms מהם and יצא (out of them came) are to be explained as a constructio ad sensum" in Biblical Commentary on the Book of Daniel, p. 294.

[3]Gesenius' Hebrew Grammar (2d ed.), p. 459 (#144). Whether this priority of masculine gender can be enforced as valid in reference to this particular case (Dan 8:9) must be left unanswered, for the grammarians do not cite this particular text.

subject is often used in the masculine singular regardless of the gender or number of the subject, especially when the latter is inanimate or animal.[1] Thus there is no syntactical anomaly.

Amazingly enough, the origin of the horn is in no way emphasized in this context, but so much more its nature, expansion, and activity.

The word מצעירה has been subject to many emendations[2] to make the passage conform to Dan 7:8 (קרן אחרי זעירה). The actual meaning is, however, brought out by several scholars. So, for instance, Zöckler translated the phrase: "out of littleness," "in a small way"--(it grew exceedingly great ותגדל־יתר).[3]

The expression מצעירה instead of presenting a synonym to זעירה, clearly emphasizes the nature of the "little horn." The fact that the "little horn" is coming forth from a small beginning is so much more striking when one considers the development that is sequentially emphasized. The expansion is brought out in the term ותגדל־יתר "grew exceedingly great" (RSV) and further specification

---

[1] Ronald J. Williams, Hebrew Syntax (Toronto: University of Toronto Press, 1967), p. 44 (#228).

[2] Bevan, Montgomery, and others have emended קרן אחת מצעירה to קרן אחרת צעירה, thus changing the -מ- in the last word to a -ת- and connecting it with אחת and adding -ר- before -ת-; see Charles, A Critical and Exegetical Commentary on the Book of Daniel, p. 203. The attempt to emendation has made the text almost to agree with Dan 7:8; see Montgomery, The Book of Daniel, p. 333. Ewald emends מָצְעִירָה into מַצְעִירָה--"showing smallness;" for this and other emendations, see Charles (ibid.).

[3] "The Book of the Prophet Daniel" in Lange's Commentary on the Holy Scriptures, 13:175; so also Payne, who translates the phrase "from the state of being little . . . meaning that from small beginnings the horn grew to great power. . . ." Encyclopedia of Biblical Prophecy, p. 378.

as to the direction of this horizontal expansion is given by the phrase: אל־הנגב ואל־המזרח ואל־הצבי. The expansion of the "little horn" is accomplished on a horizontal level and, according to the text, is reflected in three directions of the compass.

The activity of the "little horn" is elucidated from vss. 10-12. The "little horn" seems to expand on a vertical level according to vs. 10: ותגדל עד־צבא השמים. The first verb is familiar from the previous verse. The extension of power "even to the host of heaven" (RSV) is determined to a large degree by the interpretation of the phrase "the host of heaven."

George F. Moore interprets the "host of heaven" to mean: ". . . the heavenly bodies, especially as the object of heathen worship, and as the celestial rulers of the heathen world."[1]

Hasel observes that if the waw in the next phrase ותפל ארצה מן־הצבא ומן־הכוכבים is "coordinative" in function (contrary to those who give it an epexegetical value[2]) then the two expressions "may be understood to have different meanings."[3]

A careful investigation of the text leads us to the same conclusion. The two expressions do not express synonymous thoughts, but if synthetically interpreted the expressions give a vivid (negative) description of the nature and function of the activity of the "little horn."

---

[1]"Daniel 8:9-14," JBL 15 (1896):194.

[2]So, for instance, Charles, The Book of Daniel, p. 204.

[3]Hasel, "The 'Little Horn'," the Saints and the Sanctuary in Daniel 8," forthcoming.

Hasel says:

> In this case [if the waw is coordinate in function] the idea of the clause "and it grew great to the host of heaven" could mean that the little horn became strong on account of an approach to "the host of heaven" in idolatrous worship. In this case "the host of heaven" may refer either to heavenly constellations, or celestial beings or both. They are venerated in worship for purpose of gaining further power.[1]

The phrase "and some of the hosts of the stars it cast down to the ground (and trampled upon them)" is explained in vs. 24--vis-à-vis persecution of the saints of God, i.e., God's people.

With vs. 11 the verb גדל occurs anew, but as it expresses a masculine form it may be suggested that the metaphor "horn" is dropped[2] and, instead, the focus of the power behind the symbol may be coming to the forefront.

The word קרן confronts us anew as we come to the interpretive part of the vision. Twice Daniel had already been reminded that the vision had reference to the "time of the end" (Dan 8:17, 19). The dual form הקרנים, according to the interpretation, refers to the dual aspect of the Medo-Persian kingdom--a fact on which all scholars in general agree.[3] Similarly, the he-goat is the

---

[1] Ibid., forthcoming.

[2] Ibid., the elimination of the metaphor provides a natural break at this point of our investigation in order to present a removal of the focal point of this particular study.

[3] So Marti, Das Buch Daniel, p. 61; Charles, A Critical and Exegetical Commentary on the Book of Daniel, p. 216; Young, The Prophecy of Daniel, p. 178; Montgomery, A Critical and Exegetical Commentary on the Book of Daniel, p. 348; Keil, Biblical Commentary on the Book of Daniel, p. 316; Heaton, The Book of Daniel, p. 199; Jeffery, The Book of Daniel, p. 470; Walwoord, Daniel the Key to Prophetic Revelation, p. 197; Hartman and Alexander Di Lella, The Book of Daniel, p. 234; Lacocque, The Book of Daniel, p. 165; Thomson, Daniel, p. 246.

the king (or kingdom) of Greece and the רהקרן הגדולה has also been interpreted as Alexander (המלך הראשון).[1]

Though scholars disagree concerning the interpretation of the four successive beasts in Dan 7,[2] there is quite unanimous opinion in regard to the interpretation of the ram, the he-goat, and the four kings (or kingdoms) into which Alexander's empire broke up. And so the general all-embracing view has been that the four kingdoms are represented by Macedonia (Cassander), Thrace and Asia Minor (Lysimachus), "Asia" or Syria (Seleucus), and Egypt (Ptolemy).[3]

Louis F. Hartman has struck another note emphasizing the directions of the compass rather than rigidly circumscribed kingdoms for the four horns in Dan 8:22 (cf. vs. 8). The following quotation reflects his view:

> . . . our author may not have had this division [the traditional division mentioned above] primarily in mind, for the boundaries and rulers of these regions shifted. For him the four Greek kingdoms that took the place of Alexander's single one, as symbolized by the four large horns of the ram that grew up in place of its single one (vs. 22), are rather

---

[1] The commentators that agree concerning the ram as a representative for the Medo-Persian empire also agree in regard to the he-goat as representing the Grecian empire; cf. Hasel, "The 'Little Horn'," (forthcoming).

[2] The majority of scholars of differing schools of thought accept the Grecian scheme, as has already been pointed out.

[3] So, for instance, Carl A. Auberlen, The Prophecies of Daniel and the Revelations of St. John (Edinburgh: T. & T. Clark, 1856), p. 53; Montgomery, A Critical Exegetical Commentary on the Book of Daniel, p. 332; Keil, Biblical Commentary on the Book of Daniel, p. 293; Charles, The Book of Daniel, pp. 202-3; Walwoord, Daniel the Key to Prophetic Revelation, p. 184; Lacocque, The Book of Daniel, p. 161.

more generalized as occupying regions "toward the four winds of the heavens"--north, east, south, and west (cf. 11:4).[1]

This keen observation by Hartman helps us to unshackle from a too one-sided view which, no doubt, has been too emphatically articulated, namely, the identification of the "four horns" (kings or kingdoms). It might be more fruitful to consider the known, the general directions of the compass, than to speculate about the unknown "conspicuous horns." It seems sound exposition of vs. 8 to consider the expansion of the "little horn" as coming from one direction of the compass instead of searching for a circumscribed origin which is not expressed. This shift of emphasis in vs. 8 provides an important key, especially for vs. 9. But whereas vs. 8 gives a generalizing statement of horizontal occupation of regions in the four directions of the compass, i.e., the four "horns" coming from the place where the "great horn" stood and moved, as it were, or spread toward the "four winds of heaven," vs. 22 emphasizes the replacement of the one great horn that was broken, in favor of the four horns which arose. Thus it seems evident that four kingdoms take the place of the one great kingdom.

Thus we may sum up our observations in the following way: (1) the <u>origin</u> of the "four horns" is emphasized in vs. 8 with the verb תעלנה (<עלה) "to come up" in the sense of a taking over; (2) the idea of <u>replacement</u> is emphasized in vs. 22 with the phrase תחתיה . . . ותעמדנה (<עמד) "to put (or "set up") in its

---

[1]<u>The Book of Daniel</u>, p. 235.

stead";[1] (3) the idea of <u>horizontal occupation of regions</u> is emphasized by the words "toward the four winds of heaven" (vs. 8), and (4) in regard to the "little horn," the idea of <u>origin recedes into the background</u> and the idea of <u>expansion</u> has primary focus (vs. 9).

In summing up the morphological evidences of apocalyptic passages in which the word קרן occurs, we find that in Dan 7 the word קרן is used in the singular in its absolute state only once and is then qualified (Dan 7:8). In all other occurrences this singular word occurs in its emphatic state, thus denoting specific "horns" or kingdoms (Dan 7:8, 11, 20, 21). The plural is expressed by the dual absolute form once (Dan 7:7) and the other four times in the emphatic state. It is worth noticing that the dual form is used even to express plurality.

Dan 8 reveals that the singular קרן occurs several times (Dan 8:5, 8, 9, 20) and each time it is qualified. Once קרן is qualified חזות and twice הגדולה--all three times it refers to the first king of Javan or Greece, that is, not to Alexander himself, but to the first kingdom which lasted during Alexander's reign and during the reign of a few other kings who ruled before the Diadochi. Once (Dan 8:9) the קרן is qualified with a numeral (adjectivally used) and it is described as coming forth in an insignificant way (from littleness) but growing exceedingly great. Both the immediate and larger context show that this latter קרן is to be distinguished

---

[1] Koehler and Baumgartner, <u>Lexicon in Veteris Testamenti Libros</u>, p. 713. See also Brown, Driver, and Briggs, <u>A Hebrew and English Lexicon</u>, pp. 763-64 and pp. 1065-66.

from the former one (vs. 8)--a fact that is observed in general by all scholars alike.

The context of Dan 8:21-22 emphasizes that four kingdoms should arise after the first horn, i.e., after the first kingdom (of Alexander and his immediate successors) had been broken off. The four horns that arose (Dan 8:22; cf. 8:8) are, therefore, four kingdoms. Vs. 23 predicts that a king of bold countenance should arise at the latter end of their rule (i.e., after the rule of the four kings or kingdoms). According to our principle of synonymity of the terms "king(s)" and "kingdom(s)," the king with a bold countenance refers to a kingdom, i.e., a new kingdom. We are here fully accepting the view of Newton, namely, that "a horn of a beast is never taken for a single person; it always signifies a new kingdom."[1]

On the other hand, the dual appears peculiar--even anomalous as far as the vocalization goes. Though the "horns" are expressed with a dual, as one would expect, the vocalization through pointing expresses plurality.[2]

For those words omitted, but at the same time self-evident by ellipses, no absolute certainty can be expressed as to their morphological structure. However, there are, it seems, two alternatives. The word "horns" may be a clear plural (קרנות) or a dual with plural vocalization קרנים. The latter is even more probable because of this particular usage in chap. 8.

---

[1] Newton, Observations, p. 123.

[2] See Dan 8:3, 7.

However, the meaning of the horn-motif cannot be elucidated only on a structural basis, though for the sake of comparison an overview of the morphological similarities and dissimilarities is helpful. Our observation so far is that in the apocalyptic genre the general morphological pattern breaks down. We must, therefore, depend more on the context (both the immediate and the larger context) for an interpretation.

The symbolic meaning, therefore, must be briefly discussed here. Our investigation shows that the term "horn" in the singular form in the apocalypse of Daniel refers to a king, or kingdom. The same word in plural analogously refers to kings or kingdoms.

Our study in chapter three made it clear that the same interchangeable usage of the terms "king" and "kingdom" is alluded to also in nonbiblical sources of ancient Near Eastern literature. It was also shown that the earliest known pattern of government in history was that of city-kingdoms. Each city had its own deity and its own king, and each king under the protection of a special deity had his own kingdom. The king and his kingdom fused together, so to speak, with the city-god or national god as the highest authority.

The pattern of city-kingdom was replaced with the pattern of imperial rulership when Sargon the Great of Akkad founded his dynasty. The most famous king of this dynasty was, no doubt, Narâm-Sin. Iconography depicts the deified king with bull-horns on his helmet--probably to indicate both origin of power (Sin-god) and universality of rulership (world-empire) after the pattern of the universal moon-cult.

Even when Sargon's dynasty came to an end and the city-kingdoms anew took over the rulership, the deification of the kings (of the Isin dynasty) continued. Whether these kings wore "horns" or not is a question that cannot yet be satisfactorily answered. However, the symbol of the "horns" of the moon together with the "horns" of the bull continued as synonymous emblems to identify the rulership of any particular king who was devoted to the astral cult--especially to the moon-cult.

We also know that in this early time of history the cities stood for kingdoms. We need only mention some of the earliest known cities--Kish, Erech (Warka), Larsa, Eridu, Ur, and later cities such as Aššur, Babylon, Mari, Ebla, Nuzi, Ugarit, Rome, and others--to realize that "cities" and "kingdoms" were also synonymous terms. This same principle of identification seems to be carried out even in the Bible where we find Samaria as standing for Israel and Jerusalem for Judah.[1]

As the ruler or king of a city always ruled with divine power, he and his kingdom (the city) were subject to the city-god or national god. By necessity the concepts of "king" and "kingdom," therefore, fused. We also presume that multiple "horns" on a headdress, as we have seen gods and goddesses depicted in ancient Near Eastern iconography, had the meaning of authority and high position in the pantheon of gods.

The "horns" in Daniel do not, however, refer to mythological

---

[1]See, for instance, Albrecht Alt, Der Stadtstaat Samaria (Berlin: Akademie-Verlag, 1954).

gods or goddesses but to the secular rulership of kings and rulers (i.e., their kingdoms) according to the interpretations found in the context of the imagery. The "horns" may, however, presumably indicate divine authority, for the crowns or headdresses of the gods implied this concept and the gods were the rulers of the cities in earliest governmental patterns known (from Sumeria). Nevertheless, we are on safe ground in interpreting the "horns" in Daniel 7 and 8 with the meaning of "kings" with the equivalence of "kingdoms." Furthermore, on the basis of our investigation, we understand these two terms as synonymous in the particular apocalyptic context discussed here.

Moreover, it seems evident that the imagery presented in the apocalyptic book of Daniel displays its own repertory and was far removed from the imaginary motifs of the ancient Near Eastern mythology.

The Horns of Moses

There is only one passage directly involved with reference to the concept of Moses wearing horns, namely, Exod 34:29, 30, 35. The passage has been subject to controversial views through the years and there is still no consensus among scholars in regard to the proper meaning of קרן.[1]

Gressmann, for instance, assigns the role of an oracular priest to Moses and makes him, in likeness with the oracle-priest in

---

[1] See, for instance, Robert A. Cole, Exodus: An Introduction and Commentary (Downers Grove, IL: Inter-Varsity Press, 1973), p. 233.

surrounding cultures, to wear a "mask" (מסוה).[1]

Noth points particularly to Egypt where the priest assumed the "face" of his deity and identified himself with him[2] as the pattern also for Israel.

Julian Morgenstern expresses the following view:

> Moses with the shining face is thus the official, earthly representative of Yahwe with the shining face, His substitute on earth, as it were. And the conclusion is inescapable that about this representative of the Deity, himself with a face shining like that of Yahwe, upon which, too, mortals could look only with difficulty and fear, there hovered something divine. Moses had become in this story a kind of a deity, or at least a semi-divine mortal.[3]

The concept of the "divinity" of Moses was deep-rooted in the Jewish people and this concept made its impact on those in close communion with the Jews. Philo, for instance, speaks of Moses, the great legislator, as having passed "from a man into a god."[4] In another connection Philo speaking about Moses says, "for he was named god and king of the whole nation. . . ."[5] There are several such quotations by Philo which show that Moses was virtually

---

[1] "Masken-Teraphim," ZAW 40 (1922):76, 77, 82-84. So also Martin Noth, Exodus: A Commentary (Philadelphia: The Westminster Press, 1962), p. 267; Karl Jaroš, "Des Mose 'strahlende Haut'," ZAW 88 (1976):275-81; J. de Fraine, "Moses' 'cornuta facies' (Ex 34:29-35," Bijdragen Tijdschrift voor filosophie en theologie 20 (1959):28-38; John A. MacCulloch, "Horns," Encyclopaedia of Religion and Ethics, ed. James Hastings (New York: Charles Scribner's Sons, 1914), 6:791-96.

[2] Exodus, p. 267.

[3] "Moses with the Shining Face," HUCA 9 (1925):5.

[4] "Quod Omnis Probus Liber Sit," VII, in Philo, trans. T. H. Colson, 9:35, 37.

[5] "De Vita Mosis," I, ibid., 6:357, 359.

"deified" by the Jews. The horns protruding from Moses' head[1] seem, therefore, to be due not only to a mistranslation but, perhaps even more so, intentionally so placed in order to express his "divinity" just as in the case of Alexander at a later time.

Ruth Mellinkoff, in <u>The Horned Moses in Medieval Art and Thought</u>, says:

> These horns of Moses . . . have traditionally been explained as the offspring of a translator's mistake. It is said that they derive from an error made by Jerome in his translation of the Old Testament, namely, a mistranslation of the Hebrew word, <u>qeren</u>, in Exodus 34:29: ומשה לא ידע כי קרן עור פניו בדברו אתו: where <u>qeren</u> (קרן) can mean "horns" or "rays of light."[2]

It is well known, as Mellinkoff has pointed out, that Jerome translated the קרן as <u>cornuta</u> "horned." Mellinkoff also points out that "Jerome had two different translations for the Hebrew <u>qeren</u> (Exod 34:29) available to him: 'glorified' in the Septuagint, and 'horned' in the Aquila version."[3]

Thus it seems clear that it was not ignorance by any means that made Jerome follow the Aquila translation--it was a conscious choice, for he writes:

> . . . deniq post quadraginta dies, uultum Moysi uulgus ignobile caligantibus oculis non uidebat, quia "glorificata erat," siue, ut in hebraico contineretur, "cornuta," facies Moysi.[4]

---

[1] So expressed in well-known art works of Michelangelo, and Claus Sluter.

[2] Ruth Mellinkoff, <u>The Horned Moses in Medieval Art and Thought</u> (Berkeley: University of California Press, 1970), p. 1. (Mellinkoff wrongly speaks of <u>qeren</u> in all her references when here, in fact, the Hebrew expresses the <u>Qal</u> perfect.)

[3] Ibid., p. 77.

[4] S. Hieronymi Presbyteri Opera, <u>Commentarium in Hiezechielem</u>

> Finally after forty days the common people with their clouded eyes could not look at Moses' face because it had been "glorified," or as it says in Hebrew, "horned."[1]

Mellinkoff draws the conclusion that Jerome considered "glorified" and "horned" as synonyms and by his choice had a metaphorical usage in mind.[2]

Lloyd R. Bailey notes that "most modern scholars had suggested that Jerome's translation was in error and that the Hebrew original (qāran ʿôr pānāw) means, 'the skin of his face shone'."[3]

Bailey refers to the Arabic cognates qarn and qarîna as support for the "shining face" interpretation; the qarn with the meaning of "the first visible part of the rising sun"[4] and qarîna "eclampsia: medical condition which sometimes includes the perception of blinding light."[5]

Fritz Dumermuth finds evidences for the biblical phrase in the history-of-religion concepts. He says,

> In der Tat ist das Phänomen des strahlenden Gesichts religionsgeschichtlich bezeugt. Es begegnet in Märchen, Sagen, Legenden so gut wie in historisch zuverlässigen Überlieferungen.[6]

---

in Corpus Christianorum, Series Latina, 75 (Turnholti: Typographi Brepols editores Pontifici, 1964), p. 557 (lines 261-64).

[1] As translated in Mellinkoff, The Horned Moses, pp. 77-78.

[2] Ibid., p. 78.

[3] "Horns of Moses," IDBSupp (1976), p. 420.

[4] Ibid.

[5] Ibid.; cf. George Mendenhall, "On a Visit with a Druzi Witch," 1972-73 Newsletter No. 9, AASOR (April 1973):1-4; 1972-73 Newsletter No. 10, AASOR (May 1973):1-2.

[6] "Moses strahlendes Gesicht," TZ 17.4 (1961):244.

Dumermuth finds an evidence for the biblical phrase in the old legend of Daniel in the "Aqhat-Sage."[1] When Daniel received the good news that he had a son, the legend says that "Daniel's face lights up, while above his forehead shines."[2] Thus, Dumermuth compares the phrase pnm tšmh w 'l yṣhl pit as similar to the qāran 'ôr pānâw in the Exodus story of Moses.[3]

Elmer G. Suhr also puts the Exodus account on the same footing as the Grecian myths and would refer "the shining brilliance" of Moses not only to his face but that it "covered his whole body."[4]

A myth of a "shining face" and a "shining body" is thus attested in surrounding cultures. Bailey even goes so far as to consider the possibility of the melammu as comparable to kābhôdh.[5] In regard to the melammu he gives the definition, "a radiant aureole which was said to surround Assyro-Babylonian deities and (occasionally) kings; and parallels in other cultures."[6]

---

[1] For a translation, see Harold L. Ginsberg, "The Tale of Aqhat," in ANET (1969), pp. 149-55.

[2] Ibid., p. 150 (ii [8d]).

[3] "Moses strahlendes Gesicht," p. 244.

[4] See Suhr's article, "The Horned Moses," Folklore (London) 74.2 (1963):387.

[5] Bailey, "Horns of Moses," p. 420; for an exhaustive study of the meaning of כבד, see Claus Westermann, "כבד kbd schwer sein," in THAT, ed. Ernst Jenni and Claus Westermann (München: Chr. Kaiser Verlag, 1971), 1:794-811; cf. Sverre Aalen, "Ehre," Theologisches Begriffs Lexikon zum Neuen Testament, 3d ed., ed. Lothar Coenen (Wuppertal: Theologischer Verlag Rolf Brockhaus, 1972), [1]:204, II:2.

[6] Ibid. Cf. George Mendenhall, The Tenth Generation, The Origins of the Biblical Tradition (Baltimore: The Johns Hopkins University Press, 1973), ch. 2 ("The Mask of Yahweh"); Leo A.

The "melammu-concept" is reflected not only in Ugarit but in many other cultures. Leo A. Oppenheim speaks of melammu as a pre-Sumerian tradition.[1] It is most probably that the Assyrians took over this ancient Sumerian concept when they applied the melammu to their own national god Aššur.

George E. Mendenhall points out that it was in the 9th century B.C. that "the winged disk became extraordinarily common."[2] It is at that time period and even as early as the 12th century B.C.[3] that Assyrian sources record such statements as the following: "The awe-inspiring splendour of Aššur overwhelmed the men . . . and they brought tribute."[4] Or, from the time of Adad-Nirari II: ". . . the effulgence of his surpassing glory consumed all of them. The lands of the kings were distressed. The mountains trembled."[5]

Mendenhall sees a close analogy between ʿanan and melammu for he says "ʿanan is the mask, and the fire is the garment of flame called puluḫtu in Akkadian."[6]

It is, however, not the word כבוד, the ענן, nor the אש --not even מסוה --which occurs in our passage, but the word קרן.

Oppenheim, "Akkadian pul(u)ḫ(t)u and melammu," JAOS 63 (1943):31-34; idem, Ancient Mesopotamia (Chicago: The University of Chicago Press, 1964), p. 98.

[1] Ancient Mesopotamia, p. 98.

[2] The Tenth Generation, p. 48.

[3] Mendenhall refers to the time of Tiglath-Pileser I (ibid.).

[4] Ibid.   [5] Ibid.

[6] The analogy based on Exod 14:19-20 seems strange to us; cf. vs. 24.

The difficulty, of course, arises because as a Qal perfect, the word may be considered almost a hapax legomenon.[1]

When we turn to the particular passages in Hebrew and consider the context, there are a few things that must be observed. First, the phrase says עור פניו "the skin of his face," a rendering on which all scholars agree. This interpretation therefore excludes any translation which implies the "horns" growing from the mēṣaḥ "forehead." Second, the passage tells us that ומשה לא־ידע "And Moses did not know," which makes it quite obvious that קרן cannot imply literal horns. If "horns" had grown out from his head he could by touching his face know that he had horns. This, then, eliminates the concept of a "mask" מסוה. And, third, this is illogical, for it was not until his face קרן (whatever it means) that he put on the מסוה.[2]

This inconsistency in interpretation makes it clear that קרן cannot be translated with "horns" and that a "mask" (with horns) must be considered a complete misapprehension.[3] The context

---

[1] The verb form קרן is used three times in the same chapter but as the context is the same--referring to the same event--the usage of this terminus technicus can be defended. Bailey implicitly expresses the same opinion, "Horns of Moses," p. 420.

[2] If the מסוה is considered a horned "mask," according to the tradition of the oracle-priests, Moses must have put on the "horned mask" (Exod 34:33)--on the horns that already had grown out (Exod 34:29, 30) from his head (forehead!!).

[3] Cole says, "The word for 'veil' (maswēh) is unknown, except from this passage, but both the context and Jewish traditional interpretation make its meaning clear. It is quite gratuitous, with some modern editors, to translate it as a 'priest's mask' (although such are known from the ancient world), the more so as Moses is acting in a prophetic, not priestly, capacity in this context. The

of the passage excludes such a translation. The question of how to understand the passage then arises.

Though Mellinkoff has shown that Jerome understood the קרן to express a metaphor, scholars in general have accepted rationalistic views from the 18th century and combined them with the "history-of-religion" school evidences in order to give an explanation. In fact, Jerome's translation is the basis for medieval exegesis,[1] but many recent works are only adaptations on that same basis.

It is only fair to consider the Septuagint translation which was available to Jerome.[2] All the Greek versions[3] render קרן with the translation δεδόξασται "glorified."[4]

William Jenks connects the passage in Exod 34:29, 30, 35 with Hab 3:4.[5] The passage in Hab 3:4 is the only passage where a

---

whole story suggests an ad hoc experience, not a religious ritual." Exodus, p. 232.

[1] This kind of exegesis has given rise to the many art-works (and caricatures) of Moses of which Mellinkoff gives a variable presentation (The Horned Moses in Medieval Art and Thought).

[2] Cf. p. 424 (above).

[3] See Chart (appendix B) in regard to Exod 34:29, 30, 35.

[4] Perfect indicative passive third person singular δοξάζω "to glorify"; for a more exhaustive study on the word δόξα, see Leona G. Running, A Historical and Philological Study of δόξα ("Glory") in the Holy Scriptures (M.A. thesis, SDA Theological Seminary, Washington, D.C., 1955). See especially Gerhard Kittel, "δοξάξω," TDNT (Grand Rapids: Wm. B. Eerdmans Publishing Company, 1964), 2:253 where Kittel says, "While Σ and Vg have 'was horned,' the LXX has ὅτι δεδόξασται ἡ ὄψις του χρώματος, which can only denote the 'radiant shining' of the skin (as in most translations)."

[5] Jenks translates the Hebrew qaran "shone" with the meaning "to irradiate," "to shoot forth" or "emit rays of light." It is in

translation of the dual קרנים as "horns" does not fit the context. As has already been shown, the context assumes a theophany of יהוה; and as the God of the Israelites is nowhere presented with "horns," this passage must convey a different meaning which must be determined on the basis of the glorious theophany and not on a bull-concept.

Jack M. Sasson is aware of the fact that "Hab 3:4 usually is alluded to as a passage where <u>qeren</u> clearly means 'light'"[1] and which has been used to exegete Exod 34:29-36. Sasson further says,

> If this be so, then Hab 3:4 offers, to my knowledge, the only example, out of almost a hundred instances in the O.T. where such a rendering can be exegeted. . . . For this reason, it seems imprudent to insist on employing it to clarify Ex 34.[2]

Sasson has rightly observed the questionable method of connecting the two passages: the קרן in the Exodus is a <u>Qal</u>

---

the last expression he sees a connection with Hab 3:4. He also says, "The Arabs also call the first rays of the rising sun, the 'horns of the gazelle';" for the full discussion see Jenks, ed., <u>The Comprehensive Commentary on the Holy Bible</u> (Philadelphia: Lippincott Grambo & Co., successor to Grigg, Elliot & Co., 1852), 1:352-53. Many Bible versions follow the metaphorically expressed translation of the Septuagint rather than the literal and misunderstood translation of Aquila. The Interlinear Bible (Exod 34:29). The Authorized Version and the Revised Version give the same translation in all three verses, "Moses wist not that the skin of his face shone," with the marginal note for קרן "sent forth beams" (Heb. <u>horns</u>); The Companion Bible gives the following clarifying notes to Exod 34:29: "Shone = radiated, or was glorious," i.e., reflected as a mirror the Divine glory. . . . Harper Study Bible, and the RSV translates the debated phrase, "the skin of his face shone," similarly in all three verses. The Jerusalem Bible makes a little variation: vs. 29 "the skin on his face was radiant," vs. 30 "the skin on his face shone," vs. 35 "the face of Moses radiant"; the NIV has chosen the phrase, "his face was radiant" in all three verses.

[1]"Bovine Symbolism in the Exodus Narrative," <u>VT</u> 18 (1968): 386.

[2]Ibid.

perfect[1] and, furthermore, a hapax legomenon. The word in Hab 3:4 is a dual noun.

We see in these two occurrences, both of which have to be interpreted with reference to יהוה, a tentative solution by assuming another tradition on a vertical level running parallel with the many metaphors having reference to the attacking bull conveying a negative emphasis on a horizontal level.[2]

The fact that Moses' face was glorified with a transcendent glory is due to the fact that he had been in the presence of יהוה and been talking with him (בדברו אתו). We therefore consider the Greek translation (δεδόξασται) "glorified" as a reliable rendering of קרן (verb). If a more "literal" rendering is to be preferred, we would consider the locution "the skin of his face shone" as equally correct. On the other hand we think that a literal translation of קרן with "horns" does not fit the context; nor is such a translation true to the text with its verb form (Qal). As for the dual (qarnayim) in Hab 3:4 it would seem that the term "rays" is to be considered a correct rendering.[3]

---

[1] Cf. the other verb form מקרן, a Hiphil participle in Ps 69:32 where the context is literal and refers to a young bull with horns and hoofs.

[2] This solution is based on the investigation done so far; especially ancient Near Eastern literature and iconography give strong hints that quite early--already in pre-historic time--there were more than one tradition for "horns," but these traditions have fused in the lapse of time and cause confusion in interpretation even today. Mellinkoff refers to the same ambiguity when she writes: "The power of the horn or horns was vast and constant: it could be associated with good or with evil, and could be transferred to 'good' gods or 'bad' gods, 'good' men or 'evil' men." See further Mellinkoff's discussion The Horned Moses, p. 122.

[3] This translation connects the locution with the verb-form קרן in Exod 34:29-35 where קרן also can be translated "to emit

The bull worship in Israel and the ancient prophets' concern in regard to the apostate people reveal clearly that throughout their history, from the wandering in the wilderness and to the exile, the bull and Yahweh were rivals in the cult of Israel.[1]

Keil, referring to the bull worship in the wilderness, says:

> The "golden calf" (עֵגֶל a young bull) was copied from the Egyptian Apis . . . but for all that, it was not the image of an Egyptian deity,--it was no symbol of the generative or bearing power of nature, but an image of Jehovah. . . . When Aaron saw it, he built an altar in front of the image, and called aloud to the people, "<u>to-morrow is a feast of Jehovah</u>"; and the people celebrated this feast . . . in the same manner in which the Egyptians celebrated their feast of Apis.[2]

Thus it is evident that bull-worship which was so distinctive in surrounding cultures both in the third and second millennium B.C. was a continuous threat to the tribes of Israel right from the very time of the exodus from Egypt, becoming a nation in the second millennium B.C., and throughout their history.

<u>Special Usages</u>

In this section we will attempt to discuss the one passage that uses the term "horn" in an idiomatic way. A few passages with names that contain the word "horn" will also be discussed.

---

rays of light." Cf. also Sumerian <u>SI</u> with the meaning of "radiance."

[1] Manfred Weippert points out the cult-scenes depicted on the "Cappadocian" seals from the beginning of the 2d mill., on which the bull assumed a very prominent role--even in some arrangements where the bull placed on a podium is the very object of worship--not to speak of the apostate Israelite kingdom in the 10th century B.C. which under Jeroboam worshipped the bull; "Gott und Stier," <u>ZDPV</u> 77 (1961):97-98 et passim.

[2] <u>The Pentateuch</u>, 2:222; cf. also Stanley A. Cook, <u>The Religion of Ancient Palestine in the Light of Archaeology</u> (London: Oxford University Press, 1930), pp. 39-40.

Idiomatic usage. Job 16:15 presents the idiom to be discussed. In comparison with the expressions already examined, this particular passage presents a rare locution. It presents a complete synthetic parallelism of thought:

שק תפרתי עלי גלדי
ועללתי בעפר קרני

"I have sewed sackcloth upon my skin,
and have laid my strength in the dust."

The background to the experience that Job relates in the two above brief couplets portrays the experience of Job at this time. Edward J. Kissane expresses some of Job's calamities in the following words:

> God's arrows have wounded his whole body, and have penetrated his vital organs. . . . But though he is already mortally wounded, God continues to inflict wound after wound, charging against him like a frenzied warrior. . . .[1]

Without analyzing the philosophy of Job--neither in general nor in particular--we are confronted with a locution that expresses on Job's part complete defeat. Kissane says, "Against such an opponent, Job must go down to defeat." He further explains the first couplet: "I have sewn means, simply, 'I have put on' sackcloth, the garb of mourning [on my skin]." In regard to the second idiom in the next couplet he says, ". . . 'to exalt the horn' signifies joy or triumph, so 'to thrust the horn into the dust' is to acknowledge defeat."[2] Gustav Hölscher has expressed the same view but in an intensified way when he says,

"Sein Horn in die Erde boren," ein Bild der tiefsten

---

[1] The Book of Job (New York: Sheed & Ward, 1946), p. 101.

[2] Ibid.

Erniedrigung; Gegensatz "sein Horn erheben" . . . als Bild des Stolzes, ursprünglich vom Stiere genommen.[1]

Solomon B. Freehof dramaticizes the defeat of Job when he writes,

> Contrariwise [to the wild ox in the word of victory and triumph proudly lifting up its horns], the proud animal, defeated, wounded, droops its head and wallows his horn in the dust. So Job here, describing how broken he is by misfortunes, says, "I have laid my horn in the dust."[2]

Georg Heinrich A. von Ewald chooses to emphasize the humiliation in other terms:

> . . . The noble, dignified hero must surely succumb in shame and sorrow, fix a close, prickly mourning-garment of coarse hair upon his bare skin and thrust his horn, i.e., his noble, honoured head, in humiliation in the dust. . . .[3]

Franz J. Delitzsch points out the meaning of עלל to mean "to inflict pain, or scorn" and prefers the Jewish expositors' explanation: "I have misused, i.e., injured or defiled my horn with dust."[4] Delitzsch also says, "This is not equivalent to my head (as in the Syr. version), but he calls everything that was hitherto his power and pride קרני."[5]

---

[1] Das Buch Hiob, HAT (Tübingen: J. C. B. Mohr [Paul Siebeck], 1937), p. 38. So also Samuel R. Driver and George G. Gray, A Critical and Exegetical Commentary on the Book of Job, ICC (Reprint ed., Edinburgh: T. & T. Clark, 1958), p. 147; Friedrich Horst, Hiob, BKAT (1968), p. 251.

[2] Book of Job (New York: Union of American Hebrew Congregations, 1958), p. 134. Marvin H. Pope has picked up the same dramatic picture of the wounded bull; see his Job, AB (Garden City, NY: Doubleday & Company, Inc., 1965), p. 117.

[3] Commentary on the Book of Job (London: Williams and Norgate, 1882), p. 189.

[4] Biblical Commentary on the Book of Job (Grand Rapids: Wm. B. Eerdmans Publishing Company, 1961), p. 287.

[5] Ibid., pp. 287-88.

Norman C. Habel, in turn, expresses himself only in by-passing Job's experience at this point with a couple of sentences: "He [Job] has been humiliated to the point of being one with <u>the dust</u>, with death itself. He is nothing."[1]

There are clearly two specific trends among scholars: those who emphasize the bull metaphor and those who avoid using it. It is to be observed that those scholars who cling to the "horn" expressions as being derived from the animal kingdom persistingly and consistently use the same explanation wherever the "horn" appears. However, this kind of elucidation in the long run seems to be one-sided, unablance, and overemphasized, especially when the context is far removed from this kind of idea.

<u>Onomastic usage</u>. The onomastic usage of "horn" in the Hebrew Bible seems to be reflected in two ways: as a place name or as a personal name. Both of these usages have confronted us in nonbiblical literature.

Already in Gen 14:5 the onomastic usage of קרן is attested in the early part of the Abraham cycle. The Hebrew construction בעשתרת קרנים with Ashteroth in the construct form and prefixed with a -ב- seems to assume Ashteroth as being a place in Qarnaim (in Ashteroth of Qarnaim) unless it is a place name with double name. Archaeology, however, attests the Karnaim (Sheikh Sa'd) as a sister city of Ashtaroth[2]--on the upper furcation of Wadi Yarmuk

---

[1] The Book of Job, The Cambridge Bible Commentary, ed., P. R. Ackroyd, et al. (London: Cambridge University Press, 1975), p. 90.

[2] Oxford Bible Atlas, 2d ed., ed. Herbert G. May (London: Oxford University Press, 1974), pp. 132, 56. (For maps see pp. 49, 57,

in Bashan. The twin cities might at some period in history have been only one city, later divided, or then independently being built. Archaeological discoveries attest Ashtaroth as being a city or place in the late 19th century without any connection with Qarnaim.[1]

According to the Abraham pericope "Chedorlaomer and the kings allied with him came and defeated the Rephaim in Ashteroth-karnaim . . . (Gen 14:15)."[2] The separation of the two cities must have taken place early, for Ashtaroth is attested as a separate city at the time of the conquest of Canaan,[3] and according to archaeological evidences it is named separately already in the 19th century.[4] In the 8th century the prophet Amos mentions Qarnaim by itself.[5] More than half a millennium later it was again mentioned as a stronghold in the Maccabean war.[6]

62, 69, 73.) Cf. also Hans Walter Wolff, Joel and Amos (Philadelphia: Fortress Press, 1977), p. 288.

[1] Oxford Bible Atlas, p. 56. "Nelson Glueck identifies Ashtaroth Karnaim . . . as two adjacent sites in southern Syria, Tell Ashtarah and Sheikh Saʼad, which was called Carnaim in New Testament times" as quoted by Henry M. Morris, The Genesis Record (Grand Rapids: Baker Book House, 1976), p. 315.

[2] Several commentators refer to the Rephaim as a prehistoric race of giant stature. So, for instance, Ephraim A. Speiser, Genesis, AB (Garden City, NY: Doubleday & Company, Inc., 1964), p. 104; Morris, The Genesis Record, p. 314.

[3] See Deut 1:4; Josh 9:10, 12:4; 13:12, 31; 1 Chr 6:56, and Josh 21:27.

[4] Oxford Bible Atlas, p. 56.

[5] Amos 6;13; cf. James L. Mays, Amos, p. 122; Cripps, The Book of Amos, pp. 215-16; Wolff, Joel and Amos, p. 288; J. A. Motyer, The Day of the Lion: The Message of Amos (Downers Grove, IL: Inter-varsity Press, 1974), p. 142.

[6] 1 Mac 5:26, 43, 44; 2 Mac 12:21, 27; (R. H. Charles, ed. APOT [Oxford: Clarendon Press, 1913], 1:84, 85, 149).

George F. Moore, referring to the Maccabean account of the war, says that there is no reason to doubt that Qarnaim "had a temenos to which people fled for refuge when Judas advanced against the city" (1 Mac 5:43-44); and in the parallel passage (2 Mac 12:26) "the place is described as a sanctuary of Atargatis."[1]

The interesting thing is that many scholars have thought that the "two horns" (dual) "could be nothing else than the lunar crescent, and thus found in the name a welcome confirmation of the theory that Astarte--at least among the Western Semites--was a Moon-goddess."[2]

Moore further thinks that the figures of Syrian and Phoenician goddesses with two horns upon their heads were formed after the Egyptian types of Isis and Hathor and had nothing to do with the crescent moon, though they may have been so understood in Syria.

Moore also points out that the summit of the mountain on which the sanctuary stood is formed by two very sharp peaks, separated by a deep gorge. The striking feature of the mountain peaks may provide a natural explanation for the onomastic usage of Qarnaim. Moore also says that "the ancient name of the mountain is still preserved in the Arabic Jebel bū Qarnain, 'the two-peaked mountain'."[3]

---

[1] "Biblical Notes: Ashteroth Karnaim," JBL 16 (1897):156.

[2] Ibid.; Morris seems to have no doubt that "the name Astaroth comes from the name of the moon-goddess Astarte (Greek), equivalent to the Babylonian Ishtar and the Canaanite Ashtaroth, the goddess of sensual love, whose worship was one of the sources of the gross immorality of the Canaanites;" The Genesis Record, p. 315.

[3] Ibid., p. 157.

In Job 42:14 the names of Job's three daughters are recorded. Amazingly enough, the names of the seven sons and three daughters that were born to Job in the land of Uz before the unforeseen catastrophe caused by the raging wind took place and in which all Job's sons and daughters died, are not mentioned. Nor do we know the names of Job's seven posterior sons. Only the names of the three daughters born to Job after his new experience with Yahweh are recorded. The names, which were rather peculiar, may reflect their famous beauty in one way or another. Their names are given as ימימה, קציעה, and קרן הפוך, with the respective meaning of Dove (diminutive), Cassia (a kind of cinnamon), and "Schminkhorn."[1]

We are, however, apt to prefer an abstract (hidden) meaning that in accordance with ancient tradition reflected Job's own restoration and new status before Yahweh.

Evaluation and Summary

With the purpose of evaluating the horn-motif, a brief compendium of categories and usages in summarizing form will be annotated.

The horn-motif is encountered in the Hebrew Bible on a diachronic level from Genesis to Zechariah and comprises various genres.

---

[1] So Gustav Hölscher, Das Buch Hiob, HAT (Tübingen: J. C. B. Mohr [Paul Siebeck], 1937), p. 99; Samuel Terrien, "The Book of Job," IB (New York: Abingdon Press, 1939), 3:1196; Samuel R. Driver and George B. Gray, A Critical and Exegetical Commentary on the Book of Job, ICC (Edinburgh: T. & T. Clark, 1958), p. 350; Marvin H. Pope, Job, AB (Garden City, NY: Doubleday & Company, 1973), p. 352; cf. Francis Brown, Samuel R. Driver, and Charles A. Briggs, A Hebrew and English Lexicon of the Old Testament (Oxford: Clarendon Press, 1976), p. 902: קרן הפוך "horn of antimony, i.e., beautifier.

With a pure literal meaning the "horn" confronts us in but one text (Gen 22:13). The form is dual, which is the usual form when speaking of natural horns on animals. Further literal usages are found where "horn" refers to a musical instrument or a vessel.

The usage of a ram's horn as a musical instrument or as an instrument to give a signal that would catch people's attention was already known in ancient Sumeria. The Bible also seems to convey this attention-getting usage, for when important decisions were made, announcements were preceded by the blowing of the horn. Any spiritual meaning is not explicitly brought out in the Bible, but the contexts in which it is used imply times of important decisions. The meaning of the instrument itself is not discussed per se in the Hebrew Bible. We presume that the importance and meaning of horn lay in the signal it conveyed--attention, alertness, and readiness.

The horn as a vessel is also sparingly alluded to in the Bible. The few passages in which it is used show that the horn as a vessel was used in Israel in cultic contexts. The horn as a vessel containing oil was used for anointing purposes. The anointing of a prophet, priest, or king indicates dedication for a special purpose and seems to imply divine election. Though the vessel (of oil) is to be understood in the literal sense of the word, the textual context indicates an extended meaning emphasizing divine power and holiness. Furthermore, it seems self-evident that, though a horn was used, the meaning of bull-power and fertility concept, so often alluded to in the ancient Near Eastern literature, has nothing to do with these usages here discussed. On the contrary, the two traditions seem to be far removed in meaning. The biblical tradition of "horn" as a musical instrument and especially of the horn as a vessel seems to derive its meaning from a vertical tradition emphasizing transcendent concepts.

A completely different usage of "horn" meets us in the many references to the altar of burnt-offering and the altar of incense. The horns are actually projections or prolongations made in one piece with the altar--not separately attached horns (bull horns or the like). The consistent use of the plural form (construct feminine) may be accounted for on the basis of the plurality of the corners of the altar. We see, however, in the plural קרנות a <u>terminus technicus</u> with added dimensions, namely, comprising the universality and totality of provisions that the altar symbolized. As it was foursquare it faced each point of the compass telling of its "worldwide aspect and application"[1] in the cult of Israel. It was on the very horns of the altar that the atonement in Israelite religion took place (Exod 30:10).

The literal-extended meaning is <u>ad sensum</u> based on a literal presence of the "horns" (קרנת) but connected with a metaphoric act which is reflected in ritual context (alluded to above). The same literal-extended meaning is reflected in the sociological context where the law-breaker, under certain conditions, may be pardoned and find asylum from vengeance by showing his trust in divine power and in the mercy of God. We think that Noth, who has observed

---

[1] Arthur W. Pink, <u>Gleanings in Exodus</u> (Chicago: Moody Press, n.d.), p. 245.

the "horns" of the altar as a symbol of the seat of God and conveying his presence has come close to the original meaning, which, however, is nowhere explicably stated in the Bible. It seems also evident that in ritual contexts the symbolism took place on the "horns" of the altar.

The third category of the literal-extended usage presents a political context. There is only one occurrence here included (1 Kgs 22:11; 2 Chr 18:10) and the form of "horns" here referred to differs from the usages above in that the dual form is being used. These "iron-horns" (probably imitating a bull's horns) are used symbolically amplifying a false prediction which is uttered by Zedekiah, the son of Chenaaniah--apparently a false prophet in Israel.

The third section presented the horn-motif with the purely extended meaning--a section which no doubt contains the most difficult cruces interpretum. It is in this purely extended meaning where the term "horn" raises a divergence of opinions regarding its meaning. Each specific text has been thoroughly scrutinized therefore, both as to structure and style as well as to content.

We may conclude that a crux interpretum is due to applying the same metaphor, i.e., the bull metaphor, in each specific case without due regard to its fitness in the context. All references to horn have more or less been interpreted on a horizontal basis and considered as originating from the one tradition: the horned bull.

As soon as we realize that there is a parallel tradition running horizontally alongside the "traditional" usage, but with another source of origin, the interpretation has to be adjusted accordingly. There are evidences which point to the fact that the "history-of-religion" school has been too narrow in its scope by interpreting the horn-motif in the Bible as originating from the animal kingdom. The meaning conveyed has, therefore, been a one-sided emphasis with bull-power in focus. As bull-power by necessity of implications in the Near Eastern context also implied the fertility-concept, these two meanings of power and fertility run parallel in the interpretation of the "history-of-religion" school. We recognize the bull-concept and the related horn-motif as a prevalent tradition in the ancient Near Eastern context. We have to consider, however, the clear evidences of another tradition related to the horn-motif in the biblical context and of which we have discovered some reflections also in the ancient Near Eastern context. We must, therefore, avoid too narrow an interpretation lest we impose one cultural mold upon another.

Many scholars have taken for granted a uniformity of pattern in all ancient Near Eastern cultures. Our investigation of the horn-motif on a comparative basis in ancient Near Eastern literature and in the Hebrew Bible makes it evident that the latter, in many respects, contains a uniqueness reflective of its own view of reality.

We find evidences that the horn-motif in the ancient Near Eastern context relates on a horizontal level while the one in the Bible, in general, indicates a vertical level. The biblical context, however, alludes to the horn-motif on a horizontal level in several passages--so, for instance, in Ps 22:22; 1 Kgs 22:11; Deut 33:11. Its main concern, however, is the horn-motif on a vertical level. Yet it seems at times that ancient Near Eastern literature and iconography give some allusions to the horn-motif on a vertical level (though often embedded in mythological concepts); nonetheless, the main concern is that same motif on a horizontal level. Again, we conclude that these two traditions are diametrically opposed to each other.

It is noteworthy that both lines of thought or traditions employ the word "horn" with the result that the two diametrically opposed traditions are easily confused. One tradition emphasizes an evil, aggressive, brutal (and fortuitous fertility) source,[1] whereas the other tradition emphasizes a positive force which operates on a vertical axis and has its origin in the transcendent Righteous One that was promised as the "horn" of Israel and which is presented as a true antithesis to the brutal force (though often disguised) in the former. This aggressive, attacking, evil and even persecuting power operating on a horizontal level is disclosed through symbolism, especially in apocalyptic settings and literary genres, as a king or kingdom among kindred kingdoms.

---

[1] It may also be argued that the ancient Near Eastern bull-concept reveals more than one tradition. One tradition may perhaps have the wild ox motif as its original source and emphasizes an attacking, aggressive, and evil force that was opposed to the concept of divine rule. The old ancient seal of an attacking bull (wild ox) with a god as his target may suggest this. The other tradition may emphasize the brutal strength and power of the domestic ox and of fertility. The "horns" of the moon may, perhaps, be the emblem of both. As we are not focusing on the bull-motif in this dissertation we have to pass by this interesting and pregnant motif.

The vertical antithesis, with cosmic and transcendent realities, which seem most evident in the Hymnic texts, reaches its climax in the Prophetic-Messianic setting with reference to the future qeren or "Branch" or "kingdom" which was promised to the dynasty of David and to the people of Israel. We therefore suggest that these two lines of thought have to be considered as separate traditions and be interpreted in their individual contexts.

The concept of the "horns" of Moses provides a typical example of the assumption of a uniform pattern of cultural conformity. In this particular case it proved to create confusion of concepts and interpretations rather than clarification of meanings and their purpose.

The bull- and fertility-concept, which was prevalent in the ancient Near Eastern cultures in general, had its origin, it seems, in the southern part of ancient Mesopotamia and from there spread to surrounding cultures. A polytheistic concept, with a dominating astral cult in which the gods were considered as "bulls"--as is evident from respective literature where the epithet "Bull" and similar expressions are prevalent--shows that the bull-concept prevailed in the ancient Near Eastern cultures. In the Egyptian religion the worship of deity in the form of a bull appeared before Israel had been in contact with that nation. The tendency of Israel to accept the bull-image probably goes back to Israel's sojourn in Egypt. Thus a borrowing from the Egyptian prevailing god-concept may account for the report in the Sinai pericope of the "golden calf." The same Egyptian bull-worship, or the Canaanite influence with a similar cult, may account for the images set up in Dan and Bethel where bull-worship with its fertility-concept was prevalent. The preaching of the prophets of Israel was directed against this type of worship. The history of Israel and Judah, however, reveals that Northern Israel during King Jeroboam's reign accepted Yahweh worship in the form of a bull as part of the state religion.

SUMMARY AND CONCLUSION

The purpose of this section is to summarize the investigation of the "horn" and its motif as carried out in this study. We will proceed chapter by chapter with a condensed presentation. Only a tentative solution can be offered in cases where the context requires further study.

In the first chapter we provided the necessary background by way of reviewing scholarly research of the horn-motif in our century. It became immediately apparent that the meaning of the term "horn" in biblical context has, in this century, been interpreted partly on the basis of the concept of the horns of the altar held by Hugo Gressmann due to his archaeological background, and partly on the basis of the concept held by Hermann Gunkel due to his form-critical approach. These two pioneer scholars exerted a strikingly noticeable influence on later scholars advocating the hypotheses of Gressmann and Gunkel. Even the current trend of scholarship follows, with only small deviations, the pattern initiated by them.

This premise of intrinsic development from primitive to more advanced, inherited from the previous century, was generally applied on a comparative basis in all spheres of cultural and religious life. The horns of the altar had been considered as recognizable signs by which the gods could identify the food table prepared for them. The horns of the altar were thought to be connected with the godhead when in the form of a bull. The archaeological approach was more concerned with the origin of "horns" than with the meaning of "horns." The "horns" of the altar as vestiges of maṣṣēbôt was the prevailing concept until the recent studies of Paul Lapp and Carl F. Graesser in 1964 and 1969 respectively.

As for the apocalyptic emphasis of the horn-motif, it became apparent from our review of literature that the noncanonical apocalyptic works have been used as a norm by which the interpretation of the horn-motif in Daniel has been expounded. The common view that the prediction of the "little horn" has been fulfilled in Antiochus Epiphanes has been the prevailing concept among scholars in the 20th century.

Concerning qâran and maswēh ("veil," "mask"[?]) with reference to Moses, apparently two concepts were tied together and interpreted according to prevailing non-Israelite images of oracle-priests. Not only Hugo Gressmann, but Martin Noth, Anton Jirku, and other scholars have expressed such a view. The current trend among scholars is to accept the interpretation of the "horns" of Moses as etiologically correct. Archaeology supports the view that masks were used in a ritual context even in the Early Bronze Age and as late as the Late Bronze Age. Furthermore, we found that according to a number of scholars, the concept of Moses wearing "horns" presents a connecting link between Yahweh and the horned bull. Such a concept was expressed by Urs Staub as late as the year 1978. This makes it evident that the current scholarly disposition is reflected

as a status quo of the bygone interpretations of St. Jerome and
Aquila. The variances of opinions among scholars, and the often
contradictory theories presented concerning the origin, meaning, and
symbolic connotation of the term "horn" in every major category
where the horn-motif plays a crucial role, provided the stage from
which our research had to proceed.

In the second chapter, therefore, we attempted to investigate
the philological evidences for the meaning of "horn" in the ancient
Sumerian and ancient Near Eastern Semitic cognates.

The ancient Sumerian language presented an unexpected richness. Many signs displayed a variety of meanings. It became evident that confusion of signs has caused numerous difficulties in the task of interpretation. For instance, the logogram SI has been confused, at times, with the logogram ma. SI, however, means "horn" in the literal sense of the word, whereas ma means "ship." The ideogram si-sar means karnû ("horned"). Other ideograms convey the meaning of "splendor," "radiance," "light," and "brightness." This category of ideograms probably refers to the "horns" of the moon shining brightly. In an attempt to reform the language, the new meaning of "arm" seems to replace the meaning "horn." Other sign combinations seem to convey the metaphorical meaning of "strength," "straight," and "right" ("righteousness"). When all the 150 Sumerian sign combinations, with si as one component, have been analyzed, the list of meanings will, without doubt, increase.

It seems apparent that the basic meaning of the Akkadian qarnu means "horn." The term qarnu occurs not only with the literal connotation of "horns" on animals, but very frequently with a metaphorical meaning similar to the one found in Sumerian. The word "horn(s)" occurred frequently in mythological and hymnic contexts, suggesting that the word "horn(s)" was used with the meaning of "divine" or "supernatural power."

A new semantic connotation of the term "horn" is brought forth by scholars who have been preoccupied with texts from Mari. It is from this area that the variant qannu is attested. The assimilation (qarnu > qannu) has been assumed by some scholars to have taken place under Amorite influence. However, it became discernible that the origin of "horn" remains more or less obscure, though there are certain hints, especially in iconography, that suggest more than one single tradition for the origin of the horn-motif and account for its subsequent development.

As for the Ugaritic language, the investigation revealed that the word qrn was used in plural, dual, and singular forms. However, some of the texts were too fragmentary to allow for a clear picture of the usage or particular meaning of "horn." By studying the few readable texts (that have reference to "horn[s]") it seems evident that the ordinary plural form of qrn was used in a literal sense with the literal meaning of horns on animals while the dual was used with reference to "horns" on gods in the Ugaritic pantheon. One occurrence of the singular form probably accounts for the "horn(s)" of the moon, showing that also in Ugarit the moon-cult prevailed. It is also apparent that qrn in the "Baʻal and ʻAnat cycle" presents a singular form, which, in its context, suggests an optional interpretation with either singular or dual meaning. The ambiguity present in that particular passage has been an issue in which it seems all prominent Ugaritic scholars have engaged. No final consensus has been reached yet.

There were few attestations of the word qrn in the Aramaic sources apart from the Bible. It was completely lacking in Old Aramaic. Imperial Aramaic gave evidence of the usage of the term "horn" in a few passages from the book of Daniel. The literal usage was attested in Dan 3 where it signifies a musical instrument--apparently made of a ram's horn as the קרני indicates. The metaphorical usage is attested in Dan 7 and 8. The apocalyptic context of these chapters makes it evident that the word "horn" in whatever form it appears has to be interpreted symbolically. Middle Aramaic yielded no evidence apart from its occurrence in an obscure context in an incantation text.

A Punic text of a late date presented a literal usage of the word "horn(s)."

The investigation also made evident that the Greek term κέρας is used in several of the apocryphal books, some of which are known only in translation. Some scholars have considered the word κέρας to be a "Hebraism" (i.e., Hebrew or Aramaic influence on the present text), which in certain contexts seemed outdated (i.e., in the second century B.C.). A new rendering of the term κέρας (i.e., "horn" from קרן with a literal connotation) seemed to be preferred, especially in military context. On the other hand, the metaphorical usage and meaning of κέρας maintained the status quo. A slightly new nuance can be added to the previously known metaphorical terms "strength" and "power," namely, the word "triumph" (1 Mac 2:48). The late apocryphal apocalypse of Enoch attests for the usage of "horn(s)" in phrases like "horned lambs," "great horn," etc. According to Robert H. Charles, the first locution has reference to the Maccabees, while the singular form (qualified by an adjective) of the second locution refers to Judas Maccabeus, the hero of the Maccabees at Emmaus.

From our investigation of the South-Arabic language it became apparent that the word qarn has several meanings. The verbal form qarana and āqrana deviate completely from the meaning of "horn." Only in the participle form āqranu do we recognize the traditional meaning "horned" or "having horns" as having relationship to the horn-motif. The noun qern (singular, masculine) has taken on a new connotation of meaning which we do not find substantiated in other cognates where the term "horn" is used. According to authorities qern has the meaning of "one who opposes," an "opponent," a "competitor," an "adversary," or an "antagonist." It became evident that this is the basic meaning of "horn" in all of the South-Arabic texts that were investigated. In the verbal form the word "horn" has a similar connotation, i.e., the meaning of "to rebel," "to attack," or "to fight" (with or against someone).

Thus it became evident that in the South-Arabic language there is a strong adversative connotation applied to the word "horn." Our investigation shows that other terms came into usage and must be considered as synonymous expressions of the often ambiguous term "horn." This term "horn" in many cases was apparently too "weak" to express the intention of the writer. On the other hand, a positive meaning of "horn" seems to be lacking in the texts scrutinized, for apparently the context always implies aggressive military action as the Sitz im Leben.

From the investigation of the term קרן in Hebrew it is clearly perceivable that the Hebrew Bible is a unique corpus of texts in which the word "horn" is attested in a variety of contexts and with a number of diverse meanings. Furthermore, it seems evident that the various morphological forms of קרן (i.e., singular, dual, and plural) might serve as a key in contextual study to detect the basic meaning of the word "horn" in its particular form.

Apart from the literal usage of "horn" with reference to an animal, the word קרן was used also with reference to a wind instrument, to a vessel or container of oil, and with reference to the horns of the altar. The metaphorical usage of "horn" conveyed meanings of "strength," "dignity," "power," and "rays." The verbal form qâran has the meaning of "shine," "be radiant" (in Qal), and the meaning of "be with horn" (in Hiphil).

It is clear, therefore, from our investigation in the second chapter that from a philological point of view the term "horn" had more than one meaning. We are here referring to the evidence received by way of ancient writings that have come down to us in historical time and by way of iconography partly from prehistoric and partly from historic time. The incidental confusion of signs in cuneiform writing at an early period may account for the various meanings of the particular term "horn." But also in later periods new meanings and emphases were attributed to this word. This has been shown especially in the Aramaic and South-Arabic part of the study.

The word "horn" was found in each one of the languages investigated. It was also found that this particular term conveyed a literal meaning which had reference to horns on animals. However, the study also made obvious that the term "horn" is far from being restricted to this one usage and meaning.

For the sake of completeness the following list of the meanings of the word "horn" in Sumerian and ancient Near Eastern Semitic languages will be given. This list presents a summary of lexical and contextual meanings based on our inclusive research in this study. Apart from the literal meaning of the term "horns" (in any of these languages referred to) with reference to animals, the following meanings were discovered:

Sumerian and Akkadian: "splendor," "radiance," "horns" (of the moon), "straight," "right," ("righteousness"), "power," "arm," "divine power" ("supernatural power") "totality," "personality" ("character"), "skirt," "edge," "flap," "corner" (of garment), "border" ("extreme limit," or "utmost point"), "rank."

Ugaritic: "Wing."

Aramaic: "Wing," "flank," "warrior," "rebel," "adversary," "antagonist," "opponent," and "competitor." The verbal form of qrn (South-Arabic) carries the meaning of "to oppose," "to rebel," "to make war" (against someone), "to fight" (with someone).

Hebrew: The noun קרן in the Hebrew Bible is used with the following meanings: horns (on animals), horn(s) as vessel(s), horn(s) as musical or signal instruments, and horns of the altar. We found also that the word קרן has the connotation of "rays" (of brightness), "power," "strength," "refuge" ("asylum"), "attitude," "pride," "vengeance" (of Yahweh), "weapon," "horn-pair," "totality," "wing," "mountain," "hillside," "messiah," "king," and "kingdom." The verbal root קרן carries the following connotations: "to irradiate," "to shoot forth," "emit rays of light," "to shine" (Qal) and "to produce horns" (participle).

From our investigation in the third chapter, with reference to the usage and meaning of "horn," it is plain that the horn-motif was present in Sumeria and elsewhere from a very early period. Plentiful collections of ancient seals attest the horn-motif in the ancient world. The numerous depictions of horned animals seem to indicate ritualistic purposes. Soon, however, the horn-motif appeared also on depicted figures. The peculiar headdresses decorated with horns represent a variety of styles and forms apparently due to cultural changes in sundry geographical areas.

The anthropomorphic concept of the gods in Mesopotamia required some distinguishing mark to set them apart from ordinary human beings. According to many scholars the horned cap or crown remained the distinctive mark of divinity since the Jemdet Nasr period (ca. 2900 B.C.) when the horned headdress first appeared. Furthermore, it is clear that the horn-motif appeared in a variety of literary genres: hymns, prayers, legends, epics, myths, and other genres where gods and demons, beasts and monsters, and other types of beings were provided with horns to indicate their supernatural or divine power.

Of specific interest is Narâm-Sin of the Sargonic dynasty. He has become the classic example of a king who was deified in his lifetime and on account of this he has been depicted with protruding, upward bent horns. The apparent bull-horns substantiate the theory of his empire being patterned in analogy with the universal mooncult in which the "horns of the moon" and "horns of the bull" were emblems of one and the same universal religious power. "The horns suggested by the moon's crescent were probably a factor in representing him [En-zu, "lord of knowledge" = Sin (Si-in or In-su)] also figuratively as a bull. . . ."[1] It also seems evident that other rulers, subsequent to Narâm-Sin, were also deified, but many of these known rulers are depicted without the typical headgear with horns. This fact presents a riddle that is still unexplainable.

Several of the mythological and legendary motifs show a marked relationship to certain, somewhat later, religious motifs which may suggest a common source though the traditions developed independently. Table VI of the Enūma eliš epic, for instance, describes the rebellious Qingu and his followers fighting against other gods. It is obvious that this particular legend and the complex motif of the Zû-bird and his retinue, also depicting a contest, on seals, seem to complement each other. The horn-motif is here alluded to through negative evidences, i.e., the deprivation of the horn-crown from the rebel. E. Douglas Van Buren and other scholars have suggested that

---

[1]Morris Jastrow, *Babylonia and Assyria* (Philadelphia: J. B. Lippincott Company, 1915), p. 222.

the headdresses with horns indicate the divine status of some of the figures, whereas the deprivation of the same emblem suggests that someone missed out or failed to fulfill his destiny and, as a result, was deprived of the visible sign of divinity. The bird-man of darkness and storm <u>wearing</u> the horned cap of divinity became, on the other hand, the sign of the monster oppressing humanity.

It also became evident from our study that the concept of <u>pulḫu</u> ("wrap of flames") and of <u>melammu</u> ("supernatural headgear") thought to be of divine origin seems to be connected with the horn-motif--not, however, as a luminous mask but as a token of divine origin and power. A careful investigation of the usage and meaning of <u>melammu</u> as well as the notion by A. Leo Oppenheim of its pre-Sumerian origin and other such hints make us inclined to correlate the twin concepts of <u>melammu</u> and <u>pulḫu</u> with two other twin concepts: the <u>pukku</u> and <u>mekku</u> in the Gilgameš epic. These twin expressions may not express widely different concepts after all; instead, it appears that they may be used interchangeably. Oppenheim, however, points out that in religious texts the two expressions <u>pulḫu</u> and <u>melammu</u> were consistently distinguished.

Our study of the biblical text in the fourth chapter was divided into three main sections: the literal, the literal-extended, and the purely extended usages. From our investigation it soon became evident that the horn-motif used with a literal meaning caused less difficulty than the ones with literal-extended and purely extended meanings. As may be expected, the passages that inferred a metaphorical or purely extended usage and meaning of the term "horn" comprised the cruces interpretum in our discussion. A certain overlapping between the sub-sections of the classified categories is also apparent, but any grouping of texts will cause this problem since many Bible texts can be classified in more than one category.

Not until the 1970s was the solution given to the origin and meaning of the maṣṣēbôt which had been interpreted as the origin of the horns of the altar. Now it has been clearly established that the "horns" never were vestiges of maṣṣēbôt but in fact were far removed from the "standing stones" both in function and meaning. The real significance of the "horns" is still a matter of concern.

The horn-motif in the political context focuses on the meaning of "horns" in 1 Kgs 22:11. A common view among scholars sees a relationship of this passage with Deut 33:17. Many have seen the horns of the wild ox of the latter passage as an apt description of Yahweh, the God of Israel. Clearly the verb נגח ("to gore") can be used not only in literal contexts and with reference to horned animals but also metaphorically with reference to kings. Zedekiah made the iron-horns not for himself, but for Ahab, the king of Israel, to convey a symbolic and flattering meaning of victory.

From our discussion of "horns" in the sociological context it became apparent that provisions of pardon and refuge for unintentional law-breakers were uniquely applied for the Israelites at a specific place, i.e., at the "horns" of the altar. The "horns" of the altar thus functioned not only in ritualistic but also in legal-sociological contexts.

The third concern of this facet of our study addressed the category of Bible texts which had a purely extended or metaphorical meaning. Hymnic, prophetic, and apocalyptic texts were discussed. In addition, the meaning of "horns" in the pericope of Moses was briefly discussed as well as a few special usages of the term "horn." The majority of hymnic texts employed the word "horn" (singular) in combinations with a nominal form that would indicate the proper meaning of the word "horn." Where the qualifying aspect was missing, the meaning seemed more or less obscure. So, for instance, in the locution "do not lift up your horn," and other archaic expressions still in use at a later time but with the original meaning lost, revealed the tendency of obscurity.

A general observation based on our study showed that scholars, in general, have arbitrarily generalized the horn-motif in the Bible with the result that this motif has often been interpreted on à priori assumptions and thus some strange and artificial meanings have been imposed upon many texts and contexts. The bull motif, tied to the fertility concept, was applied without selection to almost all "horn" passages referred to in the Bible. Because the bull-concept and the horn-motif naturally seemed to be related in the Near Eastern context, its validity in the interpretation of biblical texts was hardly ever questioned. More recent scholars, however, have become more aware of a "missing link" somewhere and apply, rarely and with great caution, these more generalized interpretations of bull-horns.

Our study made it apparent that the term and the motif of

"horn" are best understood in their own contexts. Furthermore, it was shown that the horizontal level on which the horn-motif operates in the ancient Near East (especially in the bull-context) is diametrically opposed to another horn-motif which operates on the vertical level--especially in biblical contexts.

The study of prophetic texts soon gave evidence that each presented a particular contextual setting. Some attempted to see as an identical incident the "horns" of the altar which were cut off and the threat of the destruction of Bethel in the oracle of Amos 4:14. The verb form פקדתי (<פקד) "to visit," however, strongly suggests a retributive punishment at a future time.

The passage of Micah 4:13 has also been subject to much discussion. It has been interpreted mostly with reference to the "horn" as being presented in a dual form--and thus with the bull-motif. Our investigation, however, indicated that the horn-motif associated with the bull-concept was unnecessarily overemphasized in this particular text. Our opinion differs from the current view. We would prefer to imply the figure of speech in regard to the term "horn" as referring not to the brutal strength of the bull but rather to the divine strength of Yahweh. It is Yahweh and no one else who will fulfill his intentions in an eschatological situation at the moment when every other power will be put to shame. This seems to coincide with Ps 75:11 which declares: "All the horns of the wicked he will cut off, but the horns of the righteous shall be exalted."

The theophanic passage in Hab 3:4 has been subject to

various interpretations. Due to textual problems there is still no consensus as to the correct way in which the dual qarnayim can fit into the context. Many take a literal view, some prefer a metaphorical meaning, while some emphasize a mythological setting.

A close investigation of the practical structure reveals that the regular stress pattern of 3:3 is here evident. Furthermore, we find that the first and third tricola employ metaphors in structuring synonymous thought patterns. A third tricolon has been added which displays a synthetic relationship to the bicola. It is but natural, therefore, to expect also the second tricolon to employ a metaphor--thus harmonizing with the poetic flow of thought. If these patterns of poetic structure and context are sound, then both poetical pattern and context favor qarnayim to be translated "rays" instead of "horns."

The apocalyptic texts comprise the ambiguous passage of Zech 2:1-4 and the much-debated texts of Dan 7 and 8. A careful investigation showed that the normal morphological patterns on which the meanings of "horn" were based broke down in the genre of apocalyptic.

Paying attention especially to the context and using a step-by-step procedure, we found that the meaning of "horn," in the apocalyptic context of Daniel, unmistakably pointed to the concept of king/kingdom. Furthermore, it seemed evident that the term "king" was understood in terms of the expression "kingdom" and that the word "horn" is employed for the extended meaning of "king" in the sense of kingdom and of "kingdom" itself. The choice of locution,"kingdom," defines the intent of the author. The tone for this emphasis is provided especially in Dan 7 with its focus on the "kingdoms" and the "kingdom" on both a contrasting and comparative basis.

The fascinating drama unfolded in Dan 7 and 8 confirms our hypothesis of the horn-motif operating on both a horizontal and a vertical level. This is reflected in the struggle for supremacy between the kingdoms on a horizontal level--a struggle which will end with final victory and supremacy on the vertical level. Though the drama of human history revealed in the apocalyptic texts, and repeatedly alluded to in other types of writings in the Hebrew Bible, does not explicitly reveal the origin of the horn-motif, it does reveal the prominence and meaning of "horn(s)" in the continuous struggle for supremacy throughout the ages. The "little horn" aspired to supremacy by reaching up on the vertical axis. This makes us here suspect a power that is akin to the rebellious and attacking (aggressive) one which, in the early dynastic eras of the city-kingdoms in ancient Sumeria, attempted a universal coup d'état to usurp power for the purpose of establishing a universal moon-cult. The synonymous emblems of this cult were reflected in the "horns" of the moon and in the "horns" of the bull. It appears that it is the same God-opposing power that is revealed in the ongoing drama of human history on the horizontal level. The horn-motif reveals also, namely on the vertical axis, that a "horn" breaks into this horizontal drama of universal antagonism. There are the promises that focus on a king with a kingdom of cosmic and transcendent character that will break the uniform pattern of sequential kingdoms and powers in human history. A kingdom will be established that alone will be supreme and exalted. This transcendent "horn," operating from above, is the main focus in the various biblical contexts. Some aspects of this transcendent Reality are in retrospect alluded to in ancient Near Eastern literature and iconography.

We, therefore, suggest that the ultimate meaning of the term "horn" and its motifs is to be found in the unfolding of these two diametrically opposed traditions: the tradition concerned with the horn conceptions on the horizontal level in its connections with astral cults and bull-worship, and the "horn" tradition on the vertical level where it is connected with messianic, eschatological, and apocalyptic realities that are said to bring about something totally new. The majority of maṣṣēbôt, ancient ziggurats, bull-images, horns and masks of the oracle-priest, and similar concepts belong unmistakably to the tradition operating on the horizontal level; whereas concepts of safety, exaltation, messianic branch, and final victory are concepts connected with the tradition operating on the vertical level that intersect and ultimately bring to an end the horizontal structures of existence.

APPENDICES

APPENDIX A

CHART A

OCCURRENCES OF קרן IN BIBLICAL ARAMAIC

CHART A

Text	BHS	Aq	Sym	Hex	Theod	Syr
1. Dan 3:5	קֶרֶן			της φωνης της σάλπιγγος		
2. Dan 3:7	קֶרֶן			της σάλπιγγος		
3. Dan 3:10	קֶרֶן			της σάλπιγγος		
4. Dan 3:15	קֶרֶן			της σάλπιγγος		
5. Dan 7:7	וְקַרְנַיִן עֲשַׂר			ειχε δε κέρατα δεκα PG, Hex, LXX (εν τοις κέρασιν αυτου) PG	κέρατα δεκα αυτω	
6. Dan 7:8	בְּקַרְנַיָּא			εν τοις κέρασιν Hex, LXX εν κέρας μικρον (PG)	τοις κέρασιν αυτου	
7. Dan 7:8	קֶרֶן			εν κέρας ... μικρόν Hex, LXX εν τοις κέρασιν αυτου PG εν τοις κέρασιν Hex, LXX	κέρας ετερον μικρον	
8. Dan 7:8	קַרְנַיָּא־מִן			τρια των κεράτων	τρία κέρατα	
9. Dan 7:8	בְקַרְנָא־דָא			εν τω κέρατι τούτω	εν τω κέρατι τούτω	
10. Dan 7:11	קַרְנָא			το κέρας	το κέρας	
11. Dan 7:20	וְעַל־קַרְנַיָּא עֲשַׂר			περί των δέκα κεράτων αυτου ...	περι των κεράτων αυτου των δέκα	
12. Dan 7:20	וְקַרְנָא דֵן			το κέρας εκεινο	κέρας εκεινο	
13. Dan 7:21	וְקַרְנָא דֵן			το κέρας εκεινο	το κέρας εκεινο	
14. Dan 7:24	וְקַרְנַיָּא עֲשַׂר			τα δέκα κέρατα της βασιλείας	τα δέκα κέρατα αυτου	

Fig. 111. Occurrences of קרן in biblical Aramaic compared with some other ancient translations.

APPENDIX B

CHART B

OCCURRENCES OF קרן IN BIBLICAL HEBREW

CHART B

	Text	BHS	Aq	Sym	Hex	Theod	Syr
1.	Gen 14:5	בְּקַרְנַיִם					
2.	Gen 22:13	בְּקַרְנָיו	ἐν συγκεῶνι, ἐν κέρασιν αὐτοῦ	ἐν δικτύῳ τοῖς κέρασιν αὐτοῦ	ἐν φυτῷ σαβὲκ τῶν κεράτων	ἐν φυτῷ σαβὲκ τῶν κεράτων	
3.	Exod 27:2	קַרְנֹתָיו			τὰ κέρατα		
4.	Exod 27:2	קַרְנֹתָיו			τὰ κέρατα		
5.	Exod 29:12	קַרְנוֹת			ἐπὶ τῶν κεράτων		
6.	Exod 30:2	קַרְנֹתָיו			τὰ κέρατα αὐτοῦ		
7.	Exod 30:3	אֶת־קַרְנֹתָיו			τὰ κέρατα αὐτοῦ		
8.	Exod 30:10	עַל־קַרְנֹתָיו			ἐπὶ τῶν κεράτων		
9.	Exod 34:29	קֶרֶן (עוֹר)	κερατώδης (ἦν)		δεδόξασται		
10.	Exod 34:30	קֶרֶן (עוֹר)			δεδοξασμένη		
11.	Exod 34:35	קֶרֶן (עוֹר)			δεδόξασται		
12.	Exod 37:25	קַרְנֹתָיו			(Text corrupt)		
13.	Exod 37:26	אֶת־קַרְנֹתָיו					
14.	Exod 38:2	קַרְנֹתָיו					
15.	Exod 38:2	קַרְנֹתָיו					
16.	Lev 4:7	עַל־קַרְנוֹת			ἐπὶ τὰ κέρατα	τὰ κέρατα αὐτοῦ	
17.	Lev 4:18	עַל־קַרְנוֹת			ἐπὶ τὰ κέρατα	τὰ κέρατα αὐτοῦ	
18.	Lev 4:25	עַל־קַרְנוֹת			ἐπὶ τὰ κέρατα		
19.	Lev 4:30	עַל־קַרְנוֹת			ἐπὶ τὰ κέρατα		
20.	Lev 4:34	עַל־קַרְנוֹת			ἐπὶ τὰ κέρατα		
21.	Lev 8:15	עַל־קַרְנוֹת			ἐπὶ τὰ κέρατα		
22.	Lev 9:9	עַל־קַרְנוֹת			ἐπὶ τὰ κέρατα		

Fig. 112. Occurrences of קרן in biblical Hebrew compared with some other ancient translations.

CHART B (Continued)

	Text	BHS	Aq	Sym	Hex	Theod	Syr
23.	Lev 16:18	עַל־קַרְנוֹת			ἐπὶ τὰ κέρατα		
24.	Deut 33:17	קַרְנֵי רְאֵם			κέρατα μονοκέρωτος		
25.	Deut 33:17	קַרְנָיו			τὰ κέρατα αυτου		
26.	Josh 6:5	בְּקֶרֶן הַיּוֹבֵל	ἐν κερατίνη τοῦ ἰωβήλ	τω κέρατι τοῦ κριοῦ	τη σάλπιγγι τῆς κερατίνης		ܩܪܢܐ
27.	1 Sam 2:1	קַרְנִי בַּיהוָה			κέρας μου		
28.	1 Sam 2:10	קֶרֶן מְשִׁיחוֹ			κέρας χριστου αυτου		
29.	1 Sam 16:1	קֶרֶן שֶׁמֶן			τὸ κέρας σου ελαίου		ܩܪܢܐ ܕܡܫܚܐ
30.	1 Sam 16:13	אֶת־קֶרֶן הַשֶּׁמֶן			τὸ κέρας του ελαιου		
31.	2 Sam 22:3	קֶרֶן יִשְׁעִי			καὶ κέρας σωτηρίας μου		ܩܪܢܐ ܕܦܘܪܩܢܝ
32.	1 Kgs 1:39	אֶת־קֶרֶן הַשֶּׁמֶן			τὸ κέρας του ελαιου		
33.	1 Kgs 1:50	בְּקַרְנוֹת			των κερατων		
34.	1 Kgs 1:51	בְּקַרְנוֹת			των κερατων		
35.	1 Kgs 2:28	בְּקַרְנוֹת	ἐχόμενα τοῦ θυσιαστηρίου		των κερατων		
36.	1 Kgs 22:11	קַרְנֵי		κέρατα	κέρατα σιδηρα		
37.	Isa 5:1	בְּקֶרֶן בֶּן־שָׁמֶן	ἐν κέρατι υἱῷ ἐλαίου	ἐν κέρατι (ἐν μέσω ἐλαίων)	ἐν κέρατι ἐν τόπω πίονι	ἐν κέρατι υιω ελαιου	ܩܪܢܐ
38.	Jer 17:1	וּלְקַרְנוֹת			τοις κέρασι των θυσιαστηρίων αυτων		
39.	Jer 48:25	קֶרֶן מוֹאָב			Text Corrupt See Jer 31:12, 25		
40.	Ezek 27:15	קַרְנוֹת שֵׁן		κέρατα	οδόντας ελεφαντίνους	κέρατα	
41.	Ezek 29:21	קֶרֶן לְבֵית יִשְׂרָאֵל			κέρας παντι τω οικω Ισραηλ		
42.	Ezek 34:21	וּבְקַרְנֵיכֶם			τοις κέρασιν εκερατίζετε		
43.	Ezek 43:15	וְהַקְּרָנוֹת			των κερατων		
44.	Ezek 43:20	קַרְנֹתָיו			ἐπὶ τὰ τέσσαρα κέρατα		

469

CHART B (Continued)

	Text	BHS	Aq	Sym	Hex	Theod	Syr
45.	Amos 3:14	קרנות			τὰ κέρατα		
46.	Amos 6:13	קרנים			κέρατα		
47.	Mic 4:13	קרניך			τὰ κέρατά σου		
48.	Hab 3:4	מידו			κέρατα ἐν χερσὶν αὐτοῦ		
49.	Zech 2:1	קרנות			κέρατα		
50.	Zech 2:2	הקרנות			τὰ κέρατα		
51.	Zech 2:4	הקרנות			τὰ κέρατα		
52.	Zech 2:4	את-הקרנות			τὰ κέρατα		
53.	Zech 2:4	קרן משאים			κέρας		
54.	Ps 18:3	קרן ישעי			κέρας σωτηρίας μου		
55.	Ps 22:22	מקרני רמים			ἀπὸ κεράτων μονοκερώτων		
56.	Ps 69:32	קר מקרן	δικηλῶν κεραστης		κέρατα ἐκφέροντα καὶ ὁπλας		
57.	Ps 75:5	אל-תרימו קרן	μὴ ὑψοῦτε κέρας		μὴ ὑψοῦτε κέρας		
58.	Ps 75:6	קרנכם	μὴ ἐπαίρετε κέρας	μὴ ἐπαίρετε τὸ κέρας ὑμῶν	μὴ ἐπαίρετε τὸ κέρας ὑμῶν		
59.	Ps 75:11	כל קרני רשעים			τὰ κέρατα		
60.	Ps 75:11	קרנות צדיק	κέρατα δικαίου	κέρατα δικαίου	τὰ κέρατα (LXX) κέρατα δικαίου (PG)	κέρας δικαίων	(S² has τὸ κέρας, See HR 2:760)
61.	Ps 89:18	קרננו			τὸ κέρας ἡμῶν		
62.	Ps 89:25	קרנו			τὸ κέρας αὐτοῦ		
63.	Ps 92:11	קרני			τὸ κέρας μου		
64.	Ps 112:9	קרנו תרום			τὸ κέρας αὐτοῦ ... ἐν δόξῃ		
65.	Ps 118:27	עד-קרנות		ἕως τῶν κεράτων τοῦ θυσιαστηρίου	ἕως τῶν κεράτων τοῦ θυσιαστηρίου		

CHART B (Continued)

	Text	BHS	Aq	Sym	Hex	Theod	Syr
66.	Ps 132:17	קֶרֶן לְדָוִד			κέρας τω δαυιδ		
67.	Ps 148:14	קֶרֶן לְעַמּוֹ			κέρας λαου αυτου		
68.	Job 16:15	קַרְנִי			τὸ δέ σθένος μου		
69.	Job 42:14	קֶרֶן הַפּוּךְ	καρναφουκ	καρναφουκ	'Αμαλθαιας κέρας		
70.	Lam 2:3	קֶרֶן יִשְׂרָאֵל			παν κέρας Ισραηλ		
71.	Lam 2:17	קֶרֶן צָרָיִךְ			υψωσεν κέρας θλιβοντός σε		
72.	Dan 8:3	קְרָנָיִם			ευχε κέρατα		αυτω κέρατα
73.	Dan 8:3	הַקְּרָנַיִם			ἀκαὶ τὰ κέρατα† PG υψηλα		καὶ τὰ κέρατα υψηλα
74.	Dan 8:5	קֶרֶן חָזוּת			καὶ ην του τραγου κέρας εν ἀθεωρητον PG/ αναμεσον των οφθαλμων αυτων	καὶ τω τςάγω κέρας θεωρητὸν ανά μεσον των οφθαλμων αυτου	
					καὶ ην του τραγου κέρας εν ανα μεσον των οφθαλμων αυτου LXX		
75.	Dan 8:6	הַקְּרָנַיִם			τὰ κέρατα εχοντα	τὰ κέρατα εχοντος	
76.	Dan 8:7	קְרָנָיו			τὰ δύο κέρατα αυτου	τὰ κέρατα αυτου	
77.	Dan 8:8	הַקֶּרֶן הַגְּדֹלָה			τὸ κέρας τὸ μέγα ετερα τεσσαρα κέρατα κατόπισθεν αυτου εις τοὺς τεσσαρας ανεμους του ουρανου	τὸ κέρας αυτου τὸ μέγα κέρατα τέσσαρα υποκάτω αυτου εις τοὺς τεσσαρας ανεμους του ουρανου	
78.	Dan 8:9	אַחַת			κέρας ισχυρὸν εν	κέρας εν ισχυρον	
79.	Dan 8:20	הַקְּרָנַיִם בַּעֲלֵי			τὰ κέρατα	τὰ κέρατα	
80.	Dan 8:21	הַקֶּרֶן הַגְּדוֹלָה			τὸ κέρας τὸ μέγα	τὸ κέρας τὸ μέγα	
81.	1 Chron 25:5	קֶרֶן (קֶרֶן [app.])			υψωσαι κέρας		
82.	2 Chron 18:10	קַרְנֵי בַרְזֶל			κέρατα σιδηρα		

APPENDIX C

CHART C

STRUCTURAL FORMS OF קרן IN BIBLICAL HEBREW

CHART C

	Structural Form		Occurrences
1.	Pl. abs. with or without def. art.	הקרנות	Ezek 43:15 Zech 2:2,4*=3x
		קרנות	Zech 2:1 = 1x
2.	Pl. cs. (with suff.) with or without prefix.	ראח-קרנתיו	Exod 30:3; 37:26 = 2x
		ועל-קרנתיו	Exod 30:10 = 1x
		קרנתיו	Exod 27:2, 2; 30:2; 37:25; 38:2, 2 Ezek 43:20 = 7x
		על-קרנות	Lev 4:7, 18, 25; 16:18 = 4x
		על-קרנת	Exod 29:12; Lev 4:30, 34; 8:15; 9:9 = 5x
		את-קרנות	Zech 2:4 = 1x
		עד-קרנות	Ps 118:27 = 1x
		ולקרנות	Jer 17:1 = 1x
		בקרנות	1 Kgs 1:50, 51; 2:28 = 3x
		קרנות	Amos 3:14; Ps 75:11* = 2x
		קרנות שן	Ezek 27:15* = 1x
3.	Dual abs. with or without def. art.	והקרנים	Dan 8:3, 6, 20 = 3x
		קרנים	Dan 8:3 = 1x
		קרנים	Amos 6:13 Hab 3:4 = 2x
4.	Dual cs. (with suff.)	ובקרניכם	Ezek 34:21 = 1x
		בקרניו	Gen 22:13 = 1x
		וכל-קרני	Ps 75:11 = 1x
		מקרני	Ps 22:22 = 1x
		וקרני	Deut 33:17 1 Kgs 22:11 2 Chron 18:10 = 3x
		קרניך	Deut 33:17 = 1x
		קרניו	Dan 8:7 = 1x

Fig. 113. Structural forms of קרן in biblical Hebrew

CHART C (Continued)

5.	Onomastic usage	עשתרות קרנים	Gen 14:5 = 1x
		קרן הפוך	Job 42:14* = 1x
6.	Sg. abs. with or without def. art.	הקרן הגדולה	Dan 8:8, 21 = 2x
		קרן חזות	Dan 8:5 = 1x
		קרן-אחת	Dan 8:9 = 1x
7.	qrn as nomen regens, a nominal as nomen rectum.	קרן . . .	1 Sam 2:10 2 Sam 22:3 Ps 18:3 Lam 2:17 Jer 48:25 = 6x
8.	In posession idioms.	קרן ל . . .	Exek 29:21 Lam 2:3 Ps 132:17; 148:14 = 4x
9.	ב or את construc- tions.	בקרן . . .	Josh 6:5 Isa 5:1* = 2x
		את-קרן	1 Sam 16:13 1 Kgs 1:39 = 2x
10.	qrn governed by a verb (idiom con- struction).	הנשאים קרן	Zech 2:4 = 1x
		אל-תרימו קרן להרים קרן	Ps 75:5 1 Chron 25:5 = 2x
11.	qrn with suff.	קרני	1 Sam 2:1 Ps 92:11 Job 16:15 = 3x
		קרנך שמך	1 Sam 16:1 = 1x
		כי-קרנך	Mic 4:13 = 1x
		קרנו	Ps 89:25; 112:9 = 2x
		קרננו	Ps 89:18 = 1x
		קרנכם	Ps 75:6 = 1x
12.	Verbal form	קרן (עור פניו)	Exod 34:29, 30, 35* = 3x
		מקרן	Ps 69:32 = 1x

APPENDIX D

TABLE 1

OCCURRENCES OF "HORN" IN THE HEBREW BIBLE

TABLE 1

OCCURRENCES OF "HORN" IN THE HEBREW BIBLE[a]

M:	Gen 22:13; Exod 27:2 29:12; 30:2,3,10; 37: 26; 30:10; 37:25 ;38:2,2
L:	Gen 22:13; Exod 27:2,2; 29:12; 30:2,3,10; 37:25,26; 37: ,26; 38:2,2
(HR:)	Gen 22:13; Exod 27:2,2; 29:12; 30:2,3,10;

M:	Lev 4:7,18,25,30,34
L:	Lev 4:7,18,25,30,34
(HR:)	Lev 4:7,18,25,30,34

M:	Lev 8:15; 9:9; 16:18; Deut 33:17,17; Jos 6:5; 1 Sam 2:1,10; 16:1,13; 2 Sam	22:3
L:	Lev 8:15; 16:18; Deut 33:17,17; Jos 6:5; 1 Sam 2:1,10; 16:1,13; 2 Sam	22:3
(HR:)	Lev 8:15; 9:9; 16:18; Deut 33:17,17; 1 Sam (= 1 Kgs) 2:1,10; 16:1,13; 2 Sam (= 2 Kgs)	22:3

M:	1 Kgs 1:39,50,51; 2:28; 22:11; 1 Chr 25:5; 2 Chr 18:10; Job 16:15; Pss 18:3;	22:11,22
L:	1 Kgs 1:39,50,51; 2:28; 22:11; 1 Chr 25:5; 2 Chr 18:10; Job 16:15; Pss 18:3;	22: 22
(HR:)	1 Kgs (= 3 Kgs) 1:39,50,51; 2:28; 22:11; 1 Chr 25:5; 2 Chr 18:10; Job 42:16; (Pss 17:2) (21:	22

M:	Pss 75:5,6; 75:11; 89:18,25; 92:11; 112:9; 118:27; 132:17; 148:14
L:	Pss 75:5,6; 75:11; 89:18,25; 92:11; 112:9; 118:27; 132:17; 148:14
(HR:)	Pss 74:4,5; 74:10; (88:17,24) (91:10) (111:9)(117:27) (131:17) (148:14)

M:	Isa 5:1; Jer 17:1; 48:25; Lam 2:3,17; Ezek 27:15; 29:21; 34:21 ;43:15,20; Dan 8:3
L:	Isa 5:1; Jer 17:1; 48:25; Lam 2:3,17; Ezek 27:15; 29:21; 34:21 ;43:15,20; Dan 8:3 5,6,7,8,9,20,21
(Hr:)	Isa 5:1; (Jer 31:25) Lam 2:3,17; Ezek 29:21; 34:21,21; 43:15,20; Dan 8:3,3,5,6,7,8,9,20,21

M:	Amos 3:14; 6:13; Hab 3:4; Zech 2:1,2,4,7; Mic 4:13
L:	Amos 3:14; Hab 3:4; Zech 2:1,2,4,7; Mic 4:13
(HR:)	Amos 3:14; (6:14) Hab 3:4; (Zech 1:18,19,21,21)Mic 4:13

Additional texts not cited by standard commentaries: Gen 14:5; Exod 27:2, and Job 42:17
Summa occurrences: 82 times (Mandelkern records 79 times; Lisowsky 75 times; Hatch and Redpath 67 times [kéras from qrn]).

Key: M = Mandelkern; L = Lisowsky; HR = Hatch and Redpath
[a]For comparison the keras [when translated from qrn] in HR has been included)

BIBLIOGRAPHY

BIBLIOGRAPHY

Aalen, Sverre. Theologisches Begriffs Lexikon Zum Neuen Testament. 3d ed. Edited by Lothar Coenen. Wuppertal: Theologischer Verlag Rolf Brockhaus, 1972.

Abel, Felix M. Géographie de la Palestine. 2 vols. Paris: J. Gabalda et Cie, 1938.

Ackroyd, Peter R. The First Book of Samuel. Cambridge: The University Press, 1971.

─────. 1 and 2 Chronicles, Ezra, Nehemiah. London: SCM Press Ltd., 1973.

─────. The Second Book of Samuel. Cambridge: Cambridge University Press, 1977.

Addis, William E. "Altar." Encyclopaedia Biblica. 4 vols. Edited by T. K. Cheyne and J. Cutherland Black. London: Adam and Charles Black, 1899.

Aharoni, Yohanan. "Arad: Its Inscriptions and Temple." The Biblical Archaeologist 31 (1968):2-35.

─────. "The Horned Altar of Beersheba." The Biblical Archaeologist 37 (1974):2-6.

Ahlström, Gösta W. Psalms 89; eine Liturgie aus dem Ritual des leidenden Königs. Translated by Hans-Karl Hacker and Rudolf Zeitler. Lund: C. W. K. Gleerups Förlag, 1959.

Aimé-Giron, M. Noel. Textes Araméens d'Egypte. Cairo: Imprimerie de l'institut Français, 1931.

Aistleitner, Joseph. Die mythologischen und kultischen Texte and Ras Schamra, 2d ed. Bibliotheca Orientalis Hungarica, 8. Budabest: Akadémiai Kiado, 1964.

─────. Wörterbuch der ugaritischen Sprache. 2d rev. ed.. Philologisch-historische Klasse. Vol. 106, pt. 3. Berlin: Academie-Verlag, 1967.

Akurgal, Ekrem. Die Kunst der Hethiter. München: Hirmer Verlag, 1976. The Art of the Hittites. New York: Harry N. Abrams, Inc., n.d.

Albrektson, Bertil. *Studies in the Text and Theology of the Book of Lamentations with a Critical Edition of the Peshitta Text.* Studia Theologia Lundensia, 21. Lund: C. W. K. Gleerup, 1963.

Albright, William F. *Archaeology and the Religion of Israel.* 2d ed. Baltimore: Johns Hopkins Press, 1942.

_____. "The Babylonian Temple-Tower and the Altar of Burnt-Offering." *Journal of Biblical Literature* 39 (1920):137-49.

_____. "New Israelite and Pre-Israelite Sites: The Spring Trip of 1929." *Bulletin of the American Schools of Oriental Research* 35 (1929):1-23.

_____. "The Old Testament and Canaanite Language and Literature." *The Catholic Biblical Quarterly* 7 (January 1945):5-31.

_____. "The Psalms of Habakkuk." In *Studies in Old Testament Prophecy, Presented to Theodore H. Robinson on His Sixty-fifth Birthday, August 9, 1946.* Edited by H. H. Rowley. Edinburgh: T. & T. Clark, 1950. Pp. 1-18.

_____. *Yahweh and the Gods of Canaan.* London: The Athlone Press, 1968.

Alexander, Joseph A. *Commentary on the Prophecies of Isaiah.* Grand Rapids: Zondervan Publishing House, 1953.

Ali, Fadhil A. "Blowing the Horn for Official Announcement." *Sumer* 20 (1964):66-68.

Alster, Bendt. *Dumuzi's Dream: Aspects of Oral Poetry in a Sumerian Myth.* Copenhagen: Det Kongelige Bibliotek, 1972.

_____. *The Instructions of Suruppak.* Mesopotamia 2. Studies in Assyriology. Copenhagen: Akademisk Forlag, 1974.

_____. *Studies in Sumerian Proverbs.* Mesopotamia 3. Studies in Assyriology. Copenhagen: Akademisk Forlag, 1975.

Alt, Albrecht. *Der Stadtstaat Samaria.* Berlin: Akademie-Verlag, 1954.

Amsler, Samuel. *Amos. Commentaire de l'Ancien Testament 11.a.* Neuchatel: Delachaux & Niestle, 1965.

Anderson, Arnold A. *The Book of Psalms.* 2 vols. New Century Bible. London: Marshall, Morgan & Scott, 1972.

Archer, Gleason L. "Aramaic Language." The Zondervan Pictorial Encyclopedia of the Bible. Edited by Merrill C. Tenny. Grand Rapids: Zondervan Publishing House, 1975. 1:251-55.

_____. A Survey of Old Testament Introduction. Chicago: Moody Press, 1964.

Assyrian Dictionary of the Oriental Institute of the University of Chicago. Vol. 7. Edited by Ignace J. Gelb, Benno Landsberger, A. Leo Oppenheim. Chicago: The Oriental Institute, 1960.

Auberlen, Carl A. The Prophecies of Daniel and the Revelations of St. John. Andover: W. F. Draper, 1856.

Aufrecht, Walter E., and Hurd, John C. A Synoptic Concordance of Aramaic Inscriptions according to H. Donner and W. Röllig. Missoula, MT: Scholars Press, 1975.

Baab, Otto J. "Incense Altar." Interpreter's Dictionary of the Bible. Nashville: Abingdon Press, 1962. 2:699-700.

Bailey, Lloyd R. "Horns of Moses." The Interpreter's Dictionary of the Bible. Supplementary Volume. Nashville: Abingdon Press, 1976. Pp. 419-20.

Baldwin, Joyce G. Haggai, Zechariah, Malachi. Downers Grove, IL: Inter-Varsity Press, 1972.

Barker, Philip C. 1 and 2 Chronicles. The Pulpit Commentary. Vol. 6. Grand Rapids: Wm. B. Eerdmans, 1977.

Barnes, W. Emery. Haggai, Zechariah and Malachi. Cambridge: University Press, 1934.

Barnes, Albert. Notes on the Old Testament, Explanatory and Practical. Grand Rapids: Baker Book House, 1950. 2:83-84.

_____. Notes on the Old Testament: Psalms. Grand Rapids: Baker Book House, 1950.

Barr, James. Comparative Philology and the Text of the Old Testament. Oxford: Clarendon Press, 1968.

_____. "Daniel." Peake's Commentary on the Bible. Edited by Matthew Black and H. H. Rowley. London: Thomas Nelson and Sons Ltd., 1962.

_____. "Etymology and the Old Testament." Language and Meaning. Oudtestamentische Studien, 19. Leiden: E. J. Brill, 1976.

Barton, George A. "Daniel, A Pre-Israelite Hero of Galilee." *Journal of Biblical Literature* 60 (1941):213-25.

Bauer, Hans. *Das Alphabet von Ras Shamra.* Halle, Saale: Max Niemeyer Verlag, 1932.

Bauer, Hans, and Leander, Pontus. *Grammatik des Biblisch-Aramäischen.* Hildesheim: Georg Olms, 1962.

_____. *Historische Grammatik der Hebräischen Sprache.* Vol. 1. Hildersheim: Georg Olms Verlags-buchhandlung, 1962.

Bauer, Theo. *Akkadische Lesestücke.* 3 vols. Rome: Pontificium Institutum Biblicum, 1953.

Baumgartner, Walter. *Das Buch Daniel.* Giessen: Alfred Töpelman, 1926.

_____. "Ein Vierteljahrhundert Danielforschung." *Theologische Rundschau* 11 (1939):201-28.

Beek, Martin A. *Atlas of Mesopotamia.* London: Thomas Nelson and Sons Ltd., 1962.

_____. "Baum." *Biblisches-Historisches Handwörterbuch.* Edited by Bo Reicke and Leonhard Rost. Göttingen: Vandenhoeck & Ruprecht, 1962. 1:206-7.

Beer, Georg. *Exodus.* (Beitrag von Kurt Galling) Handbuch zum Alten Testament. Edited by Otto Eissfeldt. Tübingen: J. C. B. Mohr (Paul Siebeck), 1939.

Béguerie, Philippe. *Le Psaume d'Habacuc.* Paris: Editions du Cerf, 1954.

Behrman, Georg. *Das Buch Daniel.* Handkommentar zum Alten Testament. Göttingen: Vandenhoeck & Ruprecht, 1894.

Bell, Richard. *The Qur'an.* Edinburgh: T. & T. Clark, 1960.

Bennett, T. Miles. *The Book of Micah: A Study Manual.* Grand Rapids: Baker Book House, 1968.

Benz, Frank L. *Personal Names in the Phoenician and Punic Inscriptions.* Studia Pohl, 8. Rome: Pontifical Biblical Institute, 1972.

Bentzen, Aage. "The Cultic Use of the Story of the Ark in Samuel." *Journal of Biblical Literature* 67 (1948):37-53.

_____. Daniel. 2d rev. ed. Handbuch zum Alten Testament. Vol.
19. Edited by Otto Eissfeldt. Tübingen: J. C. B. Mohr
(Paul Siebeck), 1952.

Benzinger, Immanuel. Hebräische Archäologie. 3d. ed. Leipzig:
Eduard Pfeiffer, 1927.

Bergsträsser, Gotthelf. Hebräische Grammatik. Wilhelm Gesenius'
Hebräische Grammatik. 29th ed., with contribution from M.
Lidzbarski. Leipzig: I. C. W. Vogel, 1918-29.

Bertholet, Alfred. Deuteronomium. Tübingen: J. C. Mohr (Paul
Siebeck), 1899. [Ann Arbor, MI: University Microfilms,
1971 (Authorized facsimile).]

_____. Hesekiel. Handbuch zum Alten Testament. Edited by Otto
Eissfeldt. Vol. 13. Tübingen: J. C. B. Mohr, 1936.

Betteridge, Walter R. "The Interpretation of the Prophecy of
Habakkuk." American Journal of Theology 7 (1903):647-61.

Bevan, Anthony A. A Short Commentary on the Book of Daniel.
Cambridge: Cambridge University Press, 1892; reprint ed.,
1971.

Bevenot, Hugues. "Le Cantique d'Habacuc." Revue Biblique 42
(1933):499-525.

Beyerlin, Walter, ed. "Mesopotamische Texte." Religionsgeschichtliches Textbuch zum Alten Testament. Translated by Hartmut
Schmökel. Göttingen: Vandenhoeck & Ruprecht, 1975.

Bezold, Carl. Babylonisch-Assyrische Glossar. Heidelberg: Carl
Winter, 1926.

_____. Ninive und Babylon. 4th ed. Monographen zur
Weltgeschichte, 18. Leipzig: Velhagen und Klasing, 1926.

Biblia Hebraica Stuttgartensia. Edited by K. Elliger and W.
Rudolph. Stuttgart: Deutsche Bibelstiftung, 1967-77.

Biblia Sacra iuxta Vulgatam versionem. Edited by Robertus Weber.
Stuttgart: Württembergische Bibelanstalt, 1969.

Biggs, Robert D. "The Abū Ṣalābīkh Tablets." Journal of Cuneiform
Studies 20 (1966):73-88.

_____. Inscriptions from Tell Abu Ṣalābīkh. Chicago: University
Press, 1974.

_____. "On Regional Cuneiform Handwritings in Third Millennium
Mesopotamia." Orientalia 42 (1973):39-46.

Bittel, Kurt. Die Hethiter. München: C. H. Beck, 1976.

Bittel, Kurt; Naumann, Rudolf; and Heinz, Otto, eds. Yazilikaya. Wissenschaftliche Veröffentlichung der deutschen Orientgesellschaft, 61. Leipzig: J. C. Hinrichs, 1941.

Black, Matthew. The Scrolls and Christian Origins. New York: Scribner, 1961.

Blackman, Aylward M. "Osiris the sun-god? A Reply to Mr. Perry." Journal of Egyptian Archaeology 9 (1925):191-215.

Blackwood, Andrew W. Commentary on Jeremiah. Waco, TX: Word Books, 1977.

Blau, Joshua. A Grammar of Biblical Hebrew. Porta Linguarum Orientalum, Neue Serie, 12. Wiesbaden: Harrassowitz, 1976.

Boehmer, Rainer M. Die Entwicklung der Glyptik während der Akkad-Zeit. Berlin: Walter de Gruyter & Co., 1965.

_____. "Hörnerkrone." Reallexikon der Assyriologie. Berlin: Walter de Gruyter, 1972-75. 4:431-34.

Bonnet, Hans, ed. Reallexikon der ägyptischen Religionsgeschichte. Berlin: Walter de Gruyter & Co., 1952. S.v. "Apis."

_____. Reallexikon der ägyptischen Religionsgeschichte. Berlin: Walter de Gruyter & Co., 1952. S.v. "Buchis."

_____. Reallexikon der ägyptischen Religionsgeschichte. Berlin: Walter de Gruyter & Co., 1952. S.v. "Mnevis."

_____. Reallexikon der ägyptischen Religionsgeschichte. Berlin: Walter de Gruyter & Co., 1952. S.v. "Month."

Borger, Rykle, ed. Handbuch der Keilschriftliteratur. 3 vols. Berlin: Walter de Gruyter & Co., 1967.

Borger, Rykle. Akkadische Zeichenlisten. Alter Orient und Altes Testament, Vol. 6. Neukirchen-Vluyn: Neukirchen Verlag, 1971.

Bottéro, Jean. Textes Economiques el Administratifs. Archives royales de Mari. Edited by André Parrot and Georges Dossin. Paris: Imprimerie Nationale, 1957.

Boutflower, Charles. Dadda-ʿIdri; or The Aramaic of the Book of Daniel. London: Society for Promoting Christian Knowledge, 1931.

_____. In and Around the Book of Daniel. Grand Rapids: Zondervan Publishing House, 1963.

Bowman, Raymond A. "Arameans, Aramaic and the Bible." Journal of Near Eastern Studies 7 (1948):65-90.

──────. Aramaic Ritual Texts from Persepolis. Oriental Institute Publication, 91. Chicago: University Press, 1970.

──────. "Arameans." Interpreter's Dictionary of the Bible. New York: Abingdon Press, 1962. 1:190-93.

Briggs, Charles A. The Book of Psalms. International Critical Commentary. Edinburgh: T. & T. Clark, 1951.

Briggs, Charles A., and Briggs, Emilie G. A Critical and Exegetical Commentary of the Book of Psalms. International Critical Commentary. Edinburgh: T. & T. Clark, 1952.

Bright, John. "The Book of Joshua." Interpreter's Bible. New York: Abingdon Press, 1953. 2:541-673.

──────. Jeremiah. Anchor Bible. Garden City, NY: Doubleday & Co., 1965.

Brockelmann, Carl. Grundriss der vergleichenden Grammatik der semitischen Sprachen. 2 vols. Hildesheim: Georg Olm, 1961.

──────. Hebräische Syntax. Neukirchen: Verlag der Buchhandlung des Erziehungvereins, 1956.

Brockelmann, Karl. Lexicon Syriacum. 2d ed. Hildesheim: Georg Olms, Verlagsbuchhandlung, 1966.

Brown, John P. "The Sacrificial Cult and Its Critique in Greek and Hebrew." Journal of Semitic Studies 24 (1979):159-73.

Brown, Francis; Driver, Samuel R; and Briggs, Charles A. A Hebrew and English Lexicon of the Old Testament. Oxford: Clarendon Press, 1907. Reprint ed. 1976.

Brownlee, William H. "Ezekiel's Poetic Indictment of the Shepherds." Harvard Theological Review 51 (1958):191-203.

Brunner, Robert. Sacharja. Stuttgart: Zwingli Verlag, 1960.

Bruno, Arvid. Micah und der Herrscher aus der Vorzeit. Uppsala: Almqvist & Wiksell, 1923.

Budge, Ernest A. Wallis. Osiris and the Egyptian Resurrection. London: Philip Lee Warner, 1911.

Budge, Ernest A. Wallis, and King, Leonard W., eds. Annals of the Kings of Assyria . . . in the British Museum. Vol. 1. London: Trustees of the British Museum, 1902.

Buhl, Irants. Wilhelm Gesenius' hebräisches und aramäisches Handwörterbuch über das Alte Testament. 17th ed. 1915 reprint ed. Berlin: Springer-Verlag, 1949.

Burkitt, Francis C. "The Psalm of Habakkuk." Journal of Theological Studies 16 (1914):62-66.

Buzy, Denis. "Les symboles de Daniel." Revue Biblique 15 (1918): 403-31.

Caldecott, Shaw W. "Altar in Worship: Tabernacle and Temple." The International Standard Bible Encyclopaedia. Grand Rapids: Wm. B. Eerdmans Publishing Co., 1939. 1:110-12.

_____. "Horns of the Altar." The International Standard Bible Encyclopaedia. Grand Rapids: Wm. B. Eerdmans Publishing Co., 1939. 3:1422.

Caquot, André. "Sur les quatre bêtes de Daniel 7." Semitica 5 (1955): 5-13.

Caquot, André; Sznycer, Maurice; and Herdner, Andrée. Textes Ougaritiques. Vol. 1. Mythes et Légendes. Paris: Les éditions du Cerf, 1974.

Cassuto, Umberto. A Commentary on the Book of Exodus. Translated by Israel Abrahams. Jerusalem: The Magnes Press, The Hebrew University, 1967.

Castellino, Giorgo R. Two Šulgi Hymns (BC). Studi Semitici 42. Rome: Istituto di Studi del Vicino Oriente, 1972.

Černý, Jaroslav. "Egypt: From the Death of Ramesses III to the End of the Twenty-first Dynasty." Cambridge Ancient History. 3d ed. Vol. 2, pt. 2. Cambridge: University Press, 1975. Pp. 606-57.

Charles, Robert H., ed. The Apocrypha and Pseudepigrapha of the Old Testament in English. 2 vols. Oxford: Clarendon Press, 1913.

Charles, Robert H. The Book of Daniel. The Century Bible. Edited by Walter F. Adeney. Edinburgh: T. C. & E. C. Jack, n.d.

_____. A Critical and Exegetical Commentary on the Book of Daniel. Oxford: Clarendon Press, 1929.

Cheyne, Thomas K. Jeremiah. The Pulpit Commentary. Vol. 11. Grand Rapids: Wm. B. Eerdmans Publishing Co., 1977.

_____. The Origin and Religious Contents of the Psalter in the Light of Old Testament Criticism and the History of Religions. London: K. Paul, Trench, Trübner & Co., 1891.

Childs, Brevard S. *The Book of Exodus*. Philadelphia: The Westminster Press, 1974.

Civil, Miguel. "Lexicography." In *Sumerological Studies in Honor of Thorkild Jacobsen on His Seventieth Birthday, June 7, 1974*. Assyriological Studies, no. 20. Chicago: University Press, 1976. Pp. 123-157.

_____. "The Sumerian Writing System: Some Problems." *Orientalia* 42 (1973):21-34.

Clarke, Adam. *The Holy Bible Containing the Old and New Testament with a Commentary and Critical Notes*. London: Ward, Lock & Co., 1881.

Clarke, Arthur G. *Analytical Studies in the Psalms*. Kilmarnock, Great Britain: John Ritchie, 1949.

Coggins, Richard J. *The First and Second Books of the Chronicles*. Cambridge: Cambridge University Press, 1976.

Cole, Robert A. *Exodus: An Introduction and Commentary*. Downers Grove, IL: Inter-Varsity Press, 1973.

Collins, John J. *The Apocalyptic Vision of the Book of Daniel*. Missoula, MT: Scholars Press, 1977.

_____. "The Son of Man and the Saints of the Most High." *Journal of Biblical Literature* 93 (1974):50-66.

Conrad, Jack R. *The Horn and the Sword*. Westport, CT: Greenwood Press, 1973.

Conti-Rossini, C., ed. *Chrestomathia arabica meridionalis epigraphica*. Rome: Istituto per l'Oriente, 1931.

Cook, Stanley A. *The Religion of Ancient Palestine in the Light of Archaeology*. London: Oxford University Press, 1930.

Cooke, George A. *A Critical and Exegetical Commentary on the Book of Ezekiel*. The International Critical Commentary. Edinburg: T. & T. Clark, 1951.

_____. *A Text-book of North-Semitic Inscriptions*. Oxford: Clarendon Press, 1903.

Cooper, Jerrold S. "Bilinguals from Boghazköi." *Zeitschrift für Assyriologie* 61 (1971):1-22.

_____. "Sumerian and Akkadian in Sumer and Akkad." *Orientalia* 42 (1973):239-46.

Corpus Inscriptionum Semiticarum Inscriptionum Phoeniciae. Paris: C. Klineksieck, 1881.

Couroyer, Bernard. "Corne et Arc." Revue Biblique 73 (1966): 510-21.

Cowley, Arthur E. Aramaic Papyri of the Fifth Century B.C. Oxford: Clarendon Press, 1923.

Craigie, Peter C. The Book of Deuteronomy. Grand Rapids: William B. Eerdmans, 1976.

Crawley, Arthur E. "Anointing." Encyclopaedia of Religion and Ethics. Edited by James Hastings. New York: Charles Scribner's Sons, 1913. 1:549-54.

Cripps, Richard S. A Critical and Exegetical Commentary on the Book of Amos. London: S.P.C.K., 1969.

Cross, Frank. Canaanite Myth and Hebrew Epic. Cambridge, MA: Harvard University Press, 1973.

Cross, Frank M., and Freedman, David N. Early Hebrew Orthography: A Study of the Epigraphic Evidence. American Oriental Series, Vol. 36. New Haven, CT: American Oriental Society, 1952.

Cumont, Franz V. Die Mysterien des Mithra. Leipzig: B. G. Teubner, 1923.

Dahood, Mitchell J. "Northwest Semitic Notes on Genesis 22:13." Biblica 55 (1974):76-82.

_____. Psalms I-III. 3 vols. Anchor Bible. Garden City, NY: Doubleday & Co., 1966.

_____. Ugaritic-Hebrew Philology. Biblica et Orientalia, 17. Rome: Pontifical Biblical Institute, 1965.

_____. "Ugaritic Lexicography." Vol. 1. Studi e Testi, 231. Vatican: Biblioteca Apostolica, 1964. Pp. 81-104.

_____. "Ugaritic-Hebrew Syntax and Style." Ugarit-Forschungen 1 (1969):15-36.

Dalman, D. Gustav H. Aramäisch-neuhebräisches Handwörterbuch zu Targum, Talmud und Midrasch. Göttingen: Eduard Pfeiffer, 1938.

Das Buch der Jubiläen oder die kleine Genesis unter Beifügung des revidirten Textes der in der Ambrosiana aufgefundenen lateinischen Fragmente sowie einer von Dr. August Dillmann aus zwei äthiopischen Handschriften gefertigten lateinischen Übertragung. Edited by Hermann Rönsch. Amsterdam: Rodopi, 1970.

Davidson, Israel. "Literature, Hebrew." The Jewish Encyclopedia. 12 vols. New York: Funk and Wagnalls, 1904. 8:108-11.

Davies, G. Henton. Exodus, Introduction and Commentary. London: SCM Press Ltd., 1967.

Deimel, Anton. "Recensiones." Orientalia 6 (1937):268-77.

_____. Šumerisches Lexikon. 2d ed. Rome: Pontificium Institutum Biblicum, 1930.

_____. "Zur Erklärung sumerischer Wörter und Zeichen." Orientalia 13 (1944):321-33.

Deimel, P. Anton, and Gössmann, P. Šumerisches Lexikon. 3d ed. 4 vols. Rome: Pontificium Institutum Biblicum, 1947.

Delaporte, Louis J. Catalogue des Cylindres Orientaux. Paris: Ernest Leroux, 1910.

Delcor, M. Le Livre de Daniel. Paris: J. Gabalda et Cie Editeurs, 1971.

_____. "Les sources du chapître VII de Daniel." Vetus Testamentum 18 (1968):290-312.

Delitzsch, Franz J. Biblical Commentary on the Prophecies of Isaiah. Biblical Commentary on the Old Testament. Grand Rapids: Wm. B. Eerdmans Publishing Co., 1900.

_____. Biblical Commentary on the Book of Job. Translated by Francis Bolton. Grand Rapids: Wm. B. Eerdmans Publishing Company, 1961.

_____. Biblical Commentary on the Psalms. 3 vols. Biblical Commentary on the Old Testament. Grand Rapids: Wm. B. Eerdmans Publishing Co., 1959.

Delitzsch, Friedrich. Assyrisches Handwörterbuch. Leipzig: J. C. Hinrichs, 1896. Reprint Demokratischen Republic Zentralantiquariat, 1968.

_____. Sumerisches Glossar. Leipzig: J. C. Hinrichs, 1914.

DeVries, LaMoine F. <u>Incense Altars from the Period of the Judges and Their Significance</u>. Ph.D. dissertation, The Southern Baptist Theological Seminary, 1975.

Dhorme, Eduard. <u>A Commentary on the Book of Job</u>. London: Thomas Nelson, 1967.

Dhorme, Edouard P. "L'emploi métaphorique des noms de parties du corps en hébreu et en akkadien." <u>Revue Biblique</u> 29 (1920): 465-506.

Diakonoff, Igor M. "Ancient Writing and Ancient Written Language." In <u>Sumerological Studies in Honor of Thorkild Jacobsen on His Seventieth Birthday June 7, 1974</u>. Chicago: University Press, 1976. Pp. 99-121.

Diamant, Steven, and Rutter, Jeremy. "Horned Objects in Anatolia and the Near East and Possible Connexions with the Minoan 'Horns of Consecration'." <u>Anatolian Studies</u> 19 (1969): 147-77.

Dombart, Theodor. "Das Zikkurat-relief aus Kujundschik," <u>Zeitschrift für Assyriologie</u> 38 (1929):39-64.

_____. "Die Zikkurat-Darstellung aus Ninive." <u>Archiv für Orientforschung</u> 3 (1926):177-81.

Donner, Herbert, and Röllig, Wolfgang. <u>Kanaanäische und aramäische Inschriften</u>. 2d ed. 3 Vols. Wiesbaden: Harrassowitz, 1966.

Dossin, Georges. "Les archives épistolaires du palais de Mari." <u>Syria</u> 19 (1930):105-26.

_____. "Une mention de Hattusa dans une lettre de Mari." <u>Revue hittite et asianique</u> 35 (1939):70-76.

Dossin, Georges, and Finet, André. "Correspondance Féminine." Archives royales de Mari. Vol. 10. Edited by André Parrot and Georges Dossin. Paris: Paul Geuthner, 1978.

Driver, Godfrey R. <u>Aramaic Documents of the Fifth Century B.C.</u> Oxford: Clarendon Press, 1957.

_____. "The Aramaic Language." <u>Journal of Biblical Literature</u> 45 (1926):323-25.

_____. "The Aramaic of the Book of Daniel." <u>Journal of Biblical Literature</u> 45 (1926):110-19.

_____. <u>Canaanite Myths and Legends</u>. Old Testament Studies, no. 3. Edinburgh: T. & T. Clark, 1956.

_____. Semitic Writing. Oxford: University Press, 1976.

Driver, Samuel R. A Critical and Exegetical Commentary on Deuteronomy. 3rd ed. The International Critical Commentary. Edinburgh: T. & T. Clark, 1902; reprint ed., 1951.

_____. An Introduction to the Literature of the Old Testament. New York: Charles Scribner's Sons, 1910.

_____. Notes on the Hebrew Text and the Topography of the Books of Samuel. Oxford: The Clarendon Press, 1913.

Driver, Samuel R., and Gray, George B. A Critical and Exegetical Commentary on the Book of Job. International Critical Commentary. Edinburgh: T. & T. Clark, 1958.

Duhm, Bernhard. Das Buch Habakuk. Tübingen: J. C. B. Mohr (Paul Siebeck), 1906.

_____. Die Psalmen. Kurzer Hand-Kommentar zum Alten Testament. Edited by Karl Marti. Tübingen: J. C. B. Mohr (Paul Siebeck), 1899.

Dumermuth, Fritz. "Moses strahlendes Gesicht." Theologische Zeitschrift 17 (1961):241-48.

Eaton, John H. "The Origin and Meaning of Habakkuk." Zeitschrift für die alttestamentliche Wissenschaft 76 (1964):144-71.

_____. Psalms. Torch Bible Commentaries. London: SCM Press, Ltd., 1967.

Ebeling, Erich. Tod und Leben nach der Vorstellung der Babylonier. Berlin: Walter de Gruyter & Co., 1931.

Eberharter, Andreas. "Das Horn im Kult des Alten Testamentes." Zeitschrift für Katholische Theologie 51 (1927):394-97.

Edwards, Tryon, ed. The New Dictionary of Thoughts. Revised and enlarged by C. N. Catrevas, Jonathan Edwards, and Ralph Emerson Browns. New York: Standard Book Co., 1961.

Eerdman, Bernardus D. The Covenant at Mount Sinai Viewed in the Light of Antique Thought. Lieden: Burgerskijk & Niermans, 1939.

Eichrodt, Walther. Ezekiel. A Commentary. Translated by Cosslett Quin. London: SCM Press Ltd., 1970.

Einstein, Albert. Cosmic Religion. New York: Covici-Friede, 1931.

Eissfeldt, Otto. "Lade und Stierbild." Zeitschrift für die alttestamentliche Wissenschaft 58 (1940-41):201.

_____. "Psalm 132." Die Welt des Orients 2 (1954-1959):450-83.

Eisser, Georg, and Lewy, Julius. "Die altassyrischen Rechtsurkunden vom Kültepe." Part 4. Mitteilungen der vorderasiatisch-aegyptischen Gesellschaft 35 (1935):100-101.

Elmslie, William A. L. The First and Second Books of Chronicles. Cambridge: University Press, 1916.

Engnell, Ivan. Studies in Divine Kingship in the Ancient Near East. 2d ed. Oxford: Basil Blackwell, 1967.

Erdman, Charles R. The Book of Exodus. New York: Fleming H. Revell Company, 1949.

Erman, Adolf. Aegypten und aegyptisches Leben im Altertum. Edited by Hermann Ranke. Tübingen: J. C. B. Mohr (Paul Siebeck), 1923.

_____. A Handbook of Egyptian Religion. Translated by A. S. Griffith. New York: E. P. Dutton & Co., 1907.

_____. Life in Ancient Egypt. London: Macmillan and Co., 1894.

Euler, Karl F. "Königtum und Götterwelt in den altaramäischen Inschriften Nordsyriens." Zeitschrift für die Alttestamentliche Wissenschaft 56 (1938):272-313.

Evans, Arthur J. The Palace of Minos. 4 vols. London: Macmillan and Co., 1921-33.

Ewald, Georg H. A., von. Commentary on the Book of Job. London: Williams and Norgate, 1882.

Ewald, Heinrich. Ausführliches Lehrbuch der Hebräischen Sprache das alten Bundes. Göttingen: Verlag der Dieterichschen Buchhandlung, 1870.

_____. Die Dichter des alten Bundes. 2d. ed. Göttingen: Vandenhoeck & Ruprecht, 1866.

Falkenstein, Adam. Archaische Texte aus Uruk. Berlin: O. Harrassowitz, 1936.

_____. Das Sumerische. Handbuch der Orientalistik. Vol 2, no. 1. Leiden: E. J. Brill, 1959.

_____. "Ein sumerisches Kultlied auf Samsuʲiluna." <u>Archiv Orientální</u> 17 (1949):217-26.

_____. "Sumerische Religiöse Texte." <u>Zeitschrift für Assyriologie</u> 56 (1964):44-129.

_____. "Sumerische Religiöse Texte, 2. Ein Šulgi-Lied." <u>Zeischrift für Assyriologie</u> 50 (1952):61-91.

_____. "Untersuchungen zur sumerischen Grammatik (Fortsetzung), 3. Das affirmative Präformativ <u>na</u>." <u>Zeitschrift für Assyriologie</u> 47 (1942-43):181-223.

Falkenstein, Adam, and Soden, Wolfram von. <u>Sumerische und akkadische Hymnen und Gebete</u>. Zürich: Artemis Verlag [1953].

Farbridge, Maurice H. <u>Studies in Biblical and Semitic Symbolism</u> New York: Ktav Publishing House, Inc., 1970.

Faulkner, Raymond O., trans. <u>The Ancient Egyptian Pyramid Texts</u>. Oxford: Clarendon Press, 1969.

Feigin, Samuel I. "A Purchase Contract from the Time of Samsu-Iluna." <u>Journal of the American Oriental Society</u> 55 (1935): 284-93.

Feuillet, André, trans. "Le fils de l'homme de Daniel et la tradition biblique." <u>Revue Biblique</u> 60 (1953):321-46.

Field, Fridericus. <u>Origenis Hexaplorum quae supersunt</u>. 2 vols. 1875. Reprint, Hildesheim: Georg Olms, 1964.

Finet, André. "Lettres de Iawi-Ilâ, nos. 139-50." Archives Royales de Mari. Vol. 13: <u>Textes Divers</u>. Paris: Paul Geuthner, 1964.

Finkelstein, Jacob J. "Ammiṣaduqa's Edict and the Babylonian 'Law Codes'." <u>Journal of Cuneiform Studies</u> 15 (1961):91-104.

_____. "The So-called 'Old Babylonian Kutha Legend'." <u>Journal of Cuneiform Studies</u> 11 (1957):83-88.

Finnegan, Ruth H. "How Oral is Oral Tradition?" <u>Bulletin of the Schools of Oriental and African Studies</u> 37 (1974):52-64.

Fiore, Silvestro. <u>Voices from the Clay</u>. Norman, OK: University of Oklahoma Press, 1956.

Fish, Thomas. "The Zû Bird." <u>Bulletin of the John Rylands Library</u> 31 (1948):162-71.

Fisher, Loren R., and Knutson, F. Brent. "An Enthronement Ritual at Ugarit." Journal of Near Eastern Studies 28 (1969):157-67.

Fitzmyer, Joseph A. The Aramaic Inscriptions of Sefîre. Biblica et Orientalia, 19. Rome: Pontificial Biblical Institute, 1967.

_____. The Dead Sea Scrolls: Major Publications and Tools for Study. Sources for Biblical Study, 8. Missoula, MT: Scholars Press, 1975.

_____. The Genesis Apocryphon of Qumran Cave I. 2d rev. ed. Biblica et Orientalia, no. 18A. Rome: Biblical Institute Press, 1971.

Fitzmyer, Joseph A., and Harrington, Daniel J. A Manual of Palestinian Aramaic Texts. Biblica et Orientalia 34. Rome: Biblical Institute Press, 1978.

Flusser, David. "The Four Empires in the Fourth Sibyl and in the Book of Daniel." Israel Oriental Studies 2 (1972):148-75.

Foerster, Werner. "Keras." Theological Dictionary of the New Testament. Grand Rapids: Wm. B. Eerdmans Publishing Co., 1965. 3:669-71.

Fohrer, Georg, mit einem Beitrag von Kurt Galling. Ezechiel: Handbuch zum Alten Testament. Edited by Otto Eissfeldt. Tübingen: J. C. B. Mohr (Paul Siebeck), 1955.

Ford, Desmond. Daniel. Nashville: Southern Publishing Association, 1978.

Fraine, Jean de. "Moses' 'cornuta facies' Ex 34:29-35." Bijdragen Tijdschrift voor Filosophie en Theologie 20 (1959):28-38.

Frank, Karl. Bilder und Symbole babylonisch-assyrischer Götter. Leipzig: J. C. Hinrichs, 1906.

Frankfort, Henri. The Art and Architecture of the Ancient Orient. Baltimore: Penguin Books Inc., 1954.

_____. Cylinder Seals. London: Macmillan and Co., 1939.

_____. "The Last Predynastic Period in Babylonia." Revised and rearranged by Leri Davis. In The Cambridge Ancient History. 3d ed. Vol. 1, pt. 2. Cambridge: University Press, 1970. Pp. 71-92.

_____. Sculpture of the Third Millennium B.C. from Tell Asmar and Khafājah. Oriental Institute Publications, Vol. 44. Chicago: University of Chicago Press, 1939.

Freedman, David N. "Genesis": The New American Bible. Paterson, NJ: St. Anthony Guild Press, 1970.

_____. "Prolegomenon" to The Forms of Hebrew Poetry, by George B. Gray. N.p.: Ktav Publishing House, 1972.

Freehof, Solomon B. Book of Jeremiah. New York: Union of American Hebrew Congregations, 1977.

_____. Book of Job. New York: Union of American Hebrew Congregations, 1958.

Fretheim, Terence E. "Psalm 132: A Form-Critical Study." Journal of Biblical Literature 86 (1967):289-300.

Freytag, Georg W. Lexicon arabico-latinum. 4 vols. Halle, Germany: C. A. Schwetschke and Sons, 1830-37.

Frost, Stanley B. "Daniel." Interpreter's Dictionary of the Bible. New York: Abingdon Press, 1956. 1:761-68.

Fuerst, Julius. A Hebrew and Chaldee Lexicon to the Old Testament. 3d ed. Leipzig: Bernhard Tauchnitz, 1867.

Fulco, William J. The Canaanite God Rešep. American Oriental Series, 8. New Haven, CT: American Oriental Society, 1976.

Gadd, Cyril J. "Babylonia c. 2120-1800 B.C." The Cambridge Ancient History. 3d ed. Vol. 1, pt. 2. Cambridge: University Press, 1971. Pp. 595-643.

_____. "The Dynasty of Agade and the Gutian Invasion." Cambridge Ancient History. 3d ed. Vol. 1, pt. 2. Cambridge: University Press, 1971. Pp. 417-63.

Gadegaard, Niels H. "On the So-called Burnt Offering Altar in the Old Testament." Palestine Exploration Quarterly 110 (1978): 35-45.

Gaebelein, Arno C. The Prophet Daniel. Grand Rapids: Kregel Publications, 1955.

Gaebelein, Frank E. Four Minor Prophets: Obadiah, Jonah, Habakkuk and Haggai. Chicago: Moody Press, 1970.

Galling, Kurt. "Altar." Biblisches Reallexikon. Handbuch zum Alten Testament. Vol. 1. Tübingen: Verlag von J. C. B. Mohr (Paul Siebeck), 1937. Pp. 13-22.

_____. "Altar." Interpreter's Dictionary of the Bible. New York: Abingdon Press, 1962. 1:96-100.

_____. *Der Altar in den Kulturen des Alten Orients.* Berlin: Karl Curtis, 1925.

_____. [Ein Beitrag] in *Ezechiel.* Handbuch zum Alten Testament. Vol. 13. Edited by Alfred Bertholet. Tübingen: J. C. B. Mohr (Paul Siebeck), 1955.

_____, ed. "Altar II. In Israel." *Religion in Geschichte und Gegenwart.* 3rd ed. Tübingen: J. C. B. Mohr (Paul Siebeck), 1957. Pp. 253-55.

Gammie, John G. "The Classification, Stages of Growth, and Changing Intentions in the Book of Daniel." *Journal of Biblical Literature* 95 (1976):191-204.

Gardiner, Alan. *Egypt of the Pharaohs.* Oxford: Clarendon Press, 1961.

Garstang, John. *The Hittite Empire.* London: Constable and Co., Ltd., 1929.

Gaster, Theodor H. "The Harrowing of Baal: A Poem from Ras Shamra." *Analecta Orientalia* 16 (1937):41-48.

Gavin, Carney E. S. "The Glyptic Art of Syria-Palestine." Ph.D. dissertation, Harvard University, 1973.

Geissen, Angelo. *Der Septuaginta-Text des Buches Daniel.* 2 vols. Papyrologische Texte und Abhandlung. Vol. 5. Bonn: Rudolf Habelt Verlag GMBH, 1968.

Gelb, Ignace J. *Sequential Reconstruction of Proto-Akkadian.* Assyriological Studies, no. 18. Chicago: University Press, 1969.

Gese, Hartmut; Höfner, Maria; and Rudolph, Kurt. *Die Religionen Altsyriens, Altarabiens und der Mandäer.* Die Religionen der Menschheit. Vol. 10, pt. 2. Stuttgart: W. Kohlhammer, 1970.

Gesenius' Hebrew Grammar. Edited by Emil Kautzsch, and Arthur E. Cowley. 2d ed. Oxford: Clarendon Press, 1976.

Ginsberg, Harold L. "Baʻl und ʻAnat." *Orientalia* 7 (1938):1-11.

_____. "The Composition of the Book of Daniel." *Vetus Testamentum* 4 (1954):246-75.

_____. "The Rebellion and Death of Baʻlu." *Orientalia* 5 (1936): 161-98.

_____. "In Re My Studies in Daniel." *Journal of Biblical Literature* 68 (1949):405-06.

_____. "The Tale of Aqhat." *Ancient Near Eastern Texts*. 3d ed. Edited by James B. Pritchard. Princeton, NJ: Princeton University Press, 1969. Pp. 149-55.

_____. *Texts and Studies in Daniel*. New York: The Jewish Theological Seminary of America, 1948.

_____. "Ugaritic Myths, Epics, and Legends." *Ancient Near Eastern Texts*. 3d ed. Edited by James B. Pritchard. Princeton, NJ: Princeton University Press, 1969. Pp. 129-55.

Glueck, Nelson. "Incense Altar." *Translating and Understanding the Old Testament: Essays in Honor of Herbert Gordon May*. Edited by H. T. Frank and W. L. Reed. Nashville: Abingdon Press, 1970. Pp. 325-29.

_____. "Ramoth-Gilead." *Bulletin of the American Schools of Oriental Research* 92 (1943):10-16.

Goetze, Albrecht, trans. "The Hittite Laws." *Ancient Near Eastern Texts*. 3d ed. Edited by James B. Pritchard. Princeton, NJ: Princeton University Press, 1969. Pp. 188-97.

_____. "Istanbul Arkeoloji Müzelerinde Bulunan Boğazköy Tabletleri I, no. 30." *Journal of Cuneiform Studies* 1 (1947):90-91.

_____. "Plague Prayers of Mursilis." In *Ancient Near Eastern Texts*. 3d ed. Edited by James B. Pritchard. Princeton, NJ: Princeton University Press, 1969. Pp. 394-96.

Goetze, Albrecht. "Is Ugaritic a Canaanite Language?" *Language* 17 (1941):127-38.

_____. "The Laws of Eshunna," *Ancient Near Eastern Texts*. 3d ed. Edited by James B. Pritchard. Princeton, NJ: Princeton University Press, 1969.

_____. "The Priestly Dress of the Hittite King." *Journal of Cuneiform Studies* 1 (1947):176-85.

Goodspeed, Edgar G. *New Chapters in New Testament Study*. New York: Macmillan, 1937.

Gordon, Cyrus H. "The Aramaic Incantation in Cuneiform." *Archiv für Orientforschung* 12 (1937-39):105-17.

_____. C. H. Gordon, Ugaritic Textbook. Analecta Orientalia, 38. Rome: Pontifical Biblical Institute, 1965.

_____. Ugaritic Literature. Rome: Pontificium Institutum Biblicum, 1949.

_____. Ugarit and Minoan Crete. New York: W. W. Norton & Co., 1966.

_____. Ugaritic Textbook. Analecta Orientalia, 38. Rome: Pontifical Biblical Institute, 1965.

Gordon, Edmund I. Sumerian Proverbs: Glimpses of Everyday Life in Ancient Mesopotamia. Philadelphia: The University [of Pennsylvania] Museum, 1959.

Göttesberger, Johann. Das Buch Daniel. Die Heilige Schrift des Alten Testamentes. Edited by F. Feldman and H. Herkenne. Bonn: Hanstein, 1928.

Graesser, Carl F. "Studies in Maṣṣēbōt." PH.D. dissertation, Harvard University, 1969.

Gray, John. "Canaanite Kingship in Theory and Practice." Vetus Testamentum 2 (1952):193-220.

_____. I & 2 Kings. A Commentary. Philadelphia: Westminster Press, 1963.

_____. The Legacy of Canaan. Supplement to Vetus Testamentum 5. Leiden: E. J. Brill, 1965.

_____. "Sacral Kingship in Ugarit." Ugaritica VI. Mission de Ras Shamra. Vol. 17. Paris: Paul Geuthner, 1969. Pp. 289-302.

_____, ed. Joshua, Judges and Ruth. The Century Bible. New ed. London: Thomas Nelson and Sons, Ltd., 1967.

Greenfield, Jonas C. "Aramaic." The Interpreter's Dictionary of the Bible. Supplementary volume. Edited by Keith Crim. Nashville: Abingdon Press, 1976. Pp. 39-44.

Gressman, Hugo. "Altar." Die Religion in Geschichte und Gegenwart. Edited by Herman Gunkel. Tübingen: J. C. B. Mohr (Paul Siebeck), 1909. 1:371-73.

_____. Ausgrabungen in Palästina und das Alte Testament. Tübingen: Verlag von J. C. B. Mohr (Paul Siebeck), 1908.

_____. Der Messias. Göttingen: Vandenhoeck & Ruprecht, 1929.

_____. "Teraphim." Zeitschrift für altestamentliche Wissenschaft 40 (1922):75-137.

_____, ed. Altorientalische Bilder zum Alten Testament. 2d ed. Berlin: Walter de Gruyter & Co., 1926.

_____. Altorientalische Texte zum Alten Testament. 2d ed. Berlin: Walter de Gruyter & Co., 1926.

Grohmann, Adolf. Göttersymbole und Symboltiere auf südarabischen Denkmälern. Wien: Alfred Hölder, 1914.

Groot, Johannes de. Die Altäre des Salomonische Tempelhofes. Stuttgart: W. Kohlhammer, 1924.

Gunkel, Hermann. Ausgewählte Psalmen. Göttingen: Vandenhoeck & Ruprecht, 1904.

_____. Einleitung in die Psalmen. Göttingen: Vandenhoeck & Ruprecht, 1966.

_____. Die Psalmen. Göttingen: Vandenhoeck & Ruprecht, 1968.

_____. Schöpfung und Chaos in Urzeit und Endzeit. Göttingen: Vandenhoeck und Ruprecht, 1895.

Gurney, Oliver R. "Babylonian Prophylatic Figures and Their Rituals." Annals of Archaeology and Anthropology 22 (1935): 31-96.

_____. "Hittite Kingship." Myth, Ritual, and Religion. Edited by Samuel H. Hooke. Oxford: Clarendon Press, 1960. Pp. 103-121.

_____. "The Sultantepe Tablets 4. The Guthaean Legend of Naram-Sin." Anatolian Studies 5 (1955):93-113.

_____. "The Sultantepe Tablets VI: A Letter of Gilgamesh." Anatolian Studies 7 (1957):127-29.

Güterbock, Hans G. "Authority and Law in the Hittite Kingdom." In Authority and Law in the Ancient Orient. John A. Wilson, Ephraim A. Speiser, Hans G. Güterbock, et al. Supplement to the Journal of the American Oriental Society, no. 17. Baltimore: American Oriental Society, 1954. Pp. 16-24.

_____. "Keilschrifttexte nach Kopien von T. G. Pinches. 11. Bruchstück eines altbabylonischen Naram-Sin-Epos." Archiv für Orientforschung 13 (1939-41):46-50.

_____. "Matériaux pour l'étude des relations entre Ugarit et le Hatti." *Ugaritica III*. Edited by Claude F.-A. Schaeffer. Mission de Ras Shamra. Vol. 8. Paris: Paul Geuthner, 1956. Pp. 1-163.

Güterbock, Hans G., and Jacobsen, Thorkild, eds. *Studies in Honor of Benno Landsberger on His Seventy-fifth Birthday, April 21, 1965*. Assyriological Studies, 16. Chicago: University Press, 1965.

Habel, Norman C. *The Book of Job*. The Cambridge Bible Commentary. London: Cambridge University Press, 1975.

Hallo, William W. "Individual Prayer in Sumerian: The Continuity of a Tradition." *Journal of the American Oriental Society* 88 (1968):71-89.

_____. "On the Antiquity of Sumerian Literature." *Journal of the American Oriental Society* 83 (1963):167-76.

_____. "Toward a History of Sumerian Literature." *Sumerological Studies in Honor of Thorkild Jacobson on His Seventieth Birthday, June 7, 1974*. Chicago: University Press, 1976. Pp. 181-203.

Hammond, Joseph. *1 and 2 Kings*. The Pulpit Commentary. Grand Rapids: Wm. B. Eerdmans Publishing Co., 1977.

Harding, G. Lankester. *An Index and Concordance of Pre-Islamic Arabian Names and Inscriptions*. Toronto: University Press, 1971.

Harper, William R. *A Critical and Exegetical Commentary on Amos and Hosea*. International Critical Commentary. Edinburgh: T. & T. Clark, 1953.

Harris, Zellig S. *The Development of the Canaanite Dialects*. American Oriental Series, 16. New Haven, CT: American Oriental Society, 1939.

_____. "Expression of the Causative in Ugaritic." *Journal of the American Oriental Society* 58 (1938):103-11.

_____. "Linguistic Structure of Hebrew." *Journal of the American Oriental Society* 61 (1941):143-67.

Harrison, Roland K. "Daniel, Book of." *The Zondervan Pictorial Encyclopedia of the Bible*. Grand Rapids: Zondervan Publishing House, 1975.

_____. Introduction to the Old Testament with a Comprehensive Review of Old Testament Studies and a Special Supplement on the Apocrypha. Grand Rapids: Wm. B. Eerdmans, 1969.

_____. Jeremiah and Lamentations. Tyndale Old Testament Commentaries. Downers Grove, IL: Inter-Varsity Press, 1973.

_____. "Zechariah, Book of." The Zondervan Pictorial Encyclopedia of the Bible. Grand Rapids: Zondervan Publishing House, 1975.

Hartman, Louis F., and Di Lella, Alexander. The Book of Daniel. The Anchor Bible. Garden City, NY: Doubleday, 1978.

Hasel, Gerhard F. "The 'Little Horn,' the Saints and the Sanctuary in Daniel 8." Studies in the Sanctuary and the Atonement. Edited by Arnold Wallenkampf. Washington, D.C.: General Conference of Seventh-day Adventists, 1980. (Forthcoming.)

_____. Old Testament Theology: Basic Issues in the Current Debate. Rev. ed. Grand Rapids: Wm. B. Eerdmans Publishing Company, 1975.

_____. The Remnant. Andrews University Monographs Studies in Religion. Vol. 5. Berrien Springs, MI: Andrews University Press, 1974.

_____. "General Principles of Biblical Interpretation." North American Bible Conference 1974: Notebook Prepared by the General Conference of Seventh-day Adventists Biblical Re-Research Committee. N.p., 1974.

_____. "General Principles of Interpretation." A Symposium on Biblical Hermeneutics. Edited by Gordon M. Hyde. Washington, D.C.: The Review and Herald Publishing Association, 1974. Pp. 163-93.

Hatch, Edwin, and Redpath, Henry A., eds. A Concordance to the Septuagint and the Other Greek Versions of the Old Testament. 2 vols. Graz: Akademische Drucks-und Verlagsanstalt, 1954. Reprint ed. 1975.

Hastings, James, ed. A Dictionary of the Bible. 5 vols. Edinburgh: T. & T. Clark, 1898-1904.

Haupt, Paul. Die akkadische Sprache. Berlin: A. Asher & Co., 1883.

_____. "The Prototype of the Magnificat." Zeitschrift der deutschen Morgenländischen Gesellschaft 58 (1904):617-32.

_____. "Schmücket das Fest mit Maien." Zeitschrift für die alttestamentliche Wissenschaft 35 (1915):102-9.

Heaton, Eric W. The Book of Daniel. Torch Bible Commentary. London: SCM Press, 1956.

Heidel, Alexander. The Babylonian Genesis. First Phoenix ed. Chicago: University Press, 1963.

Heim, Suzanne M. Ladders to Heaven. Toronto: Royal Ontario Museum, 1979.

Heimpel, Wolfgang. Tierbilder in der Sumerischen Literatur. Studia Pohl, 2. Rome: Pontificium Institutum Biblicum, 1968.

Helmbold, Andrew K. "Micah the Prophet." The Zondervan Pictorial Encyclopedia of the Bible. Grand Rapids: Zondervan Publishing House, 1975. 4:214-16.

Henderson, Ebenezer. The Book of the Prophet Jeremiah and That of the Lamentation. London: Hamilton, Adams Co., 1851.

Hengstenberg, Ernst W. Christology of the Old Testament and a Commentary on the Messianic Predictions. 4 vols. Grand Rapids: Kregel Publications, 1956.

Herdner, Andrée. Corpus des Tablettes en Cunéiformes Alphabétiques. Mission de Ras Shamra, 10. 2 vols. Paris: Imprimerie Nationale, 1963.

Herodotus. Translated by A. D. Godley. Vols. 2-3. Loeb Classical Library.

Hertzberg, Hans W. Die Bücher Joshua, Richter, Ruth. Das Alte Testament Deutsch. Vol. 9. Göttingen: Vandenhoeck & Ruprecht, 1953.

_____. 1 and 2 Samuel: A Commentary. Philadelphia: The Westminster Press; SCM Press Ltd., 1964.

Hieronymus (Jerome), S. "Commentarium in Hiezechielem." In Corpus Christianorum. Series Latina, 75. Turnholti: Typographi Brepols Editores Pontifici, 1964.

Hillers, Delbert R. Lamentations. Anchor Bible. Garden City, NY: Doubleday & Company, Inc., 1972.

Hinke, William J. A New Boundary Stone of Nebuchadrezzar I from Nippur. The Babylonian Expedition of the University of Pennsylvania Series D: Researches and Treatises. Edited by H. V. Hilprecht. Philadelphia: University of Pennsylvania, 1907.

Hirzel, Ludwig. Hiob. Kurzgefasstes exegetisches Handbuch zum Alten Testament. Leipzig: Weidmannsche Buchandlung, 1839. S. Hirzel, 1869.

Hoftijzer, Jacob, and Kooij, G. Van der. Aramaic Texts from Deir ʿAllā. Leiden: E. J. Brill, 1976.

Holladay, William L. A Concise Hebrew and Aramaic Lexicon of the Old Testament. Grand Rapids: Wm. B. Eerdmans, 1971.

Hölscher, Gustav. Das Buch Hiob. Handbuch zum Alten Testament, 17. Tübingen: J. C. B. Mohr (Paul Siebeck), 1957.

Hooke, Samuel H., ed. Myth, Ritual and Kingship. Oxford: Clarendon Press, 1960.

Horst, Friedrich. Hiob. Biblischer Kommentar Altes Testament. Neukirchen, Vluyn: Neukirchener Verlag, 1968.

_____. Die Zwölf Kleinen Propheten: Nahum bis Maleachi. Handbuch zum Alten Testament, 14. Tübingen: J. C. B. Mohr (Paul Siebeck), 1938. Pp. 153-267.

Howard, G. Clavis Cuneorum sive Lexicon signorum assyriorum. London: Apud H. Milford, 1904-33.

Hoyningen-Huene, George, and Steindorff, George. Egypt. 2d rev. ed. New York: J. J. Augustin Publisher, 1945.

Hrouda, Barthel. "Tell Fechērīje," Zeitschrift für Assyriologie 54 (1961):201-39.

Huffman, Herbert B. Amorite Personal Names in the Mari Texts. Baltimore: The Johns Hopkins Press, 1965.

Hyatt, J. Philip. Commentary on Exodus. New Century Bible. London: Oliphants, 1971.

Irwin, William A. "The Psalm of Habakkuk." Journal of Near Eastern Studies 1 (1942):10-40.

Jack, J. William. The Ras Shamra Tablets and Their Bearing upon the Old Testament. Old Testament Studies, no. 1. Edinburgh: T. & T. Clark, 1935.

Jacobs, Vivian, and Isaac, R. "The Myth of Môt and ʾAlʾeyan Baʿal." Harvard Theological Review 38 (1945):77-109.

Jacobsen, Thorkild. The Sumerian King List. Assyriological Studies, no. 11. Chicago: The University of Chicago Press, 1939.

_____. "Mesopotomian Religion." An Encyclopedia of Religion. Edited by Vergilius Ferm. New York: The Philosophical Library, 1945.

_____. "Sumerian Mythology: A Review Article." Journal of Near Eastern Studies 5 (1946):128-52.

_____. "The Myth of Inanna and Bilulu." Journal of Near Eastern Studies 12 (153):160-87.

_____. "Early Political Development in Mesopotamia." Zeitschrift für Assyriologie 52 (1957):91-140.

_____. "About the Sumerian Verb." In Studies in Honor of Benno Landsberger on His Seventy-fifth Birthday, April 21, 1965. Assyriological Studies, no. 16. Chicago: University Press, 1965. Pp. 71-101.

_____. "Samuel Noah Kramer: An Appreciation." In Kramer Anniversary Volume. Alter Orient und Altes Testament 25 (1976):xiii-xvi.

Jamme, Albert. "Le panthéon sud-arabe préislamique d'après les sources épigraphiques." Le Muséon 40 (1947):57-147.

_____. Sabaean Inscriptions from Maḥram Bilqîs (Mârib). Publications of the American Foundation for the Study of Man. Vol. 3. Baltimore: The Johns Hopkins Press, 1962.

_____. Sabaean and Ḥasaean Inscriptions from Saudi-Arabia. Studi Semitics, 23. Rome: Istituto di Studi del Vicino Oriente, 1966.

_____, trans. "South Arabian Inscriptions." Ancient Near Eastern Texts. Edited by James Pritchard. Princeton, NJ: University Press, 1966. Pp. 663-70.

Jaritz, Kurt. Schriftarchäologie der altmesopotamischen Kultur. Graz: Akademische Druck-und Verlagsanstalt, 1967.

Jaroš, Karl. "Des Mose 'strahlende Haut'." Zeitschrift für die alttestamentliche Wissenschaft 88 (1976):275-81.

Jastrow, Marcus. A Dictionary of the Targumin, the Talmud Babli and Yerushalmi, and the Midrashic Literature. New York: Pardes Publishing House, Inc., 1943.

Jastrow, Morris. The Civilization of Babylonia and Assyria. Philadelphia: J. B. Lippincott Co., 1915.

Jean, Charles-F. "Arišen dans les Lettres de Mari." Semitica 1 (1948):17-21.

Jean, Charles-F., and Hoftijzer, Jacob. Dictionnaire des Inscriptions sémitiques de l'Ouest. Leiden: E. J. Brill, 1965.

Jeffery, Arthur. "The Book of Daniel: Introduction and Exegesis." Interpreter's Bible. New York: Abingdon Press, 1956. 6:341-549.

⸺. "Aramaic." Interpreter's Dictionary of the Bible. New York: Abingdon Press, 1962.

Jenks, William, ed. The Comprehensive Commentary on the Holy Bible. Philadelphia: Lippincott Grambo & Co., 1852.

Jenni, Ernst. "אצי̇ jṣʾ hinausgehen." Theologisches Handwörterbuch zum Alten Testament. Edited by Ernst Jenni and Claus Westermann. München: Chr. Kaiser Verlag, 1971.

Jenni, Ernst, and Westermann, Claus. Theologisches Handwörterbuch zum Alten Testament. München: Chr. Kaiser Verlag, 1971. 1:755-62.

Jeremias, Alfred. Handbuch der altorientalischen Geisteskultur. 2d ed. Leipzig: Walter de Gruyter & Co., 1929.

⸺. Das Alte Testament im Lichte des Alten Orients. 4th rev. ed. Leipzig: J. C. Hinrichs, 1930.

Jeremias, Christian. Die Nachtgesichte des Sacharja. Göttingen: Vandenhoeck & Ruprecht, 1977.

Jeremias, Joachim. "ποιμήν B. Transferred Usage." Theological Dictionary of the New Testament. Grand Rapids: Wm. B. Eerdmans, 1977. 6:487-88.

Jirku, Anton. "Die Gesichtsmaske des Mose." Zeitschrift des deutschen Palästina-Vereins 67 (1944-45):43-45.

Jöcken, Peter. Das Buch Habakuk. Bonner Biblische Beiträge, 48. Köln-Bonn: Peter Hanstein Verlag, GMBH, 1977.

Johnson, Aubrey R. Sacral Kingship in Ancient Israel. Cardiff: University of Wales Press, 1967.

Jones, Bruce W. "More about the Apocalypse and Apocalyptic." Journal of Biblical Literature 87 (1968):325-27.

⸺. Ideas of History in the Book of Daniel. Ph.D. dissertation, Ann Arbor, MI, 1972.

Joüon, P. Paul. Grammaire de l'Hébreu Biblique. 2d rev. ed. Rome: Institut Biblique Pontifical, 1947.

Kallas, James. "The Apocalypse--An Apocalyptic Book?" Journal of Biblical Literature 86 (1967):69-80.

Kapelrud, Arvid S. Baal in the Ras Shamra Texts. Copenhagen: G.E.C. Gad, 1952.

_____. "Ugarit." Interpreter's Dictionary of the Bible. New York: Abingdon Press, 1962. 4:724-32.

_____. The Ras Shamra Discoveries. Norman, OK: University of Oklahoma Press, 1963.

_____. "Baal and the Devourers." Ugaritica VI. Mission de Ras Shamra. Vol. 17. Paris: Paul Geuthner, 1969. Pp. 319-32.

_____. The Violent Goddess Anat in the Ras Shamra Texts. Oslo: Universitätsforlaget, 1969.

Karageorghis, Vassos. "Notes on Some Cypriote Priests Wearing Bull-Masks." Harvard Theological Review 64 (1971):261-70.

Karo, Georg H. "Altar B. Ägäischer Kreis." Reallexikon der Vorgeschichte. Berlin: Walter de Gruyter & Co., 1924.

Kaufmann, Yehezkel. The Religion of Israel's Faith. Translated by Moshe Greenberg. Chicago: The University of Chicago Press, 1960.

Kautzsch, Emil. Biblische Theologie des Alten Testamentes. Tübingen: J. C. B. Mohr (Paul Siebeck), 1911.

_____. Kautzsch, Emil. Die Apokryphen und Pseudepigraphen des Alten Testaments. 2 vols. Hildesheim: Georg Olms, 1962.

Kautzsch, Emil, and Cowley, Arthur E. Gesenius' Hebrew Grammar. 2d ed. Oxford: Clarendon Press, 1976.

Keel, Othmar. Wirkmächtige Siegeszeichen. Orbis Biblicus et Orientales, 5. Freiburg, Switzerland: Universitätsverlag Freiburg, 1974

_____. The Symbolism of the Biblical World. Translated by Timothy J. Hallett. New York: The Seabury Press, 1978.

Kees, Hermann. Die Hohenpriester des Amun von Karnak von Herihor bis zum Ende der Äthiopenzeit. Probleme der Ägyptologie. Vol. 4. Leiden: E. J. Brill, 1944.

_____. Das Priestertum im ägyptischen Staat von neuen Reich bis zur Spätzeit. Probleme der Ägyptologie. Vol. 1. Leiden: E. J. Brill, 1953.

Keet, Cuthbert C. *A Study of the Psalms of Ascents: A Critical and Exegetical Commentary upon Psalms 120-134.* London: The Mitre Press, 1969.

Keil, Carl F. *Biblical Commentary on the Prophecies of Ezekiel.* Vol. 2. Biblical Commentary on the Old Testament. Grand Rapids: Wm. B. Eerdmans, 1952.

_____. *The Book of the Kings.* Biblical Commentary on the Old Testament. Grand Rapids: Wm. B. Eerdmans Publishing Co., 1952.

_____. *The Prophecies of Jeremiah.* Biblical Commentary on the Old Testament. Grand Rapids: Wm. B. Eerdmans Publishing Co., 1960.

_____. *The Twelve Minor Prophets.* Biblical Commentary on the Old Testament. Grand Rapids: Wm. B. Eerdmans Publishing Co., 1961.

_____. *The Book of the Prophet Daniel.* Biblical Commentary on the Old Testament. Edinburgh: T. & T. Clark, 1872.

Keil, Carl F., and Delitzsch, Franz J. *Biblical Commentary on the Books of Samuel.* Grand Rapids: Wm. B. Eerdmans, 1952.

_____. *The Pentateuch.* 3 vols. Biblical Commentary on the Old Testament. Grand Rapids: Wm. E. Eerdmans Publishing Company, [1952].

_____. *The Prophecies of Jeremiah.* Biblical Commentary on the Old Testament. 2 vols. Grand Rapids: Wm. B. Eerdmans Publishing Company, 1956.

Kennett, Robert H. "Notes and Studies Zechariah 12-13." *Journal of Theological Studies* 28 (1927):1-9.

Kershaw, Norma. "The Bible Comes to Life at the Jewish Museum." *Biblical Archaeology Review* 3 (1977):45-46.

Key, Andrew F. "Traces of the Worship of the Moon God Sin among the Early Israelites." *Journal of Biblical Literature* 84 (1965):20-26.

Kidner, Derek. *Genesis: An Introduction and Commentary.* Downers Grove, IL: Inter-Varsity Press, 1974.

_____. *Psalms 73-150: A Commentary on Books 3-5 on the Psalms.* London: Inter-Varsity Press, 1975.

Kissane, Edward J. *The Book of Job.* New York: Sheed & Ward, 1946.

_____. The Book of Psalms. Dublin: Browne and Nolan, [1964].

Kitchen, Kenneth A. "The King List of Ugarit." Ugarit-Forschungen. Neukirchen-Vluyn: Neukirchener Verlag, 1970. 9:131-42.

Kittel, Rudolf. Die Bücher der Könige. Handkommentar zum Alten Testament. Göttingen: Vandenhoeck & Ruprecht, 1900.

Klein, Jacob. Šulgi D: A Neo-Sumerian Royal Hymn. Ph.D. dissertation, University of Pennsylvania, 1968.

Klostermann, August. Die Bücher Samuelis und der Könige. Nördlingen: Beck, 1887.

Knudtzon, Jørgen A. Die El-Amarna-Tafeln. 2 vols. Aalen: Otto Zeller, 1964.

Koch, Klaus. The Rediscovery of Apocalyptic. Studies in Biblical Theology, 22. London: SCM Press, 1972.

Köcher, Franz. "Ein Inventartext aus Kār-Tukulti-Ninurta." Archiv für Orientforschung 18 (1957-58):300-13.

Koehler, Ludwig, and Baumgartner, Walter, eds. Lexicon in Veteris Testamenti Libros. Grand Rapids: Wm. B. Eerdmans, 1958.

Köhler, Ludwig. "Zu Jes. 28:15[a] und 18[b]." Zeitschrift für die alttestamentliches Wissenschaft 48 (1930):227-28.

König, Eduard. Die Psalmen. Gütersloh: C. Bertelsmann, 1927.

_____. Hebräisches und aramäisches Wörterbuch zum Alten Testament. 6th and 7th eds. Leipzig: Dietrich'sche Verlagsbuchhandlung, 1936.

Koschaker, Paul. "Kleidersymbolik in Keilschriftrechten." ACTES du 20e Congrès International des Orientalistes, Bruxelles 5-10 September 1938. Louvain: Bureaux du Muséon, 1940.

Kraeling, Emil G. Aram and Israel. New York: Columbia University Press, 1918.

_____. The Brooklyn Museum Aramaic Papyri. New Haven: The Yale University Press, 1953.

_____. Rand McNally Bible Atlas. New York: Rand McNally, 1956.

Kramer, Samuel N. "A Matter of Method in Sumerology." The American Journal of Semitic Languages and Literatures 49 (1932-33): 229-47.

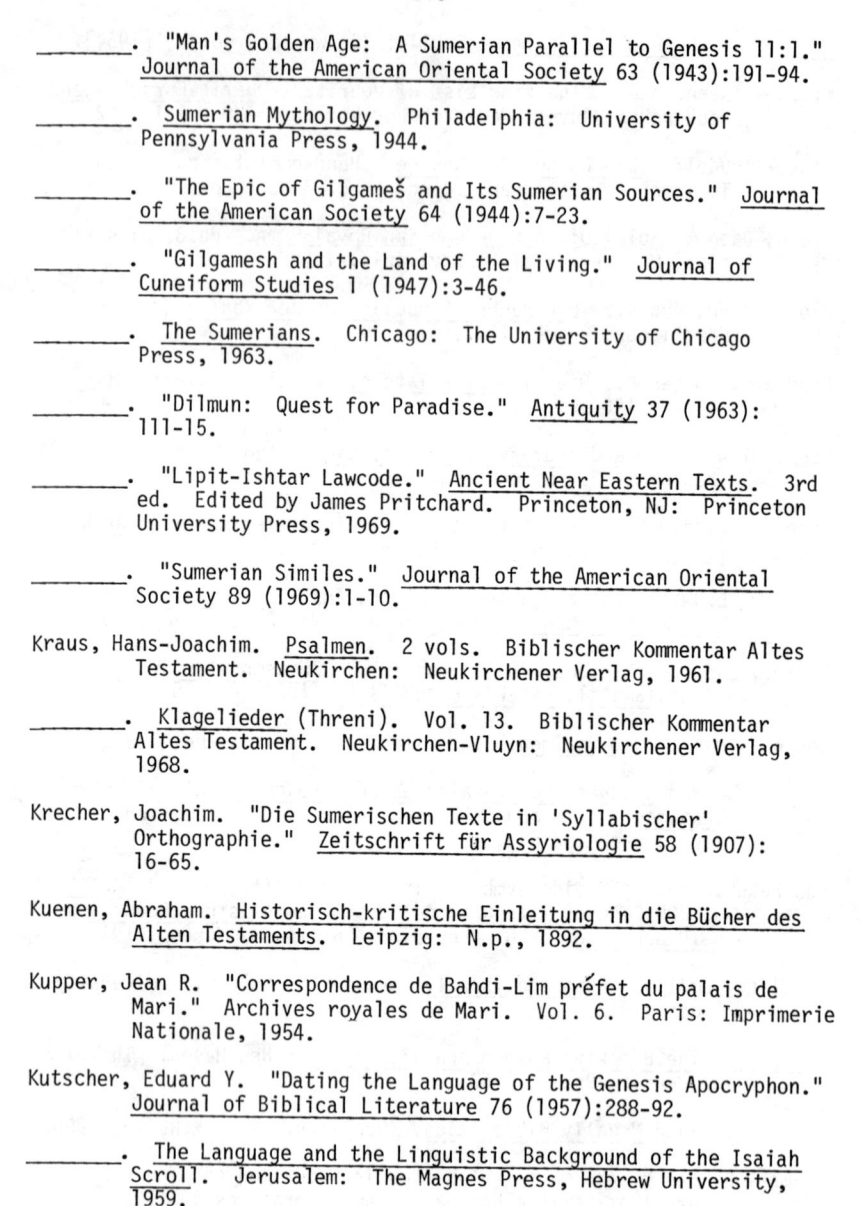

_____. "Man's Golden Age: A Sumerian Parallel to Genesis 11:1." *Journal of the American Oriental Society* 63 (1943):191-94.

_____. *Sumerian Mythology*. Philadelphia: University of Pennsylvania Press, 1944.

_____. "The Epic of Gilgameš and Its Sumerian Sources." *Journal of the American Society* 64 (1944):7-23.

_____. "Gilgamesh and the Land of the Living." *Journal of Cuneiform Studies* 1 (1947):3-46.

_____. *The Sumerians*. Chicago: The University of Chicago Press, 1963.

_____. "Dilmun: Quest for Paradise." *Antiquity* 37 (1963): 111-15.

_____. "Lipit-Ishtar Lawcode." *Ancient Near Eastern Texts*. 3rd ed. Edited by James Pritchard. Princeton, NJ: Princeton University Press, 1969.

_____. "Sumerian Similes." *Journal of the American Oriental Society* 89 (1969):1-10.

Kraus, Hans-Joachim. *Psalmen*. 2 vols. Biblischer Kommentar Altes Testament. Neukirchen: Neukirchener Verlag, 1961.

_____. *Klagelieder* (Threni). Vol. 13. Biblischer Kommentar Altes Testament. Neukirchen-Vluyn: Neukirchener Verlag, 1968.

Krecher, Joachim. "Die Sumerischen Texte in 'Syllabischer' Orthographie." *Zeitschrift für Assyriologie* 58 (1907): 16-65.

Kuenen, Abraham. *Historisch-kritische Einleitung in die Bücher des Alten Testaments*. Leipzig: N.p., 1892.

Kupper, Jean R. "Correspondence de Bahdi-Lim préfet du palais de Mari." Archives royales de Mari. Vol. 6. Paris: Imprimerie Nationale, 1954.

Kutscher, Eduard Y. "Dating the Language of the Genesis Apocryphon." *Journal of Biblical Literature* 76 (1957):288-92.

_____. *The Language and the Linguistic Background of the Isaiah Scroll*. Jerusalem: The Magnes Press, Hebrew University, 1959.

_____. "Review of <u>The Genesis Apocryphon of Qumran Cave I</u>, by Joseph A. Fitzmyer." <u>Orientalia</u> 39 (1970):178-83.

_____. "Aramaic." <u>Current Trends of Linguistics</u>. Vol. 6. Edited by Thomas A. Sebeok. The Hague: Mouton, 1970. Pp. 347-77.

_____. "Aramaic." <u>Encyclopaedia Judaica</u>. Jerusalem: Keter Publishing House, 1971. 3:259-87.

_____. <u>Hebrew and Aramaic Studies</u>. Jerusalem: The Magnes Press. Hebrew University, 1977.

Labat, René. "Elam and Western Persia." <u>Cambridge Ancient History</u>. 3d ed. Cambridge: University Press, 1975. 2:482-506.

Lacocque, André. <u>The Book of Daniel</u>. Translated by David Pellauer. Atlanta: John Knox Press, 1979.

Laessøe, Jørgen. "Literacy and Oral Tradition in Ancient Mesopotamia." <u>Studia Orientalia Ioanni Pedersen 70th Anniversary, Nov. 7, 1953</u>. Copenhagen: Einar Munksgard, 1953. Pp. 205-18.

Lagarde, Paulo de, ed. <u>Bibliothecae Syriaca</u>. Göttingen: Luederi Horstmann, 1892.

Lambert, Mayer. <u>Traité de Grammaire Hébraÿque</u>. Hildesheim: Verlag dr. H.A. Gerstenberg, 1972.

Lambert, Wilfred G. "A Catalogue of Texts and Authors." <u>Journal of Cuneiform Studies</u> 16 (1962):59-77.

_____. "The Gula Hymn of Bulutsa-rabi." <u>Orientalia</u> 36 (1967): 105-29.

Landsberger, Benno. <u>Die Fauna des alten Mesopotamia nach den 14. Tafel der Series ḪAR-ra = Ḫubullu</u>. Leipzig: S. Hirzel, 1934.

Landtman, Gunnar. "Priest, Priesthood." <u>Encyclopaedia of Religion and Ethics</u>. Edited by James Hastings. New York: Charles Scribner's Sons, 1919. 10:278-84.

Lane, Edward William. <u>An Arabic-English Lexikon</u>. London: Williams and Norgate, 1893.

Lang, George H. <u>The Histories and Prophecies of Daniel</u>. Grand Rapids: Kregel Publications, 1943.

Langdon, Stephen. *The Annals of Ashurbanipal: A Glossary in English and German and Brief Notes.* Semitic Studies Series, Vol. 2. Leiden: E. J. Brill, 1903.

_____. *Sumerian and Babylonian Psalms.* Paris: Paul Geuthner, 1909.

_____. *A Sumerian Grammar and Chrestomathy.* Paris: Paul Geuthner, 1911.

Langhe, Robert de. "L'autel d'or du temple de Jérusalem." *Biblica* 40 (1959):476-94.

Lapp, Paul W. "The 1963 Excavation at Taʿannek." *Bulletin of the American Schools of Oriental Research* 173 (1964):4-44.

Legrain, Leon. *Historical Fragments.* Publications of the Babylonian Section, Vol. 13. Philadelphia: University Museum, 1922.

_____. *The Culture of the Babylonians from their Seals.* Publications of the Babylonian Section, Vol. 14. Philadelphia: University Museum, 1925.

Leslau, Wolf. "Ethiopic and South Arabian." In *Current Trends in Linguistics.* Vol. 6. Edited by Thomas A. Sebeok. The Hague: Mouton, 1970. Pp. 467-527.

Leupold, Herbert C. *Expositions of the Psalms.* Columbus, OH: Wartburg Press, 1959.

_____. *Exposition of Daniel.* Grand Rapids: Baker Book House Co., 1969.

_____. *Exposition of Zechariah.* Grand Rapids: Baker Book House, 1978.

Lewy, Hildegard. "The Nuzian Feudal System." *Orientalia* 11 (1942):297-349.

_____. "Assyria c. 2600-1816 B.C." *Cambridge Ancient History.* 3rd ed. Cambridge: At the University Press, 1971. Vol. 1, pt. 2, pp. 729-70.

Lewy, Julius. "Some Aspects of Commercial Life in Assyria and Asia Minor in the Nineteenth Pre-Christian Century." *Journal of the American Oriental Society* 78 (1958):89-101.

Ley, Julius. *Die metrischen Formen der hebräischen Poesie systematisch dargelegt.* Leipzig: B. G. Teubner, 1866.

Lias, John J. *Joshua: Exposition and Homiletics.* The Pulpit Commentary. Grand Rapids: Wm. B. Eerdmans, 1977.

Liddell, Henry G., and Scott, Robert, eds. A Greek-English Lexicon. Rev. ed. 2 vols. Oxford: At the Clarendon Press, 1940.

Lidzbarski, Mark. Handbuch der nordsemitischen Epigraphik nebst ausgewählten Inschriften. Weimar, 1898; reprint ed. Hildesheim: Georg Olm, 1962.

_____. "König Zkr von Hamath." Ephemeris für semitische Epigraphik. Giessen: Alfred Töpelmann, 1915. 3:1-11.

_____. "Ein phönizische Inschrift aus Zendschirli." Ephemeris für semitische Epigraphik. Giessen: Alfred Töpelmann, 1915. 3:218-38.

_____. Altaramäische Urkunden aus Assur. Osnabrück: Otto Zeller, 1970.

Lieberman, J. Stephen. The Sumerian Loanwords in Old-Babylonian Akkadian. Harvard Semitic Studies, no. 22. Missoula, MT: Scholars Press, 1977.

Lipiński, Edward. "Les conceptions et couches merveilleuses de ʿAnath." Syria 42 (1965):44-73.

Lisowsky, Gerhard. Konkordanz zum Hebräischen Alten Testament. Stuttgart: Württ. Bibelanstalt, 1958.

Lohmann, Paul. "Der Altar im altbabylonischen Kulturkreise." In Kurt Galling. Der Altar in den Kulturen des alten Orients. Berlin: Karl Curtis, 1925.

_____. "Der assyrischer Altar." In Kurt Galling. Der Altar in Kulturen des alten Orients. Berlin: Karl Curtis, 1925.

Løkkegaard, Frede. "A Plea for El, the Bull and Other Ugaritic Miscellanies." Studia Orientalia Ioanni Pedersen Septuagenaria. Pp. 219-35. Copenhagen: Einar Munksgaard, 1953.

Luckenbill, Daniel D. Ancient Records of Assyria and Babylonia. Chicago: The University Press, 1926.

Lurker, Manfred. In Memorian Eckhard Unger: Beiträge zu Geschichte, Kultur und Religion des alten Orients. Baden-Baden: Valentin Koerner, 1971.

Luschan, Felix von. Die Kleinfunde von Sendschirli. Edited by Walter Andrae. Ausgrabungen in Sendschirli 5 of Mitteilungen aus den Orientalischen Sammlungen, Vol. 15. Berlin: Walter de Gruyter & Co., 1945.

McCrindle, John W. The Invasion of India by Alexander the Great. Westminster: 1896; reprint ed. New York: Barnes & Noble, 1969.

McKane, William. _1. & 2. Samuel: Introduction and Commentary._
London: SCM Press, Ltd., 1963.

McKeating, Henry. _The Books of Amos, Hosea and Micah._ The
Cambridge Bible Commentary. Cambridge: University Press,
1971.

Macalister, R. A. Stewart. _The Excavation of Gezer 1902-1905 and
1907-1909._ 2 vols. London: John Jurray, 1912.

MacCulloch, John A. "Horns." _Encyclopaedia of Religion and Ethics._
Edited by James Hastings. New York: Charles Scribner's
Sons, 1914.

MacRae, Allan. "Prophets and Prophecy." _The Zondervan Pictorial
Encyclopedia of the Bible._ Grand Rapids: Zondervan
Publishing House, 1975. 4:875-903.

Malamat, Abraham. "Aram, Arameans." _Encyclopaedia Judaica._
Jerusalem: Keter Publishing House, 1971. 3:252-56.

Mallowan, Max E. L. "The Early Dynastic Period." In _The
Cambridge Ancient History._ 3rd ed. Cambridge: At the
University Press, 1971.

Malten, Ludolf. "Der Stier in Kult und mythischem Bild." _Jahrbuch
des deutschen archäologischen Instituts_ 43 (1928):90-139.

Mandelkern, Solomon. _Veteris Testamenti Concordantiae Hebraicae
atque Chaldaicae._ 2d rev. ed. Leipzig: F. Margolin, 1925.

Margalit, Baruch. "The Geographical Setting of the Aqht Story and
its Ramification." Paper presented at the Ugarit Symposium,
Session 2: "Ugarit and the Bible," at the joint meetings
of the Middle West Branch of the American Oriental Society
and the Mid-West Region of the Society of Biblical Literature, University of Wisconsin, Madison, 25 to 27 February 1979.

_____. "Studia Ugaritica II: Studies in Krt and Aqht."
Ugarit-Forschungen. Neukirchen-Vluyn: Neukirchener
Verlag, 1970. 2:139-58.

Marti, Karl. _Das Buch Daniel._ Kurzer Hand-Commentar zum Alten
Testament. Vol. 18. Tübingen: J. C. B. Mohr, 1901.

_____. _Das Buch Jesaja._ Kurzer Hand-Commentar zum Alten
Testament. Tübingen: J. C. B. Mohr (Paul Siebeck), 1900.

_____. _Das Dodekapropheton._ Tübingen: J. C. B. Mohr
(Paul Siebeck), 1904.

Matthews, Isaac G. _Ezekiel._ An American Commentary on the Old
Testament. Philadelphia: American Baptist Publication
Society, 1939.

Mauchline, John, ed. 1 and 2 Samuel. New Century Bible. London: Oliphants, 1971.

May, Herbert G., ed. Oxford Bible Atlas. 2d ed. London: Oxford University Press, 1974.

Mays, James L. Amos: A Commentary. Philadelphia: The Westminster Press, 1976.

_____. Micah. A Commentary. Old Testament Library, 1976. Philadelphia: Westminster Press, 1976.

Meade, C. Wade. Road to Babylon. Leiden: E. J. Brill, 1974.

Meek, Theophile J. "The Book of Lamentations." Interpreter's Bible. Edited by George A. Buttrick. New York: Abingdon Press, 1956. 6:3-38.

_____. "The Code of Hammurabi." Ancient Near Eastern Texts. 3rd ed. Edited by James Pritchard. Princeton, NJ: Princeton University Press, 1969.

Meissner, Bruno. "Assyrische Jagden." Der alte Orient 13 (1911):3-32.

_____. Babylonien und Assyria. 2 Vols. Heidelberg: Carl Winter, 1920-25.

_____. Beiträge zum assyrischen Wörterbuch. Chicago: University Press, 1931.

_____. "Grundzüge der altbabylonischen Plastik." Der alte Orient 15 (1914):1-64.

_____. "Grundzüge der mittel- und neubabylonischen und der assyrischen Plastik." Der alte Orient 15 (1915):65-151.

Mellaart, James. Çatal Hüyük: A Neolithic Town in Anatolia. New York: Hill Book Company, 1967.

Mellinkoff, Ruth. The Horned Moses in Medieval Art and Thought. Berkeley: University of California Press, 1970.

Mendenhall, George. "On a Visit with a Druzi Witch." 1972-73 Newsletter No. 9. Annual of the American School of Oriental Research (April 1973):1-4.

_____. "On a Visit with a Druzi Witch." 1972-73 Newsletter No. 10. Annual of the American School of Oriental Research (May 1973):1-2.

_____. *The Tenth Generation: The Origins of the Biblical Tradition.* Baltimore: The Johns Hopkins University Press, 1973.

Mercatante, Anthony S. *Who's Who in Egyptian Mythology.* New York: Clarkson N. Potter, Inc., Publishers, 1978.

Mercer, Samuel A. B. *The Pyramid Texts in Translation and Commentary.* 4 Vols. New York: Longmans, Green and Co., 1959.

_____. *The Tell El-Amarna Tablets.* 2 Vols. Toronto: Macmillan Co., 1939.

Meshel, Ze'ev. "Did Yahweh have a Consort? *Biblical Archaeology Review* 5 (1979):24-35.

Metzger, Bruce M. "Himmlische und irdische Wohnstatt Jahwes." In *Ugarit Forschungen.* Neukirchen-Vluyn: Neukirchener Verlag, 1970. 2:193-58.

_____, ed. *The Apocrypha of the Old Testament.* New York: Oxford University Press, 1965.

Meyer, Frederick B. *The Prophet of Hope Studies in Zechariah.* London: Morgan & Scott, 1952.

Meyrick, Frederick. *The Book of Leviticus.* The Pulpit Commentary. Grand Rapids: Wm. B. Eerdmans, 1977. 2:1-427.

Michaeli, Frank. *Les Livres des Chroniques d'Esdras et de Néhémie.* Commentaire de l'Ancien Testament, 16. Neuchatel, Switzerland: Delachaux & Niestle, 1967.

Micklem, Nathaniel. "The Book of Leviticus: Introduction and Exegesis." *Interpreter's Bible.* Nashville: Abingdon Press, 1953. 2:3-134.

Migne, Jacques P., ed. *Patrologia . . . Series Graeca.* Vols. 15-16, pt. 3. Paris: J.-P. Migne, 1857-63.

Milgrom, Jacob. "Altar." *Encyclopaedia Judaica.* Jerusalem: Keter Publishing House, Ltd., 1971. 2:760-67.

Milik, Józef J. *The Books of Enoch: Aramaic Fragments of Qumran Cave 4.* Oxford: Clarendon Press, 1976.

Milns, R. D. *Alexander the Great.* London: Robert Hale, 1968.

Moeller, Joseph. "Habakkuk." *New Catholic Encyclopedia.* New York: McGraw-Hill Book Co., 1967. 6:875-76.

Mond, Robert and Myers, Oliver H. *The Bucheum.* London: Oxford University Press, 1934.

Montgomery, James A. Aramaic Incantation Texts from Nippur. The Museum Publications of the Babylonian Section. Vol. 3. Philadelphia: University Museum, 1913.

_____. A Critical and Exegetical Commentary on the Book of Daniel. The International Critical Commentary. Edinburgh: T. & T. Clark, 1950.

_____. A Critical and Exegetical Commentary on the Books of Kings. The International Critical Commentary. Edinburgh: T. & T. Clark, 1951.

_____. "Notes on Amos." Journal of Biblical Literature 23 (1904):94-96.

_____. "Some Gleanings from Pognon's ZKR Inscriptions." Journal of Biblical Literature 28 (1909):57-70.

Moore, George F. "Biblical Notes: Ashteroth Karnaim." Journal of Biblical Literature 16 (1897):155-65.

_____. "Daniel 8:9-14." Journal of Biblical Literature 15 (1896):194.

Moortgat, Anton. Vorderasiatische Rollsiegel. Berlin: Gebrüder Mann, 1966.

Morenz, Siegfried. "Das Tier mit den Hörnern, ein Beitrag zu Dan 7:7f." Zeitschrift für die alttestamentliche Wissenschaft 63 (1951):151-56.

Morgenstern, Julian. "Moses with the Shining Face." Hebrew Union College Annual 11 (1925):1-27.

Morison, James. 1 and 2 Samuel. The Pulpit Commentary. Grand Rapids: Wm. B. Eerdmans Publishing Co., 1977.

Morris, Henry M. The Genesis Record. Grand Rapids: Baker Book House, 1976.

Moscati, Sabatino. An Introduction to the Comparative Grammar of Semitic Languages. Wiesbaden: Otto Harrassowitz, 1964.

Motyer, Alex. "The Prophets, Introduction." Eerdmans Handbook to the Bible. Edited by David Alexander, Pat Alexander. Grand Rapids: Wm. B. Eerdmans Publishing Co., 1973.

Motyer, J. A. The Day of the Lion: The Message of Amos. Downers Grove, IL: Inter-Varsity Press, 1974.

Mowinckel, Sigmund. He That Cometh. Translated by George W. Anderson. New York: Abingdon Press, 1954.

_____. "Immanuelsprofetien Jes. F. Streiflys fra Ugarit."
Norsk Teologisk Tidsskrift 41 (1941):129-57.

_____. Psalmenstudien. 2 Vols. Amsterdam: P. Schippers
N.V., 1966.

_____. "Zum Psalm des Habakkuk." Theologische Zeitschrift
9 (1953):1-23.

Muilenburg, James. "The Book of Isaiah." Interpreters Bible.
New York: Abingdon Press, 1956. 5:151-773.

Murphy, James G. A Critical and Exegetical Commentary on the
Book of Psalms. Andover: Warren J. Draper, 1875.

Myers, Jacob M., ed. I Chronicles. Anchor Bible. Garden City:
Doubleday & Co., Inc., 1965.

Neil, William. "Zechariah, Book of." Interpreter's Dictionary
of the Bible. New York: Abingdon Press, 1962. 4:943-47.

Newton, Isaac. Observations upon the Prophecies of Daniel.
London: 1733. New ed. London: James Nisbet, 1831.

Nicholson, Reynold A. A Literary History of the Arabs.
Cambridge: University Press, 1966.

Nielsen, Ditlef. Die altarabische Kultur. Vol. 1 of Handbuch der
altarabischen altertumskunde. Edited by Ditlef Nielsen,
Fritz Hommel, and Nikolaus Rhodokanakis. Kopenhagen:
Arnold Busck, 1927.

_____. Die altarabische Mondreligion. Strassburg: Karl J.
Trübner, 1904.

_____. Die Religionen Altsyriens, Altarabiens und der
Mandäer. Die Religionen der Menschheit, Vol. 10, pt. 2.
Stuttgart: W. Kohlhammer, 1970.

_____. "Der sabäische Gott Ilmukah." Mitteilungen der
vorderasiatischen Gesellschaft 14 (1909):1-70.

_____. Studier over old arabiske indskrifter: Rejserne til
Sydarabien. Landets aeldste historie. Copenhagen: Det
Schønbergske forlag, 1906.

Noth, Martin. Das Buch Joshua. Handbuch zum Alten Testament.
Tübingen: J. C. B. Mohr (Paul Siebeck), 1938.

_____. Exodus: A Commentary. Philadelphia: The Westminster
Press, 1962.

_____. Könige. Biblischer Kommentar Altes Testament
Neukirchen-Vluyn: Neukirchener Verlag, 1968.

_____. The Laws in the Pentateuch and other Studies.
Philadelphia: Fortress Press, 1966.

_____. Numbers: A Commentary. Philadelphia: The Westminster Press, 1968.

Nowack, Wilhelm. Die Kleinen Propheten. Göttinger Handkommentar zum Alten Testament. Göttingen: Vandenhoeck & Ruprecht, 1922.

Obbink, Herman T. "The Horns of the Altar in the Semitic World, especially in Jahwism." Journal of Biblical Literature 56 (1937):43-49.

_____. "The 1963 Excavation at Ta'annek." Bulletin of the American School of Oriental Research 173 (1964):35-37.

Oesterley, William O. E. The Psalms. London: Society for Promoting Christian Knowledge. [1939].

Oldenburg, Ulf. The Conflict between El and Ba'al in Canaanite Religion. Leiden: E. J. Brill, 1969.

Old Testament in Greek, The. Edited by Alan England Brooke and Norman McLean. Cambridge: At the University Press, 1906.

Old Testament in Greek according to the Septuagint, The. 3 Vols. Edited by Henry Barclay Swete. Reprint ed. Cambridge: At the University Press, 1930.

Oppenheim, A. Leo. "Akkadian pul(u)ḫ(t)u and melammu." Journal of the American Oriental Society 63 (1943):31-34.

_____. Ancient Mesopotamia. Chicago: University Press, 1964.

_____. Catalogue of the Cuneiform Tablets of the Wilberforce Eames Babylonian Collection. American Oriental Series. Vol. 32. New Haven, CT: American Oriental Society, 1948.

Origenes. Origenis Hexaplorum. 2 Vols. Edited by Fridericus Field. Hildesheim: Georg Olms, 1964.

Osten, Hans H., von der. Ancient Oriental Seals in the Collection of Mrs. Agnes Baldwin Brett. Chicago: The University of Chicago Press, 1936.

_____. Ancient Oriental Seals in the Collection of Mr. Edward T. Newall. Chicago: University Press, 1934.

Otten, Heinrich. "Teschup." Biblisch-Historisches Handwörterbuch. Göttingen: Vandenhoeck & Ruprecht, 1962-66.

Otto, Eberhard. Beiträge zur Geschichte der Stierkulte in Aegypten. Untersuchungen zur Geschichte und Altertums kunde Aegyptens, Vol. 13. Edited by Hermann Kees. Hildesheim: Georg Olms, 1964.

Oxford Bible Atlas. Edited by Herbert G. May. London: Oxford University Press, 1974.

Parrot, André, ed. Studia Mariana. Documenta et Monumento Orientis Antiqui, Vol. 4. Leiden: E. J. Brill, 1950.

Paton, Lewis Bayles. "Baal, Beel, Bel." Encyclopaedia of Religion and Ethics. Edited by James Hastings. New York: Charles Scribner's Sons, 1913.

Payne, J. Barton. Encyclopedia of Biblical Prophecy. New York: Harper & Row Publishers, 1973.

Pentateuch with Targum Onkelos, Haphtaroth and Prayers for Sabbath and Raschi's Commentary. Translated by M. Rosenbaum and A. M. Silbermann, et al. London: Shapiro, Vallentine & Co., 1946.

Perowne, J. J. Stewart. The Book of Psalms. 2 Vols. Grand Rapids: Zondervan Publishing House, 1976.

Perry, Guthrie E. Hymnen an Sin. Leipzig: J. C. Hinrichs, 1907.

Perry, William J. "The Cult of the Sun and the Cult of the Dead in Egypt." The Journal of Egyptian Archaeology 11 (1925):191-200.

Pettinato, Giovanni. "The Royal Archives of Tell Mardikh." Biblical Archeologist 39 (May 1976):44-52.

Philo of Alexandria. Translated by F. H. Colson and G. H. Whitaker. The Loeb Classical Library. Cambridge, MA: 1929-62.

Piankoff, Alexander. Mythological Papyri: Texts. Vol. 3. Bollingen Series, 40. New York: Pantheon Books, 1957.

_____. The Pryamid of Unas. Vol. 5. Bollingen Series, 40. Princeton, NJ: University Press, 1968.

Pinches, Theophilus G. "Priest, Priesthood." Encyclopaedia of Religion and Ethics. 12 Vols. Edited by James Hastings. New York: Charles Scribner's Sons, 1919.

Pink, Arthur W. Gleanings in Exodus. Chicago: Moody Press, n.d.

Plöger, Otto. Das Buch Daniel. Kommentar zum Alten Testament. Vol. 18. Gütersloh: Verlagshaus Gerd Mohn, 1965.

Plumptre, Edward H. and Adeney, Walter F. Ezekiel. The Pulpit Commentary. Grand Rapids: Wm. B. Eerdmans Publishing Co., 1977.

Poebel, Arno. Grammatical Texts. Philadelphia: University Museum, 1914.

_____. Grundzüge der Sumerischen Grammatik. Rastork: By the author, 1923.

Pope, Marvin H. Job. 3rd ed. The Anchor Bible. Garden City, NY: Doubleday & Co., Inc., 1973.

_____. "The Saltier of Atargatis Reconsidered." Near Eastern Archaeology in the Twentieth Century. Edited by James A. Sanders. Garden City, NY: Doubleday & Co., 1970. Pp. 178-96.

_____. "YHWH and his AŠRT." Paper presented to the American Oriental Society, St. Louis, on 26 April, 1979.

Porada, Edit, ed. The Pierpont Morgan Library of Corpus of Ancient Near Eastern Seals in North American Collections. 2 Vols. The Bollingen Series, 14. Washington: Pantheon Books, 1948.

Porteous, Norman W. Daniel: A Commentary. Philadelphia: The Westminster Press, 1965.

Powell, Marvin A. "Sumerian Area Measures and the Alleged Decimal Substratum." Zeitschrift für Assyriologie 62 (1973):165-72.

Pritchard, James, ed. The Ancient Near East in Pictures. Princeton, NJ: Princeton University Press, 1954.

_____, ed. Ancient Near Eastern Texts. 3rd ed. Princeton, NJ: Princeton University Press, 1969.

Pusey, Edward B. Daniel the Prophet. New York: Funk & Wagnalls, 1885.

Rabin, Chaim. "Hebrew." Current Trends in Linguistics. Vol. 6. Edited by Thomas A. Sebeok. The Hague: Mouton, 1970. Pp. 304-45.

Rad, Gerhard von. Deuteronomy: A Commentary. Philadelphia: The Westminster Press, 1966.

_____. Genesis: A Commentary. Philadelphia: The Westminster Press, 1961.

_____. Old Testament Theology. Translated by D. M. G. Stalker. New York: Harper & Row, 1962-[65].

Ranke, Hermann. Early Babylonian Personal Names. Vol. 3 of the Babylonian Expedition of the University of Pennsylvania. Series D: Researches and Treatises. Edited by H. V. Hilprecht. Philadelphia: University of Pennsylvania, 1905.

Rawlinson, George. The Book of Psalms. The Pulpit Commentary. Grand Rapids: Wm. B. Eerdmans Publishing Co., 1977.

_____. Exodus: Exposition and Homiletics. The Pulpit Commentary. Grand Rapids: Wm. B. Eerdmans Publishing House, 1977.

_____. Genesis and Exodus. The Pulpit Commentary. Grand Rapids: Wm. B. Eerdmans, 1977.

_____. II Kings. The Pulpit Commentary. Grand Rapids: Wm. B. Eerdmans, 1977.

Reed, William L., and Winnett, Frederick. Ancient Records from North Arabia. Near and Middle East Series, 6. Toronto: University of Toronto Press, 1970.

Reichert, Andreas. "Altar." Biblisches Reallexicon. Tübingen: J. C. B. Mohr (Paul Siebeck), 1977.

Reicke, Bo, and Rost, Leonhard, eds. Biblisch-Historisches Handwörterbuch. 3 Vols. Göttingen: Vandenhoeck & Ruprecht, 1962.

Reiner, Erica. "Akkadian." Current Trends in Linguistics. Vol. 6. Edited by Thomas A. Sebeok. The Hague: Mouton, 1970. Pp. 274-303.

Renger, Johannes. "Überlegungen zum akkadischen Syllabar." Zeitschrift für Assyriologie 61 (1971):23-43.

_____. "Untersuchungen zum Priestertum in der altbabylonischen Zeit." Zeitschrift für Assyriologie 58 (1967):110-88.

Rhodokanakis, Nikolaus. "Altsabäische Texten." Wiener Zeitschrift für die Kunde des Morgenlandes 39 (1932):173-226.

_____. "Dingliche Rechte im alten Südarabien." Wiener Zeitschrift für die Kunde des Morgenlandes 37 (1930): 121-73.

Roberts, Jimmy J. M. The Earliest Semitic Pantheon. Baltimore: Johns Hopkins University Press, 1972.

Robinson, George L. The Twelve Minor Prophets. Grand Rapids: Baker Book House, 1926.

Robinson, Joseph A. The First Book of Kings. Cambridge: The University Press, 1972.

_____. The Second Book of Kings. Cambridge: Cambridge University Press, 1976.

Robinson, Theodor H. "Micha." Die zwölf kleinen Propheten. Handbuch zum Alten Testament. Vol. 14. Tübingen: J. C. B. Mohr, 1938. Pp. 127-52.

Rödiger, Emil. Gesenius' Hebrew Grammar. 17th ed. Translated by Thomas J. Conant. New York: D. Appleton and Company, 1875.

Roeder, Günther. "Altar C. Ägypten." Reallexikon der Vorgeschichte. Berlin: Walter de Gruyter & Co., 1924.

Rogerson, John W., and McKay, John W. Psalms. 3 Vols. Cambridge, NY: Cambridge University Press, 1977.

Rosenbaum, Morris, and Silbermann, Abraham M. Pentateuch with Targum Onkelos, Haphtaroth and Prayers for Sabbath and Rashi's Commentary. London: Shapiro, Vallentine & Co., 1946.

Rosenthal, Franz. "Canaanite and Aramaic Inscriptions." Ancient Near Eastern Texts. 3rd ed. Edited by James B. Pritchard. Princeton, NJ: Princeton University Press, 1969. Pp. 653-62.

_____. A Grammar of Biblical Aramaic. Wiesbaden: Otto Harrassowitz, 1968.

Rowley, Harold H. The Aramaic of the Old Testament. London: Oxford University Press, 1929.

_____. "Book Review: Studies in Daniel, by H. Louis Ginsberg." Journal of Biblical Literature 68 (1949):173-77.

_____. Darius the Mede and the Four World Empires in the Book of Daniel. Cardiff: University of Wales Press, 1959.

_____. "Early Aramaic Dialects and the Book of Daniel." Journal of the Royal Asiatic Society (1933):777-805.

_____. Job. The Century Bible. New York: Thomas Nelson and Sons, 1970.

_____. "A Rejoinder." Journal of Biblical Literature 69 (1950):201-03.

_____, ed. Studies in Old Testament Prophecy Presented to Theodore H. Robinson by the Society for Old Testament Study on His Sixty-Fifth Birthday. Reprint ed. Edinburgh: T. & T. Clark, 1957.

_____. "The Unity of the Book of Daniel." Hebrew Union College Annual 231 (1951):233-72.

Rudolph, Wilhelm. Amos. Kommentar zum Alten Testament. Gütersloh: Gerd Mohn, 1971.

_____. Habakuk. Kommentar zum Alten Testament. Gütersloh: Gerd Mohn, 1975.

_____. Jeremiah. Handbuch zum Alten Testament. Tübingen: J. C. B. Mohr (Paul Siebeck), 1958.

_____. Micah-Nahum-Habakuk-Zephanja. Kommentar zum Alten Testament. Gütersloh: Verlagshaus Gerd Mohn, 1975.

Running, Leona G. A Historical and Philological Study of δόξα "Glory" in the Holy Scriptures. Thesis M.A. Washington, D.C.: SDA Theological Seminary, 1955.

Rust, Eric C. The First and Second Books of Samuel. The Layman's Bible Commentary. Richmond, VA: John Knox Press, 1961.

Ryckmans, Gonzague. "Inscriptions süd-arabes." Le Muséon X 66 (1953):267-317.

_____. Les Religions Arabes préislamiques. 2d ed. Louvain: Publications Universitaires, 1951.

Sabourin, Leopold. The Psalms. Staten Island, NY: The Society of St. Paul, 1969.

Saggs, Henry W. F. The Greatness that was Babylon. New York: Hawthorn Books, 1962.

Sanda, Albert. Die Bücher der Könige. Münster: Archendorff, 1911.

Sanders, James A., ed. The Dead Sea Psalms Scroll. Ithaca, NY: Cornell University Press, 1967.

Sasson, Jack M. "Bovine Symbolism in the Exodus Narrative." Vetus Testamentum 18 (1968):380-87.

Sayce, Archibald H. The Religion of Ancient Egypt. Edinburgh: T. & T. Clark, 1913.

Schachermeyr, Fritz. "Hörnerhelme und Federkronen als Kopfbedeckungen bei den 'Seevölkern' der ägyptischen Reliefs." Ugaritica VI, pp. 451-59. Mission de Ras Shamra. Vol. 17. Paris: Paul Geuthner, 1969.

Schaeffer, Claude F.-A. The Cuneiform Texts of Ras Shamra-Ugarit. London: Oxford University Press, 1939.

_____. Le palais royal d'Ugarit II. Mission de Ras Shamra. Vol. 7. Paris: Imprimerie Nationale, 1957.

_____. "Matériaux pour l'étude des relations entre Ugarit et le Hatti." Ugaritica III. Pp. 1-95. Mission de Ras Shamra. Vol. 8. Paris: Librairie Orientaliste Paul Geuthner, 1956.

Scheftelowitz, Isidore. "Das Hörnermotiv in den Religionen." Archiv für Religionswissenschaft 15 (1912):451-87.

Scheil, Vincent. "Stèle de Narâm-Sin." Mémoirs de la Délégation en Perse. Paris: E. Leroux, 1900. Pp. 52-56.

Schmidt, Hans. Die Psalmen. Handbuch zum Alten Testament. Tübingen: J. C. B. Mohr (Paul Siebeck), 1934.

Schmuttermayr, Georg. "Die Doppeltexte." Psalm 18 und 2 Samuel 22: Studien zu einem Doppeltext. München: Kösel-Verlags, 1971.

Schramm, Gene M. "The Semitic Languages: An Overview." Current Trends in Linguistics. Edited by Thomas A. Sebeok. The Hague: Mouton, 1970. 6:257-60.

Scott, Robert B. Y. "The Book of Isaiah." Interpreter's Bible. New York: Abingdon Press, 1956. 5:151-773.

The Septuaginta. 2 Vols. Edited by Alfred Rahlfs. Stuttgart: Privilegierte Württembergische Bibelanstalt, 1949.

The Septuaginta. Vetus Testamentum Graecum. Auctoritate Academiae Scientiarum Göttingensis editum. Göttingen: Vandenhoeck & Ruprecht, 1974.

Sethe, Kurt H. Urgeschichte und älteste Religion der Ägypter. No. 4. Abhandlung für die Kunde des Morgenlandes. Vol. 18. Leipzig: Deutsche morgenländische Gesellschaft, 1928-30. Nendeln, Lichtenstein: Kraus Reprint, Ltd., 1966.

Sethe, Kurt. Untersuchungen zur Geschichte und Altertumskunde Aegyptens. Vol. 4. Hildesheim: Georg Olms Verlagsbuchhandlung, 1964.

Shanks, Hershel. "Yigael Yadin finds a Bama at Beer-sheva." Biblical Archaeology Review 3 (1977):3-12.

Shea, William H. "The Date and Significance of the Israelite Settlement at Kuntillet Ajrud." BA forthcoming.

_____. "David's Lament." Bulletin of American Schools of Oriental Research 221 (Feb. 1976):141-44.

Sheehan, Michael M. "Right of Asylum." New Catholic Encyclopedia. 14 Vols. New York: McGraw-Hill Book Co., 1967. 1:994.

Simpson, Cuthbert A. "The Book of Genesis." Interpreter's Bible. New York: Abingdon Press, 1952. 1:439-829.

Sjöberg, Åke. "Hymns to Meslamtaea, Lugalgirra and Nanna-Suen in Honour of King Ibbīsuen (Ibbīsîn) of Ur." Orientalia Suecana 19-20 (1970-71):140-70.

_____. "Miscellaneous Sumerian Hymns." Zeitschrift für Assyriologie 63 (1973-74):1-55.

_____. Der Mondgott Nanna-Su^{j}en in der sumerischen Überlieferung. Uppsala: Almqvist & Wiksell, 1960.

Sjöberg, Åke and Bergman, E. The Collection of the Sumerian Temple Hymns. In Texts from Cuneiform Sources. Vol. 3. Locust Valley, NY: J. J. Augustin, 1969.

Skinner, John, ed. A Critical and Exegetical Commentary on Genesis. 2d ed. International Critical Commentary. Edinburg: T. & T. Clark, 1951.

_____, ed. Kings: Introduction, Revised Version with Notes. New Century Bible. New York: H. Frowde [1904?].

_____. Prophecy and Religion. Cambridge: The University Press, 1940.

Smend, Rudolf. "Altar." Biblisch-historisches Handwörterbuch. Edited by Bo Reicke und Leonhard Rost. Göttingen: Vandenhoeck & Ruprecht, 1962-66. 1:63-65.

Smith, George. The Chaldean Account of Genesis. Rev. ed. A. H. Sayce. London: Sampson Low, 1880.

Smith, J. Payne. A Compendious Syriac Dictionary. Oxford: Clarendon Press, 1903.

Smith, John M. P. A Critical and Exegetical Commentary on the Books of Micah, Zephaniah, Nahum, Habakuk, Obadiah and Joel. International Critical Commentary. Edinburgh: T. & T. Clark, 1959.

Smith, R. Payne. The First Book of Samuel. Pulpit Commentary. Grand Rapids: Wm. B. Eerdmans Publishing Co., 1977.

_____. I and II Samuel. Pulpit Commentary. Grand Rapids: Wm. B. Eerdmans, 1977.

Smith, Samuel H. P. A Critical and Exegetical Commentary on the Books of Samuel. International Critical Commentary. Edinburgh: T. & T. Clark, 1951.

Smith, Sidney. "b/pukk/qqu and mekku." Revue d'Assyriologie et d' Archéologie Orientale 30 (1933):153-68.

Soden, Wolfram von, ed. Akkadisches Handwörterbuch. 2 Vols. Wiesbaden: Otto Harrassowitz, 1965-72.

Soden, Wolfram von, and Röllig, Wolfgang. Das akkadische Syllabar. 2d. rev. ed. Analecta Orientalia, 42. Rome: Pontificium Institutum Biblicum, 1967.

Soggin, J. Alberto. Joshua: A Commentary. Philadelphia: The Westminster Press, 1972.

_____. Le Livre de Josué. Commentaire de l'ancien Testament. Editions Delachaux & Niestlé, Neuchatel (Suisse), 1970.

Sollberger, Edmond. The Business and Administrative Correspondence under the Kings of Ur. In Texts from Cuneiform Sources. Vol. 1. Locust Valley, NY: J. J. Augustine, 1966.

Sollberger, Edmond, and Kupper, Jean-Robert. Inscriptions royales sumériennes et akkadiennes. Paris: Les éditions du Cerf, 1971.

Sorg, Rembert. Habaqquq III and Selah. Fifield, WI: King of Martyrs Priory, 1968.

Speiser, Ephraim A. "Akkadian Myths and Epics: The Epic of Gilgamesh." Ancient Near Eastern Texts. Edited by James Pritchard. Princeton, NJ: Princeton University Press, 1969.

_____. Genesis. Anchor Bible. Garden City, NY: Doubleday & Co., 1964.

_____. "The Myth of Zu." Ancient Near Eastern Texts. 3rd ed. Edited by James Pritchard. Princeton, NJ: Princeton University Press, 1969. Pp. 111-13.

Spurgeon, Charles A. The Treasury of David. New York: Association Press, 1913.

Stamm, Johann J. Die akkadische Namengebung. Darmstadt: Wissenschaftliche Buchgesellschaft, 1968.

Stark, Jürgen K. Personal Names in Palmyrene Inscriptions. Oxford: Clarendon Press, 1971.

Staub, Urs. "Das Tier mit den Hörnern Ein Beitrag zu Dan 7.7f." Freiburger Zeitschrift für Philosophie und Theologie 25 (1978):351-97.

_____. Die Tiervision im Danielbuch. Eine motivgeschichtliche und ikonographische Untersuchung zu Dan 7:2-8. Lizentiatarbeit, Freiburg Universität, 1977.

Steinmueller, John E. "Cities of Asylum." New Catholic Encyclopedia. New York: McGraw-Hill Book Co., 1967. 1:993-94.

Stephens, Ferris J. "The Babylonian Dragon Myth in Habakkuk 3." Journal of Biblical Literature 43 (1924):290-93.

Streck, Maximilian. Assurbanipal und die letzten assyrischen Könige biz zum Untergange Niniveh's. Vol. 2. Leipzig: J. C. Hinrichs, 1916.

Strong, James. A Commentary on the Holy Scriptures: Critical, Doctrinal and Homiletical. Vol. 13. Edited by John Peter Lange. New York: Charles Scribner's Sons, 1915.

Suhr, Elmer G. "The Horned Moses." Folklore 74 (1963):387-95.

Tallqvist, Knut. Akkadische Götterepitheta. Studia Orientalia, 7. Helsinki: Akateeminen Kirjakauppa, 1938.

Terrien, Samuel. "The Book of Job." Interpreter's Bible. New York: Abingdon Press, 1939. 3:877-1198.

Thomas, D. Winton. "The Book of Zechariah." Interpreter's Bible. New York: Abingdon Press, 1956. 6:1053-1114.

Thompson, John A. Deuteronomy: An Introduction and Commentary. Downers Grove, IL: Inter-Varsity Press, 1976.

Thompson, Reginald C. The Epic of Gilgamesh. Text, Translation, and Notes. Oxford: Clarendon Press, 1930.

_____. The Reports of the Magicians and Astrologers of Nineveh and Babylon. 2 Vols. London: Luzac and Co., 1900.

Thomsen, Peter. "Altar, D. Palästina-Syrien." Reallexikon der Vorgeschichte. Berlin: Walter de Gruyter & Co., 1924. 1:109-11.

Thomson, John E. H. The Book of Daniel. The Pulpit Commentary. Grand Rapids: Wm. B. Eerdmans, Publishing Co., 1977. 13:1-349.

Thureau-Dangin, François. Les homophones Sumériens. Paris: P. Geuthner, 1929.

Tien Khang Kiat. Genesis and the Chinese. Hong Kong: n.p., 1950.

Torrey, Charles C. "The Zakar and Kalamu Inscriptions." Journal of the American Oriental Society 35 (1915):353-69.

Tritton, Arthur S. "King (Semitic)." In Encyclopaedia of Religions and Ethics. Edited by James Hastings. New York: Charles Scribner's Sons, 1915.

Ullendorff, Edward. "Comparative Semitics." Current Trends in Linguistics. Edited by Thomas A. Sebeok. The Hague: Mouton, 1970. 6:261-73.

Unger, Eckhard. "Altar." Reallexikon der Assyriologie. Berlin: Walter de Gruyter & Co., 1932.

_____. "Altar, E. Vorderasien." Reallexikon der Vorgeschichte. Berlin: Walter de Gruyter & Co., 1924. 1:111-12.

_____. "Diadem und Krone." Reallexikon der Assyriologie. 4 Vols. Berlin: Walter de Gruyter & Co., 1932. 2:201-11.

_____. "Götterbild." Reallexikon der Vorgeschichte. Berlin: Walter de Gruyter & Co., 1926. 4:412-26.

_____. "Lebensbaum." Reallexikon der Vorgeschichte. Berlin: Walter de Gruyter & Co., 1926. 7:261-62.

_____. "Mischwesen." Reallexikon der Vorgeschichte. Berlin: Walter de Gruyter & Co., 1926. 8:195-216.

_____. "Religion, E. Mesopotamien." Reallexikon der Vorgeschichte. Berlin: Walter de Gruyter & Co., 1926. 11:115-22.

Unger, Merrill F. Zechariah. Grand Rapids: Zondervan Publishing House, 1976.

Ungnad, Arthur. Grammatik des Akkadischen. München: Biederstein Verlag (C. H. Beck), 1949.

Van Buren, E. Douglas. "Akkadian Sidelights on a Fragmentary Epic." Orientalia 19 (1950):159-74.

_____. "Concerning the Horned Cap of the Mesopotamian Gods." Orientalia 12 (1943):318-27.

Van Dijk, Johannes J. A. La Sagesse Sumero-Accadienne. Leiden: E. J. Brill, 1953.

Vaux, Roland de. Ancient Israel: Its Life and Institutions. London: Darton, Longman & Todd, 1961.

_____. ["Bulletin . . . Ras Shamra."] Revue Biblique 65 (1958):635-36.

Versteegh, C. H. M. Greek Elements in Arabic Linguistic Thinking. Leiden: E. J. Brill, 1977.

Vincent, L.-Hugues. "La Représentation divine orientale archaïque." Mélanges Syriens. Vol. 1. Paris: Paul Geuthner, 1939. Pp. 373-90.

Vischer, Wilhelm. "Sonnenstrahlen ihm zur Seite." Der Prophet Habakuk. Neukirchen: Kreis Moers, 1958.

Wainwright, Gerald Averay. The Sky-religion in Egypt. Cambridge: University Press, 1938.

Walwoord, John F. Daniel, the Key to Prophetic Revelation. Chicago: Moody Press, 1971.

Ward, William H. A Critical and Exegetical Commentary on Habakkuk. International Critical Commentary. Edinburgh: T. & T. Clark, [1959].

_____. The Seal Cylinders of Western Asia. Washington: Carnegie Institution, 1910; reprint ed., n.p. Columbia Planograph Company, 1919.

Watson, Wilfred G. E. "Ugaritic and Mesopotamian Literary Texts." Ugaritic Forschungen. Neukirchen-Vluyn: Neukirchener Verlag, 1970. 9:139-58.

Weber, Otto. "Eine neue minäische Inschrift (Glaser 1302)." Mitteilungen der vorderasiatischen Gesellschaft 6 (1901):1-34.

Weinel, Heinrich. "משח und seine Derivative." Zeitschrift für die alttestamentliche Wissenschaft 18 (1898):1-82.

Weiner, Harold M. "Altar." The International Standard Bible Encyclopaedia. Grand Rapids: Wm. B. Eerdmans Publishing Co., 1939. 1:106-10.

Weippert, Manfred. "Gott und Stier." Zeitschrift des deutschen Palästina-Vereins 77 (1961):93-117.

Weiser, Artur. Das Buch der Zwölf Kleinen Propheten. Das Alte Testament Deutsch. Göttingen: Vandenhoeck & Ruprecht, 1967.

_____. The Psalms. Philadelphia: The Westminster Press, 1962.

Weiss, Hans-Fredrich. "Baʻal." Biblisch-Historisches Handwörterbuch. Göttingen: Vandenhoeck & Ruprecht, 1962. 1:173-75.

Westermann, Claus. "Structur und Geschichte der Klage im Alten Testament." Zeitschrift für die alttestamentliche Wissenschaft 66 (1954):44-80.

Wevers, John W., ed. Ezekiel. Century Bible. London: Thomas Nelson and Sons, 1969.

_____. Genesis. In Septuaginta Vetus Testamentum Graecum. Göttingen: Vandenhoeck & Ruprecht, 1974.

Whitaker, Richard E. A Concordance of the Ugaritic Literature. Cambridge: Harvard University Press, 1972.

Whitelaw, Thomas. Genesis and Exodus. Pulpit Commentary. Grand Rapids: Wm. B. Eerdmans, 1977.

Wiedeman, Alfred. Religion of the Ancient Egyptians. London: H. Grevel & Co., 1897.

Wilcke, Claus. "Formale Gesichtspunkte in der sumerischen Literatur." In Sumerological Studies in Honour of Thorkild Jacobsen on his Seventieth Birthday, June 7, 1974. Edited by Stephen J. Lieberman. Assyriological Studies, no. 20. Chicago: University of Chicago Press, 1976. Pp. 205-80.

_____. Das Lugalbanda epos. Ph.D. dissertation. Wiesbaden: Harrassowitz, 1968.

_____. "Philologische Bemerkungen zum Rat des Šuruppag." Zeitschrift für Assyriologie 68 (1978):196-232.

Wildberger, Haus. Jesaja. Biblischer Kommentar Altes Testament. Neukirchen-Vluyn: Neukirchener Verlag, 1968.

Wilkinson, J. Gardner. The Manners and Customs of the Ancient Egyptians. 3 Vols. New rev. and corrected ed. Edited by Samuel Birch. New York: Dodd, Mead and Company, n.d.

Wilson, John A. "Egyptian Historical Texts." In Ancient Near
    Eastern Texts. 3rd ed. Edited by James Pritchard.
    Princeton, NJ: Princeton University Press, 1969.
    Pp. 234-35.

Wilson, Robert D. Studies in the Book of Daniel. New York:
    G. P. Putnam's Sons, 1917.

Winnett, Frederick V. and Reed, William L. Ancient Records from
    North Arabia. Toronto: University of Toronto Press,
    1970.

Wiseman, Donald J. "Abban and Alalaḫ." Journal of Cuneiform
    Studies 12 (1958):124-29.

_____. "Assyria and Babylon ca. 1200-1000 B.C." Cambridge
    Ancient History. 3rd ed. Cambridge: At the University
    Press, 1975.

_____; Mitchell, T. C.; and Joyce, R.; Martin, W. J.;
    Kitchen, K. A. Notes on Some Problems in the Book of
    Daniel. London: The Tyndale Press, [1965].

Wohlstein, Herman. "Die Gottheit An-Anu in sumerisch-akkadischen
    Urzeitsmythen." In memoriam Eckhard Unger: Beiträge zu
    Geschichte, Kultur und Religion des Alten Orients. Baden-
    Baden: Valentin Koerner, 1971. Pp. 55-73.

Wolfe, Rolland E. "The Book of Micah." Interpreter's Bible.
    New York: Abingdon Press, 1956. 6:897-949.

Wolff, Walter H. Joel and Amos. Biblischer Kommentar Altes
    Testament. Philadelphia, PA: Fortress Press, 1977.

Wood, Leon J. Daniel: A Study Guide. Grand Rapids: Zondervan
    Publishing House, 1975.

Wright, G. Ernest. "Sun-Image" or "Altar of Incense." The Biblical
    Archaeologist 1 (1938):9-10.

Wright, William A. "Zedekiah." A Dictionary of the Bible. Edited
    by William Smith. London: John Murray, 1863. 3:1833-36.

Wyatt, Nicolas. "Atonement Theology in Ugarit and Israel."
    Ugarit-Forschungen. Vol. 8. Neukirchen-Vluyn:
    Neukirchener Verlag, 1970. Pp. 415-30.

Yadin, Yigael. The Art of Warfare in Biblical Lands. 2 Vols.
    New York: McGraw-Hill Book Company, 1967.

_____. "Beer-sheba: The High Place Destroyed by King
    Josiah." Bulletin of the American Schools of Oriental
    Research 222 (1976):5-17.

_____. "Symbols of Deities at Zinjirli, Carthage and Hazor." In *Near Eastern Archaeology in the Twentieth Century*. Edited by James A. Sanders. Garden City, NY: Doubleday & Company, Inc., 1970. Pp. 199-231.

Yamauchi, Edwin M. "Tammuz and the Bible." *Journal of Biblical Literature* 84 (1965):283-90.

Young, Edward J. *The Prophecy of Daniel*. Grand Rapids: Wm. B. Eerdmans Publishing Co., 1949.

Young, G. Douglas. *Concordance of Ugaritic.* Analecta Orientalia 36. Rome: Pontificium Institutum Biblicum, 1956.

Zewit, Ziony. "The Structure and Individual Elements of Daniel 7." *Zeitschrift für die alttestamentliche Wissenschaft* 80 (1968):385-96.

Zimmerli, Walther. *Ezechiel*. Biblischer Kommentar Altes Testament. Neukirchen-Vluyn: Neukirchener Verlag, 1969.

Zöckler, Otto. *The Book of the Prophet Daniel*. Translated, enlarged, and edited by James Strong. *A Commentary on the Holy Scriptures* by John Peter Lange. New York: Charles Scribner's Sons, 1876. 13:1-273.